Bounty from the Box

THE
CSA FARM
COOKBOOK

Bounty from the Box

THE
CSA FARM
COOKBOOK

MI AE LIPE

Twisted Carrot Publishing LLC
www.bountyfromthebox.com

Front and back cover illustration by Mary Woodin.
Cover and book design by Mi Ae Lipe.
Printed in the USA by BookPrinting.com.

To order additional copies of this book, please visit
www.bountyfromthebox.com

To inquire about discounts, or offer your comments and suggestions,
please contact the author by email:
miae@bountyfromthebox.com

First Edition
ISBN: 978-0-9905011-0-7
Library of Congress Control Number: 2015911234

*Parts of this book were previously published in 2008
as* Tastes from Valley to Bluff: The Featherstone Farm Cookbook

To Stefan and Ryan,
who never needed any encouragement
to eat their vegetables

and to Ron,
who could sum up Brussels sprouts in two words:
Why bother?

Contents

Foreword

Will Allen is the founder and CEO of Growing Power, one of America's first urban farms. Growing Power began in Milwaukee, Wisconsin, in 1993, and has since grown into a national nonprofit organization and land trust that supports people from diverse backgrounds and the environments in which they live by helping to provide equal access to healthful, high-quality, safe, and affordable food for people in all communities. Will, who was formerly a professional basketball player and a corporate executive, decided to become a farmer specifically to meet a desperate need for nourishing food in his inner-city Milwaukee community. In 2008, Will was awarded the John D. and Catherine T. MacArthur Foundation's Genius Grant and named a MacArthur Fellow—only the second farmer ever to be so honored. Will was also one of four national spokesmen who joined First Lady Michelle Obama at the White House to launch her "Let's Move!" initiative to reverse the epidemic of childhood obesity. In May 2010, Time magazine named Will as one of the 100 Most Influential People in The World. Despite his busy schedule as an international ambassador for urban agriculture and universal food security, Will continues to farm his own property in Oak Creek and direct operations at Growing Power, still headquartered in its original location on Silver Spring Drive in Milwaukee.

I've been farming since long before Growing Power started. I was actually operating a 20-acre farm at the same time I was working in the corporate world at Procter & Gamble, but when I left P&G in 1993, I purchased the Milwaukee facility that is now known as Growing Power. At that time, my purpose was to sell my produce from my farm in Oak Creek, where I lived and cultivated 100 acres, growing primarily vegetables.

A lot of naysayers in those days told me that growing food in the city wouldn't change the dynamics of people's lives. So I kind of took that as a challenge. I like challenges. I knew that if you did it the right way, you could grow a significant amount of food in the city.

That's when I went about building the infrastructure you see today in Silver Spring, which now has 25 acres of greenhouses and 300 acres of outdoor production. The three-acre farm in the city produces enough produce to feed more than 10,000 people annually. I always liked growing food for people—that's a passion, and what it's all about. Being able to distribute that food and make it accessible for folks—now, that's another piece of the puzzle.

Not a lot of other people were doing urban agriculture back in those days. When we had a meeting, it would be attended mostly by a few crusty old farmers like myself and university researchers who would be studying the food system—maybe about 10 folks in all. Today if you called a meeting, there would be 100 people, and they're involved in every discipline there is, from engineers and truck drivers to factory workers and lawyers.

Urban agriculture has become kind of cool in food politics. I don't want to take too much credit, but

we do have the largest single urban farm in the world. And it wasn't originally intended to be that way.

A lot of things came together to create the perfect storm. One of them was First Lady Michelle Obama getting behind us, putting that garden in the White House lawn and trying to get kids to eat better. It's estimated that she inspired some 10 million people to start growing their own food. When they saw the First Family bringing their own chef on board and eating their own organic food, that helped us a lot. And that kind of leadership, along with the help of many other folks involved over the years in the local food movement, like Alice Waters, made people realize they wanted good—and better—food.

But that good food still hadn't reached the people who were the most vulnerable, like the poor. That's why we started our social justice work—because everyone deserves to eat good food. It's a matter of strategizing and coming up with ways that everyone can access it. We don't grow separate foods because that person is poor and can eat only this kind of food or that. We make our food available for everyone and get it to every sector—whether it's wholesalers, delivery services, grocery stores, CSAs, or farmers markets. Every possible way we can deliver food to the community, we're involved in.

And it's critical to do this at a reasonable price by cutting production costs, using renewable energy, and eliminating the transportation associated with moving food from California and around the country.

Another problem is that most people don't know very much about what good food actually is. It's all about not making assumptions. Just because it has a big organic label and comes from a high-end store doesn't mean that it has a high nutrition value. Good food is really determined by what soil it's grown in, and only 3 or 4 percent of all food is actually grown in decent soil. So many people think they're eating good food when they really are not. You have to know your farmers and the type of soil in which they are growing their crops before you can determine its nutritional value.

We also know that when food travels, it usually takes at least several days for it to get from California or wherever it's grown to your grocery store. We don't know how long those fruits and vegetables sat in coolers before they got moved by wholesalers into the marketplace. Then people buy them and stick them in their refrigerators for a couple more days. Often people are eating food that is at least 10 or 12 days old. By then, it has lost a lot of its nutritional value.

When you buy my salad mix and cucumbers, it's been picked just the day before. That's a much bigger difference, and that's why developing local and regional food systems is so important. Because that's where the rubber meets the road—it's really about the nutritional value of that food and its wonderful taste, which is so much better than when it's been sitting in the refrigerator.

Agriculture is part of everybody's heritage. That's because, at some point in time, everyone's family had a part in farming the land in one way or another. But we've lost that connection in modern times, and that's why people don't know much about where their food comes from or how it gets to them.

Another huge problem is when people can't afford to buy good food. Instead, they go for the cheapest, most easily available things they can eat. And even then, tonight 3 out of 10 young people in America will go to bed without a meal—that's pretty tragic. It shouldn't be that way.

It's about food inaccessibility and inequity— many poorer communities have no grocery stores, only corner and convenience stores and fast-food joints, making it very difficult to eat healthfully. It becomes a vicious cycle, because many of these folks who buy food there are not well-educated; they know a lot less about their bodies and the adverse effects of these diets than their more affluent counterparts.

Changing food and dietary habits is a long-range process that doesn't happen overnight, but it can eventually take hold once the education and availability are there. But the fact is, we've been addicted to bad food for a long time, so people need a lot of support and to be offered the means to empower themselves in their own eating. This book and others help in that effort to educate people about better food choices and more healthful eating.

One of the changes I think we need to make is to establish a federal office for urban agriculture and small-scale farming in Washington, DC. There's a big black hole in our current farm bill, and no money is available for this kind of sustainable agriculture. I'll be working over the next few years to ask for help in opening such an office where we can work directly with legislators, food distributors, and other stake-holders, so we can be ready when the next iteration of the farm bill comes up for review.

The public needs to get more involved. Be politically active. Write letters to your community leaders, elected officials, and legislators. Tell them that you want a good farm bill. Tell them that you're tired of processed, bad food, that you won't tolerate food deserts, and that you want good food for yourself and your family. Let your local grocery store know that you want it to stock locally grown produce and that you'll buy it.

Also think about where you shop. Where do most people buy their food? It's often from the convenience store, the big-box store, and other sources of bad food. As a consumer, you can—and should— vote with your pocketbook every day. Everyone complains and blames one another, but everybody from all walks of life (not just farmers and politicos) has to come to the table, so to speak, and work together. That's how change is made.

Will Allen
Founder, Growing Power
July 2015

Introduction

When I self-published *Tastes from Valley to Bluff: The Featherstone Farm Cookbook* in 2008, the organic-food movement was starting to take root across America. Now, seven years later, local and sustainable agriculture has captured the nation's imagination and bellies, with no signs of letting up. Thousands of CSA farms are thriving across the country, farmers markets are the new town squares, and consumers are increasingly exploring—and demanding—local, sustainably raised food in stores and restaurants.

I grew up in the San Francisco Bay Area only a hundred miles from one of the largest-scale, most chemical-intensive agricultural operations in the world, California's Central Valley. By pure chance would I finally get to taste vegetable bounty years later from a small organic farm in Minnesota. Once I did, I was hooked, and for several years I was a CSA (community-supported agriculture) member of Featherstone Farm, scarfing down some of the most delicious produce I had ever eaten.

I have always considered myself a far more dedicated eater than a cook of any merit. However, my lifelong passion for food, coupled with being a professional book editor and designer, inspired me to create a cookbook for Featherstone. I conceived it as a place for CSAers to get inspiring recipes and practical, comprehensive information on what to do with that eggplant or kale lurking in their boxes. I myself often had plenty of questions and little inspiration when I lugged my own boxes home, often to a hungry family begging for dinner in a hurry.

From those beginnings, *Tastes* flourished. People absolutely loved it, and I realized after countless conversations with folks from all walks of life and ages who showed up at book signings and food tastings how deep the need was for a book like this. Shoppers told me how much they wanted to support local agriculture, to improve their diets and health, and to help their children learn how to cook. The book sold phenomenally in the Upper Midwest, but distributing it nationally was always a commercial struggle because of its singular focus on the one Minnesota farm.

In 2011, I decided to revise the book in the form you're now holding in your hands. The number of fruits, vegetables, and herbs covered was expanded from 50 to 92, including special sections for Asian vegetables and tropical fruits. It now has more than 350 recipes from a variety of superb sources, many of them new to this volume. This is a truly comprehensive resource, whether your produce comes from a weekly CSA box, the supermarket, or your local farmers market.

Aside from it being a cooking resource, I wanted this book to give readers more than a passing glimpse into what it actually takes to get food from seed to plate. Many of us are familiar with the basic concepts of CSA and organic farming, but we often don't know much beyond buzzwords or the media's broad brushstrokes surrounding sustainable agriculture, which often teem with generalities and misconceptions. Like the taproot of a dandelion in drought, the issues go much deeper.

When we started this book, what my research assistants and I did not expect to encounter was the staggering diversity of CSA farms across America. They all have in common a basic mission to provide food, but we were truly stunned by their dedication to strengthening their communities, not just in terms of physical nourishment but also employment, education, outreach, housing, environmental stewardship, fellowship, compassion, and hope.

Doubtless the hardest part of putting this book together was choosing which farms to include. The four that are featured in this book's season openers are outstanding representatives, each chosen for their unique stories of challenge and triumph; the dozens of others mentioned in the book's sidebars are no less noteworthy. But in singling them out, we realize how many other incredible farms had to be omitted.

Also in this book are numerous sidebars, little essays that delve into all sorts of topics related to farming (many written by farmers themselves), cooking, nutrition, sustainable agriculture, and food politics and systems.

It is my hope that you will not only learn how to make the most of your fruits and veggies, but that you will get more curious—and informed—about how your food choices affect farmers, the environment, your health, and ultimately the well-being of both you and this earth. May you enjoy this journey.

Mi Ae Lipe
July 2015
Seattle, Washington

How to Use This Book

One of my many goals in creating this book was to assemble a truly useful and enjoyable reference for preparing many of the fruits, vegetables, and herbs from CSA farms, farmers markets, home gardens, and grocery stores across the country. Most of us want to support local agriculture, eat better, and not let our produce go to waste, but let's face it, the prospect of what to do with all that fragile, fresh food can be daunting—especially when you are not even sure what all of it actually is!

The ever-skyrocketing interest in ethnic cuisines and food in general has happily resulted in people becoming more knowledgeable and curious about different ingredients—we are unbelievably fortunate to be cooking in an age when we have so many choices. I've written this section to make sure you're making the most of your food dollars, regardless of where or how you shop.

Important Basics About *Bounty from the Box*

This book is arranged by season, to reflect the general growing cycle of most American CSA farms and to emphasize seasonality, a concept that sadly, in this age of year-round supermarket availability, is nearly unknown to many home cooks. Each season brings a unique appreciation of the jewels flowing out of fields and greenhouses, as well as a keen anticipation of future garden treats made all the more precious by their fleeting presence. The crops listed within each season may be available across more than one season; for instance, radishes appear in CSA boxes both in the spring and fall, but they are listed in this book under the Fall section, when they are far sweeter and less fibrous.

Obviously, there are vast differences in crop availability between different regions of the country—California and Florida can supply fruits and vegetables in the dead of winter that are simply not growable in Minnesota or Vermont. But part of the joy of eating mindfully is paying attention to what's good in your community when, and learning to enjoy a melon from your local farmer at its sweetest height in August, rather than a specimen that has traveled thousands of miles from Chile in January.

Within each season, every crop is listed alphabetically for easy reference. Each entry covers history, nutrition, selection, storage, trimming and cleaning, and an array of cooking techniques, including steaming and boiling, stir-frying and sautéing, baking and roasting, blanching and freezing, and microwaving. Some crops contain additional instructions for grilling or, in the case of herbs, simple drying techniques. All of the entries contain handy information on measurements, equivalents, and, where appropriate, substitutions (especially in the case of herbs).

Each vegetable or fruit crop features wonderful recipes and serving suggestions designed to highlight that particular ingredient. I've had great fun gathering these recipes. Some are from professional chefs, and others have been previously published in cookbooks or cooking magazines. Still others are from talented food bloggers, and many are the excellent recipes and suggestions from the four CSA farms featured in *BFTB* and their members.

The book also lists complementary foods, herbs, and seasonings for each crop, as well as numerous serving suggestions. My goal is to spark more cooking and preparation ideas; the idea is that, when you're too tired or rushed to shop, you can scan them to see what items you already have in your refrigerator or pantry that might work together for a quick, easy meal or pairing.

Recipe headnotes are divided into Source and Author Notes; the former reflect the comments of the recipe's original author or source, whereas the latter are my own additional comments.

Sprinkled throughout are dozens of sidebars that focus on different topics about food, CSA farms, sustainable agriculture, gardening, and nutrition; they range from a glimpse into a typical summer day on a farm to how to cool the burn of chile peppers, as well as fascinating trivia, cooking and safety tips, quotations, and further references.

The book's recipes range from traditional American classics to more eclectic and international dishes. Some recipes are simple and quick to prepare, and others are more complex. Within this book is something for everyone. Many of the recipes can be easily adapted to fit dietary preferences, with the addition or omission of meat, fowl, fish, eggs, gluten-containing ingredients, and dairy. I wholeheartedly encourage you to jump in and try some of the more unusual recipes or serving suggestions; don't be afraid to explore unexpected—or unlikely—combinations.

What Isn't Covered

This book does not extensively cover certain techniques such as canning, making jams and jellies, baking, fermenting, deep-fat frying, and drying. Countless excellent books and copious Internet resources cover these topics much more effectively than space allows here; I trust that if readers have specific interests, they will pursue that information on their own. This book is meant to provide a comprehensive overview of everyday shopping, storage, and preparation.

If you are new to cooking or have not done much of it before, you may be feeling a bit overwhelmed. With a CSA box in hand overflowing with fragile perishables, urgency is a factor, and suddenly you may need to do more meal planning and cooking to use your bounty. You may also see a number of terms in this book and not be quite sure what they mean.

Luckily, help is at hand—hundreds of great resources on every aspect of cooking, thousands of different cookbooks (including the one you're holding in your hands), and millions of recipes on the Internet and at booksellers. Thanks to a burgeoning American interest in food and cooking, an entire world of cuisines is now available at our fingertips—as are many diverse ingredients that were relatively unknown or hard to find even just a decade ago. Check out the Suggested Additional Resources section on page 659 for some of my favorites.

This book assumes that you already know many of the basics of cooking, food preparation, and related terminology, although by no means do you need to be an experienced chef to follow these recipes. I highly recommend books such as *CookWise* by Shirley O. Corriher and *Brilliant Food Tips and Cooking Tricks* by David Joachim for terrific information on cooking techniques and the science behind them. And for an everyday, practical guide to the basics, few books are better than *The Art of Simple Food* by Alice Waters.

Basic Cooking Techniques

To get you started, here is a rundown of basic cooking techniques—their definitions, their uses, and their pros and cons:

BOILING

Although you can certainly cook many foods (vegetables and even meats) by boiling them, it's not the method of choice if you want the most flavor and nutrition from your food, especially vegetables. These days, good cooks use boiling water, often salted, to cook vegetables very quickly—actually called blanching—with the goal of removing them from the water before they become waterlogged and overdone. Once blanched, your crisp-tender, brightly colored vegetables can be eaten right away, tossed into a sauté pan with a bit of oil to shine them up, or chilled for later use.

STEAMING

A good, wide steamer pot or bamboo basket will soon become your best kitchen friend, because steaming is a fantastic way to cook and eat vegetables. Steam is hotter than boiling water, so veggies cook quickly—and they also get done all at the same time. Your vegetables come out of the pot au naturel, giving you a lot of control over how to season or use them after that.

Steaming may also be used for fish: Throw some aromatics (onion, garlic, ginger, whole spices) into the water, steam a fish fillet or some prawns, and drizzle with lemon butter for a wonderful entrée.

STIR-FRYING

When we think of stir-frying, usually the first thing that comes to mind is a wok, that very wide, shallow, metal pan that originated in China. It's great if you have a wok for stir-frying, but a large sauté pan (12 inches is a common size) is a reasonable substitute. The technique of stir-frying is simply one of adding ingredients to the hot pan (usually starting with some oil or liquid), putting in the ones that take the longest to cook and ending with the quickest-cooking ingredients, tossing or stirring everything as you go. Often you'll add some final seasonings or sauce to finish.

It's important with stir-frying to know how long various ingredients take to cook and to be able to wield a knife well enough to cut even-size pieces. Because stir-frying cooks food so quickly, it is also important to have all of your ingredients already cut up and ready to go before you start heating the pan. Having said that, it seems like almost anything that comes from a stir-fry recipe tastes delicious…

SAUTÉING

Sautéing is, in a way, the French version of stir-frying. A small amount of oil or other fat is placed in a wide skillet or sauté pan and set over medium to medium-high heat. The foods—meats, fish, poultry, or vegetables—cook fairly quickly as they are tossed (probably not with the vigor of stir-frying in a wok) over the direct heat. Often sautéing produces food that is slightly browned or caramelized, giving extra flavor and dimension to just about anything.

STEWING

Almost all of us know firsthand what a stew is: a combination of meat, vegetables, and seasonings in a sauce or broth that is eaten as a hearty, stand-alone dish. The key to successful stewing is to choose the right cuts of meat, cover the solid ingredients with a generous amount of liquid, and cook them very slowly for several hours. Flavor combinations are almost endless; think of a Moroccan tagine, an Irish lamb stew, American-style beef stew, French coq au vin, and so on. Last, don't forget to use a slow cooker for your stew making—there's a lot to be said for combining all your ingredients and walking away!

BRAISING

Braising is closely related to stewing. Generally, the cuts of meat used are the same (the cheaper, tougher, more flavorsome ones)—but braising means using less liquid, keeping the pot covered, and again, cooking at a very low temperature until the luscious meat starts to fall apart. Your mom's pot roast comes under this category, as does pulled pork for barbecue. Don't be tempted, if your recipe calls for browning the meat before assembling the braise (or stew), to skip this step! You'll get tons of dark, caramelly flavor notes in the process.

FRYING (ALSO DEEP-FRYING)

Think of fried chicken cooking happily in a cast-iron pan on the stove, and you'll recognize the technique called pan-frying. It differs from sautéing in that more fat is used, often to effectively surround a bumpy, breaded piece of something tasty.

Deep-frying, of course, implies submerging the food completely in oil. And although most of us don't deep-fry food too often at home, it's a very doable process. You'll have the most success by dedicating a medium pot to deep-frying (since the oil can coat the inside of the pot and make it stubbornly sticky) and by investing in a thermometer that attaches to the side of that pot. Temperature is critical for making deep-fried foods that cook evenly and don't retain a lot of extra oil.

ROASTING

If you're not already eating oven-roasted vegetables on a regular basis, you're going to love starting! Simply cut one or more types of vegetables into even-size pieces, then toss them in a bowl with flavorful olive oil and a sprinkle of salt and pepper. Spread them out on a cookie sheet and bake them at a pretty high temperature—385°F to 425°F is about right—until they are caramel-brown and slightly crisped. Your kids will love the way this method adds sweetness to the flavor of their favorite vegetables.

Oven-roasting is also an excellent method for cooking meat and poultry. Think of that whole, golden-brown, herb-roasted chicken; a garlicky roasted rack of lamb or pork; or a beef standing rib roast. Find a respected cookbook that helps you choose the proper cut of meat for this (or any) method.

BAKING

Baking can refer to the way we cook many savory foods (anything from a single sweet potato to a casserole); it implies cooking food, usually uncovered, with dry heat. Then there's the kind of baking that we all tend to love: the kind that produces bread, pastries, cookies, and so on. This type of baking often involves very specific methods, ingredients, temperatures, and timing, depending on the final product. Take baking step by step, using trusted sources for your recipes and ideas.

MICROWAVING

Microwaving can be a big timesaver; besides reheating and defrosting, it can also be used to precook certain ingredients that are destined for the recipe you're making for dinner. Another handy use is to get a head start on baking potatoes: Microwave a baking potato for several minutes (don't forget to poke some holes in the skin first to prevent it from exploding), then transfer it to your hot oven to finish baking and dry out. You'll have eliminated perhaps half the cooking time this way!

Of course, microwaves have their drawbacks; they don't always cook or reheat things evenly, and they can toughen or overcook meat and certain other foods. You can best decide which tasks they're most suitable for, depending on your style of cooking.

Cooking Times and Methods

Many strong opinions abound about cooking times, particularly with vegetables. One person may think that broccoli is just right when it has been steamed for three minutes and still retains a bright green color; others think that this same vegetable is still raw at this stage and requires a half hour (or more) of rapid boiling to make it edible. Many boiling, steaming, and sautéing times listed in this book err on the side of al dente rather than overcooking. If you prefer your veggies more tender, adjust your cooking times accordingly. And remember that the times given in this book are only guidelines; actual times can vary tremendously depending on your equipment, the size and condition of your produce, your own personal preferences, and even the altitude at which you are cooking.

The Best Ingredients

Anything we eat, regardless of how fancy or simple it is, is only as good as its components. Make an effort to find the very best-quality ingredients you can afford, whether it is olive oil, a tomato, or a cut of beef. And that doesn't necessarily mean paying the highest price; it just means eating foods at the peak of quality, freshness, and natural flavor whenever possible.

Herbs, Garlic, Citrus Juices, Salt, and Pepper

Use fresh herbs rather than dried if possible; their oils are more potent, giving them more vibrant flavors. Herbs frozen in butter or oil are also superior to their dried counterparts. Avoid garlic powder at all costs—it's often acrid, and it's a shame to use it when fresh garlic is so inexpensive and readily available. Lemon and lime juices should be freshly squeezed; the bottled stuff can be nasty and off-tasting. When finishing a dish at the last moment, flaked sea salt can be an exquisite final touch. And use freshly ground pepper rather than that dusty preground stuff—there's no excuse!

Olive Oil

A lot of myths swirl around cooking oils, especially olive oil. Nearly all of the olive oils (even extra virgin) in supermarkets are bland and incredibly inferior, since they are often pressed and mass-blended from olives of dubious quality. Adulteration and vague labeling are rampant in the olive oil industry. This is one food where it pays to do a bit of research and locate oils of superior flavor from reputable or even local producers, many of whom do business by mail order. Top-quality, nutritious oils that are full of antioxidants often taste peppery and grassy, with numerous distinctive flavor notes. Don't waste expensive oils in cooking, frying, or baking, where their strong flavors can mar a dish; use modestly priced, mild-flavored oil instead, and save the premium oils for drizzling over finished dishes, for dipping, or in salad dressings.

Reducing Food Waste

We tend to waste a lot of food in America, and it's time to change that. It's estimated that a full 30 percent of the food that is grown and prepared goes uneaten and gets tossed in the garbage or compost. Here are some tips for getting the most out of your box and food dollars!

Get Your Produce Home and Treat It Well

Most of us, when we go shopping or pick up our CSA boxes, tend to throw our veggies into plastic bags and dump them in the refrigerator crisper, where they often sit neglected for days. Too often, by the time we get to them, they are past their prime, wilted, or even starting to rot.

If you can, make it a habit to set aside time the very day you bring your produce home to prep it right away. Excessive moisture is an enemy of most vegetables and mushrooms; many will keep far better if they remain unwashed and as dry as possible until ready to use. Carrots, celery, radishes, and other veggies can be washed, peeled, and cut ahead of time so they are ready for snacking and cooking. Slipping a few dry (or slightly damp) paper towels in with certain vegetables can help them stay fresher longer.

Different crops prefer different temperatures and storage methods. Some fruits will ripen sitting out at room temperature—or will need to do so, like pears. Others will not. Consult the storage tips in each crop chapter for specific details. The main thing is, the longer you let your produce sit around, the more likely you are to forget about it and that it will go to waste.

Fresh herbs can often be treated like cut flowers—simply snip off the stem ends, place them in a glass of water, and store them on the counter at room temperature or in the refrigerator.

Use the Whole Plant

Remember that most food plants can be eaten in their entirety; don't use just the white parts of green onions and leeks, but the whole stalk. The leaves of broccoli, kohlrabi, turnip, and beet are not only edible but delicious. The skins of most vegetables, if they are not too tough, are extremely nutritious and can add fiber and texture. Many flowers of herbs and vegetables are tasty. However, be aware that this is not necessarily universal—the leaves of rhubarb and tomato plants, for instance, should not be eaten because of their toxicity. Know your plants.

Don't Be Afraid of Blemishes

Another huge contributor to food waste in America is consumer intolerance of fruits and vegetables that have a bruise or two, some spots, wilted leaves, even a worm. Although you don't want to use food that is obviously spoi jled, don't be afraid to cut around an affected area if the rest of it is perfectly good.

Freeze Your Food

Freezing can be a godsend for busy home cooks and families, enabling them to prepare different ingredients, sauces, condiments, side dishes, and entire meals when they have more time for cooking. Then it's easy to just pull out items for lunch or dinner, thaw, heat, and eat. Single-serving portions are especially handy for quick meals. Freezing is also a great way to stock up on meat and produce when they are in season and at their most economical. Be aware that not all foods keep for an equal length of time, so be sure to write the date on all of your items. Also, food must be properly packaged to avoid ice crystals and thus freezer burn, which changes texture and hastens deterioration.

The Proper Tools

Invest in a small but efficient collection of kitchen gadgets. Nothing is more frustrating than not having the right tool for the job at the time. It doesn't mean spending a huge amount of money on every sort of gadget known to man, but at the same time, don't be afraid to splurge on a few well-chosen, frequently used items: a set of decent knives, a few good pots and pans, a sturdy vegetable peeler, a Dutch oven, a nice wok. Keep your knives sharpened, and have at the ready other essentials such as a large, good-quality cutting board, food processor, colander, garlic press, cheese slicer, whisk, and other items.

Creativity and Experimentation

Last but not least, I personally find that cooking is an organic process. Certainly, we all have occasion to strictly follow certain recipes, especially for particular dishes that call for exact proportions or techniques, like baking and deep-frying. But frequently, when we come home tired after a long workday or have a hungry family becoming crankier by the minute, we cook intuitively, throwing in a bunch of this and a pinch of that, according to whim and preference. I strongly encourage you to do this with many of this book's recipes and to be creative with various combinations of herbs, spices, sauces, and condiments.

I hope you find this book a fun, valuable resource that you will want to turn to again and again. I heartily welcome your comments, suggestions, and feedback; feel free to email me at miae@bountyfromthebox.com.

Happy cooking and eating!

Acknowledgments

It's been said that it takes a village to raise a child. It has taken an entire community to make the cookbook that you are now holding, one that was years in the making. Although it has been my vision for a long time to produce this volume, I honestly could not have done it alone.

First and foremost, my gratitude to Maureen Cooney and Martha Wagner, who spent countless hours researching, selecting, and interviewing people at CSA farms across America. Their passion, curiosity, and dedication to this enormous task can be seen throughout these pages. An additional heartfelt thank-you to Martha for her work in writing many of the topic sidebars in the book, and for her incredible eye for detail and accuracy.

And to Maureen also, who helped promote the book in its former life as *Tastes from Valley to Bluff: The Featherstone Farm Cookbook*. Her amazing enthusiasm for that book helped make it an enormous sales success, and her faith in it has helped me carry on through the years with this one, even when my energy flagged at times.

Thank you to Will Allen, whose accomplishments include starting the first urban farm in America and effecting real change in how some of the poorest people in America eat. I am humbled by his support of the book and willingness to write its foreword.

I owe an enormous debt to Lisa Gordanier, a former chef who served as my cookbook editor and recipe development tester. With this tome's recipes coming from so many different sources and cooking styles, many was the day that we discussed how to clarify a procedure or whether a recipe would actually work as listed. She also created several original recipes for this book, and it was her eye that oversaw all of the crop text and cooking information—no small task indeed.

Laurel Robinson happily served as my proofreader extraordinaire—I am deeply grateful for her editing talent and eagle eye. Thank you also to both of my sons, Ryan and Stefan Butterbrodt, for their cheerful help in proofing the recipe lists and website assistance.

A huge hug goes to Jason Ennis-Holland of Volegrand Studio, who created the gorgeous Bounty from the Box website and was not afraid to take it to a level that I never imagined—not just a place to promote the book but a lovely online ecosystem where people can share and build community.

Social media is an indispensable part of marketing a book these days, but it is not my specialty. My enormous thank-yous to Paul Anater, Nicole Crakes, and Anna Morris for their tremendous enthusiasm in launching this venture and keeping it going 24/7. It is such a lot of work, but I so appreciate you.

Thank you to all of the members of my current and former sales team— Maureen Cooney, Anna Morris, Dolores Rossman, Eric Jones, and Nancy Tudorof for their support and energy. The best is yet to come!

To my husband, Ron, for putting up with four years of my being distracted with this book and being incredibly patient with me as he wondered just when the heck it was going to finally be done.

And of course, to all the farms, stores, restaurants, organizations, and recipe contributors who agreed to be a part of the book in both its previous and current forms. There are so, so many of you, and I am grateful beyond words for your support and what you do for your communities across the country and the world. Without you, the world would be truly be an emptier—and hungrier—place.

And finally, to you—my past, current, and new readers: I thank you for giving this book a reason to exist and flourish, like peas in spring.

Spring

IN MUCH OF THE COUNTRY, SPRING CROPS ARE CONSIDERED ANYTHING HARVESTED FROM THE END OF WINTER UP THROUGH THE END OF JUNE. THEY INCLUDE PERENNIAL CROPS (ASPARAGUS, RHUBARB, AND STRAWBERRIES), ANNUAL CROPS SEEDED IN THE SPRING (SALAD GREENS, HERBS, AND PEAS), AND OTHERS PLANTED IN THE FALL AND OVERWINTERED IN THE GROUND FOR AN EARLY SPRING HARVEST (SPINACH AND GARLIC).

SPRING IS EASILY THE TRICKIEST—AND BUSIEST—SEASON FOR THE FARMER. SO MUCH DEPENDS ON THE WHIMS OF WEATHER. LATE FROSTS, TOO MUCH RAIN, NOT ENOUGH RAIN, AND UNEXPECTED APRIL OR MAY SNOWFALLS CAN ADD UP TO SERIOUS DELAYS, OR WORSE YET, THE DEATH OF ENTIRE SPRING PLANTINGS. BUT WHEN THEY DO SUCCEED, THE RESULTS ARE WONDERFUL.

EARLY SPRING ALSO MARKS A FRENZY OF CSA-SIGNUP TIME, FIELD PREPARATION, GETTING STARTS GOING IN THE GREENHOUSES, AND A GENERAL RAMP-UP OF OPERATIONS. EAGERLY ANTICIPATED BY BOTH FARMER AND SUBSCRIBER ARE THE FIRST CSA BOXES OF THE YEAR AND THE FIRST APPEARANCE AT THE LOCAL FARMERS MARKET. IT IS A TIME OF ABUNDANT HOPE FOR THE SEASON AHEAD, OF HUNGER AND GRATITUDE FOR FRESH, TENDER GREENS, HERBS, AND SHOOTS AFTER A LONG WINTER OF STARCHY ROOT AND STORAGE VEGETABLES.

FOR FARMS IN TROPICAL REGIONS, SPRING IS ACTUALLY A TIME TO WIND DOWN, BECAUSE TEMPERATURES BEGIN TO GET TOO HOT TO WORK IN THE FIELDS. FOR THEM, THIS FINALLY MARKS THE WELL-DESERVED CHANCE TO REST.

Sang Lee: Immigrant Roots to Organic Renewal

Sang Lee Farms

25180 County Road 48
Peconic, New York 11958

631-734-7001
info@sangleefarms.com
www.sangleefarms.com

If you were a Chinese man living in America in the early 1900s, your choices were decidedly limited. Most likely you had immigrated to a strange new land in search of work with the railroads or to seek potential fortune with the gold rush out West. Or perhaps racial discrimination and the Chinese Exclusion Act had forced you to flee the West Coast and head east to New York City. You didn't know the language, you were treated like a second-class citizen, and you were relegated to menial jobs in the restaurant or laundry business. You intended to stay in America for only a few years so that you could make some money, go back to China, and marry.

And how you missed the food of your homeland. Yes, rice could be had, and if you were fortunate enough to live in a large enclave of other Chinese people or in a big Chinatown, you might be able to enjoy some familiar foods—congee, Peking duck, steamed dumplings, pork buns, chicken feet, and pig's blood soup. And the vegetables—gai lan, bitter melon, napa cabbage, bamboo shoots, yardlong beans, pak choy, bok choy, Asian eggplants, garlic chives, tung ho, daikon radish, gai choy…

In the 1930s, two Chinese brothers and one cousin decided they wanted to avoid working in the hot, miserable laundries of New York City, and they established a small farm in Queens to supply NYC's

Chinatown with badly needed high-quality Asian produce. In spite of their not having had any previous farming experience, word of these delicious vegetables quickly spread. After George Kim Lee finished his navy tour of duty in World War II, he joined his brother Kim Poy Lee and cousin Hugh K. Lee on the farm. In the 1940s, they incorporated the business, naming it Sang Lee Farms, and moved it to Huntington. Although there was some competition from Chinese farms in New Jersey, the Lees' produce was in strong demand, and they began trucking it all over New York City and Boston. In the late 1950s, the farm expanded to Hobe Sound, Florida, to provide customers with vegetables in the winter and thus a year-round supply.

In 1964, in an effort to reduce expenses and find more affordable land, the New York operation was moved to East Moriches, Long Island. Over the next three decades, Sang Lee production and wholesale distribution expanded to Asian markets all along the East Coast. Tractor-trailer trucks plied the highways from Canada to Florida, delivering Asian vegetables for Chinese markets in Toronto; Montreal; New York City; Chicago; Washington, DC; Atlanta; Miami; and other cities in between.

With the sudden death of George Lee in 1980, the fate of the farm fell to his son Fred, who was attending Boston University at the time. As the only son of a Chinese family, Fred felt great responsibility for the business and was compelled to return to the farm. In addition to the cultural component that motivated Fred to return, there was the farm business aspect as well. As his wife, Karen, says, "A farm has a life of its own, and you can't just stop it—there's the crew and customers to think about and take care of."

Karen met Fred when they were both studying for MBA degrees at Boston University. She was a nurse working toward a health care management career, and he was majoring in finance. She was a city girl from Boston who had never known farm life, but that was about to change. Fred took over the Florida farm after his father's death, they married shortly thereafter and started a family, and, as she describes it, "We literally did not come up for air for 10 years."

In Florida, Karen and Fred farmed from September to May while his uncle and cousin continued to attend to the Long Island operations. It was very challenging, with farms in two states to manage, deliveries to numerous cities, and all the accompanying logistics. When his uncle and other landholding partners decided they wanted to get out of the business, Fred decided to move the operation to Peconic, on the north fork of Long Island. The land in both Florida and East Moriches was sold. Then, shortly after establishing the new base in Peconic, Fred bought out his cousin's share in the business and became the sole owner and operator of the farm.

The transition from conventional farming to organic was a gradual one, spurred on by several serendipitous factors. One is that, after Fred moved the farm to Peconic, Karen started a roadside farm stand. "I wanted to get our children involved in the business, but not directly farm," she says. The three kids were responsible for managing and selling cut flowers at a self-serve table. Visitors loved them, and ultimately 10 acres were devoted

Pak choy from Sang Lee Farms in the 1960s, after it moved to East Moriches on Long Island.

In the earlier days when the farm was at its original location in Huntington. George Kim Lee, Fred's father, poses shirtless.

George Lee on the tractor in the farm's early days.

to cultivating fresh flowers. Soon baby greens, herbs, and seasonal and Asian vegetables were added to the burgeoning stand.

One day, after spraying a field with pesticide, Fred suddenly realized that he was the only one handling these harmful chemicals. He worried about the safety of his children, and he speculated that the sudden illness and untimely death of his father, who had been strong and healthy all of his life until his diagnosis of cancer, may have been caused by the pesticides he had used on his farm. "Back in those days, farmers didn't don all of the protective gear, masks, and gloves like they do now," reflects Karen.

"Growing organically felt like the right thing to do, both for personal and business reasons," she says. "We wanted to do it for our own family and for all of the families eating our food."

Organic farming is a dynamic practice that requires the management of soil health through the application of organic matter, crop rotation, and the planting of cover crops, according to Karen. "All of these practices provide essential nutrients for the soil. Our organic certification requires that we submit a seasonal plan that outlines the rotation of our crops each year. It also requires the careful management of pests without synthetic insecticides, fungicides, or herbicides. We use 'naturally occurring' products for pest control, all of which must be approved by the Organic Materials Review Institute and inspected by the Northeast Organic Farming Association (NOFA), who comes yearly to assess, give input, and make recommendations. To supplement these natural applications, we release thousands of beneficial insects such as ladybugs and praying mantises that help maintain the natural balance of insects, keeping our crops healthy without harmful applications of systemic products. It is always difficult, however, to control the weeds. There are many tasks you can't mechanize, like weeding. We weed by hand—and it takes many hands."

As part of soil health management, it is also necessary to apply fertilizers to supplement the mulching and cover cropping that provides the foundation. "For a long time, Fred kept using chemical fertilizers because, at the time, organic alternatives cost three to four times as much and provided fewer nutrients per pound," explains Karen. "Once he made that final step of using organic fertilizers, transitioning the land and becoming certified required a final three-year waiting period. But Fred is still on a learning curve when it comes to knowing all there is to know about growing this way."

At last, in 2007, Sang Lee Farms became Certified Organic by NOFA. Karen admits that it has taken a lot of hard work and a strong commitment over the last 10 years to transform their farming practices and to establish an organic farm that is financially viable as well. But she and Fred believe it is important to the health of the soil and water in their community to grow food this way, and to be stewards of the land for future generations. They also believe it is critical to the health and well-being of their family and their customers.

At the same time that they were transitioning the farm to organic, market dynamics for fruit and vegetables were drastically changing. Wholesaling had always been Sang Lee's mainstay, but in the 1990s, the advent of the

North American Free Trade Agreement, or NAFTA, changed everything for many farmers on both sides of the border by opening trade between the United States, Mexico, and Canada. Both NAFTA and the American government economically favor farmers who grow commodity crops like corn, wheat, soybeans, and rice, not fruit and vegetable farms, which are considered specialty farms. It is these farms, especially smaller family-run operations, that have felt the worst effects, and many have been forced to go out of business altogether.

Suddenly supermarkets, food-service companies, food manufacturers, and individual consumers alike were awash in foreign produce imported from Canada and Mexico. Because labor and production costs are so much less, especially south of the border, American farmers simply cannot compete. "There used to be Polish farmers all over this area who grew huge acreages of cabbage, potatoes, and cauliflower," says Karen, "but many had to close because of competition from California and Mexico. Some of our buyers reneged on big orders from us because they were able to get cheaper produce from foreign growers. Even we were offered the opportunity to grow our vegetables in Mexico. We knew we couldn't compete in the long term, just as other growers of commodity products could not, despite the fact that we had a specialty niche market. We were working 24/7 as it was, and it just wasn't sustainable. The writing was on the wall."

"Seeing the links between farming, where their food comes from, how to grow it, and cook and eat it—that completes our customers' circle of understanding. If you have people out in the field who can see their food from plant to plate, it gets them thinking in that framework."

— *Karen Lee*

Fortunately, because the Sang Lee name had been around for so long, its produce was widely recognized and well-respected by many discriminating customers. Balducci's was a legendary specialty food market in NYC that was the first to have a top-flight butcher shop, fishmonger, delicatessen, and greengrocer all under one roof. In its halcyon days, it was renowned for the incredible quality of its foods, and it would become the model for many specialty markets today. "It was visionary for its time," Karen says, "partly because it would source the very best from specific suppliers and put their names out on signs for customers to see. Balducci's wanted to carry our mesclun salad mix in those huge bowls with the self-serve tongs. That in part led to NYC restaurants wanting to order our mesclun." Happily, it also led to people recognizing the Sang Lee name when they stopped by the farm's roadside stand to buy flowers.

Karen Lee (right) with Fong Shiu, who has worked at the farm for over 35 years. As Karen says, she is indispensable both in the kitchen and in the field.

Like so many produce farmers in recent years since foreign fruits and vegetables started flooding the market, Sang Lee has had to adapt in a rapidly changing world. It is no longer enough to grow top-quality product these days; farmers who want to survive have to be savvy at identifying and marketing new ways to package and sell their crops. In 2002, Sang Lee stopped wholesaling completely and shifted its business exclusively to retail. It now supplies farmers markets, runs a large CSA program, and produces an entire line of prepared food products and precut vegetables.

Currently, Sang Lee farms over 100 different types of vegetables on about 90 acres of land. Out of this acreage, Karen and Fred own 23, with the rest on leased property. At any given time, 65 to 70 acres are actively farmed, and the rest are planted in cover crops, which is critical for the health of the soil and pest and disease control. It is a "large small farm," as Karen puts it.

Their location between the waters of Long Island Sound and the Peconic Bay enjoys a maritime climate with mild year-round temperatures. This allows for a considerably extended growing season in this part of the Northeast. Although they do occasionally get hard frost, heavy snow, and single-digit temperatures, winters do not last as long. In a mild year, they can start cultivating outside as early as mid March and go all the way into November and December before it gets too cold.

Temperatures in the 90s, rain, and heavy humidity are typical in the summer, to the delight of funguses that attack watermelons and heirloom tomatoes. To grow certain crops year-round, such as mesclun, and also to get an early start on spring planting, they use 20 hoophouses. These also enable them to sow certain crops in October and have them ready when their farm stand opens in April.

The glacial soils are lovely here as well—rich, well-drained, sandy loam that is ideal for growing vegetables and grapes; the area is well known for its vineyards and a flourishing wine industry.

The staff of Sang Lee Farms is diverse in both ethnicity and talent, coming from America, Guatemala, Central America, China, Ireland, and Thailand. The farm has 25 to 30 employees who work in the field, the kitchen, the office, the farm stand, and at the farmers markets. Some are part-time, and many are old-timers who have been coming back for 25 or even 35 years.

An enormous part of Sang Lee's business is its line of Loca∗Lee prepared food products, which include delectable dressings, dips, jellies, pickles, sauces, pestos, soups, salads, juices, roasted vegetables, and baked goods. For customers who want fresh vegetables but don't have the time to prep them, Fresh-Lee-Cut products fit the bill nicely, with all sorts of Asian vegetables, baby greens, and herbs that are already washed, cut, and ready to eat.

Karen says that the inspiration for this came from the farm stand, when customers shopping for vegetables repeatedly asked her what dressings, dips, and sauces she would recommend to serve with them. Karen immediately recognized this need for great pairings that would inspire her customers to make the most of their veggies.

One of the farm's many Loca∗Lee prepared foods, Ginger-Scallion Dip.

The sheer array of Loca*Lee and Fresh-Lee-Cut products is astounding, especially when you consider the mind-boggling amount of work it takes to have a fully state-certified organic kitchen and to meet NOFA standards. "It is essential that we have a fully traceable product," says Karen. "There is no specific required way to do it, but you have to keep really careful records and extensive logbooks that document every ingredient, and every lot and batch. And I want to keep our quality very high, so we make everything by hand in small batches."

Labeling must be absolutely accurate, and it can be a tricky thing. A product that says "organic" must be made with no less than 95 to 100 percent certified-organic ingredients. If the label says "Made with organic," that proportion drops to 75 to 90 percent. The sourcing of certain items such as oils and vinegars can be problematic, and forecasting what will be needed in the most cost-effective quantities (drums versus jars) can be difficult, especially when they are already in scarce supply. "Organic rice wine vinegar has to be made especially for us," Karen says, "or we need to put in our order when a larger quantity is already being made for someone else."

Rules and regulations being what they are, it means that Karen is required to document cleanliness, to submit a profile for each product that outlines accurate ingredient and nutritional percentages, and properly record every supplier for every ingredient and their certification in turn. She also has to train all of her food-prep staff in many of these procedures and record-keeping. Annually their kitchen and records are checked in what is essentially a yearlong process to get through all of their products over the course of a year. Fortunately, Karen gives NOFA credit for being extremely supportive and fostering excellent communication, which helps immensely. "They take the time to get it right and help us through things—after all, they don't want to see us fail."

And she has found that all the extra work has been worth it. "People really love our prepared products, and they get really excited about them. Our customers know that I am very particular about the quality of my foods, and they appreciate that."

"People really love our prepared products, and they get really excited about them. Our customers know that I am very particular about the quality of my foods, and they appreciate that."

— *Karen Lee*

Kale growing strong and beautiful.

To offer their subscribers more options, Sang Lee has a tiered system for its CSA program. For a base price, you start by becoming a Vegetable Share member; then you can join their other CSA programs, for which Sang Lee teams up with other area farmers. You can enjoy 18 weeks of cow, goat, and sheep's milk cheeses from the East End of Long Island and Hudson Valley. Or you can add a fruit share, which may include rhubarb, berries, peaches, plums, apples, and pears from local fruit growers. And you can try Sang Lee's Value-Added Share, which, on top of the regular vegetable allotment, adds its own prepared foods, dressings, and sauces.

You can also get Home Delivery Boxes that consist solely of prepared foods, or a Roasting Box that contains one pound each of five different vegetables, cut up and prepared for cooking, along with toppings and recipes. Sang Lee also offers a Soup-Salad-Side Box with toppings and recipes. A link to a fun YouTube video created in the farm's kitchen is sent to customers to view each week with tips and suggestions on using their box selections.

Besides having its own farm stand, Sang Lee participates at four different New York farmers markets, where it sells produce, prepared foods, and nursery plants and seedlings. CSA members can also pick up their shares here. The farm has slowly been growing its nursery business, offering its own potted organic herbs, vegetable starters, an exotic selection of perennials and annuals from local greenhouses, pots, soils, tools, and other gardening supplies. It has also been offering gardening classes in organically growing your own herbs and vegetables.

As you might imagine, the transition from wholesaling to retailing has meant that the farm has stepped up its outreach efforts in recent years. For youth aged 4 to 12, the farm offers camps that gets children involved in learning where their food comes from and actively growing, exploring, harvesting, and tending to their vegetables. Cooking classes are another natural outlet for the farm, giving visitors ideas on how to improvise in the kitchen with what they might find in their CSA boxes that week, or how to preserve and can that fresh-veggie goodness in July and August.

During the summer, the farm offers tours every week to the public, kids on school field trips, scout troops, summer camp participants, and others. Open houses are held regularly as well.

Philanthropy is another issue near and dear to Fred and Karen. As a producer of perishable items, they are constantly thinking of ways to avoid wasting food, knowing that countless people need fresh food. Every week, they provide Island Harvest, a local food bank, with at least 10 to 20 crates of vegetables that will not last into the next week. In 2014, they did a campaign called Donate to Dig, where people donated money to the farm to fund the labor for digging potatoes (or came and helped dig themselves) that were then donated to Island Harvest right before Thanksgiving so that families could stock up for the holiday. Thanks to this effort, they were able to donate 1,500 pounds of potatoes!

Sang Lee also donates CSA shares that have not been picked up for the week to several nonprofits and food banks that distribute to local families in need. And every week it donates vegetables to Maureen's Haven, a local service that cooks dinner for the homeless, and to a local church that offers community suppers.

This may all sound quite exhausting to keep up with, but Karen is encouraged by the tremendous demand she sees from their customers and the public for their outreach, plant sales, and cooking classes. She has noticed a renewed interest in home gardening, and she works on plant selection with her greenhouse staff, who are particularly attuned to what people want to buy. Asian vegetables such as white and baby eggplants are fast rising on people's radar, as are seedless cucumbers and certain heirloom and cherry tomato varieties.

Karen sees her work now as much more than a farmer, grower, and purveyor; she understands keenly the need to support customers and educate them on their perceptions and expectations. "Seeing the links between farming, where their food comes from, how to grow it, and cook and eat it—that completes their circle of understanding. If you have people out in the field who can see their food from plant to plate, it gets them thinking in that framework." Karen and her farm educator Lucy Senesac find that when it comes to recipes and tastings, "people are often very challenged as to what to do with their produce, to get new ideas. So we have recipes right there available at our pickup sites. And we introduce them to different ways of eating things—people are sometimes afraid to eat raw kohlrabi or cabbage. It never occurred to them to try these vegetables this way before."

What's the hardest part of farming? "After 35 years," Karen says, "it has never gotten easier because the weather, the staff, the growing conditions, the marketing requirements—all of these are continually changing. It's a different story each year, a different combination of conditions every year. The challenge is, how do we manage it for that year? We've become used to working with this continual state of change and have learned to stay calm in the face of it. It requires a great deal of stamina, and we do worry about sustaining that energy."

Out of their three children, their son William has the most interest in continuing the family business and has been helping to manage parts of it. Still, Karen worries about the sustainability of the small family farm. "There's just not a lot of financial return for all of the effort that it requires."

Still, in spite of all the decades of hard work and challenges, she and Fred have no regrets. "We feel very blessed to have had deep insight into growing food and what it takes, and we've been very lucky to have had the energy and health to live this lifestyle," Karen says. "It's very satisfying."

"Growing organically felt like the right thing to do, both for personal and business reasons. We wanted to do it for our own family and for all of the families eating our food."

— *Karen Lee*

Artichokes

CYNARA SCOLYMUS

Spaniards, Italians, Moroccans, and Middle Easterners must often be bewildered (and disappointed) by the barrenness of artichoke choices in a typical American grocery store, which usually features exactly one type—the ubiquitous, enormous Green Globe. In other cultures, especially those of the Mediterranean, artichokes come in all sorts of delightful sizes and colors; some are so small and tender that they can be eaten raw. The other way that Americans know artichokes are as hearts, either canned or in jars, usually relegated as fancy appetizers tinged with a faint air of aristocracy. It's a shame, because artichokes can be so much more.

When we dine on artichokes, we are actually eating the flower buds of a very large thistle. Although thistles in themselves are edible, it's understandable that few people desire them outside of artichokes and their close sibling, the cardoon, which is treasured for its huge, celery-like stalks. Not many items are more delightful (and seasonal) than artichokes, which are at their best between March and May. California grows virtually 100 percent of the US artichoke crop in a narrow area around Monterey and Castroville, whose coastal fog, cool summers, and mild winters provide ideal growing conditions. Castroville, in fact, proclaims itself the Artichoke Center of the World.

Occasionally specialty and farmers markets carry so-called baby artichokes, which are often about the size of a small egg and may be dark purple or wine-red in color. These are not actually babies but entirely different varieties from Italy and France, or just younger, smaller specimens of the Green Globe variety.

Artichokes sometimes get a bad rap because they contain cynarin, which is not in itself sweet but acts chemically on our tongues to temporarily make certain foods taste sweeter. Wine pairings can be particularly problematic, but a knowledgeable cook or sommelier can actually work this to their advantage by serving dry champagne or Italian Barbera. Also, artichokes go well with foods that benefit from a touch of sweetness, like spicy curries or bitter greens.

HISTORY

The exact origins of artichokes are hazy at best, according to food historian Waverly Root, but it is likely that the plant came from the Mediterranean, possibly Sicily or North Africa. It is perhaps one of the oldest cultivated food plants, noted as far back as 500 BCE. European aristocracy ate it for centuries, but after the fall of Rome the plant was largely forgotten until Catherine de Medici, the Italian wife of King Henry II, reintroduced the artichoke to France in the mid-16th century. Her gluttonous, public love for artichokes was scandalous, as women at that time were not allowed to eat foods considered to be aphrodisiacs. But happily artichokes soon returned as a popular vegetable for both sexes. In the 1920s, Italian immigrants started growing artichokes in the northern California town of Half Moon Bay, near Castroville. Soon they were supplying a curious American public with exotic thistle buds, thus giving birth to the massive California artichoke industry.

NUTRITION

Artichokes are low in calories (a medium one has about 128) and are an excellent source of dietary fiber (no surprise to anyone who has ever plucked stray strands caught between the teeth). They also contain significant amounts of folate, vitamins C and K, and various antioxidants. Artichokes are also rich in minerals: copper, calcium, potassium, iron, manganese, and phosphorus.

SEASON

Green Globe artichokes grown in California have two seasons. The biggest is from March to May; another smaller crop is harvested from October to January.

SELECTION

Regardless of their variety, artichokes should be heavy for their size with tightly packed centers and firm stems. A sign of freshness is a distinctive squeak when squeezed; flabby ones are much quieter. Watch for signs of dehydration in the stems and pointy edges on the bracts (petals). Purple, brown, or even blistered areas on the big Green Globe variety indicate the artichoke was exposed to colder temperatures ("winter kissed"); these tend to be sweeter and tastier, so don't consider them a sign of bad quality.

STORAGE

On the outside, artichokes seem to be pretty hardy vegetables and can appear capable of being kept for weeks. However, they lose flavor as time goes on and should be used as soon as possible after purchase. To store them, slice off the ends of their stems and wrap them unwashed in a damp paper towel inside a plastic bag in the refrigerator vegetable crisper.

TRIMMING AND CLEANING

Artichokes do require careful trimming to make the most of their delectable attributes, much more so than most vegetables. As Elizabeth Schneider says in her book *Vegetables from Amaranth to Zucchini*, don't be afraid of being ruthless in the trimming process—the goal is for the vegetable to cook evenly and be tender throughout, not necessarily to maximize quantity. But don't let the preparation discourage you; the end result will be well worth it.

First, clean the artichokes by rinsing them thoroughly in lukewarm water or submerging them in a full sink while prying open the petals.

Decide first how much stem to remove. Because the stem is an extension of the choicest part (the bottom section, where the inner heart and fuzzy "choke" are located—see the illustration on the next page), you may not want to trim it excessively. But because the stem's core can taste bitter, sample it first. If you are serving artichokes whole for stuffing purposes, trim their stems as closely as possible to their bases so that the artichokes sit flat on the plate.

The next step will depend on whether you are serving them whole or using just the bottoms.

If you're serving them whole, snap off the first two or three layers of the outer bracts. Then slice off the top quarter or third of the artichoke. Finally, using kitchen scissors, trim off the tiny sharp tip of each exposed bract.

see the illustration on the next page

Spring Crops Featured

Artichokes
Arugula
Asparagus
Basil
Beans (Fava)
Chives
Green Garlic
Lettuce
Mushrooms
Peas
Rhubarb
Salad and Braising Mixes
Spinach
Strawberries
Swiss Chard

Books

Artichokes: Articles and Recipes
from The New York Times
Kindle Edition,
The New York Times Company, 2012.

Vegetable Literacy:
Cooking and Gardening with
Twelve Families from the Edible
Plant Kingdom, with over
300 Deliciously Simple Recipes
Deborah Madison,
Ten Speed Press, 2013.

The Country Cooking of Greece
Diane Kochilas,
Chronicle Books, 2012.

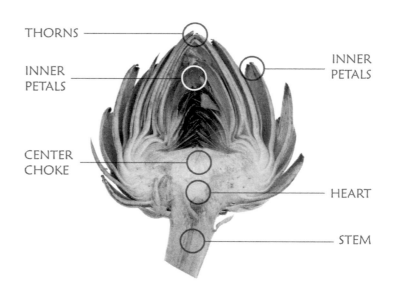

THORNS

INNER PETALS

INNER PETALS

CENTER CHOKE

HEART

STEM

If you want to extract the hearts, snap off the bracts until only the yellow-green core remains. Slice off the top third of the artichoke. Now you can pare the stem or snap it off and trim the base. Scrape off the choke, which is the layer of fuzzy fibers. What remains is the tender, pale-yellow heart.

If you want just the bottoms, follow the same trimming procedures as for the hearts, but slice off the entire cone and break off the stems, leaving just the rounded artichoke bottom. Scrape out the fuzzy choke with a melon ball cutter or grapefruit spoon. You can leave the bottoms whole or cut up as needed.

Dealing with the chokes: The actual choke part is the fine layer of velvety fuzz that sits atop the heart, exposed when all of the inner bracts are removed or pulled back. In larger artichokes, these chokes are divine to stroke with a finger (it feels like the softest fur), but it's most unpleasant if stray fuzzies get caught in the back of your throat, where they incessantly tickle and indeed make you feel like you're choking. During the trimming process, remove them by scraping them out thoroughly with a melon ball cutter or a grapefruit spoon. In smaller or baby artichokes, the chokes are fine to eat.

Cut artichokes dramatically discolor when exposed to air and other environmental conditions; see the Cooking Tips on page 13 for how to prevent this.

STEAMING AND BOILING

Steam whole trimmed artichokes by setting them stem-end up on a steamer rack over boiling water for 30 to 45 minutes, depending on their size. To add subtle flavor, you can season the water with lemongrass, ginger, garlic, and herbs.

Alternatively, boil whole trimmed artichokes in salted water to which about 2 tablespoons of lemon juice have been added for every quart of water. Bring to a boil, then reduce heat and simmer for 25 to 40 minutes, depending on the size (you can test by piercing the stem or base with a knife or toothpick; if it enters easily, they are likely done). Invert to drain, then serve promptly.

STIR-FRYING AND SAUTÉING

Unless they are very small baby specimens, artichokes generally must be precooked or blanched before being thrown into the sauté pan or wok. Once they have been precooked, they can be stir-fried or sautéed for an additional 5 to 10 minutes, depending on their size.

BAKING AND ROASTING

Roasting is a great way to prepare artichokes, a delicious alternative to the usual boiling or steaming because the roasting process concentrates the flavors of the artichoke flesh. Trim whole artichokes as instructed above, then cut them in half lengthwise. (Don't worry about removing the fuzzy chokes at this point—they are far easier to scoop out after the artichokes are cooked.) Fit them together as closely as possible in the pan (six Green Globe halves will fit in a 9-by-13-inch pan). Pour in 1 to 2 tablespoons of oil per artichoke as well as finely chopped herbs if desired, roll the artichokes in the oil, and place them cut-side down. Bake in a 375°F oven until the artichoke bottoms are tender when pierced with a knife, 40 to 50 minutes.

MICROWAVING

I find microwaving artichokes to be the fastest and easiest way to cook them. If you're preparing a single artichoke, place it in a glass bowl with ¼ cup water, ½ teaspoon salt, and ½ teaspoon olive oil. Cover the bowl with plastic wrap, and cook on high power for 6 to 7 minutes, or until the bottom of the artichoke can be easily pierced with a knife. I also get good results by just wrapping the entire artichoke in plastic wrap and microwaving without the dish. If you're preparing two artichokes, cook on high power for 7 to 10 minutes. In either case, let them stand for about 5 minutes after cooking.

BLANCHING AND FREEZING

Artichokes must be blanched or precooked before freezing; they should not be frozen raw, or they will turn brown and their taste will deteriorate considerably. There are several methods for doing this; the California Artichoke Advisory Board website (www.artichokes.org) has complete instructions, but here is one method: Trim the tops from the artichokes and rub the cut surfaces with lemon. Cook the artichokes in water to which a little lemon juice has been added; simmer only until al dente (about 20 minutes). Remove, turn upside down, and drain thoroughly. Then place the whole artichokes upside down on a tray and freeze them quickly in the coldest part of the freezer. Package the artichokes in zipper-lock freezer or vacuum food sealer-type bags, or freezer containers. Frozen artichokes will keep for up to 6 months at 0°F.

To thaw and finish cooking, wrap each frozen artichoke in aluminum foil, sealing tightly. Place them on a rack above boiling water. Cover and steam them until they are hot and cooked through.

EQUIVALENTS, MEASURES, AND SERVINGS

- One 9-ounce box frozen = one 8-ounce jar = one 14-ounce can = hearts from 6 fresh artichokes

Cooking Tips

Use stainless steel knives to trim artichokes, as carbon steel blades will darken them. The same is true for aluminum and cast-iron cookware.

To reduce discoloration, keep your artichokes in water acidified with lemon juice as you work with them.

If your artichokes turn a startling turquoise, it is because your water is unusually alkaline (hard). But the artichokes are perfectly safe to eat, in spite of what your family and guests might think!

HOW TO EAT AN ARTICHOKE

Most fruits and vegetables are pretty straightforward as to how to eat them. Artichokes, however, can be a bit intimidating for a first-timer. Serve larger artichokes whole, either hot or cold. To eat, pull off the outer petals one at a time, and dip the base of the petal into sauce or melted butter. Pull the petal between your teeth to remove the soft, pulpy portion at the base. Discard the remainder of the petal, and continue until all the petals have been removed. Now you're left with the best part—the succulent inner heart. With a spoon, scoop out the fuzzy choke and discard. The remainder of the artichoke is completely edible, and can be cut into pieces and dipped into sauce.

Baby artichokes are completely edible—no need to scoop out the fuzzy chokes inside.

COMPLEMENTARY HERBS, SEASONINGS, AND FOODS

Anchovies, arugula, asparagus, bay, beef, black pepper, butter, capers, cheese (goat, Parmesan, ricotta), chervil, cilantro, eggs, endive, fennel, hazelnut oil, honey, garlic, grapefruit, ham, Jerusalem artichokes, lamb, leeks, lemons, mayonnaise, mushrooms, olives, olive oil, onions, oranges, oregano, parsley, pasta, peas, potatoes, prosciutto, rosemary, shallots, tarragon, thyme, tuna, vinaigrette, walnuts, walnut oil.

SERVING SUGGESTIONS

- Add cooked hearts or fried whole baby artichokes to stir-fries and pasta dishes.

- Fry up whole baby artichokes until tender on the inside and crispy on the outside.

- Artichokes can be fun for kids because they are the ultimate finger food! Individual leaves are great for dipping into butter and sauces.

- Although a bit labor-intensive, stuffed artichokes make a stunning dish for fancy occasions and can be truly delicious. Typical stuffing includes breadcrumbs, garlic, oregano, parsley, grated cheese, and prosciutto or sausage. Seasoned couscous is also a tasty vegetarian alternative. Push the mixture into the spaces at the base of each leaf and the hollowed-out center before steaming or baking.

- Who could forget artichokes and dip? Often artichokes themselves are made into dip, but the petals make perfect scoops. Creamy or mustard-based dips are quite tasty with artichokes, as is a good hollandaise sauce.

ARTICHOKES STUFFED WITH HAM AND PINE NUTS
SERVES 4

Source Note: Baked this way, artichokes turn almost silky, while the stuffing browns to a nice crust. Try experimenting with this stuffing; chopped green olives are good, too.

2 tablespoons pine nuts
½ lemon
6 medium artichokes
1 garlic clove

¼ baguette, crust trimmed, bread cubed (about 2 ounces)
2 ounces ham, cubed
3 tablespoons chopped fresh parsley
1 teaspoon grated lemon zest
½ teaspoon salt
1 cup dry white wine

1. Toast the pine nuts in a small skillet over medium heat, stirring, until they are lightly browned and fragrant, about 10 minutes. Set aside.

2. Heat the oven to 350 °F. Fill a bowl with water and squeeze the lemon juice into it. Keep the squeezed-out lemon half.

3. Pull off the lower leaves and tough outer leaves from an artichoke; this will be about the first two rings. Using kitchen shears, trim the top half of the next several rings of leaves until you get to the tight central cone, where the leaves are pale green at least two-thirds of the way up. Use a knife to cut off the dark green top third. Trim the stem of the artichoke with a paring knife, making a flat base. Rub all the cut surfaces with the lemon half.

4. Place the artichoke upside down on a work surface and press firmly. Turn the artichoke right side up and use your fingers to spread the leaves as much as possible without breaking them. Use a grapefruit spoon or other small spoon to remove the innermost purple-tipped leaves and then scrape the fuzzy choke from the base.

5. Place the cleaned artichoke in the bowl of lemon water and repeat with the remaining artichokes.

6. When all of the artichokes have been cleaned, mince the garlic by dropping it down the feed tube of a food processor while it's running. Stop the machine and add the bread cubes. Pulse 2 or 3 times to break them down. Add the ham and parsley, and pulse until the bread and ham are in large crumbs, 4 or 5 times. Remove the blade and stir in the pine nuts, lemon zest, and salt.

7. Drain the artichokes and arrange them in a baking dish just large enough to hold them in a single layer. Fill the central cavity of each artichoke with some of the stuffing mixture, mounding it over the top and working a bit of it between the leaves.

8. Pour the white wine into the bottom of the baking dish and add just enough water to come to a depth of about ¾ inch. Cover the dish with aluminum foil and bake until the artichokes are tender enough that you can easily pull out one of the interior leaves (a knife will pierce the base easily as well), about 40 minutes.

9. Remove the artichokes from the baking dish and carefully pour the leftover liquid into a small saucepan. Bring it to a boil over high heat and reduce to a thin syrup. Pour the syrup over the cooked artichokes and set aside to cool to room temperature before serving.

— *Russ Parsons,* How to Pick a Peach

Where Did CSAs Come From?

Mi Ae Lipe

Although CSAs practice business in ways that feel old and traditional, their origin is surprisingly modern.

*Various community-supported agriculture models arose concurrently in Japan and Europe in the 1960s in response to rising concerns about food safety and quality. In the mid-1980s, Jan Vander Tuin from Switzerland and Trauger Groh from Germany brought biodynamic farming concepts to Massachusetts (**Indian Line Farm**) and New Hampshire (**Temple-Wilton Community Farm**), respectively.*

Biodynamic farming is an agricultural method that views soil quality, livestock, and plant growth as an integrated whole rather than as separate aspects of agriculture (see the sidebar on biodynamic farming on page 427 for more information). Variations on these biodynamic methods gave rise to such concepts as sustainable agriculture, organic produce, free-range poultry, grass-fed beef, cage-free eggs, and a host of other nonfactory-farmed agricultural products.

From those initial two farms, the movement spread down the East Coast and took off in the West, Midwest, and Canada. As the CSA movement grew, so did the variations on the economic model. Although no one knows for sure the precise number of CSAs in North America, current estimates are around 6,500 and growing. They can be supplied by a single farm or by a cooperative of several farms. As their numbers grow, so do their variations on the basic model and the foods they supply. They can be urban, rural, seasonal, or year-round.

But what all of them have in common is a commitment to bringing fresh, healthful food to their communities while connecting modern consumers with the land in ways that aren't possible for most people.

12 Reasons to Be a CSAer
Mi Ae Lipe

1. **Your food is fresher** (and thus better quality), usually because it has been picked within the past 24 hours.

2. **Your organically grown fruits and vegetables are more nutritious,** containing more antioxidants, vitamins, and minerals than produce grown on a large scale with chemicals.

3. **It makes economic sense.** Your money goes directly to the farmer (and thus the local economy), and not to distributors and shipping companies. Also, the elimination of paying these middlemen means that the farmer is able to sell below retail cost.

4. **Organic farming benefits the environment,** because the huge quantities of carcinogenic pesticides and corrosive fertilizers used in commercial, large-scale farms are not used. Also, eating local eliminates the need for so much petroleum-based fuel to be consumed in the course of shipping and distributing.

5. **Because organic farmers grow more plant varieties** than do large-scale commercial farms, consumers are exposed to fruits and vegetables that they might not otherwise discover (such as heirloom tomatoes).

6. **You protect your health as well as that of your family** by limiting your exposure to cancer-causing pesticides. Also, certain types of outbreaks, such as those caused by E. coli, are far less likely to occur because of the different growing setups of organic farming.

7. **Having a CSA share saves time,** with convenient pickup sites and prepacked boxes—

ROASTED ARTICHOKES FOR TWO   SERVES 2

Source Note: Artichokes are often steamed, but we find that roasting is the best approach for accentuating their nutty flavor. To ensure artichokes that are fully tender and nicely browned, we trim them one by one, dropping them in lemon water to prevent them from oxidizing. Next, we toss the artichokes with seasoned oil, making sure to get oil between their leaves. Finally, we roast them in a 475°F oven in a baking dish tightly crimped with foil until the leaves, heart, and stem are tender. To accentuate the rich, nutty flavor of the vegetable, we serve them with a tangy lemon vinaigrette or a garlicky butter sauce.

If your artichokes are larger than 8 to 10 ounces, strip away another layer or two of the toughest outer leaves.

> 1 lemon, plus extra lemon wedges for serving
> 2 artichokes (8 to 10 ounces each)
> 2 tablespoons extra-virgin olive oil
> Salt and freshly ground black pepper

1. Adjust the oven rack to the lower-middle position and heat the oven to 475°F. Cut one lemon in half, squeeze the halves into 1 quart water, and drop in the spent halves.

2. Cut off most of the stem of one artichoke, leaving about ¾ inch attached. Cut off the top quarter. Pull the tough outer leaves downward toward the stem and break off at the base; continue until the first three or four rows of leaves have been removed. Using a paring knife, trim the outer layer of the stem and the rough areas around the base, removing any dark green parts. Cut the artichoke in half lengthwise. Using a spoon, remove the fuzzy choke. Pull out the inner, tiny purple-tinged leaves, leaving a small cavity in the center of each half. Drop the prepped halves into the lemon water. Repeat with the remaining artichoke.

3. Brush an 8-inch square baking dish with 1 tablespoon oil. Remove the artichokes from the lemon water, shaking off the excess lemon water (some should be left clinging to the leaves). Toss the artichokes with the remaining 1 tablespoon oil; season with salt (about ½ teaspoon) and pepper to taste, gently working some oil and seasonings between the leaves. Arrange the artichoke halves cut-side down in the baking dish and cover tightly with aluminum foil.

4. Roast until the cut sides of the artichokes start to brown and both the base and leaves are tender when poked with the tip of a paring knife, 22 to 27 minutes. Transfer the artichokes to a serving dish. Serve the artichokes warm or at room temperature, passing the lemon wedges separately.

— Cooks Illustrated

PORK AND BABY ARTICHOKE SAUTÉ WITH APPLE BRANDY

SERVES 4

1 large lemon
1½ pounds (16 to 20) baby artichokes
4 ounces (one stick) butter
1 pound pork loin, cut into ½-inch slices (called scallops)
1 large, firm apple, peel on, cut into medium dice
3 green onions, thinly sliced
1 large clove garlic, minced
1 tablespoon chopped fresh sage leaves
¼ cup apple brandy, preferably Calvados
½ cup chicken stock
Salt
Sage sprigs, for garnish

1. Squeeze the lemon and add the juice to a large bowl of cold water. Drop in the lemon halves.

2. Wash the artichokes. Remove the outer leaves until pale green leaves appear; trim off the stems and top quarter of each artichoke. Cut the artichokes lengthwise into halves and drop into the lemon water to preserve the color. Set aside.

3. Heat a large sauté pan over medium heat and add half of the butter. Sauté the pork scallops until lightly browned; remove from the pan and keep warm.

4. Add the remaining butter to the pan (the butter is not just used for sautéing—it will eventually become part of the sauce). Place the artichoke halves, cut-side down, in the pan and sauté for 5 minutes.

5. Add the apples and cook until just tender. Add the onions, garlic, chopped sage, and Calvados; toss together 1 minute.

6. Add the chicken stock and cook until the artichokes are tender and the stock has mostly evaporated. Season to taste with salt.

7. Arrange the pork scallops on heated serving plates with the baby artichoke mixture and a little sauce. Garnish with sage sprigs.

— *California Artichoke Advisory Board*

LEMON ARTICHOKE SOUP

SERVES 4

4 medium to large artichokes with stems, cooked
¼ cup long-grain white rice
5½ cups chicken or vegetable broth
3 eggs

---

no more constant running to the grocery store and trying to decide what to bring home for dinner.

8. **Visiting a real working farm is fun and educational** for children and adults alike. Most CSA farms have open houses, socials, festivals, harvest suppers, and other events when you and your family can visit and actually see how your food is grown and processed.

9. **Having a CSA share cements the farmer-to-consumer connection.** Urban CSAers especially can forge closer relationships with the rural farm, seeing the origins of their food and sharing in the process.

10. **Organic fruits, vegetables, and herbs simply taste better!** That is why discriminating chefs prefer organic foods for their recipes. In turn, the richer flavor of organic produce helps encourage you to eat your veggies. And that is always a good thing!

11. **You get to try the new and unexpected.** Chances are good that in the course of your CSA subscription, you'll receive at least one vegetable or fruit that you might not ever have purchased in the grocery store or market, or even known existed. CSAs are great opportunities to break out of eating "ruts" and old habits.

12. **You get an opportunity to volunteer for the greater good.** Although many CSAs do not require it, some farms ask that you volunteer time in the form of a work shift or at events. It helps to keep costs lower and more evenly distributes the immense workload. Actively participating in your CSA further cements your connection to your food and your community.

2 to 3 tablespoons fresh lemon juice
Salt and freshly ground black pepper

1. Remove the petals and fuzzy centers from the cooked artichokes; cut the bottoms into ¼-inch cubes.

2. In a saucepan, simmer the rice in the broth for about 20 minutes, or until tender.

3. When the rice is done, add the cubed artichokes to the broth.

4. Whisk together the eggs and lemon juice.

5. Take out about 1½ cups of the hot broth and drizzle it into the egg mixture, whisking constantly. This tempers the eggs so they won't curdle. Pour this mixture back into the saucepan, still whisking.

6. Cook over low heat, stirring constantly, until the soup thickens slightly. Do not boil once the eggs have been added, or the soup will separate.

7. Season with salt, pepper, and more lemon juice if desired.

— *California Artichoke Advisory Board*

Arugula

ERUCA SATIVA

When I wrote the first edition of this cookbook in 2008, arugula was a relative newcomer to the American gastronomic scene, in spite of having been a staple in Mediterranean and Middle Eastern cuisines for centuries. Since then, it has passed through the stages of being a darling of the foodie crowd to now often being a routine, blasé addition to restaurant salads and other dishes. Although it resembles green oakleaf lettuce, this peppery green is a member of the large cress family, which also includes mustard and radish. Arugula is also known as garden rocket, rocket, rocket salad, rugola, rucola, or roquette.

In spite of its current ubiquity in the United States, arugula is deservedly popular. Its pretty leaves and pleasing bite make it an interesting addition to salads of mixed greens, and it is a natural with creamy goat cheeses and balsamic vinegar. The pepperiness of arugula varies tremendously, depending on the type and locale; in southern Italy, I ate salads made with a pungent wild species that often cleared my sinuses.

HISTORY

Arugula has been a favorite since Roman times in Mediterranean countries, where both the leaves and seeds are used in salads and in cooking. It was even favored as an aphrodisiac, dating back to the first century CE. References to arugula as food and medicine appear in many Holy Land texts, including the Talmud.

NUTRITION

Arugula is high in vitamins A and C, iron, and calcium. A half-cup serving contains only 2 calories.

SEASON

Commercially, arugula is commonly available year-round. It is a cool-growing crop, and in farmers markets and CSA farms, it peaks in spring and early summer. Hot weather usually means a more peppery, strongly flavored arugula.

SELECTION

Arugula should look fresh, with no wilted or limp leaves or stems. Avoid discolored, yellowed, or waterlogged specimens, which indicate advanced age or improper storage.

STORAGE

Store unwashed, fresh arugula wrapped in damp toweling in a plastic bag in the refrigerator vegetable crisper. Arugula does not keep well; use it within 2 to 3 days. Avoid storing arugula and other leafy greens next to apples or other sources of ethylene gas, which can hasten yellowing and decay.

The Value of Fresh Fruits and Vegetables

Mi Ae Lipe

How many of us haven't heard our parents say that we have to eat our fruits and vegetables because they are "good for us"? (And how many of us recall that this argument didn't make them taste better?)

Today, modern research continues to find that the nutritional benefits of fresh produce are even greater than previously thought. Scientists have discovered that many fruits and vegetables are exceptionally rich sources of antioxidants, chemical molecules that help prevent or retard cell deterioration by inhibiting degenerative oxidation processes that contribute to stroke, cancer, and heart disease.

Beta-carotenoids, isoflavones, lutein, zeaxanthin, sulfur compounds, and folic acid are all antioxidants that have been well-publicized in recent years, and the ingestion of specific antioxidants has been linked to the lowered incidence of certain cancers.

If prepared properly, fruits and vegetables provide many essential vitamins and minerals while remaining low in calories and fat, unlike many processed snack foods.

Consuming plenty of fruits and vegetables also ensures that you receive abundant dietary fiber, which helps guard against colon cancer and other maladies. Fiber also makes you feel fuller, which in turn means that you consume fewer calories.

Typical American diets consistently lack sufficient fiber, vitamins, and minerals such as iron and calcium, to the point that many of us are slightly malnourished. The price to pay for these long-term deficiencies—in dealing with chronic illness, medical bills, and decreased quality of life, even the shortening of life span—is difficult to swallow indeed, far more so than a nice, juicy apple.

TRIMMING AND CLEANING

Like spinach and leeks, arugula often harbors sand and other unpleasant grit. Unless you enjoy a little crunch with your greens, wash the leaves by submerging in a sinkful of water and swishing about thoroughly. Repeat as necessary, and then rinse under running water, and pat or spin dry.

STEAMING AND BOILING

Arugula responds well to a gentle, brief steaming. Wash the arugula well but do not dry. Place in a steamer basket, cover, and steam in its own moisture for 2 to 3 minutes. Boiling is not recommended for this delicate green, for overcooking will destroy its peppery, characteristic flavor and render it a watery mess.

STIR-FRYING AND SAUTÉING

Add arugula leaves near the end of cooking times of stir-fries and sautés, and cook until just wilted, usually about 1 or 2 minutes. Be careful not to overcook, or arugula's delicate flavor will dissipate.

MICROWAVING

Wash arugula but do not dry. Place in a microwave-safe dish and cook on high power for 2 to 4 minutes, or until the greens are tender.

BLANCHING AND FREEZING

Freezing arugula is not recommended because of its high water content and delicate flavor. However, if you still want to try, shred it into ½-inch ribbons; sauté in olive oil, salt, and pepper; and package 1-cup portions tightly in zipper-lock freezer or vacuum food sealer-type bags, or freezer containers. Alternatively, you can freeze arugula as pesto (see the Pesto sidebar under Basil on pages 32–33).

COMPLEMENTARY HERBS, SEASONINGS, AND FOODS

Apples, avocado, bacon, basil, butter, cheese (blue, goat, mozzarella, Parmesan, ricotta), citrus, cream, dill, eggs, fennel, fish, garlic, goat cheese, ham, hazelnuts, hazelnut oil, lemon balm, lemon juice, marjoram, mushrooms, olive oil, onions, oregano, pasta, pears, pecans, pine nuts, poultry, seafood, tarragon, thyme, tomatoes, walnuts, walnut oil.

SERVING SUGGESTIONS

- Liberally sprinkle arugula in any tossed lettuce salad to add zip and interest.
- Add arugula to stir-fries near the end of the cooking time.
- Try arugula instead of lettuce in a surprise BLT; the pepperiness of arugula pairs beautifully with good-quality, thick-cut, maple-cured bacon.
- Try using arugula sprouts in salads or sandwiches instead of alfalfa sprouts.
- Combine arugula with thinly shaved Parmesan cheese, good-quality olive oil, white wine vinegar, salt, and freshly ground black pepper.
- Substitute arugula for part or all of the basil to make a zippy, unusual pesto. (Unlike basil, arugula keeps its vibrant green color!)
- Sprinkle raw leaves over pizzas after baking.
- Arugula makes a great "mixing" green; combine with different lettuces, chicory, endive, spinach, herbs, and flowers for a salad with personality.

- Arugula goes wonderfully with fennel, apples, mandarin oranges, red onions, and pomegranates. Fruity flavors help offset its assertive pungency.
- If arugula is not available, you can substitute watercress for a similar spicy flavor, or vice versa.
- Lightly sauté arugula as a green and serve with pastas, robust meats, or a good roasted chicken.

. . . .

PASTA WITH ARUGULA   SERVES 4

2½ cups chopped tomatoes
¼ cup chopped Kalamata olives
2 tablespoons olive oil
2 cloves garlic, crushed
Salt and freshly ground black pepper
8 ounces uncooked gemelli pasta
    (or use another short, chunky pasta such as penne or fusilli)
3 cups arugula, torn and trimmed
½ cup Asiago cheese, grated

1. Combine the tomatoes, olives, olive oil, garlic, salt, and pepper in a large bowl; set aside.

2. Cook and drain the pasta. Add the hot pasta and arugula to the bowl.

3. Toss everything together, sprinkle with the cheese, and serve promptly.

— *Ruth Charles, Featherstone Farm CSA member*

. . . .

ARUGULA PESTO   MAKES ABOUT 1 CUP

Source Note: *Arugula is peppery, and with raw garlic this makes a full-flavored, intense sauce that works great on noodles or to spice up a sandwich. Blanching the arugula leaves first will keep this pesto a nice green color.*

4 cups firmly packed fresh arugula leaves
1 tablespoon finely chopped garlic
Salt and freshly ground black pepper
⅔ to 1 cup olive oil
3 tablespoons pine nuts or walnuts, toasted
½ cup freshly grated Parmesan cheese

1. Plunge the arugula into boiling water and stir to blanch it evenly, about 15 seconds. Immediately remove and plunge into ice-cold water to stop the cooking process. Drain and squeeze the water out.

2. Chop the arugula and put it into a blender. Add the garlic, salt, pepper, olive oil, and 2 tablespoons of the nuts. Blend for about 30 seconds. Add the cheese and pulse to combine.

Books

Wild Arugula Recipes
Mariquita Farm,
www.mariquita.com/recipes/
arugula.html.

The Italian Vegetable Cookbook:
200 Favorite Recipes
for Antipasti, Soups, Pasta,
Main Dishes, and Desserts
Michele Scicolone and Rux Martin,
Houghton Mifflin Harcourt, 2014.

Arugula Greats:
Delicious Arugula Recipes,
Jo Franks,
Emereo Publishing, 2012.

3. Serve immediately or refrigerate until needed; it will keep for several days. Before serving, bring to room temperature. Add the remaining nuts as desired for a garnish.

— *Nash's Organic Produce, Sequim, Washington*

ARUGULA AND GRILLED GOAT CHEESE SALAD WITH WALNUT-OIL DRESSING SERVES 4

Source Note: *Goat cheese is available in many different forms. For this recipe, look for cylinder-shaped goat cheese from a delicatessen or for small rolls that can be cut into pieces, each weighing about 2 ounces.*

CROUTONS

About 1 tablespoon olive oil
About 1 tablespoon vegetable oil
4 slices Italian bread

APRICOT SAUCE

3 tablespoons apricot jam
¼ cup white wine
2 teaspoons Dijon mustard

WALNUT-OIL DRESSING

3 tablespoons walnut oil
1 tablespoon lemon juice
Salt and freshly ground black pepper

1 (8-ounce) cylinder-shape goat cheese, at room temperature
Generous handful of arugula
3 to 4 ounces (about 4 cups) frisée (curly endive)

1. To make the croutons, heat the olive and vegetable oils in a frying pan and fry the slices of Italian bread on one side only, until lightly golden brown. Transfer to a plate lined with paper towels.

2. To make the sauce, heat the jam in a small saucepan until warm but not boiling. Push it through a strainer into a clean pan to remove the pieces of fruit, and then stir in the white wine and mustard. Heat gently and then keep warm until ready to serve.

3. Blend the walnut oil and lemon juice and season with a little salt and pepper.

4. Preheat the broiler a few minutes before serving the salad. Cut the goat cheese into 2-ounce rounds; place each piece on a crouton, untoasted side up, and spread the cheese to mostly cover the bread. Place under the broiler and cook for 3 to 4 minutes until the cheese melts.

5. Toss the arugula and frisée in the walnut-oil dressing and arrange attractively on four individual serving plates. When the croutons are ready, arrange on each plate and drizzle them with a little of the apricot sauce.

— *Christine Ingram,* The Cook's Encyclopedia of Vegetables

Arugula flourishing in the greenhouse at Teena's Pride CSA.

4. ***You can't eat everything in your box before it spoils.*** *This is probably the biggest reason why CSA subscriptions don't work out. Getting through everything before it rots can be daunting and discouraging. This book contains plenty of storage and cooking tips, as well as recipes to help you tackle this abundance, but it can still be a challenge. Some CSAs offer half or solo shares for smaller households. Or you might consider splitting a full share (and its costs) with another family. This could be a problem when deciding how to equitably split the choicest bits (such as strawberries).*

5. ***You do not have time to volunteer on the farm.*** *Although many CSAs do not require it, some ask that you volunteer time in the form of a work shift or at events. It helps keep costs lower and more evenly distributes the immense workload. But not everyone has time to get involved at this level.*

6. ***You want everything available all of the time.*** *CSAs grow and harvest what is seasonal in their local areas. If you demand eggplants in winter and you live in Maine, this could be an issue.*

7. ***You cannot afford the upfront subscription cost.*** *Different CSAs have different payment options, but many ask for the entire season's subscription costs up front in one lump sum—typically $600 to $900. Although produce through a CSA is usually no more expensive than through a grocery store, many families cannot afford the cost or can't pay the total all at once. Ask your farmers if they can work with you on this—some can.*

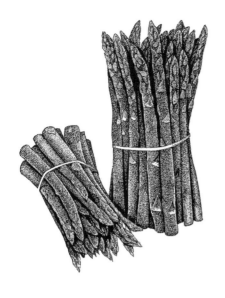

Asparagus

ASPARAGUS OFFICINALIS

Few vegetables represent spring as definitively as asparagus, with its tender shoots poking out of the moist, dark earth to meet the warm sun and lengthening days. This perennial garden favorite is a member of the lily family, one that is harvested in an all-too-brief season. Most commonly cultivated is the familiar green asparagus, but in Europe white asparagus (created by piling soil high around the emerging shoots) is a highly prized delicacy.

In some farmers markets, asparagus comes in tubs or bins where shoppers can select their own spears, stalk by stalk. People tend to have their own strong preferences about how thick the thickness of the perfect asparagus should be; it doesn't really matter, and they are all good, as long as the stalks aren't too old or woody. In some places, especially along irrigation ditches, wild asparagus still grows (or escapees of regular garden asparagus). Provided that they are not near harmful or contaminated runoff areas, don't pass these up should you spot them—they can be quite the taste treat.

HISTORY

Humans have eaten asparagus since ancient times, cultivating it 2,000 years ago in the Mediterranean and Asia Minor. The ancient Greeks and Romans were particularly fond of it; the latter even froze it! Asparagus was eaten fresh in season and dried for consumption in other times of the year. Asparagus was prized not only as a food plant but also as medicine, used to treat an array of symptoms from heart trouble to toothaches.

NUTRITION

Asparagus is high in vitamins A, B-complex (especially folic acid), and C, as well as potassium and zinc. Like most veggies, asparagus has no fat; four spears contain only 15 calories.

SEASON

Asparagus is a quintessentially spring crop, although it is grown year-round in California. It is at its best in farmers markets and CSA farms from late February to June, peaking in April.

SELECTION

Good asparagus should feel firm, not limp or shriveled (especially its tips), with an attractive green color (except for white asparagus, which is deliberately kept pale yellow to keep the stalks tender). Stalks that are large at the base may be tough or woody; such specimens should be trimmed or peeled before cooking. Thinner-stalked asparagus spears may be more tender and sweeter than larger ones; you may want to peel them as well, just to avoid the annoyance of potential long fibers.

STORAGE

Wrap unwashed, dry asparagus in a plastic bag and place it in the refrigerator vegetable crisper. Use as soon as possible, within 1 or 2 days;

the plant's sugars turn to starches very quickly. If you have to store the asparagus for more than a day, either wrap the ends in a damp paper towel or bundle the spears with a rubber band and stand them upright in a container in an inch of water.

TRIMMING AND CLEANING

Wash and thoroughly drain the spears in cool running water. (Watch out for grit trapped under the scales.) The tougher bottom ends can be either snapped or sliced off. If your asparagus spears are thicker and older, you may need to peel them first. Thin or very fresh stalks do not need peeling.

STEAMING AND BOILING

A perennial dilemma with asparagus is that the thicker bottom ends take longer to cook while the tender tips become mushy. Steaming asparagus upright in a deep steamer, double boiler, or percolator solves this problem, but then the spears lose their bright green color. Boiling asparagus uncovered in lots of salted water keeps it nice and green, but you will have to monitor for that exact moment when the spears go from being deliciously crisp-tender to mushy. Boil rapidly for 4 to 5 minutes, testing by piercing them with a fork; when they are tender, drain and plunge them immediately into cold water to stop them from cooking further.

STIR-FRYING AND SAUTÉING

Cut the spears diagonally into ½-inch pieces, leaving the tips whole. Stir-fry the pieces in butter or hot oil in a skillet or wok at medium-high heat. Stir constantly until tender-crisp, 3 to 5 minutes. For perfectly cooked asparagus, you may want to toss in the thicker stem pieces first, sauté them for a minute or so, and then add the thinner, more delicate tips.

BAKING AND ROASTING

Roasting asparagus in the oven brings out its natural sweetness and makes a sophisticated dish that is very easy to prepare. Pour in 1 to 2 tablespoons of olive oil in a baking pan, add any desired seasonings, and roll or toss the spears in the oil to evenly coat them. Roast them at 500°F for 8 to 10 minutes, depending on their thickness, or until they can be pierced easily with a knife and take on a slightly crisp and browned exterior.

MICROWAVING

Microwave fresh asparagus by placing 1 pound in a shallow, microwave-safe baking dish or serving bowl. If you are cooking whole spears, arrange with the tips in the center. Add ¼ cup water and cover tightly. Microwave on high power for 4 to 7 minutes for spears, 3 to 5 minutes for pieces and tips. Stir or turn halfway through the cooking time.

- 1 cup = 2 to 3 minutes
- 2 cups = 3 to 4 minutes
- 1 pound = 8 to 10 minutes

BLANCHING AND FREEZING

To blanch asparagus, thoroughly wash it and trim the stem ends as necessary. Sort into piles, according to stalk thickness: small, medium, and large. You may either leave the spears whole or cut them into 2-inch

Books

The Asparagus Festival Cookbook
Jan Moore, Barbara Hafly, and Glenda Hushaw;
Celestial Arts, 2003.

Asparagus Recipes: A Collection of Asparagus Recipes That Showcase the Versatility of This Spring Vegetable
Kindle Edition, Mary Miller, 2014.

lengths. Blanch in boiling water for 1½ minutes for small stalks, 2 minutes for medium stalks, or 3 minutes for large stalks. Plunge into ice water to stop the cooking process and drain, then pack in zipper-lock freezer or vacuum food sealer-type bags. Squeeze out excess air and leave ½ inch of headspace (unless you are using the vacuum sealing method). Or pack in freezer containers. Frozen asparagus will keep for up to 8 months at 0°F.

EQUIVALENTS, MEASURES, AND SERVINGS

- 16 to 20 spears = 1 pound = 2⅔ to 3 cups cut into 1- to 1½-inch pieces
- ½ pound per person (8 to 10 spears)

COMPLEMENTARY HERBS, SEASONINGS, AND FOODS

Artichokes, bacon, blood-orange juice, butter, chervil, cheese (goat, Parmesan), chicken, chives, crab, eggs, fava beans, garlic, green garlic, halibut, ham, hollandaise sauce, leeks, lemons, lobster, mushrooms, nutmeg, olive oil, onions, parsley, pasta, peanut oil, peas, potatoes, prosciutto, shallots, tarragon, vinegar.

SERVING SUGGESTIONS

- Serve cooked asparagus warm with hollandaise sauce or topped with butter and Parmesan cheese.
- Serve cooked asparagus cold with a simple vinaigrette, or olive oil, lemon juice, and sea salt. A final toss with grated lemon zest adds flavor and beauty.
- Asparagus is the ultimate finger food. Believe it or not, proper etiquette calls for eating asparagus with your fingers, not utensils! Kids love dipping spears in a little dish of melted butter, salad dressing, or mayonnaise.
- Slice into 1-inch pieces and stir-fry with other vegetables in a wok with a little corn, peanut, or sesame oil.
- Substitute asparagus for leeks in a leek tart or quiche recipe, or combine the two vegetables.
- Top pizza with very thin spears or tips of parboiled or steamed asparagus.
- Sauté asparagus in chicken broth for more flavor.
- Place parboiled asparagus spears, tomatoes, mushrooms, and shredded mozzarella cheese on top of focaccia bread for an elegant garden pizza.
- French-fry asparagus just like potato fries for a delicious and unusual dish, or try as a tempura vegetable.
- Asparagus and morel mushrooms, lightly sautéed in butter, are a magical combination, with happily synchronized market appearances in the spring.
- Add cooked asparagus to your favorite omelet, scrambled eggs, or quiche.
- If you are lucky enough to encounter young, tender asparagus the width of a pencil, try serving it raw with carrot and celery sticks and a favorite dip.
- Asparagus was born to be wrapped. I like to do it with bacon, but smoked salmon, prosciutto, Iberian ham, phyllo dough, salami, and smoked turkey are also absolutely delicious.
- Grill asparagus brushed with olive oil, vinaigrette, or your favorite dressing, plus a little salt and pepper.

Asparagus-Eating Champ

The central California city of Stockton is home to the three-day Stockton Asparagus Festival, celebrated in April.

Among the much-anticipated entertainment is the annual World Deep-Fried Asparagus Eating Competition. In 2014, competitive eater Joey Chestnut took first place by consuming over 12 pounds of the tempura-style fried stalks in 10 minutes.

ROASTED BACON-WRAPPED ASPARAGUS — SERVES 4

1 bunch asparagus (15 to 20 spears)
1 small white onion, thinly sliced
2 tablespoons extra-virgin olive oil
10 slices raw, thick-cut bacon, cut crosswise into half strips
Freshly ground black pepper and salt

1. Preheat the oven to 375°F.

2. Wash, pat dry, and trim the asparagus. Line a 9-by-13-inch pan with aluminum foil, and brush it with 1 tablespoon of the oil to keep the asparagus from sticking. Wrap each spear with a half strip of bacon, tucking the ends under the asparagus, and place it in the pan. Place the onion rings over the asparagus, drizzle with the remaining oil, and sprinkle with salt and pepper.

3. Cover and bake for 30 to 45 minutes, or until the spears are tender and the bacon is crisp on the edges.

— *Mi Ae Lipe*

ASPARAGUS AND SHRIMP SALAD — SERVES 4

Source Note: This is a wonderful spring-summer salad.

1½ pounds asparagus, washed, trimmed, and peeled
½ cup water
1 slice lemon
1 sprig fresh parsley
5 peppercorns
½ teaspoon salt
16 to 20 small shrimp, raw, unshelled
½ cup mayonnaise
½ cup sour cream
½ teaspoon fresh lemon juice
¼ teaspoon dry mustard
½ teaspoon prepared horseradish (optional)
1 tablespoon gin
Salt and freshly ground black pepper
Lettuce leaves

1. Blanch the asparagus for a few minutes in boiling water and drain it on paper towels. Cut off the tips; cut the stems diagonally into 2-inch pieces. Place the tips and stem pieces in a large bowl and set aside.

2. Combine the water, lemon slice, parsley, peppercorns, and salt in a medium saucepan. Heat to boiling; then decrease the heat. Add the shrimp and simmer, uncovered, until they turn pink, about 4

"Life expectancy would grow by leaps and bounds if green vegetables smelled as good as bacon."

— *Doug Larson,
American newspaper columnist*

Spears on the Water

Roman emperors were so fond of asparagus that they kept special boats for the purpose of fetching the vegetable, calling them the "Asparagus Fleet."

The Journey of an Asparagus Stalk

Sarah Stone
Former Featherstone Farm CSA Manager

I came to work for Featherstone because I wanted to see firsthand where my food was coming from. Picking a bunch of broccoli or a pint of cherry tomatoes from a giant mound at the market seemed too mindless. I wanted to follow the vegetables that would make up a future meal from seed to plant to harvest to package to delivery to display.

And let me tell you, after having witnessed a vegetable's journey this season, the amount of humanpower and machinery needed to bring my vegetables from seed to table is enough to make me examine my dinner with incredulity and awe before popping any veggie into my mouth.

Take asparagus, for instance. Once the sun comes out and the earth warms up a bit, asparagus grows like a tasty weed. It shoots up from the ground with amazing speed, and demands to be picked several times a day.

Think about the bunch of asparagus you received in this week's box. Let's suppose your bunch contains 15 individual stalks. Someone has hiked up to our asparagus field with a basket and a wicked-looking knife. Each stalk that stands high enough to wave at us from the field gets cut from its family cluster and placed in a basket. (Shorter stalks are left to stretch toward the sun a bit longer.) Once we've walked the length and breadth of the field and given attention to each cluster, we bring our full baskets back.

Back at the shop, each individual asparagus stalk needs to be gently wiped free of dirt before they are weighed and bound into one-pound bundles. Any stalks that are "deformed"—i.e., grown crooked—

minutes. Drain, cool slightly, shell and devein, and add them to the asparagus.

3. Combine the mayonnaise with the sour cream in a medium bowl. Beat in the lemon juice, mustard, horseradish, gin, and salt and pepper to taste. Spoon this dressing over the asparagus and shrimp, and toss well. Serve on lettuce leaves, at room temperature or slightly chilled.

— *Bert Greene,* Greene on Greens

ASPARAGUS AND SPINACH SOUP   SERVES 6 TO 8

Source Note: This is wonderful hot, but it is also excellent chilled.

1 pound asparagus, washed, trimmed, and peeled
3 cups chicken or vegetable stock
1 cup chopped fresh spinach leaves
2 tablespoons unsalted butter
10 whole scallions (green onions), bulbs and green tops,
    roughly chopped
Pinch of ground cloves
3 tablespoons cornstarch
1 cup heavy cream
Salt and freshly ground black pepper
Sour cream (optional)

1. Place the asparagus in a medium saucepan and cover with the chicken stock. Heat to boiling over high heat; decrease the heat. Simmer, covered, for 3 minutes. Remove the asparagus from the stock and set aside. Add the spinach to the saucepan and cook for 3 minutes. Drain; reserve the stock.

2. Cut the tips off the asparagus; reserve. Chop the stems into 1-inch pieces; reserve.

3. Melt the butter in a medium saucepan over low heat. Add the scallions; cook until wilted. Stir in the cloves, cooked spinach, and asparagus stems. Cook, covered, over low heat for 10 minutes.

4. Remove the cover; add the reserved stock.

5. Place the cornstarch in a small bowl. Slowly beat in the cream until the mixture is smooth. Stir this into the vegetable mixture in the saucepan. Heat to boiling; remove from the heat.

6. Cool the mixture slightly and puree it in a blender or food processor in two batches (be careful—the hot liquid will expand). Return the puree to the saucepan and reheat over low heat. Season with salt and pepper to taste; stir in the asparagus tips. Serve garnished with dabs of sour cream, if desired.

— *Bert Greene,* Greene on Greens

Spaghetti with Spring Vegetables

SERVES 6

> 5 medium tomatoes
> ¼ pound thin-stalked asparagus
> 1 medium zucchini
> ¼ pound small white mushrooms
> 1 large red or green bell pepper
> 5 tablespoons olive oil
> 1 medium onion, thinly sliced
> Salt and freshly ground black pepper
> 3 tablespoons chopped fresh parsley
> 2 cloves garlic, finely chopped
> 1 pound spaghetti

1. Peel, seed, and dice the tomatoes. Wash the asparagus and cut the tips off the stalks; cut both the stalks and tips into 1-inch-long pieces, but keep them separate. Wash and dry the zucchini and mushrooms; cut into thin slices. Wash the pepper and cut into short, thin strips.

2. Heat the oil in a large skillet. Add the pepper strips and asparagus stalks, and sauté over medium heat for 5 to 6 minutes. Add the onion, zucchini, asparagus tips, and mushrooms. Sauté 4 to 5 minutes. Add the diced tomatoes, salt, and pepper. Cook uncovered over medium heat for 10 minutes, stirring frequently. Stir in the parsley and garlic. Taste, and adjust the seasoning.

3. While the sauce finishes cooking, boil the spaghetti according to the package directions; drain and place in a warm deep dish or bowl. Pour the sauce over the spaghetti, and serve immediately.

— Jeanette Mettler Cappello; Produce for Better Health; Fruits & Veggies— More Matters; Centers for Disease Control and Prevention

Asparagus and Morels

SERVES 6

> 8 tablespoons (1 stick) unsalted butter
> 2 medium shallots, finely chopped
> 2 large cloves garlic, minced
> 1 teaspoon chopped fresh thyme, plus 6 sprigs, for garnish
> 1 pound morels, cleaned and halved or quartered lengthwise
> 1 cup dry white wine
> 1 cup vegetable or chicken stock
> Salt and freshly ground black pepper
> 1 pound asparagus

1. In a large skillet over medium heat, melt 6 tablespoons of the butter. When the butter is hot but not browned, add the shallots and garlic,

are discarded into the "dinner for Sarah" pile. (However, if that pile grows too large, I can be persuaded to share.)

Next, the ends are cleanly cut so that the stalks in each bunch are semi-uniform in length. Then the finished bunches are carried to our coolers. There they wait to be packed into your produce boxes or dropped off at your pickup site, and carried into your home. Finally, when you open your box and eat it, the asparagus stalk's journey has come to an end.

Incredibly, the journey of an asparagus stalk is significantly shorter than the sagas many other vegetables endure. I find it all amazing. The intense individual care and gentle handling each piece of produce gets before you pluck it from your box or supermarket shelf is mind-boggling. (Think about cherry tomatoes, each fruit individually picked and placed in your pint.)

Witnessing firsthand a vegetable's journey has made me more appreciative of a perfectly formed fruit, and more forgiving of the small dings and bruises that inevitably mark a road-weary traveler. It has also opened up a soft place in my heart for the deformed, and helps me remember that the asparagus with a crooked neck tastes the same as its beautiful brother.

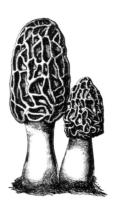

then sprinkle the thyme on top. Add the morels and cook until lightly browned, about 5 minutes, taking care not to burn the butter.

2. Pour in the wine and boil until it is almost evaporated, about 5 minutes. Add the stock, stir well, and simmer until the liquid is reduced and has thickened slightly. Season lightly with salt and pepper and swirl in the remaining 2 tablespoons butter. (You should now have about 3 cups of liquid.)

3. Meanwhile, prepare the asparagus: Cut the spears so that they are about 6 inches long; save the trimmings for another use. If the base of the spears is thicker than ½ inch in diameter, peel the bottom half of each with a vegetable peeler.

4. In a large skillet with a tight-fitting lid, bring ½ inch of water to a boil. Lay the asparagus in the pan, cover, and cook vigorously just until the bottom of a stalk can be pierced easily with a sharp knife, about 4 minutes. Drain on paper towels.

5. Divide the asparagus among 6 dinner plates and spoon the morels across the middle of the asparagus, making sure that each serving includes 1 or 2 spoonfuls of the pan juices. Garnish each plate with a sprig of thyme and serve immediately.

— *Joel Patraker and Joan Schwartz,* The Greenmarket Cookbook

Beautiful purple and green asparagus at Sang Lee Farms.

Basil OCIMUM BASILICUM

A beloved herb that is related to mint, basil is popular in Mediterranean and Asian dishes. It thrives in hot, humid weather, disliking even the coolness of spring and early summer. In northern climates, basil acts as an annual, but in its native tropical climate, it grows year-round.

Numerous types of basil grow around the world, including lemon basil, African blue basil (which smells like camphor), and licorice basil. There are the large-leaved Italian types and the smaller-leaved Asian basils that are popular in Thai and Vietnamese cuisines. Some basils are so sensitive to regional microclimates that plants of the same species grown in different locales produce distinctly different-tasting pestos.

HISTORY

A beloved kitchen herb for at least 4,000 years, basil originated in India, where it was revered and used in religious occasions and funerals. The herb later migrated to the Mediterranean through the famous Oriental spice routes. Ancient Greeks and Romans associated the plant with death and love, respectively. It was favored in England in the 16th century for a time, but its popularity eventually died out there, although it remains an essential ingredient in that country's famed turtle soup.

NUTRITION

Basil is an exceptionally rich source of vitamin K, but it also has manganese, copper, and vitamin A. Two tablespoons of the chopped herb contain a mere single calorie. Basil has many medicinal properties and is well known as a remedy for digestive upsets, and basil tea is said to dispel flatulence. It is often used to treat headaches and anxiety, and its aroma alone is reputed to have calming properties.

SEASON

Commercially, basil is widely grown and available year-round. But basil is a heat-loving plant, and you'll find it at its best at farmers markets and CSAs between June and September.

SELECTION

If possible, basil should be purchased in fresh bunches (usually these are plentiful in season, at farmers markets, or in larger natural foods supermarkets). This way you can see the condition of the leaves. Try to avoid getting basil in those tiny, flat plastic boxes; these scanty sprigs tend to be well past their prime and outrageously expensive. Avoid basil that is wilted or has large brown patches on its leaves; the darkened areas affect the flavor.

STORAGE

Store unwashed basil in a plastic bag in the refrigerator vegetable crisper, but for no longer than a few days.

Pesto

Mi Ae Lipe

That most famous of Italian condiments, pesto, was likely born in the Italian coastal city of Genoa, where the mild climate fostered verdant basil, abundant olives, and plump garlic—all key ingredients for this aromatic green sauce. In this land of seafarers and fishermen who frequently plied the ocean on long journeys, pesto was a welcome part of their homecoming, offering a taste of fresh greenery after weeks or months of a monotonous, starchy diet.

Traditionally pesto is made in a marble mortar with a wooden pestle, which is still widely considered the best way. The key to making great pesto with this method lies in the wrist action of grinding the basil leaves finely with garlic, salt, extra-virgin olive oil, pine nuts, and grated cheese (preferably Pecorino, made from sheep's milk).

In today's world, however, it can be made in a food processor or blender, although it will lack the same texture. It should always be made as quickly as possible with room-temperature ingredients, as ground basil oxidizes rapidly, turning an unappealing brown.

Although the traditional green basil–based pesto is the best-known version, other pestos exist, often created to use the freshest local ingredients particular to a specific Italian region. Even differences in the taste and smell of the basil and olives grown in different Mediterranean microclimates can be detected in regional basil pestos.

Among green pestos, sometimes broccoli, mint, or flat-leaf parsley is used in addition to or instead of basil. Red pesto, from the Italian region of the Cinque Terre, includes fresh or sun-dried tomatoes.

In areas where pine nuts are too costly, walnuts, pistachios, and even almonds are substituted and added to the traditional basil. Sicilian

TRIMMING AND CLEANING

Strip the leaves off the tough stems and wash thoroughly to rinse away any grit or sand. Then pat or spin dry.

FREEZING

You can freeze basil, either pureed with olive oil and garlic, or in leaf form (just be forewarned that the leaves will turn brown). If you don't think you will use all of your fresh basil before it goes bad, chop it finely, mix it into a paste using ⅓ cup of olive oil or cooled melted butter to every 2 cups of herbs, and then freeze the resulting mixture in ice cube trays. To thaw, simply pop out a few cubes into a strainer and let the oil melt away, or just drop them frozen into sauces or soups.

DRYING

Fresh basil is far superior to the dried version, which contains only a fraction of its distinctive flavor and fragrance. Even basil frozen in the manner described above is better than the dried herb.

If you still want to dry the herb, spread a single layer of leaves on a cookie sheet and place the sheet in a warm (up to 180°F) oven for 3 to 4 hours, stirring the herbs periodically until they are thoroughly dry. Or remove the best leaves from the stems and arrange on a paper towel so the leaves do not touch. Cover this layer with another paper towel and add another layer of leaves over the top. Up to five layers may be dried at one time in the oven using this method.

A microwave oven can also be used to dry small quantities of basil. Place 4 or 5 herb branches layered between paper towels in the microwave. Heat for 2 to 3 minutes on high power. If the basil is not brittle and dry when removed, repeat the microwave drying for 30 seconds more. Note: The heat generated during microwaving not only removes moisture but also some of the oils, so these herbs may not have as intense a flavor as herbs dried by other methods.

EQUIVALENTS, MEASURES, AND SERVINGS

- 1 tablespoon chopped fresh basil = 1 teaspoon dried basil

COMPLEMENTARY HERBS, SEASONINGS, AND FOODS

Cheese, chicken, duck, eggplant, eggs, fish, ginger, lamb, liver, marjoram, mint, olive oil, onions, oregano, pasta, pesto, pizza, pork, potatoes, rabbit, rosemary, sage, salads, shellfish, soups, summer savory, sweet peppers, tomatoes, tomato sauce, veal, vegetables, vinegars, zucchini.

SERVING SUGGESTIONS

- Basil has a famous affinity for tomatoes and cheese; a favorite Italian summer salad combines basil, olive oil, balsamic vinegar, rounds of fresh mozzarella cheese, and vine-ripened tomatoes.

- Substitute basil for parsley in meat loaf; it adds a marvelously savory, perfumed flavor.

- If you are a huge basil fan, tear off the leaves from the stems and add liberal quantities to tossed salads, just like a salad green. Leaves of fresh mint and a few thin shreds of raw ginger along with the basil make a powerful flavor combination in a salad.

- Substitute fresh basil for half of the spinach in some recipes.
- Use basil pesto to add flavor to a salmon loaf.
- Chop a few leaves into egg and cheese dishes to add flavor and color.
- Substitute basil for parsley in the filling for deviled eggs.
- Place a few leaves in sandwiches, like lettuce.
- The uses of basil pesto are numerous: for spreading on ham sandwiches, mixing into mashed potatoes, stirring into tomato or bean soup, dabbing on salmon, marinating meat kebabs, saucing pizza, adding to stuffed eggs, mixing with salad oil and using as a dressing…

SUBSTITUTIONS

If you do not have basil on hand, use oregano, parsley, or thyme.

. . . .

KAHUMANA CAFÉ PASTA WITH
MACADAMIA NUT PESTO SAUCE   SERVES 4 TO 6

Source Note: This is our signature and most popular dish served at our farm-to-table café. Traditionally you would add Parmesan cheese to the pesto, but at Kahumana we do not, to make it more versatile to meet our customers' diverse dietary needs. We make our base sauce vegan and top the final dish with freshly grated Parmesan.

PESTO SAUCE

2 cups organic olive oil
1 head garlic, cloves separated and peeled
8 ounces dry-roasted macadamia nuts
2 tablespoons coarsely ground sea salt
1 pound fresh basil leaves

In a food processor, mix the oil, garlic, nuts, and salt. Blend to a medium consistency. Gradually add the basil leaves and continue blending until you have a rich pesto paste. Transfer the pesto to a small container and lay a sheet of plastic wrap directly on top of it to help prevent discoloration. If you have extra pesto sauce, store it in the refrigerator (also with the plastic wrap on the surface) and use it within the next few days.

PASTA

1 pound organic whole-grain pasta
    (preferably spaghetti or linguine noodles)
2 tablespoons olive oil
3 carrots, julienned
1 leek, julienned
1 bulb fennel, julienned
8 ounces baby arugula leaves
Freshly grated Parmesan cheese (optional)

pestos often add capers, chilies, raisins, anchovies, and fennel; they are usually more rich and spicy than Ligurian varieties. In Liguria, a white pesto is also made with no basil or few green herbs.

A slightly different version of the sauce is made in the Provence region of France, known as pistou, which is usually made with only olive oil, basil, and garlic. Cheese is optional, but pistou generally does not contain nuts.

Pesto is a sauce best eaten as soon as possible, although it will keep a few days if it is covered with a layer of olive oil (this also preserves its green color).

It also freezes well; fill ice-cube trays with it, pop out the cubes, and place them in a zipper-lock freezer bags to use as needed for winter pasta dishes or soups. Most sources recommend preparing it without the cheese (freezing can deteriorate its taste and texture) and adding it later; others include it. Try making a batch both ways and see which one you prefer. Pesto will keep in the freezer for up to 6 months.

1. Cook the pasta al dente, or to your preference. Drain, rinse, and set aside.

2. Meanwhile, while the pasta is cooking, heat the oil in a very large skillet over medium heat. Sauté the carrots, leek, and fennel for 7 to 10 minutes, until crisp-tender.

3. Add the pasta to the vegetables and mix well. Add the arugula and mix well. Remove from the heat.

4. Add about ½ cup of the pesto sauce to the pasta and mix thoroughly. Portion the pasta on serving dishes, sprinkle generously with the Parmesan, and serve immediately.

Serving Suggestion: Here at our café, we offer this dish vegetarian, vegan (no cheese), or with a choice of sautéed chicken, garlic-butter shrimp, or seared ahi (tuna). The seared ahi option is definitely the most popular. Enjoy whichever option you choose!

— *Robert Zuckerman, Kahumana Farm Café, Waianae, Oahu, Hawaii*

DEVILED EGGS WITH SALMON AND BASIL
MAKES 24 DEVILED EGG HALVES

Author Note: The salmon and basil give a delicious, unexpected twist to these deviled eggs. Make plenty, for these never last long at parties or potlucks.

1 dozen eggs
1 (15½-ounce) can pink or red salmon, canning liquid reserved
3 tablespoons mayonnaise
½ cup onion, finely chopped
1 large clove garlic, finely chopped
1 cup loosely packed basil, finely chopped
Salt and freshly ground black pepper
Chopped fresh parsley or paprika, for garnish (optional)

1. Hard-boil the eggs, peel away their shells, and cut them in half lengthwise. Scoop out the yolks, place them in a large bowl, and mash them lightly. Set aside the egg white halves.

2. Add the salmon and reserved liquid, mayonnaise, onion, garlic, basil, and pepper to the mashed yolks. (Additional salt is usually not needed with the salmon and its canning liquid, but taste and adjust the seasoning if necessary.) Mix thoroughly, and place heaping spoonfuls into the egg white halves.

3. Garnish with parsley or paprika, if desired. For best results, chill the deviled eggs several hours before serving to let the flavors mingle.

— *Mi Ae Lipe*

REAL BASIL CHEESECAKE

MAKES 10 SERVINGS

2 tablespoons butter, softened
1 cup crushed vanilla wafers or graham crackers
2 large eggs
1 cup sour cream
¾ cup granulated sugar
1 cup stemmed, coarsely chopped basil leaves
2 tablespoons cornstarch
2 tablespoons fresh lemon juice
1 teaspoon vanilla extract
2 pounds cream cheese, at room temperature

1. Position a rack in the center of the oven and preheat it to 350°F.

2. Spread the softened butter on the bottom and halfway up the sides of a 9- or 10-inch springform pan. Cover the buttered area with the wafer or cracker crumbs, pressing to be sure they stick.

3. In a food processor, lightly beat the eggs. Add the sour cream, sugar, basil, cornstarch, lemon juice, and vanilla. Process until smooth. Add the cream cheese, ½ pound at a time, making sure after each addition that the mixture is very smooth.

4. Pour the cheesecake batter into the prepared pan and bake for 50 to 60 minutes, or until a toothpick or knife inserted into the center comes out clean. Gently run a knife around the edges of the cake as soon as it comes out of the oven to allow it to sink evenly.

5. Cool on a wire rack for 20 minutes, then remove the outside of the pan. Finish cooling; wrap well and refrigerate. To serve, use plain dental floss or a thin-bladed knife to cut into thin wedges.

— *FairShare CSA Coalition,* From Asparagus to Zucchini

GREEN BEANS IN
BASIL-WALNUT VINAIGRETTE

SERVES 6 TO 8

Source Note: *For a lovely presentation, put a couple of radicchio or red cabbage leaves on each salad plate and place the green beans on top.*

1½ pounds young green beans, trimmed

BASIL-WALNUT VINAIGRETTE

1 teaspoon chopped garlic
20 basil leaves
½ teaspoon salt
½ teaspoon freshly ground black pepper

Love and Scorpions

In Romania, when a man accepts a sprig of basil from a woman, he is officially engaged.

In Mexico, basil is carried around in the hope of recapturing a lover's roving eye.

In some cultures, basil symbolizes hatred; in others it is associated with scorpions.

2 teaspoons Dijon mustard
¼ cup white wine vinegar
½ cup olive oil
3 scallions (green onions), thinly sliced, for garnish
Chopped walnuts, for garnish

1. Bring a large pot of salted water to a rolling boil. Add the green beans and cook until they turn just tender-crisp, 3 to 5 minutes. Drain immediately into a colander and pour ice-cold water over the beans to stop the cooking process. Drain well.
2. To prepare the vinaigrette: Put the garlic, basil, salt, and pepper in a blender or food processor. Pulse on and off, then add the mustard and vinegar. Pulse until smooth. With the machine running, add the oil very slowly in a thin stream, just until blended.
3. Place the beans in a serving bowl and pour the vinaigrette over them, tossing to coat thoroughly. Garnish with the scallions and walnuts.

— *Renee Shepherd, Renee's Garden, Felton, California*

Bountiful basil at Sang Lee Farms.

Beans (Fava)

VICIA FABA

There is something strikingly sensual about fava beans—their smooth green pods fat and virile with plump seeds cradled in downy-soft interiors, promising fertile, nutritious, nutty goodness. When heaps of the pods are stacked in bins at farmers markets, they can be an impressive sight—the very picture of vegetable abundance. The plants are quite imposing too; this is not your typical delicate bean vine climber or low-lying, fluffy bush. Fava beans grow on sturdy plants that can reach 6 feet tall, with lush foliage and pretty white or purple flowers with distinctive black spots. Sometimes called broad beans, faba beans, field beans, bell beans, or tic beans, favas are extremely useful as a cover crop; they overwinter well, prevent erosion, and, like all legumes, fix nitrogen in the soil. Farmers often plow the plants under after the beans mature to enrich the earth.

A little-known fact is that the gray-green leaves of favas are also delicious, with a rich meaty texture and a nutty flavor reminiscent of the beans. Occasionally you can find them in the larger farmers markets, but they are rare ... just another reason to grow them yourself in your own garden.

HISTORY

Favas are one of the oldest foods for people; they originated in the Mediterranean, where local populations are known to have been eating them by 6000 BCE or earlier. The plants' hardiness and delectable seeds made them especially popular throughout Mediterranean Europe, the Middle East, Asia, Africa, and Latin America. Favas were the original bean in the traditional Twelfth Night cake, the festivities during which some branches of Christianity mark the coming of the Epiphany. A single dried bean was baked into the cake, and whoever found the bean in his cake would rule the feast (or at least host the next Twelfth Night party).

NUTRITION

Fava beans are incredibly nutritious; a 1-cup serving of shelled favas contains 187 calories, plus significant amounts of protein, folate, riboflavin, vitamin B6, thiamine, calcium, iron, magnesium, phosphorus, zinc, copper, and manganese. Favas are one of the richest plant sources of potassium and dietary fiber, as well as certain phytonutrients. Interestingly, favas also contain levodopa, a precursor of brain neurochemicals that regulate body movement; as a result, some medical studies are being carried out to see if favas can be beneficial for patients with Parkinson's disease.

SEASON

Favas are very seasonal, reaching their peak in April and May. They come and go quickly, so enjoy them when you see them.

SELECTION

Look for pods that are fresh, plump, and have a luminous yellow-green color. Avoid pods that show signs of shriveling or feel empty when squeezed (a sure sign of missing beans). Pods are also an indication of

Like CSAs and farmers markets, the number of community gardens across the country keeps growing. Many of them are managed by local city-parks-and-recreation departments, and others sprout up at schools, churches, nonprofits, and businesses. A garden ties communities and people together in subtle and self-empowering ways, for both the young and old, offering camaraderie and satisfaction as well as food. And if gardeners can't use everything they grow, they may have donation networks in place to contribute excess produce to food pantries and other nonprofits serving people in need.

*In Portland, Oregon, **Produce for People** does a great job of collecting fresh, organic produce weekly to deliver to local emergency food banks during the growing season. In 2013, the organization exceeded an ambitious goal of increasing donations, with 38 community garden sites donating more than 36,000 pounds of food to 30 food pantries.*

*An interesting new model of community gardening linked to both a CSA and weekly farm stands is **CityGrown Seattle**, where the "farm" consists of urban neighborhood backyard plots and unused spaces that are cultivated by farm staff and volunteers. In exchange for use of the space, landowners get a share of the produce for the season. Members pay for their subscriptions at the beginning of the farm season, but instead of receiving weekly boxes of farm-chosen produce as in the typical CSA model, they use the money in their CSA accounts to pick up fruits and veggies of their choice at farm stands in the Crown Hill and Wallingford neighborhoods.*

***Garden City Harvest** in Missoula, Montana, has multiple pro-*

bean size: Smaller favas will be more tender and delicate; larger seeds have a more robust flavor but could be prone to starchiness if they are too big or overly mature.

STORAGE

Because the bulky pods take up lots of room, you can shell the beans first. Either way, tightly wrap unwashed favas in a plastic bag and store them in the refrigerator. Use within a few days; they are not the best keepers.

TRIMMING AND CLEANING

Probably the main reason why fava beans have never really caught on in the American culinary scene is that they are extremely labor-intensive. The beans first need to be shelled; unzip the little string from the flower end of the pod downward and remove them. Then either boil them briefly (see the instructions below) or place them in a large mixing bowl and cover with boiling water. After the water has cooled enough to handle the beans, drain it off.

Now the work begins: Each bean has a thick skin that needs to be individually peeled. Very young favas can possibly be left unpeeled, but any bean more mature than that really must have these slightly bitter skins removed, otherwise chewing them is a fibrous, unpleasant task. To peel them, slit the wrinkled skin with the tip of a knife or pinch it with your fingernail, and gently slip it off the bean. As in the old days of shelling garden peas, this is a good job to do with friends, over drinks and convivial conversation; then enjoy the lovely gustatory rewards afterward.

STEAMING AND BOILING

For peeling, boil shelled favas in salted, boiling water for 30 seconds (any longer than that will render them a mushy mess when you try to peel them). Drain and remove the skins of each individual bean (see the Trimming and Cleaning instructions above). To continue cooking, steam the beans over rapidly boiling water for 6 to 10 minutes, depending on their size, or until tender. Or boil the shelled favas in several quarts of salted water until they turn just bright green and tender, 2 to 6 minutes.

STIR-FRYING AND SAUTÉING

Young favas are incredibly delicious stir-fried or quickly sautéed with light seasonings or other delicate vegetables. Sauté shelled and peeled beans for 7 to 10 minutes on medium-high heat in a wok or large frying pan. Be sure to add some liquid, such as melted butter, olive oil, or even water to the pan, or they will stick.

BAKING AND ROASTING

One unexpected twist with roasting fava beans is that if they are small and young enough, both their pods and skins may be tender enough to be edible. Toss whole, clean fava pods with olive oil and seasonings, arrange them in a single layer on a baking pan or sheet, and roast at 400°F for 25 minutes, or until tender.

GRILLING

Favas can be grilled and served whole in their pods. Toss the pods in olive oil and seasonings first, then arrange them directly on the grill in a single layer. Grill until the pods are blistered on one side, 4 to 5 minutes. Then flip and grill a few more minutes on the other side. Sample the beans from one pod first before removing them all from the heat—the favas should be smooth and creamy, not too firm. Remember that the beans will continue to cook a little longer after they are taken off the grill. Any seasonings on the pod will stick to your fingers, so when you shell them, lick your fingers—constantly.

MICROWAVING

Place shelled and peeled fava beans (see the Trimming and Cleaning instructions on page 38) in a microwave-safe dish; add ¼ cup water; cover and cook on high power.

- 1 cup = 3 to 4 minutes

BLANCHING AND FREEZING

Blanch and peel the favas (see the Trimming and Cleaning instructions on page 38). Then return them to salted boiling water for 3 minutes. Drain, then plunge them into ice water for 5 minutes to stop the cooking process. Remove and drain. Package them in zipper-lock freezer or vacuum food sealer-type bags, or freezer containers. Squeeze out any excess air and leave ½ inch of headspace (unless you are using the vacuum sealing method). Frozen favas will keep for up to 6 months at 0°F.

EQUIVALENTS, MEASURES, AND SERVINGS

- 1 pound pods = 1 to 1½ cups shelled

COMPLEMENTARY HERBS, SEASONINGS, AND FOODS

Artichokes, asparagus, bacon, beets, butter, cheese (feta, *queso anejo*, Parmesan, pecorino, ricotta), chicory, chiles, cream, cumin, eggs, garlic, green garlic, ham, leeks, lemon, mint, mushrooms, nuts, olive oil, pancetta, pasta, pea vines, prosciutto, rice, risotto, sage, savory, shellfish, shrimp, thyme, yogurt.

SERVING SUGGESTIONS

- Favas are at their best when adorned very simply—olive oil, butter, garlic, lemon juice, or chile flakes.
- A sprinkling of cooked fava beans brightens veal, seafood, roasted poultry, and sautéed meats. Or drizzle a spoonful or two of the meat's pan juices over the beans—yummy.
- Pair fresh favas with savory morel mushrooms; happily, they both appear at the same time in the spring.
- Toss favas into pasta dishes—their bright green color, nutty flavor, and creamy texture are a nice contrast with the noodles.
- Substitute rich, hearty favas for lima beans in succotash.
- Favas sprinkled with shavings of dense, rich cheeses like Parmesan, Asiago, and pecorino are a marriage made in heaven.
- Stir favas into frittatas, omelets, and other egg dishes for quick meals.
- Puree fava beans with cheese, pistachio nuts, garlic, and olive oil (in essence, a type of pesto); serve over thick slices of crusty artisan bread.
- Young favas are delicious stir-fried or quickly sautéed with light seasonings or other delicate spring vegetables like asparagus, artichokes, and mushrooms.

grams focused on building community through agriculture by growing produce with and for people with low incomes and offering education and training in ecologically conscious agriculture. Its community garden program has sites in low-income neighborhoods throughout the city, each of which provides gardeners with a 15-by-15-foot plot, tools, water, compost, straw, and the knowledge and guidance of an experienced garden coordinator. Weekly programs for young gardeners include lessons about gardening, botany, food sources, and cooking.

In Bloomington, Indiana, **Mother Hubbard's Cupboard**, a community-based food pantry serving 3,000 people every week, provides volunteers with multiple ways to help build community food security. In its 14 years, volunteers, interns, and staff have raised more than 18,000 pounds of organic fruits and vegetables. The organization has its own community garden and food forest and also partners with several community gardens managed by Bloomington Parks and Recreation, including the Banneker Green Thumbs Youth Garden.

Across America, an increasing number of companies—including Google, Kohl's, Southwest Airlines, Timberland, and PepsiCo—are providing space and time for employees to get their hands in the dirt and grow food for both themselves and people in need. Hundreds of companies are doing it, according to Fred Haberman, who maintains the **Employer Sponsored Gardens** website (www.employergardens. com). The workplace, he says, "is the ultimate 'community-based' site to offer healthier, lower-cost eating practices, especially those inspired by growing food. (Not to mention it's a great team and morale builder.)"

At **Idexx Laboratories** in Westbrook, Maine, employees grew more than 500 pounds of fresh vegetables in organic garden plots in

The fresh, green flavor of fava beans makes a hummus that is different from the usual chickpea-based ones. Mix with sour cream or a little Greek yogurt, fresh lemon juice, and lots of fresh herbs.

FAVA-STUDDED PASTA WITH RICOTTA CHEESE, PANCETTA, AND LEMON SERVES 2 AS AN ENTRÉE

Source Note: This makes one beautiful bowl of pasta! The flavor combo of mild, sweet ricotta cheese with lemon and fresh mint is classic Italian—and my American sensibility couldn't resist adding crisp, salty bits of pancetta to the mix. Use any small pasta you'd like, but the orcchiette work especially well because their "little ear" shape holds random bits of fava beans and pancetta like the bowl of a spoon. Celebrate spring with this elegant supper dish.

1 pound whole fava beans in their pods
4 tablespoons coarse salt
½ cup ricotta cheese
¼ cup plus 2 tablespoons Parmesan cheese
1 medium lemon, zested and juiced
1½ tablespoons minced fresh mint
8 medium asparagus spears
⅓ cup finely cubed pancetta or bacon
6 ounces orcchiette (or any dried, bite-size pasta)
Olive oil, for sautéing
Salt and freshly ground pepper
2 large red radishes, cut into fine julienne, for garnish

1. Shell the fava beans, discarding any that are shriveled or yellowed. You should have about 1 to 1½ cups of beans. Fill a large bowl with ice water and set it aside.

2. Fill a large pot with water and bring to a boil. Pour the beans into the boiling water and cook for 30 to 45 seconds. Drain, then put them into the bowl of ice water until cold. Prick the tough skins of the beans with a small knife or your fingernail and slip the bright green beans into a bowl; you should have about 1 or 1¼ cups, depending on the size of the beans.

3. Now, finish cooking the favas: In the same pot bring more water to a boil and add 2 tablespoons of the salt. Pour the peeled favas into the boiling water, cook for 2 to 3 minutes, and drain.

4. Put the ricotta, ¼ cup Parmesan cheese, the lemon zest, 1 tablespoon of lemon juice, 1 tablespoon of the mint, and a pinch of salt in a small bowl. Stir until well combined and set aside at room temperature.

5. Snap off the tough bottoms of the asparagus spears, rinse them, then cut the spears into 1-inch lengths.

6. Heat a large sauté pan over medium heat; add the pancetta and sauté it until slightly crisp. Remove the pancetta with a slotted spoon (keep the oil), then add the asparagus to the pan. Sauté it for several minutes, tossing, until it is tender-crisp.

7. To assemble the dish, bring more salted water to the boil, then cook the pasta according to the package instructions. Drain and shake the pasta. Put it into the sauté pan (containing the asparagus) over medium-high heat. Add the fava beans, about 3 tablespoons of the ricotta mixture, the pancetta, the remaining 2 tablespoons of Parmesan, and a generous drizzle of olive oil. Stir gently to combine the ingredients, tasting and adding more salt, pepper, or lemon juice as desired.

8. To serve, divide the pasta between two warmed bowls. Place a dollop of the ricotta mixture in the center of each serving and sprinkle with a little more mint and the julienned radishes.

— *Lisa Gordanier*

. . . .

FAVA BEAN PESTO WITH ROMAINE   SERVES 4

Author Note: This recipe is unusual in a couple of ways; instead of a pesto based on basil, this one relies on fava beans and green garlic. And the romaine lettuce is cooked briefly—on the grill. It's a lovely dish to serve with steak or chicken, as long as you have the grill going.

1 bunch green garlic scapes
1 cup fresh fava beans, shelled, blanched, and peeled
¼ cup olive oil
Fresh lemon juice (optional)
Salt and freshly ground black pepper
1 head romaine lettuce

1. Preheat the oven to 375°F. Place the garlic scapes on a cookie sheet with a little bit of oil and roast for about 10 minutes. Remove them from the oven and let cool. Once the scapes have cooled, place all of the ingredients except the romaine lettuce into a food processor and pulse until the mixture forms a smooth puree. Set aside.

2. Cut the head of romaine into 4 long wedges. Drizzle the cut sides of the wedges with olive oil and sprinkle them with salt and pepper. Grill the romaine over a hot fire, cut side down, until it is charred in spots, about 20 seconds. Turn the romaine over and grill for 20 seconds longer.

3. Transfer the romaine wedges to a platter, cut side up, and drizzle the fava bean pesto over them.

— *Karolina Tracz, Nash's Organic Produce, Sequim, Washington*

. . . .

Safety Tip

Some people, especially those of Middle Eastern descent, may be allergic to fava beans in a hereditary disorder called Glucose-6-phosphate dehydrogenase deficiency, or more simply, "favism."

Certain chemical alkaloids in favas can trigger anemia and kidney failure in these individuals. Even inhaling the plant's pollen can cause a toxic effect.

Additionally, people who take MAO-inhibitor antidepressants are advised not to eat fava beans because of their high tyramine levels.

Author Note: Given the uncertainties of cooking large dried beans like favas, you may choose to cook these ahead of time—like the day or evening before. (The cooking time can vary quite a bit, depending on the age, size, and quality of the beans.) When the beans are cooked, drain the liquid off them but don't discard it; keep it, stored separately, to add back to the soup toward the end of cooking. Refrigerate the beans and cooking liquid until ready to use.

½ cup dried skinless fava beans
2 bay leaves
1 tablespoon chopped fresh basil, or 1 teaspoon dried basil
⅓ cup vegetable oil
1 medium leek or onion, finely sliced
2 ribs celery, sliced
¼ teaspoon caraway seeds
¼ teaspoon mustard seeds
3 cloves garlic, crushed
2 medium carrots, sliced
1 medium turnip, finely sliced
4 medium potatoes, cut into eighths
4 medium beets, sliced
2 to 3 cups water
¼ cup apple cider vinegar
½ cup chopped fresh dill or parsley
Salt and freshly ground black pepper
2 cups sliced cabbage
Hot pepper sauce (such as Tabasco), for serving
Sour cream, for serving

1. Wash the favas, cover them with water, and soak them overnight. When you are ready to prepare the borscht, drain the beans, place them in a pot with 3 cups of fresh water, then add the bay leaves and basil. Bring to a boil. Cover and simmer on medium-low heat until the beans are tender (2 to 3 hours), adding more water if the level gets too low. Do not drain.

2. Meanwhile, heat the oil in a large stockpot. Add the leek, celery, caraway seeds, mustard seeds, and garlic, and cook until the leek is tender. Add the carrots, turnip, potatoes, and beets. Cook, stirring, for about 5 minutes, or until the vegetables have started to soften. Add the cooked fava beans. Add the water, vinegar, dill, and salt and pepper to taste.

3. Bring to a boil, then lower the heat and simmer for 20 to 30 minutes, or until the larger vegetables are tender. Stir in the sliced cabbage and cook until the cabbage has softened somewhat, about 5 minutes. Serve with the hot sauce and sour cream on the side.

— *Mary Wong, Nash's Organic Produce, Sequim, Washington*

Chives

ALLIUM SCHOENOPRASUM

The chive is the smallest species of the much beloved Allium (onion) family. Perennial chives grow from bulbs in dense clumps (hence the plural name) that sprout grasslike, hollow, tubular leaves. In late spring or early summer, chives bear delicate, globe-shaped pink or purple blossoms that are also edible; these are quite delicious in salads and sprinkled atop dishes.

The flavor of chives is among the most delicate in the onion family, and they are better used raw or barely cooked. They constitute one of the famous fines herbes of French cooking, along with tarragon, chervil, and parsley. One cooking tip: Their thin leaves are easier to snip with scissors than to cut with a knife.

HISTORY

Chives are thought to be native to Britain, but they also grow wild in Greece and Italy. Europeans have grown chives since the Middle Ages, although both regular chives and the closely related garlic chive *(Allium tuberosum)* have been used in Asian cuisines for centuries.

NUTRITION

Although they are not typically used in large enough quantities to be a significant source of nutrients, chives do contain vitamins A and K, potassium, phosphorus, magnesium, and calcium.

SEASON

Commercially grown chives are available year-round. In farmers markets and CSA farms, chives often arrive in late spring and continue until fall. Chives typically bloom in late May or June, and you may see these edible blossoms bunched with or without leaves.

SELECTION

Choose chives that look fresh and plump, with no signs of wilting, yellowing, or other discoloration. Thicker-tubed leaves tend to be more fibrous than smaller ones.

STORAGE

Chives that are unwashed and tightly wrapped in a plastic bag will keep for up to 1 week in the refrigerator vegetable crisper.

TRIMMING AND CLEANING

Rinse quickly and gently pat dry to avoid bruising the tender leaves. The easiest way to chop them finely is to gather up a whole bunch of stems, slightly twist them together tightly lengthwise, and snip them with a pair of kitchen scissors.

FREEZING

You can freeze chives by snipping them into small lengths and freezing them in a single layer on a baking sheet. Then they can be placed in zipper-lock freezer or vacuum food sealer-type bags. No thawing is necessary before using.

DRYING

Chives can be dried, although they lose much of their flavor this way. (If you really crave fresh chives in the winter, it's better to keep a pot growing indoors!) However, if you want to dry them, spread chives in a thin layer on a baking sheet or tray and dry them in the oven at no hotter than 100°F for 4 to 6 hours, or until crisp.

EQUIVALENTS, MEASURES, AND SERVINGS

- 1 tablespoon chopped fresh chives = 1 teaspoon dried
- 1 bunch = ½ cup chopped

COMPLEMENTARY HERBS, SEASONINGS, AND FOODS

Asparagus, butter, cheese (cottage, cream, goat, ricotta), chervil, chicken, crab, cream, eggs, fava beans, fish, ham, lemon, parsley, potatoes, salads, shellfish, soups, tarragon, vegetables.

SERVING SUGGESTIONS

- Combine chives with other herbs like chopped parsley and chervil, and sprinkle generously over scrambled eggs, omelets, and soft-boiled eggs.
- Add a tablespoon of finely chopped chives to each cup of milk when making a white sauce to add color and flavor.
- Snip a fresh spoonful over hot soups.
- Stir chopped chives into softened butter, which can then be spread over rounds or split loaves of French bread and baked like garlic bread.
- Tie up a couple chive leaves into spears, then use as a garnish atop or alongside puff pastry parcels, dumplings, deviled eggs, or open-faced crackers.
- To add a gentle oniony flavor, sprinkle a few tablespoons of chives during the last minute of cooking stir-fries.
- Give soft cheeses extra character with finely chopped chives.
- Scatter chives over buttered carrots or peas, marinated leeks, and steamed vegetables of all kinds.
- An Alpine treat is black rye bread spread with butter and chopped chives.
- Lightly chopped or whole chive flowers make a lovely, edible garnish for summer salads and chilled soups.
- Whip up a batch of chive soup by combining cooked potatoes, a handful of fresh chives, chicken stock, light cream, and seasonings in a blender or food processor.
- Liven up a bowl of cottage cheese by sprinkling a couple of tablespoons of finely chopped chives over the top.
- Salads of all sorts benefit from finely chopped chives—egg, potato, crab, chicken, Waldorf, shrimp, fava bean and pea—any where you'd want a touch of onion flavor.
- Combine chives with a touch of mayonnaise or sour cream and use as a sandwich spread along with other finely minced herbs, deviled ham, or mashed hard-boiled egg yolk.

Use green onion, finely chopped leek, or mild sweet onion.

. . . .

BABY POTATOES WITH LEMON AND CHIVES   SERVES 4

1 pound baby potatoes
2 tablespoons (¼ stick) butter
2 tablespoons coarsely chopped fresh chives
1 teaspoon grated lemon rind

1. Wash and steam the potatoes for 12 to 15 minutes until tender. (If preferred, they can be cut in half before cooking.)

2. In a separate pan, heat the butter. Add the chopped chives and lemon rind. Toss to release the flavors, then pour over the potatoes and serve.

— *Adapted from Fooddownunder.com*

. . . .

CHIVE AND PARMESAN POPCORN   SERVES 2

⅔ cup unpopped popcorn
5 tablespoons butter
Freshly ground black pepper
½ cup chopped fresh chives
1 cup finely grated Parmesan cheese
Salt

1. Pop the popcorn.

2. In a pan, melt the butter. Grind as much pepper as you want into the butter.

3. Sprinkle the chives over the popcorn along with the grated cheese. Drizzle the butter mixture over the popcorn, and salt to taste.

— *Fooddownunder.com*

. . . .

BOURSIN DIP   MAKES 1 CUP

Source Note: *Add other fresh herbs to taste—rosemary, thyme, basil, oregano, summer savory, sage—any or all, it's all good. If necessary, thin with sour cream or yogurt to the desired dipping consistency. I make this dip at least a day ahead to let the flavors mingle.*

8 ounces cream cheese, softened
1 tablespoon lemon juice

pizza, packaged and branded by a thousand nameless individuals. By making your own pizza with last season's pureed tomatoes, you are actively stepping aside from the food systems that lock us into fossil fuels and are chock-full of chemicals to enhance flavor and keep products on the shelves for a long time.

Or, to use hipster-speak, cooking is old-school DIY.

People purchase from natural-food stores and get CSAs for a variety of reasons, ranging from less exposure to pesticides to having a relationship with a local farm. Regardless of the motive, a natural outcome is that by cooking with fresh ingredients, you are freeing up capacity in the system and thereby defying the corporate food companies that want your dollar in their pockets.

It's quite liberating, once you stop to think about it. Though we may not be in the midst of a world war, we are in the midst of a food war, where politicians, lobbyists, and corporations are fighting over how to describe, produce, and market the packaged food items we put in our grocery carts.

Why not make it easier on them all and go straight to the source, roasting your winter squash and beets in the oven, then adding a bit of salt, herbs, and goat cheese after the vegetables have cooked? They'd get the message loud and clear.

1 clove garlic, minced
½ teaspoon Worcestershire sauce
½ teaspoon dry mustard
1 tablespoon chopped fresh parsley
1 tablespoon chopped fresh chives

Mix all of the ingredients together, then refrigerate. For the best flavor, serve softened at room temperature.

— *Maureen Cooney,* The Bluff Country Co-op Cookbook

LOW-FAT RANCH DIP

MAKES ABOUT 2 CUPS

2 cups cooked Great Northern beans, or 1 (15-ounce) can, rinsed and drained
1 clove garlic
¼ cup water
½ cup plain low-fat yogurt
¼ teaspoon cayenne pepper
½ teaspoon black pepper
1 tablespoon chopped fresh chives
1 tablespoon chopped fresh parsley
1 teaspoon chopped fresh tarragon
¼ teaspoon salt
1 tablespoon lemon juice

1. Blend the beans and garlic in a blender, adding enough water to coarsely puree the beans. Then blend for 2 minutes more until the mixture turns silky smooth.

2. Use a spatula to scrape the mixture into a medium bowl.

3. Stir in the yogurt, cayenne and black pepper, chives, parsley, tarragon, salt, and lemon juice, blending thoroughly. Serve with vegetables or chips for dipping.

— *Adapted from 5aday.gov, National Cancer Institute*

Green Garlic   ALLIUM SATIVUM

Green garlic is one of spring's first much-anticipated crops. Green garlic is simply the juvenile stage of the familiar cured bulb garlic that we all know so well—parts of the new plant sprouting from the cloves. Green garlic refers to the entire plant; garlic scapes are the long, curly shoots bearing immature flower clusters that form on hardneck garlic plants in early summer. (Scapes are also sometimes called whistles, stems, flowers, spears, or tops.) When recipes call for green garlic, the scapes, flowers, leaves, or very young bulbs are interchangeable. Recipes specifying scapes or whistles refer to just the long stems and flowers.

These curling flower stalks are delicious and have many uses, from soups and salads to main dishes and garnishes. Stronger and richer in flavor than chives, green garlic's pungency is milder than that of its cured-bulb siblings. Use it any way that you would use shallots or regular garlic. (Jack Hedin of Featherstone Farm claims that you have only to fill your roasting pan with meat and green garlic and cook it slowly to taste the richest roast ever made.) Garlic scapes are highly prized delicacies in European and Korean cuisine because of their subtle garlic flavor, tender-crisp texture, and nutraceutical potency.

Like most spring crops, green garlic's season is fleeting. By early June the stems and leaves start getting woody, as the plant's moisture is drawn out of the above-ground shoot and into the now-forming bulb. Its next reincarnation appears in the fall, as cured garlic in October.

HISTORY

See Garlic on page 538.

NUTRITION

See Garlic on page 538.

SEASON

Green garlic is truly a harbinger of its season. You are unlikely to find this springtime treat in large supermarkets, but you may be lucky enough to run across it at farmers markets or in your CSA box in late spring or very early summer. Blink and you might miss it, but enjoy it for the brief time it is available.

SELECTION

Choose shoots and scapes that look fresh, not wilted. Older, larger scapes and shoots (especially toward the end of the season or in the summer) tend to be fibrous.

STORAGE

Some vegetables do not store well after being washed, getting slimy if not used immediately; green garlic is one of them. To keep the scapes crisp, forgo a quick rinse and instead store them in a brown paper bag in the refrigerator, where they will last for weeks.

"No one who cooks, cooks alone. Even at her most solitary, a cook in the kitchen is surrounded by generations of cooks past, the advice and menus of cooks present, and the wisdom of cookbook writers."

— *Laurie Colwin,*
American food writer

Jack and Oscar Go to Mexico

Jack Hedin
Featherstone Farm Owner
Rushford, Minnesota

April 2015

In order to understand my relationship with the Gasca family—and the nature of my visit to Mexico last month—it would be worth a quick review of the history of employment and growth at Featherstone Farm, going back nearly 20 years.

In the year 2000 Featherstone Farm had at most three to four seasonal employees. But as the farm expanded to serve CSA and wholesale markets in Rochester and eventually the Twin Cities, it had to add more seasoned, professional farmworkers. And going with Spanish speakers seemed like a no-brainer for me; after four or five years of working with Mexican-American fieldworkers in California, I was very comfortable with the energy, the culture, the joi de vivre that comes with employees from "south of the border." Enter the Gasca family, starting in 2001 or 2002 (all blurry memory).

Initially we hired two (but eventually all five) brothers of the Gasca family. The arrangement was always—and remains—a seasonal one; these folks have their own farms, livelihoods, and extended families on their "rancho" in the

TRIMMING AND CLEANING

Like small children, green garlic tends to be grubby. Scrub the scapes slightly and rinse them under running water, especially at their bases, where sand often accumulates. You may need to remove tough or yellowed outer leaves from the stalks.

STEAMING AND BOILING

If you plan to steam green garlic, keep it brief—a few minutes at most. To add a subtle garlic touch, add some chopped scapes to the steamer basket in which other vegetables are cooking during the last couple of minutes. Boiling tends to leach out its delicate flavor.

STIR-FRYING AND SAUTÉING

Add green garlic to stir-fries during the last several minutes of preparation. To sauté green garlic, slice 6 to 8 stalks into thin rounds and sauté in a couple of tablespoons of butter or olive oil for at least 10 minutes.

MICROWAVING

Microwave green garlic like you would green onions. Chop into 1- or 2-inch pieces, place in a microwave-safe container containing ½ inch of water, cover, and microwave on high power for 3 to 5 minutes. After draining, they are ready to use in cooked dishes.

BLANCHING AND FREEZING

If you cannot use your green garlic right away, chop the scapes into 1-inch pieces, place them in zipper-lock freezer or vacuum food sealer-type bags or freezer containers, and squeeze out the excess air. They will keep for about 6 to 8 months at 0°F, if you can resist using them for that long.

EQUIVALENTS, MEASURES, AND SERVINGS

- 1 stalk green garlic = 1 or 2 regular garlic cloves

COMPLEMENTARY HERBS, SEASONINGS, AND FOODS

Beans, beef, beets, cabbage, chicken, eggplant, eggs, fish, lamb, lentils, mushrooms, pasta, pork, potatoes, poultry, rice, shellfish, spinach, tomatoes, vegetables, zucchini.

SERVING SUGGESTIONS

- Steam rice until it is about 80 percent cooked; take three green garlic shoots and place right on top of the rice; the garlic will wilt, releasing its aromatic juices down into the rice.

- Finely chop a tablespoon or two of green garlic and add it to your tuna fish salad. Delicious as a sandwich filling, or by itself!

- Combine green garlic (cut into 1-inch lengths), basil, pine nuts, olive oil, Parmesan cheese, and lemon juice in a food processor or mortar to make a delicious pesto.

- Throw sautéed green garlic into pasta salads and salad dressings.

- Chop up garlic shoots and mix with ground beef for the best grilled hamburgers you've ever tasted.

- Add green garlic at the last minute to stir-fries of all kinds.

- Sauté green garlic and add to frittatas, omelets, or scrambled eggs.
- Top potato soup with finely chopped scapes for a stronger kick than chives.
- Sprinkle chopped green garlic over pizza or Italian grinders.
- Make a delicious aïoli with green garlic, and use it as a dipping sauce, condiment, or flavoring agent with many different vegetables, meats, fish, pasta, soups, rice, sandwiches, and shellfish.

. . . .

GREEN GARLIC MASHED POTATOES   SERVES 6

1½ pounds Russet potatoes, peeled
4 tablespoons (½ stick) butter
2 bunches green garlic, green leaves only
½ cup milk
½ cup cream
Salt and freshly ground black pepper

1. Leave the potatoes whole if they are small, or cut them in half if they are large. Place them in a large saucepan with enough salted water to cover them by several inches. Bring to a simmer, cover partially, and adjust the heat to maintain a gentle simmer. Cook until a knife slips in easily, about 30 minutes. Drain, then return the potatoes to the warm pot. Return the pot to the stove and shake it until all of the moisture evaporates.

2. While the potatoes cook, melt the butter in a small saucepan over medium heat. Add the green garlic and sauté until softened, 3 to 5 minutes. Add the milk and cream. Season with salt and pepper.

3. Put the boiled potatoes through a food mill or ricer. Add the hot milk mixture and stir with a wooden spoon until smooth.

— *The Garlic Store, Fort Collins, Colorado*

. . . .

GARLIC SCAPE PIZZA   MAKES ONE 12-INCH PIZZA

6 to 8 green garlic scapes with stems
½ medium onion
½ red bell pepper
½ yellow bell pepper
1 tablespoon butter
3 to 4 cloves garlic, chopped
3 to 4 ounces (about ½ cup) tomato paste
1 (12-inch) prepared pizza crust (see Suggestions below)
½ cup grated mozzarella cheese
3 ounces spinach
½ cup grated Cheddar cheese
5-inch stick pepperoni, thinly sliced

central Guanajuato province that keep them more than busy in the off season. They are quite content to work in Minnesota for five or six months a year before returning home for the remaining months of the year . And the H2-A guest worker visa program—cumbersome and expensive as it is—does seem to fill this need fairly well.

As Featherstone Farm grew in scale and complexity, the brothers began inviting cousins, in-laws, and eventually their father and children to work here (FF is now a three-generation employer!). Women started to join the crew in 2011 or so. My own three sons spent many hours hanging around the Gascas' houses, initially for Minnesota Twins games broadcast on satellite TV (we had no television in our own house), but eventually for meals and off-hours lounging around. The Gascas are from an old-school "visiting culture" that I love, even if I have all too little time to enjoy it most days.

There is something about working with folks in the field, day after day, through good weather and bad, heavy crops and light, that makes for forging great friendships. Although I have little time for this now, I was out in the field every single day for a solid decade, planting, hoeing, picking, and packing with these folks. And although my limited Spanish was (and remains) a certain barrier to intimacy, over the past 14 years I feel like I have grown to know and appreciate and, yes, to love these folks as I would my own family.

I visited the village of Vista Hermosa for the first time in January 2008, and returned again in December 2011 with my oldest son, Emmet. I'd be dishonest if I said these trips were easy or even fun for me. Frankly, my Spanish is good enough stateside when the subjects are all familiar to me ("Weed these three rows" or "Pick all the beans"). But in the environment of the village, all its weaknesses are exposed; I go *around for three days feeling stupid and inadequate because of the language.*

Add to that the idea that my identity as patron means one thing in Rushford, and something completely different in Mexico. It's weird being hosted with the red-carpet treatment in a community that scarcely can afford it (multiple trips to the store each day to get expensive bottled juice or pop, etc.).

But these trips are not about me in any case, and so I work on putting my own discomfort aside and focus on the things that there are to enjoy while I'm there. And they are many.

On my second visit I served as Godfather of the Chains at the quinceañera celebration for Saul's youngest daughter, Xochil. My son Emmet held his breath as I entered the spotlight at that evening's celebration—surrounded by hundreds of villagers—and placed a gold chain (with an impossibly delicate clasp that I could hardly work) around her neck. What a sigh of relief we all breathed once that chain was in place and this tall patron retreated into the shadows!

That was the context for my third and most recent trip to Mexico in late March. This is why I wanted to bring my son Oscar to see the village and to meet the extended family—to see a way of life that is at some level much more sustainable—even if a great deal economically poorer—than our own. I also wanted to strengthen the connections between our families beyond the limits of work and employment.

The food!! If you've never had a handmade tortilla (homegrown corn shelled by hand and soaked overnight, milled into masa in the predawn hours, hand-formed and cooked on a colmál over a wood fire for breakfast), you have never really had a tortilla. The chiles and the móle sauce, the gordos de horno and the fresh goat (slaughtered in our honor) ... Such good eating.

10 cherry tomatoes, sliced in half
¾ cup grated Parmesan cheese

1. Preheat the oven to 350°F.

2. Slice the garlic scapes, onions, and peppers into small pieces. Put them into a medium sauté pan along with the butter and garlic. Cook until tender, and set aside to cool.

3. Spread the tomato paste over the pizza crust, and sprinkle with the mozzarella cheese.

4. Make a bed of spinach over the mozzarella cheese. Cover the spinach with the sautéed vegetables, and sprinkle the Cheddar cheese on top. Add the pepperoni slices and top with the cherry tomatoes. Sprinkle the Parmesan cheese over the top of the pizza.

5. Bake in the oven for 20 to 25 minutes.

Suggestions, Substitutions, and Additions:

- Buy prepared pizza crust or make your own.
- Use garlic scapes that are as young as possible and include the stems.
- Add hot pepper flakes while sautéing the vegetables.
- Use about 1 pound of hot Italian sausage cooked to a crisp in a skillet in place of the pepperoni, or go meatless.
- Any of the topping ingredients may be increased or decreased, depending on taste.

— *David Sutton, The Garlic Store, Fort Collins, Colorado*

GARLIC SCAPE SOUP

SERVES 4

Source Note: This soup enhances the delicate garlic-asparagus flavor of the scapes. You may use the garlic scape flowers as well.

3 cups garlic scapes, cut into 2-inch pieces
1 medium onion, chopped
1 tablespoon olive oil
1 teaspoon fresh thyme leaves or ½ teaspoon dried thyme
3 cups chicken broth, divided
1 cup cream
Salt and freshly ground black pepper

1. Sauté the garlic scapes and onion in the olive oil over medium heat until the vegetables become soft. Add the thyme at the end.

2. In a food processor, puree the vegetables and add chicken broth as needed to make a smooth paste.

3. In a saucepan, heat the vegetable puree and add the remaining

broth. Bring to a simmer and add the cream, stirring regularly. Adjust the seasoning with salt and pepper.

— The Garlic Store, Fort Collins, Colorado

. . . .

JAPANESE PICKLED GARLIC SCAPES

MAKES TWO 1-QUART JARS

Author Note: *The ingredients for this recipe can be found in Asian grocery stores or the Asian food aisle of larger supermarkets. Kombu is an edible seaweed used to flavor broths and soups and is sold dried in sheets. Shiso (sometimes called perilla) is a fresh herb of the mint family with a citrusy taste.*

The ginger in this recipe is cut into 4 bias-sliced oval pieces, 2 per jar. This makes it easier to use or remove, depending on your preference. If you want more of the ginger's spice, slice it finely into matchsticks instead.

½ pound garlic scapes
1 (3-inch) knob ginger, cut on the bias into 4 pieces
1½ cups water
1¾ cup rice wine vinegar
⅔ cup mirin rice wine
2 tablespoons granulated sugar
5 teaspoons kosher salt
1 (8-inch) sheet of kombu
4 green shiso leaves

1. Sterilize two 1-quart canning jars (along with two canning lids and two rings) by washing them and then submerging them in boiling water for 5 minutes. Dry upside down on a clean cloth.

2. If the garlic scapes are tough, blanch them for a couple of minutes in salted water, then plunge them into an ice-water bath. This will tenderize them.

3. In a saucepan, bring the ginger, water, rice wine vinegar, mirin, sugar and salt to a boil. Remove from heat. Taste and adjust flavors—sour, sweet, salty—to preference. Drop in the kombu and let sit for 10 minutes.

4. Meanwhile, crush the shiso leaves with your fingers and drop two into each jar. Stuff in the cold garlic scapes. Remove the kombu and ginger from the saucepan and drop them evenly into the jars.

5. Finish by evenly distributing the brine between the jars. Seal and let sit overnight before refrigerating. Although a week is sufficient for pickling, the flavor of the subtle kombu and shiso will intensify after a couple of months. To serve, either eat the pickled scapes whole, or chop and toss them with rice, salads, or any dish of your choosing.

— Brian Fink, The Cascadian Kitchen *blog*

We were humbled to be the recipients of all this caring.

The matriarch and patriarch, Salvador Sr., of the Gasca family. These two live surrounded by dozens and dozens of their children, grandchildren, and great-grandchildren, all within a quarter-mile radius of their home.

I was so proud of Oscar on this as well. A year ago he would have had a real tough time with the spice (HEAT!) and the lack of familiarity ("ick factor" with goat organ meat and the lack of sanitation). On this trip, he handled it all like a champ.

The community!! The progress of the Gasca family in building up their own farms and households over the past decade is incredible. And how much I truly love these people.

This is why, despite the heat, the language barrier, and the shortness of the trip (two days and three nights in Vista Hermosa, total), I considered it totally worthwhile. And thankfully Oscar shared the sentiment, too. When Jenni asked him what he thought about it, moments after stepping back through our front door, his response was a classic: "SO fun, Mom!!" It seems that Emmet and Oscar are making plans for a return trip (together, but without me!) for this coming winter. How wonderful!

And Esteban just called last night; he and Juan Gasca will be arriving Saturday morning on the bus. Another season is just beginning…

Books

The Truth About Organic
Gardening: Benefits, Drawbacks,
and the Bottom Line
Jeff Gillman, Timber Press, 2008.

The Good Food Revolution:
Growing Healthy Food,
People, and Communities
Will Allen, Gotham, 2013.

Greenhorns: 50 Dispatches from
the New Farmers' Movement
Zoe Ida Bradbury and
Severine von Tscharner Fleming,
Storey Publishing, 2012.

The Dirty Life: A Memoir of
Farming, Food and Love
Kristin Kimball, Scribner, 2011.

Farmer Jane: Women
Changing the Way We Eat
Temra Costa,
Gibbs Smith, 2010.

Fresh Fruit, Broken Bodies:
Migrant Farmworkers in the
United States
Seth Holmes, University of
California Press, 2013.

Stuffed and Starved: The Hidden
Battle for the World Food System
Raj Patel, Melville House, 2012.

Food Politics: How the Food
Industry Influences Nutrition
and Health
Marion Nestle, University of
California Press, 2013.

The Omnivore's Dilemma: A
Natural History of Four Meals
Michael Pollan, Penguin, 2007.

SPINACH, NUTS, AND CHEESE   SERVES 2

Source Note: This is a great savory dish. You can add hot chiles for added pizzazz.

> 2 slices thick-cut bacon, minced (optional)
> 1 tablespoon olive oil
> ¼ cup minced onion (red or white)
> 2 green garlic scapes, minced, or 2 regular cloves garlic
> ¼ cup walnuts
> 1 bunch spinach, coarsely chopped and washed
> ¼ cup cubed feta or fresh mozzarella cheese

1. In a medium skillet over medium-high heat, brown the bacon (if using), set it aside, and drain off the fat. Heat the olive oil on medium heat, and sauté the onion, garlic scapes, and walnuts until they soften.

2. Stir the spinach into the nut-and-onion mixture and cook down, about 5 minutes.

3. Add the bacon and cheese; cover until warmed, about 3 minutes.

— *Judy, Featherstone Farm CSA member*

Lettuce

LACTUCA SATIVA

Time was when lettuce in America meant only the anemic, tightly headed iceberg, wrapped in their lattice-woven, clear plastic bonnets and sitting huddled in the supermarket produce section. Thankfully, those days are a distant memory as we stroll through those same aisles and in farmers markets and encounter a vibrant bounty of different lettuces and other greens from which to choose for the evening's salads.

Lettuce is eaten mostly as a raw salad green in the United States, but in some countries such as France and China, it is also cooked as a vegetable in its own right. (Stir-fried iceberg is an incredibly popular dish in Hong Kong.) In America, you can still find iceberg, but also butterhead lettuces (like Boston and Bibb), romaine (famous in Caesar salad), looseleaf types (which include frilly varieties and oakleaf), and stem lettuces, which are more likely to be seen in Asian markets.

HISTORY

The exact homeland of lettuce remains lost to the ages, although many botanical authorities believe that its wild cousin originated in Europe or Southwest Asia (possibly Turkey or Iran). Lettuce was recorded growing in Babylonian gardens as early as 800 BCE, and lettuce seeds have been found in ancient Egyptian tombs. The earliest lettuces did not form heads but instead grew leaves from a tall, central stalk, which our modern lettuces mimic when they bolt—go to seed—in hot weather. Lettuce did not reach East Asia until after 30 CE, and it was slow to find favor with the French, who preferred watercress instead during the Middle Ages. Columbus probably introduced the plant to America, where Thomas Jefferson had it grown in his gardens at Monticello.

NUTRITION

The nutrient content of lettuce varies widely, depending on the type. The chlorophyll-deprived iceberg is less nutritious than romaine, but all lettuces have an extremely high water content. A 2-cup serving of shredded romaine contains 143 percent of your daily requirement for vitamin K, 60 percent of your vitamin A, nearly half of your vitamin C, over a third of your folate, and about 10 calories.

SEASON

Baby lettuce is one of the earliest available greens in farmers markets and CSAs, appearing in April or May and then throughout the summer. Lettuce dislikes hot temperatures, so the most tender, flavorful lettuces appear in the spring and fall. Commercially grown lettuce is available year-round.

SELECTION

Look for fresh, crisp heads with no signs of withering, sliminess, or discoloration. Contrary to popular belief, a brownish color on the underside of the cut stem end is not necessarily a sign of bad or old lettuce; the milky sap of cut lettuce naturally oxidizes when exposed to air.

STORAGE

To keep lettuce fresher longer, wash and dry romaine and leaf lettuce thoroughly before storing. Wrap the greens in paper towels or in a clean kitchen towel, then place in plastic bags. Seal the bags tightly and keep in the refrigerator vegetable crisper. Periodically check the bags and replace any damp towels. Butter lettuces, on the other hand, should not be washed before storing.

If you find yourself preparing a lot of lettuce or other salad greens, a salad spinner can be quite useful in removing excess moisture before serving. Salad greens should always be thoroughly dry before being dressed; otherwise the salad may end up becoming a watery mess.

If you do not have a salad spinner, placing greens in an empty pillowcase bound with a rubber band and running it in the laundry dryer for a few minutes with the heat off can be quite effective, or even swinging it around your head for a couple of minutes (the pillowcase, not the dryer). The trick to preventing bruised greens is not to pack too many greens inside the pillowcase.

Lettuce and other salad greens should not be stored next to apples or other fruits that emit ethylene gas, which will hasten spoilage and cause brown spots.

TRIMMING AND CLEANING

Lettuces, especially those from a farmers market or fresh from a field, can harbor more than their fair share of dirt and small insects. To clean, remove the outer leaves and rinse them thoroughly under running water, or submerge and swish them in a sinkful of water. Keep rinsing the inner leaves as well until all traces of dirt are gone. Then cut off the base where the leaves attach to the stem, as this tends to be bitter.

STEAMING AND BOILING

Steamed lettuce may sound strange to Americans, but the Chinese, who almost never eat vegetables raw, prefer their lettuce braised or steamed. Shredded lettuce can be briefly steamed for 2 to 3 minutes and topped with butter, or you can add lettuce toward the very end of preparation of slow-cooked meats and vegetables. Boiling is way too harsh for this delicate green.

STIR-FRYING AND SAUTÉING

Although uncommon in America, stir-fried lettuce is a favorite dish in some Asian countries. Simply place washed, dried lettuce leaves in a wok or skillet in which vegetable oil and seasoning have been heated, and stir-fry for about 1 minute, or until the lettuce just wilts. Add a bit of soy or oyster sauce, and cook for 1 more minute, or until the lettuce is tender but still bright green.

MICROWAVING

Microwaving is not lettuce's favorite treatment, although it is acceptable if the lettuce is shredded and combined with other ingredients that con-

tain a bit of cooking liquid or sauce. Microwave on high power for about 2 minutes, or until the lettuce is tender but not shriveled.

BLANCHING AND FREEZING

Freezing is not recommended for lettuce because of its high water content.

EQUIVALENTS, MEASURES, AND SERVINGS

- Leaf and romaine lettuce: 1 medium head = 8 cups leaves
- Bibb and butter lettuce: 1 medium head = 4 cups leaves
- 1 pound raw lettuce = 4 to 5 (2-cup) servings
- 5 cups raw lettuce (about ½ pound) = about 1 cup cooked
- ½ cup cooked lettuce per person
- 1 whole braised lettuce = 1 serving

COMPLEMENTARY HERBS, SEASONINGS, AND FOODS

Anchovies, apples, avocados, bacon, balsamic vinegar, cheese (blue, feta, goat, Parmesan), chicken, chives, citrus juice, croutons, eggs, garlic, greens, hazelnut oil, herbs, lemon juice, mayonnaise, meat (beef, lamb, pork), mustard, nuts, olives, olive oil, onions, oranges, peanuts, peas, pepper, raisins, rice wine vinegar, sea salt, sesame, vinaigrette, vinegar, walnuts, walnut oil.

SERVING SUGGESTIONS

- Try a truly lush taco, with plenty of shredded green leaf or Bibb lettuce.
- For fun, substitute a sturdy lettuce leaf for the seaweed wrapper in sushi.
- Cut tightly headed lettuce (like iceberg) into wedges and serve, well chilled and crisped, with salad dressing as a dip.
- Stir-fry lettuce in a little sesame oil, ginger, and soy sauce like you would spinach or other tender greens.
- Lettuce is tasty wilted with a warm onion-and-bacon dressing.
- One popular French dish combines green peas, shallots, butter, sugar, water or stock, and shredded lettuce, covered and cooked on low heat for 15 minutes or until tender.
- Put out romaine leaves along with other raw vegetables on the crudités tray, and add your favorite dips.
- The old standby: a truly good bacon, lettuce, and tomato sandwich, made with only the finest-quality bread, thick-cut bacon, farm-fresh lettuce, and vine-ripened tomatoes. Irresistible!
- Pickle lettuce with sugar, salt, and vinegar in the refrigerator the same way you would cucumbers.
- Stuff romaine or Bibb lettuce leaves with blue cheese, walnuts, and bacon. Drizzle with good olive oil or nut oil, and serve as a "hand salad."

CITRUS BUTTER SALAD   SERVES 2 TO 4

Source Note: This is a terrific beginning-of-summer salad.

CITRUS VINAIGRETTE
2 tablespoons grapefruit juice

mornings, and finding plump earthworms were simple joys that I had nearly forgotten in all those intervening years. But the body and mind have a way of remembering, and soon the front yard was riotous with vegetables and herbs and overflowing with flowers and coleus. Stepping out the front door into the lushness on bright summer days made me smile. Big-time.

Growing up, I also had a passion for foraging for wild foods, a habit that I still practice to this day. Finding miner's lettuce, blackberries, watercress, wild fennel, sea beans, rose hips, prickly pear fruits, orach, and wild nasturtiums on hikes delights me to no end, and there are places that I seek out where I know choice plants still stand. They feed my soul as well as my stomach.

When I was living at that suburban Seattle house, a young neighbor boy whose family is from the Middle East used to come over when I was tending to my garden. One day he squealed, pointing to a fat, dark eggplant hanging from a plant bending over from its weight. "We eat that!" he shouted, his big dark eyes shining brightly, and suddenly I realized that this was the first time he had ever seen one of his staple foods actually growing on the plant—at its source.

How sad, I thought: a whole generation of kids growing up with no idea of the connection between their food and the earth. Not only do gardening and foraging make these ties apparent, but they also teach us to value life, the essence of what keeps us and others existing on this wondrous planet. They remind you to get outside yourself, to nurture energies that are far bigger than yours, ones that we should not—and cannot—remain so isolated from if we are to survive and thrive.

So help a child start a lifetime of caring—by bringing home a packet of seeds and a pot of soil today. And watch their wonder unfold, as well as your own.

½ tablespoon champagne vinegar
¼ teaspoon salt
2½ tablespoons olive oil

In a small bowl, combine all of the ingredients until they are thoroughly blended. Set aside to let the flavors mingle for at least 1 hour.

Salad

1 (12-inch) stalk green garlic, finely chopped
½ tablespoon olive oil
1 head green butter lettuce, torn into bite-size pieces
¼ cup toasted pine nuts

1. Sauté the green garlic in a hot pan with the olive oil. Cook for 1 to 2 minutes, or until it turns barely brown. Cool slightly.

2. Toss all of the ingredients and top with Citrus Vinaigrette (recipe above).

— *Jan Taylor, Featherstone Farm CSA member*

MARCO'S CAESAR SALAD

SERVES 1

Source Note: This is the Caesar salad that was served for decades at the restaurant in the world-famous Wrigley Building in Chicago, home to the chewing gum company and one of the Windy City's most beautiful architectural landmarks.

Dressing

¼ teaspoon sea salt
½ clove garlic
2 to 3 anchovy fillets
Freshly ground black pepper from 5 turns of the pepper mill
¼ teaspoon red wine vinegar
Juice of ½ lemon
1 egg, coddled
½ teaspoon Worcestershire sauce
2 drops Tabasco
¼ cup olive oil
½ teaspoon spicy mustard

Whisk together all of the dressing ingredients in a bowl or blender.

Salad

Romaine lettuce, washed, dried, and chilled
Parmesan cheese
1 to 2 tablespoons croutons

"I don't think America will have really made it until we have our own salad dressing. Until then we're stuck behind the French, Italians, Russians, and Caesarians."

— *Pat McNelis*

Coarsely tear the romaine lettuce and place it in a bowl. Add the dressing and toss well. Just before serving, grate Parmesan cheese over the top and sprinkle with the croutons.

— *Maureen Cooney,* Bluff Country Co-op Cookbook

Lettuce washday at Featherstone Farm.

GRILLED ROMAINE WITH POACHED EGGS AND GREEN GODDESS DRESSING

SERVES 4

Author Note: *Enjoy this novel dish as a complete lunch or dinner. If you don't have time to make the poached eggs, just prepare the lettuce and other vegetables as your salad on the side.*

4 eggs, poached (see Cooking Note below)
2 large heads romaine lettuce
5 scallions (green onions)
1 bunch radishes, preferably French-style
1 large or 2 small kohlrabi bulbs
3 tablespoons olive oil, divided
1 tablespoon lemon juice
Zest from 1 lemon
Salt and freshly ground black pepper
Green Goddess Dressing (see recipe below)
¼ cup toasted pine nuts or sunflower seeds

1. Poach the eggs per the Cooking Note below and hold them in a bowl of cold water until needed.

2. Thoroughly wash all of the vegetables. Trim part of the bottoms off the romaine heads (but not too far up because you want them to stay

intact as heads). Cut the heads in half lengthwise, then gently wash them on the inside and between the leaves.

3. Finely chop the scallions and radishes and put them in a medium bowl. Cut the leaves off the kohlrabi and peel the bulb using a sharp vegetable peeler or knife. You should end up with a pure white, round bulb. Slice it into quarters, then cut each piece into very thin slices. Mix the kohlrabi with the other vegetables and add 2 tablespoons of the olive oil, plus the lemon juice, lemon zest, salt, and pepper. Set aside.

4. Lightly drizzle the remaining 1 tablespoon olive oil, salt, and pepper over the romaine heads. Prepare your grill and lay them open, cut side down, for 2 to 3 minutes, or until they are charred and slightly wilted. Flip them over and do the same on the other side. Set aside.

5. Put the chopped vegetables that were set aside into a grill pan (or something metal with small holes). Grill for 4 to 5 minutes over medium heat. This step is optional, as the vegetables are delicious raw as well—this just softens them a bit.

6. Reheat the poached eggs by slipping them into a pan of simmering water for several minutes.

7. To assemble the salad, place one of the romaine halves cut side up, add some of the vegetable slices, and then top with an egg. Drizzle with the Green Goddess Dressing and sprinkle with some toasted pine nuts. Add salt and pepper to taste if needed.

Cooking Note: To poach the eggs, bring a deep-sided saucepan filled three-quarters full with water to a low simmer. Make sure it never fully boils. Add 1 tablespoon of vinegar (any kind) to the pot to prevent the eggs from running. Crack open each egg one at a time into a separate bowl and then slide the egg into the pan. Cook each egg for 3 to 4 minutes, or until the whites set but the yellow is still runny. Remove them with a slotted spoon and hold them in a bowl of cold water until you're ready to reheat and serve them.

— *Sang Lee Farms, Peconic, New York*

GREEN GODDESS DRESSING   MAKES 4 CUPS

Source Note: You will have more than enough dressing from this recipe, so feel free to halve it if you want just enough for this meal. If you make the full amount, it will go great on your salads all week!

8 anchovy fillets, chopped
2 ripe avocados, peeled and diced
5 scallions, finely chopped
2 garlic cloves, minced

2 tablespoons vinegar (any type you prefer)
2 tablespoons fresh lemon juice
2 tablespoons chopped fresh flat-leaf parsley leaves
1½ tablespoons chopped fresh tarragon
1 tablespoon chopped fresh cilantro
1½ cups mayonnaise
2 tablespoons sour cream

Place all of the ingredients except the mayonnaise and sour cream into a food processor. Blend until creamy, then add the mayo and sour cream. Taste and add any spices or additional herbs that suit your fancy. If the dressing is too thick, you can add a tablespoon of milk to thin it out.

— *Sang Lee Farms, Peconic, New York*

. . . .

MYLAR'S LETTUCE WRAPS

Author Note: These Asian-inspired appetizers make fun, interactive hors d'oeuvres for kids and adults alike and are great at parties. Choices of fillings and seasonings are limited only by your imagination.

LETTUCE
Wash and thoroughly dry large lettuce leaves. Butterhead lettuces work extremely well for these wraps, but any lettuce with large, pliable leaves is suitable. Arrange on a large serving platter. Reserve 2 to 4 lettuce leaves per person.

FILLING SUGGESTIONS
- Strips of chicken, turkey, steak, barbecued beef, corned beef, ground beef, pastrami, deli meats, pepperoni, Chinese pork
- Smoked salmon, smoked carp, tuna packed in oil, anchovies, kippers, pickled herring
- Chunks of hardboiled egg
- Shredded or sliced cheese
- Green and red bell pepper slices, onion rings, tomato slices or cherry tomato halves, bean sprouts, and other vegetables
- Shredded lettuce
- Baked or fried tofu or tempeh
- Fresh herbs like cilantro, parsley, mint, basil, and shiso
- Fruit, such as apples, pears, mandarin oranges, strawberries, blueberries, and raspberries
- Roasted nuts or ground peanuts
- Tuna, ham, chicken, or egg salad
- Whole shrimp, crab, or lobster pieces
- Cooked sticky rice or sushi rice; cooked bulgur or quinoa

"Lettuce is like conversation; it must be fresh and crisp, so sparkling that you scarcely notice the bitter in it."

— *Charles Dudley Warner, American essayist and novelist*

"What is more refreshing than salads when your appetite seems to have deserted you, or even after a capacious dinner—the nice, fresh, green, and crisp salad, full of life and health, which seems to invigorate the palate and dispose the masticating powers to a much longer duration."

— *Alexis Soyer, 19th-century French chef*

Books

Salad of the Day: 365 Recipes for Every Day of the Year
Georgeanne Brennan, Williams-Sonoma, Weldon Owen, 2012.

Salad as a Meal: Healthy Main-Dish Salads for Every Season
Patricia Wells, HarperCollins, 2011.

Salad Samurai: 100 Cutting-Edge, Ultra-Hearty, Easy-to-Make Salads You Don't Have to Be Vegan to Love
Terry Hope Romero, Da Capo Lifelong Books, 2014.

CONDIMENT SUGGESTIONS

- Chili sauce, ketchup
- Mayonnaise, aïoli
- Mustard (yellow, Dijon, stone-ground, whole-seed)
- Sriracha, *romesco*, harissa
- Hummus
- Tapenade
- Hoisin sauce, soy sauce, plum sauce, oyster sauce
- Nuoc mam (Vietnamese fish sauce), nam pla (Thai fish sauce)
- Pickled ginger
- Salsas
- Whipped cream or honey (for fruit wraps)

Arrange the filling ingredients on serving platters, set out the condiments and lettuce leaves, and let the fun begin.

— *Mi Ae Lipe*

FRENCH CREAM OF LETTUCE SOUP   SERVES 6

Source Note: This savory and attractive French first-course soup sounds like it might be bland, but it isn't. It has a wonderful consistency and is distinctive enough to set up strongly flavored courses. Its texture is so silken that you'll be champing at the bit to eat more.

4 tablespoons (½ stick) butter
2 cloves garlic, finely minced
2 tablespoons minced fresh parsley
1 tablespoon minced fresh tarragon
1 cup chopped onion
2 cups finely shredded romaine lettuce
1 cup finely chopped watercress
4 cups beef or vegetable stock
2 egg yolks
2 cups light cream
Salt and freshly ground black pepper

1. Heat the butter in a large saucepan, then sauté the garlic, parsley, tarragon, and onion until the onion is transparent. Add the lettuce and watercress, and stir over low heat for 5 minutes. Stir in the stock and simmer, uncovered, for 30 minutes.

2. When ready to serve, whisk the egg yolks and cream in a separate bowl with several tablespoons of the hot soup. Then pour the mixture into the saucepan, stirring constantly over low heat until the soup thickens slightly. (Do not allow it to boil!) Season to taste with salt and pepper and serve immediately.

— *Fooddownunder.com*

Mushrooms

There is something primordial and atavistic about mushrooms. They represent a food that still connects us to the wild, and the fact that many of our most prized edible fungi resist being cultivated only deepens that mystique. Mushrooms also defy tidy classification; at least 40,000 species are known, out of which several thousand are widely eaten by humans. Very few mushroom species can actually kill you, but lots of them will give you at the very least a big stomachache or worse. Foraging for wild mushrooms is great fun and an activity well worth pursuing, but always be certain to properly identify any you put in your basket; a number of dangerous look-alikes exist. Much folklore also abounds about how to tell if a mushroom is poisonous. Nearly all of these tales are simply not true, and ignoring them can save your life.

Mushrooms are a delight gastronomically with their delicate flavors and a meaty, supple texture when cooked. Their savor partially comes from the fact that they are one of nature's richest natural sources of glutamate, an amino acid that is a component of the seasoning monosodium glutamate or MSG (seaweed and Parmesan cheese also contain significant amounts of glutamate). This chemical accounts for their meaty, savory taste property called umami, *making mushrooms delicious on their own or when combined with other foods. (But note that glutamate itself is not harmful for people with MSG sensitivities.)*

Mushrooms are extremely versatile and tasty combined with meats, poultry, pasta, vegetables, and eggs. Many wild mushrooms, like morels, are seasonal and the window of time to enjoy them is extremely brief; take advantage of it when you see them in your box or at the market.

Thousands of edible mushroom species exist, but here is a sampling of the most popular fungi available from CSA farms and farmers markets:

Chanterelle (*Cantharellus cibarius*)
These beautiful mushrooms, with their distinctive fluted trumpet-like shape, are among the most delicious ones too, with peppery, spicy, or fruity flavor notes. Chanterelles do not take to cultivation, so specimens you see have been foraged, typically from coniferous forests. Chanterelles come in several species, but the golden chanterelle is the most common. Also not to be missed is the black trumpet (*Craterellus falla*), which is actually a different genus but included in the larger chanterelle family. If you see black trumpets at your local market, do not pass them up—in spite of their unappetizing-looking dark, shriveled forms, they are among the most flavorful of all mushrooms.

Cremini and Portobello (*Agaricus bisporus*)
You may be familiar with the small white button mushrooms that are cremini, as well as the huge slab-like caps of portobellos, but not realize that they are one and the same fungi—just at different stages of development. The meaty portobellos are a treat brushed with nut or garlic-infused oil and grilled, and they are often used as a meat substitute in sandwiches.

Enokitake or Enoki (*Flammulina velutipes*)

Who doesn't smile when they see these perky, tiny, pale, long-stemmed mushrooms? They grow in very dense clumps that are sold by the piece. Their flavor is distinctive and quite unmushroomy, with hints of yeast, fruit, and acid, and their texture is crisp and surprising. These little guys deserve to be savored simply—raw in salads or appetizers, or cooked very briefly and added to soups and egg dishes. Enokis are usually farmed.

Lion's Mane (*Hericium erinaceus*)

This is a bizarre-looking fungus that looks something like a cross between a white mop and a massive grouping of impeccably neat bean sprouts hanging downward. They are often farmed, but they bruise easily and do not ship well. Their flavor is delicate and reminiscent of lobster, with a crab- or seafood-like consistency to match when cooked.

Morel (*Morchella* species)

With their wizened, deeply grooved conical caps that look like something out of a Grimm's fairy tale, morels are among the most distinctive of all fungi. As one of the very first mushrooms of spring, their appearance is heralded and as much anticipated for the sport of finding them as for eating them. Morels can be farmed, but most specimens are gathered in the woods. They have a nutty, somewhat smoky flavor, and a chewy, hearty texture that lusciously soaks up broth and sauce. They often come with quite a bit of sandy grit hiding inside their grooves, so wash them very thoroughly before cooking.

Porcini (*Boletus edulis*)

Sometimes called cèpes in French and boletes in America and elsewhere, porcinis are enjoyed the world over for their creamy texture, unique perfume, crunchy stems, and high nutritional value. Although their appearance can vary widely, they tend to have very bulbous bases and a spongy consistency; the caps of these mushrooms actually consist of tiny tubes in lieu of gills. Porcini are extremely difficult to cultivate and therefore are typically foraged. They are also one of the very few wild mushrooms that are delicious raw as well as pickled.

Oyster (*Pleurotus* species)

Oyster mushrooms cover a rather large family of fungi with many variations in color and form. However, they all grow quite densely in tightly packed clumps, with slightly flattened caps that somewhat resemble their namesake mollusk. Oysters are easily farmed, growing fast and prolifically, so they are popular for cultivation. They tend to be on the bland side but are very tender when cooked, so they make a great foil for stronger-flavored seasonings and sauces.

Shiitake (*Lentinula edodes*)

The shiitake is native to East Asia, where it is revered for its culinary and medicinal qualities. It is also immensely popular in America and a regular ingredient on the foodie circuit, prized for its meaty texture and earthy flavor. Shiitakes are extensively farmed, and their quality can vary wildly depending on the conditions under which they are grown.

HISTORY

It's probably safe to say that people have been consuming mushrooms as long as humans have been around, but there's no telling how many poor souls died from figuring out which ones were poisonous. Nearly every major world cuisine has prized its own local varieties of fungi, from the wood-ear mushroom soups of China to the pickled mushrooms of Eastern Europe. In ancient Egypt, mushrooms were valued so highly that the pharaohs proclaimed that they were a food for royalty only, thus assuring their own supply.

France became perhaps the first year-round cultivator of mushrooms in the late 1700s, where the fungi were grown in special caves near Paris that were set aside for this purpose. Since then, mushroom culture and farming have become huge industries in the Netherlands, Poland, the United States, and China, the last of which produces nearly 70 percent of the world's crop. Still, many gastronomically prized species resist cultivation (even varieties widely farmed today require exacting conditions to thrive), so the mushroom remains a food source that does not bend entirely to the will of humans.

NUTRITION

Specific mushrooms vary widely in their nutritional content, depending on their species, but overall mushrooms are excellent sources of copper, selenium, B vitamins, phosphorus, potassium, zinc, and manganese. A 1-cup serving contains about 21 calories. They also contain significant amounts of dietary fiber. Some species (especially shiitakes, which have been studied extensively for their medicinal properties) also contain cholesterol-reducing compounds like lentinacin and numerous antioxidants.

SEASON

Commercially grown mushrooms are widely available year-round. But many species are quite seasonal and are at their best in the fall and winter. In particular, morels tend to be an early spring mushroom.

SELECTION

Mushrooms of all kinds should be firm, plump, and fresh looking. Avoid specimens that are desiccated, discolored, soft, slimy, or damp. With button-type mushrooms, look for unopened "veils" underneath the caps; open veils with exposed gills (the little slats extending outward) may mean a mushroom is past its prime, but it also might indicate a richer flavor.

STORAGE

Always store fresh mushrooms dry in the refrigerator, and do not wash them until you are ready to use them. Mushrooms get slimy quickly if stored in plastic, so keep them in a paper bag, which absorbs moisture. Mushrooms prefer lots of ventilation, so refrain from packing them tightly together. They are also quite perishable; use within 3 to 5 days.

TRIMMING AND CLEANING

Mushrooms frequently harbor dirt and insects (especially morels, with their deeply grooved caps). The easiest way to wash mushrooms of all types is to immerse them in a sinkful of water and swish them gently to

What's for Dinner, Zeus?

Ancient Romans believed that mushrooms gave them strength in battle, dubbing them the "food of the gods."

Other cultures thought that mushrooms had powers to give them superhuman strength, help them find lost objects, and lead their souls to the gods.

"Nature alone is antique and the oldest art a mushroom."

— *Thomas Carlyle, Scottish philosopher*

remove debris. Or if they are not particularly dirty, you can wipe them clean with a damp cloth or a soft brush; special mushroom brushes are available in specialty stores for this purpose, but a toothbrush with soft bristles works just as well.

STEAMING AND BOILING

Steaming is a better way to cook mushrooms than boiling, which tends to make them waterlogged. Steam whole button mushrooms or quartered pieces for 6 to 7 minutes, or until they become tender.

To boil mushrooms, the key is to crowd them in a pan and use as little liquid as possible. Layer them in a sauté pan 2 to 3 deep, and add enough water to barely cover them. For 8 ounces of mushrooms, add 1 tablespoon of butter or oil and 1 teaspoon of salt. Bring to a boil over high heat, and turn down the heat once they come to a rolling boil. But don't simmer—they need to boil. Don't be alarmed at the amount of liquid in the pan—the mushrooms are simply releasing their own water. Keep them at a boil until you hear them start to sizzle—a sign that all of the liquid has evaporated. Boiling times vary widely, depending on the type of mushroom used.

GRILLING AND BROILING

Larger-capped mushrooms like portobellos and shiitakes are luscious grilled. Lightly brush the caps and stems with a little oil or dressing; season with salt, pepper, and herbs; and grill or broil about 6 inches from the heat source for 4 to 6 minutes on each side. Brush with oil once or twice to keep them from drying out.

STIR-FRYING AND SAUTÉING

Mushrooms are extremely versatile in stir-fries. Quarter or slice the mushrooms into bite-size pieces. Stir-fry the pieces in 1 tablespoon of butter or hot oil in a skillet or wok over high heat. A lot of liquid will appear in the pan as the mushrooms release their moisture. Keep cooking until barely any water remains in the pan, about 5 to 7 minutes. Once the mushrooms are tender and cooked through, it is best to set them aside in a bowl as you cook the other ingredients; this prevents them from absorbing any more oil—otherwise you'll end up with greasy mushrooms.

BAKING AND ROASTING

Most of us don't think of roasting mushrooms, but this cooking method concentrates their earthy flavors. They can be heavenly with a highly flavored fat like goose or duck.

Brush the mushrooms with oil or fat and place them in a shallow baking pan. Sprinkle with sea salt and freshly ground black pepper. Bake in a 450°F oven for about 20 minutes, stirring occasionally, until they are browned.

MICROWAVING

Place 8 ounces of thickly sliced mushrooms in a shallow, microwave-safe baking dish or serving bowl. Because mushrooms have a naturally high water content, no extra cooking liquid or fat is needed. Cover and microwave on high power for 2 to 3 minutes, stirring once.

- 8 ounces = 2 to 3 minutes

BLANCHING AND FREEZING

Most kinds of mushrooms can be successfully frozen from the raw state, as long as they are not high in moisture (in which case it is better to cook them before freezing). Regardless of whether you use cooked or raw mushrooms, it is best to freeze them individually rather than as a big clump. That way you can pour out just what you need.

For raw mushrooms: Chop or slice the mushrooms into pieces no thicker than ½ inch. Spread them in a single layer on a cookie sheet or a large plate, making sure the pieces do not overlap. Freeze for 2 hours, then transfer the frozen pieces into zipper-lock freezer or vacuum food sealer-type bags, or freezer containers. Squeeze out any excess air (unless you are using the vacuum sealing method).

For cooked mushrooms: Slice them up smaller than you would for raw ones. Heat a little butter or oil in a skillet over medium or low heat; add the mushrooms and cook, stirring frequently as the mushrooms release their liquid and reabsorb it. Once the mushrooms are cooked through, let them cool to room temperature, then transfer them to either small freezer containers (a 1-cup size works well for most recipes) or zipper-lock storage bags. Frozen mushrooms will keep for up to 1 year at 0°F.

EQUIVALENTS, MEASURES, AND SERVINGS

- 3 ounces = 1 cup
- 1 pound fresh button mushrooms = 20 to 24 medium mushrooms
- 1 pound fresh button mushrooms = 2 cups sliced and cooked
- 8 ounces sliced fresh mushrooms = 4 ounces drained, canned, sliced
- 8 ounces sliced fresh mushrooms = 1½ ounces dried mushrooms plus ¾ cup boiling water
- 4-ounce can sliced button mushrooms = ¾ cup
- 1½ ounces dried mushrooms = 8 ounces sliced fresh
- 1 tablespoon powdered mushrooms = 3 tablespoons whole dried mushrooms
- 1 tablespoon powdered mushrooms = 4 ounces fresh mushrooms

COMPLEMENTARY HERBS, SEASONINGS, AND FOODS

Arugula, asparagus, bacon, balsamic vinegar, beef, Belgian endive, butter, carrots, cashews, celery, chicken, chiles, chives, cream, duck, eggs, fennel, garlic, ginger, green onions, hazelnuts, hazelnut oil, lamb, nutmeg, olive oil, onions, palm hearts, Parmesan cheese, parsley, pasta, peppers, pine nuts, potatoes, red wine, rice, rosemary, savory, shallots, sherry, soy sauce, spinach, tarragon, thyme, tomatoes, turkey, veal, walnuts, walnut oil, white wine, wild rice, winter squash, zucchini.

SERVING SUGGESTIONS

- Braise or simmer morels in stock, cream, or broth, reducing to concentrate the flavors. Happily, they are also excellent with asparagus and peas, which are in season at the same time.
- Separate and sprinkle enoki mushrooms raw over salads, or treat them as you would sprouts.
- Mushrooms and eggs are natural mates, especially in omelets and frittatas.

ed winter market to purchase anything that Mycoterra Farm sells, or to preorder in bulk.

The Portland, Maine–based **North Spore Mushroom Company** sells their fungi both through a CSA and wholesale, and it also offers teas and tinctures made from foraged wild, medicinal mushrooms. From January to March, participants who pay for a full share ($250) get a pound of cultivated mushrooms every week and a mushroom cookbook. Half shares get you a half pound for $150 and a cookbook. North Spore also sells to about 15 restaurants.

Nantucket Mushrooms LLC of South Chatham, Massachusetts, offers 10-week CSA shares starting at a quarter pound per week. A weekly assortment may include golden oyster, pink oyster, Phoenix oyster, blue oyster, shiitake, and lion's mane, all grown without pesticides and herbicides. It also offers educational workshops throughout the year on cultivation, medicinal mushrooms, mushroom identification, and bioremediation. You can find its products online at www.efungi.com. Nantucket also sells directly to chefs, restaurants, and markets, and ships nationwide and overnight.

Cherry Tree House Mushrooms grows delicious and fresh shiitake, oyster, and other log-cultivated mushrooms in the Twin Cities region in Minnesota. It partners with several area CSA farms to provide add-on mushroom shares.

If you want to grow mushrooms yourself, the Oregon nonprofit **Fungi for the People** provides extensive education and resources for a variety of mushroom-growing projects, as well as medicinal mushroom supplies. It offers workshops in Oregon and a diversity of edible and medicinal mushroom spawn, released in the right season for using it, delivered anywhere in the mainland United States or Canada.

According to the United States Department of Agriculture, the top mushroom-producing countries include China (with 9.2 billion pounds in 2010) and the United States (896 million in 2013), followed by Italy, the Netherlands, and Poland.

In America, Pennsylvania is the leading state producing agaricus mushrooms, with almost of it centered in Kennett Square in Chester County. The county alone produced over 400 million pounds, or 47 percent of the nation's crop in 2013–2014. California comes in second, with about 18 percent.

- Season and broil or grill a whole portobello mushroom cap and use it in a sandwich or as a burger substitute.
- Stuff the caps of bigger mushrooms like cremini and portobellos with savory, herb-filled mixtures.
- Some mushrooms, like porcini, oysters, shiitakes, and chanterelles, can be pickled. Look for Polish and Russian recipes, which tend to be excellent.
- Mushrooms with risotto or polenta is another combination made in heaven.
- Porcini and other boletes are exceptional when baked in parchment, which actually bakes rather than just steams them, in contrast to aluminum foil.
- The delicate flavors and textures of mushrooms make them terrific in stir-fries. Depending on the variety of mushroom, you can cook them substantially with other ingredients or wait until the last minute to preserve their crunchiness (as with enoki).
- Pasta and mushrooms are another dreamy combination. A filling, quick dish is to sauté thinly sliced mushrooms in oil and garlic and add them to fettuccine, orecchiette, or spaghetti.
- Roasting mushrooms is sometimes overlooked, and that is a shame—it concentrates the flavors. Try using duck or goose fat for a change in flavor.
- When you soak dried mushrooms to reconstitute them for recipes, save their soaking liquid—it makes a terrific base for stock.
- Mushrooms and beef or veal are best buddies. Try this combination as a stir-fry or in stroganoff, or prepare the mushrooms as a side dish with steak.
- Wild rice has a special affinity for mushrooms; the contrasting textures and flavors can be mesmerizing.
- Try making chicken Marsala, a savory dish of chicken cutlets, mushrooms, and Marsala wine. It's an awesome comfort food dish on crisp fall and cold winter nights.
- Chop up mushrooms finely and use them in hamburgers, tacos, meat loaf, lasagna, meatballs, and pasta sauce. This will help cut the amount of ground beef used and create a more healthful dish with fewer calories.

LA PIZZA DELLA TERRA (PIZZA OF THE EARTH)

MAKES TWO 10-INCH PIZZAS

Source Note: In the fall, when chanterelles are in season, this recipe is hard to beat—and it's a nice variation from a traditional pie based on red sauce.

4 tablespoons extra-virgin olive oil, divided
8 ounces fresh chanterelles, cleaned and sliced
Salt and freshly ground black pepper
3 tablespoons finely chopped fresh thyme, divided
1 teaspoon lemon juice
3 cups thinly sliced radicchio (about 1 small head)
1 large leek, white and pale green sections only, halved lengthwise, washed, and thinly sliced crosswise
1½ pounds pizza dough, either purchased or homemade
1 cup (about 4 ounces) coarsely grated Val d'Aosta Fontina cheese
1 (8-ounce) ball fresh, water-packed mozzarella cheese, drained, halved, thinly sliced

2 ounces pancetta, coarsely chopped

1. Place a pizza stone in the oven and preheat it to 500°F.

2. While the stone is heating, heat 2 tablespoons of the olive oil in a large skillet over medium-high heat. Add the chanterelles; sprinkle with salt and pepper. Sauté until the liquid has evaporated and the mushrooms have browned, about 5 minutes. Add 1 tablespoon of the thyme; stir for 30 seconds. Mix in the lemon juice and stir briefly. Remove from the heat and transfer to a small bowl.

3. Heat the remaining 2 tablespoons of oil in the same skillet over high heat. Add the radicchio, leek, and 1 more tablespoon of the thyme. Sprinkle with salt and pepper. Sauté the vegetables until just wilted, about 2 minutes. Remove from the heat and transfer to a medium bowl.

4. Divide the pizza dough in half. Stretch and roll out each half on a well-floured work surface to a 10½-inch round. Scatter the Fontina and mozzarella on each round. Top each with the radicchio mixture, then the mushroom mixture. Sprinkle each pizza with pancetta and the remaining thyme.

5. Slide the pizzas onto the pizza stone and bake until they turn crisp and golden, about 12 minutes.

— *P. N.,* The 2013 MAJIQal Cookbook

. . . .

CHICKEN SALAD
WITH MUSHROOMS AND WALNUTS   SERVES 4 TO 6

8 to 12 ounces fresh mushrooms, cooked, or substitute
**   2 to 3 (4-ounce) cans cooked, sliced champignon mushrooms**
2 cups cooked chicken breast, finely shredded
½ cup crushed walnuts
2 to 3 tablespoons mayonnaise
½ cup finely chopped cilantro
Freshly ground black pepper, to taste

1. If you are using canned rather than the fresh mushrooms, drain and rinse them. Slice them in half if desired.

2. Combine the mushrooms with the shredded chicken and walnuts. Add the mayonnaise and mix until evenly blended. Add more or less mayonnaise, based on your preference.

3. Add the cilantro and black pepper, and do a final mix. Ready to serve!

— *Anush Oganesian and Lida Hovhannesyan*

. . . .

"Chicken salad has a certain glamour about it. Like the little black dress, it is chic and adaptable anywhere."

— *Laurie Colwin*, Home Cooking

Taking a break from tending to seedlings at Featherstone Farm.

Books

Shroom: Mind-bendingly
Good Recipes for Cultivated
and Wild Mushrooms
Becky Selengut,
Andrews McMeel Publishing, 2014.

The Mushroom Hunters:
On the Trail of an
Underground America
Langdon Cook,
Ballantine Books, 2013.

The Wild Table:
Seasonal Foraged Food and Recipes
Connie Green and Sarah Scott,
Studio, 2010.

WALNUT-MUSHROOM BURGERS   SERVES 4

Source Note: This brilliant recipe is very meaty tasting, because of the mushrooms. It is one of the best ways to work cabbage into a meal. Any spices missing from your spice rack (or that you do not like the flavor of) can be left out. I have made these burgers without rosemary, chipotle powder, and paprika—they tasted great anyway.

    1 cup walnuts (toast them for additional flavor)
    1 cup green (raw) pumpkin seeds
    1 cup mushrooms, quartered
    1 cup chopped onion
    3 cloves garlic, minced
    ½ teaspoon ground turmeric
    2 tablespoons paprika (the smoked variety adds a deeper flavor but
        regular paprika also works well)
    ¼ teaspoon chipotle pepper powder
    ⅛ teaspoon cayenne powder
    ⅛ teaspoon chopped fresh rosemary
    1½ cups coarsely chopped red cabbage
    1 egg
    ¼ cup olive oil

1. Preheat the oven to 350°F.

2. Put the walnuts and pumpkin seeds in a food processor and pulse until fine. Put them in a large bowl. Next, process the mushrooms, onions, and garlic, and then add the spices and rosemary; pulse until fine and add to the bowl with the nuts. Next, process the cabbage and pulse it until finely chopped, and then add it to the bowl. In a separate small bowl, beat the egg; then mix it in with the other ingredients.

3. Wet your hands so the mixture does not cling to your fingers. Form it into 12 patties. Brush the patties with olive oil and bake on a

greased cookie sheet for 10 minutes. Turn the patties over, and continue cooking for another 10 minutes.

4. Remove the patties from the oven and serve with a nice mustard.

— *Kathy Abascal,* The Abascal Way Cookbook

BONELESS LAMB SAUTÉ WITH OLIVES AND MUSHROOMS

SERVES 2

1 tablespoon butter
1 tablespoon olive oil
6 fresh sage leaves
1 to 2 tablespoons chopped fresh rosemary leaves
1 bay leaf
1½ pounds lamb chops, bone removed, meat cubed
3 tablespoons white wine
6 shiitake mushroom caps, sliced
¾ cup Sicilian green olives
2 tablespoons capers
¼ cup red or yellow bell pepper strips
Salt and freshly ground black pepper

1. Melt the butter and oil in a large skillet over medium heat. Add the sage, rosemary, and bay leaf.

2. Add the lamb cubes and lower the heat. Cook, stirring continuously, until the meat is well-browned.

3. When the lamb is browned, pour the wine into the pan. Add the mushrooms, olives, and capers, and simmer for 5 minutes. Then add the bell peppers.

4. Season with salt and pepper to taste. Simmer for 5 more minutes, then serve immediately.

— *Jacob Wittenberg*

Peas

PISUM SATIVUM

Peas grown on a farm and delivered to the consumer within hours of picking are truly gems of the garden. Once you taste such fresh peas, their sweetness and sheer vegetable flavor will spoil you for anything less.

These legume siblings of beans come in several forms. There is the common garden, or shelling, pea with which we are most familiar, with peas suitable for shelling, and two subspecies of edible-podded peas, the snow pea and the sugar snap. Although garden peas may be available in your CSA box, you are more likely to see sugar snaps and snow peas.

The flat pods of snow peas have a terrific pea flavor without the hassle of shelling, and they are extremely popular in stir-fries. Sugar snaps, with their juicy, fleshy pods and full-size peas, combine the best attributes of regular garden and snow peas. A cool-weather crop, all of these pea varieties are at their most succulent and sweet in late spring or early summer.

HISTORY

The garden pea is one of the oldest foods eaten by humans, and its precise origins remain so ancient that they are unknown. Popularly the pea is attributed to central Asia; indeed the oldest carbon-dated peas were found between Burma and Thailand, and are believed to be from 9750 BCE. The ancient Egyptians, Greeks, and Romans all enjoyed peas, as did King Charlemagne, who ordered them planted in his gardens in about 800 CE.

Until the time of the Italian Renaissance, however, peas were generally consumed mature and dried, and it was not until Catherine de' Medici introduced them to her court when she married Henry II of France that the fresh, young *piselli novelli* became fashionable. Subsequently they became all the rage during Louis XIV's time, so much so that both he and the ladies of his court were notoriously obsessed with them.

Snow peas and sugar snaps have existed at least since the 16th century. Sometimes called Chinese snow peas, these flat-podded legumes are not from China, nor do they have any obvious connection with snow; instead they may have been developed in Holland in the 1500s.

Varieties of the fleshy-podded sugar snap pea have been around for at least 300 years, but it was not until plant breeder Calvin Lamborn created an All-American Selection–winning hybrid in the early 1970s by crossing snow peas with a thick-walled rogue he found in his test plants that this vegetable suddenly became popular.

NUTRITION

All peas are rich in vitamin K, a nutrient essential for proper blood clotting and bone maintenance. They are also an excellent source of manganese, vitamin C, thiamine, folate, vitamin A, phosphorus, vitamin B6, niacin, iron, copper, tryptophan, and dietary fiber. A single cup of regular shell peas contains 118 calories; 1 cup of chopped snow or sugar snap peas contains 41 calories.

Snap Peas and Pesticides

Conventionally grown, imported snap peas are on the "Dirty Dozen" list—meaning they are very high in pesticide and herbicide residues.

This residue is particularly harmful to children, as well as to adults with health issues. Purchase organic, locally grown snap peas whenever possible.

SEASON

Commercially, peas are widely grown and available year-round. But peas do not like heat, and you'll find them at farmers markets and CSAs in the spring. An occasional late fall crop may appear as well, depending on the region's climate.

SELECTION

With all peas, choose fresh specimens with firm, uniformly bright-green pods. Avoid flabby, overly large, desiccated-looking, or discolored pods—all signs of old, tired peas past their prime.

STORAGE

Like all peas, use snows and sugar snaps as soon as possible, because their sugars start turning into starch at the moment of picking. If you must store them, wrap them in a perforated plastic bag and refrigerate them in the vegetable crisper for no more than 2 or 3 days.

TRIMMING AND CLEANING

Snow and sugar snap peas usually need only to be gently rinsed. Not all sugar snap peas have strings; if they do, snap off the stalk end and pull down on the thicker side of the pod to remove the central string. Test to see if the other side requires stringing as well. Garden peas should be shelled into a bowl and their pods discarded.

STEAMING AND BOILING

Overcooking is anathema to peas of all sorts. Steam shelled garden peas over rapidly boiling water for 2 to 4 minute; whole snows and sugar snaps for 4 to 6 minutes. Boiling should be kept to an absolute minimum—2 to 3 minutes.

STIR-FRYING AND SAUTÉING

Sugar snaps and snow peas are delicious stir-fried or sautéed for 2 to 4 minutes in a little water, stock, or sesame oil in a wok until they are just crisp-tender, before they turn limp.

MICROWAVING

Place shell peas in a microwave-safe dish, add 2 to 3 tablespoons water, cover, and cook on high power.

- 1 pound garden peas = 4 to 6 minutes
- 1 pound snow or sugar snap peas = 6 to 7 minutes

BLANCHING AND FREEZING

To blanch snow and sugar snap peas, wash and, if necessary, string them. Blanch them in rapidly boiling water for 1½ to 2 minutes, then plunge them into ice water for 5 minutes to stop the cooking process. Remove and drain. Package the peas in zipper-lock freezer or vacuum food sealer-type bags, or freezer containers. Squeeze out any excess air and leave ½ inch of headspace (unless you are using the vacuum sealing method). Frozen peas will keep for up to 6 months at 0°F.

"We lived very simply—but with all the essentials of life well understood and provided for—hot baths, cold champagne, new peas, and old brandy."

— Winston Churchill

"I always eat my peas with honey; I've done it all my life. They do taste kind of funny but It keeps them on my knife."

— Anonymous

For shell peas, follow the same steps except that after draining, spread them out in a single layer on a baking sheet with raised sides. Place the baking sheet in the freezer and freeze for 1 hour. Then place the frozen peas into a baggie or container. This makes it far easier to pour out just the quantity you need, rather than trying to break apart a big clump.

EQUIVALENTS, MEASURES, AND SERVINGS

- 1 pound whole peas = 1 to 1⅓ cups shelled peas
- ½ to ¾ pound whole peas = ½ to ¾ cup shelled peas = 1 serving
- 1 pound sugar snaps = 4 to 5 cups peas = 4 to 6 servings
- 1 pound snow peas = 3 servings

COMPLEMENTARY HERBS, SEASONINGS, AND FOODS

Almonds, artichokes, asparagus, bacon, balsamic vinegar, butter, carrots, chervil, chicken, chives, cilantro, citrus, cream, fava beans, fennel, garlic, ginger, green garlic, ham, leeks, lemons, lettuce, marjoram, mint, mushrooms, new potatoes, nutmeg, olive oil, onion, orange juice, parsley, peanuts, peanut oil, prosciutto, rice, risotto, rosemary, sage, salmon, sesame, shallots, sorrel, tarragon, tofu.

SERVING SUGGESTIONS

- Snow peas and sugar snaps can be tossed whole into the wok for stir-fries.
- Serve raw or lightly steamed snow and sugar snap peas on a plate with a variety of dipping sauces: mayonnaise, melted butter, salad dressing. This is a great favorite with children.
- A traditional New England Fourth of July meal is salmon, garden peas, and new potatoes. Serve with freshly made lemonade and strawberries for dessert.
- Lightly sauté sugar snaps in a little butter and salt, and serve.
- Chop herbs like tarragon, dill, mint, basil, and parsley, and combine with chopped green onions and steamed peas.
- Pickle and can snap peas just like small cucumbers, using bread-and-butter pickle recipes.
- Toss a few snow peas in with fresh pastas to add crunch, flavor, and nutrition.
- Combine snow pea pods or snapped sections of sugar peas with shredded chicken, green onion, mayonnaise, almonds, raisins, and chopped apple for a most unordinary chicken salad.
- Stir-fry snows or sugar snaps with mushrooms, or try them raw in salads.
- For an unusual hors d'oeuvre, stuff blanched sugar snap peas with cream cheese combined with chopped fresh spring radish and green garlic.
- Throw sugar snaps or snows into the soup pot during the last few minutes of cooking.
- Of course, nothing beats a handful of fresh shelled peas stripped out of their pods and popped raw right into a waiting mouth. One of the sweetest and best summertime treats!

Mushroom, Snow Pea, and Spinach Salad   Serves 6

Dressing

¼ cup olive oil
¼ cup vegetable oil
¼ cup tarragon vinegar
1 teaspoon minced fresh tarragon or ½ teaspoon dried tarragon
½ teaspoon Dijon mustard
Salt and freshly ground black pepper

1¼ pounds snow peas, strings removed
1 bunch spinach, destemmed, washed, dried, and chilled
8 ounces fresh mushrooms, sliced
4 large radishes, thinly sliced

1. Whisk the oils, vinegar, tarragon, and mustard in a small bowl. Add salt and pepper to taste.

2. Bring a large pot of salted water to boil. Add the snow peas and cook 45 seconds. Drain, run the peas under cold water, and drain again.

3. Combine the peas, spinach, mushrooms, and radishes in a large bowl.

4. Toss the salad with enough dressing to lightly coat. Pass the remaining dressing separately.

— *FairShare CSA Coalition*, From Asparagus to Zucchini

. . . .

Pamela's Fresh Pea Soup   Makes about 7 cups

1 tablespoon butter
1 tablespoon olive oil
1 clove garlic, chopped
1 large onion, chopped
1 small head Bibb lettuce, shredded
15 leaves fresh spinach
1 tablespoon chopped parsley
3 cups fresh sugar snap peas, or 5 cups young shell peas
5 cups chicken stock, divided
¼ cup uncooked white rice
2 teaspoons sugar
Salt and freshly ground black pepper
¼ cup finely chopped fresh mint
About 1 cup milk
Fresh mint sprigs, for garnish

1. Heat the butter and oil in a large pot. Add the garlic and onion, and sauté until softened.

2. Add the lettuce, spinach, and parsley; cook, stirring, until the vegeta-

neighbor or making a batch of soup for the freezer?

To compare CSA farms, here's what you'll need to consider:

Share sizes: Are the options offered a good fit for your household or do you have a neighbor or friend who might want to split a share? Some websites post photos of a typical weekly share.

Cost and payment options: It's not easy to compare the cost of a share between one farm and another because of the many variables, but you will likely spend less and get better quality produce than you'll find at the grocery store. CSA farms began with the idea that members pay for their share when they sign up so that farmers can buy what they need for the growing season, but many farms now offer payment options to help their customers, including "scholarship" shares, work-trade shares, or payment through the Supplemental Nutrition Assistance Program (SNAP, formerly known as food stamps).

If you're considering a whole diet (or full diet) CSA that supplies most of your household's food—and there are a few dozen of them—the costs are significantly higher and typically require everyone in a household to be a member.

Produce choice and add-on options: Many farms now offer some degree of free choice of produce, allowing you to switch one vegetable you're not so keen on for one that you like a lot. How important are add-on options such as meat, chicken, eggs, flowers, honey, cheese, grains, sauerkraut, or bread produced on the farm or by nearby farms and businesses?

U-pick and preserver share options: Does the farm offer CSA members free or low-cost U-pick items in season, such as apples, pears, or flowers? Does it offer preserver shares suitable for canning, pickling, and freezing in the fall?

bles wilt. Add the peas and 3 cups of the stock. Cover the pot, bring to a boil, then decrease the heat to a simmer, and cook until the peas become soft, about 5 minutes. Remove from heat.

3. In a food processor or blender, process the pea mixture in batches until coarsely blended. Pour it back into the pot. Add the remaining 2 cups stock. Bring to a boil, add the rice, decrease the heat, and cook for 15 minutes. Add the sugar, salt, pepper, and mint; stir in enough milk to reach the desired consistency. Heat slowly, stirring, until the soup is hot. Do not boil.

4. Garnish each serving with a sprig of mint.

— *FairShare CSA Coalition,* From Asparagus to Zucchini

GRILLED SUMMER CORN AND SUGAR SNAP PEA SALAD   SERVES 6 TO 8

Source Note: Buying a bag of sugar snap peas for me is like walking home with a fresh loaf of bread—I need a spare. I cannot resist crunching away on those sugary, tender green pods.

4 ears of corn, as fresh as possible
1 tablespoon olive oil
1 small red onion, diced
1 chile, diced (very hot, such as serrano, habanero, or jalapeño)
2 teaspoons cumin seed, ground
½ pound sugar snap peas, cut into thirds
⅛ cup red wine vinegar
¼ cup Italian parsley leaves, chopped
Salt and freshly ground black pepper

1. Peel the husks from the corn and remove the silk. On a very hot grill, cook the corn to blister and lightly char it. Carefully cut the corn kernels from the cob and set aside.

2. Heat a 2-quart saucepan over medium heat and add the olive oil. Add the onion and chile, cooking until the onion becomes translucent, 3 to 5 minutes. Add the cumin and cook for 30 seconds.

3. Add the sugar snap peas and cook for about 3 minutes to "off" the rawness of the peas. Remove from heat, mix in the corn, the red wine vinegar, and parsley, then season with salt and pepper. Serve warm or cold.

— *Richard Ruben,* The Farmer's Market Cookbook

Rhubarb

RHEUM RHABARBARUM

Rhubarb is a curious phenomenon, for it is one of the few plants of which we consume just the thick stalks, or petioles. Its assertive tartness is caused by large quantities of oxalic acid, which makes the leaves unpalatable and toxic. But the plant's succulent, juicy stems are delicious, especially when sweetened with plenty of sugar, strawberries, or other fruits in pies, sauces, and jams.

In the Western Hemisphere, rhubarb typically comes into season during April and May, making it one of the first fresh food plants to mature. Thus it was much welcomed in times before produce was available year-round. Rhubarb is a perennial that grows from short, stubby rhizomes into rather large plants with huge leaves that resemble giant, heart-shaped Swiss chard. It is unusual in that it does not breed true from seed, but must be propagated from cuttings of its rootstock.

HISTORY

Rhubarb is native to Asia, where the dried root has been used in traditional Chinese medicine for thousands of years. It was so revered for its healing qualities that rhubarb cost ten times as much as cinnamon in France during the mid-1500s. Although rhubarb was consumed as a food in the ancient Middle East, it did not exactly take the European or American gastronomic scene by storm. It remains a specialty food whose popularity waxes and wanes, depending on the public's attitude toward the vast amount of sweetener necessary to make it palatable.

Well known for its laxative qualities since ancient times, rhubarb was once regarded as a medicinal plant rather than as food. It was not cultivated widely for the kitchen until the 1800s in Europe; apparently the unappetizing leaves rather than the stalks were generally sampled, which may have contributed to its delay in finding culinary enthusiasts.

NUTRITION

Rhubarb contains vitamins A, K, folate, calcium, magnesium, potassium, phosphorus, dietary fiber, and a fairly significant amount of lutein, a carotenoid that benefits eye health. A 1-cup serving contains just 25 calories—without all of that added sugar, of course.

SEASON

As one of the first harvested food plants available in the spring, rhubarb has a highly defined season—mid to late spring, with the best picked in April and May.

SELECTION

Fresh rhubarb stalks should be firm, crisp, and brightly colored, with no signs of wilting and shriveling. Slender stalks are more tender than thicker ones.

Cooking Tip

If you prefer to not use large quantities of sugar in rhubarb recipes, try preparing it with sweet fruits (strawberries, raspberries, or apples), apple juice concentrate, or small amounts of honey or stevia.

Cooking Tip

The acidity of rhubarb reacts with aluminum, iron, and copper cookware, leading to discolored pans and possible leaching of the metals into the food. Use only anodized aluminum, stainless steel, or glass pans for cooking and baking rhubarb concoctions.

For More Information

The Rhubarb Compendium
www.rhubarbinfo.com

Rhubarb: Fruit or Vegetable?

Botanically and gastronomically, rhubarb is properly considered a vegetable, although it is often used like a fruit in recipes.

However, in 1947, the US Customs court in Buffalo, New York, declared it a fruit, which allowed it to pass with a smaller import duty.

STORAGE

Wrap unwashed rhubarb stalks in a plastic bag and refrigerate in the vegetable crisper, where it will keep for up to 10 days.

TRIMMING AND CLEANING

Thoroughly wash the stalks under running water to remove all traces of dirt, and trim off the stem ends and discard. Although the skins on rhubarb look quite substantial, they soften with cooking and are quite edible; peeling rhubarb is not common.

MICROWAVING

Rhubarb can be cooked by microwaving it on high power in a microwave-safe dish for about 12 to 14 minutes, or until the rhubarb is tender.

BLANCHING AND FREEZING

Save a taste of spring by freezing rhubarb for later enjoyment. Simply cut the raw stalks into ¾-inch pieces, arrange them in a single layer on a baking pan, and place in the freezer. Once they are frozen, place them in zipper-lock freezer or vacuum food sealer-type bags, or freezer containers. Squeeze out any excess air and leave ½ inch of headspace (unless you are using the vacuum sealing method).

For more tender frozen rhubarb, you can blanch the stalks by boiling them for 1 minute and quickly plunging them in ice water to halt the cooking process. Either leave them whole or cut them into desired lengths; then pack them for the freezer, leaving 1½ inches of headroom if you are using bags. Rhubarb may also be packed in a sugar syrup (see Strawberries on page 95). Frozen rhubarb will keep for up to 6 months at 0°F.

EQUIVALENTS, MEASURES, AND SERVINGS

- 1 pound = 3 cups chopped = 2 cups cooked

COMPLEMENTARY HERBS, SEASONINGS, AND FOODS

Apples, beef, berries, blackberries, black pepper, blueberries, brandy, brown sugar, butter, cake, cinnamon, citrus, cream, duck, fruit, ginger, grapefruit, honey, ice cream, lemons, limes, maple syrup, oranges, plums, raspberries, sour cream, strawberries, sugar, yogurt.

SERVING SUGGESTIONS

- Stewed rhubarb, rhubarb sauce, or rhubarb chutney makes a great counterpoint to hearty meats like duck, roast beef, corned beef, or Rock Cornish game hen.
- A light, tangy, and sweet rhubarb sauce makes a delectable topping for ice cream, pudding, custard, or pound cake.
- Top your breakfast cereal with sweetened, stewed rhubarb.
- Try English trifle with a twist, substituting rhubarb prepared with cherries or raspberries for the traditional strawberries.
- An early spring treat is a snack of washed, raw rhubarb stems and a bowl of sugar for dipping. As simple as can be, on a warm spring day.
- Add a sophisticated touch to stewed rhubarb or rhubarb sauces with the addition of fruit-flavored liqueurs such as orange liqueur, kirsch, melon liqueur, or apple schnapps. Or try brandy, port wine, or rosewater.

- Combine rhubarb with kumquats or oranges for a tasty chutney.
- Add very thin slices of rhubarb to spring soups or salads, or anywhere a bit of tartness is welcome.

....

EASY-AS-PIE RHUBARB PIE   MAKES ONE 9-INCH PIE

1 unbaked 9-inch piecrust, plus extra for top crust or lattice,
    if desired
4 cups diced rhubarb stalks
¼ cup flour
1¼ cups sugar
1 tablespoon butter, melted
4 tablespoons dry tapioca mix (Jell-O has the finest texture, but
    other brands work fine if you don't mind larger tapioca balls)
1 tablespoon fresh lemon juice
Cinnamon

1. Put the bottom piecrust into a 9-inch pie pan. If using a frozen prepared shell, allow to thaw at room temperature for about 15 minutes.

2. Mix all of the remaining ingredients together and let them stand for 15 minutes, stirring occasionally.

3. Preheat the oven to 450°F.

4. Pour the filling into the piecrust and cover with a top crust or lattice, if using. Sprinkle with cinnamon.

5. Bake for 10 minutes at 450°F, then decrease the heat to 350°F and continue to bake for 45 to 50 minutes, or until the filling is bubbly.

Cooking Note: If you prefer, you may use a graham cracker crust.

— *Rich Hoyle*

....

RHUBARB CRISP   SERVES 6 TO 8

6 to 8 cups thinly sliced and chopped rhubarb (leave it unpeeled)
1½ cups granulated sugar
2 tablespoons flour
2 to 3 teaspoons cinnamon
Pinch of salt

TOPPING

¾ cup oatmeal
½ cup unbleached flour
¼ cup whole wheat flour
½ cup brown sugar

½ cup chopped walnuts
2 tablespoons ground golden flaxseeds or wheat germ (optional)
¼ teaspoon baking soda
¼ teaspoon baking powder
⅓ cup melted butter

1. Preheat the oven to 350°F.

2. Butter a 9-by-13-inch pan. In a large bowl, mix together the rhubarb, sugar, flour, cinnamon, and salt. Place the rhubarb mixture in the pan.

3. Combine the topping ingredients in a small bowl, adding the butter last. Mix well, then spread the topping mixture over the rhubarb. Bake for 35 to 40 minutes, until bubbling.

— *Robin Taylor, Featherstone Farm CSA member*

SPICED RHUBARB CHUTNEY   MAKES ABOUT 3 CUPS

Source Note: This chutney works well as an accompaniment to chicken, duck, or lamb.

¾ cup sugar
⅓ cup cider vinegar
1 tablespoon minced peeled fresh ginger
1 tablespoon finely crushed garlic
1 teaspoon cumin
½ teaspoon ground cinnamon
½ teaspoon ground cloves
¼ teaspoon dried crushed red pepper
4 cups ½-inch cubes fresh rhubarb (about 1½ pounds)
½ cup chopped red onion
⅓ cup dried tart cherries or golden raisins (about 2 ounces)

1   Combine the sugar, vinegar, ginger, garlic, cumin, cinnamon, cloves, and red pepper in a large Dutch oven. Bring to a simmer over low heat, stirring until the sugar dissolves.

2. Add the rhubarb, onion, and dried cherries; increase the heat to medium-high and cook until the rhubarb is tender and the mixture thickens slightly, about 5 minutes. Cool completely.

Cooking Note: This chutney can be made 1 day ahead. Cover and chill. Bring to room temperature before using.

— *Bon Appétit, as appeared on Epicurious*

BALSAMIC RHUBARB COMPOTE

SERVES 4

3 tablespoons balsamic vinegar
⅔ cup sugar
¾ teaspoon peeled and grated fresh ginger
2 stalks fresh rhubarb, leaves discarded, ends trimmed,
    and stalks cut crosswise into ¼-inch-thick slices,
    or 2 cups frozen sliced rhubarb, thawed, liquid reserved

1. In a medium saucepan over medium-low heat, simmer the vinegar with the sugar and ginger, stirring until the sugar is dissolved. Then stir in the rhubarb (with reserved liquid if using frozen).

2. If you are using fresh rhubarb, simmer it until it is crisp-tender, about 1 minute, then use a slotted spoon to transfer it to a bowl, keeping the liquid behind in the pan. If you are using frozen rhubarb, transfer the rhubarb to a bowl as soon as it returns to a simmer (don't continue cooking it), also keeping the liquid behind in the pan.

3. Simmer the liquid until it thickens slightly, about 5 minutes, and then remove the pan from the heat. Stir in the rhubarb. Serve the compote warm or at room temperature.

— Produce for Better Health; Fruits & Veggies—More Matters;
Centers for Disease Control and Prevention

Seedlings in the greenhouse at Featherstone Farm.

member's garage, the club has been renting a warehouse large enough to include a small café and storefront. The next step will be transitioning from a private food-buying club to a community-owned cooperative grocery.

Why join a food-buying club? Saving money is not the only attraction, even though members might save 25 percent or more on food they might otherwise buy at a natural foods grocery. Other reasons to join are a sense of empowerment in choosing how to spend your food dollars and a social element that develops from shared work, potlucks, and other events, such as farm tours.

How can you find a club? The websites of Local Harvest (**Localharvest.org**) and the Organic Consumers Association (**Organicconsumers.org**) both list co-op groceries and food-buying clubs as well as CSAs. Google searches are another option, of course. And if you want to start your own club, you can find help online for that, too.

Salad & Braising Mixes

A riotous combination of young, tender greens makes up most salad mixes, and more hearty types of leaves constitute a braising mix. The former is best served raw as salad, whereas the latter is usually too coarse and strong-flavored for munching and is better suited for cooking.

Most CSA farms cultivate a variety of lettuces and other greens that are harvested early for salad mixes. Usually salad mix is planted only in the spring and fall because it grows better in cooler weather. The resulting greens taste sweeter and more flavorful than those maturing in the hotter summer months.

The exact makeup of braising mixes varies considerably, but generally they consist of young leaves cut, washed, and dried from several different types of kale, chard, mustard, mizuna, spinach, and sometimes cultivated dandelions. These greens are wonderful lightly steamed or braised. Braising mix is primarily available in the spring and occasionally in the fall.

HISTORY

Salad mix was virtually unknown in America before the late 1990s, when a taste for sophisticated foods and ethnic ingredients burgeoned, and mesclun was introduced to our gastronomic consciousness. Mesclun originated in southern France and refers to a mix of assorted juvenile greens that can include chard, mustard greens, endive, lettuce, dandelion, chicory, mizuna, mâche, frisée, radicchio, sorrel, spinach, arugula, various herbs, and flowers. For Americans, this combination of precut, prewashed young greens is now ubiquitous with the introduction of bagged and boxed salad and "spring" mixes in grocery stores.

NUTRITION

The nutritional content of salad mix varies widely, depending on the types of greens included, but these leaves tend to be powerhouses of nutrients, especially vitamins A and C, calcium, iron, potassium, and phosphorus. A 2-cup serving of salad mix contains about 20 calories.

SEASON

Commercially, salad and braising mixes are widely grown and available year-round. But the best mesclun and salad mixes are available at farmers markets and CSAs in the spring, early summer, and fall. Braising mixes are at their best in the spring and fall.

SELECTION

When choosing either salad or braising mix, look for greens that are fresh and not wilted, with as few bruised leaves as possible. Slimy leaves spread decay quickly, so it is wise to pick through and discard these specimens before storing. Salad mix that comes in those plastic tubs in the grocery store frequently harbor older, slimy leaves that can give the whole lot a slightly sour smell and taste, so be very selective when choosing; tubs that are stored farther back in the cooler behind the forward-facing ones are often a better bet for fresher product.

STORAGE

Salad and braising mixes usually come prewashed and dried. If you prefer, you can rinse them one more time before serving, but the greens will keep far better dry until you are ready to use them. For mixes that seem too damp, slip a couple of paper towels into the bag among the greens. This will keep them drier and less susceptible to spoilage-inducing slime. (Conversely, if the greens seem to be on the dry side, use lightly dampened paper towels.) Store them in the refrigerator crisper for up to a few days.

Salad greens should not be stored next to apples or other fruits that emit ethylene gas, which will hasten spoilage and cause brown spots.

TRIMMING AND CLEANING

Other than an optional final rinse or picking through to discard wilted or decayed leaves, salad and braising mixes need no other preparation.

STEAMING AND BOILING

Boiling is not recommended for salad mix, but a very quick steaming for 1 to 2 minutes renders the tender greens just wilted but still bright green and full of nutrients. Braising mixes, on the other hand, will need a bit longer cooking time. As their name suggests, braising greens can slowly simmer with meat or other vegetables until tender. They should be added during the last half to three-quarters of an hour of cooking, depending on the toughness of the leaves and personal preference. Braising greens can also be boiled for 8 to 10 minutes.

STIR-FRYING AND SAUTÉING

Stir-fry salad mix in much the same way as lettuce: Simply toss it into a wok or skillet in which vegetable oil and seasoning have been heated, and stir-fry for about 1 minute, or until the leaves just wilt. Add a bit of soy or oyster sauce if desired, and cook for 1 more minute, or until the salad mix turns tender but is still bright green. Braising greens will take up to 3 to 4 minutes. They also respond wonderfully to the wilted-greens treatment, with hot bacon dressing.

MICROWAVING

Salad mix can be cooked in the microwave if you do not want to bother with a steamer; place in a microwave-safe dish with a little water or cooking liquid, and microwave on high power for about 2 minutes, or until the greens are tender but not shriveled. Braising mixes require 4 to 5 minutes, or until tender.

BLANCHING AND FREEZING

Freezing is not recommended for salad and braising mixes because of their high water content.

COMPLEMENTARY HERBS, SEASONINGS, AND FOODS

Almonds, anchovies, apples, avocados, bacon, balsamic vinegar, cheese (blue, goat, Parmesan, feta, pecorino), croutons, eggs, garlic, hazelnuts, hazelnut oil, herbs, lemon juice, mayonnaise, mustard, nuts, olives, olive oil, onions, oranges, peanuts, pepper, raisins, rice wine vinegar, sea salt, sesame, tofu, vinaigrette, vinegar, walnuts, walnut oil.

"The first gatherings of the garden in May of salads, radishes, and herbs made me feel like a mother about her baby—how could anything so beautiful be mine. And this emotion of wonder filled me for each vegetable as it was gathered every year. There is nothing that is comparable to it, as satisfactory or as thrilling, as gathering the vegetables one has grown."

— *Alice B. Toklas,*
life partner of Gertrude Stein

- Fresh salad mix dressed with a light vinaigrette is hard to beat for a spring or early summer salad.

- Toss a few handfuls of braising mix in during the last minute or two of cooking a stir-fry, or sauté it on its own in a bit of butter or olive oil.

- Throw some salad mix into scrambled eggs, omelets, or frittatas.

- Substitute salad mix for lettuce in sandwiches.

- Add variety to salad mix by adding fresh herbs such as basil leaves, dill sprigs, chervil, borage, or chopped chives. Edible flowers make beautiful, tasty decorations—try pansies, violets, nasturtiums, calendulas, daylily buds, or marigolds (see pages 194–204 for ideas).

- Braising greens prepared southern-style with ham hocks, bacon, or salt pork are delicious; remember, they don't need to cook as long as collard greens.

- Boil braising greens in salted water, then lift out the greens and boil pasta in the same cooking water to increase nutrition and flavor. Combine the greens and pasta along with anchovy fillets, red pepper flakes, capers, tomatoes, garlic, and olives, for pasta puttanesca-style.

- Braising mix really shines when prepared simply—sautéed in olive oil with plenty of garlic. Serve it with a hearty meat, like rib roast or lamb, and sweet potatoes for a match made in heaven.

SEASONAL SALAD WITH VINAIGRETTE   SERVES 6

Source Note: Make the vinaigrette only a couple of hours before serving.

VINAIGRETTE

2 scant tablespoons red wine or sherry vinegar, or a combination
1 small clove garlic, peeled
Salt
6 tablespoons extra-virgin olive oil
Freshly ground black pepper

6 large handfuls salad greens, about ¾ pound
Garlic toast or croutons

1. To make the vinaigrette: Measure the vinegar into a small bowl. Crush the garlic clove and add it to the vinegar, along with ½ teaspoon salt. Set aside to let the flavors blend. After 10 minutes or so, whisk in the olive oil and a little freshly milled pepper. Taste and adjust the seasoning.

2. To make the salad, put the greens in a wide salad bowl and season with a small pinch of salt. Going back to the vinaigrette, remove the garlic clove, whisk the vinaigrette, and pour it over the greens. Toss the greens lightly, using just enough dressing to make the leaves glisten. (Your clean hands make the best salad-tossing tools.) Serve immediately with garlic toast or croutons.

— *Pam Garetto, Featherstone Farm CSA member (adapted from Alice Waters)*

TOSSED MESCLUN SALAD
SERVES 4

4 cups mesclun (small-leafed mixed greens, also known as salad mix)
2 cups romaine lettuce, torn into small pieces, washed, and dried
2 cups Boston lettuce, torn into small pieces, washed, and dried
½ cucumber, peeled, halved, and thinly sliced
½ yellow or red bell pepper, cut into very thin slivers
2 scallions (green onions), very thinly sliced
Your favorite dressing

Combine all of the ingredients except the dressing in a large salad bowl. Just before serving, toss with the dressing. Taste and add more if necessary, but be careful not to overdress the salad. Serve at once on 4 salad plates.

— *Jeanne Lemlin*, Vegetarian Classics

MESCLUN WITH MAPLE-MUSTARD TOFU POINTS
SERVES 4

1 tablespoon soy sauce
2 tablespoons Dijon mustard
1 tablespoon sweet white miso
1 tablespoon maple syrup
1 tablespoon water
1 teaspoon sesame oil
Chili oil (optional)
1 pound extra-firm low-fat tofu, drained
¼ pound mesclun or mixed salad greens
1 large roasted red bell pepper, cut into about 16 strips
Seasoned rice vinegar

1. Preheat the broiler. Line a broiling pan with aluminum foil.

2. Mash and mix the soy sauce, mustard, miso, maple syrup, water, and sesame and chili oils until thoroughly blended.

3. Press the tofu 4 or 5 times between 2 plates, until all of the water is released. Cut the tofu crosswise into 8 slices, about ½-inch thick. Cut each slice on the diagonal, creating triangles. Dip the triangles into the soy mixture and coat all sides.

4. Broil the tofu triangles until they are lightly browned and slightly crusty on the first side, about 3 to 4 minutes. Turn the tofu over. Brush on any remaining soy mixture, and broil the second side until it is browned, about 3 minutes. (For a more barbecued taste, broil the tofu until slightly blackened around the edges.)

Labor of Love

Lindsay Arbuckle Courcelle
Alchemy Gardens
West Rutland, Vermont

Every day at 3 AM, I wake up, stumble downstairs, throw on a coat and boots, and trudge out to the greenhouse to feed the woodstove. The stove is the sole source of nighttime heat in our greenhouse, which houses the baby plants that we sell to home gardeners and the seedlings that we'll transplant at our farm field in West Rutland.

My other half, Scott, has a knack for building fires. He makes sure the stove is roaring from dusk to midnight. Since I have a knack for falling asleep under adverse circumstances, I take the shift in the wee morning hours.

This labor of love lasts only a month or two each spring, depending on the weather, but this period is crucial to our farm's success every year. Most of our main crops, like tomatoes and peppers, are started in the greenhouse rather than sown as seeds directly in the field. Also, our leased land at Boardman Hill Farm has heavy soils that are often wet in the spring. Working the soil too early could damage it for decades to come. Last year, the field was tilled and ready for planting on April 8. The year before: May 23. This is the nature of farming, and as farmer Greg Cox would say, "Control is an illusion." So we wait patiently for warm, breezy days that will dry out the soil and instead focus on greenhouse production for spring income.

Like infants and small children, baby plants need to be nurtured with keen attention and awareness. When kids are hungry or sleepy, they let us know. Similarly, baby plants that are thirsty, light-deprived, too cold, or too warm will give us signals to remedy the situation. With proper care in the early stages, both humans and plants

5. Serve either warm or at room temperature on top of the mesclun and red peppers; sprinkle with rice vinegar, and serve with crusty bread.

— *Lorna Sass,* The New Soy Cookbook: Tempting Recipes for Soybeans, Soy Milk, Tofu, Tempeh, Miso and Soy Sauce, *as appeared on Fooddownunder.com*

....

POACHED EGGS WITH PANCETTA AND TOSSED MESCLUN

SERVES 4

8 large eggs
1 tablespoon extra-virgin olive oil
4 ounces thickly sliced pancetta, cut into ¼-inch dice
1 large shallot, minced
2 tablespoons white wine vinegar
2 tablespoons chopped fresh tarragon
2 scallions (green onions), thinly sliced
10 cups mesclun (about 6 ounces)
Salt and freshly ground black pepper
Toast points or steamed, sliced new potatoes, for serving

1. Bring a large, deep skillet filled with 2 inches of water to a simmer. Crack each egg into a cup and gently slide it into the water. Cook until the whites are solid but the yolks are still soft, 5 minutes. Using a slotted spoon, transfer the eggs to a paper towel–lined plate to drain; set in a warm place.

2. Meanwhile, in a large skillet, heat the olive oil until it shimmers. Add the pancetta and cook over moderately high heat until crisp, about 3 minutes. Add the shallot and cook until softened, 2 minutes. Remove from the heat and add the vinegar, tarragon, and scallions.

3. In a large bowl, toss the mesclun with the pancetta-shallot mixture; season with salt and pepper. Transfer the salad to plates, top with the eggs, and serve with toast points.

— *Chef Julie Ridlon*

....

WAKE-UP TUNA SALAD

SERVES 1

Author Note: This is my favorite salad, one that I eat most days for breakfast as an entire meal. With its bold flavors and raw hot pepper, this is definitely not a delicate salad for the faint of heart. The beauty of it is that I can vary the ingredients and proportions according to what is absolutely fresh and top-notch that day, and to my mood—and so should you.

This salad will only be as good as the quality of the ingredients used, so don't scrimp on the greens, herbs, tuna, and oil. Because the flavors are

are more likely to lead strong and healthy lives. This is what I keep in mind on the mornings when waking up at 3 AM feels like a medieval torture ritual.

But most nights, this feels like a small sacrifice to make in exchange for healthy plants. The thousands of tiny seeds we plant this spring will generate thousands of pounds of fresh vegetables later this season. Those tiny eggplant seeds that have now morphed into baby plants? In little more than three months, the plants will be loaded with shiny-skinned, heavy fruits.

Our crop of eggplant, which began as a bunch of seeds that fit easily into my palm, will stretch to cover hundreds of feet in the field, and will yield hundreds of pounds of food. This amazing transformation—from sun, water, soil, and seed, to food—is what continually inspires us to be farmers at Alchemy Gardens.

Even more inspiring are the seeds that have been saved and handed down for generations. We have several varieties of heirloom tomatoes that were originally brought to the Rutland area by Italian immigrants and have now been kept alive for decades by devoted home gardeners. These varieties have names like Menduni, Pratico, and P. Lunghi Giallo. We don't know their whole stories, but we like to imagine someone in Rutland many years ago holding those tomato seeds in the palm of his or her hand, and later harvesting bushels of ripe fruit.

I like to imagine that Scott's great-great-grandfather Arthur Courcelle may have been one of those people. Like most people of that era, his family had a large vegetable garden. He was the proprietor of Courcelle Flower Shop in Rutland, starting in the late 1800s. The business operated two large glass greenhouses and flourished for nearly 100 years before it closed during Scott's childhood. These

already so powerful, the dressing should not be a dominating one. I have found that the very best-quality hazelnut oil and a sprinkling of sea salt are the perfect accompaniments; the nutty saltiness gently mellows and enhances the greens and tuna.

A note about the tuna: Don't make this with that insipid water-packed albacore—use an oil-packed tuna that is richly flavored. The extra calories are well worth it.

Salad mix or mesclun (can contain any proportions of baby
    lettuces, mizuna, tatsoi, spinach, escarole, radicchio, arugula)
Fresh basil leaves, torn
Fresh herbs (oregano, chives, tarragon, or whatever you fancy)
Jalapeño or serrano pepper, thinly sliced or diced, to taste
Hazelnut oil
Sea salt
1 (5-ounce) can Italian oil-packed tuna (Genova brand
    is my favorite)

1. Place a generous handful of salad mix in a large bowl or on a plate. Add the torn basil leaves and sprinkle with whatever fresh herbs you desire. Add the jalapeño. Gently toss together to combine.

2. Drain the tuna (save the tasty oil and use it within a day or two for adding to a pasta dish or as a treat for a lucky cat) and add it to the top of the salad. Drizzle a generous amount of hazelnut oil all over the salad, then finish with a sprinkling of sea salt. Enjoy immediately.

Variations: Instead of tuna, substitute canned salmon or chicken. Add finely chopped green onions, shallots, or onion rings. Substitute the very best extra-virgin olive oil you can afford for the hazelnut oil.

— *Mi Ae Lipe*

legacies—of family trade and of seeds—remind us daily of those who've come before us and our connection through food and agriculture.

The next time you eat, let your mind wander to these transformations from seed to food—whether you're eating a carrot, a bowl of cereal, or a cheeseburger. What seeds were sown to yield that food? What labor, or labor of love, was done to transform sun, water, soil, and seed into the bites you take, day in and day out?

Spinach

SPINACIA OLERACEA

Succulent spinach is one of the best-known vegetables in America, loved for its versatility in the kitchen but sometimes not so enjoyed by juveniles. Belonging to the same family as beets, Swiss chard, and amaranth, spinach comes in several different forms: savoy, which has very crinkly leaves and is often the one available fresh in bunches; flat or smoothleaf, which has broader, smoother leaves; and semi-savoy, a hybrid type that combines the texture of savoy but is not nearly as difficult to clean.

Do not confuse spinach with New Zealand spinach or water spinach, which are entirely different plants.

In recent times spinach has unfortunately been associated with E. coli outbreaks, the result of central California–grown plants tainted by irrigation water contaminated with manure runoff. Although the chances are extremely remote that spinach grown locally in small-scale operations for farmers markets and CSAs would be similarly contaminated, periodic outbreaks on lettuce, alfalfa sprouts, and certain fruits are a good reminder to thoroughly wash or cook our produce before using it, regardless of the source.

HISTORY

Spinach has a rich history as a favored vegetable. Its wild form originated in ancient Persia (now modern-day Iran), and the Arabs likely introduced the plant from Asia to Europe. Oddly, unlike many other modern vegetables, the ancient Italians and Greeks did not seem to know anything about it, even though spinach is common in many traditional Greek dishes. By the 1500s spinach was a favored Lenten food because of its early spring availability. When the Italian Catherine de' Medici married King Henry II of France, she introduced spinach to the French court, and to this day the phrase *à la florentine* signifies a dish containing the vegetable (in France, but not in Florence).

Exactly how spinach got to America is a mystery, but it was growing in several American gardens by the early 19th century. In the late 1800s, a misplaced decimal point in a European publication pegged spinach's iron content as 10 times too high, and it was not until 1937 that German chemists corrected the mistake. But by then the cartoon character Popeye was already extolling the muscle-building properties of this wonder vegetable.

NUTRITION

A strong, muscular Popeye made the nutritional qualities of spinach famous, and indeed a 1-cup serving of spinach does contain almost 40 percent of your daily adult requirement for iron (at only 7 calories). Unfortunately, its naturally occurring oxalic acid binds with the iron, rendering much of this nutrient unusable. But spinach has plenty of other nutritional redemption, with enormous amounts of vitamins K, A, and C; the B vitamins (especially folate); calcium; potassium; and manganese. Spinach is also one of the richest natural sources of lutein, a carotenoid that protects against degenerative diseases of the eye. It is also rather high in sodium for a vegetable, accounting for its slightly salty taste.

SEASON

Commercially, spinach is widely grown and available year-round. But spinach is a cool-season plant that dislikes heat, and you'll find the tenderest, most succulent specimens at farmers markets and CSAs in the spring (mid-May to June) and again in the fall (mid-September until frost).

SELECTION

All spinach, whether in the form of bunches or washed, bagged leaves, should look fresh and bright green, free from yellowing or wilting leaves, slime, or decay.

STORAGE

Spinach should be stored unwashed and wrapped in a perforated plastic bag in the refrigerator vegetable crisper until ready to use; depending on its condition, it will keep for 3 to 5 days. Before storing, inspect the bunch to make sure no slimy leaves are present, as rot will spread to other leaves quite quickly. Excess moisture tends to promote sliminess; slipping a dry paper towel among the leaves can help keep things drier.

Spinach and other salad greens should not be stored next to apples or other fruits that emit ethylene gas, which hastens spoilage and causes brown spots.

TRIMMING AND CLEANING

Spinach loves sandy soil, and plenty of it often remains lodged in its crinkly leaves, sometimes even after several rinsings. The easiest way to wash spinach is to fill a big sink or bowl full of water, separate the leaves from the bunches, and completely submerge them, swishing vigorously. Inspect especially crinkly leaves and stems, where telltale brown grit may persist. Then rinse under cold running water, and repeat if necessary. To dry, use a salad spinner or gently pat the leaves dry between a couple of clean dish towels.

STEAMING AND BOILING

Steaming is an excellent way to cook spinach, which tends to be more watery when boiled. About 1½ pounds of freshly washed (but not dried) raw spinach will steam in its own moisture if placed in a steamer basket, covered, and cooked for 5 to 8 minutes.

If you prefer, boil spinach by dropping it into a large pot of boiling water and cooking it for 3 to 5 minutes. Be sure to drain it really well, even squeezing out some of the excess moisture, or the result will be a watery mush.

STIR-FRYING AND SAUTÉING

Spinach is delicious in a stir-fry, especially when young leaves are tossed in during the last few minutes of cooking. To sauté spinach in quantity, put a little oil or stock into a broad pan, and place about a quarter to a third of the total amount of spinach you plan to use into it. Cook these leaves down a bit, letting them wilt; then add the next third, and repeat the process until all of the spinach is used up.

At Least the Bugs Will Stay Away

Conventionally grown spinach contains some of the highest levels of pesticide residue of any fruit or vegetable, according to the Environmental Working Group. Refrain from buying spinach unless it is organic or you've grown it yourself.

Cooking Tip

Spinach reacts adversely with certain metals, discoloring them. Use stainless steel knives (not carbon-steel blades), and avoid cooking it in aluminum pans or serving it in sterling silver dishes.

Safety Tip

Some controversy exists about whether leftover spinach can be safely reheated and eaten, as bacteria can convert its naturally occurring nitrates into harmful compounds called nitrites.

Most of us have survived eating spinach that has been reheated at least once, but regardless, it is probably best not to serve such spinach to infants under six months or to very young children.

Add more oil or stock as necessary. Toward the end of the cooking time, season with garlic, black pepper, nutmeg, salt, butter, or whatever seasoning you desire.

EQUIVALENTS, MEASURES, AND SERVINGS

- 1 pound raw spinach = 1 cup cooked
- ½ cup cooked = 1 serving

MICROWAVING

Wash and rinse, but do not dry. The water that clings to the leaves is enough moisture for it to cook in. Place the leaves in a microwave-safe dish, cover, and cook on high power, stopping to stir the spinach occasionally.

- 1 pound = 4 to 6 minutes

BLANCHING AND FREEZING

To blanch, bring salted water to a boil. Drop the spinach into the boiling water for 15 to 30 seconds until it turns bright green. Remove the spinach and immediately plunge it into ice water to stop the cooking process. Squeeze the excess water from the spinach, then place the spinach in zipper-lock freezer or vacuum food sealer-type bags, or freezer containers. Squeeze out any excess air and leave ½ inch of headspace (unless you are using the vacuum sealing method). Frozen spinach will keep for up to 6 months at 0°F.

COMPLEMENTARY HERBS, SEASONINGS, AND FOODS

Almonds, anchovies, bacon, basil, butter, cardamom, carrots, cheese (Cheddar, feta, goat, mozzarella, Parmesan, pecorino), chiles, chives, citrus, cream, cumin, curry, dill, eggs, fish, garlic, ginger, ham, hollandaise sauce, horseradish, hot peppers, leeks, lemons, lemongrass, mace, marjoram, mint, miso, mushrooms, mustard, nutmeg, nuts, olive oil, olives, onions, oranges, parsley, pasta, peaches, pepper, pine nuts, polenta, potatoes, raisins, raspberries, rice vinegar, sesame, sour cream, soy, strawberries, sugar, tarragon, tomatoes, vinegar, walnuts, yogurt.

SERVING SUGGESTIONS

- Mix baby spinach with various lettuces, arugula, endive, dandelion greens, and fresh herbs for lush tossed salads bursting with different flavors and textures.
- Spinach combines wonderfully with pasta; toss it with cooked noodles, or use it in gnocchi or for ravioli fillings.
- Add a few spinach leaves in place of lettuce in your sandwiches, or add to tacos and burritos.
- Throw in a few handfuls of spinach leaves toward the end of cooking a stir-fry.
- Sprinkle some thinly sliced strawberries over your spinach salad and serve with a balsamic vinegar dressing. Mandarin oranges (either fresh or canned) and peaches are delicious too.
- Perk up your frittatas and crêpes with steamed spinach leaves.
- A classic recipe of old called for adding 8 tablespoons of butter every day for 4 days to a pot of cooked spinach, pureeing the mixture into a velvety

Books

Spinach and Beyond: Loving Life and Dark Green Leafy Vegetables
Linda Diane Feldt,
Moon Field Press, 2003.

The Leafy Greens Cookbook: 100 Creative, Flavorful Recipes Starring Super-Healthy Kale, Chard, Spinach, Bok Choy, Collards and More!
Kathryn Anible,
Ulysses Press, 2013.

Greene on Greens
Bert Greene,
William Morrow Cookbooks, 2001.

One Bite Won't Kill You:
More than 200 Recipes to Tempt Even the Pickiest Kids on Earth
Ann Hodgman,
Houghton Mifflin, 1999.

green soup, and finishing with nutmeg. Not exactly the most healthful, but certainly the richest and most sinful—a spinach soup decidedly for adults.

- One of the classic spinach preparations is still the best: a wilted spinach salad made with hot bacon dressing, garnished with toasted almonds.

- Middle Eastern and Greek cuisines make use of spinach in many forms. Try it in rice dishes, or combine it with feta cheese, pomegranate seeds, garlic, and preserved lemon.

- Spinach is very popular in Indian dishes such as curries, as saags (Indian-style creamed spinach), and with paneer (cheese).

. . . .

GRANDMA'S SPINACH SOUFFLÉ   SERVES 4

Source Note: Don't be put off by the word "soufflé"—this is very easy! Call it baked spinach if you feel more confident with that. The main trick here is to call everyone to the table just before you take the dish from the oven, so they can admire the puffy, golden top. My children, sadly, lack appreciation. They just see the green bits.

1 bunch fresh spinach
    (about 6 ounces leaves, or 4 cups firmly packed)
2 tablespoons flour
1 cup milk
1 teaspoon salt
Freshly ground black or white pepper
3 eggs, whites and yolks separated
¾ to 1 cup grated or crumbled cheese (feta, sharp Cheddar,
    smoked anything, blue cheese, Parmesan)

1. Preheat the oven to 350°F. Butter a 2-quart casserole dish and set aside.

2. Wash the spinach leaves and spin them dry. Heat a large sauté pan with a small amount of oil or butter; put all the spinach in and cook, turning, until the leaves are fully wilted, about 4 minutes. Spread the cooked spinach on a plate and allow it to cool somewhat, then squeeze all the moisture from it. Chop finely.

3. In a small saucepan, whisk the flour into the milk. Set the pan over medium-low heat and simmer, stirring frequently, until it thickens and has a smooth consistency. Pour the mixture into a large bowl; stir in the salt and pepper, and allow to cool somewhat.

4. In a large, very clean bowl, whip the egg whites until soft peaks form.

5. Whisk the egg yolks into the milk-flour mixture. Add the chopped spinach and grated cheese; stir to combine. Using a rubber spatula, gently fold in the egg whites; pour into the casserole dish and spread evenly.

6. Bake for 40 to 45 minutes, or until puffed and golden. Serve immediately.

— *Margaret Houston, Featherstone Farm CSA member*

"This recipe is certainly silly. It says to separate the eggs, but it doesn't say how far to separate them."

— *Gracie Allen, comedienne*

Sweet, succulent spinach growing in Featherstone Farm's greenhouse in early spring.

GOMAE (SESAME SPINACH)   SERVES 2

Source Note: This is a traditional Japanese dish of cooked spinach prepared with a sesame dressing, usually served at room temperature.

   12 ounces (1 large bunch) fresh spinach
   1 to 2 tablespoons dark sesame oil
   ½ teaspoon soy sauce or tamari
   1 teaspoon toasted sesame seeds

1. Bring a small pot of salted water to a boil. Drop the spinach into the boiling water for 1 to 2 minutes; it will turn bright green. Immediately remove the spinach and plunge it into ice water for 1 minute to stop the cooking process. Drain it thoroughly, then squeeze out the excess water.

2. Mix the sesame oil and soy sauce in a bowl. Toss the oil mixture with the spinach and top with toasted sesame seeds. Serve warm or cold.

— *Featherstone Farm, Rushford, Minnesota*

SAAG PANEER   SERVES 2 TO 4

Source Note: Saag paneer is a delicious Indian vegetable dish made with spinach, mustard greens, and paneer (Indian cheese). This wonderful dish is smooth, creamy, and full of warm spices. Serve saag paneer with fragrant basmati rice and fresh naan.

   4 tablespoons ghee, or 2 tablespoons mustard oil plus
       2 tablespoons vegetable oil
   Green chiles (as many as you want), split lengthwise
       (remove the seeds for less heat)
   1 onion, grated or finely chopped
   1 teaspoon fenugreek seeds
   2 (3-inch) sticks cinnamon
   5 cardamom pods
   5 whole cloves
   4 cloves garlic, minced
   1½ tablespoons grated ginger
   1 teaspoon ground cumin
   1 teaspoon ground coriander
   1 tablespoon tomato paste
   Two (16-ounce) bags frozen chopped spinach, thawed and liquid
       squeezed out, or 4 pounds fresh whole-leaf spinach, chopped
   1 bunch kale or mustard greens, stems removed, chopped
   ⅓ cup heavy cream (optional)

"On the subject of spinach:
Divide into little piles.
Rearrange again into new piles.
After five or six maneuvers,
sit back and say you are full."

— *Delia Ephron*,
How to Eat Like a Child

1 portion paneer, cubed (either homemade or store-bought)
Salt

1. In a large Dutch oven, heat the ghee over medium heat. When it is hot, add the chiles, onion, fenugreek, cinnamon, cardamom, and cloves. Sauté until the onion begins to brown slightly. Adjust the heat if necessary to prevent burning. Add the garlic and ginger and continue to cook for about 1 minute. There should be a nice fragrance coming from the pot.

2. Add the dry spices and mix to thoroughly combine. Add the tomato paste, spinach, and fresh greens. Mix well. Add 1 to 2 cups water (the amount will depend on how big your pot is) to give about ½ inch of liquid above the greens. Bring to a boil, then lower the heat to allow the greens to simmer, partially covered, for 30 to 45 minutes (longer is better). Stir occasionally. When the water has evaporated, add either the cream or a little more water. By the end of the cooking time, the greens should be tender and most of the liquid should be evaporated.

3. Turn off the heat, cover the pot, and allow it to sit for about 15 minutes. Add salt to taste.

4. Let the spinach cool enough so that you can remove the cinnamon stick and cardamom pods. Using a food processor or a stick blender (also called an immersion blender), puree the mixture until it is very smooth; this is optional, but doing so will yield the perfect, creamy consistency.

5. Before serving, fry the paneer cubes in a little bit of oil (or ghee) until they are browned on all sides. Drain on paper towels. Check the saag again to make sure it is the consistency you want. If you prefer, add a little more water to thin it out. Add the paneer to the saag and mix gently.

— *Foodista.com*

. . . .

SPANAKOPITA (GREEK SPINACH PIE)   SERVES 6 TO 10

Source Note: This is a traditional Greek dish. You can find phyllo dough at most supermarkets in the frozen pie and pie dough section.
Frozen spinach is actually preferred for this recipe over fresh spinach, which must be meticulously cleaned, chopped, wilted, and then squeezed dry, all of which takes time. And to get the quantity the recipe requires, you must use a huge amount of fresh spinach. Frozen spinach is already cleaned and that large amount is already compressed into bags or boxes, plus it is chopped more evenly and thus mixes and cooks better with the rest of the filling.

    2 tablespoons olive oil
    1 medium yellow onion, chopped

Eating Tip

Serve spinach with meats, vitamin C–rich fruits and vegetables, or white wine to help the body absorb more of its iron, which occurs in a less-accessible chemical form.

Martha Wagner

Zenger Farm is one of the largest farm education centers in the country, comprising 4 acres of organic farmland and 10 acres of wetland in the outer southeast quadrant of Portland, Oregon. A nonprofit today, Zenger Farm was a dairy farm for many years before being purchased in 1994 by the City of Portland's Bureau of Environmental Services (BES), which saw an opportunity to promote environmental stewardship in a way that would complement its long-term conservation plans for the area.

Zenger Farm is guided by the mission of promoting sustainable food systems, environmental stewardship, and local economic development through a working urban farm. The mission is fulfilled in multiple, noteworthy ways. On-staff farmers and interns raise a variety of food crops, laying hens, and seasonal turkeys using sustainable farm practices.

They grow about 24,000 pounds of food annually that are sold to colleges and restaurants, through its Farm Shares CSA and through the Lents International Farmers Market, a nearby market that the farm helped establish and whose vendors and customers include people from the local Hmong, Latino, and Russian communities.

Of the 60 CSA members, 40 are neighbors living within five miles of the farm and 30 pay for their weekly shares with SNAP funds, formerly known as food stamps. (Zenger ran a pilot SNAP payment program that has become a model for other Oregon CSAs.)

Programs for Children and Families

More than 7,000 children and adults visit the farm for field trips, children's vacation camps, classes, and workshops every year. Experiential and science-based programs

Two (16-ounce) bags frozen spinach (do not thaw),
    or 4 pounds fresh whole-leaf spinach, chopped
1 pound feta cheese
2 eggs
1½ teaspoons dry dill, or 1 tablespoon chopped fresh dill
Salt and freshly ground black pepper
4 ounces (1 stick) unsalted butter, melted
One (1-pound) box phyllo dough, thawed overnight
    in the refrigerator

1. Preheat the oven to 400°F.

2. If you are using fresh spinach, blanch it first. Bring salted water to a boil. Drop the spinach into boiling water for 15 to 30 seconds until it turns bright green. Remove the spinach and immediately plunge it into ice water to stop the cooking process. Thoroughly squeeze the excess water from the spinach.

3. In a large, heavy-bottomed pot or Dutch oven, heat the olive oil (it should be enough to cover the bottom of the pan) on medium heat. Add the onion and sauté it, stirring occasionally, until it turns translucent, about 2 minutes.

4. Add the frozen spinach and stir it with the onion, cooking it until it is thawed but not hot. If you're using fresh spinach, heat it through until it wilts (about 1 minute).

5. Transfer the onion and spinach to a colander. When it is cool enough to handle, squeeze it with your hands or press with a spoon to extract as much water as possible. Set the mixture aside to cool completely.

6. Crumble the feta into a large bowl, add the eggs, and stir well. Add the dill, then salt and pepper to taste. Add the spinach and onions and combine well.

7. To make individual triangles: Brush one or two sheets of phyllo with melted butter. Fold the sheets lengthwise twice (so they are long and thin-shaped), and place a heaping teaspoonful of the spinach mixture at one end in the corner of the dough. Then fold the dough into a triangle over the spinach mixture, creating a little pocket. Repeat folding the pocket of spinach until no more dough remains to fold. (There may be a little flap of dough left, which you can cut off with a knife.)

8. A much easier method is to make a spanakopita casserole: Using scissors or a sharp knife, cut the sheets of phyllo so that they will fit into a 9-by-13-inch baking pan or Pyrex dish. Brush each sheet with butter; continue this until you've used up half of the sheets (8 to 10), and lay them flat in the bottom of the dish. Add the spinach mixture and gently spread it into an even layer. Then stack the rest of the sheets on top, buttering each one as you go.

9. Score the layers of phyllo before baking—otherwise it will be very hard to slice, as it gets so flaky. Bake the casserole for about 25 min-

utes; if you've made the triangles, bake them on a greased baking sheet for about 15 minutes. Check often—spanakopita is ready when the dough is golden brown; if it gets too dark, it is overdone.

— *Jen Vassili*

. . . .

SPINACH AND WARM SUNGOLD TOMATO SALAD

SERVES 4

2 large bunches spinach
1 pint (2 cups) Sungold cherry tomatoes
3 tablespoons olive oil
1 clove garlic, minced
Salt and freshly ground black pepper

1. Wash the spinach, removing and discarding the thick stems. Dry the spinach thoroughly, and divide it among 4 large plates.

2. Wash the tomatoes and cut them in half through their stem ends.

3. In a saucepan, heat the olive oil over medium-high heat and add the garlic and halved tomatoes. Cook for 3 to 5 minutes, until the tomatoes soften and release some of their juices (but do not overcook, as the tomatoes should hold their shape).

4. Season with salt and pepper. Spoon the warm tomatoes, garlic, and pan juices evenly over the spinach. Serve immediately.

— *Colleen Wolner, Blue Heron Coffeehouse, Winona, Minnesota*

teach youth and adults the importance of food, farming, wetland conservation, and environmental stewardship in healthy urban communities.

The farm's Healthy Eating on a Budget workshops, which are funded through a grant, engage more than 500 families annually from nearby diverse and under-served communities. It trains 20 volunteers and six interns to lead 50 workshops and demonstrations annually. Many families participate in multiple programs and have become volunteer leaders. Programs take place at the farm and out in the community at schools, churches, housing complexes, and farmers markets. (See the sidebar on classes, page 162.)

Farmer Training and an Urban Grange, Too!

Other opportunities at the farm include The Outer Southeast Farmer Training Project, a collaboration between Zenger Farm and the nearby Powellhurst-Gilbert Neighborhood Association. This program is designed to support skill building in gardeners and small-scale farmers. The project is community-based, so that participants decide upon and design training curricula and networking opportunities. Workshops are held once a month.

Historically, Grange halls were gathering places for rural people to break bread, support one another in times of need, and celebrate the bounty of the land. With this vision in mind, Zenger Farm broke ground in 2014 on a $2.3 million, 6,660-square-foot Urban Grange building that will enable the organization to double the number of people it serves with the addition of a new classroom, kitchen, and workspace. Local businesses as well as grants from the Murdock Trust and the Meyer Memorial Trust enabled the farm to meet its fund-raising goal.

Strawberries   FRAGARIA × ANANASSA

June spells summer weddings, the end of school, and delicious, sweetly fragrant strawberries. Although strawberries are commonly available now throughout the year, thanks to harvests from Chile and California, these big, beautiful berries often sadly disappoint. They lack nearly all of the flavor and scent that their smaller, less picture-perfect cousins deliver for just a few rapturous weeks of the year. Wild strawberries carry the most intense flavor and perfume of all, but beating the birds and squirrels to them is a challenge.

A member of the vast rose family, strawberries are one of nature's oddities in that they are among the very few fruits with external seeds (the cashew is another). In fact, strawberries are actually not true berries at all but are considered "accessory fruits," meaning that the fleshy parts are not derived from the flower's ovaries, but from the peg at the bottom of a receptacle that contains the ovaries. Therefore, the seeds are the strawberry's true fruit, with that succulent, perfumed flesh serving merely to support them.

Anatomy aside, strawberries come in a surprising number of forms. Some 600 varieties are grown in the United States alone. The variety with which we are most familiar is the garden strawberry, which spontaneously came into being when two Fragaria *species crossed.*

HISTORY

Humans have treasured the diminutive but strongly flavored wild strawberry for millennia. Strawberries appear to have originated in both the Old and New Worlds but were cultivated only relatively recently. Wild varieties (likely *Fragaria vesca*) were first documented in gardens in the early 1300s, most likely as transplants. American or Virginia strawberries *(Fragaria virginiana)* shocked European explorers with their abundance and comparatively large fruit size.

Our modern strawberries resulted purely by accident in France in the early 1700s, when a French explorer brought back several specimens of a Chilean *Fragaria* species that bore enormous fruits with acceptable flavor. These all-female (unbeknown to anyone) plants flourished but failed to set fruit until some male Virginian strawberries happened to be planted nearby. At last consummation took place, producing a fruit that has since become the world's most widely grown strawberry. Still, those lucky enough to have tasted the intense flavor of its wild cousins still believe that no garden berry holds a candle to its untamed counterparts.

NUTRITION

A 1-cup serving of strawberries provides more than an adult's daily requirement for vitamin C, as well as 20 percent of manganese, all for just 43 calories. Strawberries also contain significant amounts of folate, potassium, iodine, dietary fiber, and antioxidants, including anthocyanin, which gives the fruit its scarlet color.

SEASON

Commercially, strawberries are often available year-round, thanks to staggered plantings in California and South America. But a strawberry out of season never tastes as good. You'll find the choicest berries at farmers markets and CSAs in April, May, and June.

SELECTION

A bright, even shade of red with fresh green caps and an enticing scent promise ripeness. Locally grown strawberries are almost always a better bet, as truly ripe berries do not travel well. Avoid unripe berries that are greenish or yellow, as well as fruit with soft spots or wrinkled skins, which may signal mold or dehydration.

STORAGE

Before storing them in the refrigerator, check the fruit for signs of mold, bruising, or overripeness. Remove any spoiling or soft berries immediately, so their malaise does not spread to their neighbors. If you spread the berries on a layer of paper towels on a plate or flat pan, they'll keep much better than all piled up in a small container. Ripe strawberries are very perishable, and they should be eaten within 1 to 2 days. Keep them unwashed until ready to use.

TRIMMING AND CLEANING

Before using, wash fresh strawberries by floating them in a bowl of water or rinsing them briefly. Lightly pat them dry with a paper towel.

BLANCHING AND FREEZING

Thoroughly wash, dry, and hull strawberries before freezing. To freeze whole berries without sweetening, place them in a single layer on a cookie sheet in the freezer; once they are frozen, transfer them to zipper-lock freezer or vacuum food sealer-type bags, or freezer containers. Squeeze out any excess air and leave ½ inch of headspace (unless you are using the vacuum sealing method).

Sliced berries should be sprinkled with a little lemon juice or ascorbic acid dissolved in water before freezing; the acid will help retain the berries' color.

Adding sugar to the berries before freezing also improves their color, flavor, and shape, and can be done either as a dry-pack (slice or halve the berries, sprinkle ½ to ¾ cup of sugar per quart of fruit, then package, and freeze), or syrup-pack, which is especially good for whole berries.

To make the sugar syrup, dissolve 1¾ cups of sugar in 4 cups of water in a pot and bring it to a boil. (If you prefer a less sweet syrup, you can try 1 cup of sugar in 4 cups of water.) Once the sugar has dissolved, remove the syrup from the heat and skim off the foam. Chill, then pour ½ cup of syrup into a zipper-lock freezer bag, jar, or freezer container, add the berries, and keep adding syrup until the fruit is covered. Leave ½ inch of headspace for pints, 1 inch for quarts.

Frozen strawberries should last for up to 1 year at 0°F.

MEASURES AND EQUIVALENTS

- 6 or 7 strawberries = 1 cup

A Lot of a Good Thing

California grows enough strawberries in a year that if they were all laid end to end, they would circle the world 15 times.

Florida, the next-largest US strawberry producer, grows nearly all of the country's winter crop.

Books

Berries: A Country
Garden Cookbook
Sharon Kramis,
Collins Publishers, 1994.

Strawberry Recipes: Top 50 Most
Delicious Strawberry Recipes
Julie Hatfield,
Otherworld Publishing, 2015.

High Turnover

Strawberries are treated as an annual crop in California, meaning that the plants are replaced every year to maintain optimal yields.

In other US states such as Oregon, they are treated as perennial crops and are allowed to bear for four to five years before being replaced.

- One 16-ounce clamshell container = 1 quart = 15 to 18 whole berries = 3 to 4 cups sliced or chopped
- 1 pint = 7 to 12 whole berries = 1½ or 2 cups sliced or chopped

COMPLEMENTARY HERBS, SEASONINGS, AND FOODS

Almonds, apricots, balsamic vinegar, bananas, basil, black pepper, brown sugar, caramel, champagne, cheese (Brie, cottage, cream, ricotta, goat), chocolate, cinnamon, coconut, cognac, cream, créme fraîche, currants, figs, grapefruit, guavas, kirsch, kiwi, lemon, lime, maple syrup, mascarpone, nuts, oranges, orange liqueur, passion fruit, peaches, pepper, pineapple, port, raspberries, rhubarb, sambuca, sherry, sour cream, sugar, vanilla, violets, wine, yogurt.

SERVING SUGGESTIONS

- Few pleasures in life beat ripe strawberries with thick Devonshire cream or whipped cream on a warm summer day.
- Pair strawberries with stir-fried scallops and sugar snap peas for a sumptuous yet simple light lunch or supper.
- Try warming a wedge or wheel of Brie cheese, then sprinkling with sugar and serving with fresh, ripe strawberries for a luxurious treat.
- Slice a fresh, ripe papaya or cantaloupe in half, scoop out the seeds, and fill the hollows with sliced strawberries and grapes.
- Melt good-quality chocolate over very, very low heat or a fondue burner, serve with strawberries and champagne, and enjoy with friends.
- Add sliced strawberries to lettuce and fruit salads.
- Make fruit kebabs by skewering chunks of pineapple, bananas, strawberries, melon, grapes, other berries, and papaya. Great for kids and grown-ups alike, with or without whipped cream or maple syrup for dipping.
- Toss sliced strawberries over cereal, pancakes, fruit salads, ice cream, oatmeal, and yogurt.
- When local strawberries are in abundance, buy a half flat, puree them, strain out the seeds, and freeze the puree as a cure for the midwinter doldrums. The sauce can be used to drizzle over desserts or waffles.
- Crush the berries with a little sugar and other berries or pineapple, and serve over ice cream, yogurt, cottage cheese, or pound cake.
- Strawberries can be a lovely surprise ingredient in salsas and chutneys.
- Puree fresh strawberries in smoothies and milkshakes.
- Make strawberry shortcake! Jam! Jelly!

SWEET-TART FRESH STRAWBERRIES   SERVES 12

Source Note: The lightly acidic balsamic vinegar and the sweet brown sugar add refreshingly sweet yet tangy flavor notes to enhance the berry flavor. You can also try adding a little freshly cracked black pepper.

2 quarts fresh strawberries, hulled
1 cup packed light brown sugar
¼ teaspoon salt
½ cup balsamic vinegar

About 1 to 2 hours before serving time, toss the strawberries with the brown sugar, salt, and vinegar in a large mixing bowl. Refrigerate and toss again. Drain and serve cold in a clear glass container.

— *Shirley Corriher,* CookWise

. . . .

STRAWBERRY SHORTCAKE   SERVES 8

Source Note: This is a real American classic—shortcake made with a rich biscuit base, lots of fresh strawberries, and a reasonably lavish hand with the whipped cream.

SHORTCAKE

1¾ cups all-purpose flour
2 teaspoons baking powder
Pinch of salt
4 tablespoons (½ stick) lightly salted butter, cut into pieces
⅔ cup whipping cream

TOPPING

1 quart fresh strawberries, washed, dried, hulled, and halved
2 tablespoons sugar for sprinkling, plus 2 teaspoons
    for whipped cream
1½ cups whipping cream

1. Preheat the oven to 425°F. Butter an 8-inch round cake pan.

2. Mix the flour, baking powder, and salt in a bowl. Combine the butter pieces into the flour mixture with a pastry blender, two knives, or your fingers until the mixture resembles coarse meal. Add the cream and stir until the mixture just comes together. Shape the dough into a flat disk and press it lightly into the prepared pan, patting it evenly to the edges. Bake on the center rack for about 20 minutes; the top should be lightly colored and feel firm to the touch. Turn the cake out of the pan and set it right side up onto a cake rack to cool.

3. When the shortcake is completely cool, slice it in half horizontally with a long, thin knife. Slice the strawberries in half and sprinkle them with 2 tablespoons of the sugar; set aside for about 30 minutes.

4. When ready to assemble, whip the cream with the remaining 2 teaspoons of sugar. Spread two-thirds of the strawberries with their juice over the cut surface of the bottom half, then cover them with about two-thirds of the whipped cream. Set the top half over the filling and press lightly. Spoon the berries onto the center of the top layer only, and top with the remaining whipped cream.

— *Rolce Redard Payne and Dorrit Speyer Senior,* Cooking with Fruit

For More Information

Strawberry Sue
www.strawberrysue.com

California Strawberry Commission
www.calstrawberry.com

Freshly picked strawberries at Featherstone Farm.

Hope They Don't All Germinate

On average, each strawberry has 200 tiny seeds on its exterior.

STRAWBERRY AND GOAT CHEESE PIZZA

MAKES FOUR 8-INCH PIZZAS

Source Note: This nontraditional take on pizza will have your taste buds exploding with savory goat cheese and strawberries marinated in a white balsamic vinaigrette.

PIZZA DOUGH

½ ounce (two 0.25-ounce packets) active dry yeast
1 tablespoon sugar
3 to 4 cups all-purpose flour
2 teaspoons kosher salt
1 tablespoon olive oil

PIZZA TOPPINGS

3 tablespoons white balsamic vinegar
3 tablespoons extra-virgin olive oil
¼ cup aged balsamic vinegar
½ cup (4 ounces) softened goat cheese
4 cups fresh strawberries, hulled and quartered
¼ cup (2 ounces) crumbled goat cheese
Coarsely ground black pepper
Baby arugula and frisée, for garnish

1. To make the pizza dough: In a mixer bowl, sprinkle the yeast and sugar over 1 cup of warm water; let stand until foamy, about 10 minutes. Add 3 cups of the flour, the salt, and olive oil; mix with a dough hook until the dough is stretchy and no longer sticky, adding more flour if necessary. Divide the dough into 4 equal portions. Refrigerate, covered, until needed.

2. To make the white balsamic vinaigrette: In a small nonreactive saucepan, simmer the white balsamic vinegar until it reduces to 1½ tablespoons. Whisk in the extra-virgin olive oil.

3. To make the aged balsamic reduction: In a small nonreactive saucepan, simmer the aged balsamic vinegar until it reduces to about 1½ tablespoons.

4. Heat the oven to 400°F. On a lightly floured surface, roll each piece of the pizza dough into an 8-inch circle. Place on a baking sheet; bake in the oven for 10 minutes, or until firm and slightly brown.

5. Spread the pizza crusts with the softened goat cheese, leaving a ½-inch border. In a bowl, toss the strawberries with the white balsamic vinaigrette; arrange the strawberries evenly on the goat cheese. Bake for 10 minutes more.

6. Remove the pizzas from the oven; scatter the crumbled goat cheese on top. Drizzle with the aged balsamic reduction; sprinkle with black pepper. Garnish the pizzas with a few leaves of arugula and frisée.

— *California Strawberry Commission*

"Doubtless God could have made a better berry, but doubtless God never did."

— *William Butler on the wild strawberry*

STRAWBERRY NACHOS   SERVES 6

3 cups sliced strawberries
⅓ cup sugar, plus 2 tablespoons for the cream
¼ cup amaretto (almond-flavored liqueur)
½ cup nonfat sour cream
½ cup frozen reduced-calorie whipped topping, thawed
⅛ teaspoon ground cinnamon
6 (7-inch) flour tortillas, cut into 8 wedges
Butter-flavored vegetable cooking spray
2 teaspoons cinnamon sugar
2 tablespoons sliced almonds, toasted
2 teaspoons shaved semisweet chocolate

1. Combine the strawberries, ⅓ cup sugar, and amaretto in a bowl; stir well. Cover and chill for 30 minutes. Drain, reserving the juice for another use.

2. Preheat the oven to 400°F.

3. Combine the sour cream, whipped topping, the 2 tablespoons of sugar, and cinnamon in a bowl; stir well. Cover and chill.

4. Arrange the tortilla wedges on two baking sheets; lightly coat with cooking spray. Sprinkle evenly with the cinnamon sugar. Bake for 7 minutes or until crisp. Cool on a wire rack.

5. To serve, arrange the 8 tortilla wedges on a serving plate; top each with about ⅓ cup of the strawberry mixture and 2½ tablespoons of the sour cream mixture. Sprinkle with the almonds and chocolate.

— *Roz Kelmig, California Strawberry Commission*

PAUL'S STRAWBERRY JAM   MAKES EIGHT (8-OUNCE) JARS

Source Note: Making strawberry jam is easy and simple. For a lot of people it's their first stab at home canning—I know it was for me, thanks to my sister Adele and her boundless love of strawberries.

There are two schools of thought when it comes to jam making. The first says that adding pectin is okay because it speeds up the process and the second says that it's cheating. Pectin is a gelling agent that is a naturally occurring saccharide in many plants. When you make cranberry sauce from fresh berries, it gels all on its own from the high level of pectin in the cranberries.

But not all fruit has high enough natural levels of pectin to allow it to gel when it's cooked through. So the options with a low-pectin fruit like strawberries are to either add a lot of sugar and cook them for a long time, or to add less sugar, use some pectin, and cook them for less time.

I come from the "add pectin" school. With that said, here's my simple recipe for strawberry jam.

2 quarts fully ripe strawberries (yields 4 cups crushed berries)
7 cups sugar
½ teaspoon butter
1 (1¾-ounce) pouch powdered pectin

1. Bring a large canning pot, filled half full with water, to a simmer. Wash the jars and screw-bands in hot, soapy water; rinse with warm water. Pour boiling water over the flat lids in a separate pan. Let the lids stand in hot water until ready to use. Drain the jars well before filling.

2. Wash, stem, and crush the strawberries thoroughly. Measure exactly 4 cups crushed strawberries into a 6- or 8-quart saucepot.

3. Add the sugar to the berries and stir. Add the butter to reduce foaming. Bring to a full rolling boil (a boil that doesn't stop bubbling when stirred) on high heat, stirring constantly. Stir in the pectin. Return the mixture to a full rolling boil and boil exactly 1 minute, stirring constantly. Remove from the heat. Skim off any foam with a metal spoon.

4. Immediately ladle the jam into the prepared jars, filling them to within ¼ inch of their tops. Wipe the jar rims and their threads. Cover with the 2-piece lids and screw the bands tightly. Place the jars on an elevated rack in the canner, and lower the rack into the canner. (The water must cover the jars by 1 to 2 inches. Add more boiling water if necessary.) Cover the pot and bring the water to a gentle boil. Process for 10 minutes.

5. Remove the jars and place them upright on a towel to cool completely. After the jars have cooled, check the seals by pressing the middle of the lid with a finger. (If a lid springs back, it is not sealed, and refrigeration is necessary.)

— *Paul Anater*

Swiss Chard

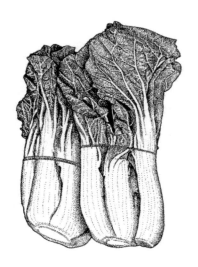

Swiss chard is closely related to beets. Like its cousin, it consists of two edible parts: its meaty dark-green leaves, which are reminiscent of sturdy spinach, and its large, flat, celery-like stems or ribs, which can be cooked and served like asparagus. Young chard leaves are tender enough to eat raw, or they can be briefly steamed or blanched and used in most preparations that call for spinach. Rich, earthy, slightly salty, and yet bitter, chard makes a delicious, nutritious addition to soups, salads, quiches, and stir-fries.

You may see several varieties in your CSA box or the farmers market: a green Swiss chard with white stems; a variety with red stems called Ruby Red; and Bright Lights, whose brilliantly colored stems glow in shades of orange, red, and yellow (sometimes informally called rainbow chard). The stems of white chard are better for eating than the colored ones, which can be quite stringy.

HISTORY

Paradoxically, Swiss chard does not have much to do with Switzerland; it is actually native to Sicily, Italy. The ancient Romans, Greeks, and Arabs ate chard and its beety cousins, but it was a Swiss botanist by the name of W. D. J. Koch who classified the plant in the 1800s; thus, the name of his homeland became part of the plant's common name.

NUTRITION

Chard is one of nature's nutritional powerhouses—it's an outstanding source of vitamins A, C, and K, as well as magnesium, potassium, iron, copper, and dietary fiber, all for only 35 calories per cup. Research studies have found that its phytonutrients, particularly anthocyanins and carotenoids, may significantly reduce one's risk of colon cancer.

SEASON

Commercially, Swiss chard is widely grown and available year-round. But its peak season at farmers markets and CSAs is during the summer months, from June to August.

SELECTION

Chard should be fresh, crisp, and unwilted. Avoid stems with cracked or brown ribs or leaves that are yellowing or drooping. For eating raw, choose chard with the smallest, tenderest greens. Larger leaves will be somewhat tougher and should be cooked.

STORAGE

Refrigerate unwashed chard in a perforated plastic bag in the vegetable crisper, where it will keep for several days.

TRIMMING AND CLEANING

Chard's large, rumpled leaves make great hiding spots for dirt and resting insects, so a thorough wash in a sink or large bowl of water is a must.

Grasp the stems and vigorously swish the leaves in the water several times. Grit will sink to the bottom, and a little extra help from fingers may be in order for the deeper crevices. The stems, which often harbor sand, can be scrubbed lightly with a soft vegetable brush.

STEAMING AND BOILING

The stems take longer to cook than the leaves, so trim and cook them separately. Colored chard stalks lose much of their color when boiled or steamed, so avoid overcooking them. To steam chard, either use a steamer or place freshly washed greens in a saucepan, cover tightly, and steam, using just the water clinging to them, for about 5 minutes. Stems will take a little longer, 7 to 8 minutes, depending on their size. Whole chard leaves can also be boiled for 5 to 7 minutes, depending on their size and condition, but take care to check frequently for signs of overcooking and too much loss of color in the ribs. Or slice chard leaves into 1-inch strips and stems into ½-inch pieces and boil for 3 minutes.

STIR-FRYING AND SAUTÉING

Chard responds well to being cooked briefly over high heat. Add freshly washed (but not dried), shredded chard leaves by the handful to the pan, stir, cover tightly, and cook for 5 to 8 minutes, or until they are wilted but still bright green. Chard stems, cut into 1-inch pieces, will take longer, 7 to 10 minutes, but their time varies, depending on their size and thickness. To avoid an extra step, start by cooking the stem pieces for a few minutes, then add the leaves to the same pan and finish them together.

BRAISING

Chard stems are delicious when braised in broth or other flavored cooking liquid for 20 to 25 minutes; the leaves can be added during the last 10 minutes of cooking time.

MICROWAVING

Wash and rinse, but do not dry. The water that clings to the leaves is enough moisture for them to cook in. Place sliced, freshly washed, shredded chard leaves in a microwave-safe dish, cover, and cook on high power for about 5 minutes. Stems cut into 1-inch pieces require a little longer time, about 8 minutes, but this will vary, depending on their size and the microwave's wattage. Check the stems frequently and remember that they will continue to cook while they are standing.

BLANCHING AND FREEZING

Unlike many greens, chard leaves do freeze acceptably well (but not the stems, which will turn soggy). To prepare the leaves, trim them away from the stems and blanch in boiling water for 2 minutes, then plunge them into ice water for 2 minutes to stop the cooking process. Drain and squeeze excess water out of the leaves. Then place in zipper-lock freezer or vacuum food sealer-type bags, or freezer containers. Squeeze out any excess air and leave ½ inch of headspace (unless you are using the vacuum sealing method). Frozen chard can keep for up to 1 year at 0°F.

- 1 pound = about ½ pound ribs and ½ pound leaves = 2 cups cooked
- 1 pound whole chard = 2 to 3 servings
- 1 pound leaves = 2 to 3 servings
- 1 pound ribs = 3 to 4 servings

Complementary Herbs, Seasonings, and Foods

Bacon, basil, beef, butter, cheese (Gruyère, Parmesan), cilantro, cream, cumin, duck, eggs, garbanzos (chickpeas), garlic, ham, lamb, lemons, lentils, nutmeg, olive oil, onions, pasta, peppers, pine nuts, pork, potatoes, prosciutto, quinoa, raisins, red wine vinegar, rice, saffron, sesame, tahini, thyme, tomatoes, turkey, walnuts, white beans.

Serving Suggestions

- Very young leaves can be eaten raw in salads, or used like lettuce in sandwiches. Try a BCT (bacon-chard-tomato sandwich).
- If you love the taste of southern-style greens but don't have nearly enough time to leisurely boil greens for hours, do a quicker version with chard. Boil it for 1 hour with a ham hock, some salt pork, or several strips of bacon (or even liquid smoke flavoring), along with a little vinegar, hot pepper sauce, salt, and sugar.
- Roasting the stems caramelizes them; drizzle with olive oil, garlic, salt, and pepper and roast for 20 minutes at 400°F.
- Boil chard leaves and stems separately and pat dry. Add diced bacon, pancetta, or prosciutto, and reheat.
- Wrap the big leaves around small fish for steaming or roasting on the grill.
- Use the finely shredded leaves as a substitute for lettuce in tacos or fajitas.
- Prepare lightly steamed chard with a hot bacon dressing, as you would wilted spinach.
- The robust, substantial leaves of chard complement equally robust meats—duck, ham, pork, pot roast, and lamb.
- Wrap lightly steamed chard leaves around your favorite vegetable or grain salad and roll into individual packages, like grape leaves in dolmas. Bake in a medium-hot oven and enjoy this nutrient-superstar alternative to stuffed cabbage.

Chard with Raisins and Almonds
Serves 4 to 6

Source Note: This recipe uses the colorful "rainbow chard" with its red, yellow, and orange stems. This is a wonderful dish for kids, who love its sweetness and bright colors.

> ¼ cup slivered almonds
> 2 pounds rainbow chard (or use red-stemmed chard)
> ½ cup water
> ½ cup apple juice
> ½ cup raisins
> 2 tablespoons butter

out of that temperature range as quickly as possible.

4. **Wash produce properly, even if you're going to peel it.** *Harmful bacteria and other nasties (including salmonella, listeria, and E. coli) may lurk on the outside of fruits and vegetables, including melons and spinach. Bacteria on the surface of, say, a melon, can easily be transferred into its interior by a knife slicing into it. Wash produce in very cold running tap water or distilled water; no soap or detergent is needed. And no need to purchase those expensive veggie washes either—although they are effective, cold, clean running water works nearly as well.*

5. **Never store raw garlic in oil at room temperature.** *Even in the refrigerator this is chancy, as sulfurous compounds in garlic provide ideal conditions for breeding botulism, the most deadly natural toxin known to humans. However, garlic can be safely stored in vinegar (not balsamic) if refrigerated; the high acid content of the vinegar prevents the formation of botulism.*

6. **When it comes to canning green beans and other low-acid veggies, pay close attention to established canning standards** *and do not try to shortcut any steps.*

7. **Refrain from washing raw meat, poultry, or eggs**, *in spite of what you may have heard in the past. Washing these foods can spread bacteria to sinks, faucet handles, countertops, and other kitchen surfaces. A better way to deal with potential contamination is to make sure you wash your work surfaces and tools after*

8. **Don't put cooked meat back on a plate that held raw meat or the marinade in which it was standing.** *This can result in cross-contamination. Always use separate dishes for raw and cooked flesh foods.*

9. **Reusing raw marinade on cooked foods is a no-no,** *since germs and bacteria from the raw meat may still be lurking there. If you want to reuse the marinade, heat it to a boil, then use it immediately.*

10. **Uncooked eggs can be a problem.** *Although salmonella is nowadays actually very rare in commercial egg production, it can still turn up occasionally. If you want to be extra safe, avoid eating products with raw eggs, such as Caesar salad dressing made with raw eggs, and (sorry, cookie-dough lovers!) cookie dough.*

11. **When you freeze foods, be sure to write the date on the package** *so you'll know whether to use or discard the food. (See the link below for some guidelines on how long to keep frozen foods.)*

12. **If in doubt, throw it out.** *Leftovers gone bad don't always smell that way—it's better to be safe than sorry. For a handy, reliable chart on food storage times, see Foodsafety.gov's website: www.foodsafety.gov/keep/charts/storagetimes.html.*

1. In a pan or using your oven broiler, toast the almonds.

2. Wash the chard, but do not dry it. Cut the leaves away from the stems, stack several of them in a neat pile, and roll the leaves up like a cigar. Slice crosswise to shred the leaves. Then cut the stems into ½-inch pieces.

3. In a large pan, cook the chard stems in the water for about 4 minutes; add the leaves and cook until they turn tender, 5 to 8 minutes. Stir in the apple juice and raisins, heating them thoroughly.

4. Top the chard with the butter and almonds, and toss lightly. Serve at once.

— *Ruth Charles, Featherstone Farm CSA member*

SWISS CHARD WONTON RAVIOLIS   SERVES 8

Source Note: Wonton skins are such a versatile product. Outside of Asian markets, you can find them in the refrigerated section of the grocery store. If they are difficult to find, you may want to buy a small supply of them when you get the chance, and freeze them. To thaw, place the package of wontons in the refrigerator and let them defrost for about 2 hours.

These uncooked raviolis themselves freeze very well, although you must freeze them in a single layer before storing them in a plastic bag or freezer container. Otherwise, they will stick to each other and you will find yourself serving very large raviolis.

> 2 bunches red or white Swiss chard
> 2 tablespoons plus ½ cup olive oil
> 2 cloves garlic, finely minced
> ¾ cup Parmesan cheese
> Salt and freshly ground black pepper
> 1 package wonton wrappers (approximately 50)
> ¼ cup cornstarch

1. Remove the ribs from the leaves of the Swiss chard. Wash both, but keep them separate.

2. Bring a 4-quart pot of water to a boil and cook the leaves for 3 to 4 minutes. Drain. Roughly chop the leaves. Meanwhile, dice the ribs into small pieces and sauté in the 2 tablespoons of olive oil, along with the garlic, for 5 minutes. Drain the ribs through a fine sieve over a large bowl, collecting and reserving the liquid.

3. Toss the Swiss chard leaves, ribs, and Parmesan cheese together. Taste and correct the seasoning with salt and pepper.

4. Place about 1 tablespoon's worth of the Swiss chard mixture in the center of a wonton skin. Lightly dampen the edges with water and lay another wonton skin on top. Carefully squeeze out any air from the ravioli and pinch the edges to seal. Place the completed raviolis

on a tray lightly dusted with cornstarch (this helps prevent the ravio-lis from sticking to the surface). Continue with the rest.

5. Preheat the oven to 350°F.

6. Lightly oil a baking tray and lay the raviolis down in a single layer. Lightly brush the tops of the raviolis with olive oil. Place them in the oven and bake for 10 minutes, or until golden brown.

7. Bring the reserved Swiss chard liquid to a boil, season it with salt and pepper, and add the remaining oil to the liquid. Drizzle over each serving.

Cooking Note: You may use any green leafy vegetable in this recipe. If you are using a thin-leafed green like spinach, blanch it in boiling water, drain, and squeeze out the excess water. Then assemble the raviolis as described.

— *Richard Ruben,* The Farmer's Market Cookbook

Swiss chard growing huge at Teena's Pride CSA.

Cooking Tip

The oxalic acid in chard will react with aluminum and iron cookware, staining the greens a dark color and lending a metallic taste.

MARINATED TOFU WITH MIZUNA OR SWISS CHARD

SERVES 2

Source Note: This savory vegan dish calls for marinating the tofu a few hours ahead. It can be served over white or brown rice, or with any type of noodles.

½ pound firm tofu

MARINADE

1 tablespoon balsamic vinegar
2 tablespoons olive oil
2 teaspoons sesame seed oil

2 tablespoons minced garlic chives (or substitute regular chives)
2 teaspoons minced or grated fresh ginger
Pinch of red pepper flakes
1½ tablespoons tamari sauce or Bragg Liquid Aminos

1 medium bunch mizuna or Swiss chard, washed, stems removed,
    leaves torn into pieces
1 tablespoon sesame seeds

1. Drain the tofu and cut it into cubes.

2. In a medium bowl, mix all of the marinade ingredients.

3. Set the tofu cubes in the marinade, toss gently, and marinate for at
    least 2 hours at room temperature, turning the cubes over occasional-
    ly.

4. Setting aside the tofu, pour the marinade into a skillet on medium
    heat; simmer 1 to 2 minutes, until reduced by about half.

5. Add the mizuna or Swiss chard and cover the pan. Continue sim-
    mering, stirring occasionally, until the greens wilt.

6. Add the tofu back in, sprinkle with the sesame seeds, stir to com-
    bine, and heat through. Serve immediately.

Cooking Note: You may substitute soy sauce for the tamari sauce;
they have a similar flavor and are both vegan friendly. However, soy
sauce is usually derived from both wheat and soy, so if you are sensitive to wheat products or gluten, choose the tamari sauce.

— *Adapted from Seabreeze Organic Farm, San Diego, California*

Summer

WE OFTEN THINK OF THE RIPENING OF THE FIRST TOMATOES AND SWEET CORN IN THE GARDEN AS THE START OF THE SUMMER PRODUCE SEASON. CERTAINLY, FEW OTHER CROPS ARE GREETED WITH SUCH FRENZIED ANTICIPATION. BUT A SINGLE-MINDED FOCUS ON THE FRUITS OF HIGH SUMMER—TOMATOES AND MELONS IN PARTICULAR—OVERLOOKS SOME OF THE WONDERFUL CROPS OF EARLY SUMMER. BEGINNING IN EARLY JULY, A BROAD NEW ARRAY OF PRODUCE BECOMES AVAILABLE IN FIELDS AND GARDENS ALIKE.

SUMMER'S SHEER ABUNDANCE MAKES IT CHALLENGING FOR EVERYONE TO KEEP UP. AS THE DAYS LENGTHEN AND THE HEAT RISES, CSA BOXES AND FARMERS MARKET STANDS ARE OVERFLOWING, WEEDS AND BUGS THREATEN TO OVERRUN THE ROW CROPS, FARMWORKERS LABOR 16-HOUR DAYS TO KEEP EVERYTHING WATERED AND HARVESTED, AND KITCHENS ARE ABUZZ AS OVERWHELMED COOKS WONDER WHAT TO DO WITH YET ANOTHER PINT OF PEACHES OR BUSHEL OF TOMATOES.

YET, JUST LIKE A FRAGRANT CANTALOUPE OR A FRAGILE SQUASH BLOSSOM, SUMMER'S HALCYON DAYS ARE ALL TOO FLEETING. TIME SEEMS TO SPEED UP, AND IN THE BLINK OF AN EYE, TEMPERATURES START COOLING DOWN. BY THE TIME SCHOOL IS BACK IN SESSION, FARMERS ARE EXHAUSTED, LOOKING FORWARD TO THE MOMENT THEY CAN BEGIN TO CATCH THEIR BREATH. LATE SUMMER FOR FARMERS ALSO COMES NONE TOO SOON FOR ANOTHER REASON—THESE HARVESTS BRING IN THE BIGGEST INCOME OF THE YEAR, A HUGE RELIEF IN THE FACE OF DWINDLING FINANCIAL RESERVES.

Jack Hedin of Featherstone Farm.

Featherstone Farm: Lessons in Perseverance

Corn. Miles and miles and miles of it, interspersed with the occasional soybeans or alfalfa, ripple across a rolling land dotted with picturesque barns and silver silos. Just when you think that no more corn could possibly exist in the world—well, there it is, hundreds more acres, standing tall, lush, and proud.

This is the bluff country of southeastern Minnesota, a stone's throw from where the Mississippi River glides through deeply carved river valleys between Wisconsin and Minnesota. This Driftless Area, as it is known, was bypassed by the last continental glacier, and a unique, rugged landscape has emerged from the resulting millions of years of weathering and erosion. Majestic bluffs up to 600 feet tall line both sides of the mighty river, whose rhythms of life, nature, commerce, and recreation dominate every season.

This area's distinctive karst topography features soluble bedrock (especially limestone and sandstone); numerous sinkholes, caves, and fissures; and vast areas of underground water and ice. Together, this complex geology and the lush river basin harbor many diverse microclimates with their own flora and fauna, wildly varying soil types, and fluctuating air temperatures. In the spring, rain and snowmelt swell several smaller rivers that drain into the Mississippi, and seasonal flooding is common. The climate here is extreme, with the temperature differences between the hot, humid summers and bone-chilling winters often spanning more than 120 degrees Fahrenheit in the course of a year.

These same conditions make wonderfully rich soils and fantastic growing environments. The high-grass prairies were cleared more than a century ago for dairy and meat production, but in recent decades, the pastures have been converted into annually tilled fields of mostly corn and soybeans, even on the hillsides. Coupled with the land's porous bedrock and intricate water systems, soil erosion and agricultural runoff are huge problems, with serious consequences for the nearby Mississippi all the way to the Gulf of Mexico.

The name "Featherstone" comes from a township in Goodhue County, not far from the Mississippi River town of Red Wing, where the world-famous shoes of the same name are made. It was in this township that a certain Alexander Pierce Anderson was born in 1862. His parents were first-generation Swedish immigrants who homesteaded here on a 160-acre farm, and young Alex grew up keenly attuned to farm life and the natural world. After his parents' early death, his life was a fascinating one that led to, among other things, botanical studies in Munich and his invention of puffed cereals and the equipment to manufacture them.

But he never forgot his roots. As a trained botanist and early conservationist, he knew all too well how the clear-cutting and prairie-burning agricultural practices of his youth had wrought environmental havoc on delicate ecosystems. In his later life, he bought back his parents' former farm, plus hundreds of acres of nearby bottomland, and established them into self-sufficient working farms. He also experimented with conservation tillage and a number of grain cultivars, and planted thousands of trees and shrubs to restore some of the original habitat. In 1932, he wrote and self-published the *Seventh Reader*, a memoir of his life that is also a chronicle of late-1800s pioneer life in Minnesota.

From firsthand experience, Alex described how he helped his father break the primeval forest and prairie to make new land for grain and corn: "I remember to this day the thousands of trees ... that we grubbed up, chopped up and burned, except those that had straight trunks from which firewood and fence posts were made." He spoke of the backbreaking work of plowing, seeding, and threshing by hand with only the help of one or two horses. And he recalled the annual worry about the crops "next year" and about paying the interest on the mortgage and loans.

It was this memoir and its musings on nature, agriculture, and humanity's place in the environment that, nearly 50 years later, would inspire his great-grandson Jack Hedin to start his own Featherstone Farm about 80 miles downriver.

The history of the modern Featherstone Farm began in the late 1980s, when Jack embarked on a series of farm internships that took him from New England to Pennsylvania to California. During this time, he acquired the practical knowledge of vegetable production as well as a love of agriculture that would be the foundation of his work in Minnesota. It was also when Jack's vision for Featherstone began to take shape.

A primary element of this vision that Jack and his wife, Jenni McHugh, shared from the outset was the desire for an organic farm to be the center of a rural community. As a young couple, they had lived and worked in two such places—Full Belly Farm near Davis, California, and the Wiscoy Community Co-op in Winona County, Minnesota. In 1994, they were among six founding members of the Zephyr Valley Land Community Co-op near Winona, a river town in southeastern Minnesota.

In its first seasons as a certified-organic producer, the farm was quite small—one greenhouse, five acres on a single site, one tractor, and a few part-time employees. The main outlets for its crops were the nearby Rochester farmers market and 20 CSA members in Winona. However, applying knowledge gained in other parts of the country to the unique microclimates of this Minnesota bluff country proved far more daunting than expected. Humility and a sense of humor were essential to survive those early days.

The years from 2000 to 2007 saw rapid growth in all aspects of Featherstone's operations. The acreage under cultivation rose from 10 to 40 and then to 80 acres, as new farm sites were rented to ensure a more predictable, high-quality crop. Tractors, equipment, and greenhous-

Alexander Pierce Anderson, whose farming philosophies inspired his great-grandson Jack Hedin to start Featherstone Farm.

Cultivate. Cultivate. Cultivate. If we keep on top of it, it means less hand weeding later.

es were added to support production. More full-time employees and seasonal workers alike were hired (see the Jack and Oscar Go to Mexico sidebar on page 48). From the beginning, Jack paid his employees well above the average, knowing that farm labor is among the most grueling on earth and such workers are often unfairly compensated (see the sidebar on immigrant farmworkers on page 408). In July 2007, the farm became one of four in Minnesota at the time that were certified and labeled fair-trade.

The Minnesota CSA grew to 200 shares in Winona, Rochester, and Minneapolis–Saint Paul. Then a wholesale business supplying food co-ops and natural-food stores from Minneapolis to Chicago began flourishing as more places called for Featherstone produce. In one season alone, Featherstone shipped 12 tons of broccoli to Whole Foods locations in the Chicago area.

Maintaining this steady growth and commercial success was anything but easy, however. The diverse microclimates and topography of southeastern Minnesota's bluff country meant wildly different degrees of sun, wind, temperatures, and soils. The rich silt loam and cool, moist conditions of the area's bottomlands made it ideal for growing sweet, tender salad mix and delicious peas, but it was awful for heat-loving crops like tomatoes and winter squash, which had to be planted on the surrounding bluff ridges for maximum sun and air movement. Floodplain land along the nearby Root River basin provided fertile, sandy loam soil and a warm, dry spot for melons and potatoes, but it also required more expensive irrigation.

To raise such a wide range of crops and provide a reliable supply of high-quality produce for commercial accounts meant identifying optimal growing conditions. At one point, Featherstone was farming five different sites miles apart, which exponentially complicated the logistics of equipment, transport, labor, and timing.

There were other unexpected problems. One of the biggest obstacles in CSA farming is a lack of access to land. And not just any land will do—great fruits and vegetables can't be grown just anywhere. But there is often a shortage, as established farmers look to expand and developers snap up the most prime acreage for nonagricultural use. The cost of purchasing land is often prohibitive, so renting it from other farmers or landowners, or through a land trust is often the only viable option. (See the Stewarding Farmland and Saving Farms sidebar on page 557.)

In the spring of 2007, Jack rented 25 acres on two nearby corn farms, knowing that his own 100 acres would not be enough to keep up with commercial and CSA demand for his produce. He plowed under the alfalfa hay established there and planted watermelons, tomatoes, and vegetables. Everything went smoothly until early July, when the two landowners were notified by the Farm Service Administration, the United States Department of Agriculture (USDA) branch that runs the commodity farm program, that there was a problem.

American agriculture is heavily subsidized by the federal government in favor of commodity crops such as corn, soybeans, wheat, rice, and cotton. The Farm Commodity Program started as a way to support farmers nationwide in the 1930s as part of the New Deal. At the time, farmers were often poor, and crop prices often fell below production costs; the program served as a valuable safety net as it enabled the government to set optimal crop pricing by controlling demand and supply. Since then, this system has become dominated by large-scale industrial agriculture, antiquated policy, and powerful lobbying interests, and it financially rewards the farmer who grows these commodity crops—to the exclusion of others.

Evaluating plant and soil health.

It turned out that this rented land on which Jack was growing his vegetables had been designated as "corn base acres," meaning that they were intended for commodity crops only. The penalties included the loss of not only the subsidy but also the market value of the produce grown, and Jack had to pay the landowners nearly $9,000 (see My Forbidden Fruits [and Vegetables] sidebar on page 518).

Sustainability was another issue as well, on multiple levels—not the kind of marketing-driven buzzword that is sometimes promoted as a half-hearted move toward being certified organic, but the kind of sustainability Jack had studied in college anthropology courses: farmers in Peru and Indonesia who have grown crops on terraces or paddies for thousands of years without depleting the soil, without hybrid and genetically modified organism (GMO) technology and, most importantly, without fossil fuels and their attendant pollution.

To this end, Featherstone worked on implementing sustainable methods whenever possible, rotating crops, integrating forage and grain crops to replenish soils, and using integrated growing methods of pest control. But running a produce farm is an object lesson in juggling expenses, marketing, production, people, labor, time, land, credit, and highly seasonal cash flow, all the while knowing that your fate is always at the mercy of unanticipated sweeps of nature, weather, pests, and plant disease. It was often a struggle just to keep up with the day-to-day workload and logistics, let alone be progressive year after year.

And, finally, as any fruit-and-vegetable farmer knows, running an operation this large is not just about the land, labor, soil, and plants—good packing, reliable refrigeration, and sound storage facilities are absolutely crucial to ensuring that its hard-won crops reach consumers in optimal condition. But such infrastructure is expensive and difficult to implement, especially when profit margins are already razor-slim. With its

Getting ready to roll on the CSA line.

This young man is excited to pick his own vegetables on a school tour.

marginal warehouse and constant juggling of logistics and finances, the farm was getting by, but utter failure could be just one disaster away.

On Saturday, August 18, 2007, a warm front pushed over Iowa, Minnesota, Wisconsin, Indiana, and Illinois, stalling as cool Canadian air poured over it. Although turbulent summer thunderstorms are common in this part of the Midwest, this system persisted, dropping torrential rain, the likes of which had never before been recorded in Minnesota and Wisconsin. With the area's steep topography, deep valleys, porous rock, thin soils, and high water tables, it was a catastrophe waiting to happen.

When it was all over, 8 to 24 inches of rain had fallen in southeastern Minnesota in less than 36 hours, creating flash floods. Roads had washed out, levees had given way, railroad tracks were ripped up, thousands of acres of cropland lay ruined underwater, seven people had died, hundreds of homes and businesses were flooded, mudslides covered roadways, and seven Minnesota counties were considered federal disaster areas. As luck would have it, Featherstone was at ground zero, with many of its operations in a vulnerable valley where much of the flooding occurred, and right next to a little stream called Money Creek that overflowed into a raging river.

The flooding couldn't have come at a worse time. Near the end of August is when farms are typically running on credit, awaiting harvests that will fetch most of the year's income. Fields are full of ripening vegetables and fruit growing fat and sweet in the last weeks of sun and warmth. In early September, harvesting is at its height, and then the cash comes in.

The day the rain began to fall, Jack and his crew had picked 10 pallets of melons and put them in a cooler for safekeeping. But the storms knocked out power overnight, and by the time a generator could be rigged up the next day, the melons were rotten.

"The flooding that followed essentially erased our farm from the map," Jack said. "Fields were swamped under churning waters, which in places left a foot or more of debris and silt in their wake. Cornstalks were wrapped around bridge railings 10 feet above normal stream levels. We found butternut squashes from our farm two miles downstream, stranded in sapling branches five feet above the ground. A hillside of mature trees collapsed and slid hundreds of feet into a field below."

The machine shed and warehouse facilities were engulfed in mud. The season's work was destroyed. Jack estimates that they lost about $500,000 in crops in those terrible hours. They were not the only ones; the area is home to an unusually high concentration of organic produce farmers who grow for CSAs and food co-ops and retailers in Minneapolis–Saint Paul and Chicago. All of them were pummeled by the ill-timed storms. Harmony Valley alone, one of the biggest produce farms in the area, lost nearly two-thirds of its annual total revenue.

A few of Featherstone's crops remained unscathed—the ones up on the ridges and hillsides had escaped the valley flooding. Jack estimated that he could salvage about $90,000 worth, but they had to be picked and sold right away if they were to make that income. Other farms were in the same position.

Jack checks on the carrots.

One of Featherstone's cornfields hours after the devastating 2007 flood.

The local community sprang into action. Within hours, the food co-ops and retailers that these farms supplied started buying all the produce they could, informing customers that it was from hard-hit farms and marking them up by only a few cents per item. The co-ops also started a nonprofit called Sow the Seeds Fund, which, along with the Institute for Agriculture and Trade Policy, began a fundraising campaign to help the area's farmers. Whole Foods donated to the campaign and did a matching grant with their customers.

Fiercely loyal CSA subscribers also pitched in and raised money, and co-op customers donated as well, some of them writing large checks right at the cash register. It was an unprecedented demonstration of what can happen when strong relationships have been forged between farmers, customers, and retail partners, and how tightly that community fabric can pull together in times of trouble.

Nature does not discriminate, and all of the farmers in the region, regardless of what they grew, sustained enormous losses and damage that year. The federal response for commodity-crop farms growing corn and soybeans included a robust safety net of taxpayer-subsidized crop insurance and farm support programs. But market-produce farmers like Featherstone received none of this help. The aid Featherstone received, as a business but not as a farm, came from agencies other than the USDA.

The crops demand not only harvesting, but cooling, packing, and shipping as well.

After the 2007 floods, Jack thought that Featherstone might be finished. Crop insurance didn't cover the farm's vegetables, and although he was able to get a small loan from the Minnesota Department of Employment and Economic Development, it didn't cover even half of his losses. Floodwaters had cracked his packing warehouse's foundation, and the resulting runoff into the fields now jeopardized the farm's ability to be certified organic. The struggles of the previous years had also left the farm with significant debt, the payback of which had been just within sight when the floods hit.

"There were many weeks when I thought it was gonna literally put our farm out of business," he said. "We'd be done and have to liquidate and sell everything at the time."

But something amazing happened. The same network that had pitched in during the weeks right after the storms stepped forward again, volunteering time, money, and expertise. Partners who had been loyal to Featherstone for years—both commercial retailers and CSA subscribers who had willingly shared the risk along with Jack—launched a capital campaign effort to save the farm. Preorders for the next year's CSAs came pouring in, loans were pledged, and gradually hope began seeping back in that the farm might not be lost after all.

"We had an immense amount of help, and I am incredibly grateful," Hedin said. "It is very, very humbling to have so many people voluntarily come forward and help you."

In a way, the flood had a silver lining; it finally forced Jack to make the difficult decisions he'd been putting off for years—to move the entire farm to a more stable location, build better packing and warehouse facilities, and make other necessary investments to streamline the operation as a viable business. But it was an incredibly painful lesson, one that he still has nightmares about to this day.

Eight years later, as of 2015, Featherstone had grown fourfold, becoming one of the largest certified-organic, fresh-market–produce farms in Minnesota, growing over 30 crop varieties. Its CSA program has swelled to nearly 1,000 members, it hires about 60 people yearly, and it is closing in on $2 million in sales. What used to be 80 acres is now 250, with most of it in the drier, less flood-prone town of Rushford. The soils include some of the richest, most fertile loam in the area, enabling Jack to grow even better vegetables than before. Unlike many CSAs that grow trendier vegetables and fruits, Featherstone continues to focus on what Jack calls "bread-and-butter crops"—just good, solid-tasting produce, like broccoli, corn, melons, and cauliflower.

"Jack talks about food as though it is his children. I never thought about food so much in my life," says Katie Sherman, the farm's former community outreach coordinator and CSA manager. "He knows food so well, and I think that transfers down into what's in the CSA box."

With the opportunity to build anew after the floods, Featherstone made a solid leap toward the sustainability that Jack had always strived for by installing solar panels on the machine shed roof in the fall of 2011. This system produces over half of the electricity consumed in the farm's packing shed, machine shop, offices, and irrigation plant—a major step toward reducing the farm's carbon footprint and a high-profile statement to the community about Featherstone's commitment to green energy.

The challenges continue. Climate change has definitely arrived in Minnesota; since 2007, the weather has dramatically oscillated between cold, wet springs; more catastrophic, flooding rains; and searing, withering droughts (see An Almanac of Extreme Weather sidebar on page 444). Farmers are used to dealing with bad weather, but this is a new kind of roller coaster, one that causes delayed CSA boxes and wholesale shipments, mounting crop losses, and profoundly challenging adjustments to planting, growing, and harvesting schedules.

Labor alone to move irrigation pipes during drought periods has sometimes cost more than $4,000 a week, and the farm has spent $30,000 over a season for extra irrigation as a climate adaptation. Again, as a produce farmer, Featherstone is not entitled to any of the crop insurance or government benefits that his commodity crop–growing colleagues enjoy, and Jack cannot pass on all of these costs to his customers. Farmers like him must absorb many of these unanticipated expenses. In the end, they may not be nimble enough to adjust to such extreme environmental fluctuations.

Land, or the lack of it, still poses huge problems. Although moving the farm after the floods reduced many risks and improved growing conditions, Featherstone still rents the majority of its vegetable acres from neighbors on year-to-year licenses because their commercial zoning designation keeps them open to development. And although this new land is on some of the best soil for growing vegetables that Jack has ever seen, there are rumblings that it may be developed. A capital campaign is underway for the farm to purchase land to ensure its long-term stability and survival.

Farming remains an extraordinary labor of love for Jack and his crew. Indeed, after everything that has happened, how could it not? In some ways, Alexander Pierce Anderson could never have imagined the modern world in which his great-grandson farms—surrounded by big agriculture, GMOs, and climate change. But over a century later, he'd understand the ever-constant worry about the crops, living at the mercy of the weather, and the niggling financial stress.

The longer one farms, the more some things stay the same.

The Featherstone Farm team, July 2015.

Asian Greens

Even a casual stroll through the produce section of an Asian market makes it apparent that the world of Asian vegetables is an enormous one, big enough on its own to fill up a book of this size. You will see strange-looking piles and heaps of greens, roots, stems, and tubers that rarely reach mainstream American supermarkets, from lotus root to countless brassicas. But, if you're game, this bounty can open whole new doors to cuisines vast and unfamiliar, yet incredibly delicious and healthful.

This book covers only a few of the Asian greens that are most commonly available at farmers markets and some CSAs, so be sure to consult the cookbooks recommended in this section for more information on these and other Asian vegetables. It's a culinary universe well worth discovering.

AMARANTH (MCHICHA) MIZUNA
BOK CHOY TATSOI
CHINESE BROCCOLI WATER SPINACH

AMARANTH AMARANTHUS SPECIES

Amaranth is not widely known in America except for its seeds, which are eaten as a grain or cereal. The plant, with its large, succulent-looking leaves splashed with fuchsia, purple, and pink, is often popular in decorative plantings. But those leaves are delectable, tasty, and highly nutritious—it's high time that Americans catch up to what their Far Eastern, African, and Caribbean neighbors have known for centuries.

The term "amaranth" is just one of many names sometimes assigned to the plant, among them callaloo, quelite, Chinese spinach, pirum, chaulai, Joseph's coat, namul, and vegetable amaranth. (It doesn't help that some of these names can refer to other greens or even dishes in their home cuisines.) But amaranth by any other name is just as delicious; the greens are like the brightest spinach—and taste like it, sometimes with an earthy flavor. Cooked, they have a slightly slippery texture like asparagus.

HISTORY

Amaranth originated in Peru, where it was a major food crop for the Aztecs along with maize and potatoes. It was also used in their religious rituals; the seeds were combined with honey to create images of their deities, a practice that horrified the conquering Spaniards. In their attempts to convert the Aztecs to Christianity, they forbade anyone to possess or even grow amaranth upon punishment of death. Today, the plant is widely grown in China, Russia, Thailand, Nigeria, Mexico, and sub-Saharan Africa, and it is especially valued for its ability to grow in drought-prone areas.

NUTRITION

Amaranth greens are a nutrient powerhouse, packing astonishing amounts of calcium, iron, magnesium, phosphorus, potassium, manganese, folate, and vitamins A, C, and K. A 1-cup serving of cooked amaranth greens contains about 28 calories.

SEASON

Commercially, amaranth is available year-round, depending on the geographical region. But its peak season at farmers markets and CSAs tends to be during the warmer months of spring and summer.

SELECTION

Look for fresh-looking bunches, free from yellowing, wilting leaves or sliminess.

STORAGE

Store amaranth with their stem ends wrapped in damp paper towels in a perforated plastic bag in the refrigerator vegetable crisper; use within 1 to 2 days. Or trim off the stem ends and place upright in a glass of water, like cut flowers.

TRIMMING AND CLEANING

Trim off the roots (if any) or stem ends. Like spinach, amaranth tends to hide a lot of sand and soil in its crinkly leaves. The easiest way to wash amaranth is to fill a big sink or bowl full of water, separate the leaves from the bunches, and completely submerge them, swishing vigorously. Rinse under cold running water and repeat if necessary. To dry, use a salad spinner or gently pat the leaves dry between a couple of dish towels.

Before cooking, trim the leaves off the stalks and discard the stalks. Very large leaves may need their tough central veins cut out.

STEAMING AND BOILING

Steaming is an excellent way to cook amaranth. About 1¼ pounds of freshly washed (but not dried) raw amaranth will steam in its own clinging water droplets if placed in a large pan, wok, or steamer basket, covered, and cooked for 2 to 5 minutes.

Because of its high water content, amaranth should not be boiled; it will turn into a watery, tasteless mush.

STIR-FRYING AND SAUTÉING

Like many delicate greens, amaranth is truly at its best when lightly stir-fried with savory seasonings. Add to the sauté pan or wok only in the last 2 to 3 minutes of cooking, as the greens cook down very quickly.

MICROWAVING

Wash and rinse, but do not dry. The water that clings to the leaves is enough moisture for them to cook in. Place the leaves in a microwave-safe dish, cover, and cook on high power.

➤ 1 pound = 3 to 4 minutes

Summer Crops Featured

Asian Greens
Amaranth
Bok Choy
Chinese Broccoli
Mizuna
Tatsoi
Water Spinach
Avocados
Beans (String)
Cantaloupes
Celery
Cilantro
Corn
Cucumbers
Dill
Eggplants
Flowers (Edible)
Honeydew Melons
Lemongrass
Mint
Okra
Onions (Green)
Oregano
Parsley
Peaches and Nectarines
Peppers (Sweet)
Peppers (Hot)
Raspberries and Blackberries
Rosemary
Savory
Shallots
Squashes (Summer)
Tarragon
Thyme
Tomatoes
Tomatillos
Tropical Fruits
Bananas
Cherimoya
Citrus
Coconuts
Kiwifruits
Lychees
Mangoes
Papayas
Pineapples
Watermelons
Zucchinis

BLANCHING AND FREEZING

To blanch, bring water to a boil. Drop the amaranth into the boiling water for 20 to 30 seconds. Remove the greens and immediately plunge them into ice water to stop the cooking process. Squeeze out the excess water from the amaranth, then place it in zipper-lock freezer or vacuum food sealer-type bags, or freezer containers. Squeeze out any excess air and leave ½ inch of headspace (unless you are using the vacuum sealing method). Frozen amaranth will keep for up to 6 months at 0°F.

EQUIVALENTS, MEASURES, AND SERVINGS

- 1 pound raw amaranth = 1 cup cooked
- ½ cup cooked = 1 serving

COMPLEMENTARY HERBS, SEASONINGS, AND FOODS

Bacon, beans, black pepper, cheese (Cheddar, goat, ricotta, sheep's milk), chiles, cloves, coconut, coconut milk, coriander, corn, cream, cumin, curry, garlic, hominy, onions, oyster sauce, peanuts, plantains, shellfish, soy sauce.

SERVING SUGGESTIONS

- Amaranth is traditionally added to many curries in India.
- Cooked amaranth can be substituted for spinach in many recipes. Try it in lasagna or other pasta dishes.
- Use raw young leaves in salads (the red variety is visually stunning).
- Amaranth with bacon! Try it wilted with hot bacon dressing, too, just like spinach.
- Add handfuls to stir-fries at the last minute. The hearty texture and brilliant color of amaranth make it a gorgeous—and nutritious—addition.
- Cooked amaranth and soft cheeses like ricotta or goat make a nice pairing baked together and finished with a little cream and seasoning.
- Try amaranth Korean-style—boil and season with sesame oil, sesame seeds, and fresh chiles or chile paste.
- Make a creamy amaranth soup with potatoes, celeriac, chicken stock, and heavy cream.
- Cook amaranth greens with hearty grains like wheat berries, millet, hominy, and quinoa for a hearty, satisfying meal.
- Blanch and freeze amaranth greens in serving-size portions to add to stir-fries, soups, and side dishes on busy days.

TANZANIAN SPINACH AND PEANUT CURRY (MCHICHA)

SERVES 4 TO 6

Source Note: Mchicha, *which means "amaranth" in Swahili, is a very traditional dish in Tanzania. It can be made like this with peanut butter—homemade or natural is best—or it can be made with a whole coconut (grated flesh and milk) instead. This dish makes a lovely side dish that can also be eaten with rice,* ugali *(a cornmeal porridge), or* samp *(hominy) and beans to form a delicious main course.*

1½ ounces (3 tablespoons) peanut butter

1 cup unsweetened coconut milk

3 tablespoons ghee or 3 tablespoons (about ⅓ stick) butter

1 medium tomato, peeled and chopped

1 medium onion, peeled and chopped

2 teaspoons curry powder

1 teaspoon salt

2 pounds amaranth (mchicha) or spinach, roughly chopped

1. In a bowl, mix the peanut butter with the coconut milk. Set aside.

2. In a large frying pan, heat the ghee over medium heat. Add the tomato, onion, curry powder, and salt and sauté for 5 minutes, or until the onion becomes soft.

3. Add the amaranth and continue cooking for 15 to 20 minutes, or until the greens are cooked.

4. Pour the peanut butter and coconut milk mixture into the pan and stir gently to mix.

5. Simmer for another 5 minutes, stirring constantly to ensure that the mixture does not stick to the pan. Serve immediately.

— *Michael Tracey,* Afri Chef: African Recipes: Cooking Real Food from Africa

BOK CHOY   BRASSICA RAPA, VAR. CHINENSIS

Bok choy by any other name may or may not be the same. Confusion reigns over the many varieties of this traditional Asian stir-fry vegetable, their interchangeable labels, and regional differences (think Chinese cabbage, Shanghai bok choy, Taiwan bok choy, pac choi, bok choi, *and* bak choy, *to name just a few). The bok choy referred to here looks like a miniature Swiss chard, with broad, dark green leaves; satiny, fat white stalks; and a delicate cabbage flavor. Both the stems and leaves are edible, making it ideal as a lightly cooked vegetable.*

HISTORY

Bok choy is native to China, where it makes a frequent appearance in the wok. Although bok choy and other closely related Asian brassica cultivars have been a part of the Asian diet for centuries, they did not find their way into Europe and North America until the 1800s, where they are still not widely used outside of ethnic restaurants. Bok choy is very popular in the Philippines, where it was introduced by immigrant Chinese who settled there after Spain conquered the islands in the 1500s.

NUTRITION

Like other members of the cabbage family, bok choy packs a nutritional wallop, with significant amounts of vitamin C, folic acid, iron, and dietary fiber at only 24 calories per cup.

Bak choy fields at Sang Lee Farms.

SEASON

Commercially, bok choy is widely grown and available year-round, especially in Asian markets and specialty food stores. But the best bok choy can be found at farmers markets and CSAs from spring through midsummer.

SELECTION

Choose bunches with firm stems and fresh-looking leaves. Very large stems may be somewhat tougher; the general rule is that the smaller the vegetable, the more tender and sweet it will be. Very small bunches may be cooked whole.

STORAGE

Fresh bok choy will keep tightly wrapped, unwashed, in a plastic bag in the refrigerator vegetable crisper for up to a week, although it may start to yellow after 3 days.

TRIMMING AND CLEANING

Bok choy tends to collect sand and grit at the base of its stalks, so a thorough cleaning or at least inspection is in order. Separate the stalks from the central stem and rinse under running water, or if they are particularly dirty, scrub them gently with a vegetable brush.

STEAMING AND BOILING

With its high water content, bok choy tends to collapse and go limp very quickly when cooked. Overcooking makes it quite watery, so keep this in mind when you choose your cooking method (steaming is preferable to boiling). The leaves cook much more quickly than the stalks, so if you want both of them to be present in the finished dish, put the stems in first, then add the leaves 1 or 2 minutes later. Steam bok choy stalks for about 6 minutes, or until tender, and leaves for about 4 minutes. As for boiling, cook the stems in salted water for 4 minutes and leaves for 2 to 3 minutes.

STIR-FRYING AND SAUTÉING

Stir-frying and sautéing bring out the best in bok choy. Cut the stalks into ½-inch pieces and stir-fry or sauté over high heat for about 6 minutes and the leaves for 3 minutes, or until just wilted.

MICROWAVING

Rinse but do not dry the bok choy. Place it in a microwave-safe dish; cover and cook on high power.

- 2 cups = 2 minutes
- 1¼ pounds = 7 to 10 minutes

BLANCHING AND FREEZING

Freezing is not recommended for bok choy because of its high water content.

EQUIVALENTS, MEASURES, AND SERVINGS

- 2 cups leaves = ½ cup cooked greens
- 1 pound bok choy = 4 to 5½ cups shredded = ¾ cup cooked

COMPLEMENTARY HERBS, SEASONINGS, AND FOODS

Bacon, beef, black bean sauce, chicken, chiles, fish, garlic, ginger, mushrooms, onion, oyster sauce, pork, rice (brown or white), sesame, soy sauce, sweet and sour seasonings, tofu.

SERVING SUGGESTIONS

- Swirl leaves and stems into stir-fries.
- Bok choy's watery texture and mild flavor best complement savory seasonings and rich meats, such as roast pork. Try braising it with duck legs or fish.
- Bok choy can be used in any recipe calling for Swiss chard.
- The tender stalks lend themselves quite well to dip, as an alternative or complement to carrot and celery sticks.
- Try substituting bok choy stems for celery; chop into egg and chicken salads, or spread peanut butter in them.
- Stir-fry with asparagus and garlic, or sugar snap peas and ginger.
- Bok choy's delicate flavor combines exceptionally well with mushrooms. Braise or stir-fry with porcinis, oyster mushrooms, thinly sliced portobellos, shiitakes, or morels.
- Stir-fry with shrimp or crab for a quick, delicious meal.
- Try wilting bok choy leaves as you would spinach, adorned with hot bacon dressing.
- Use bok choy in the filling for eggrolls and spring rolls.
- Shred raw bok choy for a crunchy Asian salad with ramen noodles and slivered almonds.
- Bok choy blends well with cheese and eggs. Sauté until soft and beginning to brown, then add it to gratins, omelets, frittatas, scrambled eggs, and casseroles. This is a good way to get kids to eat their veggies!

> "Omit and substitute! That's how recipes should be written. Please don't ever get so hung up on published recipes that you forget that you can omit and substitute."
>
> — *Jeff Smith, American chef and TV cooking personality of* The Frugal Gourmet

TRITICALE BERRIES WITH BABY ARTICHOKES, BABY BOK CHOY, AND DILL OIL   SERVES 4

Author Note: Triticale is a hybrid of wheat and rye; its berries look similar to those of wheat but they have a subtle rye flavor.

DILL OIL
1 bunch baby dill
¼ cup extra-virgin olive oil
Salt

To clean the dill, trim off the stem ends, rinse under cold water, and let the sprigs dry on a cloth. Chop the foliage coarsely. Use a blender to puree the dill with the olive oil and a little salt to taste.

1¼ pounds baby artichokes
3 cups ice-cold water mixed with the juice from 2 fresh lemons
    (about 3 tablespoons), or an equal amount of vinegar
1 cup water
½ cup olive oil, divided
2 cups triticale berries, cooked
3 cloves garlic, minced
1 bunch baby bok choy, chopped
1 tablespoon lemon juice or balsamic vinegar
½ teaspoon salt
Dash of freshly ground black pepper
Fresh spinach for serving (optional)

1. Rinse the artichokes. Set out a bowl with the ice-cold lemon water.

2. Working on the artichokes one by one, cut off the stem to ¼ inch
   from the base; peel back and remove the bottom leaves until only
   the top third of the pale-green cone tip remains. Cut off the pale
   green tips. Trim off any remaining dark green from base of artichoke.

3. Halve or quarter the artichokes (depending on their size) and drop
   them in the bowl of acidified water (to prevent discoloration).
   Drain.

4. In a large skillet, heat the artichokes with 1 cup of water to boiling.
   Cover and simmer 3 to 5 minutes, depending on the size of the
   artichokes. Drain well.

5. In a medium skillet, heat 2 tablespoons of the olive oil, add the
   cooked triticale berries and garlic, and sauté. Once the berries start
   to turn golden brown, add the artichokes and bok choy and cook for
   another 10 minutes. When everything is cooked through, toss with
   the lemon juice, salt, and pepper. Serve the berries, bok choy, and
   artichokes on a bed of fresh spinach drizzled with the dill oil.

— *Karolina Tracz, Nash's Organic Produce, Sequim, Washington*

. . . .

BALLISTIC BABY BOK CHOY AND FRIED TOFU   SERVES 4

*Source Note: Because tofu soaks up so many flavors and seasonings, it is ideal
to use in many dishes that have a strong flavor base. If it is used and cooked
properly, even your most carnivorous friends can be persuaded to try it.
Seduce them with this recipe.*

1½ cups raw rice (about 4 cups cooked)
16 ounces firm tofu
3 tablespoons chile oil, or 3 tablespoons corn oil mixed with
    1 teaspoon crushed and dried santaka or Thai chile,
    or 2 teaspoons New Mexican red chile powder

1½ pounds baby bok choy, washed and coarsely chopped
4 cloves garlic, minced, or several stalks of chopped green garlic
6 scallions (green onions), sliced
1 red bell pepper, julienned
¼ cup water
¼ cup soy sauce
2 dried shiitake mushrooms, rehydrated and sliced
¾ cup water chestnuts or jicama, coarsely chopped
3 teaspoons sugar
2 teaspoons crushed and dried santaka or Thai or New Mexican
     red chile powder, or to taste
1½ teaspoons cornstarch or arrowroot mixed
     with 2 tablespoons water

1. Cook the rice and set it aside to keep warm.

2. Cut the tofu into 1-inch slices and place them on paper or linen towels; cover with more towels. Place a cookie sheet on top of the tofu and place several weights (such as canned goods) on top to help squeeze the excess liquid out of the tofu. Let sit for 15 to 20 minutes. Cut the tofu into 1-inch cubes.

3. Heat the pepper oil in a large sauté pan or wok on medium-high heat. Sauté the tofu cubes, turning them when necessary, until they become golden brown. Drain the tofu cubes on paper towels and set aside.

4. In a large skillet with a cover, add the bok choy, garlic, scallions, bell pepper, and water. Cover and steam until the bok choy is tender, about 5 minutes. Add the soy sauce, tofu, mushrooms, water chestnuts, sugar, chile powder, and the cornstarch mixture and toss to mix. Stir lightly until the sauce boils, decrease the heat, and allow it to simmer for 1 minute. Serve the mixture immediately over the hot cooked rice.

— *Dave DeWitt*, 1,001 Hot & Spicy Recipes

"I came to all the realizations about sustainability and biodiversity because I fell in love with the way food tastes. That was it.

And because I was looking for that taste I feel at the doorsteps of the organic, local, sustainable farmers, dairy people, and fishermen."

— *Alice Waters, American chef*

CHINESE BROCCOLI   BRASSICA OLERACEA

If you like brassicas, then Chinese broccoli may become one of your favorites, if it is not already. It is quite distinctive looking, with thick, fleshy stems; broad collard-like leaves; and clusters of broccoli-ish flower buds (usually white, but sometimes yellow). It tastes similar to broccoli, but sweeter and brighter. When quick-cooked or stir-fried, it retains a succulent, juicy crunch and somewhat bittersweet flavor that was born to frolic with soy, oyster, black bean, and other savory cooking sauces. Aside from farmers markets and certain CSAs, it can be readily found in Asian markets, often under the name of pak choi *or* gai lan. *Do not confuse it with broccoli rapini or broccoli raab, with which it is sometimes mislabeled; the three of them are entirely different vegetables.*

HISTORY

In spite of its name, Chinese broccoli is not from China but probably originated in the Mediterranean from a close cousin of our modern European broccoli. It was introduced to China in ancient times, where it remains an extremely popular vegetable—but curiously not so outside of that country.

NUTRITION

Like all brassicas, Chinese broccoli is packed with nutrition, rich in vitamins A, B12, C, and K, as well as folate, fiber, phosphorus, potassium, and manganese. A 1-cup serving of cooked Chinese broccoli contains 20 calories.

SEASON

Commercially, Chinese broccoli is widely grown and available year-round. But, as a cool-weather crop, its peak season is during the fall and winter months.

SELECTION

Choose specimens that are firm and fresh looking, with no signs of wilting, yellowing, sliminess, or stinkiness. The flower buds should be mostly unopened, and the stalks should be fairly thin, with no fibrous white core showing at the base of the cut stems.

STORAGE

Store Chinese broccoli unwashed and wrapped in slightly damp paper towels in a perforated bag in the coldest part of the refrigerator. It will keep for up to 1 week.

TRIMMING AND CLEANING

Rinse the stalks well to dislodge any insects or dirt, or immerse in a sinkful of water and swish vigorously. The stalks may need to be peeled if they are very thick.

STEAMING AND BOILING

Steaming is the best way to cook Chinese broccoli to preserve its nutrients. Steam for 4 to 5 minutes; or boil for 2 to 3 minutes, depending on your preference for doneness. Remember that the vegetable will continue to cook as it cools down, so it is better to slightly undercook than overdo it.

STIR-FRYING AND SAUTÉING

Chinese broccoli is ideal for stir-frying, but blanching it first helps to retain its color and juiciness. To blanch, drop the whole vegetable into a large pot of boiling, salted water. Cover the pot and return to a boil for 1 to 2 minutes. Then drain. Once this blanching step is complete, slice the Chinese broccoli into 1-inch pieces, separating the leaves and stalks. Stir-fry the stems in oil for 1 to 2 minutes on high heat in a wok or large frying pan, or until the pieces are crisp-tender. Then add the leaves and sauté for another 30 seconds to 1 minute.

Microwaving

Peel the largest stalks (if desired) and arrange the pieces in a single layer in a microwave-safe dish. Add 1 tablespoon water, cover, and cook on high power. Alternatively, you can wrap the bunches in plastic cling wrap and place them in the microwave; they will steam inside the wrap.

- 1 bunch or ½ large bunch = 2 minutes
- 2 small bunches = 2 to 3 minutes

Blanching and Freezing

To blanch, drop the whole vegetable into a large pot of boiling, salted water. Cover the pot and return to a boil for 1 to 2 minutes, then plunge into ice water for several minutes to halt the cooking process. Drain and place in zipper-lock freezer or vacuum food sealer-type bags, or freezer containers. Squeeze out any excess air but do not leave any headspace. Chinese broccoli frozen at 0°F should keep for up to 6 months.

Equivalents, Measures, and Servings

- 1 pound Chinese broccoli = 4 to 5½ cups chopped = ¾ cup cooked

Complementary Herbs, Seasonings, and Foods

Almonds, anchovies, bacon, balsamic vinegar, beef, black bean sauce, carrots, chicken, chile, citrus, fish, garlic, ginger, grains, ham, hot peppers, lemons, mushrooms, olives, onion, oyster sauce, pasta, peanuts, pine nuts, pork, raisins, sausage, sesame, soy sauce, sweet and sour seasonings, tamari, tofu, tomato, walnuts.

Serving Suggestions

- Chinese broccoli is a natural for stir-fries. Cook the stalks first and add the leaves near the very end, as they will cook faster than the stems. Oyster sauce, soy sauce, black bean sauce, and miso are all classic Asian condiments that complement this vegetable.

- Pasta and Chinese broccoli go together wonderfully, the same way that broccoli raab does. Keep the flavors bright and uncomplicated: chile, garlic, and lemon. Italian sausage is especially good with this.

- Chinese broccoli takes to vinaigrette like a duck to water. This is a good dish to serve either hot or cold, like asparagus.

- Combine tofu and Chinese broccoli with yakisoba noodles and sesame oil for a delicate, nutritious dish.

- Add very thinly sliced coins of cooked Chinese broccoli stems and shredded leaves to fried rice.

- Make meatballs from ground chicken and ginger, then serve with cooked Chinese broccoli in a delicate broth.

- Like bok choy, Chinese broccoli combines well with mushrooms. Braise or stir-fry with porcinis, oyster mushrooms, thinly sliced portobellos, shiitakes, or morels.

- Stir-fry with shrimp, lobster, or crab for a quick, delicious meal.

- Try wilting Chinese broccoli as you would spinach, adorned with hot bacon dressing.

- Use thinly shredded Chinese broccoli leaves in the filling for eggrolls and spring rolls.

◢ Crush pine nuts, almonds, or walnuts, then sprinkle over lightly oiled and salted blanched Chinese broccoli.

Books

Asian Greens: A Full-Color Guide, Featuring 75 Recipes
Anita Loh-Yien Lau,
St. Martin's Griffin, 2001.

The Serious Eats Field Guide to Asian Greens (website)
www.seriouseats.com/2014/05/asian-green-guide.html
Ben Jay; Serious Eats, 2014.

A Cook's Guide to Asian Vegetables
Wendy Hutton,
Tuttle Publishing, 2004.

CHINESE BROCCOLI IN SESAME-SICHUAN VINAIGRETTE

SERVES 4

Source Note: Chinese broccoli stems have a pickle-ly crunch par excellence, but their dark green becomes a bit drab in the presence of acid—although far less so than other brassicas. The shorter the marinating time, the brighter the color. Serve with barbecued meats or mix into grain salads. Or top with peanuts and chiles to serve as a side dish to an Asian meal.

¾ teaspoon Sichuan pepper
¼ teaspoon anise seeds
¼ teaspoon kosher salt
1 or 2 small dried chiles (optional)
¼ teaspoon minced garlic
2 tablespoons rice vinegar
2 teaspoons honey
1 tablespoon soy sauce or tamari
1 tablespoon peanut oil
1 tablespoon Asian (dark) sesame oil
1 pound Chinese broccoli
3 medium-large carrots
¼ cup chopped roasted peanuts (optional), **for garnish**

1. In a small pan over low heat, stir the Sichuan pepper, anise seeds, salt, and optional chiles until fragrant and crisp, about 3 minutes. Transfer to a suribachi or mortar; cool slightly. Crush the spices finely. Add the garlic and crush. Stir in the vinegar, honey, and soy sauce, blending well. Add the peanut and sesame oils.

2. Rinse the Chinese broccoli in a sinkful of water. Cut the leaves with their stems from the stalks. Halve the smaller leaves; quarter the larger ones and cut from stems. Peel the base of the larger stalks. Cut the stalks on the diagonal into 1½-inch pieces. Peel the carrots and halve crosswise. Halve the wider top parts lengthwise, then cut all of them into diagonal slices ¼ inch thick.

3. Drop the broccoli into plenty of boiling salted water. Return to a boil, covered. Uncover and boil 1 minute. Add the carrots. Return to a boil and cook just until the slices lose their raw crunch, less than a minute. Drain and refresh in cold water. Spread the vegetables on a towel to dry.

4. Combine the vegetables and dressing and toss. Serve at room temperature or chilled. If desired, sprinkle with peanuts.

— *Elizabeth Schneider,* Vegetables from Amaranth to Zucchini: The Essential Reference

WILTED GREENS WITH COCONUT   SERVES 4

Source Note: I lived in Australia for a couple of years, and my palate has never been the same. I grew to enjoy the intermingling of sweet, sour, and salty flavors as well as the mix of slightly bitter with sweet in a savory dish. If you do not have access to a coconut tree to make your own fresh coconut (and how many of us do?), head to any Indian or Southeast Asian market or natural foods store to find unsweetened coconut.

What greens you decide to use will determine the cooking time. Spinach takes about 3 minutes, whereas Chinese broccoli will take at least 5 minutes.

2 tablespoons sesame oil
2 pounds greens, such as spinach, bok choy, or Chinese broccoli
¼ cup unsweetened shredded coconut
Salt and freshly ground black pepper

Heat a 12-inch sauté pan or wok until hot, and add the oil. Cook the greens until just wilted, then add the coconut and toss to combine. Season with salt and pepper. Serve immediately.

— *Richard Ruben,* The Farmer's Market Cookbook

MIZUNA   BRASSICA RAPA NIPPOSINICA

Mizuna is a relatively new green to American shores, brought by the Japanese, who use it extensively in soups, stir-fries, and as a pickled vegetable, but not as a raw green. Like all mustard greens, mizuna packs a peppery bite and a full-bodied flavor in its delicate-looking, heavily incised leaves, which resemble those of an elaborate dandelion. Young mizuna is zesty in salads and often used as a beautiful garnish; larger specimens are best cooked. It is often found in mesclun, that European mix of baby salad greens, and is sometimes known as Japanese mustard, mizu-na, kyona, *or California pepper.*

HISTORY

Mizuna is thoroughly associated with Japanese cooking, but the plant may have originated in China. Many mustard greens are thought to have grown wild in parts of Asia and India, where they have been eaten for thousands of years.

NUTRITION

As a cruciferous vegetable (a member of the cabbage family), this delicate green pulls its own weight nutritionally, containing folic acid, carotene, vitamin C, and a number of antioxidants. A 1-cup serving of chopped, raw mizuna contains 15 calories.

Farming Food in the City: Urban Agriculture

Mi Ae Lipe

As world populations mushroom, more people are moving to cities. According to the UN Food and Agriculture Organization, it is estimated that by 2030, 60 percent of people in developing countries will live in cities. Already, urban farms are supplying food to about 700 million city residents—about a quarter of the world's urban population.

To meet this massive demand for food, urban farms and gardens are sprouting faster than dandelions after a spring rain. And it is not just in the United States—countries all over the world are figuring out innovative, intensive ways to cultivate the maximum amount of food in the tiniest spaces.

This book mentions several noteworthy urban farms across America: **Heritage Point Urban Farm** (page 565), **Zenger Farm** (92), **New Roots for Refugees** (433), **Growing Power** (352–353), **CityGrown** (38), **The Growing Experience** (486), **Growing Home** (343), and **B.U.G. (Backyard Urban Garden Farms)** (488).

What is urban agriculture, exactly? In its most essential form, it is the practice of cultivating, processing, and distributing food in a village, town, or city. But the term has very different meanings, depending on the socio-economics of a region. In more affluent areas, urban agriculture often takes the form of a social movement that creates a hub for sustainable farming, around which locavores, foodies, and organic growers can share their common desire for community and fresh, natural food. However, in developing countries (and economically depressed areas in nondeveloping ones), urban agriculture serves much more elemental needs for food security, nutrition, and income.

From New York to Tokyo to South Africa, urban farms come in

SEASON

Commercially, mizuna is widely grown and available year-round. But its peak season at farmers markets and CSAs is during the spring and summer months.

SELECTION

Like a dress uniform, mizuna should look fresh and crisp. Pass up slimy, wilted, or discolored leaves. The pepperiness of mizuna varies widely from plant to plant, depending on its growing conditions, so sample a few leaves before purchasing if you want to be sure of its flavor qualities.

STORAGE

Refrigerate fresh mizuna unwashed in a perforated plastic bag in the vegetable crisper for up to 5 days. If the greens are particularly wet, insert a dry paper towel in the bag to absorb excess moisture and prevent rotting.

TRIMMING AND CLEANING

Mizuna should be thoroughly washed before using, preferably by submerging and swishing it in a sinkful of water to remove all impurities and stray insects. The stem ends are often woody and should be trimmed and discarded.

STEAMING AND BOILING

Mizuna can be steamed briefly for 2 to 3 minutes, or until it is just wilted. If you are steaming it in quantity, it may benefit from a slight squeezing and draining after cooking to remove excess water. To boil, mizuna should be plunged into rapidly boiling water for 1 minute, or until just tender; then drain and use either whole or cut into bite-size pieces.

STIR-FRYING AND SAUTÉING

Mizuna responds to light stir-frying extremely well, maintaining its crisp texture and spicy flavor if added to the wok or sauté pan during the last 1 or 2 minutes of cooking.

MICROWAVING

Place mizuna in a microwave-safe bowl, add a few drops of water, and cover. Microwave on high power for 2 to 3 minutes, or until it is wilted; the greens will steam in their own moisture this way.

BLANCHING AND FREEZING

Freezing is not recommended because of mizuna's high water content and delicate texture.

COMPLEMENTARY HERBS, SEASONINGS, AND FOODS

Almonds, apples, chestnuts, chiles, crab, fish, garlic, ginger, ham, lemon, lettuce, lobster, mustard, peanuts, rice, scallops, sesame, shrimp, soy sauce, spinach, tofu, vinegar, walnuts.

SERVING SUGGESTIONS

- Mizuna's assertive flavor makes it a good addition to mixed salads, combined with milder lettuces and spinach.

- Mizuna adds sophistication, elegance, and surprising flavor to seafood salads. Its zestiness provides a great contrast to milder shellfish, such as scallops and lobster.
- Combine mizuna in a salad with toasted almonds, slivered green apples, and a little grated pecorino or other hard cheese; lightly toss with walnut oil.
- Slice mizuna leaves and add to stir-fries during the final minutes of cooking.
- Add mizuna leaves to freshly made miso soup or dashi broth.
- Mizuna's highly decorative appearance and surprising durability make it a great garnish. Use larger leaves as a bed for meats, seafood, and poultry.
- Substitute a few leaves of mizuna for the usual lettuce in tacos and sandwiches.

MIZUNA AND SUMMER SQUASH
SERVES 2 TO 4

3 tablespoons olive oil
1 to 2 cups summer squash (such as zucchini or yellow crookneck), thinly sliced
3 to 4 cloves garlic, chopped
1 bunch mizuna, roughly chopped
Salt and freshly ground black pepper
Hard cheese for grating, such as Parmesan

1. In a large saucepan, heat the olive oil over high heat, then add the summer squash and cook for 3 to 4 minutes, stirring a bit.

2. When the squash is somewhat cooked, add the garlic, mizuna, salt, and pepper. Cook for 2 to 3 minutes longer. Sprinkle with cheese to finish off the dish.

— *Mariquita Farm, Watsonville, California*

SPINACH, ROCKET, AND MIZUNA SALAD
SERVES 4

Author Note: This nutritious salad is enhanced by colorful, in-season, edible flowers. Try Johnny jump-ups, calendula petals, nasturtiums, or chive blossoms (see the Edible Flowers chapter on page 194).

¾ pound spinach leaves
¾ pound arugula leaves
¾ pound mizuna leaves
2 to 3 ounces smoked streaky bacon (not too lean)
Cider vinegar
Walnut or extra-virgin olive oil (optional)
Edible flowers

1. Quickly wash the greens and shake or towel them dry. Tear any large leaves into manageable pieces. Place all of the leaves in a salad bowl.

remarkable forms, sizes, and locations. They may be maintained by volunteers or paid staff, and have a budget of hundreds or thousands of dollars. Some begin as a concerted effort by community leaders or even a single individual, whereas others are spearheaded by non-profits, charity organizations, institutions (such as hospitals, prisons, and public housing), for-profit companies, schools, state and city agencies, or a combination of the above.

A hallmark of urban ag are very intensive, efficient growing methods such as raised beds, aquaponics, composting, rainwater collection, vertical and container gardening, and edible landscaping. Urban waste is frequently recycled through filtration systems, and animals are often part of the equation—think chicken coops, beekeeping operations, backyard goats, and fish tanks.

Urban farms take the form of rooftop gardens atop skyscrapers, unused city lots, public school plots, communal growing areas, container gardening, interior greenhouses with special lighting, edible sidewalk gardens, and home and office vertical gardens. And urban farming doesn't just have to be a farm operation per se; residents who have their own vegetable gardens and fruit trees or cultivate their own crops in community gardens are a vital part of this food network as well.

The benefits of urban farming are many. Fossil fuel consumption is a growing problem, with its costs and contribution to climate change. By growing food at or near the places where it is consumed, urban ag reduces or eliminates the need for fuel usage. It also helps reduce nutrient loss from long shipping times. Another big problem is the prevalence of so-called "food deserts," in which city dwellers cannot access high-quality, fresh food at affordable prices. Most urban farms and gardens can fill this need with remarkably little up-front cost and investment, providing food security even in winter.

2. Cut the bacon into matchsticks. First render it slowly in a frying pan, then raise the heat and cook it more quickly to make it crispy.

3. Pour the hot bacon and its fat over the greens and toss quickly.

4. Sprinkle with a little cider vinegar, drizzle with oil if desired, and scatter the flowers over the greens. Serve immediately.

Cooking Note: For a vegetarian salad, omit the bacon and simply dress the salad, then add the flowers.

— *Fooddownunder.com*

TATSOI   BRASSICA RAPA, NARINOSA GROUP

Tatsoi (pronounced taht-SOY) is a newcomer to the American gastronomical scene but a common fixture in Asian cuisine, especially in China, where it originated. It is a member of the cabbage family, closely related to bok choy, which it somewhat resembles in flavor and texture; it is occasionally called rosette bok choy. To add to the confusion, horticulturists sometimes classify it as a type of mustard green.

Whatever its true nomenclature, tatsoi is a stunning plant, with shiny, dark-green, spoon-shaped leaves that grow in a beautifully shaped rosette. Its flavor is pleasantly vegetable, reminiscent of spinach, with a spicy hint of mustard. Its juicy leaves are usually eaten raw but can be used in stir-fries or added to soups and stews at the end of cooking.

HISTORY

Tatsoi is native to China, where it and legions of other Asian brassicas have been enjoyed for centuries as cooked vegetables. The tatsoi that is gradually becoming available in the United States is a Japanese variant. Recently tatsoi has begun to show up in commercial prewashed salad mixes, as its sweet, mild, durable personality blends well with other greens.

NUTRITION

Like all brassicas, tatsoi is an extremely nutritious green, an excellent source of vitamins C and E, fiber, folate, calcium, iron, magnesium, potassium, and B6. A 1-cup serving of raw tatsoi leaves contains about 30 calories.

SEASON

Commercially, tatsoi is widely grown and available year-round. But its peak season at farmers markets and CSAs is during the spring and summer months.

SELECTION

Tatsoi leaves should be fresh and intact, with no signs of yellowing or wilting.

STORAGE

Tatsoi is not the most durable of vegetables and should be used within a few days. Store the entire head tightly wrapped and unwashed in the refrigerator vegetable crisper.

TRIMMING AND CLEANING

Like all ground-level vegetables, tatsoi benefits from a thorough washing to remove dirt and insects. If the head is small enough, submerge the entire rosette in a sinkful of water, swish, and rinse. If the rosette is too large to fit into the sink, cut it into sections, or pull off and rinse individual leaves briefly.

STEAMING AND BOILING

Steaming is a gentle way of cooking that brings out the best in tatsoi without making it too watery. Place detached leaves or small halved or quartered bunches in a vegetable steamer and cook for about 5 minutes. Or place a whole small head of tatsoi in a steamer basket or rack inside a larger pot filled with 1 inch of water brought to a boil.

STIR-FRYING AND SAUTÉING

Tatsoi should be added to stir-fries near the very end of cooking (within the last 2 minutes or so) and sautéed only until it just wilts but is still crisp. Small bunches can be halved or quartered and stir-fried without detaching the leaves.

MICROWAVING

Place the leaves in a microwave-safe dish or zipper-lock freezer bag and add about ½ inch of water. Either cover lightly with a paper towel or leave an opening in the bag and microwave on high power for 5 to 7 minutes, or until tender.

BLANCHING AND FREEZING

Because of its high water content, freezing is not recommended for tatsoi.

COMPLEMENTARY HERBS, SEASONINGS, AND FOODS

Bok choy, chicken, chiles, fish, garlic, ginger, mushrooms, onions, oyster sauce, peanuts, scallops, sesame, shallots, shrimp, soy sauce.

SERVING SUGGESTIONS

- Serve the tender young leaves raw, tossed with a little vinaigrette dressing.
- Shred the leaves into fine strips and sprinkle them with finely diced mushrooms on top of miso soup.
- Stir-fry tatsoi with a bit of sesame oil and soy sauce.
- Tatsoi can be used as a substitute for baby or frozen spinach in many recipes. Try experimenting!
- Mushrooms and tatsoi make an irresistible combination, with their meaty textures and robust flavors. Try sliced portobellos, oyster mushrooms, or porcinis.
- Lightly stir-fry or steam tatsoi, toss in a reduced savory sauce, and use the leaves as a bed for roast chicken, pork loin, filet mignon, braised lamb, or a fine fish.

Farm to Table ... By Bike!

Martha Wagner

You can reduce your carbon footprint by joining a CSA. Reduce it even further by having your share delivered to your doorstep from the farm or your regular pickup site by bike in places like Chicago, Boston, and Seattle.

Loaded Bikes (www.loadedbikes.tumblr.com), located in the Chicago area, will work with your choice of CSA at rates that start at $8 per week for the full season, depending on the distance. It will even pick up your compostable food scraps.

In Boston, **Metro Pedal Power** (www.metropedalpower.com) delivers weekly farm shares from eight metro-area CSA farms. Other delivery options include a monthly "farm-to-glass" wine delivery service from local and regional vineyards and a weekly farm-to-table meal delivered to your door.

Clean Greens Farm and Market (www.cleangreensfarm.com), a nonprofit owned and operated by African-American residents of Seattle's Central District, partners with **Fork + Frame** pedal-powered CSA delivery in central Seattle. Delivery is free! Sign up with this CSA program and you'll not only support local agriculture but also help low-income families by keeping farm stand prices low and supporting a CSA giveback program.

In Burlington, Vermont, **One Revolution**'s bike delivery service partners with two farms as well as the Intervale Food Hub, which markets and distributes food through a multifarm CSA.

And what better place for bike delivery than congested New York! **Brooklyn Bike Armada** (www.brooklynbikearmada.com), a worker collective, partners with two CSAs to bring customers their shares for $8 per delivery.

TENDER TATSOI
WITH SESAME OIL VINAIGRETTE

SERVES 4

> 8 cups tatsoi leaves or other tender salad greens
> 2 scallions (green onions) (including some of the greens),
>   thinly sliced
> 1 tablespoon thinly sliced garlic chives or regular chives
> 1 tablespoon toasted sesame seeds

> *SESAME OIL VINAIGRETTE*
> 2 teaspoons rice vinegar
> 2 tablespoons sesame oil
> 1 tablespoon dark sesame oil
> ½ teaspoon sea salt

1. Sort through the greens; then trim, wash, and dry them well. Toss the greens with the scallions and chives.

2. To make the vinaigrette: In another bowl, whisk together the vinegar, oils, and salt. Taste the dressing on a leaf and adjust the oil or vinegar if necessary.

3. Pour the dressing over the salad, toss well, add the sesame seeds, toss again, and serve.

— *Deborah Madison,* Vegetarian Cooking for Everyone

FARMERS MARKET GREEN SALAD WITH
FRIED SHALLOTS

SERVES 6

Source Note: Although we used Asian greens and radish sprouts for our salad, we encourage you to explore your local farmers market and use whatever small young greens (baby spinach, arugula, or watercress, for example) and other fresh goodies you find.

> ½ pound (4 large) shallots
> 1½ cups vegetable oil, for frying
> 6 ounces mizuna
> 6 ounces tatsoi (about 6 cups total of mixed greens, loosely packed)
> ⅓ cup radish sprouts
> 1 tablespoon white-wine vinegar
> Sea salt to taste

1. Cut the shallots into ⅛-inch-thick slices. In a heavy-bottomed 10-inch skillet, cook the shallots in oil over moderate heat, stirring occasionally, until they turn golden, 15 to 20 minutes. With a slotted spoon, transfer the shallots to paper towels to drain; season them

"I feel that good food should be a right and not a privilege, and it needs to be without pesticides and herbicides. And everybody deserves this food. And that's not elitist."

— *Alice Waters, American chef*

with salt. Reserve 3 tablespoons of the oil for dressing the salad, and cool the shallots to room temperature. (The shallots may be fried 2 days ahead and kept in an airtight container at room temperature.)

2. Just before serving, toss together the greens, sprouts, reserved oil, vinegar, and sea salt in a large bowl. Sprinkle the shallots over the salad.

— Gourmet, *June 1999, as appeared on Epicurious*

WATER SPINACH   IPOMOEA AQUATICA

This tasty vegetable, a relative of the sweet potato and a member of the morning glory family, grows rampantly in tropical freshwater lakes, ponds, and riverbanks all over Southeast Asia, China, South America, Australia, and Africa. Sometimes called swamp cabbage or kangkong, *it is uncommon to find it commercially in the United States except at farmers markets and Asian grocery stores in tropical areas like Hawaii and Florida. But if you see it, don't pass up the opportunity to try this distinctive leafy green. The flavor of water spinach is very mild indeed, with sometimes nutty overtones, but its hollow stems have a succulent crunch that is luscious raw or very lightly stir-fried with savory Asian sauces. Its young shoots and leaves are especially favored because their flavor is sweeter and their texture more tender than the mature leaves.*

HISTORY

Water spinach grows widely in tropical and subtropical regions throughout the world, although its exact origin is unknown. It has served as a valuable food plant throughout wartime Asia, especially during the Vietnam War, when North Vietnamese soldiers dropped stems of water spinach along with a few fish into the water-filled craters left by bombs, thus ensuring a constant food supply along the Ho Chi Minh Trail. It a fast-growing plant (sometimes growing up to 4 inches a day) that is considered an invasive species in many areas, including the Philippines and Florida.

NUTRITION

Like many leafy greens, water spinach is very nutritious and an excellent source of vitamins A and C, magnesium, calcium, iron, and potassium. The plant also has medicinal properties and has been used to treat constipation, fever, high blood pressure, ringworm, and opium poisoning.

SEASON

Commercially, water spinach is not widely available in regular supermarkets, but you can find it sporadically at farmers markets and Asian grocery stores, especially in tropical places like Hawaii and Florida.

SELECTION

Choose large, tight bunches that look fresh and lush, with no wilted, discolored, or slimy leaves or stems, which tend to hide in the center of the bunch.

STORAGE

Water spinach should be stored unwashed and tightly wrapped in damp toweling in the refrigerator vegetable crisper. Or snip the stem ends and store upright in a vase of water at room temperature, like cut flowers. Use within 1 week.

TRIMMING AND CLEANING

Water spinach should be thoroughly rinsed to remove any hidden grit or mud, especially in its hollow stems. Fill a sink or large bowl with water, submerge the bunch, and swish it vigorously. Repeat if necessary, then drain and gently pat it dry with paper or cloth towels. Snap off the fibrous bases of the stems and trim to the desired length.

STEAMING AND BOILING

Water spinach is a much more delicate green than it appears, so it should be served either raw or very lightly cooked to preserve its essential character and wonderful crunch. Thus boiling is not recommended, and even steaming yields a vegetable that is more watery and less flavorful than stir-frying or sautéing in oil or seasonings.

STIR-FRYING AND SAUTÉING

Stir-frying is where water spinach truly shines. It maintains its crisp texture if added to the wok or sauté pan during the last 1 or 2 minutes of cooking.

MICROWAVING

Wash and rinse, but do not dry. The water that clings to the leaves is enough moisture for it to cook in. Cut the stems into 2-inch segments, place the leaves and stems in a microwave-safe dish, cover, and cook on high power.

- 1 pound = 2 to 3 minutes

BLANCHING AND FREEZING

Because of its high water content, freezing is not recommended for water spinach.

EQUIVALENTS, MEASURES, AND SERVINGS

- 1 pound = 4 servings

COMPLEMENTARY HERBS, SEASONINGS, AND FOODS

Beef, black bean sauce, chicken, chiles, citrus, fish, fish sauce, garlic, ginger, mushrooms, onions, oyster sauce, peanuts, pork, scallops, sesame, shallots, shrimp, shrimp paste, soy sauce, tofu, vinegar.

SERVING SUGGESTIONS

- Water spinach is unparalleled in stir-fries of all kinds. Add the delicate leaves and stems only in the last 1 to 2 minutes of cooking.
- Float young, tender leaves over rich broths and simple soups.
- Add raw shoots and young leaves to salads.
- Mix stir-fried stems and leaves into curries.

- Serve stir-fried water spinach with delicate fish like halibut, sole, and sea bass.
- Thinly sliced flank steak pairs deliciously with blanched water spinach cooked quickly with fish sauce, chopped garlic, and fresh chiles.
- Toss a few water spinach leaves in with fresh pastas to add crunch, flavor, and nutrition.
- In Vietnamese cuisine, the larger, crisp, drinking-straw-type stems are more popular than the leaves. Cut the stems with a vegetable peeler into long strips and toss with seasonings like ginger, sugar, salt, pepper, and white vinegar.
- Sauté water spinach with mustard seeds and coconut flakes for an unexpected, flavorful dish.

. . . .

MALAYSIAN SAMBAL KANGKONG (WATER SPINACH WITH SAMBAL)

SERVES 4

Author Note: Sambal is a popular, fiery condiment in Indonesian and Javanese cuisines, made from chile peppers, shrimp paste, fish sauce, garlic, ginger, shallot, green onions, sugar, lime juice, and rice vinegar. It is usually served with fish or fried chicken, but it makes a great stir-fry sauce as well. You can find it in bottled form in Asian markets or online.

2 shallots, diced
1 clove garlic, finely minced
1 tablespoon vegetable oil
1 bunch water spinach (*kangkong*), leaves and stems chopped
     into 1-inch pieces
1 tablespoon sambal paste (store-bought or homemade)

1. Using a mortar and pestle, pound the diced shallots and garlic into a coarse paste.

2. In a skillet, heat the oil over low to medium heat; sauté the shallot-and-garlic paste until it turns aromatic, about 3 minutes. Be careful not to burn the garlic, or it will turn bitter.

3. Stir in the sambal paste and sauté until aromatic.

4. Add the water spinach leaves and stems to the pan, stirring until they are thoroughly coated with the garlic, shallots, and sambal. Cook until the water spinach is slightly wilted, 2 to 4 minutes (the stems should remain a bit crunchy). Serve immediately.

— *Foodista.com*

Togo, and Uzbekistan, bringing with them decades of experience working the land and growing diverse crops. The fruits and vegetables they grow are sold at a downtown public market and also through CSA Phoenix.

Intervale Community Farm (ICF) began in 1990 on a small field in the Intervale, an agricultural neighborhood that sits on an ancient floodplain in Burlington, Vermont. Originally conceived as a reliable local source of fresh organic produce when such options were difficult to find, the farm organized around the CSA model. In the late 1990s, demand led it to expand to 44 acres. The nonprofit Intervale Center owns, leases, and manages 350 acres in the Intervale, and subleases land to more than a dozen independently owned farms, of which the ICF is the oldest and largest.

Unlike a typical CSA farm, the farmers are hired employees and have no ownership interest in the business, which is instead owned by CSA members through a consumer cooperative. Also distinctive is that all of the CSA shares are distributed right at the farm, not at outside pickup locations. As a result, the farm is considered an approachable and engaging destination for all ages. In the planning stages are a greenhouse complex, expanded pick-your-own fields, and new storage and distribution facilities to enable a 12-month CSA share option.

Bayfield Food Producers Cooperative was formed to develop a regional identity for foods produced by 18 small- to medium-size farms and other food businesses in Ashland and Bayfield counties in Wisconsin, and to help them with marketing. Member-producers include a family-owned nursery and orchard; a farmer producing grass-fed, organically raised beef cattle; and a fourth-generation wholesale fish house selling fresh, frozen, and smoked Lake Superior whitefish, trout and herring.

Avocados

A most curious fruit is the avocado, sometimes dubbed "nature's butter" for its unctuous, creamy texture, or called "alligator pear" for its nubby skin and obvious shape. The avocado is a member of the Lauraceae family, whose other well-known species include bay and camphor.

A native of Mexico and Central America, the avocado grows only in very warm climates. Over 400 varieties of avocados exist, but only a few are commercially popular. Most common is the dark green–skinned Hass avocado, which accounts for about 95 percent of the total crop grown annually in California. You may find different varieties offered by your CSA or local farmers market, including the Gem, Gwen, Lamb Hass, Bacon, Fuerte, and Reed.

HISTORY

Avocados are believed to have come from Mexico, although some species may have originated as far north as California.

NUTRITION

Avocados are unique in the plant world for their extraordinarily high levels of both unsaturated and saturated fat, which can range from 10 to 30 percent, depending on the species. The unsaturated fat is primarily in the form of linoleic and linolenic acids, and it can help counteract the effects of harmful saturated fats. Avocados are also rich in lecithin, potassium, magnesium, vitamins D and E, niacin, and the antioxidants lycopene and beta-carotene. A 1-cup serving of slice avocado contains about 234 calories.

SEASON

Commercially, avocados are available year-round, but California avocados are in their best season from spring through fall. Farmers markets in California, Hawaii, and Florida will carry avocados according to local varieties and seasons.

SELECTION

Avocados are typically harvested while they are unripe and rock-hard, and they ripen after harvest. They are at their best when the fruits yield to a gentle squeeze. The skin of some avocados, such as the Hass variety, darken as they ripen, but color is not always a reliable indicator of ripeness. Avoid fruits with obvious bruising and desiccation, or that are overly soft or unusually light for their size.

STORAGE

If your avocados need to ripen, do not store them in the refrigerator (and see the ripening tip on page 137). Once they are ripe, keep them in the refrigerator for 2 to 3 days. Even with refrigeration, they tend to spoil quickly, however, so enjoy them promptly.

TRIMMING AND CLEANING

An avocado is quite simple to prepare; however, it does have that one single big seed at its center. Slice the avocado in half lengthwise until the knife hits the seed, then cut into the rest of the fruit around it. Then turn the avocado by a quarter and cut it in half lengthwise again. Rotate the avocado halves in your hands and separate the quarters; then remove the seed by pulling it away gently with your fingertips.

Also, peel avocados carefully to minimize the loss of the very nutrient-rich flesh just under the skin. You can actually nick the thin skin and peel it back just as you would a banana.

Avocados have a nasty habit of darkening unpleasantly once cut, the result of enzymes reacting to exposure to air. You can prevent this by squeezing a little lemon or lime juice immediately over all of the cut surfaces, then covering them tightly in plastic wrap. If you make guacamole and it turns black in the refrigerator, just remove the darkened top layer and discard.

STIR-FRYING AND SAUTÉING

Most people don't think of cooking avocados, but they take beautifully to light sautéing in a little olive oil. Keep the seasonings simple (cumin, chile flakes, and cilantro are all good) and sauté for just a few minutes on medium heat. Don't overcook, or the avocados will start to fall apart and become mushy.

FREEZING

You can freeze avocados, but only the puree, not whole specimens. Add 1 tablespoon of lemon or lime juice per avocado to prevent darkening, and puree the avocado in a food processor or blender to evenly distribute the juice throughout. Place the pureed avocado into an airtight container, leaving ½ to 1 inch of headspace to allow for expansion. Frozen puree can be stored for up to 5 months at 0°F.

EQUIVALENTS, MEASURES, AND SERVINGS

- 1 large avocado = 8 ounces = 1 cup pulp

COMPLEMENTARY HERBS, SEASONINGS, AND FOODS

Bacon, bread, chicken, chile, chocolate, cilantro, citrus, corn, cumin, eggs, garlic, grapefruit, hot sauce, lobster, olives, onions, lemon, lime, pasta, pork, potatoes, shrimp, tomatoes.

SERVING SUGGESTIONS

- Make guacamole, of course.
- The smooth texture of avocados can be a nice contrast in salads; try using it in creamy salads such as potato, tuna, egg, seafood, or chicken, or with other fruits like raspberries and oranges.
- A traditional and very popular street drink in Indonesia is avocado blended with a little chocolate syrup and crushed ice. A surprising but divine combination (see the recipes on pages 138 and 139).
- Avocados are a nice textural foil in a bacon, lettuce, and tomato sandwich.
- Avocados on toast with fried eggs make a fantastic, easy breakfast or snack.
- Puree avocados and add to creamy soups.

Ripening Tip

You can persuade avocados to ripen faster by placing them inside a brown paper bag with a ripe apple or banana, which gives off ethylene gas. Store the bag at room temperature; the avocados should be ripe in two to five days.

- Avocados can be a nice alternative nutritionally to butter or oil in baking recipes. Their high fat and water content make them ideal substitutes in cookies, cakes, or muffins. The Avocado Central website (www.avocadocentral.com) has a good selection of baking recipes.
- A filling and nutritious lunch or snack is avocado halves in which a scoop of tuna or chicken salad is stuffed into the hollowed area remaining after the seed is removed.
- Consider using avocados wherever a creamy consistency is desired; it makes a nutritionally superior substitute for butter or mayonnaise in many dishes, including salad dressings and dips.
- Avocados are surprisingly good grilled. Try them in kebabs or grilled whole on the "half shell."
- Add chunks of avocado to pitas, and to burritos, fajitas, and other Mexican dishes.
- A traditional Mexican dish is the shrimp cocktail, made with shrimp, tomatoes, cilantro, onions, and avocado combined in a parfait glass. Perfect for a hot summer day.
- Avocados make a terrific natural baby food. Kids love them also for their mild flavor and creamy texture.

Books

Mexican Everyday
Rick Bayless, Christopher Hirsheimer, and Deann Groen Bayless,
W. W. Norton, 2005.

Guac Off!
Nathan Myers,
Chronicle Books, 2009.

Absolutely Avocados
Gaby Dalkin,
Houghton Mifflin Harcourt, 2013.

INDONESIAN AVOCADO AND CHOCOLATE SHAKE

MAKES 1 LARGE OR 2 SMALL SHAKES

1 small ripe Hass avocado
1¼ cups milk
3 tablespoons sweetened condensed milk
5 ice cubes
A few squirts of chocolate syrup

1. Add the avocado, milk, condensed milk, and ice cubes to a blender and process until smooth and foamy.

2. Squirt the chocolate syrup onto the sides of a clear glass, making a pretty design if you wish. Then carefully pour in the avocado shake.

— *Linda Shiue,* Spicebox Travels *blog*

CALIFORNIA AVOCADO HUMMUS

SERVES 8

Source Note: This avocado hummus is simple to prepare, creamy, and a delicious change from classic hummus recipes. Large avocados are recommended for this recipe. A large avocado averages about 8 ounces. If you use smaller or larger avocados, adjust the quantity accordingly.

2 ripe avocados, peeled and seeded
1½ cups cooked garbanzo beans (chickpeas), or 1 (15-ounce can), rinsed and drained
1 large clove garlic, minced

2 tablespoons fresh lemon juice, divided

2 tablespoons avocado oil or extra-virgin olive oil,
    plus additional for garnish (optional)

½ teaspoon salt, or to taste

1. Dice half of the avocado and squeeze 1 tablespoon of the lemon juice
   over it to keep it from darkening. Set aside.

2. Mash the remaining avocado, garbanzo beans, garlic, lemon juice,
   avocado oil, and salt together until smooth. (You may also puree in a
   blender or food processor.)

3. Gently stir the diced avocado into the hummus mixture.

4. Drizzle with avocado oil if desired; serve.

Serving Suggestion: Mold into a 2-cup ring mold lined with plastic
wrap or waxed paper. Unmold onto a serving platter, drizzle with
avocado or olive oil, and sprinkle with chopped flat-leaf parsley. Serve
with toasted pita chips or carrot chips, and enjoy with a full-bodied
red wine.

— *Marji Morrow, California Avocado Commission*

For More Information

Avocado Central
www.avocadocentral.com

California Avocado Commission
www.californiaavocado.com

. . . .

DARK CHOCOLATE AVOCADO COOKIES

MAKES ABOUT
TWELVE 1-INCH COOKIES

*Source Note: These sumptuous cookies are both gluten- and dairy-free, with
avocado and dark chocolate as the main ingredients. If you're feeling fancy,
you can add chopped, roasted nuts too.*

½ cup mashed avocado

½ cup turbinado sugar

2 teaspoons vanilla extract

1 teaspoon cider vinegar

½ teaspoon baking soda

2 tablespoons unsweetened cocoa powder

1 teaspoon cinnamon

¾ cup gluten-free flour mix (or whole wheat flour)

3½ ounces dark chocolate chips

1. Preheat the oven to 350°F.

2. In the bowl of a food processor, combine the avocado and sugar.
   Blend until well incorporated. (If you don't have a food processor, go
   for a good ol' bowl and mixing spoon. Just mix very, very well!)

3. Add the vanilla, cider vinegar, baking soda, cocoa powder, and cinnamon; mix to combine.

4. Add in the flour; mix until the batter is smooth and the ingredients
   are evenly incorporated.

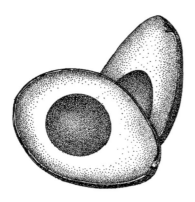

5. Take the cookie dough out of the food processor and put it into a mixing bowl. Stir in the chocolate chips.

6. Line a baking sheet with parchment paper. Spoon out approximately 1-tablespoon-size scoops of the dough, and flatten into even, cookie-like shapes (the dough will not spread when it bakes).

7. Bake for 10 minutes, turning the tray around halfway through.

8. Allow the cookies to sit for 3 to 4 minutes before transferring them to a cooling rack.

— *Greatist, adapted from* Cooking with Dia, *by Kate Morin*

. . . .

CLASSIC GUACAMOLE

SERVES 8

4 ripe avocados, seeded and peeled
2 tablespoons lemon juice
1 clove garlic, crushed
1 tomato, finely chopped
¼ cup finely chopped onion
⅛ teaspoon ground cumin
3 drops hot pepper sauce
Salt

1. Using a fork, coarsely mash the avocado with the lemon juice and garlic.

2. Stir in the remaining ingredients to blend thoroughly. Season to taste with salt.

— *California Avocado Commission*

Beans (String)

PHASEOLUS VULGARIS

Often called green beans or snap beans in America, string beans are one of the most common garden vegetables in the United States. String beans come in many forms—some 130 in all—ranging from the petite, delicately flavored French variety called haricot verts to the broader, meaty Italian specimens. String beans are divided into two categories: bush beans, which have a long, slender, rounded pod, and pole beans, which are usually large and quite flat.

Decades ago, string beans were named for the tough fibers that ran from one tip to the other. Although these strings have long been bred out of most varieties, the moniker has stuck. The pods of these beans can be green, yellow (referred to as wax beans), purple, red, or streaked. String beans are actually immature seeds and pods; if left on the bush, the seeds swell and the pods become too fibrous to eat. However, they do not mature to become "shell" beans; string beans are bred specifically for their youthful succulence and tenderness and are meant to be eaten pods and all.

HISTORY

The haricot bean (which includes string beans) had long been a domesticated staple in Central and South American Indian diets by the time Columbus arrived and introduced the vegetable to Europe. Seeds have been found in Peru with a radiocarbon dating of nearly 8,000 years ago. Precisely when humans began consuming the immature, green pods is impossible to know, but the modern, truly stringless varieties have been bred only within the past 100 years.

NUTRITION

Like most vegetables, green beans are low in calories (43 per cup) but pack lots of fiber and nutrients. A cup's worth provides about 25 percent of your daily supply of vitamin K and 20 percent of vitamin C, as well as manganese, vitamin A, potassium, and folate.

SEASON

Commercially, string beans are widely grown and available year-round. But their peak season at farmers markets and CSAs is during the summer and early fall months.

SELECTION

Look for beans that are firm, crisp, velvety to touch, and not too swollen, which may indicate that the beans inside are getting too mature to be at their tastiest. Supermarket green beans are often dehydrated or old; watch out for pods that are limp toward their ends, are starting to shrivel, or are easily bendable. Such beans often have little gustatory or nutritive value. Also beware of beans that are overly large, or worse yet, whose pods have a rough, spongy texture.

Cooking Tip

Green beans cooked in hard water can become very tough because the calcium in the water reacts with the pectic substances in the beans.

STORAGE

Refrigerate unwashed beans in a paper or perforated plastic bag in a warmer section of the refrigerator. Use within 2 or 3 days. If they start to wilt, soaking in ice water may rehydrate them.

TRIMMING AND CLEANING

Wash the beans in cool water. "Top and tail" them (snap off the top stem ends and bottom curved tips). With modern varieties, no destringing is necessary.

STEAMING AND BOILING

Boil green beans in several quarts of salted water until they turn just tender and have lost their raw taste, 6 to 8 minutes. Steam green beans over rapidly boiling water for 10 to 12 minutes, or until tender.

STIR-FRYING AND SAUTÉING

Green beans are delicious stir-fried or sautéed for 7 to 10 minutes on medium-high heat in a wok or large frying pan. Be sure to add some oil to the pan (plus, perhaps, a few tablespoons of water or stock at the beginning of sautéing), or they will stick. In the last couple of minutes of cooking, toss with soy sauce or sesame oil.

BAKING AND ROASTING

When preparing green beans in the oven, make sure they are topped with or immersed in other ingredients, so they do not dry out. If you want to roast just the beans, drizzle them with a nut oil or dressing of your choice and roast them for 20 to 25 minutes in a 425°F oven. They'll brown slightly and take on a rich flavor.

MICROWAVING

Cut or snap beans into 1-inch pieces, then place them in a microwave-safe dish; add ¼ cup water; cover and cook on high power.

- 1 cup = 3 minutes
- 1 pound = 7 to 12 minutes

BLANCHING AND FREEZING

Blanch green beans in salted boiling water for 3 to 4 minutes, or until they are crisp-tender. Drain, then plunge them into ice water for 5 minutes to stop the cooking process. Remove and drain. Package them in zipper-lock freezer or vacuum food sealer-type bags, or freezer containers. Squeeze out any excess air and leave ½ inch of headspace (unless you are using the vacuum sealing method). Frozen green beans will keep for up to 6 months at 0°F. Rubbery green beans, when thawed, often mean they were past their prime to begin with or were cooked too long.

EQUIVALENTS, MEASURES, AND SERVINGS

- 1 pound = 3½ cups whole = 4 cups cut into 1-inch pieces = 3 to 4 servings

COMPLEMENTARY HERBS, SEASONINGS, AND FOODS

Almonds, artichokes, asparagus, bacon, basil, béchamel sauce, butter, cheese (Parmesan, feta, goat), chicory, chiles, cream, crème fraîche, curry, dill, garlic, green garlic, ham, hazelnuts, hazelnut oil, lamb, leeks, lemons, marjoram, mint, mushrooms, mustard, nutmeg, nuts, olive oil, onions, orange, oregano, parsley, pine nuts, prosciutto, rosemary, shallots, soy sauce, tarragon, tomatoes, tuna, vinegar, walnuts, walnut oil, Worcestershire sauce.

SERVING SUGGESTIONS

- Toss freshly boiled or steamed green beans with soy sauce, sesame oil, extra-virgin olive oil, pesto, lemon juice, Italian dressing, or vinaigrette.

- Munch raw beans with various dips. Kids like these as a finger food!

- Sprinkle chopped fresh herbs over steamed or boiled green beans; dill or mint are pleasant surprises with green beans.

- Stir-fry or sauté green beans with a mixture of peanut or sesame oil, soy sauce, green onions, garlic, ginger, chili paste, sugar, salt, and pepper for Szechuan-style beans.

- Drop a handful into stir-fries at the last minute to add flavor and crunch. (This works best with young, tender beans.)

- Serve salade niçoise, that hearty, traditional cold salad with tuna, hard-boiled eggs, olives, and green beans. There's nothing better for supper on a warm summer evening.

- Treat your string beans as you would southern-style greens—cook them slowly in lots of water with a ham hock or piece of pork fatback, and finish off with a dose of vinegar and a dash of hot pepper sauce.

- Add interest to cooked green beans by tossing them with a light vinaigrette and slivered almonds or chopped hazelnuts.

- Create a colorful vegetable julienne with green and yellow string beans, carrot strips, golden beets, and red or orange bell pepper strips steamed or boiled briefly.

- Pickle green beans for a crunchy, juicy change from regular cuke pickles.

- Green beans go well with just about every sort of nut and nut oil. Try 'em with walnuts, almonds, pecans, hazelnuts, and macadamias. They're also great with dried fruits like cranberries and cherries.

- Remember the old green-bean casserole standby? You know, green beans with a can of cream of mushroom soup poured over them, and crisp-fried onions sprinkled on top? Don't be ashamed to admit you like it!

CREAMY GREEN BEAN AND MUSHROOM SOUP

SERVES 8

  2½ cups finely chopped onion
  5 tablespoons butter
  1 pound mushrooms, diced
  ⅓ cup flour
  1 teaspoon paprika
  6 cups vegetable stock

Part of the pleasure of buying food from a CSA farm is connecting to the farm and the farmers growing food for you through events at the farm or your weekly box pickup. The connection is deeper yet when you belong to a whole-diet (also known as full-diet) CSA that supplies most of your household's food needs.

The concept was pioneered in 2004 at **Essex Farm** in upstate New York by Kristin and Mark Kimball, who produce food for more than 220 families on their 600 acres. Kristin's 2011 book The Dirty Life: A Memoir of Farming, Food, and Love has brought considerable media attention to CSA farming.

"There's a reason there aren't that many completely diversified farms out there, and it's because they're so challenging to manage," Mark Kimball has acknowledged. Nine draft horses, 10 full-time farmers, three tractors, and 15 solar panels are what it takes to supply Essex Farm's year-round CSA. The farm produces grass-fed beef, pastured pork, chicken, eggs, 50 different kinds of vegetables, milk, grains and flour, fruit, herbs, maple syrup, and soap.

Members come to the farm on Friday afternoons and take what they need for the week in any quantity or combination they choose, except when items are scarce (like maple syrup or the year's first tomatoes), but most food is available on an all-you-can-eat basis. Members are encouraged to take extra produce during the growing season for freezing or canning to supplement what's available from the root cellar in winter and early spring.

Most whole-diet CSA farms pride themselves on producing everything or nearly everything right on the farm and keeping their carbon footprint low through selling shares locally. Some offer delivery; some offer pickup at the farm. Memberships vary greatly in size. **S&S Homestead Farm** in Washington State offers 15 shares to neighbors on Lopez Island.

The cost of year-round whole-diet membership shares may seem steep compared with short-season CSAs or weekly grocery store trips, but if it is averaged out by the week, the charge carries less sticker shock. Memberships range from about $3,000 to $5,000 per year for a single subscriber, with discounts for additional family members and lower prices for children. Some farms offer membership by the season. At Essex Farm, payments can be made annually, quarterly, monthly, or weekly. Most whole-diet CSA farms require that all members of a household be subscribed to the CSA.

Whole-diet CSAs nationwide are scarce, numbering in perhaps the dozens in the United States compared with an estimated 6,000-plus more-traditional CSA programs. **Rainshadow Organics** in central Oregon offers traditional vegetable CSA shares as well as separately priced mixed meat shares, plus summer and winter full-diet shares.

Full-diet summer shares consist of vegetables, meat, freshly milled flour, and wheat berries. Monthly winter shares consist of winter greens, stored potatoes, onions, garlic, winter squash, and 10 pounds of frozen mixed meats, including whole chickens and various cuts of pork and beef.

At **Green Mountain Girls Farm** in Vermont, the Omnivore's Farm Share provides local, organically managed—although not certified-organic—meat (pork, chicken, turkey, lamb, and goat), eggs, vegetables, and goat milk in a free-choice model year-round. Members choose the volume and exact items from the meat, vegetables, eggs, and milk

1 pound fresh green beans, cut into 1-inch pieces
1¼ cups heavy cream
Pinch of nutmeg
Salt and freshly ground black pepper
Pinch of cayenne pepper

FRIED SHALLOTS

⅓ cup flour
½ teaspoon paprika
¼ teaspoon salt
Pinch of freshly ground black pepper
1 cup shallots, thinly sliced and separated
1 cup vegetable oil

1. Prepare the soup: In a large stockpot, sauté the onion and butter for 10 minutes over medium-low heat. Add the mushrooms, flour, and paprika, and stir until the butter is absorbed.

2. Add the vegetable stock and green beans, and bring to a simmer, stirring occasionally. Simmer 10 minutes, or until the beans are tender.

3. Add the heavy cream, nutmeg, salt, and black and cayenne pepper. Heat through, and adjust the seasonings to taste.

4. Prepare the fried shallots: Toss the flour, paprika, salt, and black pepper with the shallots to coat. Remove the shallots from the mixture, shaking off excess flour. Fry in hot oil in a skillet until crisp and golden brown. Then drain the shallots on a paper towel.

5. Top the soup with the fried shallots, and serve.

— *Blue Heron Coffeehouse,* The Bluff Country Co-op Cookbook

BASIC LO MEIN
SERVES 4

Source Note: Lo mein doesn't take much effort and uses up loose odds and ends of vegetables in the refrigerator, and everyone loves it. It lends itself to many variations and can be made either with meat or as a vegetarian dish using tofu.

MEAT OR TOFU AND MARINADE

8 ounces beef, pork, or boneless, skinless chicken sliced into
    thin strips (or use 8 ounces extra-firm tofu, cubed)
1 piece fresh ginger (½ inch long), peeled and minced
1 clove garlic, minced
1 tablespoon soy sauce
½ tablespoon oyster sauce
½ tablespoon Chinese rice wine or dry sherry
½ teaspoon dark sesame oil
2 teaspoons cornstarch

Noodles and Vegetables

12 ounces fresh Chinese egg noodles,
   or 8 ounces thin spaghetti noodles (dry)
2 tablespoons peanut oil, divided
½ medium onion, halved and cut into slivers, or 1 leek,
   white and tender green parts only, thinly sliced
1 cup chopped or julienned firm vegetables
   (asparagus, broccoli, baby corn, green beans, snow peas,
   or sugar snap peas, alone or in combination), corn kernels,
   or shelled peas
⅓ cup plus 1 tablespoon stock (chicken, beef, or vegetable all
   work well)
1 small carrot, cut into matchsticks
2 tablespoons soy sauce, divided
2 cups thinly sliced greens, such as bok choy, broccoli raab,
   cabbage, chard, escarole, or kale, alone or in any combination
3 tablespoons oyster sauce
½ cup mung bean sprouts

1. To marinate the meat or tofu, combine it in a bowl with the ginger, garlic, soy sauce, oyster sauce, wine, and sesame oil. Toss to mix well. Sprinkle with the cornstarch and toss to mix. Set in the refrigerator while you prepare the remaining ingredients.

2. Cook the noodles in plenty of boiling salted water until al dente. Drain well.

3. Heat a large wok over high heat. Add 1 tablespoon of the peanut oil (alternatively, put the oil into a large, nonstick sauté pan and heat over medium-high heat). Add the meat and marinade; stir-fry until the meat is cooked through (or the tofu is browned), 4 to 8 minutes. Scrape the mixture from the wok into a bowl and keep warm.

4. Reheat the wok over high heat. Add the remaining 1 tablespoon of oil, reduce the heat slightly, and add the onion. Stir-fry until tender, about 4 minutes. Push the onion to the sides of the wok and add the firm vegetables. Add the stock and stir-fry until the vegetables are slightly tender, about 2 minutes. Add the carrot, another tablespoon of stock, and 1 tablespoon of the soy sauce. Continue to stir-fry until the carrot is almost tender, about 2 minutes. Add the slivered greens and the remaining 1 tablespoon of soy sauce, and stir-fry until all of the vegetables are tender, 3 to 5 minutes.

5. Add the noodles, meat, oyster sauce, and bean sprouts to the wok. Toss and stir-fry until the ingredients are thoroughly mixed and heated through, 3 to 4 minutes. Taste and add more soy sauce and oyster sauce, if desired. Serve hot.

— *Adapted from Andrea Chesman's* The Garden-Fresh Vegetable Cookbook

that are on offer each week. Winter veggies include stored, dried, and frozen options as well as some fresh winter greens. Summer veggies are also turned into salsas, pickles, tomato puree, and tomato paste for the winter season. Monthly adult and child shares are individually priced and must be purchased on a full-year basis. A Farmstand membership provides the same range of food, but without the same level of financial commitment or as much of a discount.

Other whole-diet CSA farms include **Moutoux Orchard**, Purcellville, Virginia; **Oakhill Organics**, Grand Island, Oregon; **Dandelion Spring Farm**, Newcastle, Maine; **Sawyer Farm**, Worthington, Massachusetts; and **Greyrock Farm**, Cazenovia, New York.

Source Note: Do not toss this salad; it should look arranged. This Riviera favorite goes best with vinaigrette dressing. You don't have to cook much— just boil the eggs and potatoes and steam the green beans (or pick them up at a salad bar for a no-cook meal). Then open a can and a couple of jars, chop, stir, assemble, and it's done. It's a fun finger-food meal for kids too!

Serve with good sliced French bread, warmed or toasted, and maybe even a chilled dry rosé wine.

½ pound green string beans
4 small red or white potatoes
1 head Boston or red leaf lettuce
1 (6-ounce) can albacore or other high-quality tuna, drained
3 to 4 tomatoes, quartered, or 1 cup cherry tomatoes, halved
2 to 3 hard-boiled eggs, peeled and halved
1 green or yellow bell pepper, seeded and cut into thin rings
16 to 20 herbed black olives (Niçoise olives are the classic choice)
2 tablespoons capers
8 anchovy fillets (optional)

SALADE NIÇOISE VINAIGRETTE

1 tablespoon white-wine vinegar
1 tablespoon fresh lemon juice
½ teaspoon Dijon mustard
1 clove garlic, minced
Pinch of fresh tarragon or basil
Salt and freshly ground black pepper
½ cup extra-virgin olive oil

1. Steam the string beans until just crisp-tender. Cool them quickly in a bowl of ice water to stop the cooking, then trim as needed.

2. Bring a medium saucepan of lightly salted water to a boil. Add the potatoes and cook for 6 minutes, or until fork-tender.

3. Meanwhile, prepare the vinaigrette. In a small bowl, stir together the vinegar, lemon juice, mustard, garlic, tarragon, and salt and pepper to taste. Slowly add the olive oil, whisking until the mixture is well-blended.

4. Peel the cooked potatoes, if desired, and cut into ¼-inch slices while still very warm. Douse with 2 tablespoons of the vinaigrette and allow to cool.

5. Thoroughly wash and spin-dry the lettuce. Place in a large bowl, add 3 tablespoons of the vinaigrette, and toss lightly.

6. Place the lettuce on a platter. Arrange the string beans, potatoes, tuna, tomatoes, eggs, and bell pepper on top of the greens in a decorative fashion. Sprinkle the olives, capers, and anchovies over the salad, drizzle with the remaining vinaigrette, and serve.

— *Fooddownunder.com*

"It's so beautifully arranged on the plate you know someone's fingers have been all over it."

— *Julia Child, American chef and TV cooking personality*

DELICIOUS GREEN BEANS

SERVES 4

Source Note: Don't underestimate this simple dish; it's easy and quick but positively bursting with flavor. It's light yet flavorful, and it makes a great side for almost any meal. It can be served warm or cold.

2 pounds green beans, washed, ends trimmed off
¼ cup butter
¼ cup chopped fresh basil
Salt to taste

1. Wash the green beans. If the beans are extra long, cut them in half.

2. Place the beans in a pot and add the butter and salt. The trick to the dish is adding the right amount of water when cooking; you don't want too much—add just enough to nearly cover the beans.

3. Cover and cook on low heat until the beans are soft and most of the water has evaporated—but do not drain.

4. Add the chopped basil. Mix well and continue cooking, uncovered, on low heat for another 5 minutes, until the water has evaporated and the flavors have blended.

— *Anush Oganesian and Lida Hovhannesyan*

JESSE'S CHICKEN STEW

SERVES 4

2 tablespoons olive oil
2 boneless, skinless chicken breasts, sliced
2 carrots, chopped
¾ cup fresh or frozen corn kernels
4 new potatoes, chopped
¾ cup fresh or frozen peas
1 rib celery, chopped
3 cloves garlic, minced
1 cup sliced fresh okra (frozen or canned is also acceptable)
1 cup sliced fresh mushrooms
Green beans (about 20 young, tender specimens)
Tarragon, thyme, parsley, basil, oregano, or other chopped fresh
    herbs, to taste
Water
2 chicken bouillon cubes
½ cup rotini pasta
Cornstarch (optional)
Tamari sauce
Oyster crackers, for garnish
Chopped fresh parsley, for garnish

"Ripe vegetables were magic to me. Unharvested, the garden bristled with possibility. I would quicken at the sight of a ripe tomato, sounding its redness from deep amidst the undifferentiated green. To lift a bean plant's hood of heart-shaped leaves and discover a clutch of long slender pods hiding underneath could make me catch my breath."

— *Michael Pollan, author*

1. Put the olive oil into a large roasting pan or Dutch oven over medium heat. Add all of the ingredients except for the bouillon cubes, rotini, cornstarch, and tamari sauce. Sauté the chicken and vegetables until they are lightly golden.

2. Cover with water, then add the bouillon cubes and rotini. Simmer until everything is tender and the flavors have blended, about 1 hour. Add some cornstarch if you'd like a thicker sauce. (Start with 1 tablespoon cornstarch that's dissolved in several tablespoons water; add and simmer until the sauce thickens. Repeat this process if you want a thicker stew.)

3. Serve tamari sauce at the table, and garnish with the oyster crackers and fresh parsley, if desired.

— *Jesse Smith,* The Bluff Country Co-op Cookbook

Seedlings in the greenhouse at Featherstone Farm.

Cantaloupes

Like sweet corn and tomatoes, melons herald the arrival of summer plenty—plump balls of juicy refreshment best savored on sweltering evenings or warm early mornings. Melons belong to the Cucurbitaceae family, a large group of vine-type plants that also include squashes, luffas, and cucumbers.

Although the terms "cantaloupe" and "muskmelon" are sometimes used interchangeably in the United States, they are completely different fruits in Europe. Cucumis melo var. reticulatus, *commonly called cantaloupe in the United States, is called muskmelon in Europe. The American varieties have netted rinds and a round or oval shape, but they often have regional differences; some of the eastern types are larger and have skins that are divided into deep ridges by long sutures.*

*In Europe, the true cantaloupe (*Cucumis melo var. cantaloupensis*) looks completely different, with deep grooves, a hard, warty rind, and orange or greenish flesh. They are little known outside their home countries.*

HISTORY

Although its exact origins are unclear, melons probably first grew in the Middle East, near Persia. Early Egyptians and Sumerians displayed melons in their art around 2200 BCE, and the Greeks had melons by the third century BCE. At the peak of their power, the Romans imported melons from Asia to Europe, but after the Empire fell, melons disappeared from European tables until possibly the 14th century.

Throughout recorded humanity, melons seem to have aroused passionate feelings, including a French obsession with the fruit at the end of the 15th century. In the 16th century, melon seeds were brought from Armenia to the papal domain of Cantalupo, near Tivoli—hence the name "cantaloupe." Melons did not arrive in the United States until the late 1800s.

NUTRITION

Cantaloupe is rich in vitamin A (a 1-cup serving contains an adult's complete daily allowance) and vitamin C, and provides some potassium, folate, vitamin B6, and dietary fiber. A single cup contains 56 calories.

SEASON

Commercially, cantaloupe is widely grown and available year-round. But its peak season at farmers markets and CSAs is during the height of summer and in the early fall months.

SELECTION

Once picked, cantaloupes do not continue to ripen, even in the sun. (They may continue to soften slightly but will not produce more sugars.) For full flavor, choose perfectly ripe specimens. One dead giveaway is that unmistakable, mouthwatering aroma wafting from the blossom end. Also, fully ripe cantaloupes easily separate from the vine with very light pressure, so a melon showing signs of damage in that area was plucked unripe. Cantaloupes should be firm and heavy, with no soft or depressed areas. Very ripe specimens are yellowish around the "netting" on their skins; a jaundiced cantaloupe with a strong smell is probably overripe.

STORAGE

You can store melons at room temperature, but they are quite susceptible to spoiling if kept too long. (A little cloud of fruit flies hovering over the melon is a giveaway.) Store them in the refrigerator if you can; they keep a bit longer this way and are extremely appetizing chilled on a hot summer day.

TRIMMING AND CLEANING

Bacteria sometimes grow on the outside of melons (a major 2001 US salmonella outbreak was traced to cantaloupe), so a thorough washing is a good idea before slicing into the fruit. Once the luscious orange flesh has yielded to the blade, scoop out the seeds and get ready for a taste treat.

STEAMING AND BOILING

Cantaloupe is usually eaten fresh, but it can be cooked to make jam, melon chutney, bread, or even pie. Low heat is best, to preserve its delicate flavor and aroma.

FREEZING

Cantaloupe and other types of melon can be frozen as-is, or prepared in a light sugar syrup to better preserve their flavor and color. Peel and cut melons into ½- or ¾-inch cubes or balls. To make the syrup, combine 9 cups of water or fruit juice with 2¼ cups of sugar in a pot, and bring to a boil until the sugar dissolves. Chill, then pour ½ cup of syrup into a freezer container, jar, or zipper-lock freezer bag. Add the melon and keep adding syrup until the fruit is covered. Leave ½ inch of headspace for pints, 1 inch for quarts.

You can also prepare your fruit unsweetened by arranging pieces on a single layer on a cookie sheet and freezing. Transfer the frozen pieces into zipper-lock freezer or vacuum food sealer-type bags, or freezer containers. Squeeze out any excess air and leave ½ inch of headspace (unless you are using the vacuum sealing method). Frozen cantaloupe should keep for up to 1 year at 0°F.

EQUIVALENTS, MEASURES, AND SERVINGS

- 1 pound = ½ medium cantaloupe = 1½ cups cubed

COMPLEMENTARY HERBS, SEASONINGS, AND FOODS

Bacon, balsamic vinegar, basil, black pepper, champagne, chiles, cognac, cream, cucumber, ginger, grapefruit, ham, honey, ice cream, kirsch, lemon, lime, mangoes, mint, oranges, orange liqueur, pear, prosciutto, raspberries, sea salt, sherry, strawberries, vanilla, wine.

SERVING SUGGESTIONS

- Combine different types of melons, along with mango, pineapple, and pomegranate seeds for an exotic fruit salad.

- Use pureed cantaloupe in your favorite homemade sorbet or ice pop recipe.
- Wrap cantaloupe with prosciutto and sprinkle lightly with a high-quality balsamic vinegar and coarsely ground black pepper for a taste explosion. Or try really ripe melon with a bit of sea salt.
- Chop cantaloupe with diced kiwi and strawberries for a fun fruit salsa.
- Combine pureed cantaloupe with orange and lemon juice, candied ginger or ginger ale, and whole milk for a refreshing soup.
- Get kids to drink their fruit by combining cantaloupe, milk, and honey in a blender to make a tasty melon milkshake.
- If you can find it, cantaloupe with genuine Devonshire clotted cream is a memorable treat.

BACON, LETTUCE, AND CANTALOUPE SANDWICH

MAKES 4 SANDWICHES

12 bacon slices (about ¾ pound)
6 tablespoons mayonnaise
2 tablespoons Dijon mustard
2 teaspoons fresh lemon juice
2 teaspoons honey
½ cantaloupe
8 soft lettuce leaves, such as Boston or Bibb
8 slices crusty bread

1. Preheat the oven to 425°F.

2. In a shallow baking pan, cook the bacon in one layer in the middle of the oven, turning occasionally, until golden and crisp, 16 to 18 minutes. Transfer to paper towels to drain.

3. In a small bowl, whisk together the mayonnaise, mustard, lemon juice, and honey until smooth. Seed the cantaloupe. Cut the melon into 12 thin slices and discard the rind. Cut out and discard the lettuce ribs.

4. Spread the mayonnaise mixture on all 8 slices of bread. Stack the lettuce, melon, and bacon on 4 of the bread slices, and top with the remaining slices, gently pressing them together.

— Gourmet, *August 1999, as appeared on Fooddownunder.com*

SPICY CANTALOUPE SALSA

MAKES ABOUT 4 CUPS

1 medium cantaloupe, peeled, seeded, and finely chopped
½ habanero chile, finely chopped
½ red onion, finely chopped
⅛ cup chopped cilantro
½ red bell pepper, roasted and chopped

Imagine walking out your front door and down the street to your neighborhood farm stand to pick up your weekly CSA share grown and raised a stone's throw from your house. Who would have guessed a decade ago that housing developers would be building sub-urban subdivisions with a working farm as a centerpiece instead of a golf course or clubhouse? At least a dozen "agrihoods" are offering a taste of farm life to nonfarmers from Virginia to Hawaii, according to a 2014 article on farm-to-ta-ble living in The New York Times *(www.nytimes.com/2014/03/12/dining/farm-to-table-living-takes-root.html).*

One such community is **Agritopia** *in Gilbert, Arizona, out-side of Phoenix. A family farm be-gun in 1927 has been transformed into a 16-acre certified organic farm alongside 452 single-family homes on a total of 160 acres. On Wednesday evenings, residents go to the farm stand in their commu-nity "square" to pick up their box of produce, eggs, and honey. On the way home, they may also stop at the neighborhood's farm-to-table restaurant. The farm grows row crops, fruit trees (citrus, nectarine, peach, apple, olive, and date), and livestock (chickens and sheep).*

Residents pay $100 a month for a CSA membership or buy what they want at the farm stand's own farmers market. Other CSA subscribers include 20 restaurant chefs. Agritopia is not an upscale development, like some agrihood communities; its home prices are comparable to others in the area. The farm is self-sustaining through its local sales.

Agrihoods—both existing and under development—vary tremen-dously in size, cost of housing, and amenities. Some offer cooking class-

½ papaya, chopped
½ tablespoon pineapple juice
½ tablespoon fresh lemon juice
½ tablespoon rice vinegar
¼ teaspoon salt
½ tablespoon sugar

Mix all of the ingredients together (wear gloves when handling the habanero chile, because it can burn your skin and eyes). Chill and serve.

— *Davis Farmers Market, Davis, California*

. . . .

CANTALOUPE PIE   MAKES ONE 9-INCH PIE

Source Note: It's said that all you have to do is take one whiff of a Pecos cantaloupe to know it's the real deal. That seductive smell equals summer in certain parts of Texas, inspiring folks to hop in their cars and make a beeline for roadside stands heaped high with the homely orbs, their sturdy countenance belying the creamy, coral-hued sweetness inside. No doubt you've indulged in wedges sprinkled with a little salt or hollowed-out halves filled with vanilla ice cream, but who among you has had a slice of cantaloupe pie?

As anachronistic as the elegant railroad dining car for which it was created, it's an uncommon confection attributed to Edward Pierce, a College Station native and 42-year employee of the Texas and Pacific Railway. (It was the T&P, in fact, that introduced the country to the Pecos cantaloupe roughly a century ago when its dining service contracted to buy the fruit from M. L. Todd, a local farmer whose little patch of alkaline soil in arid West Texas was producing some mighty fine specimens.) A resourceful sort, Pierce couldn't tolerate the wasteful disposal of overripe cantaloupes and came up with a dessert that quickly became a menu favorite.

1 very ripe cantaloupe (2 to 2½ pounds)
½ cup sugar
½ cup all-purpose flour
¼ teaspoon salt
3 egg yolks
2 tablespoons water
1 tablespoon butter
¼ teaspoon butter-flavored extract or vanilla extract
1 tablespoon fresh lemon juice
1 (9-inch) piecrust, baked
3 egg whites
6 tablespoons sugar
¼ teaspoon cream of tartar

1. Cut the cantaloupe in half, remove the seeds, and scoop the pulp into a saucepan. Place the pulp over medium heat until it comes to

a simmer. Mash the cantaloupe as it heats. This should make about 2 cups of pulp.

2. Combine the ½ cup sugar, flour, and salt. Add to the heated cantaloupe pulp and cook, stirring constantly until thick, about 2 minutes. (The amount of flour seems large, but it takes considerable thickening to achieve the correct consistency.)

3. Preheat the oven to 400°F.

4. In a large bowl, beat the egg yolks; add the water to the yolks. Add a little of the cantaloupe to the yolks in order to temper them, then stir the yolk mixture back into the cantaloupe mixture. Over medium-low heat, continue cooking, stirring constantly, until the mixture becomes thick and creamy. Remove from the heat. Add the butter, flavoring, and lemon juice to the cantaloupe mixture. Pour into the baked pie shell.

5. Beat the egg whites and cream of tartar together until frothy. Continue beating, adding the 6 tablespoons of sugar gradually; beat until thick peaks form. Top the pie with this meringue.

6. Bake at 375°F until the meringue turns delicately brown on top.

— *Adapted from Edward Pierce's original recipe, as appeared in the* Fort Worth Star-Telegram

. . . .

CANTALOUPE AND CUCUMBER SALAD   SERVES 4 TO 6

Source Note: This is a refreshing and light summer salad for all occasions. The lime juice adds a note of tartness that brings out the cantaloupe's sweet side. Add a dash of cayenne pepper for a bit of heat or a sprinkle of smoked paprika to pair with barbecued meats or poultry.

1 tablespoon honey
2 tablespoons fresh lime juice
½ cup plain yogurt
1 cantaloupe, peeled and roughly chopped
1 large cucumber, peeled and chopped
2 teaspoons chopped fresh mint leaves
⅓ cup chopped roasted pistachios
Salt

1. In a large serving bowl, whisk together the honey and lime juice until well blended.

2. Add the yogurt and whisk it in. Add the cantaloupe, cucumber, and mint; toss to combine.

3. Sprinkle with the pistachios; salt to taste and serve.

— *Gabriel Avila-Mooney, Full Circle Farm, Seattle, Washington*

es. Others offer community garden plots and opportunities to help tend bees and chickens.

Existing communities include **Serenbe** in Georgia, **Hidden Springs** in Idaho, **South Village** in Vermont, **Willowsford** in Virginia, **Kukul'ula** in Hawaii, and **Prairie Crossing** in Illinois. Communities being developed include **Bucking Horse** in Colorado, **Harvest** in Texas, and **Skokomish Farms** in Washington State.

The developments aren't just idyllic—there's also an economic benefit for developers. "They've figured out that unlike a golf course, which costs millions to build and millions to maintain, they can provide green space that actually earns a profit," Ed McMahon, a senior fellow for sustainable development at the Urban Land Institute, told The New York Times.

Celery

APIUM GRAVEOLENS

Celery's role is muddled in the American culinary landscape, simultaneously considered essential in flavoring homemade stocks and soups and on a crudités platter, yet largely ignored as a featured vegetable in its own right. At one point it was quite fashionable as a tonic (remember Dr. Brown's Cel-Rey soda?), and at times it has been ridiculed as rabbit or diet food.

Yet this venerable member of a vast plant family that includes carrots, parsley, fennel, and dill was once highly valued on the groaning Roman table, especially in its wild form. Wild celery has thinner, stringier stalks and is much stronger-tasting; even to this day Italians still prefer it, considering it "cooking celery" as opposed to the milder, cultivated "eating celery." Our modern cultivated forms are usually blanched, a process whereby soil is heaped around the developing stalks to protect them from the sun so they remain pale, sweet, mild, and more succulent.

HISTORY

Celery is thought to be native to the Mediterranean, where it still grows wild in brackish waters (not surprising to home gardeners, who know the plant is a tricky, slow-growing crop that loves wet roots and fertile soil but hates heat). Wild celery was prized by Romans and Greeks not only for eating but also as medicine; the seeds were used as a painkiller, and modern laboratory testing reveals they contain a chemical that reduces blood pressure. In classic Greece, the leaves were used as garlands for the dead.

NUTRITION

Celery is well known for being extremely low in calories (16 calories per cup), but it also contains surprising amounts of vitamin K, manganese, folate, potassium, beta-carotene, and phytonutrients. And anyone who has gotten celery strings stuck in the teeth will not be surprised to learn that celery is an excellent source of dietary fiber. However, celery (along with spinach, carrots, and bok choy) has naturally high levels of sodium, so people on sodium-restricted diets may want to avoid it.

SEASON

Commercially grown celery is available year-round, but because of its very long growing time, homegrown and CSA-farm celery typically comes into season in later summer, around August or even September.

SELECTION

Celery that looks crisp, firm, and succulent is usually a good bet; avoid specimens with shriveled stalks or wilting leaves. Bunches should be fairly firm and compact, with bright-green leaves. Celery can also be susceptible to blackheart, which results in blackened or yellow discoloration at its heart; check for this by splaying out the stalks during selection.

You Might Not Want To Eat That

Celery is one of the best vegetables to buy organic; some samples of conventionally grown celery have been found to have trace residues of over 60 pesticides.

STORAGE

Celery is best stored tightly wrapped in a plastic bag in the refrigerator. The stalks will keep for 5 to 7 days, after which they will start to lose flavor and nutrients. The leaves often last less time than the stalks, so it's good to use them sooner if you have a recipe calling for them.

TRIMMING AND CLEANING

The same stalk shape that is tailor-made for holding peanut butter also can harbor lots of sand and soil. To avoid a mouthful of unpleasant grit, separate the stalks and individually rinse and scrub them. To prepare the stalks, slice them about 1 inch from the white base and remove the leafy tops (but reserve these tops for flavoring, seasoning, and decorative purposes). If you are preparing celery sticks as a raw vegetable, you may want to remove its fibrous strings by slitting the ends of the stalk and peeling away the fibers.

STEAMING AND BOILING

Celery's high water content does not lend itself well to boiling, which creates an even soggier vegetable. Steaming is a better alternative; cut the stalks into ½-inch thick slices and steam for 4 to 9 minutes.

STIR-FRYING AND SAUTÉING

Cut celery into very thin slices or julienne it into strips that can cook quickly and evenly; stir-fry for 3 to 5 minutes on medium heat, depending on how crisp you want it.

EQUIVALENTS, MEASURES, AND SERVINGS

- 1 bunch = about 1 pound
- 1 pound celery = 4 cups chopped or sliced
- 1 pound prepared celery = 4 servings
- 4 cups raw = approximately 3 cups cooked
- 3 medium ribs = 1 cup, diagonally sliced
- Average serving size = 1½ ribs

MICROWAVING

Slice celery into 1-inch pieces, then place them in a microwave-safe dish; add ¼ cup water; cover and cook on high power. Test for doneness with a fork.

- 1 cup = 2 to 3 minutes
- 2 cups = 5 to 6 minutes

BLANCHING AND FREEZING

Because of its high water content, celery should not be frozen; it will turn mushy.

COMPLEMENTARY HERBS, SEASONINGS, AND FOODS

Apples, butter, capers, carrots, cheese, chervil, chicken, chives, cream, Dijon mustard, dill, dried beans, eggs, fennel, garlic, lemon juice, mayonnaise, olives, onions, parsley, peanut butter, pepper, potatoes, seafood, shrimp, tarragon, thyme, tomatoes, vinegar, white wine.

"There ought t'be some way t'eat celery so it wouldn't sound like you wuz steppin' on a basket."

— Frank McKinney (Kin) Hubbard

Safety Tip

Celery can trigger severe allergic symptoms in some people, especially those sensitive to birch pollen or mugwort.

Better than Tomatoes

One of English football's weirder traditions is for fans of the Chelsea team to throw celery sticks onto the field during play while chanting a rather raunchy tune, a peculiar practice that started during the 1980s but was banned in 2007 because of safety concerns.

- Combine celery and green olives for a refreshing, unusual salad.

- A traditional Italian dish is braised celery with tomato sauce—a surprisingly good combination.

- Celery, along with carrots and onion, forms the flavoring trinity called mirepoix, the basis of many top-notch stocks, broths, soups, and stews.

- Use the pretty, yellow-green celery leaves, finely chopped, in place of or alongside parsley as a flavoring agent in salads and cooked dishes. Be careful—a little can go a long way, depending on the age and strength of the leaves.

- Who can forget the time-honored classic of celery stalks heaped with peanut butter? Uphold it! (Add raisins and it becomes "ants on a log.") Same goes for soft cheeses, Boursin dip, flavored mayonnaise, sour cream, yogurt, hummus, even Nutella.

- Celery can be a terrific kid-friendly vegetable, especially if it is served with lots of tasty dips and dressings, or if the stalks are holders for other foods, like little grape tomatoes, raisins, olives, etc. The fact that it's an ultimate finger food helps too!

- Chopped celery is a great way to add crunch to pasta, tuna, and egg salads.

- Celery is a terrific but often overlooked addition to stir-fries—add a couple of chopped stalks to add crunch and texture.

- Add celery (chop it first to shorten its fibers) to tomato- or carrot-based vegetable juice blends.

- Celery makes a great pickle; try using Japanese seasonings like rice vinegar, shiso, and soy sauce in the brine.

FENNEL AND CELERY SALAD WITH ASIAGO CHEESE

SERVES 4

3 medium fennel bulbs, trimmed, some fronds reserved
6 celery stalks, trimmed, some leaves reserved
¼ cup extra-virgin olive oil
3 tablespoons fresh orange juice
½ teaspoon salt
¼ teaspoon freshly ground black pepper
Freshly shaved Asiago or Parmesan cheese

1. Cut the fennel bulbs lengthwise into quarters, discarding the outermost layer if it is exceedingly tough. Use a mandoline, a chef's knife, or a box grater to slice the quarters thinly; slice the celery equally thinly.

2. Put the sliced fennel and celery into a large bowl and drizzle with the olive oil and orange juice. Season with salt and pepper, then toss gently to combine. Top with lots of Asiago cheese, chopped celery leaves, and chopped fennel fronds.

— *Paul Anater*

Soupe au Pistou (French Vegetable Soup with Pesto)

Serves 12 (Makes 6 cups)

Source Note: This Provençale "Soup with Pesto" is a casual, family-style soup that is frequently featured in cafés and even fine-dining restaurants in the south of France. With vegetables, beans, and pasta drifting around in a pesto-laced broth, the soup reflects the cultural connection between the Côte d'Azure (or French Riviera) and Liguria, the region of Italy that lies just around the bend. Italians call Nice "La Bella Nizza" and seem barely cognizant of the fact that this part of the Mediterranean coast slipped out of their grasp a few hundred years ago to become a part of France. Serve the soup hot with a spoonful of pesto on top of each bowlful.

For the Beans

4 cups water, plus additional water if needed
1 cup dried white beans
1 bay leaf
1 teaspoon salt

To Complete the Soup

¼ cup olive oil
1 medium onion, peeled and thinly sliced
1 large leek, white and pale green end only, split, rinsed, and sliced
2 ribs celery, sliced
3 cloves garlic, peeled and thinly sliced
1 medium zucchini
2 medium Yukon Gold or other thin-skinned, waxy potatoes, scrubbed
1 (14½-ounce) can diced tomatoes in their own juice
8 cups water, plus more if needed
Salt
1 teaspoon freshly ground black pepper
2 cups (about ¼ pound) haricots verts (tiny French-style green beans)
¼ pound spaghetti noodles, broken into 2-inch lengths
Prepared pesto, for garnish

1. Presoak and cook the beans: In a large kettle over high heat, bring the water to a boil. Add the beans, bay leaf, and salt, and as soon as the water returns to a boil, turn off the heat. Cover the pan and leave undisturbed for 1 hour.

2. When the hour has passed, turn the burner on high heat and bring the beans to a boil again, then decrease the heat to medium-low. Cook, adding more water if necessary to keep the beans barely covered, until the beans are tender, about 90 minutes.

3. While the beans are cooking, prepare the other elements of the soup. In a very large, heavy-bottomed Dutch oven or soup pot, heat the

6. **Arrive early at the market for the best picks, or leverage closing times for a good deal.** *Farmers don't want to leave with a full truck. Be careful not to barter too much; farmers are primarily interested in building long-term customer relationships, and they have worked hard to bring their products to market. Try out something like "I see that you have some food left over, and I want to help out. What can you give me for $20?" By initially offering a set amount of money and giving the farmer a choice in what to sell you, the farmer will be inclined to give you both a good deal and the best of what his or her table has to offer.*

7. **Many farmers sell fresh herbs, vegetables, and fruits that you can take home and plant yourself!** *Consider starting a small box of herbs or some frequently used veggies, such as salad greens (which you can cut and they'll regrow).*

8. **Consider raising your own small animals in your backyard,** *such as chickens, turkeys, dwarf goats, ducks, and rabbits. You can harvest eggs, milk, and meat from these animals, ensuring that you know where the food is coming from and that it is healthy.*

9. **Instead of just car-pooling, consider "cow-pooling."** *Get together with friends or neighbors to purchase healthy, grass-fed beef, pork, and lamb from local farmers. Ask questions about how the farmers are raising their animals and if they are free of antibiotics or hormones.*

10. **Many farmers markets are sponsored by local organizations that need volunteers**

olive oil over medium heat, and sauté the onion, leek, celery, and garlic until the vegetables are tender and just beginning to color, about 10 minutes.

4. While the onion mixture is sautéing, prepare the zucchini. Cut the sides of the vegetable away from the seedy center and discard the center. Cut the sides into matchsticks about 2 inches long and ¼ inch wide. Add the cut zucchini to the pot. Cut the potatoes into matchsticks the same size as the zucchini and stir them in.

5. Stir the tomatoes and water in with the sautéed vegetables and increase the heat to high. Bring the soup to a full rolling boil and add a little salt; taste to make sure the salt is correct, then stir in the green beans and spaghetti noodles. Cook until the spaghetti is tender, then stir in the cooked beans with their cooking liquid. Decrease the heat to low, and allow the soup to simmer until the flavors merge and the broth surrounding the vegetables thickens slightly, about 10 minutes.

— *Greg Atkinson,* Northwest Essentials: Cooking with Ingredients That Define a Region's Cuisine

11. **Bring your favorite farmer or producer a cup of hot coffee or a taste of something** *you just whipped up in the kitchen with fresh ingredients. Compliment them if you enjoyed their food and let them know you appreciate their hard work. You may end up saving some money!*

12. **Inquire at your local state health and human services office or senior center about WIC [Women, Infants, and Children] and senior nutrition programs.** *You might be eligible to receive free vouchers that are redeemable for fresh fruit and produce at farmers markets.*

13. **Buy veggies, grains, and fruits in bulk with family and friends** *to save significant money.*

14. **Offer the farmers more than cash.** *Farmers are independent and sometimes unconventional. Bartering is second nature to them. A farmer, like anyone else, specializes in a certain trade or skill. If you also have a skill or service that you can offer—website design, carpentry, tax preparation—a farmer may be willing to trade for your services.*

15. **Participate in local gleaning or community gardening opportunities.** *A little donated time can provide a welcome wealth of local food in your life.*

Cilantro

CORIANDRUM SATIVUM

Cilantro has a bright, assertive, sage-citrus flavor that people either love or hate. (Those of the latter persuasion say it tastes like soap or rubber, and there is actual scientific evidence to support their taste buds' reaction.) Resembling flat-leaf parsley but with leaves that are more rounded, it is an essential ingredient in many world cuisines, including Vietnamese, Middle Eastern, Indian, and Latin American. Cilantro is sometimes called Chinese parsley, Mexican parsley, or Vietnamese mint. It is one of the few herbs in the world that has different names for the leaf and spice forms: The seeds of fresh cilantro are called coriander.

HISTORY

Coriander is one of humanity's earliest spices, and it is probably safe to assume that the leaves were also used. The plant likely originated in North Africa or the Middle East, but it also grows wild in Mediterranean Europe.

Coriander seeds have been found in Bronze Age ruins and Egyptian tombs, are mentioned in the Bible, and were brought to northern Europe by the Romans. Spanish conquistadors introduced it to Latin America, where, paired with chiles and tomatoes, it became a staple.

NUTRITION

Cilantro is a good source of vitamins A and K, as well as dietary fiber, potassium, calcium, phosphorus, magnesium, and trace amounts of B vitamins. Coriander and cilantro have both been used as an aphrodisiac, diuretic, and appetite stimulant. Cilantro leaves contain an antibacterial agent in their essential oils. A quarter cup of fresh cilantro contains a single calorie. (Dieters, if you can figure out how to survive solely on cilantro and water, you're in luck.)

SEASON

Commercially, cilantro is widely grown and in season year-round. You'll find it at its best at farmers markets and CSAs from spring through early fall.

SELECTION

Look for very fresh bunches, with no signs of bruising, yellowing, or sliminess.

STORAGE

Handle cilantro carefully, for its leaves wilt and bruise easily. Cilantro is often bunched, with the root ends conveniently close together. If the roots are still attached, you can place your cilantro bouquet in a small glass of water, cover it loosely with plastic, and store it in the refrigerator or on your countertop at room temperature. If you change the water every few days, your cilantro should last for up to 2 weeks.

Alternatively, if you can't store it this way, cilantro will keep better if it is washed and dried right away after purchase; otherwise it tends to

Do not confuse cilantro with culantro (*Eryngium foetidum*), which is an entirely different herb used mainly in Mexican and Caribbean cuisines.

rot and turn yellow rather quickly. When you get your cilantro home, immediately free it from the bonds of its tight wire or rubber-band binding. Cilantro's finely notched leaves can conceal plenty of sand, soil, and insects, so it is best to wash it just like you would spinach. Fill a big sink or bowl full of cold water and completely submerge the cilantro, swishing vigorously. Remove any questionable stems and leaves that are on the edge of decline, and inspect for persistent telltale brown grit. Then rinse under cold running water, and repeat if necessary. Spin or vigorously shake the cilantro dry, then spread it out on a paper towel or two. Roll the paper towel loosely and slip the whole bundle into a plastic bag. The cilantro will keep for up to 1 week—and it will be clean and just slightly damp (perfect!), ready for you when you need to grab a lot or a little for cooking.

TRIMMING AND CLEANING

If you have thoroughly washed your cilantro as listed in the storage instructions above, you can skip this step. Remove any yellow or slimy leaves, give the rest of the leaves a quick rinse under running water, and lightly pat dry. The stems can be a bit tough and unpleasant to chew, so unless they are being cooked as a vegetable on their own (they are great with lamb!), it is best to tear the leaves off the stems when using cilantro in dishes.

BLANCHING AND FREEZING

Arrange dry cilantro leaves in a single layer on a cookie sheet and place it in the freezer. When the leaves are frozen, place them in zipper-lock freezer or vacuum food sealer-type bags and return them to the freezer immediately. Frozen cilantro will keep for up to 6 months at 0°F. Do not thaw before using.

DRYING

Because cilantro almost completely loses its fragrance and flavor when dried, drying is not recommended.

EQUIVALENTS, MEASURES, AND SERVINGS

- 3 teaspoons fresh cilantro = 1 teaspoon dried

COMPLEMENTARY HERBS, SEASONINGS, AND FOODS

Avocado, basil, beef, black beans, borage, chicken, chiles, coconut, curry, fish, garbanzos (chickpeas), garlic, ginger, honey, ice cream, lamb, lentils, lime, mayonnaise, mint, onions, peppers, pork, potatoes, rice, salads, salsas, shellfish, shrimp, tomatoes, turkey, yogurt.

SERVING SUGGESTIONS

- Use cilantro generously in fresh salsa, pico de gallo, and chutneys.
- Add several tablespoons of chopped fresh cilantro to green salads.
- Try tossing it into your potato salad or adding it to soups for a fresh zing.
- Use cilantro instead of basil to make pesto.
- Cilantro and fresh lime juice are nonnegotiable ingredients in guacamole.
- Use cilantro like dill—in dips, hummus, and butters.

- In Vietnamese and Thai cuisines, cilantro is one of the several raw green herbs that accompany savory dishes (basil and mint are popular too).

- Mix cilantro with lime juice, honey, and shredded cabbage to make an unusual coleslaw.

- Cilantro makes an interesting addition to stir-fries. Toss in fresh leaves at the very end of cooking to preserve its distinctive flavor and oils.

- Add a handful to a smoothie or when making juice blends. Especially good in tomato juice!

- Curries and cilantro harmonize together better than most siblings. Coconut and cilantro are an especially wonderful combination.

- Cilantro makes a nice herbal counterpoint to rich meats like beef and pork.

- It may sound a little odd, but cilantro stems can actually be an interesting vegetable on their own. Cut them into short pieces and add them to stir-fry dishes; they remain a bit crunchy and tasty, providing a neat texture. They're especially good with lamb and flank steak.

- Coriander is a staple in Indian cooking along with cumin and cardamom.

- Use coriander seeds in pickling solutions, to spice a pot of beans or chili, or even to flavor home-brewed beer (along with orange peel).

- Toast coriander seeds in a dry pan on the stove (the toasted seeds take on a flavor that is completely different from untoasted), grind them finely, and add them to mashed potatoes along with some butter, salt, and freshly ground black pepper. A terrific and unexpected dish!

SPAGHETTI WITH CILANTRO, CORN, AND TOMATOES

SERVES 2

Source Note: Fragrant cilantro, sweet corn, and summer tomatoes have so much color and flavor that you may be surprised to find that this is a low-calorie meal.

2 very ripe medium tomatoes, stem ends removed
1 medium ear fresh corn, husked
½ pound spaghettini
1 egg
1 tablespoon red wine vinegar
½ teaspoon sugar
Salt and freshly ground black pepper
1 to 2 tablespoons full-flavored oil
¼ cup cilantro, finely minced
⅛ cup chopped red onion

1. Drop the tomatoes and corn into a large pot of salted, boiling water; return to a boil on the highest heat. Boil 15 seconds. Remove the tomatoes; let the corn boil 1 minute, then remove. Cover the pot and lower the heat.

2. Peel the tomatoes, halve them, and squeeze out the seeds. Cut one of the tomatoes into ½-inch cubes. Cut off the corn kernels from the cob.

Books

The Art of Mexican Cooking
Diana Kennedy,
Clarkson Potter, 2008.

Into the Vietnamese Kitchen:
Treasured Foodways, Modern Flavors
Andrea Nguyen,
Ten Speed, 2006.

The Best of Lord Krishna's Cuisine:
Favorite Recipes from The Art
of Indian Vegetarian Cooking
Yamuna Devi,
Plume, 1991.

3. Whirl the egg in a food processor until it turns pale and fluffy; cut up the remaining tomato and add with vinegar, sugar, salt, and pepper to taste. Whirl to blend well.

4. Boil the spaghettini until it becomes just barely tender. Toss the drained pasta in a warm serving dish with the oil, to taste. Add the egg-tomato sauce and toss to coat. Add the cilantro, onion, corn, and remaining tomato; toss gently and serve at once.

— *Elizabeth Schneider,* Uncommon Fruits & Vegetables

MEXICAN BLACK BEAN AND TOMATO SALAD

SERVES 4

Source Note: You can vary the spices to suit your palate. This salad tastes best when refrigerated for an hour or two before serving.

DRESSING
2 tablespoons olive or vegetable oil
2 tablespoons fresh lemon or lime juice
1 to 2 cloves garlic, crushed
1 to 2 teaspoons cumin powder
1 to 2 teaspoons chili powder
Pinch of salt

1½ cups cooked black beans, or one (16-ounce) can, rinsed and dried
1 to 2 chopped fresh tomatoes (or a pint of halved cherry tomatoes)
1 green bell pepper, chopped
A little red onion or a couple of green onions, chopped
Several sprigs of fresh cilantro, chopped

In a medium bowl, mix the dressing ingredients. Then add the remaining ingredients and toss thoroughly.

— *Robin Taylor, Featherstone Farm CSA member*

CARROT AND RED LENTIL CURRY

SERVES 4 TO 6

Source Note: Berbere *is an Ethiopian spice blend that is a key ingredient in many Ethiopian and Eritrean dishes. Not for the faint of heart, this spicy mixture usually includes chile peppers, garlic, ginger, basil,* korarima, *rue,* ajwain *or* radhuni, nigella, *and fenugreek. You can either make your own (good recipes exist on the Internet) or you can buy it online from specialty-food retailers.*

2 tablespoons peanut oil, divided

1 teaspoon black mustard seeds

1 teaspoon cumin seeds

6 to 8 carrots, grated

Garlic, to taste

Ginger, to taste

Jalapeño, to taste

Fresh turmeric, to taste

Berbere, to taste

4 cups chicken or vegetable stock

1 cup split red lentils, washed

1 to 2 tablespoons crunchy peanut butter

1 tablespoon curry powder

Salt and freshly ground black pepper

½ cup chopped cilantro, plus 2 tablespoons for garnish

Yogurt, to garnish

8 to 12 nice sprigs cilantro, for garnish

1. Heat 1 tablespoon of the oil in a large nonstick frying pan. Add the mustard and cumin seeds. Fry until the mustard seeds start to pop. Add the carrot and stir. Let the carrot "sweat" for 10 minutes.

2. In a separate pan, sauté the garlic, ginger, jalapeño, and turmeric in the remaining 1 tablespoon oil for 3 minutes, add a little berbere and salt, then mix everything with the carrots.

3. Add the stock, lentils, and more berbere; then simmer for 30 minutes. Add more stock if the pan starts to get too dry.

4. Add the peanut butter, curry powder, salt, and pepper. Simmer until the lentils are cooked through (they'll break down a little) and the soup is a thick consistency. Right before serving, add the ½ cup chopped cilantro and stir to combine.

5. Serve the soup in individual bowls, garnishing each with the yogurt, chopped cilantro, and cilantro sprigs. Serve with rice, naan, or pita bread.

— *Allison, Featherstone Farm, Rushford, Minnesota*

from field to table at **Gathering Together Farm** in Philomath (population: 2,145), Oregon. The farm had one of the first CSAs in the state, and is still going strong with 350 shares. In 2003 it opened a small, seasonal restaurant at its farm store that's known as the Farm Stand, serving lunch Tuesday through Friday, dinner on Thursday and Friday, and breakfast on Saturday. Longtime chef J. C. Mersmann writes charming entries about what's being served each week on his blog at http://barnandtable.wordpress. com. Everything is made from scratch from locally sourced ingredients, the atmosphere is casual, and the menu is somewhat upscale.

Kahumana Farm on Oahu, Hawaii, has been using organic and biodynamic methods since the Kahumana community was started in 1977—four distinct campuses on more than 50 acres in the Lualualei Valley. The farm is a place of vocational learning for families transitioning from homelessness, people with disabilities, and youth. It produces a prodigious amount of food, a CSA being just one part of the operation. The on-farm Kahumana Farm Café serves lunch and dinner five days a week, using fruits, vegetables, herbs, eggs, tilapia, and more from the farm. It also provides vocational training in culinary arts and hospitality services for participants in the nonprofit's social programs. A large commercial kitchen on another campus prepares 5,000 organic meals per week to deliver to 35 schools on the west side of Oahu (see pages 384–394 for more information on Kuhumana).

Numerous small farms host multicourse, white-tablecloth dinners out in the field in summer and fall to raise money for special causes, typically related to farming, hunger, or land conservation. Menus pairing local food and wine with top chefs and a farm tour lead to sold-out events. Organizations like **Connecticut Farmland Trust** and **Maine Farmland Trust** each host an annual series of farm dinners, as does the **Chicago Botanic**

Garden, hosting at its fruit and vegetable garden. Farmers and chefs are typically on hand to talk about the food.

Plate & Pitchfork has been handling the logistics of summer dinners at farms in and around Portland, Oregon, for more than a decade. Its 2013 series raised funds for Farmers Ending Hunger, an Oregon nonprofit. The season's proceeds covered the cost of more than one million servings of vegetables for people needing emergency food assistance.

HOMEMADE SALSA

MAKES 2 CUPS

1 cup finely chopped, peeled tomato
½ cup tomato sauce
¼ cup finely chopped yellow or red onion
¼ cup finely chopped green bell pepper
2 tablespoons vinegar
2 cloves garlic, minced
1 to 3 jalapeño peppers (depending on how much heat
    you want in the final salsa), seeded and chopped
½ cup chopped fresh cilantro

Mix all of the ingredients in a glass bowl. Refrigerate until you are ready to serve.

— *Produce for Better Health; Fruits & Veggies—More Matters;
    Centers for Disease Control and Prevention*

Staking tomatoes at Featherstone Farm.

Corn

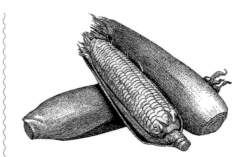

Corn has a long history as a staple food for humans, especially for the peoples of the New World. Also known as maize, corn has evolved into an astonishing number of forms, from plants growing 2 to 20 feet tall and ears measuring anywhere from the length of a thumbnail to 2 feet long. One characteristic common to all of them is the placement of seeds in orderly rows along a central cob.

Maize's value to modern humanity is inestimable. Most of the corn grown in the United States and Canada is used for livestock feed; the making of that ubiquitous sweetener, corn syrup; and for grain alcohol and its sister product, the fuel alternative ethanol.

Sweet corn is a relatively recent phenomenon. The Iroquois were raising it in central New York by the early 1600s, but it was not widely cultivated until after the Civil War. Selective breeding has elevated the sugar levels of this crop to new heights, with "supersweet" and "sugar-enhanced" varieties available with higher sucrose levels than that of standard sweet corn (at the expense of traditional corn flavor, according to some).

HISTORY

Maize is native to the Americas, where it has been cultivated for thousands of years. The earliest maize probably came from Mexico, and pollen has been found in Mexico City dating 60,000 to 80,000 years ago. Native Americans have long cultivated maize, which is one in the famous trio of vegetables (corn, beans, and squash) that contain complementary vegetable proteins. Wherever maize was grown, it became a staple food, and it is no exaggeration to say that the Incan empire was built on the prosperity that corn provided.

When Europeans encountered maize in the New World in the 1500s, they were not so impressed, for its gluten-free seeds lacked the rising and baking qualities of their more familiar grains such as wheat. In many areas, like Russia, where maize was imported in 1921 to ward off starvation, people stubbornly viewed it as food for swine and consumed it only because they had no choice.

NUTRITION

One medium ear of sweet corn offers 80 calories, with lots of dietary fiber, a few grams of protein, and a fair amount of vitamin C, vitamin A (unless it is white corn), potassium, niacin, and folate.

SEASON

Commercially, sweet corn is widely grown and in season year-round. At farmers markets, CSAs, and roadside stands, however, its season is extremely brief, from early July through mid-August.

SELECTION

Try to buy corn with the husk on, and pierce a kernel with a fingernail to see what spurts out. If you can puncture the kernel easily and a trans-

> "Sex is good, but not as good as fresh, sweet corn."
>
> — *Garrison Keillor,*
> *American humorist*

lucent, milky juice emerges, the corn is likely to be fresh. If you have a hard time piercing the kernel, and little or no juice comes out, pass it up for a better, more youthful ear. Both the husks and tassel should be light green and moist, not dried out, brown, or mushy.

STORAGE

Cook your corn promptly; its sugars start converting to starch as soon as the ears are picked, although the newer supersweet hybrids may retain their sweetness for several days. Always refrigerate your corn until you are ready to cook it; this chilling slows down the sugar conversion. Keep the husks on to retain freshness.

TRIMMING AND CLEANING

If you are preparing the ears for boiling, peel back the husks like a banana, pulling off the silks as you go. Then break off the whole kit and caboodle along with its stalk as close to the end of the ear as possible. You can rinse the ear under running water or wipe it with a damp paper towel to help clear off any remaining silks. Corn destined for the barbecue grill should stay protected in its husks.

There are so many ways to use fresh, cut-off-the-cob corn kernels. After removing the husks and silks, cut the skinny stalk as close to the end of the ear as possible. Stand the ear of corn on its cut end (it should be pretty flat and stable). Use a sharp knife to cut down the length of the ear, slicing off several rows of kernels at a time. Rotate the ear until it's bare. This method works equally well with raw or cooked corn.

STEAMING AND BOILING

Steam or boil corn for as little time as possible to maintain that crisp sweetness characteristic of this summer treat. To steam, place shucked whole or half ears in a steamer and cook, covered, for 6 to 10 minutes.

To boil, place the ears in a large pot of boiling water, add a spoonful of sugar if desired (but no salt, which toughens corn), and boil for 3 to 7 minutes, depending on the size of the ears. Drain and serve immediately.

STIR-FRYING AND SAUTÉING

Use either fresh or frozen corn kernels in stir-fries or sautéed dishes, adding them in the last 3 minutes of the cooking time to preserve their texture and flavor.

GRILLING

You can make delicious corn on the cob on the grill. Pull back the husks, but do not remove them. Remove and discard the silks, and then soak the whole cobs in a pot of cold water for 15 minutes. Preheat the grill to a medium temperature. Remove the corn from the water, shake off the excess, and brush the kernels with olive oil. Add whatever seasonings you desire. Then reposition the husks over the kernels and tie each ear with a piece of loose husk or cotton twine. Place the prepared ears on the grill over medium heat, turning every 2 minutes. After a couple of turns, place the corn on indirect heat or on the top shelf of your grill and close the cover. Allow the corn to slowly roast for another 15 minutes. The corn is done when the pierced kernels squirt a sweet liquid. The kernels will be lightly charred or brown in spots—this is perfectly normal.

MICROWAVING

Rinse the shucked ears and wrap each one in a damp paper towel. Microwave on high power for 3 to 4 minutes. Then turn the cobs over and microwave an additional 3 to 4 minutes, depending on how tender you want them.

- 1 ear = 2 to 3 minutes
- 2 ears = 3 to 4 minutes
- 4 ears = 8 to 10 minutes
- 2 cups kernels = 3 minutes

BLANCHING AND FREEZING

To prepare corn for freezing, it should be blanched first, preferably in a 12- to 15-quart pot. Blanching times will vary, depending on the thickness of the cob. Blanch several cobs at a time in boiling water for 4 to 6 minutes. (Some supersweet varieties require only a 4-minute blanching.) Then submerge the ears immediately in ice water for about 20 minutes to stop the cooking process and allow the cobs to cool.

You can either freeze the corn while it is still on the cob or remove the kernels first. Place the corn in zipper-lock freezer or vacuum food sealer-type bags, or freezer containers, and squeeze out any excess air. For the best flavor, frozen corn should be used within 3 months, but it will keep for up to 1 year at 0°F.

EQUIVALENTS, MEASURES, AND SERVINGS

- 2 medium ears, kernels scraped = 1¼ cups kernels

COMPLEMENTARY HERBS, SEASONINGS, AND FOODS

Bacon, basil, bell pepper, black pepper, butter, cayenne pepper, chiles, cream, cumin, curry powder, dill, green beans, hazelnuts, lima beans, lime juice, lobster, Old Bay seasoning, onions, paprika, parsley, peas, pepper, salt, seafood, seasoned salts, sugar, tarragon, thyme, tomatoes, walnuts, zucchini.

SERVING SUGGESTIONS

- It's awfully hard to beat simple, freshly boiled corn on the cob served with nothing but butter and salt and pepper. An interesting variation is corn on the cob with thick cream, ground chile powder, and lime juice.
- A popular street food in Japan is fresh sweet corn on the cob grilled with miso, butter, and soy sauce.
- If you actually get tired of fresh corn on the cob or find that you have a lot of corn on your hands, try making something sweet and creamy, like corn pudding, corn au gratin, scalloped corn, creamed corn, or corn soufflé.
- Combine sweet corn kernels and lima beans with bits of onion and bacon for that traditional American dish, succotash.
- In a Boston baked beans recipe, substitute fresh sweet corn kernels for the beans.
- Barbecue corn on the grill, along with potatoes, onions, and meat.
- Strip off the kernels from older corn and use them in chowders, soups, stews, omelets, quiches, fried rice, and pancake batter.
- Add fresh, whole kernels to cornbread batter.

Farms That Sell Nursery Plants, Seeds, and Services

Martha Wagner

One of the many ways smaller family farms are generating income today is through growing plants for sale to nurseries and home gardeners, and providing landscaping services, workshops, and more.

Gardens of Eagan (see page 564) in Minnesota has grown its own transplants since 1974. It prides itself on having the Midwest's only certified-organic plug program—plugs being field-ready young plants raised in small, individual cells, ready to be transplanted into containers or gardens. Hybrid and heirloom veggie favorites and culinary herb varieties are what the farm is best known for. Plants are sold through the farm's website and at several farmers markets.

Crown Point Ecology Center in Ohio sells organic plant starts at a weekend sale for gardeners every May that includes heirloom and hybrid varieties. Its Slow Food USA's Ark of Taste heirloom breeds are selected for their taste, beauty, and overall contribution to American cuisine and culture. Also offered are perennial native prairie flower seedlings that are not easily found anywhere else. After the sale, Crown Point donates leftover plants to not-for-profit gardens associated with schools, social service agencies, and community gardens in low-income neighborhoods.

Appalachian Seeds Farm and Nursery, a sustainable family farm with a produce and flower CSA in North Carolina, has been selling certified-organic, heirloom tomato seeds and plants since 1998. It also sells medicinal and culinary herbs, a diverse selection of heirloom vegetable plants, and open-pollinated bedding plants mainly to regional garden centers and organically minded stores. Edible landscaping plants include elderberries, blueberries, grapes, and figs in gallon containers. The farm also generates income through workshops for gardeners as well as landscape consultations and design and installation services.

A plant nursery at **Shambala Permaculture Farm** on Camano Island in Washington State sells edible plants and trees, perennial vegetables, and herbs. It also serves as a go-to resource for permaculture education: workshops, permaculture design certification programs, food forest garden and farm animal tours, and edible landscaping and permaculture design services. The farm has shifted from selling produce through a CSA to selling through the Puget Sound Food Hub, an online ordering system enabling restaurants and institutions to place a single weekly order from multiple sustainable local farms. Its produce is also available at its café, Shambala Ancient Grain Bakery and Farm Fresh Bistro in nearby Sedro Wooley.

Some of the farms featured in this book have thriving seed businesses, too. **Nash's Organic Produce** in Sequim, Washington, has been preserving and selling seed for years. Owner Nash Huber believes that seed saving is a necessary skill for every organic farmer. He started seed breeding on a modest scale in the 1970s with Forest Shomer of Abundant Life Seed Company in nearby Port Townsend, Washington. Shomer was interested in "wild crafting," or collecting wild seed for sale. Huber helped him fill an order for dandelion seed by putting together a special harvesting machine and later started breeding an overwintering cauliflower and a heritage variety of cabbage.

Abundant Life was eventually sold to the **Organic Seed Alliance (OSA)**, which works closely with Huber and his crew to develop new varieties and maintain existing ones. Nash's grows seed for sever-

- If the corn is really fresh and just-picked, try enjoying a tender, sweet ear raw.
- Corn soup can be a nice change, served either hot or chilled. Try flavorings like vanilla, pancetta, chipotle chiles, paprika, feta cheese, and bacon.
- Sprinkle corn kernels in salads; they go especially well with basil, blue cheese, tomatoes, and red onions.
- Try making a soothing sweet, hot corn porridge that is an adaptation of the Brazilian corn dish *canjica*, made with milk, sugar, cinnamon, cloves, coconut or coconut milk, and sweetened condensed milk.

CORN CHOWDER
SERVES 6

Source Note: This is a lower-calorie version of the traditional corn chowder that is usually made with lots of cream and butter. If you are on a sodium-restricted diet, omit the salt.

2 pounds white potatoes, diced
1 bay leaf
4 cups water
3 teaspoons margarine or butter
3 medium onions, chopped
4 ribs celery, chopped
2 teaspoons cumin seeds
3 tablespoons all-purpose flour
1 teaspoon chopped fresh sage, or ½ teaspoon crushed dried sage
½ teaspoon crushed white pepper
2 cups skim milk
1⅓ cups cooked fresh or frozen whole-kernel corn
Salt
Parsley, for garnish (optional)
Red bell pepper slices, for garnish (optional)

1. In a large saucepan, combine the potatoes, bay leaf, and water; bring to a boil. Cover and cook for 15 minutes, or until the potatoes are tender. Discard the bay leaf. Drain the potatoes, reserving the liquid. Set both aside.

2. In the same saucepan, melt the margarine. Add the onions, celery, and cumin seeds; cook until the onions are tender. Stir in the flour, sage, and white pepper. Stir in enough reserved potato liquid to make a smooth paste, then stir in the remaining potato liquid and potatoes, and heat through. Stir in the milk and corn, season to taste with salt, and heat thoroughly.

3. If desired, top with snipped parsley and bell pepper slices.

— *Produce for Better Health; Fruits & Veggies—More Matters; Centers for Disease Control and Prevention*

Raw Corn Summer Salad with Apples and Jicama

SERVES 4 AS A SIDE DISH

Author Note: We don't often think of eating corn raw but—especially in the height of summer when quality is high and quantity abounds—it can be a sublimely sweet, crisp, juicy treat. This salad abounds with crunchy textures, contrasting flavors, and wonderful color. Besides serving it as is, you can vary the presentation (and use more items from your summer CSA box) by julienning several leaves of leaf lettuce (dark red varieties such as Red Oak or Lolla Rossa are great), dress them lightly with oil and vinegar, and make a bed for the corn salad on individual plates.

Jicama is a root vegetable that resembles a turnip-shaped potato. Its juicy, creamy white flesh has a delicate, sweet flavor and a lovely, crisp texture that resembles a water chestnut or raw potato. It is usually eaten raw in salads or with salsa, chile powder, lime juice, or other seasoning.

DRESSING

¼ cup plain yogurt
2 to 3 teaspoons fresh lime juice or apple cider vinegar
2 teaspoons honey
Salt and freshly ground pepper

SALAD

2 large ears fresh corn, kernels stripped off (refer to the Trimming and Cleaning instructions on page 166)
½ small jicama
1 sweet-tart apple (preferably organic), skin left on
⅓ cup walnuts or pecans, lightly toasted
2 teaspoons chopped fresh tarragon or basil
Tarragon or basil sprigs, for garnish

1. To make the dressing, whisk the yogurt, lime juice, and honey in a small bowl until smooth (if you're using creamed or semisolid honey, melt it in the microwave before whisking). Add a bit of salt and pepper; taste and adjust the seasoning.

2. Peel the jicama, being sure to get the thin layer of stringy flesh off as you go (it's right below the tan skin). Cut the jicama into ¼-inch slices, then cut each slice into small cubes.

3. Stand the unpeeled apple on its end and cut it into ¼-inch slices, as you did with the jicama. Cut each slice into thin strips so that you end up with apple matchsticks.

4. Put the corn kernels, jicama, apple, walnuts, and tarragon into a medium bowl. Drizzle most of the dressing over the ingredients and toss gently. Add the remainder of the dressing if you'd like more. Spoon the salad onto individual plates and garnish with a few herb sprigs.

— Lisa Gordanier and Mi Ae Lipe

al companies and for the Family Farmers Seed Cooperative.

Adaptive Seeds, founded in 2009, grows certified-organic seed at **Open Oak Farm** in Sweet Home, Oregon. The farm grows grains, beans, and winter vegetables for its CSA. Adaptive Seeds is one grower in the **Seed Ambassadors Project**, a small group of Oregon-based seed stewards committed to increasing the diversity of locally adapted varieties in this bioregion. Some members have spent several winters traveling through Europe and Asia sharing seed, collecting hundreds of varieties of food plants, and teaching seed-saving skills. The Seed Grower Network includes a number of local organic farms, such as **Uprising Organics** and **Wild Garden Seed** at **Gathering Together Farm**.

CORN SALSA

Source Note: This is a great summer dish for all those family potlucks. Feel free to vary the proportions of any of the ingredients listed here, based on what's in your CSA box or your garden. This combo works great, but there are almost endless possibilities for making fresh, colorful salsas.

2 tablespoons good-quality olive oil
1 tablespoon red wine vinegar (or use fresh lime juice)
1 cup grilled corn, removed from the cob
2 grilled serrano peppers, chopped fine
1 large ripe tomato, diced
Fresh basil leaves, chopped roughly
Freshly ground black pepper
Salt

Whisk the olive oil slowly into the vinegar. Add everything else. Mix and refrigerate until well chilled. This salsa is great on many things (with chips, pita, hummus, grilled veggies, and meat) or all by itself.

— *Amy Chen, Featherstone Farm CSA member*

FLAVORED BUTTERS FOR FRESH CORN

Source Note: It can be fun for you and your guests or kids to create flavored butters in which to roll delicious, fresh corn on the cob! And of course, these are delectable on all sorts of other vegetables too—potatoes, carrots, brassicas, parsnips, artichokes, green beans—the possibilities are endless.

The only slightly technical point to remember is to buy good-quality, salted butter and have it at room temperature before mixing it with your seasonings. (If you try melting the butter and then combining it with the flavorings, the butter will separate into an oily portion and a milky liquid portion—not so pretty.) Here are a few of our favorite combinations.

CURRY-LIME BUTTER

Curry seasonings are dynamite with sweet corn! Since curry powder—actually a mix of typical Indian spices, not a single spice in its own right—varies a lot from brand to brand, add the amount that seems right for you. A little finely chopped cilantro will boost flavor and color as well.

4 tablespoons (½ cube) salted butter
1 teaspoon curry powder
1½ teaspoons freshly squeezed lime juice

CHIPOTLE CHILE BUTTER

Look in the Latin American or international section of your grocery store for small cans of chipotle chiles in adobo sauce. These are jalapeños that have been smoked and processed to a soft, unctuous consistency. They're usually a little spicy-hot, and their smokiness is a perfect partner with corn—kind of like grilled corn without the fuss!

4 tablespoons (½ cube) salted butter
1 tablespoon chopped chipotle chiles in adobo sauce

MISO BUTTER

Yes, even Japanese soybean paste can complement the sweet, nutty flavors of fresh corn! Use mild, white miso paste (as opposed to hatcho or red miso, both darker and stronger-tasting varieties); you'll be intrigued by its round, mushroom-like taste.

4 tablespoons (½ cube) salted butter
2 teaspoons white miso
Dash of soy sauce (optional)

— *Lisa Gordanier*

SWEET CORN PUDDING   SERVES 4

½ cup milk
½ cup heavy cream
½ cup shredded Cheddar cheese
½ teaspoon cayenne pepper
2 eggs, beaten
Salt and freshly ground black pepper
Kernels scraped off the cobs of 6 medium ears of sweet corn
Crispy fried onion rings

1. Heat the oven to 350°F. Butter a medium casserole dish.

2. In a large bowl, combine the milk, cream, cheese, cayenne, eggs, salt, and pepper. Add the corn and mix well.

3. Pour into a casserole dish and bake for 35 minutes, or until set and golden brown.

4. Let cool slightly, then top with the crispy onion rings and serve.

— *Marybeth, Foodista.com*

Books

Vegetarian Cooking for Everyone
Deborah Madison,
Broadway Books, 1997.

Vegetables from Amaranth to
Zucchini: The Essential Reference
Elizabeth Schneider,
William Morrow Cookbooks, 2001.

Uncommon Fruits and Vegetables:
A Commonsense Guide
Elizabeth Schneider,
William Morrow Cookbooks, 2010.

The New Enchanted Broccoli Forest
Mollie Katzen,
Ten Speed Press, 2000.

The Farmer's Market Cookbook:
Seasonal Dishes Made from Nature's
Freshest Ingredients
Richard Ruben,
The Lyons Press, 2000.

Northwest Essentials: Cooking with
Ingredients That Define
a Region's Cuisine
Greg Atkinson,
Sasquatch Books, 2010.

The Renee's Garden Cookbook
Renee Shepherd,
Shepherd Publishing, 2014.

HEATHER'S QUINOA SAUTÉ

SERVES 6

2 cups uncooked quinoa
4 cups water
1 teaspoon sea salt
2 to 3 tablespoons extra-virgin olive oil
1 shallot, minced
1 cup corn, fresh or frozen
1½ cups finely chopped kale, spinach or other hearty green
2 cups extra-firm tofu, browned in a skillet a bit
⅓ cup basil pesto (homemade or purchased)
⅓ cup pumpkin seeds, toasted
¼ cup roasted tomatoes or chopped sun-dried tomatoes
Cherry tomatoes, for garnish

1. To cook the quinoa: Rinse the quinoa in a fine-meshed strainer. In a medium saucepan, heat the quinoa with the water and salt until boiling. Reduce the heat and simmer until the water is absorbed and the quinoa fluffs up, about 15 minutes. The quinoa is done when you can see the curlicue in each grain; it should be tender, with a bit of pop to each bite. Drain any extra water and set the quinoa aside.

2. In a big skillet or pot, heat the olive oil and a bit more salt over medium-high heat. Stir in the shallot and cook for 1 or 2 minutes. Stir in the quinoa and corn and cook until hot and sizzling. Add the kale and then the tofu, cooking until the tofu is heated through. Remove the skillet from the heat and stir in the pesto and pumpkin seeds. Mix well so the pesto is spread throughout the mixture. Add the roasted tomatoes.

3. Turn everything out onto a platter and top with the cherry tomatoes.

— *Featherstone Farm, Rushford, Minnesota*

Cucumbers

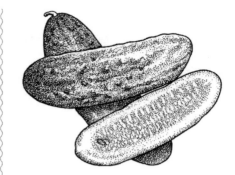

The Cucurbits are a large, sprawling family that includes pumpkins, squashes, melons, gourds, and yes, cucumbers. The cucumber is beloved the world over for its cool, crisp, thirst-quenching flesh and clean flavor when raw and for its capacity to absorb salt, vinegar, water, and spices as a delectable pickle.

Cucumbers come in two major varieties: pickling and slicing. Pickling types include the tiny gherkin and the French cornichon, as well as the American dill; all have skins with warts or spines.

Slicing varieties are bigger, ranging about 8 to 15 inches in length, and have smooth, dark-green skins. Older American varieties of slicing cucumbers used to have rather tough, thick skins full of spines; most modern varieties today lack the spines and are considered more digestible (or "burpless") than their cousins of yesteryear.

It is well worth venturing from the typical bland, thick-skinned American slicers (which were bred for optimal shipping) and trying their Armenian, Middle Eastern, Oriental, and European greenhouse counterparts, which practically explode with flavor and crunch in comparison. These cukes are often narrower, feature thinner ribbed skins, and have flesh that is far less watery and more strongly perfumed. Try these personality-filled guys and you may never want to eat another blah American cucumber again.

HISTORY

Cucumbers are believed to be native to India, although seeds have been found near Thailand that carbon-date to nearly 10,000 years ago. Cucumbers were brought from Asia to Europe, where the Romans became particularly fond of them, even soaking the seeds in honeyed wine in the hope of sweetening the resulting fruit. The Spaniards brought cucumbers to America, where they were received so enthusiastically by some of the indigenous peoples that the Pueblo Indians were falsely reported as using it as a native food.

NUTRITION

Cucumbers are lower in nutrients than many vegetables, but they do contain some vitamin C, dietary fiber, potassium, and magnesium. Cucumbers also contain significant amounts of silica, water, and caffeic acid, all of which benefit the skin—one reason why cucumber slices are often recommended for treating swollen eyes and topical burns. A ½-cup serving contains only 8 calories.

SEASON

Commercially, cucumbers are widely grown and in season year-round. The tastiest specimens at farmers markets and CSAs typically appear from early summer to early fall.

SELECTION

Cucumbers should be uniformly firm with no soft spots or shriveled ends. Yellowing cucumbers (except lemon cucumbers) may be too old, and large cukes may not have the best flavor. Winter is also a problematic time for commercially grown cukes—watch out for soft specimens that may have been slightly frozen and will deteriorate quickly into mush.

STORAGE

Supermarket cucumbers are usually coated with a food-grade wax that allows them to be stored for about 1 week in the refrigerator vegetable crisper. Unwaxed cucumbers should be used within a few days.

TRIMMING AND CLEANING

Whether to peel a cucumber depends on your personal preference and whether it is waxed or not. Supermarket cucumbers usually have a thin, edible wax coating, but if you don't enjoy ingesting unknown substances, you should peel them first. An advantage to obtaining unwaxed or organic cucumbers is that no peeling is necessary, so you also get the benefit of the nutrient-rich skin (in any case, be sure to wash them well before consuming). You may want to peel unwaxed cucumbers anyway if the skin is tough or bitter, or if the skin's presence would detract from its texture (such as in thinly sliced cucumbers for tea sandwiches).

STEAMING AND BOILING

Sliced cucumbers can be steamed for 5 to 8 minutes, or until just tender. Boiling cucumbers makes them soggy and is not recommended.

STIR-FRYING AND SAUTÉING

Although we tend to think of cucumbers as exclusively a vegetable to be eaten raw or pickled, cucumbers do respond well to a light, quick sauté in butter or olive oil for a few minutes, and flavored with fresh herbs.

MICROWAVING

Cut cucumbers into slices or chunks and microwave on high power for 7 to 9 minutes, depending on the thickness of the pieces.

BLANCHING AND FREEZING

Because of their high water content, cucumbers should not be frozen, or they will turn mushy.

MEASURES AND EQUIVALENTS

- 1 medium cucumber = 1 cup chopped
- 2 medium cucumbers = 1 pound = 4 cups cubed = 3 cups sliced = 2 cups shredded
- 1 pound peeled, seeded, sliced, salted, drained, pressed cucumber = about 1⅓ cups

COMPLEMENTARY HERBS, SEASONINGS, AND FOODS

Apples, butter, buttermilk, cayenne pepper, chervil, chile, chives, cilantro, cream, cream cheese, cumin, curry powder, dill, fromage blanc, garlic salt, hummus, lemons, lima beans, lime juice, lovage, melon, mint, Old Bay seasoning, paprika, parsley, pears, peas, pepper, quinoa, rice, salmon, salt, smoked fish, sour cream, sugar, tarragon, watermelon, yogurt.

Cooking Tip

You can revive most of the crispness of a wilted cuke by soaking it in salted ice water for 1 to 2 hours.

SERVING SUGGESTIONS

- Cooked cucumbers go well with white-fleshed fish or diced pork; cut them into strips or cubes and sauté in butter until tender.

- For an unusual alternative to zucchini, try thin-slicing cucumbers and deep-frying them.

- Make little sandwiches by cutting cucumbers into ¼-inch-thick slices and pressing deviled ham or chicken spread between them.

- Add bits of diced cucumber, tomato, and onion to a chilled gazpacho soup just before serving.

- Make fun cucumber boats by splitting a large cucumber lengthwise, then filling it with cheese, onions, or meat, and broiling until lightly browned.

- Place a few slices of cucumber in a glass of ice water for a refreshing drink.

- The traditional English cucumber tea sandwich is made with peeled, thinly sliced cucumber on white bread spread with the finest sweet butter you can afford, and with the crusts cut off.

- Puree cucumber in a blender, then press the water out for drinking or adding to a summer spritzer or cocktail; it adds a refreshing flavor to chilled beverages.

- Liven up the usual carrots and celery on the relish tray by adding cucumber sticks.

- Combine diced cucumbers, sugar snap peas, and mint with Italian dressing or sour cream for a refreshing summer salad.

- Cucumbers and ginger are an irresistible, zingy combination that is refreshing on a sweltering day.

- Make a delicious cold, creamy cucumber soup with herbs. Julia Child has a fantastic recipe in her classic *French Chef Cookbook*.

- Cucumber—cooked or raw—pairs well with delicate seafood like scallops, octopus, lobster, and crab.

- Cucumber and fruit are unsung couples in the kitchen. Try apples, pears, watermelon, and cantaloupe.

BARELY PICKLED CUCUMBERS   MAKES ABOUT 3 CUPS

Author Note: Kids love these crisp, salty, slightly acid, and yet sweet cucumber slices, which make excellent refreshers on hot summer days. You can make this recipe with whatever ingredient proportions best tickle your taste buds.

Several large cucumbers
3 parts water
1 part white wine vinegar or apple cider vinegar
Sea salt, to taste
Sugar, to taste
Freshly ground black pepper
Generous amount of fresh dill, slightly crushed

1. Fill a large container that has a cover about half full of water. Add the vinegar, salt, sugar, pepper, and dill in the proportions desired (taste a few times to check acidity, sweetness, and saltiness).

2. Wash and dry the cucumbers (peeling is optional). Slice the cucumbers as thinly as possible and add to the brine.

3. Cover and refrigerate. Chill for at least 1 hour before serving. These cucumbers taste better on the second day, and will keep for 3 to 5 days. As you use up the slices, you can add fresh cucumber to the brine.

✒ Variation: For spicier cucumbers, add 2 or 3 slices of jalapeño pepper.

— *Mi Ae Lipe*

AGUA DE PEPINO (CUCUMBER LIMEADE) · MAKES 2 LARGE GLASSES

Source Note: This is a very refreshing drink. You can add a section of ripe pineapple as an alternative to using so much sugar.

> 4 cucumbers, cut into chunks
> 2 apples, cored
> 3 to 4 mint sprigs
> Juice of 2 to 3 limes
> Sugar (about 3 tablespoons is enough unless you like it sweeter)
> Ice
> Mint sprigs, for garnish
> Cucumber slices, for garnish

Put the cucumber, apples, and mint through a juicer. Add the remaining ingredients, and blend well. Pour over ice and garnish with mint sprigs and cucumber slices.

— *Chef Gary Masterson, Fire and Ice Café, Midleton, County Cork, Ireland*

VEGETABLE SUBS · MAKES 2 SANDWICHES

Source Note: Depending on what part of the country you live in, this popular vegetarian sandwich could be called a sub, a hero, or a grinder. Whatever its name, it is always made with a long sandwich-bread roll. In this case, it is stuffed with salad vegetables and sliced cheese.

This delicious sandwich has become a staple in my house because I can easily keep the rolls in the freezer to have on hand, and my vegetable bin always contains some lettuce and other salad ingredients. Don't hesitate to improvise here. You can include sliced olives, roasted red peppers, scallions, hot peppers, sprouts, mushrooms, and your favorite cheese.

Books

Perfect Recipes for Having People Over
Pam Anderson,
Rux Martin/Houghton Mifflin Harcourt, 2005.

Sacramental Magic In a Small-town Cafe: Recipes and Stories from Brother Juniper's Cafe
Peter Reinhart,
Addison Wesley, 1994.

The Greenmarket Cookbook
Joel Patraker and Joan Schwartz,
Viking Penguin, 2000.

Ottolenghi: The Cookbook
Yotam Ottolenghi and Sami Tamimi,
Ten Speed Press, 2013.

The Abascal Way Cookbook
Kathy Abascal,
Tigana Press, 2011.

2 submarine (grinder) rolls, sliced horizontally almost all of the
    way through
2 tablespoons mayonnaise (see Variations note below)
Freshly ground black pepper
4 lettuce leaves
4 thin slices tomato
2 thin slices red onion
4 thin rings green or red bell pepper
8 thin slices cucumber
6 thin slices smoked Gouda cheese (see Variations note below)

1.   Spread the bread halves with the mayonnaise, then season generously
    with pepper.

2.   Divide the ingredients in half. Layer them in each sandwich and close
    tightly, pressing down on the bread gently to help it adhere. Slice
    each sandwich in half.

Variations: Smoked cheese gives this sandwich a rich, dynamic flavor
that is hauntingly good. Other cheeses will also work well, such as
Muenster, provolone, Monterey Jack with jalapeño peppers, and Swiss.
Vinaigrette dressing is a wonderful substitute for the mayonnaise.

Cooking Note: If you are going to pack these sandwiches for lunch or
a picnic, wrap the tomato slices separately and then place them in the
sandwiches just before eating.

— *Jeanne Lemlin,* Vegetarian Classics

"Seventy years ago, farmers
were seduced into going for
mechanization and, later, the
use of chemicals, because these
practices gave good returns.
No one could have foreseen
the damage that this approach
to growing food would wreak."

— *Bryan Lynas,*
science writer and farmer

SAUTÉED EASTERN CUCUMBER SLICES   SERVES 2 TO 3

Source Note: Oriental, Middle Eastern, and Armenian cucumbers
demonstrate their bright coloring, sweet and green flavor, and solid crunch
when merely sliced, salted, and quick-sautéed. Both the look and taste suggest
the very best of cuke and zuke—a superior quick-cooked side dish for seafood,
poultry, veal, or pilafs.

¾ to 1 pound slim Oriental, Middle Eastern, or Armenian cucumbers
½ teaspoon kosher salt
1 tablespoon butter
Chervil leaves, snipped dill, and chives (optional)

1. Rinse the cucumbers. Cut into ¼-inch slices. Sprinkle with salt and toss. Let them stand 15 to 30 minutes, as convenient.

2. Rinse the cucumber slices in a sieve, bouncing so all are well rinsed. Spread out on a towel. Pat dry.

3. Melt the butter over moderate heat in a skillet large enough to hold the slices in a single layer. Add the cucumbers and toss often, shaking the pan until the slices are lightly speckled with gold and the raw taste disappears, about 3 minutes or so, or somewhat longer for the Armenian type.

4. Sprinkle sparingly with the optional herbs. Serve hot.

— *Elizabeth Schneider,* Vegetables from Amaranth to Zucchini: The Essential Reference

. . . .

SEEDLESS CUCUMBERS, YOGURT, MINT, AND GARLIC SALAD

SERVES 4 TO 6

2 European cucumbers or 3 medium regular Persian cucumbers
1 clove garlic mashed with ½ teaspoon salt, minced
1 pint nonfat plain yogurt
2 to 3 tablespoons fresh chopped mint, or 1 tablespoon dried mint

Peel and slice or dice the cucumbers. Mash the garlic with salt and add to the yogurt. Add the cucumbers and mint to the yogurt, and gently stir until the cucumbers are well-dispersed throughout the salad.

— *From Produce for Better Health; Fruits & Veggies—More Matters; Centers for Disease Control and Prevention*

Dill

ANETHUM GRAVEOLENS

Familiar to most of us as the seasoning of the ubiquitous pickle bearing its name, dill is a much-loved fixture in a number of world cuisines, particularly Polish, Russian, and Scandinavian. An annual member of the Apiaceae or Umbelliferae family, which includes such familiar plants as Queen Anne's lace, carrot, celery, fennel, and parsnip, dill is grown for its feathery, caraway-tasting leaves in the spring and early summer, and harvested for its seeds in late summer. Its name comes from the Old Norse word dylla, *meaning to soothe or lull, and the herb has long been used as a digestive tonic and for its calming effects.*

HISTORY

Dill hails from Asia and southern Europe, where the Romans reveled in its springy, ferny fronds, even making wreaths of it to wear at their feasts. In the Middle Ages, dill was thought to protect from the effects of witchcraft. Beverages made from dill seeds were drunk, and charms created from the leaves were worn as an antidote to spells.

Dill has been valued for its cleansing and digestive properties for centuries. In America during the 1700s and 1800s, both dill and fennel seeds were given to children to chew on during church services to keep them calm and quiet, hence the moniker "meetin' seeds."

NUTRITION

Dill has long been used as medicine; it contains carvone, which relieves intestinal gas. The seeds are high in calcium, with 1 tablespoon containing the equivalent of a third of a cup of milk. Fresh dill (sometimes called dill weed) is also a decent source of manganese and iron. A single cup of fresh dill sprigs contains 4 calories.

SEASON

Commercially, dill is widely grown and in season year-round. You'll find it at its best at farmers markets and CSAs from spring through early fall.

SELECTION

Dill weed should be bright green and fresh, not wilted or yellowish. Avoid slimy, yellowing, or tired-looking dill.

STORAGE

The leaves wilt quickly upon harvesting, but this will not affect their flavor. To store, mist the whole stems lightly with a fine spray of water, wrap them loosely in paper towels, place them in a plastic bag, and store in your refrigerator crisper drawer. Dill should last up to 1 week or longer, although its distinctive flavor will fade as it sits. You can also trim the stems, place them in a glass with an inch of cold water, loosely wrap the top with a damp paper towel, and place a plastic bag over the herbal bouquet; store it in the refrigerator.

Cooking Tip

The flavor of dill weed diminishes greatly the longer it is cooked, so add it at the last minute for full flavor and aroma.

TRIMMING AND CLEANING

Dill benefits from a quick rinse under running water. To dry, gently roll up the stems in a paper towel. Then snip or trim sprigs with a pair of kitchen scissors.

BLANCHING AND FREEZING

Although fresh is always best, the flavor of frozen dill is superior to that of the dried form. Fresh dill sprigs can be frozen for up to 2 months, but their color will darken. To freeze, place the entire stalk with its leaves still attached in a zipper-lock freezer or vacuum food sealer-type bag or freezer container. Squeeze out the excess air. To use, simply snip off the leaves.

Or you can snip off the leaves, spread them out on a cookie sheet to dry overnight, then package them for the freezer the next day. They do not need to be thawed before using.

Another terrific way to freeze dill is to chop it finely and place some in ice cube trays. Add a little water, oil, or butter, and freeze. To thaw, simply pop out a few cubes into a strainer and let the liquid melt away, or you can just drop them frozen into sauces, soups, stews, casseroles, and other cooked dishes. Dill frozen this way will keep for up to 1 year at 0°F.

DRYING

You can easily dry dill; however the dried herb contains only a fraction of the flavor of its fresh counterpart and is vastly inferior for cooking.

If you want to dry dill, tie fresh sprigs into a bunch and hang in a cool, dark place with good ventilation. You can cover the bunches with small paper bags to keep dust off them, but make sure the bags have adequate holes for proper ventilation. Once the dill has dried, seal the bunches tightly in a container with a lid or a zipper-lock plastic bag and store away from light and heat.

You can oven-dry dill by spreading a single layer of cut-up sprigs on a cookie sheet and placing it in a warm (up to 180°F) oven for up to 2 hours, checking the herbs every 30 minutes or so for doneness.

A microwave oven can also be used to dry small quantities of dill. Place a single layer of sprigs in the microwave between paper towels. Heat for 1 minute over high power. If the dill is not brittle and dry when removed, repeat the microwave drying for 30 seconds more. (Be aware that the heat generated during microwaving removes not only moisture but also some of the oils, so these herbs may not have as intense a flavor as herbs dried by other methods.) Keep dried dill in a cool, dark place away from light and heat, and use within 6 to 9 months.

MEASURES AND EQUIVALENTS

- 3 teaspoons chopped fresh dill = 1 teaspoon dried

COMPLEMENTARY HERBS, SEASONINGS, AND FOODS

Beets, bread, cabbage, carrots, chicken, cream cheese, cream sauces, cucumbers, dips, dressings, eggs, fish, garbanzos (chickpeas), hazelnuts, lamb, mild cheeses, pickles, potatoes, salads, salmon, scallops, seafood, soups, sour cream, tomatoes, veal, vinegar.

SERVING SUGGESTIONS

- Snip dill sprigs and add to your favorite tossed green salad for extra flavor.

- Make dill butter by adding ¼ cup minced fresh dill to ½ cup softened butter. Mix well, cover, and refrigerate at least 2 hours before using to let the flavors blend.

- Dill is a vital ingredient in the beloved Swedish dish gravlax. Fresh, raw salmon fillets are layered with generous amounts of salt, sugar, and dill weed, and cured for several days.

- Snip bits of dill over summer potato, beet, and tomato soups for a zingy flavor.

- Add freshly minced dill weed to chilled tomato juice.

- Stir minced dill weed and other fresh herbs into cottage cheese.

- When both the cucumbers and dill are overflowing from the garden or your CSA box, the solution is obvious—make pickles!

- Dill has a natural affinity for citrus. Try finely chopped dill in a refreshing summer salad with oranges, or combine dill with fresh lemon juice as a dressing for vegetables.

- Dill and yogurt are primary ingredients in the ubiquitous creamy Mediterranean tzatziki sauce, which is served with grilled meats and as a dip.

- Enliven hot cooked cabbage by adding a generous sprinkle of chopped fresh dill.

- Make an interesting dish by combining a couple of members of the Umbelliferae family—dill with fennel, dill with carrots, or dill with parsnips.

- Fresh dill goes well with eggs and cheese. Try it in scrambled eggs or frittatas.

- An unexpected use for dill is in savory baked goods like cheese biscuits or scones.

- Dill is quite versatile in creamy dips and spreads of all kinds. Use your imagination—yogurt, cream cheese, Boursin, sour cream, goat cheese—and don't be afraid to try it with other fresh herbs on hand. Serve with raw vegetables and high-quality crackers or breads.

DILLED VEGETABLE-BARLEY SOUP   SERVES 6

Source Note: This soup tastes best the day after it is made. However, as it sits around, the barley expands, so it usually needs a little additional water upon reheating. Adjust the seasonings, if necessary.

½ cup uncooked pearl barley
5½ cups water, divided
2 to 3 tablespoons butter or vegetable oil
2 cups minced onion
1½ to 2 teaspoons salt
1 bay leaf
2 medium carrots, diced
1 medium rib celery, minced
1 pound mushrooms, chopped
6 tablespoons dry white wine (optional)
1 tablespoon fresh lemon juice

agriculture for new entrants, welcome them to our community, and build cultural solidarity for this new farmers movement. We are deeply committed to the rebuilding of rural economies through sustainable agriculture, to small business entrepreneurship, and to teamwork."

The Greenhorns produced an eponymous documentary in 2009, and in 2012 three founding members edited a book of member essays titled Greenhorns: 50 Dispatches from the New Farmers' Movement (Storey Publishing). One of the three editors, Severine von Tscharner Fleming, is the cofounder of **Farm Hack**, an online, open-source platform for appropriate and affordable farm tools and technologies, as well as an adviser to the Agrarian Trust, a new organization focused on land access for next-generation farmers.

The **National Young Farmers Coalition**, founded in 2009, has chapters in 25 states and is committed to supporting practices and policies that will sustain young and independent farmers now and in the future.. It's a farmer-led partnership between young farmers and innovative beginning farmer service providers and is fiscally sponsored by **The Center for Rural Affairs.**, a 501(c)(3) nonprofit organization. Guiding principle of NYFC include creating independence for family farms, affordable land for farmers, fair labor practices, apprenticeship farmer education, and diversity of gender, race, and sexual orientation in the farming profession.

3 tablespoons minced fresh dill, or 1 tablespoon dried dill
½ cup minced fresh fennel fronds (optional)
2 large cloves garlic, minced
Freshly ground black pepper

Optional Toppings: Sour cream or yogurt, toasted sunflower seeds, minced fresh parsley, and chives.

1. Place the barley and 1½ cups of the water in a small saucepan. Bring to a boil, cover, and lower the heat to a simmer. Cook about 30 to 40 minutes—until tender.

2. Melt the butter in a soup pot or Dutch oven. Add the onion, salt, and bay leaf, and cook over medium heat until the onion begins to soften (5 to 8 minutes).

3. Add the carrots, celery, and mushrooms, and cook over medium heat, stirring occasionally, for about 10 minutes. Add the remaining 4 cups water, wine, lemon juice, and cooked barley. Lower the heat to a quiet simmer. Cover, and let it bubble peacefully for about 30 minutes. The soup will thicken, and you might want to add more water.

4. Shortly before serving, stir in the dill, fennel, garlic, and black pepper. Taste to adjust the seasonings. Serve hot, with all, some, or none of the optional toppings.

— *Mollie Katzen,* The New Enchanted Broccoli Forest

SALMON, CUCUMBER, AND DILL SALAD   SERVES 4

Source Note: This very summery dish is light and refreshing. The dill complements the rich taste of salmon beautifully.

1 large cucumber, peeled, cut in half lengthwise, seeds scooped out, diced in ½-inch cubes (3 cups)
1 large ripe tomato, seeds and excess pulp removed, diced
1 medium-ripe but firm avocado, diced into ½-inch cubes
2 tablespoons chopped chives
3 medium cloves garlic, pressed
1½ tablespoons chopped fresh dill
2 tablespoons plus 1 tablespoon fresh lemon juice
1 tablespoon extra-virgin olive oil
Salt and cracked black pepper
1½ pounds salmon fillet, cut into 4 pieces, skin and bones removed
½ tablespoon honey
1 tablespoon Dijon mustard

1. Mix together the cucumber, tomato, avocado, chives, garlic, and dill in a bowl and set aside at room temperature.

2. Whisk together the 2 tablespoons lemon juice, olive oil, salt, and pepper in a separate bowl. Toss with the cucumber mix when you are ready to serve.

3. Preheat a stainless steel skillet over medium-high heat for 2 minutes. Rub the salmon fillets with the remaining 1 tablespoon of lemon juice and season them with salt and pepper. Place in the hot pan, bottom side up. Cook for 2 minutes.

4. While the salmon is cooking, mix together the honey and mustard. Turn the salmon and spread the honey mustard over the top of the fish. Continue to cook for another 2 minutes, depending on how thick the salmon is (it should still be pink on the inside). Season with a bit more pepper and set the pan off the heat.

5. Gently toss the lemon dressing with the cucumber mixture. Divide it between 4 plates and serve with the salmon alongside.

— *World's Healthiest Foods*

CARAMELIZED CABBAGE

SERVES 4

¼ cup (½ stick) butter
1 large onion, sliced
1 bunch dill, chopped
1 small cabbage, cored and sliced
Salt and freshly ground black pepper
1 bunch spinach, washed and dried
Carrot Slaw (see recipe on page 529)

1. Heat a skillet over medium heat and add the butter. Sauté the onion and dill in the butter until the onion is just translucent.

2. Add the sliced cabbage. Place the lid on the skillet to allow the cabbage to soften. Cook 4 to 5 minutes, stirring occasionally. Turn the

heat up to high and stir-fry for a few minutes. The cabbage should begin to color and caramelize with the onions.

3. Season with salt and pepper. Make a bed of the raw spinach and top it with some of the carrot slaw. Arrange the hot cabbage on top and serve.

— *Karolina Tracz, Nash's Organic Produce, Sequim, Washington*

. . . .

CREAMY DILL DRESSING   MAKES 1½ CUPS

Source Note: This creamy dressing has no added oil; it is made with silken tofu, which has a softer texture than regular tofu.

1 (10½-ounce) package firm silken tofu
2 cloves garlic, or ½ teaspoon garlic powder
1½ teaspoons chopped fresh dill, or ½ teaspoon dried dill
½ teaspoon salt
2 tablespoons water
1½ tablespoons fresh lemon juice
1 tablespoon seasoned rice vinegar

Combine all of the ingredients in a food processor or blender, and blend until completely smooth. Store any extra dressing in an airtight container in the refrigerator.

— *Amanda Formaro,* The Chamomile Times and Herbal News

. . . .

GRAVLAX (SALMON MARINATED IN DILL)   SERVES 8 TO 10

Source Note: This cured salmon is one of the greatest Scandinavian delicacies. Prepared with sugar, salt, white pepper, and dill, this moist, tender, springlike dish is also relished in Denmark. The fish is not technically cooked but cured by the salt and sugar; the timid can take courage from the fact that pickled herring is not cooked either.

3 to 3½ pounds fresh wild salmon, center cut, cleaned, and scaled
1 large bunch dill
¼ cup coarse (kosher) salt, or if unavailable, substitute regular salt
¼ cup sugar
2 tablespoons white peppercorns (or substitute black), crushed

1. Ask the fish dealer to cut the salmon in half lengthwise and to remove the backbone and the small bones as well.

2. Place half of the fish, skin side down, in a deep glass, enamel, or stainless-steel baking dish or casserole. Wash and then shake dry the bunch of dill, and place it on the fish. (If the dill is of the hothouse

variety and not very pungent, chop the herb coarsely to release its flavor and sprinkle it over the fish instead.)

3. In a separate bowl, combine the salt, sugar, and crushed peppercorns. Sprinkle this mixture evenly over the dill. Top with the other half of the fish, skin side up. Cover the fish with aluminum foil and on it set a heavy platter slightly larger than the salmon. Pile the platter with 3 or 4 cans of food; these make convenient weights that are easy to distribute evenly.

4. Refrigerate for 48 hours (or up to 3 days). Turn the fish over every 12 hours, basting it with the liquid marinade that accumulates, and separating the halves a little to baste the salmon inside. Replace the platter and weights each time.

5. When the gravlax is finished, remove the fish from its marinade, scrape away the dill and seasonings, and pat it dry with paper towels. Place the separated halves skin side down on a carving board and slice the salmon halves thinly on the diagonal, detaching each slice from the skin.

6. Gravlax is typically served as part of a Swedish smörgåsbord or as an appetizer, and is accompanied by mustard sauce. When presented as a main course, it is garnished with lemon wedges as well as the mustard sauce, and served with toast and perhaps a cucumber salad.

— *Dale Brown,* Time-Life Foods of the World: The Cooking of Scandinavia

> "I don't like gourmet cooking or 'this' cooking or 'that' cooking. I like good cooking."
>
> — *James Beard,*
> *American chef and food writer*

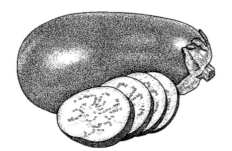

Eggplants

SOLANUM MELONGENA

Eggplants are a curiosity, since they are neither much like a vegetable nor much like a meat but are blessed with the personality traits of both. They also suffer from a popularity complex, since they are either much loved or quite neglected. This may be partly because they are a member of the Solanaceae family, which includes such common vegetables as the potato, tomato, and pepper, but also the infamous deadly nightshade. This kinship caused many to believe for centuries that eggplants and tomatoes were both poisonous.

Happily, eggplants are not, and they are much beloved in Asia and the Middle East, where they are a staple in those cuisines. Although their American name (they are called aubergines in Europe) comes from the fact that some varieties resemble the chicken's rounded ovum, Asian eggplants are slender and elongated, perfect for slicing into stir-fries. Modern hybrids come in different colors as well, with beautiful green, pure white, and delightfully speckled varieties.

A versatile vegetable, eggplant can be baked, sautéed, grilled, broiled, steamed, or braised in a sauce. They also adapt beautifully to roasting. One rule of thumb about this vegetable is that it should never be undercooked; a tough eggplant is an unappetizing eggplant.

HISTORY

India is the eggplant's ancient homeland, where it is believed to have been cultivated over 4,000 years ago. Despite its modern-day association with Mediterranean cuisines, eggplant's trek to southern Europe was a slow journey, and the vegetable always seemed to be more popular in the Middle East. (The Turks claim they know a thousand ways to prepare it.) The French blamed eggplant for causing epileptic seizures, but southern Italians happily adored it. Eggplant also found favor with Thomas Jefferson, American Founding Father and amateur horticulturist, who had it grown in his extensive gardens at Monticello, Virginia.

NUTRITION

Eggplants contain modest nutrition, mostly in the form of dietary fiber, potassium, manganese, copper, and some B vitamins. A single cup of cubed eggplant contains 20 calories. Recent research has revealed that eggplant skins contain a potent antioxidant, as well as phenolic compounds that possess anticancer and antiviral properties.

SEASON

Commercially, eggplants are widely grown and in season year-round. But they remain a warm-weather crop, and you'll find them at their best at farmers markets and CSAs from July through October.

SELECTION

Choose eggplants that are uniformly firm and heavy for their size. Avoid lightweights that have soft spots, signs of shriveling, or brown patches on

Cooking Tip

Sliced eggplant will discolor when exposed to air; to avoid this, brush the freshly cut slices with lemon juice or water acidulated with vinegar or lemon juice.

Also, use a stainless steel knife to cut eggplant; carbon steel knives discolor the flesh.

their skins. Smaller eggplants are generally much sweeter and less bitter than overly large ones.

STORAGE

Refrigerate eggplants in a perforated plastic bag in the refrigerator vegetable crisper. They do not keep well and should be used within a few days.

TRIMMING AND CLEANING

Thoroughly wash the outside of eggplants before slicing, then trim off the stem end. The skins are edible, but they may be tough on older, larger specimens or white eggplants. You may peel the skins before cutting, or, if you are baking the eggplant, scoop the flesh out of the shell after cooking.

Some people think that salting and rinsing eggplant slices before cooking removes bitterness and makes them more tender. The effectiveness of this method is debatable in some circles, and it generally applies only to larger, older fruits. If you'd like to try this method, slice eggplants into ½-inch-thick rounds, sprinkle with salt, and let the slices sit in a colander in the sink for 30 minutes to "sweat." Before cooking, rinse the slices briefly under running water to remove the salt.

STEAMING AND BOILING

Whole eggplants can be steamed for 15 to 20 minutes; slices or cubes should be steamed only 4 to 8 minutes, or until meltingly tender. Boiling eggplant results in an icky, watery vegetable, so steaming is preferable, especially if garlic, black tea, or other herbs and seasonings are added to the cooking water; the eggplant will absorb these flavors.

STIR-FRYING AND SAUTÉING

Eggplants have an insatiable thirst for oil, which their porous flesh soaks up like a sponge. This should be taken into account when cooking. If you keep adding more oil, the eggplant will get greasier. Sauté or stir-fry cubed eggplant in a well-oiled pan over high heat for 7 to 10 minutes, or until tender. Take care the eggplant doesn't burn, and stir often to keep the heat distributed, or the vegetable may come out unevenly cooked.

BAKING AND ROASTING

Eggplants respond very well to roasting in the oven. To roast whole, pierce an eggplant several times with a fork to allow steam to escape, then bake at 350°F for 15 to 25 minutes, depending on its size. Test for doneness by inserting a knife or fork, which should pass through easily.

BRAISING AND STEWING

Because eggplants readily absorb the flavors of whatever food or sauces they come into contact with, they can be excellent braised in a highly flavored sauce, heated to boiling for a few minutes, then allowed to cook on decreased heat for 12 to 15 minutes, or until tender. Eggplants can also be stewed, either on their own with savory seasonings or in combination with other vegetables, on medium-low heat for about 30 minutes.

MICROWAVING

Placed cubed or whole eggplant (pierced with a folk) in a microwave-safe

> "When I was alone, I lived on eggplant, the stovetop cook's strongest ally. I fried it and stewed it, and ate it crisp and sludgy, hot and cold. It was cheap and filling and was delicious in all manner of strange combinations. If any was left over, I ate it cold the next day on bread."
>
> — *Laurie Colwin, American food writer*

Cooking Tip

Eggplants absorb astonishing amounts of oil; baking results in fewer calories than frying.

dish, add 2 tablespoons of water, cover, and cook on high power, rotating every 2 minutes.

- 1 pound, cubed = 6 to 8 minutes
- Whole 1-pound eggplant = 4 to 7 minutes for scooping out the flesh, 8 to 9 minutes for pureeing

BLANCHING AND FREEZING

Eggplants can be frozen if blanched first. Peel them if desired, then slice them into ⅓-inch-thick rounds or cubes. Bring a pot of water to a rapid boil, add ½ cup of lemon juice to the water, drop in the eggplant, cover, and boil for 4 minutes. Then plunge the eggplant into ice water for 5 minutes to stop the cooking process. Drain and pack in zipper-lock freezer or vacuum food sealer-type bags, or freezer containers. Squeeze out any excess air and leave ½ inch of headspace (unless you are using the vacuum sealing method).

If you are preparing slices for frying, pack with sheets of wax paper or freezer wrap between the drained slices. Frozen eggplant will keep up to 1 year at 0°F.

MEASURES AND EQUIVALENTS

- 1 medium eggplant = about 1 pound = 4 to 6 servings
- 1 pound eggplant = 3 to 4 cups diced = 1½ cups cooked
- 1 serving = ⅓ pound as a side dish
- 1 serving = ½ to ¾ pound as a main dish
- 6 cups raw cubed flesh = 3 cups cooked = 2 cups pureed
- 1½ pounds raw = 2 to 2¼ cups mashed or pureed

COMPLEMENTARY HERBS, SEASONINGS, AND FOODS

Aïoli, anchovies, bacon, balsamic vinegar, basil, béchamel sauce, breadcrumbs, capers, chard, cheese (feta, goat, Gruyère, Parmesan, mozzarella, ricotta), cream, cumin, garbanzos (chickpeas), garlic, ginger, ham, lamb, lemon, lentils, mint, miso, mushrooms, olive oil, olives, onions, oregano, parsley, peanut oil, peppers, pesto, pine nuts, potatoes, rice, rosemary, sesame, shallots, soy sauce, thyme, tomatoes, vinegar, walnut oil, walnuts, white beans, yogurt, zucchini.

SERVING SUGGESTIONS

- Here's a salty, savory, simple dish: Heat a preferred oil in a saucepan until hot (peanut or vegetable are good choices). Add eggplant that has been cut into 1-inch chunks, and brown them on each side. Then add garlic, shallots, and tamari or soy sauce. Top with chopped green onions and serve hot or cold.
- Because of their substantial, rich texture, eggplants have been used as a meat substitute for centuries. Try using grilled, seasoned slices in sandwiches, lasagna, and casseroles.
- Grill or broil eggplant slices and use them in combination with mushrooms in sandwiches or other dishes.
- Top a pizza with strips of precooked eggplant, roasted sweet red peppers, and ripe tomatoes.
- Eggplants stuffed with crustaceans (such as shrimp, crab, and lobster) and combined with a cream sauce make a delicious, filling meal, rounded out with a green or tomato salad and good crusty bread.

- For a twist on a traditional dish, mash and whip eggplants the same way you'd prepare mashed potatoes.

- Baba ghanoush, that traditional Middle Eastern preparation of pureed, roasted eggplant, makes a delicious dip or sandwich filling. Combine the eggplant with garlic, tahini, lemon juice, sea salt, and olive oil.

- Add tender eggplant cubes to an Indian curry or Asian stir-fry.

- Hollow out eggplant "shells," stuff them with ground meat and spices, and bake them in the oven.

- Create a delicious, hearty, vegetarian spaghetti sauce by steaming eggplant slices until tender; sautéing garlic, onion, and Italian-style stewed tomatoes; combining the eggplant with the tomato mixture and adding chopped fresh basil; and simmering on low heat for 20 minutes.

MIDI-POCHE (EGGPLANT BAKE)　　　　　SERVES 4

Source Note: This dish is a staple in Provence, served up at least once a week for dinner, supper, and sometimes next morning's breakfast as well. It is good both cold and hot.

2 small eggplants (about ¾ pound total), sliced
2 tablespoons lemon juice
1 tablespoon plus ½ teaspoon salt
4 tablespoons (½ stick) unsalted butter, divided
2 tablespoons olive oil, divided
1 shallot, minced
1 small onion, finely chopped
1 clove garlic, minced
3 cups chopped, seeded tomatoes (about 2 pounds)
Pinch of sugar
½ teaspoon chopped fresh thyme or a pinch of dried thyme
1 tablespoon minced fresh basil or 1½ teaspoons dried basil
1 teaspoon crushed allspice
¼ cup all-purpose flour
1 cup cooked rice
¼ cup freshly grated Parmesan cheese

1. Place the sliced eggplant in a colander. Sprinkle it with the lemon juice and 1 tablespoon salt; let stand 30 minutes to "sweat" the eggplant, and drain.

2. Meanwhile, heat 2 tablespoons of the butter with 1 tablespoon of the oil in a medium saucepan over medium heat. Add the shallot and onion; cook 2 minutes. Stir in the garlic; cook 1 minute longer. Add the tomatoes; sprinkle with sugar. Add the thyme, basil, allspice, and ½ teaspoon salt. Cook, uncovered, over medium-low heat 20 minutes. Set aside.

3. Preheat the oven to 350°F.

4. Brush the eggplant with paper towels to remove the salt; pat dry. Dust the eggplant slices lightly with the flour. Heat the remaining butter and oil in a heavy-bottomed skillet and sauté the eggplant over medium heat until golden on both sides. Drain on paper towels.

5. Spoon ¼ of the tomato sauce over the bottom of an ovenproof baking dish or casserole. Layer half of the eggplant over the sauce. Sprinkle the eggplant with half of the rice and then spoon half of the remaining tomato sauce over the rice. Top with half of the grated cheese. Repeat the layers of eggplant, rice, tomato sauce, and cheese.

6. Bake until bubbly, about 15 to 20 minutes. Serve hot or at room temperature.

— *Bert Greene*, Greene on Greens

ROASTED EGGPLANT SALAD WITH BEANS AND CASHEWS

SERVES 6

2 medium globe eggplants diced into 1-inch cubes
3 tablespoons olive oil
1 teaspoon coarse salt, divided
½ pound green beans, cut into 1-inch pieces
3 tablespoons fresh lime juice
2 tablespoons vegetable oil
1 teaspoon curry powder
¼ teaspoon freshly ground black pepper
½ cup roasted cashews, chopped
½ cup chopped fresh cilantro

1. Preheat the oven to 475°F.

2. Toss the eggplant with the olive oil and ½ teaspoon of the coarse salt. Place the eggplant in a single layer on a cookie sheet in the oven for 25 to 30 minutes or until it becomes golden brown.

3. Cook the green beans in a large saucepan of boiling salted water until they become crisp-tender, about 2 minutes. Drain. Transfer them to a bowl of ice water to stop the cooking process. Drain, and pat dry with paper towels.

4. In a large bowl, whisk together the lime juice, vegetable oil, curry powder, the remaining salt, and pepper. Toss the eggplant, green beans, cashews, and cilantro with the dressing and serve immediately.

— *Featherstone Farm, Rushford, Minnesota*

GRILLED EGGPLANT QUESADILLAS

SERVES 8

2 large eggplants, grilled (recipe below)
1½ cups vinaigrette made with red wine vinegar
8 ounces low-fat, shredded Monterey Jack cheese
1 bunch fresh basil, chopped
2 to 3 tomatoes
2 cups assorted roasted peppers (green or red bell, jalapeños, poblanos)
4 (12-inch) flour tortillas
Vegetable oil

FOR THE GRILLED EGGPLANT

Slice the eggplant into ½-inch rounds. Brush the slices with some red wine vinaigrette. Grill the eggplant over hot coals, turning and basting occasionally with more vinaigrette until the slices turn very soft. Cover the eggplant until ready to use.

FOR THE QUESADILLAS

1. If you are using an oven rather than a griddle to cook the tortillas, preheat the oven to 400°F.

2. Layer the cheese, basil, grilled eggplant, tomatoes, and peppers inside the tortillas. Fold the tortillas in half. Brush the outside of the tortillas with oil.

3. Bake the tortillas or cook them on a hot griddle until their centers are hot and their exteriors are brown and crisp. While the tortillas are still hot, brush the quesadillas with a bit more oil.

— *Marc Casale of Dos Coyotes Border Café, for Davis Farmers Market*

BABA GHANOUSH (EGGPLANT DIP)

SERVES 8

2 large eggplants (about 1¼ pounds)
2 level tablespoons tahini
4 cloves garlic, crushed with salt
½ cup diced onion
1 cup chopped tomato
3 tablespoons fresh lemon juice, or more to taste
3 to 4 tablespoons cold water
¼ teaspoon salt
Dash of freshly ground black pepper
1 teaspoon olive oil
Chopped parsley, for garnish
Finely diced tomatoes, for garnish

Apothecary in Portland, Oregon, specializes in community-supported herbalism (CSH), explained by owner Lara Pacheco as a monthly pickup of herbal preparations from her neighborhood, derived from medicinal plants that she grows organically in her yard or ethically harvests from nearby forests. Her CSH shares are seasonally based preparations with educational material included. A customized option provides a consultation with Pacheco and individualized herbal preparations.

Other noteworthy medicinal herb CSAs include **Blue Turtle Botanicals** in Tucson, Arizona (available for pickup either in Tucson or by mail order); **For the Love of Dandelions** in Cambridge, Minnesota (besides herbs, it offers handcrafted lotion, tinctures, salves, jelly, pesto, soap, lip balm, and more); **Morgan Botanicals Herbal CSA** in Loveland, Colorado (which also has classes in herbalism, soap and medicine making, gardening, and health and nutrition; and **Herbal Revolution** in Lincolnville, Maine (which also takes custom requests).

> "The smell of manure, of sun on foliage, of evaporating water, rose to my head; two steps farther, and I could look down into the vegetable garden enclosed within its tall pale of reeds—rich chocolate earth studded emerald green, frothed with the white of cauliflowers, jeweled with the purple globes of eggplant and the scarlet wealth of tomatoes."
>
> — *Doris Lessing, author*

1. Pierce the eggplants in several places with a toothpick. If you are cooking indoors, wrap the whole eggplants in aluminum foil and place them over the open flame of a gas burner; or place them under your oven broiler to cook on all sides until they collapse and begin to release steam. If you are cooking outdoors over coals, grill the eggplants until blackened, collapsed, and cooked through.

2. Remove the foil and place the cooked eggplants into a basin of cold water; peel them while they are still hot, and allow them to drain in a colander until they are cooled. Squeeze the pulp to remove any extra juices—they may be bitter. Then mash the eggplant to a chunky consistency.

3. In a food processor, mix the tahini with the garlic, onion, tomato, and lemon juice until the mixture turns into a uniform puree. Thin with water. With the machine still running, add the eggplant, salt, pepper, and oil. Taste and adjust seasonings.

4. Spread the mixture evenly in a shallow dish and garnish with more pepper, parsley, and tomatoes.

— Produce for Better Health; Fruits & Veggies—More Matters; Centers for Disease Control and Prevention

EGGPLANT, TOMATO, AND RED POTATO CASSEROLE

SERVES 6 TO 8

Source Note: This is hearty for a vegetarian dish and even satisfies folks who usually prefer meat dishes.

2 to 3 medium red potatoes, cut into 1-inch cubes
½ cup cooked garbanzo beans (chickpeas)
⅛ cup olive oil
1 medium onion, sliced
½ head of garlic, cloves quartered
½ red bell pepper, sliced into small pieces
5 to 7 cremini mushrooms, thickly sliced
1 medium eggplant, cut into ½-inch cubes
3 medium tomatoes, diced
Oregano, fresh or dried
Basil, fresh or dried
Salt and freshly ground black pepper

1. Preheat the oven to 350°F.

2. Slice all of the ingredients in advance, preparing the mushrooms and eggplant last to minimize discoloration.

3. Place the eggplant, potatoes, and garbanzo beans in a large casserole dish.

4. Heat the olive oil in a large skillet and sauté the onion until it is nearly translucent. Add the garlic, bell pepper, and mushrooms. Cook until softened, but do not brown. Add the tomatoes and sauté just until they are heated through. Add generous amounts of oregano, basil, salt, and pepper to taste.

5. Pour the skillet ingredients over the casserole ingredients and mix them all together. Cover the casserole and bake for 45 minutes.

— *Nelda Danz*

The succulent Asian eggplants of Sang Lee Farms.

Books

The Food of Morocco
Paula Wolfert
Ecco, 2011.

Totally Eggplant Cookbook
Kindle Edition,
Helene Siegel,
Random House, 2014.

Jerusalem: A Cookbook
Yotam Ottolenghi and Sami Tamimi,
Ten Speed Press, 2012.

Flowers (Edible)

Few people realize the bounty and variety of edible flowers growing all around them in the spring and summer. Many common garden blossoms are tasty and add wonderful colors, textures, and dimension to salads, drinks, sandwiches, desserts, and other dishes. That said, not all flowers are safe to eat, so it is important to know which ones are not. Even many edible flowers can cause allergic reactions in some people, or should not be consumed in large quantities because of stomach upsets. Also, not all flowers of a specific family can be eaten: begonias (not recommended) and chrysanthemums (fine to eat) are good examples.

Below is a partial list of the more common edible varieties. Thompson & Morgan has a good list with considerable notes and details (www.thompson-morgan.com/edible-flowers), as does About.com's Home Cooking section (http://homecooking.about.com/library/weekly/blflowers.htm).

FLOWER	NOTES
Angelica (*Angelica archangelica*)	Flavor is similar to licorice.
Apple (*Malus* species)	Delicate floral flavor. Use in moderation, as the flowers have cyanide precursors.
Arugula (*Eruca sativa*)	Nutty, spicy flavor, similar to the leaves.
Banana (*Musa × paradisiaca*)	These huge, purplish buds are eaten cooked or raw in salads and Asian dishes.
Basil (*Ocimum basilicum*)	Reminiscent of basil. Flavor varies by basil variety.
Bee balm (*Monarda* species)	Makes tea similar to Earl Grey.
Borage (*Borago officinalis*)	Tastes like cucumbers.
Broccoli (*Brassica oleracea*)	Tastes like broccoli.
Burnet (*Sanguisorba minor*)	Also a cucumber-like flavor.
Calendula (*Calendula officinalis*)	Spicy, peppery. One of the most popular edible flowers because of their cheerful orange hue.

Carnation (*Dianthus caryophyllus*)	Spicy, clove-like flavor.
Chervil (*Anthriscus cerefolium*)	Very delicate, anise-like flavor. Excellent used raw in salads.
Chives (*Allium schoenoprasum*)	Mild oniony flavor. The flowers of both garden and garlic chives are tasty.
Chrysanthemum (*Glebionis coronarium*)	Slightly bitter. Eat only the *G. coronarium* type.
Cilantro (*Coriander sativum*)	Strong herbal flavor reminiscent of the herb. Use in salads and bean dishes.
Clover (*Trifolium* species)	Some digestibility issues with raw flower heads.
Cornflower (*Centaurea cynaus*; also known as bachelor's buttons)	Sweet to spicy flavor, clove-like.
Dandelion (*Taraxacum officinale*)	Best used when young. Cooked buds taste like mushrooms.
Dianthus (*Dianthus* species)	Spicy, floral, clove-like taste.
Daylily (*Hemerocallis* species)	Crisp texture, sweet flavor. Buds are terrific in stir-fries.
Dill (*Anethum graveolens*)	Flavor is reminiscent of dill and more powerful than the seeds. Good in pickles and vegetable dishes.
Elderberry (*Sambucus* species)	Sweet flavor and aroma. Used in cordials, jellies, and desserts, or fried as a fritter.
English daisy (*Bellis perennis*)	Tangy, vegetable taste.
Evening primrose (*Oenothera* species)	Sweet, mild flavor.
Fennel (*Foeniculum vulgare*)	Sweet, licorice flavor. Sprinkle fennel pollen (the tiny yellow florets of the umbrella blossoms) on fish dishes, salads, and vegetables.

Fuchsia (*Fuchsia* × hybrida)	Acidic flavor.
Garlic (*Allium sativum*)	Very garlicky flavor that is milder than the bulb. Excellent in salads.
Ginger (*Zingiber officinale*)	Spicy, gingery taste.
Gladiolus (*Gladiolus* species)	Tastes similar to lettuce. Individual petals make a colorful addition to salads.
Grapefruit (*Citrus* × *paradisi*)	Citrus-like, highly scented, waxy. Use sparingly.
Hibiscus (*Hibiscus rosa-sinensis*)	Tastes slightly lemony. Excellent in teas and cold drinks.
Hollyhock (*Alcea rosea*)	Bland flavor. Use for color in salads and crystallized in desserts.
Honeysuckle (Japanese) (*Lonicera japonica*)	Sweet flavor reminiscent of honey. Flowers only are edible; berries are poisonous.
Hyssop (*Hyssopus officinalis*)	Good for soups, salads, and meat and fish dishes. Also excellent for making tea.
Impatiens (*Impatiens walleriana*)	Bland flavor.
Jasmine (*Jasminum officinale*)	Intensely fragrant, sweet flavor. Excellent in teas.
Jasmine (Arabian) (*Jasminum sambac*)	Delicate, sweet flavor. Excellent in teas.
Johnny-jump-up (*Viola tricolor*)	Resembles miniature pansies. Sweet, bland flavor.
Kumquat (*Citrus japonica*)	Citrus-like, highly scented, waxy. Use sparingly.
Lavender (*Lavandula* species)	Florets may be used in both sweet and savory dishes.
Lemon (*Citrus* × *limon*)	Citrus-like, highly scented, waxy. Use sparingly.

Lemon verbena (*Aloysia triphylla*)	Delicate, lemony flavor. Especially good in custards and desserts.
Lilac (*Syringa vulgaris*)	Lemony, floral flavor.
Lime (*Citrus × aurantifolia*)	Citrus-like, highly scented, waxy. Use sparingly.
Linden (*Tilia* species)	Fragrant, honey-like flavor. Use in teas or infused as syrup.
Marigold (*Tagetes tenuifolia*)	Spicy to bitter flavor.
Marjoram (*Origanum majorana*)	Flowers taste like the leaf, although with a milder flavor.
Mallow (*Malva sylvestris*)	Sweet, delicate flavor.
Mint (*Mentha* species)	Flowers taste minty, like the leaves, and reflect the subtleties of different varieties.
Mustard (*Brassica* species)	Bright, peppery flavors reminiscent of kale, chard, and mustard greens.
Nasturtium (*Tropaeolum majus*)	Sweet, pungent, and peppery flavor. Among the most popular edible flowers. Buds are sometimes pickled like capers.
Okra (*Abelmoschus esculentus*)	Similar to squash blossoms.
Orange (*Citrus × sinensis*)	Citrus-like, highly scented, waxy. Use sparingly.
Oregano (*Origanum vulgare*)	Milder flavor than the leaf.
Pansy (*Viola × wittrockiana*)	Mild, sweet to tart flavor.
Primrose (*Primula vulgaris*)	Bland to sweet flavor.
Radish (*Raphanus sativus*)	Tastes like radishes. Can be peppery.
Rose (*Rosa rugosa* or *Rosa gallica officinalis*)	Sweet, aromatic, rose flavor. Use in salads, jellies, jams, and syrups.

Rosemary (*Rosmarinus officinalis*)	Piney, sweet taste. These flowers taste strongly of rosemary and are beautiful when scattered on a salad or a pasta dish. Also fun to use in flavored butters.
Pea (*Pisum* species)	The flowers of the garden pea are slightly crunchy and reminiscent of peas. The flowers of ornamental sweet peas are poisonous.
Perennial phlox (*Phlox paniculata*)	Slightly spicy taste. Use only this variety of phlox (not the annual or creeping varieties).
Runner bean (scarlet) (*Phaseolus coccineus*)	Bean-like, sweet flavor. Also a little crunchy with a spectacular bright orange color!
Safflower (*Carthamus tinctorius*)	Slightly bitter flavor. Historically marketed as "poor man's saffron" for its color and appearance. Dye extracted from its flowers is used in butters, confections, and liqueurs.
Sage (*Salvia officinalis*)	Reminiscent of sage. Their sometimes strong flavor varies by sage variety. These flowers are beautiful when scattered on a salad or a pasta dish. Also fun to use in flavored butters.
Scented geranium (*Pelargonium* species)	Ranges from lemon to mint flavor. Varieties include rose (one of the oldest and most popular), lemon, mint, and pineapple.
Snapdragon (*Antirrhinum majus*)	Bland to bitter flavor.
Sorrel (*Rumex acetosa*)	Tart, lemony flavor. Delicious in salads and in cucumber dishes.
Squash blossom (*Cucurbita pepo* species)	Sweet, vegetable flavor.
Strawberry (*Fragaria* × *ananassa, Fragaria vesca*)	Light strawberry flavor. Excellent in drinks.

Summer savory (*Satureja hortensis*)	Mildly peppery, spicy flavor reminiscent of the herb.
Sunflower (*Helianthus annuus*)	Mild, nutty taste.
Sweet cicely (*Myrrhis odorata*)	Sweet, anise-like flavor.
Thyme (*Thymus vulgaris*)	Tastes like the herb and, in the case of lemon thyme, a bit citrusy.
Tuberous begonia (*Begonia × tuberosa*)	Sour, lemony flavor with a crisp texture. Should not be eaten in large quantities; other begonia species are poisonous.
Tulip (*Tulipa* species)	Sweet, pea-like flavor with a crisp texture.
Violet (*Viola* species)	Sweet flavor.
Yucca (*Yucca baccata*)	Mild, sweet, fresh flavor with a crunchy texture.

HISTORY

Humans have probably been using flowers as food, medicine, and perfume for as long as both have existed together. The earliest recorded mention is 140 BCE; to this day flowers have played remarkable culinary and medicinal roles. For instance, Chartreuse, that classic green liqueur developed by French monks in the 17th century, contains carnation petals as part of its highly secret formula, which uses 130 different herbs, plants, and flowers. In the American Civil War, calendulas were prized for their antihemorrhagic and antiseptic properties on open wounds, and they are still used in alternative and homeopathic medicines today. Marigold petals are commonly added to the commercial feed of chickens to boost the color of their egg yolks. And rose petals are revered for their fragrance—in fact, attar of rose continues to be among one of the most widely used essential oils in the world today—and they make delectable jams, jellies, and soups.

NUTRITION

Like herbs, flowers are often a rich source of antioxidants, phytonutrients, bioflavonoids, and beta-carotene—the very sources of their many colors and flavors. Some flowers also contain significant amounts of vitamins A, C, and E, as well as calcium, potassium, and iron.

SEASON

Flowers are most commonly available at CSA farms and farmers markets during the spring, summer, and early fall. Exact seasons vary widely, depending on the flower species. Some farmers markets offer bags or clamshell boxes with flower-petal mixes, which often include a mix of calendulas, pansies, and nasturtiums.

SELECTION

When choosing or foraging flowers for eating, be careful that they have not been treated with any sort of harmful pesticides, been artificially dyed, or been exposed to pollution or runoff. Avoid using commercially grown florist flowers for this purpose (they almost always have heavy pesticide residue). Instead either grow your own organically or buy them from your CSA farm or farmers market (but if you buy from the latter, make sure they are safe for eating).

Choose flowers the same way you would choose fresh salad mix: They should be fresh and springy, with no traces of slime, decay, or wilting. If you harvest your own, pick them early in the morning just after the dew has dried; they have the most flavor at this time of the day.

STORAGE

Keep flowers unwashed until you're ready to use them. They are highly perishable and should be used within a day or two of buying or picking. If you can't use them immediately, wrap them between two dampened paper towels and store them in a plastic bag in the refrigerator. If you are lucky enough to have cut flowers, trim the stems and place them upright in a glass or a vase of water at room temperature until you're ready to use them. They are flowers, after all.

TRIMMING AND CLEANING

Flowers are extremely fragile and bruise easily, so keep your handling of them to an absolute minimum. Shake them lightly and inspect them closely to make sure no insects are lurking or debris or dirt is present. If they need washing, set the loose flowers or petals in a colander and run them briefly under the finest, softest spray of water possible. Then drain them on kitchen or paper towels and allow them to air-dry; do not try to wipe them down, or they will bruise.

Depending on the type of flower, you may need to remove the stamens, pistils, bits of stem, or bases of the petals (such as with roses).

BLANCHING AND FREEZING

Because of their fragility, freezing is not recommended for flowers.

SERVING SUGGESTIONS

- Daylily buds are fabulous in stir-fry and vegetable sautés. They also make an interesting addition to the raw vegetable tray, served alongside old favorites such as carrots, celery, cauliflower, and broccoli. For the best texture, it's important to pick them when they're nice and fat but before they've begun to break open into a blossom.

- Flowers are a garnish that is sure to make everyone smile. Try them sprinkled over salads, soups, and stews. They are really great sprinkled on pasta dishes, too, which usually provide a great neutral background from which to appreciate them. Or tuck them into appetizers and sandwiches.

- Make a vinaigrette using nasturtiums, shallots, oil, and vinegar.

- Some flowers take really well to being boiled down to make syrups, which can then be used in desserts and cocktails. Have fun experimenting with different flavor combinations.

- The large, showy petals of pansies, hollyhocks, tulips, and gladioli are simply stunning in salads.

- Mix calendula petals into soup, egg, and pasta dishes to brighten them up and add color and flavor.

- Lavender is one of the most versatile of the edible flowers. The buds are terrific when used to flavor sugar; to use in sorbets, ice creams, jams, and jellies; and to add to vegetable stock and sauces for duck, chicken, or lamb dishes. They are also fantastic in mixed drinks, and they give an unexpected flavor to salad dressings. Be especially careful when choosing to cook with lavender blossoms, as some will smell (and taste) quite sweet and floral, whereas other varieties will smell more soapy and almost medicinal. Generally for culinary purposes, you'll want your lavender to lean toward the first category.

- A great use for some flowers is in teas (both hot and iced) and punches. Borage, hibiscus, jasmine, lilac, and strawberry are all excellent.

- Jams and jellies and flowers were made for one another. Choose flowers with sweet or spicy scents, such as geraniums, roses, jasmine, and carnations.

- Crystallizing petals and leaves is a favorite way to add flowers to desserts. Good candidates are angelica, borage, rose, violets, and scented geraniums.

- Make fried squash blossoms! This is a delicious summer treat. See the recipe on page 299.

- Consider the vibrant colors of flowers and how they can visually enliven dishes. Try sprinkling bright blue flowers over a gazpacho or tomato soup, or red and orange flowers over deep-green vegetables or egg dishes.

- Chive flowers can be added to any dish where a light, oniony taste is desired. Sprinkle over soups and casseroles, toss into green salads, or add to pasta dishes. They go great in egg and potato salads as well.

- Use violets and pansies to decorate baked goods like cupcakes, bars, and sheet cakes. Or candy them.

- Scarlet runner beans, with their distinctive red flowers, make a beautiful garnish for deviled eggs, pasta salads, and cold soups.

- Dried rose petals make a wonderful Middle-Eastern–style dip when combined with Greek yogurt, dried fruit, toasted walnuts, and olive oil.

- Infuse vinegars and oils with fresh flowers.

- Add flavorful flowers to pancake, scone, or biscuit batter for a surprise—kids love them!

- Freeze flowers in ice cubes to add color and visual interest in cold beverages.

tion of local agriculture, which reduces the reliance on monoculture—single crops grown over a wide area to the detriment of soils.

8. **Attracts tourists.** Local foods promote agritourism, in which farmers markets and opportunities to visit farms and local food producers help draw tourists to a region.

9. **Preserves open space.** Buying local food helps local farms survive and thrive, keeping land from being redeveloped into suburban sprawl.

10. **Builds more connected communities.** Local foods create more vibrant communities by connecting people with the farmers and food producers who bring them healthful local foods. As customers of CSAs and farmers markets have discovered, they are great places to meet and connect with friends as well as farmers!

A SALAD OF HERBS AND FLOWERS WITH FRESH RASPBERRY AND BASIL VINAIGRETTE   SERVES 6

Source Note: Summer salads in the Northwest are regularly filled with tiny violas, yellow and orange nasturtiums, and the occasional petals of a daylily. In spring, don't put it past a Northwest chef to serve the petals of unsprayed tulips in a salad. They taste like snow peas and have the texture of the best

Let's say you want to start a CSA vegetable farm. You have always wanted to be a farmer, work with the land, and grow great food for people. Maybe you've already had farming experience working as an apprentice on another farm. You have the ambition and idealism, and you're ready to work hard.

But first there are a few things to attend to. You need land, of course. But you can't grow great produce just anywhere; you need soil that is well suited to what you grow, or to be willing to cultivate plants ideal for your conditions. If you want to be certified organic, you'll need land that has not been exposed to synthetic fertilizers or pesticides over the past three years. You'll also need to think about soil fertility, drainage, water supply, irrigation, potential runoff from neighboring farms, land topography, and sunlight and wind conditions.

Financing and credit are constant issues. Banks may be reluctant to finance you because they know how risky these business ventures are. If you are just starting out, chances are that land is too expensive to buy or simply unavailable, so you will have to rent acreage from another farm or access it through a land trust. Or maybe you are lucky enough to inherit land.

Much depends on the scale of your operation. You'll also need to think about equipment and facilities; tractors are expensive, not to mention all the other tools and implements needed to cultivate. Although a few CSA farmers do their planting and tilling by horse, the vast majority use motorized equipment. If you want your farm to be eligible for organic certification, you'll need to use organic fertilizers and natural pesticides to get good

butter lettuce. Experiment with other edible flowers in season, but be sure to use only unsprayed garden flowers and avoid experimenting with blossoms that are of dubious edibility.

> 6 to 8 cups mixed salad greens, washed and dried
> 2 to 3 tablespoons Fresh Raspberry and Basil Vinaigrette (recipe below)
> 24 to 36 basil leaves
> 6 tulips (in spring) or daylilies (in summer)
> 18 nasturtium blossoms
> 18 violas, Johnny jump-ups, or pansies
> 3 chive blossoms
> 1 cup fresh raspberries

1. Pick through the salad greens, removing any undesirable leaves. Pile them into a large salad bowl and toss with the vinaigrette.

2. Add the basil leaves and toss lightly to avoid bruising the basil.

3. Arrange the petals of the tulips or daylilies on each of 6 chilled salad plates, then divide the dressed greens evenly among them. Tuck 3 whole nasturtium blossoms into each salad, scatter the petals of the violas over the greens, and then pluck the petals from the chive blossoms and scatter those over as well.

4. Finally, sprinkle each salad with a few raspberries and serve at once.

— *Greg Atkinson,* Northwest Essentials: Cooking with Ingredients That Define a Region's Cuisine

. . . .

FRESH RASPBERRY AND BASIL VINAIGRETTE   SERVES 6

Source Note: Ordinarily a raspberry vinaigrette is made with raspberry-flavored vinegar. This dressing incorporates whole raspberries, and the pulp of the berries allows the oil and vinegar to emulsify to a creamy consistency.

> ½ cup raspberries
> 3 tablespoons rice vinegar
> 1 tablespoon sugar
> ⅔ cup light olive oil or vegetable oil
> 1 teaspoon kosher salt
> ½ teaspoon freshly ground black pepper
> 12 leaves fresh basil

1. In a blender, combine the raspberries, rice vinegar, sugar, oil, salt, and pepper and puree the mixture at high speed. Force the puree through a fine strainer to remove seeds.

2. Cut the basil into fine ribbons and stir in. Use 2 to 3 tablespoons for each salad. The dressing keeps, refrigerated, for at least 1 week.

— *Greg Atkinson*, Northwest Essentials: Cooking with Ingredients
    That Define a Region's Cuisine

Blossom Tea Sandwiches   SERVES 8

1 large cucumber, peeled, seeded, and finely chopped
8 ounces cream cheese, at room temperature
¾ teaspoon Worcestershire sauce
¼ teaspoon minced garlic
1 teaspoon salt
¼ cup finely chopped chives or scallions (green onions)
Thinly sliced cracked wheat or white bread, crusts removed
Lots of edible blossoms: nasturtiums, chives, borage, calendula,
    bean flowers, or herb blossoms, rinsed and patted dry

1. Squeeze the chopped cucumber in a kitchen towel to remove as much
    moisture as possible; set aside.

2. In a bowl, blend the cream cheese, Worcestershire sauce, garlic, salt,
    and chives. Add the cucumber and combine well but do not overmix.

3. Spread on the bread and cut into finger-size open sandwiches.

4. To serve, decorate the tops of the sandwiches with the petals of vari-
    ous edible flowers.

— *Renee Shepherd, Renee's Garden, Felton, California*

Lavender-Mint Tea Punch   SERVES 8

Author Note: *The vibrant flavors of fresh mint and lavender will surprise and
delight those who are fortunate enough to sip this punch on a warm summer
day.*

harvests attractive enough for consumers to want to buy.

You will need a place to properly
process, wash, pack, and refrigerate
your produce. How will you get it to
market and to your customers? A
refrigerated delivery truck, although
pricey, is almost indispensable.

And chances are that you will
need help—and a lot of it, depending on the size of your operation.
How many people? And should
they be employees or apprentices?
Where do you find them? Who is
most reliable? What do you pay
them in terms of money, housing,
a stipend, or a combination of all
of the above?

What is your business and marketing plan? How will you get customers? Will it be all CSAers, or will
you sell to restaurants, wholesale,
and at farmers markets as well?
How will you get the word out, attract new business? Do you have
competition from other farms?
How will you position yourself to
distinguish yourself from them?

You will need to seriously think
about the business path you take
and how quickly you want to expand. Grow too fast and too much,
and you may not be able to keep
up with your customers' expectations for reliable produce of consistent quality. And in a bad harvest
year, they may not be too forgiving;
worse yet, they may not want to return the next year.

Late frosts, spring floods, summer droughts, and sudden storms.
And if a weather disaster does
strike, you will usually have no re-
course in terms of crop insurance
or federal aid; it can be a total loss.
Equipment breaks down, workers
don't show up, and bugs and blights
threaten to ravage your hard-won
crops. And oh, the cursed weeds! Be
prepared to work 17-hour days and
even then, hardly clear enough to
live on.

It's a true wonder that any CSA
farms manage to survive—let
alone thrive.

1 bottle sparkling grape juice (about 4 cups)
6 cups boiling water
½ cup fresh mint leaves, firmly packed, or 3 tablespoons dried mint leaves
2 tablespoons fresh lavender florets (see Cooking Note below) or 1 tablespoon dried lavender

1. Refrigerate the sparkling grape juice and be sure to have ice on hand before serving. Large cubes are better than small because they'll melt more slowly.

2. In a medium pot or bowl, pour the boiling water over the mint leaves. Let steep for about 10 minutes. Add the lavender blossoms and allow to cool. Strain the mixture and refrigerate until very cold.

3. Pour the lavender-mint tea into a punch bowl, then add the sparkling grape juice. Stir gently to combine and add ice.

Cooking Note: To prepare the fresh lavender, pull the tiny, individual florets off the main flower stalk.

If you can't find sparkling grape juice, combine 3 cups white grape juice with 1 cup (or more, as desired) sparkling water. Alternatively, use ginger ale or another neutral-flavored soda.

— *Lisa Gordanier and Mi Ae Lipe*

Nasturtiums grown for their edible flowers at Teena's Pride CSA.

Honeydew Melons

CUCUMIS MELO,
INODORUS GROUP

This alabaster, smooth-skinned beauty is a close cousin of the crenshaw, casaba, Persian, and winter melon, and is considered the sweetest of all melons. Honeydews can be round or oval and weigh up to 4 to 8 pounds, with sweet, juicy, pale-green flesh that can be absolutely scrumptious when ripe. Determining ripeness can be tricky, because unlike muskmelons, the stem does not "slip" or separate cleanly from the fruit. Honeydew maturity is not based on size, but rather on the fruit's skin color (ripe melons are creamy yellow, not greenish white) and sometimes exterior texture (often an extremely subtle, almost undetectable wrinkling of the skin is perceptible).

HISTORY

Like its melon cousins, honeydews or their forerunners probably originated in Persia (now modern-day Iran). Confusion runs as rampant in melon history as its vines, and the name has frequently referred to multiple types of melons or sometimes even to gourds. It is, however, known that the honeydew was imported to the United States around 1900 by the French, who call it the White Antibes winter melon.

NUTRITION

Like many melons, honeydews are mostly water and have a mildly diuretic effect. They do contain significant amounts of vitamin C, potassium, and folate. A 1-cup serving contains about 64 calories.

SEASON

Commercially grown honeydews are in season from August through October. You'll find them at their best at farmers markets and CSAs in mid to late summer.

SELECTION

A choice honeydew should be uniformly firm and heavy for its size, and its skin more on the yellow than white side. A ripe honeydew may have a faint, characteristic perfume, plus a slight wrinkling on its skin. Avoid melons with cracks, soft spots, or other surface blemishes.

STORAGE

Fresh honeydews can be stored for a week or two at room temperature, provided that they are not overripe and have no cracks or blemishes. Cut melons will keep in the refrigerator for up to a few days, but wrap the pieces well or store the melon in tightly sealed containers, as their odor tends to permeate other nearby foods and vice versa.

TRIMMING AND CLEANING

Bacteria sometimes grow on the outside of melons, so washing the skin thoroughly with warm, soapy water before slicing into the fruit is a good idea. Scoop out the seeds, and the melon is ready to enjoy.

BLANCHING AND FREEZING

Honeydew and other types of melon can be frozen as is, but preparing them in a light sugar syrup can enhance their flavor and color. Peel and cut melons into ½- or ¾-inch cubes or balls. To make the syrup, combine 9 cups of water with 2¼ cups of sugar in a pot, and bring to a boil until the sugar dissolves. Chill, then pour ½ cup of syrup into a freezer container, jar, or zipper-lock freezer bag. Add the melon, and keep adding syrup until the fruit is covered. Leave ½ inch of headspace for pints, 1 inch for quarts.

If you prefer your fruit unsweetened, arrange cut pieces in a single layer on a cookie sheet and freeze. Transfer the pieces into zipper-lock freezer or vacuum food sealer-type bags, or freezer containers. Squeeze out any excess air and leave ½ inch of headspace (unless you are using the vacuum sealing method). Frozen honeydew will keep for 8 months at 0°F.

EQUIVALENTS, MEASURES, AND SERVINGS

- 1 pound = ¼ medium honeydew = 1 cup cubed

COMPLEMENTARY HERBS, SEASONINGS, AND FOODS

Berries, cantaloupes, cheese (Brie, Camembert), cilantro, ginger, honey, ice cream, lemon, lime, mint, orange, other melons, pineapple, prosciutto, rum, salami, smoked fish, tequila, watermelon, yogurt.

SERVING SUGGESTIONS

- Wrap thin slices of honeydew with prosciutto, salami, or other high-quality charcuterie meats.
- Cut a honeydew in half, scoop out the seeds, and fill the cavity with berries or other cut fruit. Then drizzle honey, maple syrup, a little lemon or lime juice, or whipped cream over the top, and break out the spoons.
- Dice honeydew and add to your favorite salsa recipe; its sweetness helps balance out an especially fiery salsa.
- Honeydews make wonderfully refreshing sorbets and sherbets.
- For the ultimate in sophistication, serve thin slices of honeydew with the finest smoked salmon.
- Honeydew pairs well with rustic foods like artisan cheeses, crusty breads, and cured meats. Use it as a palate cleanser between tastings.
- Combine balls or chunks of honeydew with cantaloupe, crenshaw or casaba melons, watermelon, berries, mandarin oranges, pineapple, guava, and kiwi. This can be great fun for kids, especially with "dipping sauces" such as yogurt, honey, or maple syrup.
- Melon wedges can be grown-up, even sophisticated, when dressed up with vanilla ice cream, bits of candied ginger, orange-flavored liqueur, rosewater, or lavender syrup.
- Combine pureed honeydew and blueberries with lemon yogurt, frozen yogurt, or Greek yogurt to make a tart, refreshing cold soup.

Honeydew and Cucumber Salad with Sesame Dressing

SERVES 4 TO 6

Sesame Dressing

1 tablespoon plus 2 teaspoons rice-wine vinegar

1 tablespoon peeled and minced fresh ginger

2 teaspoons tamari or soy sauce

1½ teaspoons sugar

1 teaspoon toasted sesame oil, or to taste

¼ teaspoon dried hot red pepper flakes, or to taste

¼ cup vegetable oil

Salad

1 seedless cucumber, halved lengthwise and thinly sliced
   (about 2 cups)

2 cups (1-inch) cubes honeydew melon

2 scallions (green onions), minced

1 tablespoon sesame seeds, toasted lightly and cooled

1. In a bowl, whisk together the vinegar, ginger, tamari, sugar, sesame oil, red pepper flakes, and the vegetable oil until the dressing is well combined.

2. Add the cucumber, melon, and scallions. Toss the salad until it is well combined. Sprinkle with sesame seeds.

— *Pillsbury Most Requested Recipes, as appeared on Fooddownunder.com*

Fruit Kebabs

SERVES 2

Author Note: Simple, easy, with no cooking required! Perfect for a hot summer day when you just want to feel cold fruit juice running down your chin. Great for kids too.

4 cantaloupe chunks

4 honeydew melon chunks

4 watermelon chunks

2 tablespoons orange juice

2 teaspoons chopped fresh mint

1. Thread 2 cantaloupe, 2 honeydew, and 2 watermelon chunks alternately onto each of 2 (10-inch) skewers.

2. Place the kebabs in a shallow, airtight container. Drizzle the orange juice over the kebabs, and sprinkle with the mint. Cover and chill.

— *Noviceromano, Foodista.com*

The Honeydew Diet

Honeydew melon is supposedly one of the few foods that has a negative calorie value; that is, one expends more calories to eat and digest it than the melon actually contains.

HONEYDEW BUBBLE TEA

Author Note: Bubble tea is a cold, sweet drink that originated in Taiwan in the 1980s. Most varieties consist of some sort of tea base mixed with fruit or milk to which large, chewy tapioca balls or fruit jellies are added. It's like eating your drink! Be sure to use straws that are big enough to suck the tapioca balls through.

You can buy black tapioca (sometimes called "boba" on the package) in Asian markets or online. Note that these are much larger than baking tapioca pearls, but they're both made from cassava starch. They don't have much taste in themselves, but the thrill is in chewing these gelatinous "eyeballs."

> 1 cup black tapioca pearls
> 2 green tea bags
> ½ honeydew melon, peeled, seeded, and cut into bite-size pieces
> 1 cup milk or plain soy milk
> Agave syrup, to taste

1. In a large pot, bring 10 cups of water to a boil. Add the tapioca pearls and boil until they turn plump, about 5 minutes. Cover and reduce the heat to medium; simmer for 5 minutes. Drain the tapioca pearls and set them aside.

2. In the meantime, bring 2 cups of water to a boil and steep the 2 bags of green tea. Place in the refrigerator until cool.

3. Place the honeydew melon in a food processor and pulse it until smooth. Refrigerate.

4. When the tea and melon puree are both cold, combine them in a large jug. Add the milk and sweeten to taste.

5. To serve, place 2 to 3 tablespoons of the tapioca pearls in a glass and top with the honeydew tea. Drink with an extra large straw (big enough to accommodate the tapioca pearls).

— *Kris, Foodista.com*

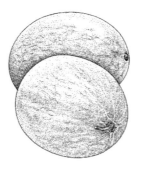

Lemongrass

CYMBOPOGON CITRATUS OR C. FLEXUOSUS

Until Americans' interest in ethnic cuisines exploded about two decades ago, lemongrass was little known outside of its home countries in Southeast Asia, Africa, and the Caribbean. This plant is a type of perennial grass related to citronella, grown for its aromatic, citrusy flavor that adds a refreshing touch to teas, soups, marinades, curries, meats, vegetables, desserts, and beverages. Its essential oils (including citral, its main aromatic compound) are also widely used in perfumes, soaps, and cosmetics, often substituting for more expensive oils like lemon verbena or lemon balm. Lemongrass is also extensively used in aromatherapy and valued as an insect repellent.

The edible portion of the plant is its stalk, which is extremely tough and fibrous. To render its lemony pulp and fragrant oils, these stalks must be thoroughly crushed or bruised. Cooked pieces, unless very finely chopped or crushed to a pulp, are too fibrous to eat and should be removed before serving.

HISTORY

Cymbopogon citratus, or West-Indian lemongrass, is a tropical plant assumed to be native to Malaysia. East-Indian lemongrass, or *C. flexuosus*, is native to India and Sri Lanka. The species are used interchangeably, but *C. citratus* is considered culinarily superior, valued as a food, medicine, perfume, and antiseptic for centuries. The earliest-known written report of lemongrass was its being distilled in the Philippines in the 17th century; subsequently it was imported to Jamaica around 1800 and to the United States in 1917.

NUTRITION

Lemongrass is not usually consumed in large enough quantities to be nutritionally significant, but it does contain folate, iron, calcium, magnesium, phosphorous, manganese, zinc, and potassium. A 1-tablespoon serving contains 5 calories. The distilled oils of this versatile plant are highly valued for their antibacterial and antiviral qualities that rival many antibiotics; traditional Indian Ayurvedic medicine has long employed lemongrass in treating infection and fevers. In aromatherapy, the stimulating yet soothing scent of lemongrass is used to treat depression.

SEASON

Commercially, lemongrass is widely grown and in season year-round. You'll find it at farmers markets and CSAs throughout the summer and fall.

SELECTION

Lemongrass should have plump bases and green, fresh-looking leaves. Avoid specimens that are brown, discolored, or dried out. If you happen to find a stalk with roots attached, you can place it in water and grow it into a plant.

Books

Pok Pok: Food and Stories from the Streets, Homes, and Roadside Restaurants of Thailand
Andy Ricker and J. J. Goode,
Ten Speed Press, 2013.

Burma: Rivers of Flavor
Naomi Duguid,
Artisan, 2012.

STORAGE

Lemongrass stalks will keep for up to 2 weeks individually wrapped in plastic wrap or aluminum foil in the refrigerator.

TRIMMING AND CLEANING

Lemongrass requires some preparation to release its lemony scent and flavor. If you are using it fresh, remove the tough outer leaves until you reach the more tender inner core, and cut off the bottom root end. Diagonally slice the bulbous stalk into ¼-inch rings if you are serving it in well-cooked dishes; otherwise, you can slice long strips if you plan to just infuse your food with its oils—just be sure to remove these tough pieces before serving. If you want to mince lemongrass, use only the bottom 4 inches of the stalk. To release its fragrant, flavorful oils, bruise the peeled stalks with the side of a cleaver or knife, a mortar and pestle, or a rolling pin.

BLANCHING AND FREEZING

Lemongrass does freeze well, with no need for blanching first. You can either freeze the stalks whole (freezing also softens the tough fibers a bit, making them easier to slice and chop) or just prepare them as you would normally for cooking, finely chopping the stalks first. Then pack them in zipper-lock freezer or vacuum food sealer-type bags, squeezing out excess air. Frozen lemongrass will keep for up to 5 months at 0°F.

DRYING

Dried lemongrass lacks the full potency of the fresh herb, but it is acceptable when fresh or frozen alternatives are unavailable. You can air-dry it by hanging bunches of stalks in a well-ventilated, dark place for a few weeks. Or place the stalks on a screen and store them in a dark, airy area for several days, then finish them in a 120°F oven for a few minutes. The herb is dry when the stems crumble easily. It should then be stored in an airtight container away from light and heat.

When you are ready to use it, reconstitute dried lemongrass in a little warm water or simmering liquid first to release its oils. Be aware that the dried product usually cannot be softened enough to chew and should be strained out before serving in a finished dish.

EQUIVALENTS, MEASURES, AND SERVINGS

- 2 stalks lemongrass = 1 tablespoon finely chopped
- Zest from 1 lemon = 2 stalks lemongrass

COMPLEMENTARY HERBS, SEASONINGS, AND FOODS

Broccoli, butter, chicken, chiles, cilantro, citrus, coconut milk, cucumbers, fennel, fish, fish sauce, galangal, garlic, geraniums, ginger, green tea, honey, Kaffir lime leaves, lavender, limes, melon, orange juice, peaches, peanuts, pears, pineapple, pork, rosemary, roses, seafood.

SERVING SUGGESTIONS

- If you are making ice cream, add a lemongrass simple syrup: Boil a cup of water with minced lemongrass, add the sugar required for the ice cream recipe, and cook to the desired strength. Then chill the mixture and add to the remaining ingredients. This syrup is especially good for poaching pears or peaches.

- Crush lemongrass into a glass of homemade lemonade.
- Pound stalks to a pulp for stir-fries.
- Use lemongrass to add flavor and life to marinades, clear soups, and sauces.
- Lemongrass-infused butter (using the most tender parts ground with a mortar and pestle and blended with butter) makes a perfect complement to lightly steamed broccoli or young, tender peas.
- Lemongrass tea is a relaxing, calming beverage: Bruise a 2-inch section of the stalk and drop it into a pot of steeping tea.
- As an antidote to colds and flu, infuse clear chicken broth or a light chicken soup with plenty of garlic, ginger, hot peppers, and lemongrass.
- Lemongrass provides the delicate flavor of lemon without the sourness and bite of the citrus fruit; add finely chopped stalks or pulp to seafood dishes.
- For a surprising twist, add a tablespoon or two of finely mashed lemongrass to your favorite salsa recipe.
- Lemongrass and rose petals make a fantastic tea—or a hot bath.
- Finely ground lemongrass is an invigorating addition to salads, especially those containing cold meat, fish, and hot peppers.
- Try using lemongrass in almost any preparation calling for lemon rind, zest, or juice. The herb has the same lemony flavor but is less harsh and acid than the fruit.

MAINE LOBSTER CHOWDER WITH COCONUT, CORN, AND LEMONGRASS

SERVES 8

Source Note: Galangal is a spicy root that resembles ginger and lends a pungent flavor to many Southeast Asian dishes. You can find it fresh or frozen in Asian markets or through online merchants.

2 tablespoons vegetable oil
4 ounces shallot, thinly sliced
6 cloves garlic, sliced
2 tablespoons minced lemongrass
2 teaspoons red chile flakes, dried
½ teaspoon chili paste
1-inch piece frozen or fresh galangal or ginger, thinly sliced
4 cups lobster stock
2 cups chicken stock
4 cups (two 15-ounce cans) unsweetened coconut milk
2 Kaffir lime leaves, center rib removed, crushed (or zest of 1 lime)
4 tablespoons fish sauce
2 teaspoons granulated sugar
1 pound Maine lobster tail meat, cooked and cut into ¾-inch dice
2 cups sweet corn kernels
½ cup enoki mushrooms
1 cup cherry tomatoes, halved
2 tablespoons fresh lime juice
Maine lobster claw meat, cooked whole and shelled, for garnish
12 cilantro sprigs, for garnish

12 Thai basil leaves, halved, for garnish
4 tablespoons fried shallots, for garnish

1. Heat the oil in a saucepan over medium heat until moderately hot. Add the shallot, garlic, lemongrass, chile flakes, and chili paste, and brown slightly, about 30 seconds.

2. Working quickly and without burning the spices, add the galangal, lobster stock, chicken stock, coconut milk, and Kaffir lime leaves. Bring to a boil and let simmer for 5 minutes so the flavors can meld.

3. Add about half of the fish sauce and sugar; stir and taste. Add more of either one if desired. Add the lobster tail meat. Bring to a simmer and let the lobster heat through.

4. Add the corn and mushrooms. As soon as the mixture comes to a second boil, turn off the heat and add the tomatoes and lime juice.

5. Garnish with the lobster claws, cilantro, Thai basil leaves, and fried shallots. Serve immediately.

— *Maine Lobster Promotion Council, from* Simply Seafood *by Pamela Eimers*

LEMONGRASS HALIBUT

SERVES 6

Author Note: Fresh lemongrass skewers add a fragrant citrus note to halibut. Green curry paste, Thai fish sauce, and toasted sesame oil are available in the Asian section of the store. Serve with jasmine or coconut rice, if desired.

2 tablespoons extra-virgin olive or macadamia nut oil
1 tablespoon green curry paste
1 teaspoon turmeric
1 tablespoon freshly grated fresh ginger
1 tablespoon rice wine vinegar
1 teaspoon nam pla (Thai fish sauce)
4 (6-ounce) skinless, boneless Alaska halibut fillets
4 fresh lemongrass stalks, each about ¼ inch in diameter and 6 inches long

1. In a small bowl, thoroughly blend the oil, curry paste, turmeric, ginger, vinegar, and fish sauce. Brush the paste on the halibut; cover and refrigerate for 30 minutes to let the flavors mingle.

2. Preheat the grill to medium high. Thread the halibut onto the lemongrass skewers, 1 fillet per skewer. Place the skewers on a well-oiled grill or a greased broiling pan.

3. Grill the halibut directly above the heat source for 4 to 5 minutes per side, turning once during cooking. Cook just until the fish is opaque throughout.

— *Vital Choice Seafood*

ICED GREEN TEA
WITH LEMONGRASS AND GINGER
MAKES 4 CUPS

1 stalk fresh lemongrass
1 (1-inch) piece peeled ginger, cut into 4 slices
2 green tea bags
¼ cup honey
4 cups boiling water
¼ cup fresh lemon juice
Ice cubes

1. Cut the dry ends off the lemongrass stalk, peel off the stalk's outer layer, and discard. Cut off the top half of the lemongrass stalk and save it to use as swizzle sticks, wrapping it in a damp paper towel and refrigerating until needed. Split the remaining portion of the lemongrass and cut it into 4 pieces, bruising it a bit.

2. Place the lemongrass, ginger, tea bags, and honey in a heatproof container or bowl. Pour boiling water over them. Let steep and cool to room temperature.

3. Remove the tea bags and stir in the lemon juice. Chill until ready to serve.

4. When you're ready to serve, separate the inner layers of the reserved lemongrass stalk into 4 stir sticks. Pour the tea through a fine mesh strainer to remove the ginger and lemongrass pieces. Serve the tea in tall glasses over lots of ice with the lemongrass sticks.

— *Fooddownunder.com*

Wake Up and Smell the Grass

Inhaling a few drops of lemongrass oil in a tissue during long car trips or a day at the office will help stimulate, soothe, and invigorate.

Mint

GENUS MENTHA

Many of us experience daily exposure to mint as a flavoring—in toothpaste, mouthwash, chewing gum—and hardly think about this ubiquitous taste at all. We should reconsider, for its culinary uses are many. Middle Eastern cuisines use huge quantities of the herb in various cooling dishes as well as in their famous hot tea, which is served strong and very sweet. In Vietnam, many varieties of mints are used in the repertoire of fresh greenery that accompanies nearly every meal. And in North African and Indian cuisines, mint can be found in everything from chutneys to beverages.

Spearmint and peppermint are the most widely known mints, but we should not forget the deliciously fragrant pineapple mint, orange mint, curly mint, pennyroyal, chocolate mint, apple mint, and ginger mint, to name a few. This plant family has many members, and it has been difficult for botanists to classify all of its distinct species because the plants tend to crossbreed very easily. In spite of their variations, what gives all mints their distinctive aroma is the presence of menthol and other essential oils, which have numerous medicinal and antiseptic properties.

HISTORY

Mint originated in Asia and the Mediterranean, where it has a long history as food, fragrance, and medicine. The ancient Greeks wore wreaths of it, decorated their banquet tables with it, and used it in their baths as a refreshing stimulant. One of the earliest recorded uses of mint was as a room freshener by the Romans, who also grew it in their gardens as a ground cover that would smell sweetly when walked upon.

Medicinally, peppermint and spearmint have been used extensively to treat stomachache, bad breath, flatulence, nausea, and heartburn. The United States produces about 75 percent of the world's peppermint oil, which is used in candy, toothpaste, soap, mouthwash, chewing gum, cough syrup, liqueur, and many other preparations. This little-known American tradition of producing peppermint oil for the gum and candy industries has been documented in the film *American Mint* by California history professor Dr. Ephraim K. Smith.

NUTRITION

Mint is a good source of vitamin C, B2, manganese, and copper, as well as several phytonutrients that help relieve digestive upsets. A 2-tablespoon serving contains 2 calories.

SEASON

Commercially, mint is widely grown and in season year-round. You'll find it at farmers markets and CSAs throughout the spring, summer, and fall.

SELECTION

Mint should be vibrantly green and fresh looking, with stiff stems and perky leaves. Avoid bunches with signs of wilting, yellowing, or dark spots.

 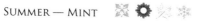

STORAGE

Wrap mint in a damp paper towel and store it in a perforated plastic bag in the refrigerator vegetable crisper, where it will keep for up to a few days. Or you can treat fresh mint sprigs like any other living flower or plant cutting; just snip off the stem ends and place them in a glass of water.

TRIMMING AND CLEANING

With its finely grooved leaves, mint can sometimes harbor dirt and bugs. Rinse fresh mint thoroughly under running water or submerge the leaves in a sink filled with water. Pat dry, then strip the leaves from the tough, woody stems.

FREEZING

An easy way to freeze fresh mint is to freeze whole leaves. Wash and thoroughly dry the sprigs and strip them of leaves. Then stack the whole leaves in ice cube trays (about 8 leaves will fit into each section of the tray); pour water over them and freeze. After the cubes are frozen, pop them out and place them in zipper-lock freezer bags.

DRYING

Mint takes to drying quite readily, although fresh mint is definitely preferable to the dried version when it comes to flavor.

If you still want to dry the herb, tie fresh, dry sprigs that are free of dew and moisture into a bunch and hang in a cool, dry, dark place with good ventilation. You can cover the bunches with small paper bags to keep dust off them, but make sure the bags have adequate holes for proper ventilation. Once the bunches are dried, seal them tightly in a container with a lid or in a zipper-lock plastic bag and store away from light and heat.

Or dry mint in the oven: Spread a layer of leaves on a cookie sheet and place the herbs in a warm (up to 180°F) oven for 30 minutes; then check them every 15 minutes, until they are thoroughly dry.

A microwave oven can also be used for small quantities of mint, although this method tends to evaporate more of the oils than does air-drying. Strip the leaves off the stems, and place on a microwave-safe plate. Mint is among the quickest herbs to dry, so microwave on High for 10 seconds at a time, then check to see if the leaves are getting brittle. They should remain fairly bright green even when fully dried, and should be completely dry in 15 to 45 seconds.

EQUIVALENTS, MEASURES, AND SERVINGS

- 1 tablespoon chopped fresh mint = 1 teaspoon dried
- 1 cup fresh = ¼ cup dried leaves

COMPLEMENTARY HERBS, SEASONINGS, AND FOODS

Apples, basil, cantaloupe, carrots, chocolate, cilantro, coconuts, cucumbers, fennel, garlic, honey, lamb, lemons, limes, oranges, papaya, pasta, peas, pineapple, tomatoes, watermelon, yogurt, zucchini.

SERVING SUGGESTIONS

- Make mojitos and mint juleps!

"How sweet I roam'd
from field to field
And tasted all the
summer's pride."

— William Blake,
Poetical Sketches

R-evolution Gardens— Challenges and Rewards of a Mostly Off-Grid Farm

Martha Wagner

Ginger Edwards has referred to herself as a crazy upstart farmer and she considers it an asset: "It may be the best set of skills I can have as the climate begins to change on planet Earth."

Like many younger-generation farmers, she came to farming from an unlikely background, having grown up in Detroit, Michigan. She moved to Oregon and chose an unlikely location—Oregon's cool, rural north coast—to start a CSA farm on a small, off-grid parcel of land. With "crazy-upstart" hard work and determination, she was growing for restaurants and 50 CSA customers in just a few years, and getting power from solar panels and a micro-hydro generator on the creek that runs through the property.

Today, Edwards and her husband, herbalist Brigham Edwards, have a four-season (spring, summer, late summer, and fall), 24-week CSA with 65 members. They also sell produce at the nearby Manzanita Farmers Market. Workshops in the spring and fall bring people to the five-acre homestead part of the farm to learn about topics as diverse as renewable energy, medicinal herbs, natural building, and mushroom foraging, taught by expert instructors. Visitors also come to the farm for a peaceful overnight stay at the Japanese Forest House, a unique off-grid Airbnb rental, handbuilt with mostly salvaged materials by Brian Schulz, friend and co-founder of the farm.

Deep Organic Practices

Hand-scaled farming is what we do, says Edwards, explaining that the farm crew "pays close attention to the flavor, color, selection, and diversity of veggies in each CSA box" and "uses deep organic farming practic-

---

- Mint leaves, when frozen as ice cubes (see the freezing instructions on page 215), are delightful when added to glasses of water, tonic, or mixed drinks.

- Perk up fruit salads with a few chopped or whole leaves of fresh mint.

- The cool sweetness of mint balances the acidity of tomatoes.

- Make a cup of mint tea, either hot or iced; it can help soothe an upset stomach. Fresh mint makes a stronger-tasting tea than dried, and it is a must for traditional Moroccan mint tea.

- Chop herbs like tarragon, dill, mint, basil, and parsley, and combine with chopped green onions and steamed peas.

- Whole sprigs of raw cilantro, basil, and mint are served by the handful with Vietnamese dishes; they make a refreshing foil for this cuisine's traditional sour, sweet, and piquant flavors.

- Mint jelly is a classic accompaniment to roast lamb, and mint chutney accompanies many Indian curries.

- Mint can be a pleasant surprise when added to otherwise common dishes—try mixing finely chopped leaves with rice, quinoa, couscous, and pasta.

- Add finely chopped mint and fresh lime or lemon juice to salad dressings.

- Mint goes great with peas of all kinds—sprinkle it in with sugar snaps or snow peas in the final minute of cooking.

- A few judiciously used leaves of mint, finely chopped, can be refreshing in green salads.

- Mint and chocolate, of course, are a most delicious pairing. Cookies, cakes, puddings, mousses, ice creams, brownies … Need I say more?

- Tabbouleh, the famous Middle Eastern herb salad, combines chopped mint, parsley, tomatoes, cucumbers, and bulgur wheat.

- Whole mint leaves are sometimes used in Thai and Vietnamese spring rolls.

· ·

JULIA CHILD'S BUTTERED PEAS WITH MINT
SERVES 2 TO 4

Source Note: This recipe is based on the Buttered Peas II recipe from Julia Child's Mastering the Art of French Cooking.

3 cups shelled fresh green peas
1 to 2 tablespoons sugar
6 tablespoons (¾ stick) butter
Kosher salt
Freshly ground black pepper
2 tablespoons finely chopped fresh mint

1. Drop the peas in boiling water and boil uncovered for 5 to 10 minutes, or until the peas are almost but not quite tender (they will finish cooking later). Drain.

2. Roll the peas in the saucepan over moderate heat for a moment or two to evaporate their moisture. Then roll them with the sugar, butter, salt, and pepper. Cover and cook over very low heat for about 10 minutes, tossing occasionally, until they are tender.

3. Toss in the fresh mint, transfer to a heated vegetable dish, and serve as soon as possible.

— *Foodista.com*

. . . .

MOROCCAN MINT TEA   SERVES 4

Source Note: In Morocco, tea is served very sweet. Decrease the amount of sugar if you prefer.

2 tablespoons Chinese green tea or Chinese gunpowder tea
5 cups boiling water
1 large bunch fresh mint
1 cup sugar, or to taste

1. Place the tea in the teapot. Pour in the boiling water. Cover and steep 2 to 3 minutes.

2. Wash the mint under running water and add to the pot. Steep for 3 to 5 minutes. Add the sugar and stir thoroughly to dissolve.

3. Serve immediately in small heatproof tea glasses or small cups.

— *MsAnthea, Foodista.com*

. . . .

SABZI (HERB SALAD)   SERVES 3 TO 4

Source Note: Sabzi refers to a mix of greens or potherbs, usually a Middle Eastern combination of dill, parsley, and mint. Serve sabzi with a warm cheese-filled turnover or falafel, or add it to a pita sandwich along with tomatoes and feta cheese or ricotta salata.

3 cups small spinach leaves
1 cup arugula
¼ cup flat-leaf parsley leaves
¼ cup cilantro leaves
¼ cup dill sprigs
6 mint leaves, torn into small pieces
Several celery or lovage leaves, torn
2 scallions (green onions), including a few inches of the greens, thinly sliced
Salt
1 tablespoon extra-virgin olive oil, or as needed
Fresh lemon juice

1. Carefully sort through the greens, then wash and dry them well. Tear or cut the spinach and arugula into bite-size pieces and toss with the herbs, scallions, and a few pinches of salt.

es," including biodynamics, focused on building soil health and quality. The crew uses hand tools and no-till or minimal-till techniques to reduce the farm's carbon footprint.

Perennials and medicinal herbs are grown on the homestead acreage with some row crops mixed in. Other row crops are grown on a nearby two-acre vegetable field leased from neighbors. The leased acreage is not fully off-grid—electricity is used for running a well pump and for powering a walk-in cooler in a packing shed inside a rented barn space. Edwards says she'd like to make these parts of the farm off-grid or at least powered by renewable energy. "The future is in renewable energy, not in fossil fuels, so I am always thinking of ways we can do things on the farm with less energy inputs," she explains.

Coastal climates have their own particular challenges. Edwards says she's learned to flow with the climate and accept crop losses when they occur with a Zen attitude. "We have a long, rainy spring and get over 80 inches of rain annually. Twenty percent of what we grow is under high plastic tunnels—a lot of kale, chard, spinach, and root veggies. In summer we put the heat-loving crops in there."

Edwards's passion for growing food extends to educating and supporting others who want to grow food. She's a founding board member of a local nonprofit, the Nehalem Valley Farm Trust. Its plans include helping new farmers acquire land and purchasing a 100-year-old homestead across the road from her farm to educate the public about renewable energy, homesteading skills, and local food; use for classes and for making value-added products; and offer farm stay accommodations.

Have there been challenges related to being a woman farmer? "Anyone who can make it as a farmer gets respect because it's a hard job," she says. "My interns ap-

preciate my being a woman. That's been important to them. One intern now has her own farm down the road. The biggest lesson for me has been managing the stress level that comes with this job—it's hard physically and mentally. To find a sense of enjoyment and know how important the work is—that's the challenge. It doesn't pay well but the rewards are there. The rewards are many, including great food, a wonderful community, and being in nature every day."

2. Drizzle on enough oil to lightly coat the leaves, then squeeze on a little lemon juice and toss again.

— *Deborah Madison,* Vegetarian Cooking for Everyone

Tractors awaiting duty at Featherstone Farm.

Okra

ABELMOSCHUS ESCULENTUS

Okra is a vegetable sometimes unfairly maligned for the very characteristic beloved by many: its slippery texture, thanks to the clear, mucilaginous juice lurking in its distinctively shaped, narrow seedpods. Pickling or frying the whole pods can reduce this slipperiness, but generally it's a futile thing to hide—best to appreciate this unique vegetable with its slightly tart, distinctive clean taste for what it is.

This tropical, heat-loving plant is actually a member of the Hibiscus family, with beautiful yellow or pink blossoms that are reminiscent of its more flashy cousins. Okra is a popular vegetable in African, Indian, Middle Eastern, Asian, and Caribbean cuisines, and in America, it is closely associated with the Deep South and African-American soul food. Okra, because of its mucilaginous qualities, has long been valued as a thickener in soups and stews. In fact, gumbo, the famous Louisiana stew, relies on either okra or filé powder as a thickening agent (but never both).

Okra's meaty texture makes it a remarkably versatile vegetable that behaves well whether it is pickled, steamed, breaded and fried, grilled, sautéed, stewed, braised, or even roasted. Both red and green forms of okra exist; the scarlet pods will usually turn green when cooked. The young leaves can be eaten raw in salads or cooked, and, interestingly, okra seed oil is also being explored for potential biodiesel production.

HISTORY

Some controversy exists about the precise origins of the plant, but many sources believe okra came from Africa, specifically the area around Ethiopia and Eritrea. South Asia is also a possibility, but regardless, okra has covered many thousands of miles around the globe, having been brought to Europe by the Arabs and to both North and South America by African slaves who carried seeds with them from their homelands.

NUTRITION

Okra is an outstanding source of dietary fiber, as well as folate, thiamine, vitamins C and K, magnesium, calcium, and potassium. A 1-cup serving contains 33 calories.

SEASON

Although most larger supermarkets carry okra year-round, the pods are at their prime in the mid to late-summer months. Okra is an incredibly prolific vegetable, and the home gardener must be quick to harvest the fast-growing pods before they get too big—sometimes a single day or two makes a difference.

SELECTION

With okra, size does matter—the smaller, the better. Okra pods are actually at their sweetest and tenderest when they are only 2 to 3 inches long;

Books

Okra: A Savor the South Cookbook
(Savor the South Cookbooks)
Virginia Willis,
The University of North
Carolina Press, 2014.

The Glory of Southern Cooking:
Recipes for the Best Beer-Battered
Fried Chicken, Cracklin' Biscuits,
Carolina Pulled Pork, Fried
Okra, Kentucky Cheese Pudding,
Hummingbird Cake, and Almost
400 Other Delectable Dishes
James Villas,
Houghton Mifflin Harcourt, 2013.

Afro-Vegan: Farm-Fresh
African, Caribbean, and
Southern Flavors Remixed
Bryant Terry,
Ten Speed Press, 2014.

5:30 AM

It's already light out by the time I come down to the shop office to open things up. This is my best chance to get my thoughts together for the day and to check over affairs in the office—I won't be back here much today. Checking on lettuce orders for the day, phoning in a compost order (two semi-trailer loads to be delivered tomorrow), noting a few phone calls to be returned later, and, above all, prioritizing the various projects of the day … I have to be ready for the crew by 6:00.

5:58 AM

Everyone is in early as usual. I give a quick outline of the day's work for everyone in a mixture of English and Spanish (and hope the Hmong speakers have understood!). I set a number of people to preparing the field wagons for the lettuce harvest (120 cases for the food co-ops). Then I outline jobs for a number of others: one guy will be chisel plowing and making beds at the Lacher farm on the ridge. Two others will be cultivating winter squash with the Regi weeder all morning. I tell these two I'll be by to check on their progress if I can; if they finish the field before I get there, they can start laying out tomato trellis stakes in a nearby field. I hear several motors starting up as I dash back up to the office to call home and let my family know where I'll be if they want to find me.

6:35 AM

Ten people are now out picking lettuce. It is an experienced crew, but this is only our third cutting of the season and I want to make sure there are no surprises and everyone

pods that are longer may still be quite edible, but they may be less flavorful and are more likely to be woody. Look for bright-colored, fresh-looking pods that are firm and crisp when snapped open, with no signs of shriveling or flabbiness.

STORAGE

Okra is surprisingly perishable and should be used within a few days of purchase. Store the dry, unwashed pods in a paper bag in the warmer part of the refrigerator (usually the upper area). Okra, in keeping with its tropical origins, does not like temperatures below 45°F.

TRIMMING AND CLEANING

Wait to wash okra until right before you use it. Small okra pods need nothing more than a little stem trimming, whereas you should cut the caps off larger okra pods if they are to be used whole. For dishes calling for sliced okra, cut off the cap or whole top end and slice the pods crosswise.

STEAMING AND BOILING

Okra takes beautifully to steaming. To minimize sliminess, steam the pods whole, about 3 to 8 minutes, depending on their size. They should remain bright green for best texture and flavor; do not overcook.

STIR-FRYING AND SAUTÉING

Okra takes well to stir-frying and sautéing. Cooking whole pods rather than slices will reduce the sliminess a bit, and it is important that you start with okra that is dry on the outside (not still wet from washing)—otherwise you may end up with a mushier result. Cook small whole pods for 4 to 6 minutes or until tender on medium-high heat in a wok or large frying pan. Sliced okra may cook even more quickly. Be sure to add a bit of oil or melted butter to the pan, or they will stick.

BAKING AND ROASTING

Roasting okra is an unusual way to prepare okra, but it produces great results. It also reduces some of its sliminess. Trim off the stems and caps, and place whole pods on a baking sheet or pan. Drizzle olive oil or seasonings over the pods, then roast for 10 to 15 minutes in a 425°F oven.

MICROWAVING

Trim stems and caps; then either leave the pods whole or cut them into slices. Place in a microwave-safe dish; add ¼ cup water; cover and cook on high power.

- 1 pound = 7 to 9 minutes

BLANCHING AND FREEZING

Trim the stems and caps off the okra, but be careful not to cut into the seed cell area, as that will release the vegetable's slippery juices. Blanch small whole pods in salted boiling water for 3 minutes and larger ones for 4 minutes. Drain, then plunge them into an ice-water bath for a few minutes to stop the cooking process. Drain thoroughly, then package them in zipper-lock freezer or vacuum food sealer-type bags, or freezer containers.

Squeeze out any excess air and leave ½ inch of headspace (unless you are using the vacuum sealing method). You can also quick-freeze individual pods by placing them on a tray lined with parchment paper and putting the tray into the freezer for a few hours. Once they are frozen, transfer them into freezer bags. Frozen okra will keep about 10 months at 0°F.

EQUIVALENTS, MEASURES, AND SERVINGS

- 1 pound, fresh = 35 pods = 10 to 12 ounces trimmed
- 1 pound, fresh = 3 to 4 cups sliced
- 1 pound = 3 to 4 servings

COMPLEMENTARY HERBS, SEASONINGS, AND FOODS

Apricots, chiles, cinnamon, citrus, coconut, coriander, corn, cumin, curry, garam masala, garlic, ginger, lamb, lemon, lime, mangoes, mustard, nutmeg, onions, oranges, shallots, soy sauce, tomato, turmeric, vinegar, wasabi.

SERVING SUGGESTIONS

- Okra makes a great finger food, for obvious reasons. Lightly steam very young pods and have on hand little bowls of hollandaise sauce, melted butter, or mayonnaise for dipping—it could become a hit with children when served this way.
- Breaded, deep-fried okra is a southern favorite. Dredge okra slices in either plain or Cajun-seasoned cornmeal.
- Okra is a staple in Indian cuisine, where it combines well with all sorts of spices and piquant sauces.
- Okra is a natural with acidic foods like tomatoes and vinegar; it is also excellent in sweet-and-sour dishes.
- Pickle okra just like small cucumbers.
- Add okra to stews or soups as a surprise vegetable—its viscous texture can pleasantly thicken the dish.
- Add sliced, sautéed okra to omelets and quiches.
- Cook sliced okra in butter with onions and ham. Combine with cooked rice, then use to stuff hollowed-out tomatoes. Bake until nice and hot.
- Steam okra and combine with oranges baked with nutmeg for a simple, delicious side dish.
- Add okra to rice and azuki beans for a twist on the traditional rice and beans of the American South. This is a popular celebratory dish in Japan.
- In Morocco, okra is combined with braised lamb and pears in a savory stew.
- Caribbean cooking frequently uses okra, which combines it with cornmeal in a dish called *coo-coo*, a Creole version of polenta.

OKRA, CORN, AND TOMATOES   SERVES 8

Source Note: Almost too pretty to eat, this recipe is seasoned with bacon, hot pepper sauce, onions and garlic—creating a beautiful dish for family gatherings large or small. You can reduce the fat by using turkey bacon instead of regular pork bacon; it has the same smoky flavor but much less fat.

knows the system: cut, field-pack, and get the heads to the wagon for washing and case-packing ASAP. When 30 or more cases are done, we have to get them back to the cooler in a hurry. The forecast is for heat, and the lettuce quality depends on the whole process—128 cases—being done by 10 AM. Everything is going well. I pick for 20 minutes myself, sampling all of the varieties to make sure they are all top quality. The red leaf seems to be heat-stressed; I make a mental note to have Esteban get irrigation going in here tomorrow. And the deer have knocked down part of the temporary fence and are nibbling the romaine. A crew will have to repair and check the entire fence this afternoon, or we could lose hundreds of heads in a single night.

8:15 AM
Back in the shop to check on fencing supplies—sure enough, we're short on ground rods to put up another deer fence. Someone will have to pick them up before the fence can go up—a very high priority. Just calling to see if the hardware store in Rushford has any around (to save a trip to Winona) when CSA managers come in to the office to ask for consultation. The three of us head out to the east end of the farm to evaluate planting conditions for carrots, which are notoriously difficult to establish. We're looking at soil moisture, cover crop residue on the beds, and the forecast. We decide to wait on the planting until conditions are better but to move forward on beets and summer salad crops instead. I remind the CSA people to check on how the specialty melons got transplanted yesterday at the Highum farm—they could need water.

9:00 AM
Returning to the shop on foot when Hugo passes by on the 4020 John Deere on his way to the ridge farm. He stops and reports that the trans-

mission's power shift has been slipping more and more recently. This will require evaluation by a mechanic in town—we discuss the options for a farm call or taking the tractor to Rushford on the trailer (which would take it out of commission at a busy time). We decide to have the tractor finish chisel plowing at Lacher's, then to substitute the new McCormick for making planting beds later in the day so Evan can take the John Deere into Hammel's in the afternoon. Tractor troubles at this time of year are stressful.

9:24 AM

Back in the shop, everything is quiet. I call Jim to make sure he can look at the 4020 if we get it to him in the afternoon. The lettuce crew will be finished before long. I've got only a few minutes to sneak home to get breakfast and to check on the kids. I pedal up to the house and have a quick bite and catch up on the news with a three-day-old Star Tribune *that's lying around. Then the boys interrupt me with a request to throw the baseball a bit. I indulge myself for a few minutes in a game of catch, feeling guilty that I should be in the shop getting ready for the lettuce crew.*

9:55 AM

In the shop, the wagons stacked with boxed lettuces are just rolling in. I check with the pickers about quality issues and their ideas about the next harvest volume. We agree that work on the fence must happen today—two guys want to go after it right away and start looking for supplies. The beds for transplanting cabbage will not be ready until later in the day, so I send the remaining crew out to hoe garlic until lunch. I then zip up to the office to talk with Larisa about lettuce availability for later in the week, so she can update her faxes to the co-ops in the Twin Cities. Larisa has other questions, and we go over a number of billing issues.

Author Note: You can make this either with fresh tomatoes, corn, and okra, or use canned tomatoes and corn and frozen okra. If you use frozen okra, it does not need to be thawed first.

> 4 slices bacon
> 1 cup coarsely chopped onion (1 large)
> 2 cups fresh cherry or grape tomatoes, halved
>   (or 2 cups canned diced tomatoes, undrained)
> 2 cups fresh corn kernels, or two (15.25-ounce) cans
>   whole-kernel corn, drained
> 2½ cups cut fresh okra, or one (1-pound) bag frozen okra
> 1 teaspoon seasoned salt
> ¼ teaspoon garlic powder
> ½ teaspoon hot pepper sauce
> Freshly ground black pepper

1. Fry the bacon in a large skillet over medium heat for 8 to 10 minutes, turning occasionally, until crisp. Remove the bacon, but leave 1 tablespoon of the bacon drippings in the pan. Drain the bacon on paper towels, crumble it, and set aside.

2. Cook the onion in the bacon drippings over medium heat, stirring occasionally until tender, 3 to 5 minutes.

3. If you're using fresh tomatoes, corn, and okra: Add the okra and corn kernels to the pan and sauté 2 to 3 minutes. Then add the tomatoes and seasonings and sauté for another 5 to 7 minutes, stirring often, or until all of the vegetables are tender. Sprinkle with the bacon.

4. If you're using canned tomatoes and corn and frozen okra: Stir in all of the ingredients except the bacon. Heat to boiling. Reduce the heat to low; cover and simmer 6 to 8 minutes, stirring occasionally, until the okra is tender. Sprinkle with the bacon.

— Adapted from Betty Crocker

OKRA PICKLES

MAKES 6 PINTS

Source Note: Okra is one of the few vegetables whose flavor and texture are upheld and nicely modified—not lost—in the pickling process. If available, use red okra, which pinkens prettily in vinegar. Serve the pickles with smoked or boiled beef or pork, beans and rice, or sweet dishes of Indian, Southeast Asian, or Japanese descent.

> 2½ pounds very small, bright okra pods (green or red)
> 6 to 12 tiny dried chiles
> 3 teaspoons mustard seeds, bruised
> 1½ teaspoons dill seeds
> 1½ teaspoons coriander seeds, bruised
> 1 very small red onion, sliced, separated into rings

2 cups cider vinegar
2 cups distilled white vinegar
2 cups water
¼ cup kosher salt

1. Rinse the okra. Dry on a soft towel. Trim the stems, leaving a little stub of cap on each and being careful not to pierce the caps or pods.

2. Divide the spices evenly among 6 sterilized, wide-mouth pint canning jars. Pack the okra upright in the jars, placing the tip and stem ends in alternating positions and interspersing the onion rings—pack tightly enough to keep the pods upright, but do not crush or jam them.

3. In a nonaluminum pot, combine both vinegars, water, and salt. Bring to a boil. Fill the jars to within ½ inch of rims. Place a scalded two-piece lid on each, then fasten the screw-bands.

4. Set the jars on a rack in a deep pot half filled with boiling water. Add boiling water to cover the jars by 2 inches. Bring back to a boil, cover, and boil for 5 minutes. Transfer the jars to a towel to cool completely. Store about a month before serving.

— *Elizabeth Schneider,* Vegetables from Amaranth to Zucchini: The Essential Reference

. . . .

SPICED OKRA AND TOMATOES OVER TOASTY CRACKED WHEAT   SERVES 4 AS A MAIN DISH

Source Note: Sliced, spiced, and braised, okra is quite different from the whole and perky vegetable, softening to a sauce-like consistency. Tomatoes, chile, and cinnamon are traditional Middle Eastern enhancements for this stewy style, which I like to freshen with mint and parsley. Technically, bulgur wheat has been precooked, whereas cracked wheat is raw, but packaging information does not always make this clear. If you cannot find cracked wheat, substitute coarse-grain bulgur wheat.

2 tablespoons olive oil, divided
1¼ cups cracked wheat (or coarse-ground bulgur)
¼ teaspoon cinnamon
¾ teaspoon kosher salt, divided
3 tablespoons raisins
2½ cups water or vegetable broth, divided
1 pound okra, rinsed
1 or 2 small fresh green chiles
1 medium red or white onion
2 medium-large firm tomatoes
1 tablespoon balsamic vinegar
About ¼ cup chopped fresh parsley leaves, divided
About ¼ cup chopped fresh mint leaves, divided

I've forgotten about the squash crew at the Lacher farm, so I get in the truck and drive up on the ridge to check in as I'd promised. The squash cultivating is done, and the two guys have moved over to caging tomatoes. The squash looks magnificent in the early summer sun, and I take a moment to walk through and admire their work. My reverie is interrupted by bad news: cucumber beetles are attacking the buttercups (the most susceptible of the squashes) in force. I know from experience that this is the crop's most vulnerable time, but if we can use an organic spray to control the beetles for a week and follow it up with foliar feed to rejuvenate the damaged leaves, the crop will be fine. I will have to communicate this plan to Salvador, the spray manager.

I decide to check on Hugo and the 4020. Walking over the ridge takes me past the field of tomatoes. This too looks beautiful—no disease or weeds. I'm surprised at how much progress the crew has made on trellising the cherry tomatoes in the last week. I remind myself that this year we need to irrigate the toms before they show heat stress … It won't be long now.

Hugo is doing well on the chisel plowing, so I don't interrupt him. Walking out into the field to see if the quack grass is under control, I happily find few white succulent roots being turned up. This old hayfield has come around nicely in three seasons. Next I spend 20 minutes mounting the bed maker on the McCormick—luckily both were left up here last week—so it will be ready for Hugo after lunch. I call Evan on his cell phone and ask him to get the 4020 loaded onto the trailer and down to Rushford after lunch.

12:25 PM
I look up to realize that everyone has returned to the home farm but

me. I take this opportunity to visit with Henry and Violette Lacher, the retired owners of this farm, at their home across the road. I ask Henry about truck access through his farmyard for compost delivery. I spend a few minutes with Violette, admiring her fabulous perennial flower garden, and I'm reminded of how much I enjoy senior farmers like the Lachers, and how important their support and advice is for our farm.

1:15 PM

I'm startled once again when I check my watch—I've got to get back to the home farm and make sure everything is on track. On the way back down the valley I pass first a truckful of guys on the way back to the tomatoes—they've determined that the tom cages should be finished today, and that they need five people to do it. Great—this crew runs itself with few snags! I mention to Salvador that he will have to spray the buttercup squash in the evening, when the beetles are more active. Then I pass Evan in the big truck and trailer, on his way to get the John Deere. Things are taking care of themselves.

Back in the shop, I try to catch up on a couple of phone calls and emails. I work on the plan to transplant broccoli over the next few weeks—numbers of beds, varieties, and timing—before being interrupted by the CSA crew, who have finished their planting. We discuss the next generations of salad crops, but they don't have the beds ready to plant yet. So I ask them to set up the irrigation in the lettuce for running overnight. This reminds me that we need new pipe gaskets. I drop 20 minutes calling around to find them at an irrigation supplier.

2:45 PM

It is now midafternoon, and I'm in distinct danger of not getting to the

(continued on page 226)

1. Heat 1 tablespoon oil in a heavy saucepan. Add the cracked wheat and stir over moderate heat for several minutes to toast lightly. Add the cinnamon, ¼ teaspoon of the salt, and raisins. Add 2 cups of the water and bring to a full boil. Turn the heat to its lowest point. Cook, covered, for 15 minutes. Turn off the heat and let stand, covered, 15 minutes or longer.

2. Meanwhile, trim the caps from the okra. Cut the pods into ½-inch slices. Seed and mince the chile. Peel and dice the onion. Peel the tomatoes, then cut into ¾-inch dice.

3. Heat the remaining 1 tablespoon oil in a heavy medium-large pot. Stir in the okra, chile, and remaining ½ cup water. Simmer, covered, for 5 minutes. Add the onion, tomatoes, vinegar, and remaining ½ teaspoon salt. Simmer until the vegetables are soft and almost saucy, about 5 minutes. Season to taste.

4. In a heated dish, toss the cracked wheat with 3 tablespoons each parsley and mint, then add more to taste. Spoon the okra mixture over each serving.

— *Elizabeth Schneider,* Vegetables from Amaranth to Zucchini: The Essential Reference

Onions (Green)

ALLIUM CEPA OR A. FISTULOSUM

In the kitchen, green onions are often overshadowed by their bigger, bolder *Allium* siblings—onions, shallots, leeks, and garlic—but these slim little guys should not be ignored. Indeed, their delicate flavor gives them an advantage over their harsher cousins, and sometimes they're just the thing when all you need is a gentle whisper of onion flavor, not a loud shout.

Green onions are simply the immature young shoots of regular bulb onions (yellow, white, red—it doesn't matter). They are sometimes called scallions, especially in the northeastern United States (people outside Boston or New York may not know what you're talking about when you mention scallions). Or you may see them in the markets labeled as spring onions, bunching onions, or salad onions. They are all the same, although bunching onions can also refer to a specific type of Asian onion that looks similar to green onions but has thicker, longer white stalks. Contrary to many dictionary definitions, however, green onions are definitely not shallots, which are a completely different form of *Allium* (see pages 287–294).

Some people prefer to use only the white bulbs and lighter-colored parts of the stalks, but the entire plant is edible and should not be wasted, in my opinion. When they are in season and at their very best, they deserve to be treated as a vegetable in their own right, not just as a garnish or seasoning.

HISTORY

Precisely where humans ate their first onions (and green onions) remains a matter of some dispute. Several wild species exist, and they were probably foraged by ancient peoples long before domestication occurred. The first known record of them comes from Mesopotamia. The ancient Egyptians valued onions not only as food but as currency, for the pyramid builders were partially paid with these aromatic vegetables along with garlic. Onions quickly spread throughout the rest of Europe and were often associated with the lower classes, who depended on them as a staple in their frugal diet.

NUTRITION

Green onions are good sources of vitamins A, C, and K, and they also contain some potassium, iron, calcium, and manganese. You will never get fat on a diet of green onions; a single stalk contains only 25 calories.

SEASON

Commercially, green onions are widely grown and in season year-round. You'll find them at their best at farmers markets and CSAs in the spring and early summer.

(continued from page 224)

corn cultivating and fertilizing that I've been intending to do all day. So I make a quick trip through the field to make sure everything is on track—the fence repair and the ir-rigation. The garlic-hoeing crew has moved on to other things: picking asparagus and then weeding the new strawberry planting. Every-thing seems to be going smoothly. So I return to the shop, load the truck with bagged fertilizer (pellet-ized poultry compost), throw the bike on top, and drive out to the field. Leaving this rig on the side of the road, I pedal back to get the tractor. Saul has removed two of the cultivator shoes from the bar, and it takes me 15 minutes to find and mount them.

The tractor and cultivator are ready. But suddenly the truck rolls in from the Lachers' site with a crew of five—they're out of cages and they still have two rows to go. We talk about staking those rows instead. Three of them go back up to finish. I ask the other two to spend the rest of the afternoon moving plant trays around in the greenhouse.

4:00 PM

I'm finally in the field cultivating corn. The fertilizer side dressers are working well, and I might even have time to finish this afternoon. Then my cell phone rings—Evan is in Rushford and needs me to discuss options for the 4020. Just then I see Hugo drive by, on his way back from making beds on the ridge. Waving him down, I ask him to finish the corn cultivating. I need to jump in my truck and go down to Rushford to look at the tractor.

4:45 PM

I'm at the tractor shop in town, look-ing over the John Deere with Evan and Jim. The options aren't good; the transmission will have to be opened up. I talk with Mike about

SELECTION

The leafy tops and middle stalks of green onions should be bright green and fresh-looking all the way through, with no chartreuse, yellow, or slimy areas; the white bases should be firm, white, plump, and sturdy.

STORAGE

When you get green onions home, peel off the thin outer skins from the bases of their roots and also the outermost layers of leaves if they appear compromised (but leave the roots themselves intact). This reduces the likelihood of the green onions turning prematurely slimy. Then wrap them unwashed in a paper towel and store them in a plastic bag in the coldest part of the refrigerator, where they will keep for 2 to 3 days. They are quite perishable, so use them as soon as possible. Don't store them next to corn or mushrooms; these vegetables will absorb their odor.

TRIMMING AND CLEANING

If you have already trimmed your green onions before storing them, as outlined above, all you will need to do is slice off the root end and quickly rinse them under running water to remove any bugs or sand.

STIR-FRYING AND SAUTÉING

Green onions are exceptionally suited to stir-frying and sautéing; their delicate texture and small size allow them to cook quickly. An easy way to slice them is to snip them with kitchen shears, like chives. Toss them in the wok or pan during the last few minutes of cooking to preserve their color and crunch.

BAKING AND ROASTING

As with all vegetables, roasting caramelizes and concentrates the natural sugars in green onions, heightening their flavor. Arrange washed, trimmed, whole green onions in a single layer on a shallow baking pan, drizzle a lit-tle oil and seasoning over the top, and toss to coat, making sure that each onion is covered in oil. Roast in a 400°F oven for 10 to 15 minutes.

GRILLING

Like other members of the onion family, green onions behave beautifully on the grill. Keep them whole and either thread them on skewers or ar-range them on a lightly oiled grill pan. Either way, toss them with a little oil and seasoning to prevent them from burning, and cook on the cooler side of the grill for 3 to 4 minutes total, turning once or twice, until they are tender and charred in spots. They are rather delicate and cook quick-ly; keep an eye on them to make sure they don't burn.

MICROWAVING

To microwave, place washed, trimmed whole green onions in a micro-wave-safe dish in a single layer, add ½ cup of water, cover, and cook on high power for 4 to 6 minutes.

BLANCHING AND FREEZING

Freezing green onions will change their texture, so reserve them for dishes in which they will be cooked rather than served raw. They can be frozen without blanching. Simply wash, trim, and chop or snip them finely. Then spread the chopped green onions in a single layer on a tray and freeze them for 30 minutes. Package them in zipper-lock freezer or vacuum food sealer-type bags or freezer containers. Squeeze out any excess air and leave ½ inch of headspace (unless you are using the vacuum sealing method). Frozen green onions will keep for up to 12 months at 0°F. They do not require thawing before using.

EQUIVALENTS, MEASURES, AND SERVINGS

- 1 pound green onions = 8 to 10 ounces trimmed = 2 to 2½ cups chopped

COMPLEMENTARY HERBS, SEASONINGS, AND FOODS

Bacon, beef, butter, cheese (Gruyère, Parmesan), chicken, eggs, fish (sole, salmon, trout, tuna), garlic, mushrooms, olive oil, parsley, pasta, pepper, pork, potatoes, rice, salads, sesame, shellfish, soft cheeses, soups, soy sauce, stews, tacos, tomatoes, vegetables, vinegar.

SERVING SUGGESTIONS

- Plain rice can be a delicious treat with a generous sprinkling of chopped green onions and sesame seeds.

- Serve whole raw green onions along with other raw vegetables such as carrots, celery sticks, quartered fennel pieces, cherry tomatoes, cucumber slices, and broccoli and cauliflower florets. Set out little bowls of different dressings and dips, and watch the fun begin. (You might even get children to eat their veggies this way.)

- Combine generous amounts of green onions with finely diced pork to make wonton fillings. Serve with a dipping sauce of soy sauce, garlic, and more green onions.

- Float pieces of green onion over hot consommé or chicken broth for a comforting dish when you're not feeling well.

- Snip slices of green onion onto stir-fries, tacos, pastas, casseroles, salads, or anywhere you want a little zippy onion flavor and bright green color.

- Fold chopped green onions into omelets and scrambled eggs.

- An old-fashioned way of eating green onions is between two thick slices of good white or dark bread heavily spread with good salted butter.

- Pickled small green onions make a tasty treat.

- If you're making a pasta or rice salad, toss the chopped green onions into the mix before the pasta cools completely; that little bit of warmth will soften the onions and considerably mellow their raw, pungent character.

SUNGOLD SALAD WITH FETA AND CUMIN-YOGURT DRESSING

SERVES 6

2 pints (4 cups) Sungold cherry tomatoes
½ teaspoon salt
¼ cup plain yogurt, drained about 30 minutes, liquid discarded
1 tablespoon olive oil
1 tablespoon fresh lemon juice

renting another fieldwork tractor while this one is laid up ... We need equipment in the field this time of year. We agree that Evan can bring a big Case tractor back to the farm this afternoon, but it will be a full load even for the fifth wheel. It will be expensive, but it will keep us going in the field.

5:20 PM

I realize that I haven't thought about my family once in hours. I call home to see if I can bring anything home from town when I return. I drop by the IGA grocery for a few things, including a 12-pack of Pepsi (their favorite) for the crew. They're getting a lot done, working long hours, and it's hot. I depend on and appreciate them immensely. Driving home, I realize that I haven't eaten anything myself since 10 this morning. I've been so busy that I've completely forgotten about lunch. I see Salvador leaving the farm to spray the cucumber beetles as I come in. I hand him a cold Pepsi as we pass in the driveway ...

Someone Open a Window

If you've been eating a lot of garlic and onions, chew slowly on several sprigs of parsley or other fresh herbs. The chlorophyll helps absorb the noxious odors.

Making Vegetables Attractive to Children

Mi Ae Lipe

Do you have young, fussy eaters (or older adult ones) in the house who won't eat their vegetables? Won't even look at them? Do they make faces at the mere mention of broccoli, asparagus, or spinach?

Most of us have childhood memories of certain foods that our parents made us eat, or traumatizing moments when we were not allowed to leave the table or have dessert unless we finished whatever ghastly pile was on our plate. Vegetables often end up on that list, which is unfortunate.

Our tastes and food preferences are strongly shaped by the eating habits of family and friends, our innate preferences, and our culture's social attitudes toward different types of foods. Our lifelong diet is profoundly shaped by what we are exposed to at a young age—even in the womb.

Whereas many American children prefer potato chips to carrots, vegetables and fruits play a much larger role in the daily diets of kids in other parts of the world. A common snack for the young and old alike in France is radishes with butter and salt; in Italy pieces of raw fennel (which taste like licorice) are served for dipping in olive oil. Young Korean children and babies are routinely given plain cooked potatoes or corn on the cob to nibble on between meals, rather than salty or sweet snacks.

Here are some ideas to tempt kids to eat more fruits and veggies:

* *Offer raw vegetables (and fruits) with dips.* *Kids love dipping things, and just about any fresh produce is more enticing if it is simply washed, cut up, and served with little bowls of dressings, dips, salsas, spreads, hummus, nut butters, even honey.*

1 clove garlic, minced
1 teaspoon ground cumin
3 green onions, white and green parts, thinly sliced
1 tablespoon chopped fresh oregano leaves
Freshly ground black pepper
1 small chunk (about 3 ounces) feta cheese

1. Stem and halve the tomatoes and toss them with the salt in a large bowl. Let them rest until a small pool of liquid accumulates—15 to 20 minutes.

2. Meanwhile, whisk the drained yogurt, oil, lemon juice, garlic, cumin, green onions, oregano, and pepper together in a small bowl. Pour the yogurt mixture over the tomatoes and accumulated liquid. Toss everything to coat. Set aside to blend the flavors, about 5 minutes.

3. Crumble the feta over the tomatoes and toss to combine. Adjust the seasonings and serve immediately.

— *Colleen Wolner, Blue Heron Coffeehouse, Winona, Minnesota*

. . . .

GREEN ONION PANCAKES   MAKES TWO 8-INCH PANCAKES

Source Note: Flour tortillas make this dish easy, and they work perfectly when filled with green onions and sesame seeds, then pan-fried in peanut oil.

1 large egg
2 teaspoons sesame oil
4 (8-inch) flour tortillas
2 teaspoons sesame seeds, toasted
⅓ cup finely chopped green onions, white and green parts
1 tablespoon peanut or vegetable oil, or more as needed

1. In a small bowl, lightly beat the egg with the sesame oil. Brush each tortilla with the egg mixture and then sprinkle two of the tortillas with the sesame seeds and green onions. Place one of the plain tortillas over each of the sprinkled tortillas and sandwich them together, pressing down to seal, forming two whole pancakes.

2. Heat the peanut oil in a sauté pan over medium heat. When hot, add a pancake to the pan and cook until lightly browned on both sides, about 2 minutes per side. Repeat with the remaining pancake, using more oil if needed.

3. Slice each pancake in half and serve one or two halves to each person.

— *Chef Tom Douglas*

* *Recipe Note:* The uncooked green onion pancakes will hold a day in the refrigerator, wrapped well in plastic. Or pan-fry them an hour

ahead. Keep them at room temperature and rewarm them in a preheated 350°F oven for 5 minutes before serving.

. . . .

SHRIMP PAD THAI

SERVES 2 TO 3

Source Note: Pad thai is one of my all-time favorite Asian dishes. I find it hard to resist ordering nearly every time I dine at a Thai restaurant, and until recently I was unable to re-create it in my own kitchen to the standards that I would have liked. It never tasted quite right … until now.

PAD THAI SAUCE

2 tablespoons tamarind paste concentrate
2 tablespoons packed light brown sugar
1½ tablespoons fish sauce

PAD THAI

6 ounces dried rice noodles (sometimes called "rice stick"), medium or large width
1 to 2 tablespoons vegetable oil, or more as needed
4 cloves garlic, minced
12 to 14 large shrimp, thawed if frozen, peeled and deveined
2 eggs, beaten
2 cups mung bean sprouts
2 green onions, light and dark green parts only, thinly sliced
¼ cup roughly chopped peanuts
    (pulsing in a small food processor or chopper works great)
Lime wedges, for serving

1. To make the sauce, whisk together the tamarind paste, brown sugar, and fish sauce until smooth.

2. Add the rice noodles to a pot of boiling water. Lower the heat and boil for 4 to 5 minutes (err on the longer side if using wider noodles—or follow the directions on the package). The noodles should be softened but still firmer than al dente; they will continue to cook later. Drain and rinse them well with cold water. Use kitchen shears to snip the noodles a couple of times. This will make it a lot easier to fry and eat them.

3. Heat a wok or large sauté pan over high heat and add 1 to 2 tablespoons of oil (if you're using a nonstick wok you won't need a lot). Once the oil begins to shimmer, add the garlic and stir-fry it for no longer than a minute, to keep it from burning.

4. Add the drained noodles and stir for another minute. Add the sauce and keep stirring the noodles until they begin to absorb some of the sauce and continue to soften. (I use a nonstick wok, but if your noodles start to stick, you can add more oil.) Add the shrimp and keep stirring until they begin to turn pink, a couple more minutes.

- ✒ **Make it a fun finger food.** Asparagus and green beans are delightful to eat with the fingers. And don't forget carrot and celery sticks, bell pepper strips, pea pods, cherry tomatoes, radishes, broccoli and cauliflower florets, corn on the cob, apples, pears, orange sections, cherries, and berries of all kinds.

- ✒ **Don't mix things up.** Young children often dislike their foods all mixed together, as in a casserole, but instead prefer separate, identifiable items.

    I found that salade niçoise, the French salad of whole green beans, tomatoes, tuna, and hardboiled eggs served over lettuce leaves, was a big hit with my kids because its ingredients are arranged separately and not tossed together, with dressing served on the side. They loved being able to serve themselves buffet-style, which gave them the satisfaction of making their own decisions and having control.

- ✒ **Use bright or novel colors to attract and entice.** Try serving red, green, orange, and yellow bell peppers, carrots, green-and-red-striped heirloom tomatoes, blue potatoes, purple broccoli, red-and-white-ringed slices of Chioggia beets, or the brilliantly colored stems of the Swiss chard variety known as Rainbow Brights.

- ✒ **Make it sweet.** It's no surprise that children are attracted to sweet-tasting foods. Try red bell pepper strips, beets, carrots, heirloom and Sungold cherry tomatoes, and sugar snap peas.

- ✒ **Don't cook them.** Many vegetables, such as broccoli and cauliflower, smell strong and unpleasant when cooked.

5. Push the noodles and shrimp to one side (the shrimp will continue to cook, so don't worry if they aren't completely pink yet) and pour the beaten eggs into the empty space in the wok. Allow the eggs to set for a minute and then stir to scramble them with the rest of the ingredients.

6. Add the bean sprouts and stir-fry for another minute or two, incorporating the rest of the ingredients in the wok, until they are crisp-tender and the noodles have a nice, chewy texture. Add half the green onions, toss one final time, and remove the pan from the heat.

7. Divide the pad Thai evenly between two or three plates. Garnish with the remaining green onions, chopped peanuts, and slices of lime. Serve immediately.

— *Victoria,* Mission: Food *blog*

Cooking and Variation Notes: I once made the mistake of doubling a pad Thai recipe to make more servings. It was extremely difficult to properly stir-fry all the ingredients in the wok without ending up with slightly mushy noodles and poorly distributed ingredients. If you intend to feed a larger group, stir-fry the pad Thai in batches. You'll thank me.

You can easily make chicken pad Thai by replacing the shrimp with thinly sliced chicken breast. Cook the chicken breast first, then remove it from the wok, continue with the recipe as directed, and add the cooked chicken back when you incorporate all of the ingredients with the bean sprouts.

. . . .

CLASSIC WEDGE SALAD   SERVES 4

Author Note: This dressing recipe makes more than enough for this salad, but it will keep well in your refrigerator for at least a few days. You can make another similar salad or (your friends will secretly love you for this) use the delicious, retro-style dressing as a dip for raw vegetables, chicken wings, or potato chips!

BLUE CHEESE DRESSING

¾ cup mayonnaise
¾ cup buttermilk
½ cup crumbled blue cheese
¼ teaspoon garlic powder
     (or use 1 small clove garlic, crushed)
¼ teaspoon onion powder (or use ½ shallot, finely minced)
¼ teaspoon freshly ground black pepper

SALAD

6 slices bacon
½ head iceberg lettuce, cut into quarters
½ cup crumbled blue cheese
1 cup grape tomatoes, cut into halves
3 green onions, thinly sliced

1. Mix all the dressing ingredients and set the mixture aside.

2. In a large pan, cook the bacon until it is crisp. Place it on a paper towel to drain. Once it has cooled, crumble the pieces.

3. Arrange a single lettuce wedge on each of four plates. Sprinkle the blue cheese, tomatoes, green onions, and bacon over the wedges. Drizzle the dressing over the top.

— Foodista.com

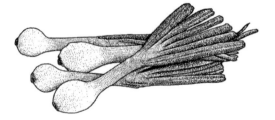

a treat. Also try combining cooked sweet potatoes with coconut milk and honey for delicious ice pops.

- **Serve a new vegetable with a familiar one.** Kids may be more willing to try the unfamiliar veggie if they know they will like the other one, and having this option assures that they won't leave the table hungry.

- **Roasting vegetables intensifies their flavors,** makes them soft, and also caramelizes their sugars, giving them a sweeter taste. Almost any vegetable prepared this way (tossed with oil, salt, and pepper, then cooked at high heat) tastes great!

- **Have cut-up prepared vegetables and fruits ready and waiting in the refrigerator at all times,** so that when your child is looking for a snack, they are available without extra hassle and fuss.

- **Most kids love bacon.** Try dressing a salad with a warm bacon dressing, adding bacon bits (and nuts), or using some bacon fat when roasting or sautéing vegetables.

Oregano

ORIGANUM VULGARE

This perennial member of the mint family is sometimes almost indistinguishable in taste from marjoram, another staple herb in Italian and Greek cooking whose name is often incorrectly used in conjunction with oregano. And Mexican oregano is actually not an oregano at all, but a plant closely related to lemon verbena, with a sweeter, more subtle flavor.

Treasured for its aromatic, warm, spicy taste with a touch of bitterness, oregano is one of the very few herbs whose flavor is actually stronger in dried form than when fresh. Its name comes from a Greek word meaning "joy of the mountains," and it grows abundantly in that country's hillsides. Surprisingly, this heat-loving plant also grows wild in cool climates, such as in England.

HISTORY

Oregano was born in the Mediterranean region, whose arid climate concentrates this hardy herb's oils. Certainly the ancient Greeks and Romans knew this showy, purple-flowered herb and used it in not only their cuisines but also their wedding ceremonies, as it was believed it would banish sadness.

Oregano has also been widely cultivated for its essential oil, which is used to flavor food and as a fragrance for soaps, detergents, and perfumes. Interestingly, oregano was virtually unknown in America until World War II, when returning soldiers craved the pizza they had eaten in Italy. In fact, this demand for pizza caused oregano sales to skyrocket 5,200 percent in the late 1940s and early 1950s.

NUTRITION

Normally, oregano is not consumed in large enough quantities to make it nutritionally significant, but 2 teaspoons of the dried herb do contain nearly one quarter of the adult daily requirement for vitamin K, as well as significant amounts of manganese, iron, and dietary fiber—all for a mere 5 calories. Oregano has also been found to have incredibly high levels of antioxidants—42 times more than apples and 12 times more than blueberries.

SEASON

Commercially, oregano is widely grown and in season year-round. You'll find it at its best at farmers markets and CSAs throughout the summer and fall.

SELECTION

Fresh oregano should be uniformly bright green, with no signs of wilting or yellowing.

STORAGE

Treat fresh oregano sprigs like any living flower or plant cutting: Just snip off the stem ends, place them in a glass of water, and store on the counter at room temperature or in the refrigerator. You can extend the life of oregano by wrapping it in damp paper towels and storing it in a plastic bag in the refrigerator vegetable crisper, where it will keep for 3 to 4 days.

TRIMMING AND CLEANING

Wash the sprigs under running water and strip the leaves off the stems. Pat dry with a soft cloth.

BLANCHING AND FREEZING

To prepare oregano for freezing, thoroughly wash and dry the oregano sprigs. Strip the leaves from the stems, place them loosely in a zipper-lock freezer or vacuum food sealer-type bag, and gently squeeze out the air.

A terrific way to freeze oregano is to chop it finely, mix it into a paste using ⅓ cup of olive oil or cooled melted butter to every 2 cups of herbs, and then freeze the resulting mixture in ice cube trays. To thaw, simply pop out a few cubes into a strainer and let the oil melt away, or just drop them frozen into sauces, soups, stews, casseroles, and other cooked dishes. Frozen oregano will keep for up to 1 year at 0°F.

DRYING

Tie fresh sprigs into a bunch and hang in a cool, dark place with good ventilation. Once they are dried, seal them tightly in a container with a lid or in a zipper-lock plastic bag, and store away from light and heat.

Or you can oven-dry oregano by spreading a layer of leaves on a cookie sheet and placing it in a warm (up to 180°F) oven for 3 to 4 hours, stirring the herbs periodically until they are thoroughly dry. Or remove the best leaves from the stems and arrange them on a paper towel without letting them touch. Cover this layer with another paper towel and add another layer of leaves. Five layers may be dried at one time using this method.

A microwave oven can also be used to dry small quantities of herbs. Place 4 or 5 herb branches in the microwave between paper towels. Heat for 2 to 3 minutes over high power. If the herbs are not brittle and dry when removed, repeat the microwave drying for 30 seconds more. (Be aware that the heat generated during microwaving removes not only moisture but also some of the oils, so these herbs may not have as intense a flavor as herbs dried by other methods.) Keep dried oregano in a cool, dark place away from light and heat, and use within 6 to 9 months. Keep dried oregano in a cool, dark place away from light and heat, and use within 6 to 9 months.

EQUIVALENTS, MEASURES, AND SERVINGS

- 1 tablespoon fresh oregano = 1 teaspoon dried
- 1 ounce fresh oregano = ½ cup chopped

COMPLEMENTARY HERBS, SEASONINGS, AND FOODS

Basil, beans, breads, broccoli, capers, cauliflower, chili, eggs, eggplant, garbanzos (chickpeas), garlic, green beans, lemon, marjoram, mushrooms, olives, olive oil, onions, parsley, pasta, pizza, pork, poultry, spaghetti sauce, thyme, tomatoes, veal, zucchini.

Gratitude

Jack Hedin
Featherstone Farm Owner
Rushford, Minnesota

I had an experience yesterday that reminded me how fortunate I am to be doing what I do, at this particular time and place, with the people I'm lucky enough to be working with. It was one of those moments of revelation when one feels equal parts of exhilaration and humility. The telling of the tale requires a little bit of context.

After being away from the farm for three days at the end of the previous week, visiting store customers and making commercial deliveries with my son Jasper (10 years old), I returned Friday evening to a farm where heat and heavy rainfall had thrown many things into disarray—schedules, harvests, and field-work plans for the weekend.

Having been away for so long, I was feeling a need to get grounded once again in the life of the farm, to catch up on where things stood in the field, and to get back to work in the basic sense of growing and maintaining crops. With more rain (and heat!) forecast for Saturday afternoon, I made a plan on the phone with Esteban Friday evening to start early the following morning, hand weeding what we could before the first showers of the day.

The first light of day was barely showing in the sky when I arrived at the shop Saturday at 5:45. A heavy fog obscured almost everything, and it was hot, with the dew point in the low to mid 70s, I'm sure. Earlier this summer I reread Heart of Darkness, and this Saturday morning reminded me very much of Marlow's descriptions of the oppressive heat of the central African rainforest: "The air hung on us as a steam blanket."

The 24 Spanish-speaking members of the farm crew showed up in a small caravan of vehicles just *before 6 AM, and we all assembled in the break room for a quick meeting. Everyone looked tired and run-down from late-summer stress.*

I'm not quite sure, but I believe that these folks have had no more than a couple of full days off over the past month. I can relate to this, of course, essentially working seven days a week myself for most of the year (what small-business owner does not, really?). But I still felt somewhat sheepish reporting to them about my three days in the air conditioning of the truck and the stores. Day after day after day harvesting heavy crops in the full sun is something I've done mainly as an apprentice farmworker two decades ago, but it's been enough to give me a huge respect for the folks who continue to do this work at Featherstone and other farms every day.

We filled the Gatorade cooler and headed out to the field with little fanfare; by 6:15 we were spread out over a dozen or so long beds of four-inch-tall carrots that were in danger of being overrun by purslane, crabgrass, and pigweed. We'd cultivated the areas on top of and between the beds several times with the tractor over the past two to three weeks, and these parts of the field were clean and black. The carrot rows themselves, however, were short, riotous Mohawks of green—only 50 percent carrots in places—and badly in need of hand weeding. No matter how sophisticated or mechanized a modern organic vegetable farm is, the problem of weeds-in-the-row still demands hand labor. There is no substitute.

We weeded silently for 20 minutes, the only sound that of someone's shirt-pocket cell phone broadcasting a tinny mariachi band. Not even the birds were stirring this foggy morning. It was satisfying to clean up the weeds, no doubt, but my mind was focused with worry. Are we pushing these folks too

SUBSTITUTIONS

If your recipe calls for Italian oregano and you do not have any on hand, substitute thyme, basil, or marjoram.

SERVING SUGGESTIONS

- Few self-respecting pizzas reach their full flavor potential until they've been baptized with a couple of generous shakes of the oregano jar.
- For a delicious twist to homemade garlic bread, add chopped fresh oregano and basil to the bread just after seasoning it with garlic and before toasting.
- Add oregano or oregano-infused oil to salad dressings.
- Oregano is the quintessential ingredient in Italian dishes—sprinkle it in pastas, pizza, sauces, meat dishes, and lasagna.
- Add a touch of oregano to egg dishes such as omelets, frittatas, or just plain old scrambled eggs.
- Toss in fresh or dried oregano with roast chicken, lamb, and meat loaf.
- Oregano is a vigorous must-have in making sausages or meatballs.
- For tasty oven-fried potatoes, season them with a mixture of finely chopped oregano and rosemary.
- Add 1 cup of fresh oregano (tie the sprigs into a rough bundle for easier removal) to the water in which you boil spaghetti or your favorite pasta. You can discard the oregano after cooking, but the pasta will remain delicately perfumed.
- Fresh oregano makes an unexpected taste surprise in pasta salads and potato salads.
- Sprinkle fresh oregano atop lightly cooked vegetable side dishes such as green beans or summer squash.
- Add oregano to light soups for a clean, slightly spicy taste.
- Drape or wrap whole sprigs of oregano and other herbs onto other foods on the grill, such as chicken or potatoes.
- Make an especially robust pesto with oregano, or a mix of oregano and basil.

....

S. NARDECCHIA'S SPAGHETTI SAUCE   SERVES 4

SAUCE

1 large yellow onion, sliced
5 tablespoons olive oil, divided
1 tablespoon salt, plus more as desired
Freshly ground black pepper
2 large cloves garlic, minced
1 (12-ounce) can tomato paste
1 medium green bell pepper, minced
1 (28-ounce) can tomatoes
2 cups water
1 cup red wine (optional)
3 bay leaves
⅓ cup fresh chopped parsley, or ¼ cup dried parsley
1 teaspoon ground fennel seed

1 tablespoon chopped fresh basil, or 1 teaspoon dried basil
1 tablespoon chopped fresh oregano, or 1 teaspoon dried oregano
1 tablespoon chopped fresh rosemary, or 1 teaspoon dried rosemary
2 pounds ground beef chuck

2 pounds thin spaghetti
Parmesan cheese, for serving

1. In a large saucepan over medium heat, sauté the onion in 3 tablespoons of the olive oil until it turns limp.

2. Add 1 tablespoon of the salt, pepper to taste, and the garlic, tomato paste, and green bell pepper. Stir and cook for 15 minutes.

3. Add the tomatoes, water, wine, bay leaves, parsley, fennel, basil, oregano, and rosemary. Simmer for 3 hours or longer, stirring occasionally.

4. Meanwhile, in a large skillet, cook the ground chuck in the remaining 2 tablespoons olive oil. Add more salt and pepper to taste. Brown the meat until all of the liquid in the pan evaporates, then add the meat to the sauce 1 hour before the end of the sauce's simmering period.

5. Cook the spaghetti according to the package instructions. Serve with the sauce and Parmesan cheese.

— *Maureen Cooney,* The Bluff Country Co-op Cookbook

. . . .

OREGANO AND ZUCCHINI PASTA

SERVES 4

Author Note: Campanelle pasta are small and fluted, resembling little tubular flowers, whereas orecchiette look like tiny ears or bowls. Both pastas are excellent with chunky, heartier sauces.

Pecorino is a type of hard cheese made from sheep's milk. Like Parmesan, it has a strong, salty flavor that pairs well with pasta dishes dressed with robust sauces. If you cannot find genuine pecorino, substitute a good-quality Parmesan instead.

1 pound campanelle or orecchiette pasta
6 tablespoons extra-virgin olive oil, divided
2 pounds (about 3 medium) zucchini, trimmed and cut into
⅓-inch-thick slices
6 cloves garlic, chopped
2 tablespoons chopped fresh basil
2 tablespoons chopped fresh oregano
Dash red pepper flakes or hot pepper sauce (optional)
Salt and freshly ground black pepper
½ cup grated pecorino cheese, plus additional for sprinkling

hard this season? Sure, they always volunteer—without hesitation, it seems—for overtime despite the heat, the nature of the work, and their recent history of rest (or lack of it!). And Esteban had been enthusiastic about finishing the carrot weeding while it was still possible ... before another heavy week of harvesting began again on Sunday morning. But when is enough really enough? I was concerned that the tired faces and lack of conversation this morning was answer enough.

Then little by little a quiet chatter broke out, spreading slowly over the entire group. My Spanish is too rudimentary to understand exactly what they were talking about, but my sense was that it was good-natured kidding around between family members. As the conversation gained momentum, there was a lot of laughter; I would look up and see one person or another straighten their back, look up into the fog, and chuckle heartily. These folks were not exactly enjoying the work, I believe, but they were definitely making the best of a tough situation.

My heart lightened, and I'm sure the pace of my weeding quickened a bit. My thin Scandinavian blood is poorly suited for this kind of steam bath, I'll admit. And at this point in my farming career, I'm not accustomed to hours and hours stooped over a row, the heavy heat surging up and off my chest, sweat bleeding from every pore on my head, shoulders, and upper body. But the light joking of the farmworkers around me—the essential optimism of their response to a tough situation—was completely contagious.

We finished the acre of carrots and stopped for a moment to stretch, standing at the end of the field. I took out my cell phone to capture the scene with its camera, but the steam and humidity made focusing all but impossible; there was nothing with which I could dry the lens. The Gascas laughed heartily when they saw me trying to do so.

1. Cook the pasta in a large pot of boiling salted water until its texture becomes al dente, stirring occasionally. Drain, reserving ½ cup of the cooking liquid. Return the pasta to the pot.

2. Heat 2 tablespoons of the olive oil in a large skillet over high heat. Add the zucchini and sauté until tender, 3 to 4 minutes. Add the garlic, basil, oregano, and red pepper flakes; remove from the heat.

3. Combine the zucchini mixture with the pasta, adding the reserved pasta cooking liquid as needed to moisten. Season to taste with salt and pepper. Add the pecorino cheese, stirring until melted and ready to serve. Sprinkle on additional cheese for garnish.

— *Mi Ae Lipe*

MARINATED BEAN SALAD   SERVES 4

Source Note: *This is a healthful, fresh-tasting bean salad that will give you an easy way to enjoy the many nutritional benefits of beans with little effort. The fresh herbs make it very flavorful, and it will keep in your refrigerator for up to 3 or 4 days. In fact, it actually gets better as it marinates. The lima beans and fresh herbs add a nice twist to the more traditional version.*

2 cups fresh green beans
1½ cups cooked lima beans, or 1 (15-ounce) can
1½ cups cooked kidney beans, or 1 (15-ounce) can
2 tablespoons minced onion
3 medium cloves garlic, pressed
1 large ripe fresh tomato, seeds and excess pulp removed, diced
2 tablespoons chopped fresh basil
1 tablespoon chopped fresh oregano
1 tablespoon chopped fresh parsley
3 tablespoons fresh lemon juice
2 to 3 tablespoons extra-virgin olive oil
Salt and cracked black pepper

1. In a pan, bring several inches of lightly salted water to a boil. Trim the green beans by cutting off the ends a handful at once (this saves time). Boil them for 3 to 5 minutes, or until they are tender. Drain and pat them dry with paper towels so that the excess water does not dilute their flavor. Cut the beans into 1-inch lengths.

2. Rinse the canned beans under running water in a colander, letting them sit for a couple of minutes to drain the excess water.

3. In a large bowl, mix all of the ingredients together. If you have the time, let this salad marinate for at least 15 minutes before serving

— *World's Healthiest Foods*

GREEK SALAD

SERVES 8

GREEK SALAD DRESSING

MAKES 3 CUPS

1 cup extra-virgin olive oil (Kalamata if available, otherwise any
    variety)
⅓ cup red wine vinegar
⅓ cup fresh lemon juice
¼ cup Greek Kalamata olive brine
14 pitted Greek Kalamata olives
3 large cloves fresh garlic
¾ cup crumbled feta cheese
¼ medium onion
¼ teaspoon whole peppercorns
1 teaspoon chopped fresh oregano, or ¼ teaspoon dried oregano

Puree all of the ingredients except the oregano in a blender or food
processor until smooth. Stir in the oregano. Store unused dressing,
covered, in the refrigerator. It will keep for up to 2 weeks.

SALAD

1 large or 2 small heads fresh lettuce, such as romaine, green leaf,
    red leaf, or any combination, or mesclun
4 tomatoes, each cut into 8 wedges
½ red onion, thinly sliced
32 Greek olives, preferably Kalamata
1 pound Greek feta cheese, crumbled
1 cucumber, peeled and cut into 32 slices
16 pepperoncini (pickled peppers)
Greek Salad Dressing (recipe above)
8 pinches dried oregano (or minced fresh oregano or marjoram)

Assemble the ingredients in the order given, or create your own pattern. Like most other salads, this can be mixed as one large salad and
then tossed, but my preference is to arrange it on individual plates.
Drizzle the dressing over the top and sprinkle the oregano over all.

— *Peter Reinhart,* Sacramental Magic in a Small-Town Café

thing of the past, permanently. But weather and crops and environmental fluctuations (deer detected in the corn on a Friday evening) conspire to make this difficult indeed.

Perhaps in California a predictable 7-to-5 schedule is possible, with weekend work limited to watering in the greenhouse or perhaps monitoring an irrigation pump; there is no "weather" in its Central Valley eight months of the year. But not here in the Midwest. I know this ... I "signed up for it," as my family rightly reminds me. But I'll be perfectly honest—the long hours and lack of real days off wear on a person after a time. Especially in the dog days of August, it's easy to lose perspective and go negative.

Which is why the good spirits and quiet determination of the Gasca crew is all the more inspiring. Why I found myself so buoyed by their chatter on such a hot, heavy morning.

Thank goodness for agricultural fieldworkers here at Featherstone Farm, and on every farm across the country. I believe we owe these folks a debt of gratitude.

Parsley

On American tables, the familiar curly leaves of parsley have long been a fixture as a tired garnish on a thousand mediocre restaurant plates and faceless buffet spreads, but rarely has it been taken seriously enough for its own culinary value. Happily, other cultures recognize its distinctive flavor and healthful properties, especially Middle Eastern, European, and Brazilian cuisines, which respect it as an herb, spice, and vegetable.

Five kinds of parsley exist: the plain-leaf (or flat-leaf), the curly-leaf, the fern-leaf, the celery-leaf, and the turnip-root. Of these, the first two are the most commonly known in America, whereas the root form, which looks like very small parsnips, is frequently eaten in Eastern Europe.

Parsley is one of the essential herbs of bouquet garni, that little bundle of herbs tied together with string that is instrumental in flavoring soups, stews, and stocks. The flat-leaf form of parsley is sometimes thought to be stronger-tasting than its curly-leaved cousin, which is cultivated more for its attractive appearance. Flat-leaf parsley may also be a bit more pleasant to eat—the curly form can be a fluffy, stickery mouthful.

HISTORY

Although the Italian island of Sardinia is sometimes attributed as the birthplace of parsley, most likely the comely herb originated in the mainland Mediterranean area, where it grows wild to this day. It is thought to have been used first as a medicinal herb rather than as food for its effectiveness in treating urinary tract infections, kidney stones, gastrointestinal disorders, anemia, high blood pressure, and menstrual issues. Ancient Greeks revered the herb, decorating tombs and athletes alike with wreaths of parsley. King Charlemagne ordered that it be grown in his gardens during the Middle Ages, and it is likely that from there, the plant entered the larger European culinary scene.

NUTRITION

Parsley is rich in many flavonoids, antioxidants, and volatile oils, plant compounds prized for their potential anticancer properties. It also contains significant amounts of folic acid and vitamins A, C, and K. A single tablespoon of raw parsley contains barely 2 calories.

SEASON

Commercially, parsley is widely grown and in season year-round. You'll find it at farmers markets and CSAs throughout the spring, summer, and fall.

SELECTION

As with all herbs, freshness is key. Look for lush, stiff stems with crisp, perky greenery. Avoid wilting or yellowing foliage, or bunches with any slimy or rotting leaves.

238   SUMMER — PARSLEY      BOUNTY FROM THE BOX

STORAGE

Parsley will keep better if it is washed and dried right away after purchase; otherwise it tends to rot and turn yellow rather quickly. When you get your parsley home, immediately free it from the bonds of its tight wire binding. Parsley's finely notched leaves can conceal plenty of sand, soil, and insects, so it is best to wash it just like you would spinach. Fill a big sink or bowl full of cold water, and completely submerge the parsley, swishing vigorously. Remove any questionable stems and leaves that are on the edge of decline, and inspect for persistent telltale brown grit. Then rinse under cold running water, and repeat if necessary. Spin or vigorously shake the parsley dry, then spread it out on a paper towel or two. Roll the paper towel loosely and slip the whole bundle into a plastic bag. The parsley will keep for up to 1 week—and it will be clean and just slightly damp (perfect!), ready for you when you need to grab a lot or a little for cooking.

TRIMMING AND CLEANING

See above for cleaning instructions. To prepare for cooking, strip the leaves off the tough stems, then chop or mince as needed.

FREEZING

To prepare parsley for freezing, thoroughly wash and dry the sprigs. Strip the leaves from the stems, place them loosely in a zipper-lock freezer or vacuum food sealer-type bag, and gently squeeze out the air.

A terrific way to freeze parsley is to chop it finely, mix it into a paste using ⅓ cup of olive oil or cooled melted butter to every 2 cups of herbs, and then freeze the resulting mixture in ice cube trays. To thaw, simply pop out a few cubes into a strainer and let the oil melt away, or just drop them frozen into sauces, soups, stews, casseroles, and other cooked dishes. Frozen parsley will keep for up to 1 year at 0°F.

DRYING

Tie fresh, dry sprigs that are free of dew and moisture into bunches and hang in a cool, dark place with good ventilation. You can cover the bunches with small paper bags to keep the dust off them, but make sure the bags have adequate holes for proper ventilation; parsley is especially susceptible to mold. Once the bunches are dried, seal them tightly in a container with a lid or in a zipper-lock plastic bag and store away from light and heat.

You can oven-dry parsley by spreading a single layer of leaves on a cookie sheet and placing it in a warm (up to 180°F) oven for 3 to 5 hours, stirring the leaves periodically until they are thoroughly dry.

A microwave oven can also be used to dry small quantities of parsley. Place 4 or 5 sprigs in the microwave between paper towels. Heat for 2 to 3 minutes over high power. If the parsley is not brittle and dry when removed, repeat the microwave drying for 30 seconds more. (Be aware that the heat generated during microwaving evaporates not only moisture but also some of the oils, so parsley dried in the microwave may not have as intense a flavor as it would dried by other methods.) Keep dried parsley in a cool, dark place away from light and heat, and use within 6 to 9 months.

Getting Kids Engaged in the Kitchen

Mi Ae Lipe

One way to instill good eating habits in children is to involve them in the kitchen. Learning how to plan meals, and shop for and cook their own food helps them help themselves to be healthier, and provides great lessons that will serve them their whole lives!

Here are some ideas for engaging your children in the kitchen:

1. **Involve them in meal planning.** Having kids do some of their own meal planning sends a powerful message that they matter, and it gives them an opportunity to pick and choose the foods and dishes they want. It also teaches them decision-making skills and how to make choices.

2. **Let kids pick out their own food at the grocery store.** Whether it is a cucumber or a cut of meat, learning how to properly pick out different foods is a great education for kids that will stay with them for their entire lives.

3. **Have them help with chopping, mixing, and pouring.** Even young children can help out in the kitchen by slicing veggies or fruit, measuring out ingredients, washing greens, mixing batter, arranging items on a tray to be baked in the oven, snipping herbs from the kitchen garden, and decorating foods. Use child-safe cutting utensils and common sense to avoid kitchen-related burns and injuries.

4. **Teach them kitchen safety.** Make sure they are aware of the dangers of hot stoves, ovens, and dishes; knives, food processors, and choppers; and

---

potential contamination of cutting surfaces and counter-tops from raw meat, poultry, and eggs.

5. **Grow your own herbs or vegetables.** *Fresh herbs perk up the taste of food immense-ly, and nothing delights a child more than plucking the first ripe cherry tomatoes off the vine. Children have a natural curiosity for new, nurturing experiences, and gardening— even if it is a single pot of chives on a windowsill—is a great way for kids to see where their food comes from and how it grows. It also gives them the satisfaction of knowing that they raised it themselves.*

6. **Have children help clean up.** *One of the least exciting parts of cooking is the clean-ing. It is best to clean up as you go along, so it is not so over-whelming at the end. Children can help by wiping up coun-tertop spills or messes on the floor, loading the dishwasher, putting away clean dishes and silverware in the draw-ers they can reach, and other simple tasks. If they balk, you can point out that the sooner everyone can get out of the kitchen, the more time there will be for eating, reading sto-ries, or other, more fun activ-ities!*

7. **Have them set the table and help out with serving.** *Younger children can set out the silverware, dishes, cups, and napkins. This task might be more fun if they and their siblings have special, personal plates or cups. School-age chil-dren can help bring out the food and serve it.*

8. **Keep it positive and don't be a perfectionist.** *When you cook with your kids,*

EQUIVALENTS, MEASURES, AND SERVINGS

- 1 tablespoon (2 sprigs) fresh parsley, chopped = 1 teaspoon dried
- 1 ounce = 1 cup chopped
- 1 bunch fresh parsley = 1½ cups chopped

COMPLEMENTARY HERBS, SEASONINGS, AND FOODS

Anchovies, anise, bay, beans, beef, beets, caraway, carrots, chervil, chicken, chives, duck, egg, fennel, fish, garlic, grains, lamb, lemon, liver, mint, onions, oranges, parsnips, pasta, pork, potatoes, tarragon, thyme, tomatoes, veal, venison.

SERVING SUGGESTIONS

- Blend it with other green herbs and vegetables into a salsa verde.
- If you can find parsley root, you're in for a treat. Use it with other hearty roots like potatoes, parsnips, and carrots; combine it with beans; or braise it on its own as a distinctive vegetable.
- Deep-fried parsley is delicious and makes a great surprise appetizer.
- Combine with bay, thyme, chervil, and other herbs to form a bouquet garni for making soups, stews, and stocks.
- Add parsley to fresh basil pesto right before serving or cooking to add flavor and texture.
- Sprinkle finely chopped parsley on top of salads, egg dishes, potatoes, casseroles, and any vegetable dish for additional color, flavor, and nutrition.
- Parsley makes a great addition to just about any dressing or dip.
- In salads, make parsley a featured ingredient, not just an afterthought garnish.
- Make gremolata, an Italian condiment made with parsley, garlic, and lem-on zest.
- Adding finely chopped fresh parsley, basil, and oregano to bottled or canned tomato or pasta sauce can help eliminate that "store-bought" taste.
- The sprigs of curly-leafed parsley, with all of its frills, are especially useful for holding lots of sauce or oil when dipped. Challenge your children to eat their "forest" of parsley "trees" by serving it with dips, flavored oils, or sauce.

TABBOULEH   SERVES 4

Source Note: This tabbouleh recipe is heavy on the parsley and light on the bulgur—closer to the way it is typically presented in Lebanon, its homeland. Go ahead and play with the proportions, though. If you have lots of cucumbers in your garden or CSA box, use twice the amount. If you're a nut for fresh mint, boost it right up. You really can't go wrong with tabbouleh's refreshing, tangy flavors as an accompaniment to just about any grilled meat or vegetable, but do note that it is best served the same day it is made.

BULGUR WHEAT
½ cup bulgur (cracked wheat)
½ cup water or chicken stock
3 to 4 tablespoons fresh lemon juice, divided
⅛ teaspoon kosher salt

SALAD

1 large bunch flat-leaf parsley
2 large Roma tomatoes, cut into ¼-inch dice
½ English cucumber, cut into ¼-inch dice
2 green onions, very thinly sliced
2 to 4 tablespoons chopped fresh mint
2 tablespoons extra-virgin olive oil
Kosher salt

1. Heat the water and 2 tablespoons of the lemon juice in a small saucepan over medium-high heat. Add the bulgur and salt; bring to a simmer, cover, and cook for 3 minutes. Take the pan off the heat and let it stand, still covered, for about 10 minutes. Transfer the bulgur to a bowl, stir in a drizzle of olive oil, and put it in the refrigerator for about 15 minutes to cool.

2. Meanwhile, wash and dry the parsley, then pull off all the leaves. You should have at least 3 cups, loosely packed. Chop the leaves until they are quite small (I find this easiest to do in two batches).

3. In a large bowl, combine the bulgur, parsley, tomatoes, cucumber, green onions, mint, 1 tablespoon of the lemon juice, and the olive oil. Season to taste with salt, pepper, and more lemon juice or oil if desired.

— *Lisa Gordanier*

. . . .

PARSLEY SALAD WITH OLIVES AND CAPERS   SERVES 6

½ cup oil-cured black olives, pitted and halved
1 cup flat-leaf parsley, coarsely chopped
½ cup red onion, coarsely chopped
¼ cup capers, rinsed
2 large garlic cloves, finely chopped
5 anchovy fillets, chopped
Freshly grated zest of 1 lemon
¼ cup olive oil
Freshly ground black pepper
Lemon juice
Sea salt
Thin slivers of Pecorino Romano cheese
Toasted bread, brushed with olive oil, for serving

1. Just before serving, combine the olives, parsley, onion, capers, garlic, anchovies, and lemon zest in a bowl, and toss well to combine. Add the olive oil and black pepper, and mix well. Add the lemon juice and salt to taste (the capers and anchovies are very salty, so you may need only a small amount, or even none at all).

schedule enough time so you are not in too much of a hurry. Remember that they are still learning new skills, so they won't be as quick in doing things as you are—or do them as perfectly as you might. It's also very important that they not associate the kitchen and cooking with negative feelings, getting yelled at, anxiety, and stress; these associations may stay with them for a lifetime.

9. **Make them truly a part of the kitchen, with their own tools.** *Children love to take ownership of their destiny, so provide them with a supportive environment. It might be in the form of their own apron, a recipe box with cards they can write on, child-size kitchen utensils, special kitchen towels, or colorful measuring cups and spoons.*

10. **Praise them.** *Be sure to let your children know when they've done a great job, and thank them for it. Then enjoy your meals together!*

2. Spoon onto a serving plate, scatter with the Pecorino Romano cheese, and serve with toasted bread.

— Paul Anater

. . . .

ARMENIAN STEAK TARTARE (CHI KOFTE)   SERVES 3 TO 4

Source Note: Some people have an aversion to eating raw meat and fish. I laugh in the face of it. Bring on the steak tartare, the carpaccio, the sushi, and sashimi—I fear you not!

To be specific, I have long been a lover of chi kofte, or Armenian steak tartare. If you live in Los Angeles and are hankering to make or buy some chi kofte, you are seriously in luck. Visit any Armenian market and you can buy chi kofte meat artfully prepared for this use (they have special machines). Otherwise, you will need to ask your butcher to grind your trimmed beef top round meat multiple times to achieve a similar texture, or grind it at home the same way. (If you grind at home, grind the paprika directly into your meat instead of mixing it in later.) It takes extra work, but it's vital to get the silky texture of the chi kofte meat. It should not be chunky like a French tartare, but smooth like a paste.

GHEYMA

½ tablespoon unsalted butter
½ pound ground beef round
1 small onion, finely chopped
Kosher salt and freshly ground black pepper
Paprika
¼ cup chopped flat-leaf parsley

SALATA

1 green Italian pepper (similar to an Anaheim), chopped
1 cucumber, peeled and chopped
4 plum tomatoes, chopped
4 scallions (green onions), sliced
½ cup chopped flat-leaf parsley
1 teaspoon paprika
¼ cup lemon juice
2 tablespoons olive oil
1 teaspoon sumac (optional)
Kosher salt and freshly ground black pepper

CHI KOFTE

1½ cups grade #1 fine bulgur (cracked wheat)
1½ cups cold water
1½ pounds very fresh top round, trimmed of all fat and ground
    four times until fine like a paste
1 tablespoon plus 1 teaspoon kosher salt

Books

Herbal Kitchen Cooking With Fragrance And Flavor
Jerry Traunfeld,
Macmillan, 1993.

The Herbfarm Cookbook
Jerry Traunfeld,
William Morrow & Company, 2005.

A Celebration of Herbs: Recipes from the Huntington Herb Garden
Shirley Kerins and Peggy Park Bernal,
Huntington Library Press, 2002.

Rodale's Illustrated Encyclopedia of Herbs
Rodale Press, 2000.

The Encyclopedia of Herbs, Spices, & Flavorings:
A Cook's Compendium
Elisabeth Lambert Ortiz,
DK Adult, 1992.

1 tablespoon paprika
½ teaspoon freshly ground black pepper
½ cup sliced scallions (green onions), divided
¼ cup plus 1 tablespoon chopped flat-leaf parsley

GARNISH

Extra-virgin olive oil, for serving (optional)

1. Start by making the *gheyma*. Heat the butter in a medium skillet over medium-high heat. When the butter has melted, add the ground beef, stirring and breaking it up into small pieces. When the beef has started to brown but is not completely cooked yet, add the onions and season with salt, pepper, and paprika. Continue to cook until the beef is well-browned and cooked through. Taste and adjust seasoning as desired. Stir in the parsley and remove from the heat. The *gheyma* can be made ahead and reheated as needed. It can also be frozen.

2. For the *salata*, mix together all the ingredients and set aside until you're ready to serve.

3. To make the *chi kofte*, first fill a small bowl with some water to use to wet your hands as needed during the mixing and shaping process. In a large mixing bowl, soak the bulgur in the cold water for about 15 minutes, until it has absorbed all of the water but is still wet. Add the ground round and mix everything thoroughly with your hands. Season with salt, paprika, and pepper and mix well. Mix in ¼ cup of the scallions and ¼ cup of the chopped parsley.

4. To shape the *kofte* (see the Cooking Note below), dip your hands in the water and grab a small handful of the meat mixture. Form it into a ball and then lightly begin to make a fist with your hand to make it a bit more oblong (but not completely flat), leaving finger imprints on one side. Place it on a serving dish, then dip your hands in the water again and repeat the process until all of the meat mixture has been used. Garnish with the remaining scallions and parsley and serve with the *gheyma*, *salata*, and olive oil on the side for topping.

🥄 *Cooking Note:* To make a more Lebanese-style *chi kofte*, omit the herbs from the *chi kofte* mixture and instead of forming it into log shapes, pat the entire mixture flat on a large, flat serving dish and serve with a cake server for cutting. Serve to individual plates.

— *Victoria,* Mission: Food *blog*

. . . .

HERBED RICE SALAD   SERVES 10

Source Note: You can make this very quickly if you use your favorite bottled dressing and just toss all of the herbs with the vegetables and rice. This makes a great potluck salad.

DRESSING

2 to 4 tablespoons olive oil

Zest of 1 lemon

Juice of 2 lemons

1 generous bunch parsley, washed well, leaves removed
    and chopped

1 teaspoon chopped fresh rosemary

1 teaspoon chopped fresh thyme

½ teaspoon finely chopped fresh sage

1 small garlic clove, finely chopped

Salt and freshly ground black pepper

4 cups cooked firm brown or white rice (not sticky rice)

4 to 6 green onions, chopped

Grated carrots and radishes (or substitute other vegetables
    as the season and your garden or refrigerator dictate)

Grated hard cheese, such as Parmesan (optional)

1. To make the dressing, put the oil, lemon zest, lemon juice, parsley,
    rosemary, thyme, sage, garlic, salt, and pepper into a blender and
    whirl until smooth.

2. Be sure you've made the rice enough ahead to let it cool to room
    temperature before tossing it with the rest of the fresh ingredients.
    (However, don't be tempted to make it the day before and refriger-
    ate it, as chilled rice becomes dehydrated and somewhat crunchy.)
    When ready to serve, toss the dressing with the rice, green onions,
    and vegetables. Sprinkle the grated cheese on top.

— *Mariquita Farm, Watsonville, California*

Peaches & Nectarines

PRUNUS PERSICA
AND
PRUNUS PERSICA
NECTARINA

There is simply nothing that compares with a perfectly ripe peach at the peak of its dripping juiciness, a sweetness heightened with well-placed acid and a heady fragrance—it is the essence of summer itself, and every bit as fleeting. But this classic experience of the fruit is increasingly rare, and surprisingly not one that everyone embraces. In recent years, consumers have shown a distinct preference for firm flesh rather than melting, for extremely sweet fruit (the skyrocketing sales of the less acidic white-fleshed peaches and nectarines attest to this), and fruit that is as red as possible on the outside (in fact, golden background tones are the best predictors of fruit quality). Consumers also strongly prefer freestone fruits rather than clingstone varieties; apparently we don't want to deal with any extra work or messiness to extricate that central pit from the flesh.

In spite of our ignorance, great peaches are still to be had, especially in Washington State, Georgia, and California. And farmers markets and CSAs are more likely to have better-tasting fruit, because it is local, can be picked when more fully ripe, and is not subject to the indignities of long-distance packing and shipping.

Only a single recessive gene separates peaches and nectarines, but the latter are completely smooth-skinned whereas peaches usually sport a distinctive fuzz. Nectarines also tend to be smaller and somewhat more acidic, but the two fruits can be used interchangeably.

HISTORY

China is the peach's original homeland, where it has been enjoyed and revered since at least 2000 BC. From there it traveled to Persia, and Alexander the Great brought the fruit to Europe after he conquered the Persians. Not surprisingly, ancient Romans loved the fruit, and Spanish explorers introduced it to the Americas in the 1500s. Commercial peach production began in the United States in the 1800s in Georgia and Virginia.

Peaches and nectarines are quite exacting in their growing conditions, since they require a period of chilling in the winter and sufficiently hot summers for the best blossom and fruit development. However, they are also vulnerable to early spring frosts and a number of blights and pests, so their growing range is rather limited.

Peaches have long been beloved and thought to have magical properties; their flowers, branches, and fruit were used to ward off and exorcise evil spirits, especially in Chinese, Japanese, Korean, and Vietnamese cultures. Represented in many realistic still-life and Impressionistic paintings alike, ripe peaches have symbolized good health, a kind heart, and honesty in western European art.

NUTRITION

Peaches and nectarines pack a lot of nutrition in their succulent beings—they are rich sources of vitamins A, C, E, and K, as well as niacin, potas-

Conventionally grown peaches are on the "Dirty Dozen" list—meaning they are very high in pesticide and herbicide residues. This residue is particularly harmful to children, as well as to adults with health issues. Purchase organic peaches whenever possible.

sium, copper, manganese, phosphorus, magnesium, and dietary fiber. A single large peach contains about 70 calories.

SEASON

Whether at supermarkets, farmers markets, or CSAs, peaches and nectarines are still a highly seasonal crop, at their best from June through the end of August.

SELECTION

When choosing nonwhite-fleshed peaches and nectarines, most consumers make the mistake of equating red color with ripeness or quality. What you should really look for is the fruit with the most golden-yellow or even orange undertones; this signifies a higher sugar content and overall a more peachy flavor. Peaches and nectarines are typically picked when they are firm-ripe, to allow time for them to fully ripen and soften between the tree and the consumer's mouth. Both yellow and white peaches and nectarines should give slightly when gently pressed with a finger (but don't overdo it—they bruise extremely easily, and you should be considerate of those shopping after you). A rich fragrance is also an excellent sign. Avoid fruit that has large bruised areas (although keep in mind that minor bruises or soft spots can easily be cut away), as well as obvious signs of mold, rotting, or shriveling.

STORAGE

Peaches and nectarines both continue to ripen after picking. If your fruit is firm when you get it home, leave it out at room temperature until it begins to ripen. Wait to refrigerate it only after it ripens; moving it into cold temperatures any sooner is a sure way to ruin a peach, rendering it dry and mealy.

TRIMMING AND CLEANING

If you are eating peaches and nectarines raw, you can choose to peel them or not. Leaving the skins on means you will get more dietary fiber and nutrients, but be aware that conventionally grown fruits also contain some of the highest pesticide residues of any produce—another reason to buy organic. Peaches should be peeled before cooking; otherwise their skins will slip off on their own and may be messy to retrieve. Nectarines don't require peeling, since their skins are thinner and break down during cooking.

To peel a peach, cut a little X on one end, then blanch it in boiling water for 30 seconds to 1 minute, depending on how ripe it is (very ripe fruits may not require blanching at all). Remove it and immediately plunge it into a bowl of ice water to stop the cooking; you should be able to easily slip off the skin with your fingers or a knife.

To remove the pits, cut the fruits in half along their naturally occurring clefts, then gently twist in opposite directions to separate the halves. (Clingstone peaches will probably require you to cut the fruit away from the pit in smaller slices.)

Like apples and avocados, peaches and nectarines discolor after being cut; treat them with a light sprinkling of sugar or dip them in a mixture of water and lemon juice to stop them from browning.

A Little Jaundiced, My Dear?

Shoppers frequently make the mistake of choosing yellow-fleshed peaches and nectarines based on the redness of their characteristic blush.

In fact, one of the most reliable signs of a peach or nectarine's goodness is how yellow their underlying skin appears. The more golden they appear, the higher their sugar content is sure to be.

BLANCHING AND FREEZING

Peaches and nectarines can easily be frozen for enjoying all year long, and indeed it is almost a necessity with their all-too-brief season. Wash, blanch, peel, and slice them, discarding the pits. To prevent them from turning an unsightly brown, dip each slice in a bowl of water mixed with either ascorbic acid (vitamin C crystals) or lemon juice, or brush them with the mixture. Arrange them in a single layer on a tray lined with parchment or wax paper and freeze. Package the slices in zipper-lock freezer or vacuum food sealer-type bags, or freezer containers. Squeeze out any excess air and leave 1 inch of headspace (unless you are using the vacuum sealing method). Frozen peaches will keep for 10 to 12 months at 0°F.

You can also freeze peaches using sugar syrup. To make the sugar syrup, put 2 cups of sugar in 4 cups of water in a pot and bring it to a boil. Once the sugar has dissolved, remove the syrup from the heat and skim off the foam. Refrigerate until cold. Place the peach slices in zipper-lock freezer bags, jars, or freezer containers, and pour in enough syrup to cover the slices (allow ½ to ⅔ cup syrup for every 2 cups peaches). Squeeze out any excess air and leave ½ inch of headspace for pints, 1 inch for quarts.

EQUIVALENTS, MEASURES, AND SERVINGS

- 1 pound fresh = 3 to 4 medium peaches = 2 cups peeled and sliced
- 10 ounces frozen = 1 cup slices
- 16-ounce can = 6 to 10 slices = 2 cups slices
- 1 pound dried = 2¾ cups dried = 5¼ cups rehydrated

COMPLEMENTARY HERBS, SEASONINGS, AND FOODS

Almonds, anise, apricots, balsamic vinegar, basil, blackberries, black pepper, blueberries, brown sugar, butter, buttermilk, carrots, cheese (Brie, cream, goat, mozzarella), cherries, chicken, cinnamon, citrus, cloves, coconut, cream, ginger, hazelnuts, honey, hyssop, jalapeños, lemon verbena, lemons, limes, mangoes, maple syrup, mint, nutmeg, oranges, pecans, pineapple, pistachio, pork, prosciutto, raspberries, sour cream, wine (champagne, Muscat, Riesling), rum, tomatoes, vanilla, watermelon, yogurt.

SERVING SUGGESTIONS

- A truly ripe peach is one of summer's greatest (and briefest) of pleasures. Enjoy it on its own or with shortbread—or shortcake.
- Peel and slice peaches and marinate them briefly in sweetened wine.
- Make the famous dessert of Peach Melba. Poach peaches in a sugar syrup, then serve over vanilla ice cream with raspberry sauce made from raspberries, sugar, and lemon juice.
- Make gelatos and ice creams from luscious summer peaches and nectarines.
- Take advantage of succulent summer peaches to make fabulous smoothies.
- Peaches or nectarines make ideal fillings for pies, tarts, cobblers, and crisps.
- Combine peaches and nectarines with berries of all sorts—raspberries, blackberries, blueberries, and strawberries. Children adore these simple, flavorful fruits, either by themselves or with a little whipped cream or honey.
- Peaches can be a delicious and unexpected addition to salads. Great pairings include prosciutto, mozzarella cheese, and arugula.

"A Georgia peach, a real Georgia peach, a backyard great-grandmother's orchard peach, is as thickly furred as a sweater, and so fluent and sweet that once you bite through the flannel, it brings tears to your eyes."

— *Melissa Fay Greene*, Praying for Sheetrock

"An apple is an excellent thing— until you have tried a peach."

— *George du Maurier*

- Grilled peaches make a lovely accompaniment to steak and pork, or to salads, especially when seasoned with sweet-and-sour condiments like balsamic vinegar and tamarind.
- The sweet, acidic flavors of peaches make delicious salsas and chutneys.
- Peaches and nectarines are fantastic in mojitos with fresh mint and lime.
- Make an unusual gazpacho from tomatoes, peaches, cucumbers, apple cider vinegar, and yogurt.
- Thinly sliced peaches or nectarines make a surprise pizza topping along with tomatoes and mozzarella cheese.
- Cool off with summer punches of peaches, pineapple, iced tea, and lemonade combined.
- Alternate chunks of peaches with pieces of pork and bell pepper as kebabs.

- -

SUMMER FRUIT IN WINE DESSERT   SERVES 2 TO 3

> 1 stalk lemongrass, dry outer layers removed
> 1 to 2 tablespoons sugar, honey, or other sweetener
> ½ cup water
> Mixed summer fruits: melon balls or chunks, strawberries, blueberries, currants, cherries, plums, peaches, nectarines, apricots, raspberries (plan on about 1 cup of fruit per person)
> White wine (Riesling, Gewürztraminer, or Muscat Canelli)
> Mint or lemon balm sprigs
> Edible flowers (nasturtium, pansy, violet, mint, lavender, calendula, borage, rosemary, etc.)

1. Chop the lemongrass and make a simple syrup by boiling it with the sweetener and water until the sweetener is dissolved. Remove the syrup from the heat and let it cool. Steep for a few hours or overnight.

2. In the meantime, wash and stem, pit, slice, and chop the fruit into bite-size pieces, and place the pieces in a nonreactive bowl.

3. Strain the lemongrass syrup and combine it with enough wine to barely cover the fruit; pour the mixture over the fruit. Chill for several hours.

4. The fruit can be served in large wine goblets or clear glass dessert bowls. Or for a fancy presentation, use a melon shell. Garnish with herb sprigs and flowers.

Variation: Instead of the lemongrass, use lemon balm, mint, lemon or regular thyme, sweet woodruff, or rosemary.

— *Melinda McBride*

NECTARINES AND BLACKBERRIES IN ROSE GERANIUM SYRUP

SERVES 6

1 cup water
½ cup sugar
2 tablespoons chopped rose geranium leaves
4 nectarines, pitted and cut into ¾-inch wedges
1 cup blackberries

1. In a small saucepan, whisk the water and sugar over high heat until the sugar is in suspension and no longer mounded on the bottom of the pan. Bring the mixture to a boil and cook until all of the sugar is dissolved, about 5 minutes. If the sugar dissolves before the water boils, heat to a boil anyway.

2. When the water comes to a boil, remove the pan from the heat and add the rose geranium leaves. Let the mixture steep for at least 10 minutes.

3. Combine the nectarines and blackberries in a large bowl or divide them evenly among 6 small ones. Ladle the warm syrup through a strainer over the fruit. (This can be done up to 2 hours in advance and held at room temperature until serving.)

— *Russ Parsons,* How to Pick a Peach

COLD CREAM OF TOMATO AND PEACH SOUP

SERVES 2

1 onion, chopped
2 tablespoons butter
2 pounds tomatoes, chopped
½ pound peaches, peeled and chopped
½ cup cream (optional)
Tarragon, for garnishing

It also helped that a group of local consumers asked him to grow a wider array of produce specifically for them. Alan was pleased to meet this demand and added about 40 crops to his production repertoire. Since then it has grown to over 300 different crops and varieties.

Because of his research efforts, he farms mostly on conventional land, but Alan has become a big supporter of organic and grows most of the CSA and farmers market produce on organic land. The farm's way of doing CSA is a bit different as well; members can order both conventional and organic produce online from a list that the farm emails out. Members choose what crops they want, the quantity, and which farmers market they'll pick it up from (as Alan says of their arid Eastern Washington location, "We're out in the middle of nowhere"). Payment is a flat rate that is due when an order is placed, an arrangement that allows for maximum flexibility for consumers: It enables them to get exactly what they want when they want and to pay as they go, without having to fork out a hefty sum up front at the beginning of the season, unlike most CSAs.

What is Alan's mission in all of this? "We really believe in eating local," he says. "It's good for the economy, for agriculture, for the community. There is so much that we could grow here that you don't see at the supermarket. For example, we grow artichokes and keep them in cold storage for six months; same with leeks. This year we have over 400 separate items.

"I really want more people to eat local. Ninety percent of our customers have told us that produce being local rather than organic is the most important factor to them. We're also GAP-certified [Good Agricultural Practices] for food safety. We had to get certified to do a wholesale business, and we were the first farm to do so in the state."

Books

The Perfect Peach: Recipes and Stories
from the Masumoto Family Farm
David Mas Masumoto
and Marcy Masumoto,
Ten Speed Press, 2013.

Peaches and Other Juicy Fruits:
From Sweet to Savory,
150 Recipes for Peaches, Plums,
Nectarines and Apricots
Olwen Woodier,
Storey Publishing LLC, 2004.

Stone Fruit: Cherries, Nectarines,
Apricots, Plums, Peaches
Cynthia Nims,
Westwinds Press, 2003.

How to Pick a Peach: The Search
for Flavor from Farm to Table
Russ Parsons,
Mariner Books, 2008.

1. In a large saucepan over medium heat, cook the onion in the butter for 5 minutes.

2. Add the tomatoes and peaches.

3. Simmer until the tomatoes break up.

4. Add the cream (optional but good). Use a blender or food processor to puree the mixture. Chill.

5. Garnish with chopped tarragon, and serve.

— *Mark Bittman,* New York Times

Peppers (Sweet)

CAPSICUM ANNUUM

Even if they weren't edible, humans might cultivate peppers just for their beautiful colors and shapes. But happily this is not the case, and peppers of all kinds—sweet and hot—add taste, texture, color, and a little (or a lot) of zip to our gustatory lives.

All peppers are members of the genus Solanaceae, the same family as tomatoes, potatoes, eggplants, tobacco, and deadly nightshade. The pepper family is a vast one, with literally thousands of varieties, many of them spicy ones. Bell peppers simply refer to a subset of capsicums whose fruits are typically bell-shaped and taste sweet, with none of the sharp bite that characterizes their spicy cousins. (The latter warrant such different culinary treatment that they appear in a separate section in this book, on pages 259–270.)

All bell peppers start out green and slowly change to red, yellow, or orange as they mature, depending on the variety, so do not be surprised if the peppers in your CSA box are "blushing." As their color changes, they become milder and sweeter. Most CSA farms grow a mix of red, yellow, and green bell peppers. Another variety may be lurking in your box as well—the apple pepper, which is a small, heart-shaped, sweet red pepper with fleshy walls.

HISTORY

Peppers originated in South and Central America, where they have been a part of the human diet for over 7,500 years—and domesticated nearly as long. Dried peppers have been found in Incan tombs, and it is thought that chile peppers were one of the first cultivated crops on that continent. Christopher Columbus brought peppers back to Europe, and Spanish and Portuguese trade routes quickly spread both sweet and hot peppers to the Philippines, India, and the rest of Asia.

NUTRITION

Bell (sweet) peppers are outstanding sources of vitamin C (a 1-cup serving contains 300 percent of the adult daily requirement) and vitamin A. They also contain significant amounts of vitamin B6, folate, vitamin K, and dietary fiber. Red, yellow, and orange bell peppers are higher in vitamins A and C than green ones, since their color comes from antioxidant compounds called beta-carotenes. Red peppers are one of the few vegetable sources of lycopene, which may help prevent prostate and bladder cancers.

SEASON

Commercially, bell peppers are widely grown and in season year-round. But all peppers are heat-loving plants, and although they are available year-round in supermarkets, their best season is mid to late summer and early fall.

SELECTION

Choose bell peppers that are heavy for their size and firm all over, with no soft spots, bruises, or signs of shriveling or decay. Red bell peppers are just green bells that are fully ripened; the redder the pepper, the sweeter it is.

STORAGE

Store peppers unwashed in the refrigerator in a perforated plastic bag in the vegetable crisper, where they will keep for a few days. If you're storing a pepper that's been cut open, just let it lie loose, cut side up, in your vegetable drawer (if it's bagged, the edges will quickly turn slimy).

TRIMMING AND CLEANING

Wash peppers well before cutting. Supermarket peppers may be covered with a fine coating of food-grade wax; be sure to scrub these well. To prepare, cut around the stem and gently lift this "cap" out; most of the pepper's seeds are attached to this inside stem end and will be removed this way. Then reach inside and clean out any stray seeds and white inner ribs.

STEAMING AND BOILING

Bell peppers can be steamed whole or in strips. Place whole peppers in a steamer basket or pan above boiling water and steam for 10 minutes; strips will be done in about 5 minutes. Boiling is not recommended for bell peppers, since this makes them watery.

STIR-FRYING AND SAUTÉING

Bell peppers love the wok or sauté pan: Slice them into rings or strips, and stir-fry or sauté them in a little butter or oil, either by themselves or with other vegetables, for 2 to 4 minutes. Great stir-fry accompaniments for bell peppers include onions, leeks, snow peas, tomatoes, green beans, cabbage, mustard greens, or tiny broccoli or cauliflower florets.

BAKING AND ROASTING

Bell peppers respond well to oven baking, although for stuffed-pepper preparations, bells benefit from a parboiling in salted water for 5 minutes before baking. Bake at 400°F for about 20 minutes, or until the peppers are soft but not collapsing. For nonstuffed-pepper recipes, cut the peppers into 1½- to 2-inch chunks, combine them with other vegetables and ingredients if desired (like onions and potatoes), and bake for 20 to 30 minutes at 425°F, or 40 minutes at 375°F.

Roasting peppers caramelizes their natural sugars, making them sweeter and more complex. To roast on the grill, halve or quarter them, depending on their size, remove their seeds and ribs, and brush the pieces with olive oil. Place the peppers directly on the grill on medium heat, and cook for 6 to 10 minutes, turning them over at least once during the cooking time. When done, the peppers should be browned but still somewhat crisp. Or you can roast whole peppers in the oven at 400°F for 40 minutes, turning at least once, until the skins are well charred.

Once they have finished roasting, place the peppers in a large bowl, seal the bowl tightly with plastic wrap, and let them stand for about 20 minutes. The trapped steam within the bowl will loosen the skins from the peppers. Then cut the peppers open and remove the ribs, seeds, stems, and skins. Now they are ready for use in dishes calling for roasted peppers.

BLANCHING AND FREEZING

Blanch peppers if you want to use them in heated dishes; for uncooked preparations, don't blanch if you want a more crispy texture. To blanch,

Peppers and Pesticides

Conventionally grown bell and hot peppers are on the "Dirty Dozen" list—meaning they are very high in pesticide and herbicide residues.

This residue is particularly harmful to children, as well as to adults with health issues. Purchase organic peppers whenever possible.

wash the peppers and remove their seeds. Blanch halved peppers in boiling water for 3 minutes; sliced or diced ones for 2 minutes. Then plunge them into ice water for 5 minutes to stop the cooking process. Remove and drain. Pack in zipper-lock freezer or vacuum food sealer-type bags, or freezer containers. Squeeze out any excess air and leave ½ inch of headspace (unless you are using the vacuum sealing method). Frozen peppers will keep for up to 12 months at 0°F.

MICROWAVING

Microwave stuffed bell peppers (fillings should be precooked) over high power for about 10 to 15 minutes, depending on the size of the pepper. Pepper chunks can be microwaved in a little liquid on high power for 6 to 8 minutes, or until tender-crisp.

COMPLEMENTARY HERBS, SEASONINGS, AND FOODS

Anchovies, anise, basil, cheese, chiles, coriander, corn, crab, cumin, eggplants, fennel, fish, garlic, ginger, goat cheese, green beans, lemons, lobster, marjoram, olive oil, onions, parsley, pasta, pork, potatoes, rice, saffron, sausage, sesame, smoked salt, soy sauce, summer squash, tamari, tomatoes, veal, vinegar, winter squash.

EQUIVALENTS, MEASURES, AND SERVINGS

- 1 large bell pepper = 1 cup chopped
- 3 medium bell peppers = about 1 pound = 2 cups chopped

SERVING SUGGESTIONS

- Thinly slice fresh bell peppers into rings or strips and serve with a favorite dressing as a dip. Kids especially love sweet red and orange bell peppers.
- Roasted peppers, although they are a bit time-consuming to prepare, instantly enrich any dish with their rich, sweet flavors.
- Make salsa! Fresh bell peppers give a wonderful flavor without adding heat—a good option for children.
- Dice bell peppers to use in fajitas, tacos, and other Mexican dishes.
- Bell peppers are wonderful stewed or cooked in sauces, and have a wonderful affinity for rich meats like sausage, veal, and steak.
- Add roasted or sautéed bell peppers to your favorite pasta dish.
- Grill bell peppers that have been marinated in olive oil, garlic, and herbs.
- Add chunks of bell pepper, onion, and tomatoes to kebabs.
- Combine bell peppers with other vegetables (broccoli, onions, greens, mushrooms, cabbage, tomatoes, carrots) for tasty, colorful stir-fries.
- That old classic, stuffed peppers, can be livened up from its traditional ground-beef-and-rice filling with different ingredients, like cooked cracked wheat berries, sliced jalapeños, barbecued chicken, sweet onions, eggplant, breadcrumbs, deep-fried parsley sprigs, miniature meatballs…
- Thinly slice bell peppers and add them to sandwiches as a substitute for lettuce. (Great with onions and cucumbers!)
- For a crunchy texture and distinctive flavor, add finely chopped bell peppers to tuna, ham, chicken, or egg salad.

Cooking Tip

To transport and serve stuffed peppers, use a Bundt cake pan.

"Food is our common ground, a universal experience."

— James Beard,
American chef and food writer

VEGGIE-STUFFED BELL PEPPERS   SERVES 6

3 small Asian eggplants, unpeeled and thinly sliced
1 teaspoon kosher salt
3 bell peppers (any color)
4 to 5 medium potatoes, peeled and thinly sliced
3 small summer squashes, thinly sliced
2 tablespoons olive oil
2 cloves garlic, minced
½ medium leek, finely sliced
1 small jalapeño pepper, minced
2 tablespoons mixed fresh herbs, finely chopped
1 cup panko breadcrumbs
½ cup grated Parmesan cheese, divided
Salt and freshly ground pepper

1. Place the sliced eggplant in a strainer or colander. Toss it with the kosher salt and let it sit for 10 minutes to draw out its moisture.

2. Meanwhile, preheat the oven to 375°F. Cut the peppers in half lengthwise and remove the seeds and inner white ribs. Place the halves on a foil-lined baking dish that is thinly coated with olive oil.

3. Rinse the salt off the eggplant and pat it dry with a towel. Chop the eggplant, potatoes, and squash very small, keeping each vegetable separate from the others; try to make them all similar in size so that the stuffing blends well and cooks evenly.

4. Over medium-high heat, add the olive oil and heat for a minute. Add the garlic and leek and sauté for 1 to 2 minutes, then add the potatoes. After 3 minutes, add the eggplant, squash, and jalapeño pepper, stirring frequently until the vegetables are soft but not mushy. Turn off the heat and add the herbs, breadcrumbs, ¼ cup of the Parmesan cheese, and salt and pepper to taste.

5. Stuff the peppers with the vegetable mixture and place them in the oven for 25 to 30 minutes. A few minutes before they are done, sprinkle the remaining Parmesan cheese over the top. Enjoy!

— *Sang Lee Farms, Peconic, New York*

RATATOUILLE NIÇOISE   SERVES 4

Source Note: *In this recipe, quantities depend on what you have, and varying the proportions doesn't matter—it is great no matter what!*

1 onion, chopped
2 tablespoons olive oil

3 cloves garlic, chopped
1 eggplant, cut into thin rounds, each slice quartered
1 medium zucchini, sliced
1 large tomato, chopped
1 green bell pepper, chopped
Handful of fresh basil, chopped
Salt and freshly ground black pepper

1. In a large saucepan, sauté the onion over medium heat in the olive oil until it turns translucent. Add the chopped garlic and sauté briefly.

2. Add the eggplant, then the zucchini and tomato, and finally the green bell pepper. Add the basil and season the mixture to taste with salt and pepper. Simmer until the liquid given off by the vegetables has mostly evaporated. Serve warm or at room temperature, adding an additional swirl of olive oil on top if you'd like, with crusty bread.

Variation: You can also put some ratatouille in the bottom of a baking pan, make indentations in the vegetables, and then crack an egg into each indentation. Bake in a 350°F oven for about 15 minutes, or until the eggs are cooked to your taste. Then sprinkle grated cheese (you could use Parmesan, mozzarella, or Fontina) over all of this— the benefits of the veggies far outweigh the fat in the cheese!

— *Margaret Houston, Featherstone Farm CSA member*

VEGETARIAN PAELLA WITH BROWN RICE   SERVES 6

Source Note: If you'd like to make a more traditional paella, switch to short-grain white rice and add several pinches of saffron threads.

1½ tablespoons olive oil
1 large onion, chopped
3 cloves garlic, chopped
½ teaspoon paprika
1½ cups long-grain brown rice, uncooked
3¾ cups low-sodium vegetable broth
¾ cup dry white wine
1 (14-ounce) can tomatoes, chopped, with juice
1 tablespoon tomato paste
½ tablespoon chopped fresh tarragon, or ½ teaspoon
    dried tarragon
1 tablespoon chopped fresh basil, or 1 teaspoon dried basil
1 tablespoon chopped fresh oregano, or 1 teaspoon dried oregano
1 red bell pepper, roughly chopped
1 green bell pepper, roughly chopped
3 ribs celery, finely chopped
3 cups mushrooms, washed and sliced

that has become a mecca of urban farming with 20 farmers markets and dozens of popular farm-to-table restaurants. What makes the project unique is that the 65 farmers who work for it all have developmental disabilities—from autism to Down syndrome. Founded by the Cuyahoga County Board of Developmental Disabilities and SAW, Inc., Cleveland Crops began with a single acre in 2010 and plans to be farming 40 acres at a dozen locations within a few years. The farm sites—which include a 15,000-square-foot greenhouse and half a dozen hoop houses—grow pesticide-free produce for local restaurants, farmers markets, and a large CSA.

Traditionally, Cleveland residents with developmental disabilities were trained for jobs in manufacturing, but those jobs have been disappearing. Cleveland Crops provides temporary training for jobs primarily in urban farming and the food service industry, equipping trainees with transferable skills. The organization has opened a 5,000-square-foot Food Innovation Center, where trainees produce dehydrated and packaged food products under the Cleveland Crops brand, as well as process food for other food-related businesses, including growers and restaurants. Some organizations that hire people with developmental disabilities get a federal waiver to pay them below the minimum wage, but that is not the case here.

In Lake County, Illinois, north of Chicago, the **Prairie Farm Corps** helps lay the groundwork for a more resilient local food system by immersing youth in sustainable agriculture. A diverse group of young people from local high schools and a local college are provided with a paid work experience on the **Prairie Crossing Learning Farm**, gaining job skills applicable to any career, an ability to grow and cook fresh vegetables, and a hands-on introduction to sustainable agriculture.

½ cup snow pea pods
⅔ cup frozen peas, thawed
⅓ cup cashew nut pieces
Salt and freshly ground black pepper

1. Heat the oil in a large, deep skillet, and sauté the onions and garlic over medium heat until they become soft.

2. Add the paprika and rice and continue to cook for 4 to 5 minutes, or until the rice becomes transparent. Stir occasionally.

3. Add the broth, wine, tomatoes, tomato paste, and herbs. Simmer for 10 to 15 minutes.

4. Add the peppers, celery, mushrooms, and pea pods. Continue to cook for another 30 minutes, or until the rice is cooked through.

5. Add the peas, cashews, salt, and pepper to taste. Heat through and place on a large heated serving dish.

Nonvegetarian Variation: Add chopped country ham, clams, mussels, cooked shrimp, chunks of crab, lobster, andouille or chorizo sausage, or rabbit.

— *Produce for Better Health; Fruits & Veggies—More Matters; Centers for Disease Control and Prevention*

Bell peppers at Featherstone Farm.

SPICY ROASTED VEGETABLE SOUP   SERVES 8 TO 10

1 medium eggplant, cut into 1-inch dice
2 red or green bell peppers, cut into 1-inch dice
2 large sweet onions, cut into 1-inch dice
3 large carrots, peeled and cut into ½-inch slices
1 medium zucchini, cut into ½-inch slices

1 head garlic, peeled, cloves minced
1 large sweet potato, peeled and cut into ½-inch dice
    (or substitute winter squash)
¼ cup olive oil
½ pint cherry tomatoes, or 1 cup diced tomato
1 tablespoon ground cumin seed
1 tablespoon ground coriander seed
1 tablespoon fennel seed
1 teaspoon red pepper flakes
3 tablespoons balsamic vinegar
¼ cup tamari sauce
1 tablespoon brown sugar or honey
3 tablespoons tomato paste
3 tablespoons dried currants
12 cups vegetable stock
Salt and freshly ground black pepper

1. Preheat the oven to 400°F.

2. In a large roasting pan or Dutch oven, toss the eggplant, peppers,
    onions, carrots, zucchini, garlic, and sweet potatoes with the olive oil.
    (If you have enough oven space, you may wish to divide the mixed
    veggies into two portions and spread them onto 2 baking sheets or
    roasting pans.) Bake for 30 minutes, stirring a few times, until the
    vegetables start to brown.

3. Remove the vegetables from the oven and place them in a large stock-
    pot. Add all of the remaining ingredients and stir gently to combine.
    Place the pot over medium-high heat and bring to a boil; quickly
    lower the heat and simmer for 10 to 15 minutes. Add additional salt
    and pepper to taste.

— *Colleen Wolner, Blue Heron Coffeehouse, Winona, Minnesota,*
    The Bluff Country Co-op Cookbook

"An old-fashioned vegetable soup,
without any enhancement, is a
more powerful anticarcinogen
than any known medicine."

— James Duke, MD,
USDA medicinal
phytochemicals expert

HARISSA

MAKES 1 CUP

*Author Note: Traditionally, this piquant red pepper sauce developed as an
accompaniment and flavor enhancer to North African stews and couscous
dishes. It can make any such warm, complex dish burst with flavor. It also
makes a lively spread for sandwiches and a killer addition to hummus.*

*This recipe features sweet red bell peppers over hot peppers, a departure from
authentic North African harissa. But feel free to bump up the amount of red
pepper flakes to suit your need for fire.*

2 to 3 whole roasted red bell peppers, skin and seeds removed,
    or 1 cup roasted red bell peppers from a jar
2 cloves garlic
2 tablespoons apple cider vinegar

¼ cup extra-virgin olive oil (see Variation note below)
1 or more teaspoons red pepper flakes
1 teaspoon salt
1 teaspoon caraway seeds
¾ teaspoon ground cumin
½ teaspoon ground coriander

Combine all the ingredients in the bowl of a food processor or
blender. Puree, pausing to scrape down the sides as necessary, until
the mixture is very smooth. Transfer the harissa to a bowl and store
it, covered, in the refrigerator for up to one week. If you can, bring
it to room temperature before serving—it will have more flavor that
way, and the cold sauce won't cool down hot foods.

Variation: Nuts go so well with roasted red peppers that your harissa
can be enhanced by using part nut oil in this recipe. For example,
use 2 tablespoons hazelnut or walnut oil, plus 2 tablespoons extra-virgin olive oil to equal the ¼ cup olive oil.

— *Lisa Gordanier (Adapted from* Pure Beef *by Lynne Curry)*

*Sweet corn just about ready for eating
at Teena's Pride CSA.*

Peppers (Hot) CAPSICUM ANNUUM OR C. FRUTESCENS

How boring and bland our gastronomic universe would truly be were it not for the fiery heat and distinctive flavors of hot peppers, those brazen denizens of the vegetable world. Nearly 4,000 varieties of hot peppers exist, in all shapes, colors, flavors, and sizes, from the diminutive Thai bird peppers to the mild, fleshy poblanos. In such a large family, botanical confusion runs rampant, for all peppers cross-pollinate easily to form new varieties, and common names may refer to completely different peppers in various countries.

What is common to all hot peppers (often called chiles) is the presence of capsaicin, a fat-soluble compound that reacts with pain receptors in the mouth and throat to produce that characteristic burning sensation. If we eat a lot of hot pepper–seasoned foods over time, these receptors become desensitized, which is why we often need to consume increasing amounts to get the same kick.

Capsaicin has a long history as medicine, valued for its antibacterial and anti-inflammatory properties. It is also used as a circulatory stimulant and pain reliever in dermatological ointments. And despite popular belief, hot peppers do not cause ulcers or hemorrhoids; in fact, they may actually help relieve those conditions.

The heat of peppers is most commonly measured in Scoville units. Bell peppers have a Scoville rating of zero; pure capsaicin has 16 million. High-performance liquid chromatography, developed in the 1980s, is a more accurate way of measuring capsaicin levels, but the Scoville scale remains popular.

The world of hot peppers is a dazzlingly colossal one, and it's worth checking out chile authority Dave DeWitt's wonderfully thorough books on the subject (see the Books sidebar on page 265). You may find many varieties of hot peppers in your CSA box or at the farmers market over the course of a season. Here are just a few of the more common ones:

Ancho
This is the dried version of the poblano pepper (see page 260). They are smoky and sweet, with a somewhat raisin-like flavor. These mild, deep reddish-brown peppers are typically used for sauces (including the famous Mexican *mole*), spice rubs, chili, and tamales.

Chipotle
The chipotle is a jalapeño that has been allowed to ripen fully and turn red. It is then picked, dried, and smoked, resulting in a distinctive fiery, smoky flavor. Their heat varies widely, from mild to hot (2,500 to 10,000 Scoville units). Chipotles are available as dried whole peppers, ground into powder, or concentrated bases. They impart a mild spiciness and earthiness in many cooked dishes in Mexican cuisine, including meats, soups, stews, beans, chili, and barbecue and hot sauces.

Bhut Jolokia
You are perhaps not likely to see the small wrinkled red fruits of this pepper at your local farmers market, but it is worth mentioning here

Will the Real Pepper Please Stand Up?

Hot peppers (*Capsicum annuum*) should not be confused with black or white pepper, which are the berries (peppercorns) of an entirely different plant (*Piper nigrum*).

because of its recent meteoric rise to culinary fame. Sometimes called the ghost pepper or Naga jolokia, it has the distinction of being named the hottest pepper in the world in 2007, at over 1 million Scoville units, or 900 times hotter than Tabasco sauce. Since then, two other varieties have surpassed the jolokia (the Trinidad moruga scorpion in 2012 and the Carolina Reaper).

In its native India, bhut jolokia is used in curries, pickles, and chutneys, and also in combination with pork and dried or fermented fish. In northeastern India, the peppers are smeared on fences or incorporated in smoke bombs as a safety precaution to keep wild elephants at a distance.

Cayenne

These long, tapered green or red chiles are usually dried and ground, but you may find them fresh in your CSA boxes or at the farmers market. They are instrumental in Asian cuisines and are a common ingredient in the spicy Buffalo wing sauce.

Habanero

These very distinctive, lantern-shaped peppers are usually bright orange or yellow, and are sometimes confused with or mislabeled as Scotch Bonnets, which have a slightly different-shaped pod. Habaneros also happen to be the hottest commonly available chile in the United States, with a Scoville rating of 100,000 to 350,000 units—at least 40 times hotter than a jalapeño.

Jalapeño

These medium-size, plump, conical green peppers are probably the most well-known hot chiles in America. Depending on their growing conditions, jalapeños range from mild to hot (2,500 to 10,000 Scoville units). They have a distinctive, fresh flavor that is ideal for salsas, pico de gallo, and grilling whole.

Piquin, Thai, Bird Pepper, Chiltepin, Tabasco

These are all diminutive peppers that pack mighty heat—the general rule with chiles is that the smaller the pepper, the hotter it is. Depending on their variety and growing conditions, they vary tremendously but often range between 50,000 and 100,000 Scoville units. These guys are tiny, some only as big as the fingernail on your little finger, but don't be fooled. They can be green, yellow, orange, and red, and just a few thin slivers can easily spice up a meal.

Poblano

The Poblano is a large green chile that is used most often in chile rellenos. It is usually mild (1,000 to 2,000 Scoville units), although it can be unpredictably hot. This pepper is especially good roasted or in *mole* sauce.

Serrano

The Serrano is a fleshy green, red, brown, orange, or yellow hot pepper that resembles a jalapeño, but with a longer, more slender pod. It is considerably hotter than a jalapeño, with a Scoville rating of 10,000 to 25,000 units, and it's popular for salsas, pico de gallo, marinades, and chili.

Shishito

These beautiful, finger-long green peppers have become recent darlings of the American food scene, and for good reason—they're crunchy, savory, and mostly sweet and mild. But beware—about 1 in every 10 peppers has some heat to it, which can take diners by surprise. Their most common preparation is to toss them in a little garlic and seasoning, pan-fry them in oil until they turn tender but are still crisp, finish them with sea salt, and serve them right away as an appetizer.

HISTORY

Peppers originated in South and Central America, where people have been eating them for over 7,500 years and domesticating them for nearly as long. Dried peppers have been found in Incan tombs, and chiles may have been one of the first cultivated crops on that continent.

Christopher Columbus brought peppers back to Europe, and Spanish and Portuguese trade routes quickly spread both hot chiles and bell peppers to the Philippines, India, and the rest of Asia. Since then, hot peppers have become one of the world's most universal seasonings—an indispensable part of the cuisines of China, Korea, Southeast Asia, Africa, and the Middle East.

NUTRITION

Hot peppers are usually not consumed in large enough quantity to be nutritionally significant, but they do contain huge levels of vitamins A and C, as well as some B6 and vitamin K. A ½-cup serving of chopped or diced hot peppers contain 30 calories (imagine eating that much in one meal!). Capsaicin, the substance that gives chiles their heat, has its own health benefits—helping to lower cholesterol, reduce pain (especially arthritis), possibly prevent stomach ulcers, and stimulate blood circulation.

SEASON

Commercially, hot peppers are widely grown and in season year-round. They are a heat-loving crop, however, and you'll find them at their best in farmers markets and CSAs throughout the summer and early fall.

SELECTION

Choose peppers that are heavy for their size (signaling a greater proportion of flesh to hollow spaces) and firm all over, with no soft spots, bruises, or signs of shriveling or decay.

STORAGE

Do not wash peppers until you are just about to use them. Store them in the refrigerator vegetable crisper in a perforated plastic bag, where they will keep for up to 1 to 2 weeks. If you're storing a pepper that's been cut open, just let it lie loose, cut side up, in your vegetable drawer (if it's bagged, the edges will quickly turn slimy).

TRIMMING AND CLEANING

Wash and dry the peppers. The trickiest part of handling hot peppers is to avoid direct skin contact with its innards; its fiery capsaicin can severely

Cooking Tip

When you cook with hot peppers, taste-test the pepper (and the dish, if feasible) during preparation, and adjust the seasoning accordingly.

The heat of individual peppers (even ones of the same species and from the same plant) varies tremendously. Peppers exposed to more sunlight, hotter temperatures, or drier soil often pack a lot more heat than less stressed plants.

Your diners will appreciate not being unpleasantly surprised at the table!

irritate skin and mucous membranes. Some cooks protect their hands, eyes, noses, and mouths by wearing thin gloves and face masks while preparing chiles.

To deseed hot peppers (and if you are not planning to peel them), slice off the stem end and then cut them in half lengthwise. With the halves exposed, carefully scrape off the seeds, cut out the whitish inner ribs (which contain the highest capsaicin concentration), and discard both.

If, on the other hand, you wish to preserve or boost the available heat of your peppers, leave the membrane and seeds intact and just chop the whole pepper.

After cutting peppers, always thoroughly wash your hands, utensils, and cutting surfaces with plenty of soap and water to prevent the capsaicin from inadvertently burning your skin, coming into contact with your face, or contaminating other foods on the cutting surface. For more tips, see the Chile Handling Safety sidebar on page 260.

STEAMING AND BOILING

For a bit of zip, add a few slices of jalapeño or other hot pepper to the steam basket or pan while other vegetables are steaming or boiling. The longer the pepper cooks, the milder it will become (although you may not notice much difference with the hottest chiles!).

STIR-FRYING AND SAUTÉING

Thinly sliced or slivered fresh hot peppers add a lovely bite to stir-fries or sautéed mixtures. Add to a stir-fry or a sauté in the last 2 to 4 minutes of cooking.

ROASTING AND BROILING

Roasting peppers in the oven or over a grill gives them a luscious, smoky flavor. It also loosens the tough skins, making them easier to remove and discard so that the pepper flesh can be used in recipes and for canning.

To roast on the grill, place whole or cut-up peppers directly atop a charcoal or gas grill 5 or 6 inches above the coals. Use tongs to constantly turn the peppers on all sides until their skins start to blacken and blister, 2 to 3 minutes.

To roast in the oven or broiler, preheat to 425°F, and use tongs to turn the peppers constantly until their skins blister on all sides. To roast on the stovetop, place the peppers on a wire mesh rack directly atop the electric or gas burner, and roast and turn until the skins are evenly blistered and somewhat charred.

Once the peppers are blistered, place them in a large bowl, seal the bowl tightly with plastic wrap, and let them stand for about 20 minutes. The trapped steam within the bowl will loosen the skins from the peppers. Then cut the peppers open and remove the ribs, seeds, stems, and skins. Now they are ready for use in dishes calling for roasted chiles.

Be sure to handle these peppers carefully, avoiding direct contact with the skin (see Trimming and Cleaning, above).

MICROWAVING

Microwave hot peppers to soften their skins: Place the peppers in a microwave-safe container, then cover with a tight-fitting lid to allow steam to build up inside. Microwave on high power for 7 to 8 minutes, then allow the steam to accumulate inside the dish for another 1 to 2 minutes. Be careful when you open the dish, as the steam will be extremely hot and may burn on contact. The skins will not appear blistered, but they will be tougher and more brittle, making them easier to peel.

BLANCHING AND FREEZING

Blanch peppers if you want to use them in cooked dishes; for uncooked preparations, do not blanch if you want a more crispy texture. Whole peppers that will not be blanched do not need any preparation; simply insert them into zipper-lock freezer bags and freeze.

To blanch peppers, wash them and remove their seeds. Cut the peppers into halves or slice them into rings. Blanch halved peppers in boiling water for 3 minutes and sliced ones for 2 minutes (chopped or diced peppers do not require blanching). Then plunge them into ice water for 5 minutes to stop the cooking process. Remove and drain. Pack them in zipper-lock freezer or vacuum food sealer-type bags, or freezer containers. Squeeze out any excess air and leave ½ inch of headspace (unless you are using the vacuum sealing method). Frozen hot peppers will keep for up to 1 year at 0°F.

DRYING

Drying is a very popular method of preserving hot peppers. Using string and wire, tie quantities of whole, fresh, unblemished peppers into a long, layered bunch called a *ristra,* and hang it up to dry in a cool, well-ventilated spot away from heat, humidity, and sunlight.

Peppers also dry well in a food dehydrator. Simply wash them, slice them into desired lengths, and dry them on the dehydrator shelves until they turn brittle. Then package the dried chiles into plastic bags or glass jars for later use, or crumble or grind them into a powder (but beware of the dust produced in the process, which can severely irritate eyes and throats).

EQUIVALENTS, MEASURES, AND SERVINGS

- 1-inch segment = 2 teaspoons finely chopped
- 20 peppers 3 to 6 inches long and ½ to ¾ inch in diameter = ½ pound

COMPLEMENTARY HERBS, SEASONINGS, AND FOODS

Beans, beef, cabbage, cheese, chocolate, chutney, cilantro, citrus, corn, crab, cream, cumin, eggs, eggplant, fish, fish sauce, fruit, garlic, ginger, honey, ketchup, lemon, lime, lobster, mangoes, mint, onions, oranges, pineapple, pork, potatoes, rice, shrimp, sweet peppers, tomatoes, vinegar, yogurt.

SERVING SUGGESTIONS

- Make salsa or pico de gallo! Although the classic ingredients are chiles, onions, cilantro, garlic, and tomatoes, feel free to mix it up (so to speak) a bit with finely chopped cucumbers, mangoes, papayas, apples, jicama, and even radishes.
- Preserve hot peppers in vinegar or oil for a spicy seasoning that is handy for sprinkling over cooked dishes or to use in dressings. To make pepper vinegar, put enough fresh, sliced hot peppers in a sterilized Mason-type jar

Eat more hot peppers. *Over time, humans often become desensitized to the effects of capsaicin if they repeatedly consume quantities of hot peppers, gradually needing to eat more to feel the same burn (and that peculiar high that accompanies it). So go ahead and indulge!*

Turning Up the Heat

If you are looking to add more fire to a recipe, use more of the seeds and white inner ribs, where the fiery capsaicin is concentrated.

Conversely, if you prefer a milder dish, use just the flesh instead.

to fill it about a quarter- to half-full. Then add enough white vinegar to fill the jar, add a little salt and powdered cayenne if desired, and seal. Let the vinegar stand for several weeks; it will keep for up to 6 months. For a recipe to create the oil, see Chili Oil on page 264.

- For a tossed salad sure to wake up your taste buds, add a few very thinly sliced hot pepper rings and finely shredded or slivered fresh ginger.

- Add a teaspoon or more of finely chopped chiles to your favorite cornbread recipe, or even cookies, macaroons, and turnovers.

- Add thinly sliced jalapeños or serranos to soups, stews, casseroles, omelets, and stir-fries, or grill them whole to go with steaks, roast meats, or chicken.

- Combine hot peppers with garlic, olive oil, coriander, cumin, peppermint, and other herbs and spices to make harissa, a Tunisian hot pepper paste that is commonly used in North African cuisines (see the recipe on page 257).

- Add a little chopped hot pepper to yogurt- and sour cream–based dips.

- Use hot peppers when making Southeast Asian, Szechuan and Hunan Chinese, Korean, and Latin American dishes.

- If you feel a cold coming on, make hot cayenne lemonade. It may sound gross, but it really can help make you feel better. Combine 1 cup of boiling water with the juice of 1 lemon and 2 to 3 dashes of ground cayenne. Stir and sweeten with honey or stevia.

- Search out chipotles canned in adobo sauce in the international section of your supermarket. They're easy to use and add a toothsome smokiness and depth to meats, beans, stews, marinades, and sauces.

- If you've got poblano peppers, make chile rellenos tonight. Roast the peppers first on a grill or under an oven broiler; then stuff them with cheese, coat them in an airy egg batter, and fry.

- Spice rubs, marinades, seasoning pastes, jerks, mole sauce, adobo sauce, barbecue sauce, harissa, romesco, chile Colorado, Thai curry paste—the list of chile-based sauces goes on and on. And they are delicious not just with meats but also with potatoes and other vegetarian alternatives.

- If you have a lot of cayenne peppers, garlic, and napa cabbage on hand, make kimchi—that fiery, pickled, fermented condiment that is a national staple of Korea.

- Add hot peppers to your favorite beverages and cocktails—Bloody Marys and vodka come to mind, but remember that the ancient Incans enjoyed their hot chiles mixed with their hot chocolate, which remains a surprisingly delicious combination today. Experiment with anchos and habaneros in cider, rum fruit punches, or daiquiris.

- Breakfast burritos!

- Rice and chiles complement each other extremely well, especially with beans and hearty seasonings.

- The judicious use of chiles can be fantastic in summer sorbets. Think blood orange, Meyer lemon, key lime, ginger, mango, coconut…

Hot Peppers by Any Other Name

Hot peppers are called many names throughout the world, depending on where you are.

In Mexico, they are *chiles*. In parts of South America, they are known as *aji*.

In the United States, they are chile/chiles, chili/chilies, or chili/chile pepper (with a single *l*).

In the United Kingdom, India, and Canada, they are chilli/chillies or chilli peppers (with a double *l*).

CHILI OIL

MAKES ABOUT 1 CUP

1 medium jalapeño with half of the seeds and veins removed, minced
1 shallot, minced
⅓ cup peanut, corn, or blended vegetable oil

3 tablespoons water
½ teaspoon sugar
1 teaspoon salt
¼ teaspoon freshly ground white pepper

1. Heat the jalapeño, shallot, and oil in a small saucepan over medium heat for several minutes. Let stand for 5 to 10 minutes for flavors to meld.

2. While the oil is still warm, stir in the water, sugar, salt, and pepper.

3. When ready to serve, spoon the flavored oil over steamed vegetables and toss gently.

— *Shirley Corriher,* CookWise

. . . .

BRAISED WATER BUFFALO STEW WITH CHILES (SEUM SIN KUAI)

SERVES 6

Source Note: Don't let the use of water buffalo meat in this recipe from Laos prevent you from making it. Simply substitute buffalo meat that is available from specialty markets and through mail-order merchants, or you can use good-quality, grass-fed beef. The use of eggplant is typical in Laotian cuisine; eggplant thickens and adds richness to stewed dishes. This dish's heat scale is medium.

2 pounds buffalo meat, cut into ¾-inch cubes (or substitute beef)
7 slices galangal (or substitute 3 tablespoons minced fresh ginger)
1 onion, peeled and sliced
½ teaspoon salt
Water
2 tablespoons fish sauce
1 large Asian eggplant, washed and sliced
1 small head garlic, roasted, peeled, and chopped
1 cup sliced green beans
3 to 4 fresh red serrano or jalapeño chiles, stems and seeds removed, cut into rings
Juice of 1 fresh lime
½ cup chopped green onions, white and light green parts only
¼ cup chopped fresh mint or basil
Chopped fresh cilantro, for garnish
Freshly ground black pepper, for garnish
Thin slices of cucumber, for garnish

1. Put the meat, galangal, onion, and salt in a large, heavy soup pot and add water to cover. Bring to a boil and add the fish sauce and eggplant. Reduce the heat and cook at a rolling simmer for 10 minutes or until the eggplant is tender. Remove the eggplant from the pot, mash it, and set it aside. Cover the meat and continue to simmer until it is tender, about 1 hour.

Books

1,001 Best Hot and Spicy Recipes
Dave DeWitt
Agate Surrey, 2010.

Rick Bayless's Mexican Kitchen
Rick Bayless, Deann Groen Bayless, and Jean Marie Brownson, Scribner, 1996.

The Complete Chile Pepper Book: A Gardener's Guide to Choosing, Growing, Preserving, and Cooking
Dave DeWitt and Paul W. Bosland, Timber Press, 2014.

The Art of Mexican Cooking
Diana Kennedy, Clarkson Potter, 2008.

Hot Sauces

Peppers, in Rehoboth Beach, Delaware, is the world's largest hot sauce museum, with 6,500 different kinds on exhibit.

Its retail store offers 1,500 to 2,000 brands for sale, with 100 to 150 available for tasting at any given time.

Visit their entertaining website to find out more about hot peppers and order from their vast selection of chile-related products:

www.peppers.com

2. When the meat is tender, add the mashed eggplant, garlic, green beans, chiles, and lime juice. Cook at a low boil, uncovered, for 10 minutes or until the beans are done and the sauce has thickened slightly.

3. Stir in the green onions and mint, and divide the stew among large soup bowls. Garnish with the cilantro, black pepper, and cucumber.

— *Dave DeWitt*, 1,001 Hot & Spicy Recipes

RAINY NIGHT CHILI

SERVES 6 TO 8

Source Note: Blackened poblano chiles—not too hot, but full of earthy flavor—give this chili a richness that is unique and satisfying. Serve with fresh, out-of-the-oven corn muffins. As with most chilies and stews, this one improves after lounging in your fridge for a day or two.

2 large fresh poblano peppers
1 large yellow onion, diced
4 cloves garlic, minced
1 (15-ounce) can kidney beans, with juice
1 (15-ounce) can fire-roasted diced tomatoes, with juice
1 (6-ounce) can tomato paste
1 bottle light-bodied beer
1 tablespoon chopped fresh thyme
2 teaspoons crumbled dry oregano
2 teaspoons ground cumin
2 teaspoons chili powder (see the Cooking Note below)
1½ to 2 teaspoons salt
1 pound ground beef, preferably grass-fed
Chicken stock or water, optional, for thinning
Fresh lime juice, for finishing

1. Use the open flame of a gas burner to directly roast the peppers, turning them so they cook evenly until completely blackened and somewhat soft. (Alternatively, place the peppers on a cookie sheet under the oven broiler set on high heat. Turn them as they roast.) Put them in a bowl and cover with a plate. Let stand for about 15 minutes; they will continue to cook and become more compliant. Now peel away the blackened skin. Split them open, remove the seeds and membrane, and cut into ½-inch dice. Set aside.

2. In a large stewpot over medium heat, cook the onion and garlic, stirring, until softened and slightly browned. Add the roasted peppers along with the beans, tomatoes, tomato paste, beer, thyme, oregano, cumin, chili powder, and salt.

3. In a large sauté pan, brown the beef over medium-high heat, seasoning it with salt and pepper as it cooks. Add the meat to the pot.

4. Simmer, partially covered, over low heat for about 1 hour. If you'd like the chili to be thinner, add a bit of chicken stock or water. Check for seasoning, adding salt, pepper, or more cumin and chili powder to taste. Fresh lime juice adds zip and sparkle at the very end of cooking.

Cooking Note: There are many types of chile powders, including pure ground versions of dried chiles and blends of different chiles and spices. Choose a fragrant version that suits your taste buds; we like to use one that includes smoked paprika—it bumps up the slightly smoky smell and taste of the blackened poblanos and diced tomatoes.

— *Jim Richards and Lisa Gordanier*

. . . .

GALLAGHER'S BAR SPAGHETTI   SERVES 8

Source Note: This may very well be the best spaghetti you ever eat. The sauce has a bit of bite and a lot of depth, thanks to the jalapeño and chipotle. This is a wonderful, time-consuming recipe that I have always made from scratch every time.

Each time involves some experimentation, and the uniqueness is totally dependent on time, mood, setting, and the alcohol being ingested. I suggest starting with a martini while crafting the meatballs and switching to red wine when finishing the sauce. By the time the meal is actually served, you will be opening that second bottle of wine to enjoy with your mate and friends.

My preference is to cook all of the ingredients, allow to cool, and reheat before serving, although you can just cook and serve it also. Try it both ways.

MEATBALLS
1 pound ground beef, buffalo, or elk
1 egg with 2 to 3 tablespoons Worcestershire sauce, mixed together in a small cup
¾ cup Italian breadcrumbs
¾ cup grated Parmesan cheese
2 tablespoons fresh oregano
½ cup minced onion
¼ cup garlic powder
2 teaspoons ground cumin
1 tablespoon freshly ground black pepper
Olive oil, for sautéing

1. In a large bowl, mix all of the ingredients by hand, working the mixture like bread dough. Form the mixture into ½- to 2-inch meatballs.

2. In a large skillet or nonstick pan, heat enough olive oil to cover the bottom of the pan. Then sauté the meatballs over medium to medium-high heat. When they're crisp but not burned on the outside, remove and drain the meatballs on paper towels.

"No man is lonely eating spaghetti; it requires so much attention."

— *Christopher Morley, American journalist and novelist*

Comforts of Home

Katie Sherman
Former Community
Outreach Coordinator
Featherstone Farm
Rushford, Minnesota

The Gasca brothers know how to bring Mexico to Minnesota. I'm not referring to the pictures of Guanajuato on their walls or the mariachi music resounding gaily from the boom boxes in the cool room (although there is that). I'm talking about food.

Every day at noon without fail, when it is 100 degrees outside, the kitchen and office area at the farm begins to fill with the scent of warm, toasted corn tortillas. Amidst laughter and the clattering of plates and spoons, the brothers and other family members sit around the lengthy folding tables and pile grilled pork, vegetables, hot sauce, and other sundries onto their round pieces of corn.

I received an education in hot sauce just recently when the brothers divulged how they make their special brew with the dried Featherstone Ring of Fire cayenne peppers or, as the brothers call it, cola de rata—rat's tail. Both names for this small scarlet red pepper seem appropriate.

Salvador conjured up a handful of cilantro and a jar of tomato puree, then called me out from the office to see how it was done. Ole was at the stove roasting nine chiles on the skillet, covering his mouth with the neck of his shirt. I was just about to ask why he was doing that when I caught the whiff of intense flame in the place where the back of my tongue meets my throat. They chuckled as my eyes widened and I considered the seeds that could emit such a powerful heat. I coughed a bit, backed up, and watched the rest of the process.

Ole tossed the roasted chiles (seeds and all) into a blender with

Spaghetti Sauce

4 cloves garlic, minced
1 large onion, diced
1 green bell pepper, seeded and diced
1 red bell pepper, seeded and diced
1 jalapeño pepper, seeded and diced
3 to 4 tablespoons chopped fresh oregano
2 tablespoons fresh thyme
¼ cup molasses or honey
2 (16-ounce cans) tomato sauce
1 (16-ounce can) diced tomatoes
1 (6-ounce) can tomato paste
⅓ bottle red wine (1¼ cups)
⅓ cup Marsala or Madeira wine
2 teaspoons cinnamon or allspice
2 teaspoons powdered chipotle pepper

1. Mix all of the ingredients together in a large pot, and bring to a slow boil over medium heat. Reduce the heat to a simmer. Simmer, partially covered, with the meatballs for 2 hours.

2. Turn off and leave to cool for several hours, stirring regularly, or transfer to a large, shallow pan and refrigerate. Reheat ½ hour before serving.

— *J. Michael Gallagher,* The Alcoholic's Cookbook

JALAPEÑO CREAM SAUCE

SERVES 6 TO 8

Source Note: All these rich sauces start out with butter, cream, and Madeira. You can use port or cognac, but I think those flavors have a tendency to overpower whatever it is you are trying to achieve with your sauce.

With this sauce, I was trying to do something unique with elk tenderloin or backstrap. The backstrap on game animals is the choicest cut of meat; it is the most tender and usually the most flavorful. Nevertheless, a sauce gives it the zip to really make your dinner special. Beef doesn't usually need a sauce, since it has all that interlaced fat to flavor it.

My personal assistant at the time, Lynsey, and I were preparing dinner for party guests several years ago. On this evening, I explained to Lynsey what we were doing. We were going to sauté the jalapeños, without seeds, to reduce the heat while retaining the flavor. We were then going to add the other ingredients, reducing the sauce and ultimately pureeing the whole thing in a blender before reducing it even further.

We started out and the sauce smelled awesome. We removed it from the stove and put it in a blender, turned it on, and watched as the hot liquid

created a vacuum and sucked the plastic lid into the rotating blades. F___!

I had no more jalapeños, no more cream. I got out a sieve and strained the sauce, hoping to remove any pieces of plastic. It worked, and we never told anyone what happened.

The sauce was a hit, and not one person complained about it being a little grainy...

> 4 to 6 jalapeños, seeded and chopped
> 1 cup minced onion
> 2 cloves garlic, chopped
> 1 cup cream
> ¼ cup currants
> 1 teaspoon freshly ground white pepper
> 1 teaspoon curry powder
> ½ teaspoon salt
> 2 tablespoons (¼ stick) unsalted butter
> 1 shot (3 tablespoons) Madeira wine

1. In a medium saucepan, sauté the jalapeños, onions, and garlic until the onions turn translucent.

2. Add the cream and cook on medium heat until the mixture is reduced by a third. Add the currants, pepper, curry, and salt. Cook another 5 minutes.

3. Remove from the heat and allow to cool somewhat. Pour the mixture into a food processor and process until the ingredients are well blended.

4. Return the sauce to the pan and cook for another 5 minutes. Remove from the heat. Just before serving, return to the heat to warm the sauce.

— *J. Michael Gallagher,* The Alcoholic's Cookbook

. . . .

MEXICAN HOT DISH   SERVES 12

Author Note: *This recipe comes from a small-town Minnesota cookbook, and it is a classic example of the food genre colloquially known as "hot dish," an indispensable fixture at Midwest potlucks, funeral and church suppers, and family picnics. Hot dish is essentially a hearty casserole, made with simple but satisfying ingredients, often along the lines of comfort food. True to its era, this recipe is made with a fair number of processed ingredients, but feel free to substitute with fresh vegetables and different seasonings.*

> 2 pounds ground beef
> 1 medium onion, chopped
> 1 (10-ounce) can diced tomatoes with green chiles, or 1½ cups
>   fresh, chopped, cooked tomatoes
> 2 (4-ounce) cans chopped green chiles, or 8 ounces
>   fresh mild green chiles, chopped
> 1 (8-ounce) jar taco sauce

about ½ cup of water and blended it thoroughly to a liquidy pulp. This mixture went into a bowl with a container of tomato puree and about a teaspoon of salt, then a healthy handful of chopped cilantro and another of diced onion.

Salvador dropped a spoonful into his palm and licked it off, then encouraged me to try some. Now was my moment of truth; I copied Salvador and licked my hand, not dying as I thought I might. I even took another bite, and then put some in a tortilla.

But I found out that this was the kind of heat that takes a while to fully accumulate in the mouth. The bridge of Salvador's nose began to bead with sweat, and I started to get the hiccups. "Sabroso, no?" Ole said between laughs, and I agreed—it tasted great.

For those who would like a milder version of this hot sauce, the Gascas recommend using five peppers instead of nine (or even fewer if you're very unsure) and taking out all the seeds instead of leaving them in.

Do this with gloves, though, and make sure your hands don't touch your face. Then, you too can add a little bit of Guanajuato to your 5-degree winter day. Enjoy!

1 (10½-ounce) can condensed cream of mushroom soup
1 (10½-ounce) can condensed cream of chicken soup
1 (12-ounce) small can evaporated milk
1 small package flour tortillas
2 (16-ounce) cans chili beans
1 (8-ounce) package shredded Cheddar cheese
Sour cream (optional)
Crushed Fritos (optional)

1. Heat the oven to 375°F.

2. In a large sauté pan, fry the hamburger with the onion until the onion is soft and some of the liquid has evaporated.

3. In a large bowl, mix together the tomatoes, chiles, taco sauce, soups, and evaporated milk. Add the hamburger and stir to combine.

4. Cut the flour tortillas into 2-inch squares. Layer the pieces on the bottom of a 9-by-13-inch cake pan. Pour half of the hamburger mixture over the tortilla squares, spreading it evenly. Drain the beans. Spread 1 can of the beans over the hamburger mixture, then sprinkle half the cheese over that. Layer the tortilla squares, hamburger mixture, beans, and cheese again.

5. Bake for 45 minutes, or until everything is hot and bubbling. Let stand for 10 minutes. Serve with sour cream and Fritos on top, if desired.

— *Janie Helgeson,* Hills Centennial Cookbook

Cayenne pepper seedlings in one of Featherstone Farm's greenhouses, awaiting transplanting.

Raspberries & Blackberries

RUBUS STRIGOSUS
AND
RUBUS FRUTICOSUS

Few fruits bring instant delight to the eye and palate as raspberries and blackberries do. These soft, delicate morsels, with their luscious perfume and melting texture, have been enjoyed by humans and animals alike throughout history, although mostly in their wild forms. Only relatively recently have raspberries and blackberries been cultivated and new varieties developed.

Raspberries and blackberries are both botanically classified as aggregate fruits, meaning that they consist of smaller fruits called drupelets. What distinguishes a raspberry from a blackberry is that its torus (the little whitish core) remains on the plant when the fruit is picked or drops off, whereas the toruses stay with the fruit on blackberries.

Red and yellow raspberries taste similar, but black and purple ones have a stronger, often more tart flavor. Orange and yellow (often referred to as golden) raspberries tend to be sweeter and less acidic than their crimson counterparts. Raspberries are divided into two categories: everbearing, which produce fruit in both the summer and fall, and summer-bearing, which fruit only in the summer.

Blackberries tend to be slightly tarter than raspberries, but their distinctively rich berry flavor is like no other. They are sweet only when fully ripe, often when the berries are nearly falling apart. Over 2,000 varieties of blackberries grow around the world, especially in cooler, northern regions. Nearly all of the US commercial crop is grown in Mexico, but happily, plenty of wild blackberries still ramble about, their drooping loads of plump fruit awaiting foragers' buckets in the heat of August.

HISTORY

Raspberries and blackberries are native to Asia, but the Rubus family is vast and complicated, with wild species growing throughout Asia, Europe, and North America. Wild raspberries and blackberries have been eaten by humans since antiquity, but the plants have been cultivated only during the past few centuries. Raspberries were gathered on Mount Ida in Turkey and have been popular in spots in Europe, although until very recently they were almost unheard of in some countries such as Italy. Despite the New World's own native species, European colonists in America preferred to import their own raspberry varieties. To this day, "wild" European canes still run rampant in some eastern US states, having escaped from early colonial gardens.

NUTRITION

Like most berries, raspberries and blackberries are antioxidant power-houses, in particular containing anthocyanins (which give red and purple raspberries their color) and ellagic acid. A single cup of raspberries contains over 60 percent of an adult's daily supply of manganese, as well as 50 percent of vitamin C, for only 60 calories; they are also very high in dietary fiber and contain B vitamins, potassium, and magnesium. Blackberries contain significant amounts of vitamins A, C, E, and K, magnesium, dietary fiber, and manganese. They are especially rich in numerous phytonutrients, anthocyanins (which give them their dark color), and flavonoids, compounds that may help fight cancer.

SEASON

Blackberries and raspberries remain truly seasonal crops; blackberries are at their peak from August through September. With raspberries, it depends on the type; June-bearing types are just that—June and early July are typically when they start—whereas fall everbearing varieties start in late July and late August and continue until frost.

SELECTION

With both raspberries and blackberries, choose firm, intact fruits that show no signs of mold or sliminess, which can spread quickly among crowded fruits. When choosing berries that are packaged in those clear plastic boxes in the supermarket, check all sides of the box to make sure no crushed or moldy fruits lurk within.

STORAGE

Raspberries and blackberries are among the most perishable of fruits, so great care must be taken to store them properly. They should remain unwashed in the refrigerator and kept as dry as possible. (Sunlight, moisture, and warm temperatures all cause berries to spoil quickly.) Moldy or soft berries tend to infect their companions, so be vigilant about promptly removing these specimens. In fact, make it a habit—as soon as you get home with your fresh raspberries and blackberries— to remove them from their original containers, sort through them, and place them on a dish lined with dry paper towels. Use within 1 to 2 days.

Raspberries and blackberries are both at their fullest flavor at room temperature, so take them out of the refrigerator about an hour before serving.

TRIMMING AND CLEANING

Raspberries and blackberries should remain unwashed until right before serving. Because they are so delicate, place them in a colander and use the sink sprayer so as not to crush them. Then spread them out on a plate lined with paper towels, and very gently pat dry. Blackberries may need to have their hulls removed but not their stem cores.

MICROWAVING

Place separated frozen berries in a single layer with plenty of space between them on a plate lined with a paper towel. They should be microwaved on the lowest power setting just long enough to defrost mostly but not completely, and when done, should retain their shape and appear slightly frosted. Remove the berries immediately when they have finished microwaving, so they stop cooking. *Note: Because of their shape, frozen raspberries are especially prone to throwing sparks, even igniting momentarily, in the microwave, so be warned! If you can plan ahead a little, it's*

better to thaw berries by spreading them on a plate or cookie sheet and letting them stand at room temperature for an hour or so.

- ¼ cup = cook on defrost setting for 30 seconds
- ½ cup = 50 seconds
- 1 cup = 1 minute, 20 seconds

BLANCHING AND FREEZING

Raspberries and blackberries can be frozen as whole fruits or in a sugar syrup. To freeze whole, wash the berries, pat them dry, place them in a single layer on a tray, and freeze them until they are solid. Then package them in zipper-lock freezer or vacuum food sealer-type bags, or freezer containers. Squeeze out any excess air and leave ½ inch of headspace (unless you are using the vacuum sealing method). Frozen raspberries and blackberries will keep for up to 1 year at 0°F.

To package raspberries for jam, wash the berries and put them in a syrup. To make the sugar syrup, put ½ to ¾ cup of sugar to 4 cups of water in a pot and bring it to a boil. Once the sugar has dissolved, remove the syrup from the heat and skim off the foam. Chill, then pour ½ cup of syrup into a zipper-lock freezer bag, jar, or freezer container, add the berries, and keep adding syrup until the fruit is covered. Leave ½ inch of headspace for pints, 1 inch for quarts.

MEASURES AND EQUIVALENTS

- 1 pint = 1½ to 2 cups
- 4 cups berries = 1 quart

COMPLEMENTARY HERBS, SEASONINGS, AND FOODS

Almonds, apricots, bananas, brandy, brown sugar, buttermilk, caramel, champagne, chocolate, cinnamon, cognac, cream, cream cheese, currants, honey, kirsch, lemon, mangoes, melons, mint, oranges, orange liqueur, other berries, peaches, pears, peppers, pineapple, pistachios, red wine, sour cream, sugar, vanilla.

SERVING SUGGESTIONS

- Few dishes are as simply good as a big bowl of chilled raspberries or blackberries sprinkled with sugar or drizzled with honey, and flooded with thick cream.
- Combine lightly crushed fresh raspberries with other berries, like blueberries, strawberries, and blackberries, as a topping for cold cereal, oatmeal, parfaits, ice cream, pudding, or chilled fruit soup.
- Sprinkle a few drops of high-quality balsamic vinegar over fresh, ripe raspberries. The taste combination is unusual but highly addictive.
- Liven up a raspberry or blackberry sauce by adding a little orange liqueur, apricot brandy, or cherry kirsch.
- Raspberries and sponge or pound cake were made for each other; garnish the cake with whole berries, or lightly crush them with a little sugar or honey for a delicious topping.
- If you have an ice cream maker at home, try this for a show-stopping combination: Infuse your egg-and-cream custard with fresh basil leaves, then add blackberry puree and make blackberry ice cream. Heavenly.
- Scatter a handful of raspberries or blackberries in a tossed green salad.

Cooking Tip

Whole raspberries will stay firmer in a sauce if you add a tablespoon of brown sugar.

Blackberries in the War

During World War I, children were sent off to gather wild blackberries for the commercial production of juice for soldiers.

- Dip raspberries and blackberries into warm, melted chocolate for a luxurious treat.
- When ephemeral summer fruit is around, shortcake and cobbler always seem like a good idea.
- Blackberries and raspberries make a fabulous topping for panna cotta or flan.
- Blackberries shine in cakes: Try adding them to a torte, coffee cake, upside-down cake, or *clafouti*, a traditional dessert from the Limousin region of France.
- Blackberry pie—need I say more?
- Capture a taste of summer with homemade jellies, jams, and preserves.
- Raspberries and blackberries both add a rich, fruity dimension when reduced in sauces along with red wine and balsamic vinegar; try them with robust meats like beef, pork, and duck.
- Make zabaglione, that refreshing Italian custard dessert with egg yolks, sugar, Marsala wine, heavy cream, and fresh berries.

....

CHOCOLATE-RASPBERRY STRATA   SERVES 6

Source Note: This dessert is actually a type of bread pudding. The combination of vanilla-scented egg custard, dark chocolate, and fresh raspberries is irresistible. Serve it warm, with a dollop of sweetened whipped cream, for maximum rapture.

> 6 cups Hawaiian monkey bread, challah, or brioche, cut into 1-inch cubes
> 1½ cups semisweet chocolate chips
> 1½ cups fresh raspberries (do not use frozen), rinsed and drained
> ½ cup heavy cream
> ½ cup milk
> 4 eggs
> ¼ cup sugar
> 1 teaspoon vanilla extract
> Sweetened whipped cream, for serving

1. Preheat the oven to 350°F.

2. Place half of the bread cubes in a well-buttered 8-by-8-inch baking pan. Sprinkle with half of the chocolate chips and raspberries. Cover with the remaining bread cubes, then top with the remaining chocolate chips and raspberries.

3. In a medium bowl, whisk together the cream, milk, eggs, sugar, and vanilla until well blended. Pour this evenly over the bread mixture. Press lightly, making sure that all of the bread and the raspberries are moistened by some of the custard mixture.

4. Cover the pan with foil and bake for 45 minutes, or until the custard is mostly set. Uncover the pan and continue to bake for about 15 more minutes to crisp and brown the bread. Serve garnished with the whipped cream.

"O, blackberry tart, with berries as big as your thumb, purple and black, and thick with juice, and a crust to endear them that will go to cream in your mouth, and both passing down with such a taste that will make you close your eyes and wish you might live forever in the wideness of that rich moment."

— *Richard Llewellyn,*
How Green Was My Valley

Cooking Note: You may cook this strata in a 3½-quart slow cooker if you'd like. Layer the ingredients as above, pour on the custard, and cook, covered, on medium heat for about 2 hours. Let stand for at least 10 minutes before serving.

— *Adapted from Razzle Dazzle Recipes*

BAKED RHUBARB WITH RASPBERRIES   SERVES 4

1⅓ cups raspberries (about 6 ounces)
¾ cup firmly packed light brown sugar
¼ cup very hot water
2 tablespoons unsalted butter, cut into bits
¼ teaspoon vanilla extract
1 pound rhubarb, trimmed and cut into ½-inch pieces
    (about 4 cups)
8 scoops low-fat frozen yogurt

1. Preheat the oven to 350°F.

2. In a blender, puree the raspberries with the brown sugar and hot water; strain the puree through a sieve into a bowl, pressing hard on the solids. Stir in the butter, vanilla, and rhubarb.

3. Transfer the mixture to an 11-by-7-inch baking dish and bake in the middle of the oven for 30 minutes, stirring once very gently after 15 minutes.

4. Cook until the rhubarb is soft. Let the mixture cool for 10 minutes and serve it over the frozen yogurt.

— *Produce for Better Health; Fruits & Veggies—More Matters;*
    Centers for Disease Control and Prevention

PEA PODS WITH RASPBERRIES   SERVES 4 TO 6

Source Note: *This unusual pairing is visually spectacular with a refreshingly different flavor. A great color and taste accent for a chicken salad, this recipe works equally well with grilled fish or poultry.*

½ pound snow pea pods
1 tablespoon balsamic vinegar
2 tablespoons olive oil
¼ teaspoon salt
Freshly ground black pepper
¾ cup raspberries, at room temperature

1. Wash and remove the tips and strings from the pea pods.

2. Bring a large saucepan of water to a rapid boil and add the pea pods. After the water returns to a full boil, cook the pods for 3 minutes. Drain them well in a colander, then toss them in a serving bowl with the vinegar, oil, salt, and pepper until they are well coated. Gently stir in the raspberries, taking care not to mash them. Serve warm.

— *Rolce Redard Payne and Dorrit Speyer Senior,* Cooking with Fruit

. . . .

BLACKBERRY-LAVENDER POPSICLES   8 (2.5-OUNCE) POPS

¾ cup superfine sugar or agave nectar
1 heaping pint (2 cups) fresh blackberries
1 tablespoon lavender buds, fresh or dried
3 tablespoons freshly squeezed lemon juice
1 cup cold water

1. In a saucepan, stir the sugar into the blackberries and allow to sit for 5 minutes. Add the lavender and bring to a boil. Reduce to a simmer and allow to bubble gently for 10 minutes. Remove from the heat.

2. Smoosh up the berries with a potato masher to release all of their juices. Stir the lemon juice and water into the mixture. Taste and add more sweetener, if you think it needs it. Refrigerate until cold, about 30 minutes.

3. Set a strainer over a large mixing bowl (preferably one with a pour spout). Strain the mixture, pushing down with a rubber spatula to extract all of the juices.

4. Pour into ice pop molds, adding the sticks at the correct time for your molds. Freeze until solid.

— *Heather Schmitt-Gonzalez, the* Girlichef blog

. . . .

BLACKBERRY-WALNUT MESCLUN SALAD   SERVES 4

DRESSING

3 tablespoons balsamic vinegar
1½ tablespoons olive oil
2 teaspoons brown sugar
1 clove garlic, minced
Salt and freshly ground black pepper

SALAD

6 cups mesclun (small-leaf mixed greens) or other salad greens
¾ cup chopped yellow bell pepper

¼ cup chopped fresh mint
1 cup fresh blackberries
1 tablespoon toasted black walnuts (see the Cooking Note below)
2 tablespoons crumbled blue cheese

1. To make the dressing, whisk together the vinegar, oil, sugar, and garlic in a large salad bowl; add the salt and pepper.

2. Add all of the salad ingredients to the bowl. Toss gently and serve immediately.

Cooking Note: To toast the walnuts, heat a small, dry skillet over medium heat. Add the walnuts and toast, stirring often to prevent burning.

— *Fooddownunder.com*

....

POLKA DOT CLOUDS   SERVES 4

Source Note: A fun fruit dish for kids and adults too. You can also use éclair rounds or waffles instead of the melba toast.

40 red or golden raspberries, blueberries, and blackberries
Whipped cream
8 melba toast rounds
Honey (optional)

Arrange the melba toast rounds in a single layer on a big plate. Place a dollop of whipped cream on each round (or use store-bought canned whipped cream), then dot with the raspberries and blueberries to form "polka dots." Drizzle with a little honey, if desired.

— *Mi Ae Lipe*

Rosemary

ROSMARINUS OFFICINALIS

In the Mediterranean climates where this perennial herb grows rampantly, it can be hard to walk past it and resist plucking a sprig or crushing a few of its evergreen, needle-like leaves and inhaling its distinctive, pungent, piney-sweet scent. Rosemary seems equally happy growing wild in sprawling bushes or contained in considerably more restrictive environments in the home garden, where it can be shaped into topiaries or grown as a potted plant. It definitely prefers a hot, arid climate where it is watered only by the moisture from daily morning fog or dew; constantly wet feet quickly kills rosemary.

Humans have treasured rosemary throughout history as a culinary herb, a decorative ornamental, and a valuable medicine. Along the way, the herb became associated with remembrance and memory, for which it still remains a symbol. Christianity favored it, and it was once believed that rosemary never grows taller than the height of Jesus Christ, nor after 33 years (the age of Jesus when he was crucified).

HISTORY

Rosemary's native shores lie in the Mediterranean region, where the hot, dry climate richly concentrates the herb's aromatic oils. Ancient Greeks used to wear rosemary wreaths while studying, to enhance their memory. In ancient Rome, sprigs of the herb were placed in the hands of the dead for remembrance. In fact, rosemary symbolized both love and death in ancient Europe, where it was carried in wedding bouquets and laid on coffins. Rosemary was imported to England in the mid-1500s.

NUTRITION

Rosemary contains fiber, iron, calcium, and vitamins A and C, as well as 2 calories per tablespoon. It is also rich in certain antioxidants, especially carnosol and ursolic acid.

SEASON

Commercially, rosemary is widely grown and in season year-round, since it is an evergreen plant. You'll find it at its best in farmers markets and CSAs throughout the spring, summer, and fall.

SELECTION

Choose sprigs that look fresh and green, with no limp or discolored branches. Fresh rosemary's flavor is far superior to the dried form. If you are using the dried version, remember to crush the now-prickly needles between your fingers, as they won't soften much during cooking.

STORAGE

An easy way to store fresh rosemary (and many other cut herbs) is to treat them like flowers: Simply trim the stem ends, strip off the leaves from the bottom several inches of the stems, place them in a glass of water, and store on the counter at room temperature or in the refrigerator.

Cooking Tip

Rosemary is a powerful herb with a strong personality. It goes best with other robust foods and seasonings that can stand up to its distinctive scent and flavor, and it should not be used in dishes that are very delicate or where it may overpower.

Or wrap the herb in damp paper towels and place in a plastic bag in the refrigerator vegetable crisper, where it will keep for up to 1 week.

TRIMMING AND CLEANING

Rinse fresh rosemary branches under running water briefly before patting dry. For recipes calling for just the leaves, grasp the stem between your forefinger and thumb and pull down, stripping the leaves off. Or use entire sprigs for grilling and roasting.

FREEZING

An easy way to freeze rosemary is to place whole sprigs in a zipper-lock freezer bag, freeze, and then run a rolling pin over the unopened bag. This removes many of the leaves from the stems. You can either continue to store the leaves in the freezer in the zipper-lock bag, package them in a vacuum food sealer-type bag, or place them in a tightly lidded canning jar. Rosemary should keep well this way for up to 1 year.

A terrific way to freeze rosemary is to chop it finely, mix it into a paste using ⅓ cup of olive oil or cooled melted butter to every 2 cups of herbs, and then freeze the resulting mixture in ice cube trays. To thaw, simply pop out a few cubes into a strainer and let the oil melt away, or just drop them frozen into sauces or soups.

DRYING

Rosemary can be dried, but its flavor deteriorates tremendously. Freezing the freshly chopped raw herb in olive oil or butter in ice cube trays yields a far better, full-flavored product (see the Freezing section above)

If you still want to dry the herb, tie fresh, dry sprigs that are free of dew and moisture into a bunch and hang in a cool, dry, dark place with good ventilation. You can cover the bunches with small paper bags to keep dust off them, but make sure the bags have adequate holes for proper ventilation. Once the bunches are dry, seal them tightly in a container with a lid or in a zipper-lock plastic bag; store the bags away from light and heat.

You can also dry rosemary in the oven: Spread a single layer of leaves on a cookie sheet and place the sheet in a warm (up to 180°F) oven for 1½ to 2 hours, stirring the herbs periodically until they are thoroughly dry. Or remove the best leaves from the stems and arrange them on a paper towel so the leaves do not touch. Cover this layer with another paper towel and add another layer of leaves over the top. Up to five layers may be dried at one time in the oven using this method.

A microwave oven can also be used to dry small quantities of rosemary. Place four or five herb branches layered between paper towels in the microwave. Heat for 2 minutes on high power. If the rosemary is not brittle and dry when removed, repeat the microwave drying for 30 seconds more. Note: The heat generated during microwaving removes not only moisture but also some of the oils, so these herbs may not have as intense a flavor as herbs dried by other methods.

EQUIVALENTS, MEASURES, AND SERVINGS

- 1 medium fresh sprig = 1 teaspoon fresh
- 3 medium fresh sprigs = 1 tablespoon fresh = 1 teaspoon dried

Women in Farming Today

Martha Wagner

Women around the world have always been involved in growing food, either independently or alongside their male partners. In North America today, an increasing number of farmer training programs and support organizations for women in farming make female farmers more visible, but their numbers have not grown dramatically. Exact numbers are difficult to assess because of the use of changing research methods.

Data from the 2012 Census of Agriculture, compiled every five years by the US Department of Agriculture, found more ethnic minorities entering farming, especially Hispanic and Hmong immigrants and refugees who bring with them strong agrarian roots and agricultural skills.

Data on women showed that the number of women farmers classified as principal operators decreased at a higher rate than their male counterparts over the previous five years—by 6 percent, compared with a 4 percent decrease in farms overall. Women made up 14 percent of principal operators, but 30 percent of all operators. Organic farms also showed more gender and age diversity than that seen on nonorganic farms, and tended to be operated by younger farmers.

Higher percentages of women farmers were found in Texas and Arizona, followed by the New England states, California, Oregon, Washington, and parts of the Southwest. Of women entering farming, the biggest increase was in women 55 to 75, which may suggest that many are choosing farming as a second career or are inheriting farms. Women continue to own and operate smaller farms than men, and they earn less income, a finding that does not surprise.

Apples, bay, beans, beef, cheese, chervil, chives, eggs, fruit, garlic, lamb, lentils, mint, mushrooms, onions, parsley, pork, potatoes, poultry, sage, spinach, thyme, tomatoes, veal.

SERVING SUGGESTIONS

- Rosemary has a surprising affinity with fruit. Try sprinkling finely chopped fresh leaves over fruit salad, or simmering fruit juice with rosemary, straining and cooling it, and pouring it over fresh fruit such as melon, oranges, peaches, and pears.

- Infuse soups and stews by adding a sprig during the last half hour of cooking.

- Flavor butter by adding 2 teaspoons of finely chopped fresh rosemary to ½ cup softened butter.

- Place rosemary sprigs in vinegar for sprinkling over salads or meats.

- Insert whole sprigs under the skin of chicken or turkey, or into lamb or beef roasts, along with slivers of fresh garlic and whole baby onions, before cooking.

- Finely chopped rosemary is heavenly with potatoes, pastas, and root vegetables.

- Besides culinary uses, the scent of rosemary is stimulating and yet soothing, useful for relieving headaches and tension. Place a few sprigs in a muslin bag when drawing a hot bath, or make tea from the fresh herb.

- Rosemary and apples are yummy together. Try sautéed caramelized apple slices with rosemary.

- Rosemary bushes abound with beautiful, orchid-like blossoms in the early summer. Pluck the violet flowers and sprinkle them over pasta or sweet vegetables such as carrots or snap peas.

SUBSTITUTIONS

If you happen to be out of rosemary, substitute thyme, tarragon, or savory.

. . . .

ROSEMARY- OR BASIL-INFUSED OIL   MAKES 1 CUP

1 cup mild olive oil or vegetable oil
¼ cup packed, chopped fresh rosemary leaves
**   or ½ cup packed, roughly chopped fresh basil leaves**

1. Place the oil and rosemary or basil in a 3½- to 4-quart slow cooker. Cook uncovered over high heat for 1 hour, then turn the cooker off.

2. Allow the oil to cool to room temperature; then pour it through a sieve lined with a clean paper towel (or a paper coffee filter) into a clean glass jar or bottle.

3. Cover the jar tightly and refrigerate for up to 2 months. (After that, the flavor may fade.) The oil may cloud under refrigeration, but it will become clear again at room temperature.

— Kylan, CD Kitchen

Cane Creek Farm *in Cummings, Georgia, was the realization of a dream Lynn Pugh had for many years—a vision of a more sustainable lifestyle, surrounded by a community of people interested in the same pursuit. She gardened on a small scale during the 18 years she taught high school and college-level science while she and her husband raised their family. In 2001, as the children left home, Lynn began applying her knowledge to transform their 17-acre property into the productive CSA farm it is today, growing flowers, vegetables, and fruit for 100 members and offering a varied educational program.*

Betsy Harrison raised her two daughters, Abby and Zoë Bradbiru, on a 90-acre farm in rural, coastal southwest Oregon, where she grazed a herd of sheep in the early 1970s. After obtaining an Ivy League education, Abby returned to the farm and began a salad greens business in 1997, developing a loyal following of chefs, retail stores, and salad lovers. Ten years later, Zoë returned with a Stanford degree and experience working for organic farms and nonprofits.

Soon **Valley Flora Farm** *was born, a two-generation CSA collective. Zoë manages the berries, flowers, asparagus, and other outdoor row crops. Abby is the "Greens Queen," overseeing salad greens production and the orchards. Their mother, Betsy, manages the greenhouses, producing tomatoes, peppers, cucumbers, basil, and summer squash. Zoë is among the 30 women farmers profiled in the book* Farmer Jane: Women Changing the Way We Eat, *by Temra Costa.*

Green Mountain Girls Farm *in central Vermont was a mid-career shift for Vermonters Mari Omland and Laura Olsen, who returned to their home state in 2007 to develop*

MYLAR'S ROSEMARY POTATO WEDGES   SERVES 4

4 medium or large baking potatoes
2 to 4 cloves garlic, finely chopped
2 to 3 large rosemary sprigs, leaves stripped off stems
**   and finely chopped**
Olive or sesame oil
Sea salt
Freshly ground black pepper

1. Preheat the oven to 450°F.

2. Cut the potatoes into wedges.

3. Strip the rosemary off its stems and coarsely chop the leaves. Finely chop the garlic. (If you have one of those little miniature food processors, you can throw the garlic cloves and rosemary together into the machine.)

4. Place the potatoes in a big bowl and toss lightly with the oil (sesame adds a deliciously nutty flavor), garlic, rosemary, salt, and pepper.

5. Line a large shallow baking dish or sheet with aluminum foil, then place the potatoes in a single layer on top. Bake for 30 to 45 minutes, or until the potatoes are nicely golden brown on the outside but still moist inside. Serve immediately.

— *Mi Ae Lipe*

ROSEMARY-LEMON CROCKPOT CHICKEN   SERVES 4

1 whole roasting chicken (3 to 4 pounds)
2 sprigs fresh rosemary
2 stalks celery with leaves, cut into pieces
2 small onions, quartered and divided
16 cloves garlic, divided
2 tablespoons fresh lemon juice
½ teaspoon salt
½ teaspoon pepper
½ teaspoon paprika

1. Remove and discard the chicken giblets and neck, or freeze them for making broth another time. Trim the excess fat and discard. Rinse the chicken and pat it dry, inside and out.

2. Place the rosemary, celery, 4 of the onion wedges, and 4 of the garlic cloves in the cavity of the chicken. Tie the legs together with string. Place the chicken, breast side up, in a slow cooker. Add the remaining onion and garlic to the pot.

a CSA farm with event and retreat space, plus cooking classes, after 15-year careers in conservation and smart-growth nonprofits.

Bridget Holcomb, executive director of Iowa-based **WFAN (Women, Food, and Agriculture Network)**, says that women often face a double whammy when they begin farming. "First, women often have trouble accessing the same resources that men do, whether those resources are information or bank loans. Second, women are more likely to try nontraditional farm operations, like diversified vegetable farms or honey from bees that feed on prairie plants, and resources for nontraditional farms are much harder to come by." WFAN, founded in 1997, helps raise the voices of women working in agriculture and assists with training and networking.

Struggle Not Necessarily a Given

Mari Omland of Green Mountain Girls Farm says that she and her partner, Laura Olsen, have been surprised by how few struggles they've had as women new to farming. "Peer to peer, we've been welcomed in our state and in our neighborhood. Whether it's our particular community or the overall culture of Vermont, we feel really lucky and respected. In our sector of farming—organic gardening small-scale—there is substantial support and assistance from other farms. Farm conferences here offer spectacular opportunity, too. This year participation was 50/50 men and women."

Are women just as capable of the hard work of farming as men? "Sure, there's a lot of heavy lifting, but there's an enormous variety of tasks," says Omland. "We probe very deeply in interviews, looking for people with a great deal of stamina. We need taller people at times, and people good with detail, not necessarily stronger."

3. Drizzle lemon juice over the chicken; sprinkle with salt, pepper, and paprika. Cover and cook on low heat for 8 hours, or until the chicken is cooked all the way through.

— *Harmony, CD Kitchen*

. . . .

ROSEMARY-ROASTED SALMON

SERVES 4

4 wild Alaskan salmon fillets, about 6 ounces each
4 medium garlic cloves, minced
2 tablespoons extra-virgin olive oil
1 tablespoon Dijon mustard
1 tablespoon chopped fresh rosemary
¼ teaspoon sea salt
¼ teaspoon freshly ground black pepper

1. Heat the oven to 475°F.

2. Place the salmon, skin side down, on a small, rimmed baking sheet.

3. Combine the garlic, oil, mustard, and rosemary in a small bowl. Sprinkle the salmon with salt and pepper; spoon the rosemary mixture over the salmon. Refrigerate for 10 minutes to let the flavors mingle.

4. Bake the salmon for 8 to 10 minutes, or until it can be flaked with a fork.

— *Vital Choice Seafood*

Savory

SATUREJA HORTENSIS

Savory is a spicy, distinctive herb reminiscent of a combination of sage and thyme—somewhat minty, green, spicy, and medicinal-tasting. The name can refer to two different species: Summer savory (Satureja hortensis) *is an annual herb with a sweet, delicate flavor preferred for sausages, cabbage rolls, or any other dish benefiting from the use of the fresh herb. There is also winter savory* (Satureja montana), *which is a perennial, semiwoody shrub whose robust, tough leaves are more suitable for long cooking with meats such as chicken and beef. The small leaves of both herbs share a similar aroma and flavor, and they are often a part of herb mixtures such as* herbes de Provence *and* bouquet garni.

Although savory is used primarily as a culinary herb, it contains oils and tannins with mild astringent and antiseptic properties that can be useful in medicines. Rubbing a sprig of crushed savory on a wasp or bee sting provides quick relief.

HISTORY

Savory originated in the Mediterranean, where the ancient Romans, including Pliny, regarded the herb as an effective aphrodisiac. Although this use is somewhat questionable, the herb is well-known for its warming qualities and was used as an expectorant. It was also used to cure flatulence and colic, to soothe earaches, and even to restore vision. Shakespeare mentioned it, along with mint, marjoram, and lavender in his play *The Winter's Tale*. Early English colonists brought savory to America to remind them of their home country.

NUTRITION

Savory is not usually consumed in large enough quantities to be of nutritive value, but 1 tablespoon of the ground herb contains about 12 calories and significant amounts of vitamins A, C, and B6, as well as calcium, iron, magnesium, potassium, and manganese. The plant does contain essential oils with warming properties, and it is reputed to be good for digestive upsets and flatulence. Early California settlers made a tea from the herb.

SEASON

Commercially, both summer and winter savory are in season year-round. You'll find summer savory at its best in farmers markets and CSAs throughout—can you guess?—the summer, whereas winter savory is available throughout the year. It can, however, be difficult to find savory in grocery stores; it just doesn't seem to be popular enough. If you want a consistent supply—especially in the winter—you might want to grow this herb in your backyard garden or indoors as a container plant.

SELECTION

Savory should be vibrantly green and fresh looking, not wilted or discolored. Avoid specimens with dark spots, yellowing leaves, mold, or slime.

How Sweet It Is

In the first century BCE, Virgil grew savory for his bees, believing that it made their honey taste better.

STORAGE

Store the fresh herb unwashed and wrapped in a damp paper towel in a plastic bag in the refrigerator vegetable crisper for up to a few days. Or you can treat fresh savory sprigs like any living flower or plant cutting: Just snip off the stem ends, place them in a glass of water, and keep either on the counter or in the refrigerator.

TRIMMING AND CLEANING

Rinse fresh savory thoroughly under running water, dry it, and strip the leaves from the stems before using.

FREEZING

You can freeze fresh savory in leaf form by washing and thoroughly drying the sprigs, stripping them of leaves, and placing them in zipper-lock freezer bags. Or package them using vacuum food sealer-type bags. Frozen thyme will keep for up to 6 months at 0°F.

A terrific way to freeze savory is to chop it finely, mix it into a paste using ⅓ cup of olive oil or cooled melted butter to every 2 cups of herbs, and then freeze the resulting mixture in ice cube trays. To thaw, simply pop out a few cubes into a strainer and let the oil melt away, or just drop them frozen into sauces, soups, stews, casseroles, and other cooked dishes.

DRYING

Spread a single layer of leaves on a cookie sheet and place it in a warm (up to 180°F) oven for 3 to 4 hours, stirring the leaves periodically until they are thoroughly dry. Or remove the best leaves from the stems and arrange them on a paper towel without letting them touch. This layer is covered with another paper towel and a second layer of leaves is added. Five layers may be dried in the oven at one time using this method.

A microwave oven can also be used for small quantities of savory. Place four or five herb branches in the microwave between paper towels. Heat for 2 to 3 minutes on high power. If the herbs are not brittle and dry when removed, repeat the microwave drying for 30 seconds more. (Be aware that the heat generated during microwaving evaporates not only moisture but also some of the herb's oils, so savory dried in the microwave may not have as intense a flavor as it would dried by other methods.)

EQUIVALENTS, MEASURES, AND SERVINGS

- 1 tablespoon fresh chopped savory = 1 teaspoon dried

COMPLEMENTARY HERBS, SEASONINGS, AND FOODS

Basil, beans, beef, beets, Brussels sprouts, cabbage, carrots, cheese, chervil, chives, cucumbers, eggs, fish, game, kale, lamb, legumes, lemon, marjoram, mushrooms, olives, oregano, parsley, peas, peppers, pork, potatoes, poultry, rabbit, sage, sausage, soups, tarragon, thyme, tomatoes, turnips, veal.

SERVING SUGGESTIONS

- Add chopped fresh savory to your favorite stuffing, marinade, or gravy. It's a classic along with sage in poultry stuffing.

- Fry pork sausage in a bit of savory and sage, or add the herb to hamburgers.
- Fresh savory is delectable mixed with goat cheese and served with crackers.
- Add savory near the end of the cooking time to soups and stews.
- Use savory in making a bouquet garni, that little bundle of fresh or dried herbs added to dishes as they cook and removed just before serving.
- Try using strong-flavored savory as a salt substitute.
- Slow-cook winter savory with dried beans and peas.
- Sprinkle chopped fresh savory, basil, oregano, and marjoram over pizza.
- Combine fresh savory and tarragon with a little lemon or lime juice, and sprinkle over sole, halibut, or other delicate white fish.
- A little chopped fresh savory livens up steamed green beans, peas, broccoli, and summer squash.
- Use savory in marinades or in poultry herbal rubs, or in concert with other herbs for flavoring stocks, soups, and stews.
- Tomatoes have an affinity for savory—use the herb the next time you make spaghetti sauce!
- Marinate goat cheese rounds in olive oil and savory; this is a popular dish in the south of France.

SUBSTITUTIONS

Use thyme, rosemary, marjoram, or sage instead.

. . . .

BLACK BEAN SOUP
WITH GARLIC AND SUMMER SAVORY   SERVES 6

2 tablespoons olive oil
1 cup onion, finely chopped
1 small jalapeño pepper, finely chopped
3 cloves garlic, minced
¼ cup summer savory leaves, divided, plus additional,
    chopped, for garnish
6 cups cooked black beans, divided (if canned, drain well)
2 cups water
4 cups chicken or vegetable stock
Salt and paprika

1. In a very large saucepan, heat the olive oil and sauté the onion and jalapeño pepper for 3 minutes. Add the garlic and ¼ cup of the summer savory; sauté for another 3 minutes.

2. Add 2 cups of the black beans and 2 cups water. Cook, mixing constantly, until the water has reduced, the beans are very soft, and the mixture is thick. Add the chicken or vegetable stock and boil for 5 minutes.

3. Strain the mixture through a sieve, pressing all of the ingredients so that they pass through the sieve. Return the liquid to the pot and add the remaining 4 cups of beans, plus the salt and paprika. Boil for another 5 minutes.

producers and food communities on six continents. The program of conferences, taste workshops, classes, and more combine to reveal the impacts our eating and consumption habits have on the welfare of the planet's ecosystems, people, and animals. Terra Madre refers to the world meeting of food communities to address topics such as climate change, population growth, animal welfare, food waste, land grabbing, and much more.

The **Ark of Taste** was created to catalog the unique fruits, vegetables, animal breeds, cheeses, breads, sweets, and cured meats that are distinctive in their home countries and regions, yet may disappear in another generation or two if action isn't taken. The Ark of Taste designation highlights the existence of these products, draws attention to their risk of extinction, and invites people to take action to support their continuation either by consuming them, telling others about them, seeking them out in the marketplace, or in some cases involving endangered species, actually eating less or none of them to help conserve them.

To be awarded Ark of Taste status, foods and food products are nominated and must meet the following criteria:

1. They must be food products, and may include domestic species (plant varieties, ecotypes, indigenous animal breeds and populations), wild species (only if tied to traditional methods of harvesting, processing, and uses), and processed products (such as cheeses and cured meats).

2. Products must be of distinctive quality in terms of taste. "Taste quality" here is defined in the context of local traditions and uses.

3. Products must be linked to a specific area, to the memory

and identity of a group and to local traditions.

4. Products must be produced in limited quantities.

5. Products must be at risk of extinction.

Some examples of Ark of Taste foods you may see in your CSA box or at your farmers market are Algonquin squash, Amish deer tongue lettuce, Radiator Charlie's Mortgage Lifter tomatoes, Tennessee fainting goats, American shad (a native fish), Hawaiian 'ulu (a type of breadfruit), Midget White turkeys, Moon and Stars watermelon, Inchelium Red garlic, and Newtown Pippin apples.

The Big Three

In Bulgaria, three seasonings regularly appear on the table: salt, paprika, and savory.

4. Divide into serving bowls and sprinkle some finely chopped fresh summer savory leaves over the soup. Serve with tortilla chips.

— *Brenda Hyde, Old Fashioned Living*

. . . .

SUMMER SAVORY SOUP   SERVES 4

1 tablespoon olive oil
2 small cloves garlic, minced
½ sweet onion, chopped
2 cups mixed vegetables (such as cabbage, cauliflower, green beans, spinach)
3 cups vegetable or chicken broth
¾ cup orzo or other small pasta
½ teaspoon minced fresh basil
½ teaspoon minced fresh oregano
1 tablespoon flour
¼ cup milk or half-and-half
½ teaspoon minced fresh summer or winter savory
Salt and freshly ground black pepper

1. Heat the oil in a medium saucepan. Add the garlic and onion, and cook until the onions have softened. Add the chunkier vegetables that will need extra time, and cook for 5 to 7 minutes on low heat, stirring occasionally.

2. Add the broth and any remaining vegetables. Bring to a boil. Add the orzo, basil, and oregano. Simmer for about 15 minutes.

3. In a separate bowl, whisk the flour into the milk until well combined. Decrease the heat and stir in the flour mixture. Add the savory. Stir frequently while the soup thickens. Add salt and pepper to taste.

— *Brenda Hyde, Old Fashioned Living*

Shallots

Until relatively recently, shallots were exotic, expensive, and hard to find in mainstream supermarkets. Happily, much has changed since the days when television chef and personality Julia Child often substituted green onions for shallots because of the latter's scarcity—but perhaps there are still too few American cooks familiar with this stellar member of the onion family. This should be rectified immediately, for shallots are great companions in the kitchen, possessing a flavor milder, yet much more delicate and complex, than that of onions. In France and Asia, they are a staple and a flavoring base for many dishes and are often treated as an elegant vegetable side dish in their own right.

Shallots may not be what they seem in the market. True shallots, with their thin, coppery skins, grow from bulbs only, not from seed; a central bulb forms, and off it grows other bulbs. In France it is illegal to sell shallots propagated from anything other than bulbs. But you may encounter small onions, long onions, onion-shallot crosses, or pseudo-shallots that are improperly labeled as shallots or seed shallots. It doesn't help that historically the name "shallots" has often been used interchangeably with the term "scallions," further muddying the onion-scented waters.

HISTORY

Confusion abounds in shallot history, as its name has been commonly interchanged with scallions (green onions), onions of various types, and other members of the large Allium family. They most likely originated in central or Southeast Asia and were then brought to the Mediterranean and India. The aromatic bulb was mentioned in the Bible, and its name (as well as that of the scallion) derives from the ancient city of Askalon, an Israeli coastal city where it is thought to have originated.

NUTRITION

Like other members of the onion family, shallots are rich in antioxidants and phytonutrients that give them their distinctive aroma and flavor—especially allicin, which can reduce blood cholesterol and also has antibacterial properties. A single tablespoon of chopped shallots contains 7 calories, as well as vitamins A, C, and B6, folate, and potassium.

SEASON

Commercially, shallots are widely grown and in season year-round. You'll find them at their best in farmers markets and CSAs throughout the summer and early fall.

SELECTION

Shallots should be firm, plump, and heavy for their size. Avoid shallots that are shriveled, lightweight, or show signs of dampness or softness. They are very prone to mold, so watch for telltale signs of gray fuzziness lurking around the tips. Sometimes a shallot past its prime, when prodded, will explode in a poof of gray spores—most disappointing indeed. Their papery skins are protective and should be present, broken or unbroken.

STORAGE

Shallots keep best when they are not stored in the refrigerator. They require proper ventilation, so spread them out in a basket and keep them in a cool, dry place. They can keep for weeks, but you should check them every so often to make sure they are not rotting; a good sniff and a quick squeeze (not at the same time) will do the trick.

TRIMMING AND CLEANING

Carefully peel off the coppery outer skins. Leave the root end intact, so that the shallot hangs together while you slice, mince, or chop it.

If you need to peel significant quantities of shallots for roasting, loosen their skins by immersing them in boiling water for 5 minutes. Remove from the water, then trim ¼ to ½ inch from both ends (this should include the neck and the root stub), and peel off the thin outer skin.

STEAMING AND BOILING

Shallots are not at their best when steamed or boiled, as this tends to exacerbate their already high moisture content and make them watery. Baking, braising, roasting, grilling, sautéing, and frying all concentrate their sugars and thus their flavor.

STIR-FRYING AND SAUTÉING

Shallots are a natural sautéed or stir-fried. Heat oil or butter in a pan over medium-high heat, thinly slice or chop the shallots, and sauté for 3 to 5 minutes, or until they turn limp and translucent. If you want to use shallots for a quiche or as a filling in another dish, cook them slowly on lower heat; they will caramelize and develop a much richer flavor.

BAKING AND ROASTING

Roasting caramelizes and concentrates the natural sugars in shallots, heightening their already rich, complex flavor. Peel and halve the shallots, toss with a little seasoning and oil, and spread a little more oil or butter on the bottom of a baking pan to prevent scorching. Roast in a 375°F oven for 45 minutes to 1 hour, or until they become tender, depending on the size of the shallots.

GRILLING

Like other members of the onion family, shallots love the grill. You can keep them whole, leaving the skins on, or cut them in half and grill them skin side down. Either way toss them with a little oil and seasoning to prevent them from burning, and cook on the cooler side of the grill for 10 to 15 minutes, or in a grilling basket over medium-high heat for 6 to 8 minutes, depending on their size, or until they become tender. They are a bit delicate and cook faster than onions; stir constantly to keep them from burning.

Braising and Stewing

Shallots take very well to braising and stewing. One method is to braise shallots in broth, wine, or water into which butter, herbs, salt, and pepper have been added. Bring to a boil, cover, decrease the heat, and simmer over low heat for 15 to 25 minutes, or until the shallots are tender.

An alternative method is to sauté the shallots in butter until they brown in spots, then add the broth mixture and cook as described above. These browned shallots can then be added to a roast toward the end of the roast's cooking time.

Microwaving

To microwave, peel the shallots (but leave them whole), place them in a microwave-safe dish, add 1 tablespoon of butter or olive oil, cover, and cook on high power.

- 1 pound = 5 to 7 minutes

Blanching and Freezing

Shallots can be frozen without blanching. They will be slightly mushy when thawed, but their flavor will remain good and they will be fine for cooked dishes. Simply package them whole in zipper-lock freezer or vacuum food sealer-type bags, or freezer containers. Squeeze out any excess air and leave ½ inch of headspace (unless you are using the vacuum sealing method). Frozen shallots will keep for up to 3 months at 0°F.

Equivalents, Measures, and Servings

- 1 medium shallot = approximately 2 tablespoons, chopped

Complementary Herbs, Seasonings, and Foods

Apples, balsamic vinegar, bay, beef, Brussels sprouts, buckwheat, butter, carrots, cheese (blue, Gruyère, Cheddar), chicken, cinnamon, cloves, cream, fish, ham, hazelnuts, hazelnut oil, lamb, mustard, olive oil, onions, parsnips, pasta, potatoes, prunes, red wine, rosemary, rutabaga, savory, sherry, sweet potatoes, tarragon, thyme, veal, vermouth, vinegar, walnuts.

Serving Suggestions

- Crispy deep-fried shallots are a highly popular topping on noodles, stir-fries, rice, fish, and other Asian dishes.

- Shallots have a natural reddish-pink coloring between their layers. If you marinate bits of shallot in a little rice vinegar or white wine vinegar, the color ascends to a beautiful magenta and will provide an electric accent to, say, blanched green beans or fresh peas.

- It's hard to beat the classic French vinaigrette, made with minced shallots, vinegar, mustard, oil, salt, and pepper.

- Caramelized, roasted shallots are a sumptuous treat with meats, poultry, and potatoes, or as a luxurious side dish in their own right.

- Chop shallots finely and use in a favorite tuna, egg, chicken, or potato salad.

- Use shallots in almost any preparation calling for onions; expect the resulting flavor to be richer, sweeter, more complex, and subtler.

- Shallots make good company with fall and winter vegetables; try them braised or roasted with Brussels sprouts, parsnips, carrots, rutabaga, and sweet potatoes.

Books

Onion: The Essential Cook's Guide to Onions, Garlic, Leeks, Spring Onions, Shallots and Chives
Brian Glover.
Lorenz Books, 2001.

Onion Delights Cookbook
Karen Jean Matsko Hood.
Cookbook Delights, 2014.

Mastering the Art of French Cooking, Volume I: 50th Anniversary
Julia Child, Louisette Bertholle, and Simone Beck.
Alfred A. Knopf, 2001.

The French Kitchen Cookbook: Recipes and Lessons from Paris and Provence
Patricia Wells.
William Morrow Cookbooks, 2013.

- Shallots make a wonderful sauté base instead of onions.
- Try a thinly sliced shallot in your favorite salad. They are dynamite with fresh avocado and a squeeze of lemon juice.
- A twist on the Swedish smörgåsbord treat: a little finely chopped shallot atop pickled herring on slices of dark rye bread thickly spread with good butter.
- Shallots are delicious in compound butters; mix with your favorite herbs.
- For a dish that delights and surprises, make fried shallot rings rather than onion rings.
- Instead of garlic mashed potatoes, substitute finely chopped, sautéed shal-lots for the garlic.
- Roast whole shallots with potatoes and rosemary for a hearty, satisfying winter meal. Great with a little balsamic vinegar, too.

SAUTÉED CHICKEN WITH SHALLOTS AND ARTICHOKE HEARTS (POULET SAUTÉ À LA BORDELAISE)   SERVES 4

Author Note: *This is a lovely traditional, provincial French dish that is typical of its cuisine in that it does not demand complicated ingredients, just the best-quality ones for its simple savoriness to shine through.*

> One 2½- to 3-pound frying chicken, cut up
> 6 tablespoons (¾ stick) butter, divided
> 2 tablespoons vegetable oil
> 16 to 24 large whole peeled shallots, or 16 one-inch peeled white onions
> Salt and freshly ground black pepper
> 2 bay leaves
> 1 teaspoon fresh lemon juice
> One 9-ounce package frozen artichoke hearts, defrosted and drained (or about 6 to 8 fresh artichoke hearts, depending on size)
> ½ cup chicken stock, fresh or canned

1. Wash the chicken quickly under cold running water and dry the pieces thoroughly with paper towels; if they are damp, they won't brown well. In a heavy 10- to 12-inch enameled or stainless-steel skillet or sauté pan, melt 4 tablespoons of the butter and the 2 table-spoons of oil over moderately high heat. When the foam begins to subside, brown the chicken a few pieces at a time, starting them skin side down and turning them with tongs. As the pieces become a rich golden brown, remove them to a plate.

2. When all of the chicken is browned, add the shallots or onions to the skillet and cook them, shaking the pan to color them lightly and as evenly as possible. Pour off all but a thin film of fat and return the chicken to the skillet. Season with salt and pepper, lay the bay leaves on top, and cover the pan. Cook over high heat until the fat splut-

ters. Reduce the heat at once and cook the chicken slowly, using a bulb baster or spoon to baste it with pan juices every 7 or 8 minutes.

3. Meanwhile, melt the remaining 2 tablespoons of butter in an 8- to 10-inch enameled or stainless-steel skillet. When the foam subsides, stir in the lemon juice. Add the artichoke hearts and toss them in the lemon butter until they glisten. Season them with salt, cover the skillet, and cook over low heat for 10 to 15 minutes or until the artichoke hearts are tender.

4. After the chicken has cooked for about 30 minutes, it should be done, and its juices will run yellow when a thigh is pierced with the tip of a sharp knife. Remove the chicken from the skillet and arrange the pieces attractively on a large heated platter with the shallots or white onions and the artichoke hearts around them. Discard the bay leaves.

5. Pour the chicken stock into the juices remaining in the skillet and bring to a boil over high heat, scraping in any browned bits clinging to the bottom and sides of the pan. Boil for 2 or 3 minutes until the sauce is reduced to about ⅓ cup. Pour it over the chicken and serve at once.

Variation: If you like, you may cook the artichoke hearts with the chicken. In that case, omit the 2 tablespoons of butter and the lemon juice from the recipe. Add the artichoke hearts to the chicken after they have cooked with the shallots for 15 minutes and baste them well with the pan juices. Cover and cook, basting every 7 or 8 minutes, for 15 minutes longer, or until the chicken is done and the artichoke hearts are tender.

— *M. F. K. Fisher and Julia Child,* Time-Life Foods of the World, The Cooking of Provincial France

. . . .

POTATO AND BACON PIEROGIES WITH CARAMELIZED SHALLOTS AND WALNUTS

MAKES 24 PIEROGIES

Author Note: Pierogies are small dumplings stuffed with a filling such as potato, ground meat, or cheese; they are typically served with onions and sour cream. Please note that the dough should be made the night before.

THE DOUGH (PREPARE THE NIGHT BEFORE)

3 cups all-purpose flour
1 teaspoon salt
2 tablespoons salted butter, melted
1 cup plain yogurt
2 eggs
1 teaspoon vegetable oil

1. In a large bowl, combine the flour and salt. Set aside.

to talk to farmers and get to know just how they raise their crops and animals.

Organic food labeling is trickier. In America, there are three levels of organic foods. According to the USDA, products made entirely with certified organic ingredients and methods can be labeled "**100% organic**," and only products with at least 95 percent organic ingredients may be labeled "**organic**." The remaining 5 percent of ingredients must be on a USDA–approved list. Both of these categories may display the USDA Organic seal.

A third category, containing a minimum of 70 percent organic ingredients, can be labeled "**made with organic ingredients**," but the products may not display the USDA Organic seal. Products made with less than 70 percent organic ingredients cannot be advertised as "organic," but they can list individual ingredients that are organic as such in the product's ingredient statement. Also, ingredients from plants cannot be genetically modified.

Remember that "certified organic" and "organic" often mean different things in different countries; produce from China, Mexico, or South America may contain levels of pesticides (including some banned in the United States) or other chemicals that don't meet stricter American standards, and it is impossible for more than a tiny fraction of it to be properly inspected or verified. It's a safer bet to buy produce from local growers (and it helps support domestic family farmers as well).

Conventional farming, modern agriculture, and **industrial farming** are all essentially the same thing—a way to raise food on a massive scale using synthetic inputs such as chemical fertilizers, pesticides, and fossil fuels; high-yield hybrid and GMO strains; a reliance on monoculture, or growing a single crop repeatedly over many years; animals raised in confined, concen-

2. In a medium bowl, combine the butter, yogurt, eggs, and oil. Whisk until smooth and fold the liquids into the flour mixture. Stir the mixture until the flour is fully integrated and a light and sticky dough forms.

3. Cover the bowl with a cloth and let it stand for 1 hour at room temperature. Wrap the dough in plastic wrap and refrigerate it overnight.

THE FILLING

3 large potatoes
3 slices bacon
1 tablespoon olive oil
2 shallots, finely sliced
½ green apple, peeled and finely diced
2 tablespoons cottage cheese
1 tablespoon milk
1 tablespoon butter
1 tablespoon walnuts, finely ground in a food processor
¼ cup shredded sharp white Cheddar cheese
¼ cup crumbled Gorgonzola cheese

1. Peel and boil the potatoes until tender—about 15 to 20 minutes, depending on the size. Drain and set aside.

2. In a large pot or Dutch oven, cook the bacon until crispy. Remove from the pan, chop into small pieces, and set aside.

3. Add the olive oil to the bacon fat and heat over medium-high heat. Sauté the shallots in the oil for 1 minute, then reduce the heat to low and allow them to simmer for 20 to 25 minutes, or until they begin to caramelize.

4. Add the diced apple to the pan and continue to cook on low heat until the apples are tender. Remove from the heat.

5. Return the bacon and potatoes to the pan and mash until the shallots, bacon, and apples are equally distributed.

6. Add the cottage cheese, milk, butter, walnuts, and Cheddar and Gorgonzola cheeses, and continue to mash until almost smooth and fully combined. Set aside.

7. To assemble the perogies, sprinkle flour over a large workspace. Roll out the dough until it is ¼ inch thick.

8. Using a round cookie cutter or the top of a wine glass, cut out rounds of dough and place 1 tablespoon of the filling in the middle. Wet the edges of the dough and fold in half, pressing the sides to seal in the filling. I like to use a fork to press down the edges so the filling is securely inside.

9. If you are going to cook the pierogies right away, proceed to Step 10. Otherwise, arrange them on a cookie sheet lined with parchment paper and place in the freezer for about 2 hours. Once they are frozen, move the pierogies to a freezer bag and store them frozen

until they will be used. Thaw by spreading them in a single layer and placing them in your refrigerator for several hours (or overnight) before you plan to bake them.

10. To cook the pierogies: Warm the olive oil over medium heat and sauté some onions and garlic. Add the pierogies to the oil and fry until they are hot and golden brown. Serve with sour cream.

— *Kris, Foodista.com*

. . . .

BALACHAUNG (BURMESE DRIED SHRIMP RELISH)   YIELDS 2 CUPS

Source Note: This is a traditional Burmese condiment that can be served as a topping on fish, vegetables, or even with plain rice. You can find ngapi *(shrimp paste) in an Asian grocery store or online at specialty-food retailers.*

    ½ cup vegetable or peanut oil
    5 shallots, finely sliced
    5 cloves garlic, finely sliced
    1 tablespoon *ngapi* (shrimp paste)
    ¼ cup white wine vinegar
    1 cup dried prawns, soaked in warm water
    1 tablespoon turmeric
    1 tablespoon chile powder

1. In a large saucepan, heat the oil over medium heat and fry the shallots until they turn golden. Remove them with a slotted spoon to a bowl.

2. Fry the garlic in the same oil until golden, then remove and add to shallots.

3. In a separate dish, dissolve the *ngapi* in the vinegar.

4. Drain the prawns and place them in a food processor; grind them until coarsely shredded or ground. Then fry the prawns in the same shallot-garlic oil for 3 to 4 minutes. Add the turmeric, chile powder, and *ngapi* to the prawns. Fry until crisp and golden. Allow to cool.

5. Add the prawn mixture to the shallots and garlic and mix well.

6. Store in an airtight jar; the *balachaung* will keep for months.

— *Evelyn Ong, Foodista.com*

. . . .

SHALLOT SALAD DRESSING   YIELDS 1 CUP

Source Note: This is a super-easy dressing to make; you control the quality of the ingredients.

and had access to grass or pastureland as opposed to a feedlot, where it would have eaten mostly or all grain. The term "grass-fed" often appears along with "free range," suggesting that the animal was allowed to roam freely, linking the two in consumers' minds. However, the two are not related because animals can be fed grass but still be contained. The appeal of grass-fed meat is that animals raised on grain in feedlots are usually less nutritious, have inferior flavor, and contain significant residues of antibiotics to help them cope with this unnatural diet. The USDA does not regulate "grass-fed" in any way other than food labeling, so unscrupulous producers can easily deceive or mislead consumers.

It is also important to remember that just because an animal was raised cage-free, free-range, or grass-fed, it does not mean that it is necessarily organic. And the terms "**hormone-free**" or "**antibiotic-free**" simply mean that the animal must never have been fed hormones or antibiotics, and the producer must provide documentation to substantiate this. But again, such products do not need to be organic.

In recent years, so-called "**local food**" has become a huge movement. There is no standard definition or distance for what constitutes local, but generally it assumes a system that connects producers and consumers in the same geographic region to build more self-reliant food systems and networks, strengthening local economies and communities. "**Locavore**" is a word invented in 2005 by three San Francisco Bay Area women who challenged residents to be locavores by eating only foods grown or raised within a 100-mile radius of San Francisco for an entire month. The term caught on like wildfire and is used widely today.

What are average shoppers to do when navigating this confusing landscape? Carefully read and

1 shallot, chopped
⅓ cup vinegar (we use champagne or sherry vinegar)
1 tablespoon Dijon mustard
Salt and freshly ground black pepper
¾ cup good olive oil

Whirl everything in a blender or food processor. Taste and adjust the seasoning, adding more of any of the ingredients to achieve the balance of flavors you prefer.

— *Julia Wiley, Mariquita Farm, Watsonville, California*

A summer CSA harvest basket from Valley Flora Farm.

Squashes (Summer)

VARIOUS CUCURBITA PEPO
AND
CUCURBITA MOSCHATA
SPECIES

A dizzying variety—over 600 types—of summer squash exist, each with distinctive colors, shapes, and sizes. Some are round and elongated, and others are scalloped and pear-shaped, with flesh that ranges from ivory to green to brilliant orange.

The terms "summer" and "winter" for squash can be confusing, as the summer types (zucchini, pattypan, and yellow) are frequently in supermarkets all winter, and winter types can be found in late summer and fall. The difference lies in how long they can be stored. Summer varieties have thin skins and are highly perishable, whereas the thick-skinned winter squashes can be stored unrefrigerated for months at a time.

For all of their visual diversity, summer squashes for the most part share a similar flavor—a light, slightly sweet vegetable taste that is delicate and takes well to fresh herbs, butter, good-quality oils, and other light seasonings. Roasting or grilling concentrates the flavors in summer squash, evaporates some of their high water content, and renders the vegetables soft and creamy—much more appetizing than the product you get from steaming or boiling.

Summer squashes commonly found in your CSA box and at farmers markets typically come in several varieties: the scallop or pattypan, a flattish, light-green or yellow squash with crimped, pie-like edges; the yellow straightneck, crookneck, and semi-straightneck, so common that it is what most people think of when they hear "summer squash"; and zucchinis, which range from small green globes to those familiar cylinders so large that you just might be able to carve a canoe from them.

For more information on zucchini, see pages 376–382. For information on winter squashes, see pages 586–597.

HISTORY

The history of squash is tangled and confusing, as references to this New World vine have intertwined it since antiquity with the closely related gourds and pumpkins, some of which may have originated in the Old World. It is thought that most modern-day summer squashes came from a wild variety that grows between Guatemala and Mexico.

Squashes are possibly one of humanity's earliest cultivated foods, with seeds found in Mexican caves dated around 9000 BCE. Christopher Columbus brought squash back from the New World to Europe in the 1400s; subsequently Portuguese and Spanish explorers introduced squash to many other parts of the world.

NUTRITION

A 1-cup serving of summer squash contains nearly one-fifth of the adult daily requirement for manganese, as well as significant amounts of vitamins A, C, and K, magnesium, potassium, copper, folate, phosphorus, and dietary fiber, all for only 36 calories.

SEASON

Commercially, summer squash is widely grown and in season year-round. But it is a warm-weather crop, and you'll find it at its best in farmers markets and CSAs from midsummer through early fall.

SELECTION

Summer squashes are best when they are still young, tender, and small. Avoid overly large squashes, for they may be bitter, tough, and tasteless. Choose firm, plump, heavy specimens with unblemished skins and no soft, bruised, shriveled, or watery spots.

STORAGE

Summer squashes are surprisingly perishable; avoid washing them until just before using, and keep them wrapped in a plastic bag in the refrigerator vegetable crisper for up to 4 days. Try to avoid bruising or puncturing the delicate skin, which will lead to decay.

TRIMMING AND CLEANING

Summer squash requires little preparation. Just wash thoroughly and slice into the desired-size pieces; if they are young and tender, peeling their thin skins is unnecessary. If you want to reduce the soft, watery aspect of summer squash, remove the seeds and cores before cooking.

STEAMING AND BOILING

Summer squashes often become watery when cooked, so either choose cooking methods that dry them out a bit, or avoid those that may exacerbate this characteristic. For this reason, steaming summer squash is preferable to boiling it, which yields a more waterlogged product. Steam 1-inch chunks over rapidly boiling water for 10 to 12 minutes, or until the squash is tender.

STIR-FRYING AND SAUTÉING

Cut the squash into thin strips or rounds. Sprinkle with oil, butter, broth, or soy sauce, and stir-fry or sauté it over high heat for about 3 to 6 minutes, or until the squash is tender and its edges are lightly browned.

BAKING AND ROASTING

Roasting summer squash is a better alternative to boiling or even steaming, as the oven or broiler heat helps evaporate its copious moisture. Squashes do well fixed as casseroles with other ingredients, or you can cut them in half lengthwise, drizzle them with olive oil, butter, or a marinade, and roast at 350°F for 25 to 30 minutes.

GRILLING

Summer squash responds well to grilling, especially the larger fruits. Use about twice what you think you will want, as they will soften and shrink considerably. Trim the ends from about 2 pounds of summer squash;

cut them into ¼-inch slabs and slather them with olive oil (you'll need salt and pepper, too), ½ cup Italian salad dressing, or other vinaigrette if desired. Grill over a medium-hot fire until they are soft and somewhat charred, 2 to 3 minutes per side.

MICROWAVING

Trim off the ends; cut into ¼-inch rounds and place in a microwave-safe dish with ¼ cup water; cover and cook on high power.

- 1½ cups = 3 to 4 minutes
- 1 pound = 6 to 7 minutes

BLANCHING AND FREEZING

Summer squash can be frozen, but its high water content causes it to turn mushy when thawed. To freeze raw squash, it must be blanched first. Wash it, trim off the stem ends, and cut it into rounds or strips. Blanch in rapidly boiling water for 3 minutes, then plunge the squash into ice water for 5 minutes to stop the cooking process. Remove and drain. Package the squash in zipper-lock freezer or vacuum food sealer-type bags, or freezer containers. Squeeze out the excess air and leave ½ inch of headspace (unless you are using the vacuum sealing method).

Pureed or sautéed squash tends to freeze somewhat better. Frozen summer squash will keep for up to 3 months at 0°F.

MEASURES AND EQUIVALENTS

- 1 pound squash = about 3½ cups sliced = 4 cups grated = 2 cups salted and squeezed = 2 to 3 servings

COMPLEMENTARY HERBS, SEASONINGS, AND FOODS

Balsamic vinegar, basil, beans, beef, butter, capers, cheese (Asiago, feta, goat, Monterey Jack, Parmesan), chicken, chives, cilantro, cinnamon, cloves, corn, cream, curry, dill, eggs, eggplant, garlic, lemons, marjoram, mint, nutmeg, olive oil, onions, oregano, parsley, pasta, peppers, pine nuts, rice, rosemary, sage, sausage, tarragon, tomatoes, walnuts, yogurt.

SERVING SUGGESTIONS

- Add peeled summer squash cubes to soups, stews, beans, gratins, and vegetable ragouts.
- Serve chunks or thin rounds of raw, tender summer squash with other fresh vegetables and your favorite dips and dressings.
- Finely grate or shred summer squash, sauté with onion in butter, and combine with milk, eggs, and seasonings. Top with butter and cracker crumbs; bake in a 450°F oven for 15 minutes, or until the casserole is golden brown.
- Make a hearty one-dish meal of squash lasagna, combining slices of summer squash with layers of meat, cheese, and noodles. Serve with salad and fruit.
- Shred summer squash with carrots, cucumbers, and cabbage for an unusual coleslaw.
- Thinly slice summer squash to substitute for cucumbers in sandwiches.
- Slice summer squashes in half and grill for 3 to 4 minutes on either side on the hottest part of the grill. Chunks of squash are terrific in kebabs.
- Make ratatouille by combining summer squash, eggplant, tomatoes, onions, garlic, herbs, and olive oil, and cooking slowly to reduce the liquid.

Books

Smitten with Squash
Amanda Kay Paa,
Minnesota Historical
Society Press, 2014.

The Classic Zucchini Cookbook:
225 Recipes for
All Kinds of Squash
Nancy C. Ralston, Marynor
Jordan, and Andrea Chesman,
Storey Publishing, 2002.

Too Many Tomatoes, Squash,
Beans, and Other Good Things:
A Cookbook for When
Your Garden Explodes
Lois M. Landau
and Laura G. Myers,
HarperPerennial, 1991.

- Roast zucchini or other summer squash in the oven with sliced onions, olive oil, salt, pepper, and other herbs and seasonings.

- Add diced, sautéed summer squash to salads and pasta dishes.

- Sauté coins of summer squash with zucchini and other squashes of contrasting colors—yellow and light green, for instance—and dress with fresh herbs (mint gives a wonderful, surprising burst of flavor) and garlic for a lovely summer dish.

- If you find yourself with extra marinated and grilled summer squash, add it to almost any type of sandwich the next day for a burst of smoky flavor.

- Combine with eggs, tomatoes, and basil to make a summer frittata.

- Of course, if all else fails, make that old standby—squash bread or muffins.

STUFFED SQUASH WITH BASIL AND HONEY
SERVES 4 TO 6

> 2 pounds summer squash (4 to 6 squashes)
> Olive oil
> 1 small Walla Walla onion, finely chopped
> 1 clove garlic, crushed
> 1 tablespoon honey
> 1 teaspoon light soy sauce
> 1 tablespoon tahini (sesame seed paste)
> ⅓ cup fresh basil
> 1 tablespoon toasted sesame seeds

1. Boil, steam, or microwave the squash whole until it is tender. Drain and cool. Slice the whole squash so it can sit flat (either like a canoe for the zucchini and yellow squash, or like a chair for the pattypan). Scoop a shallow hole from the top of each squash. Set the shells aside, and finely chop the scooped pieces.

2. Preheat the oven to 375°F.

3. Heat some olive oil in a small saucepan and add the onion and garlic. Sauté over medium heat until they become soft, about 2 minutes. Add the chopped squash, honey, soy sauce, tahini, and basil, and cook for 1 more minute. Place the squash shells onto an oven tray, spoon the basil mixture into the hollows, and sprinkle with sesame seeds.

4. Bake for 10 minutes, or until heated through. Serve the individual squashes on their own plates.

— *Featherstone Farm, Rushford, Minnesota*

FAVORITE BAKED SUMMER SQUASH
SERVES 4

Source Note: This is an adaptation of a Joy of Cooking *recipe that I prepare often during the summer.*

3 cups any kind of summer squash, cut into strips or thin rounds
2 tablespoons unsalted butter, sliced into pats
½ teaspoon salt
¼ teaspoon paprika
1 teaspoon fresh lemon thyme or chopped fresh parsley (optional)
¼ cup milk
1 teaspoon grated onion (optional)
Crisp, crumbled bacon for garnish

1. Preheat the oven to 350°F.

2. Place the squash into a shallow, greased baking dish and dot with pats of butter. Sprinkle with the salt and paprika. Add the lemon thyme. Pour the milk over the mixture and add the grated onion.

3. Cover and bake for 20 to 30 minutes, until tender. Garnish with the bacon bits and serve.

— *Marianne Streich*

Savory Summer Squash Muffins   Makes 12 muffins

Source Note: These muffins are great for breakfast or as a substitute for bread with a colorful summer meal. Also, by using the microwave oven to cook the muffins, you won't heat up your kitchen!

1 cup all-bran cereal
¾ cup skim milk
2 cups grated zucchini or other summer squash
    (8 ounces, or about 1 medium)
½ cup whole wheat flour
½ cup all-purpose enriched flour
1 teaspoon baking powder
1 teaspoon baking soda
1 teaspoon ground cinnamon
½ teaspoon ground ginger
⅛ teaspoon salt
2 tablespoons frozen orange juice concentrate
2 tablespoons vegetable oil
1 tablespoon fresh lemon juice
1 medium egg, beaten

1. Line a microwave-safe muffin tin (such as silicone) with 2 paper liners per cup.

2. In a large bowl, combine the bran with the milk and grated squash. Let stand for 5 minutes, stirring once more to make sure the bran is evenly wet.

3. In a medium bowl, mix the dry ingredients. In a small bowl, whisk the orange juice concentrate, oil, lemon juice, and egg. Add the wet

---

Fifth, immediately after picking the flowers, you must lightly spray the inside of each one with cool water to remove any soil or creatures that may still be inside.

Sixth, hold each flower firmly by the stem and gently shake off all the excess water. Place a layer of paper towels on the bottom of a large, shallow plastic container. Line up the flowers (give each one a bit of room) in rows on top of the paper towels. Gently cover each row with more toweling, tightly wrap the container with aluminum foil, and refrigerate until ready to use.

When packaged this way, the flowers will maintain their peak condition for up to several weeks. It's all a matter of picking, washing, drying, toweling, and sealing with foil as quickly as possible to keep them fresh.

Fried Squash Blossoms

Serves 4 as an entrée and 8 as an appetizer

½ cup milk
⅔ cup flour
⅔ cup beer (not dark) or club soda
Salt and freshly ground pepper
Oregano or other herbs
1 teaspoon olive oil (more for frying)
1 teaspoon lemon juice
20 to 24 squash blossoms, trimmed
    and washed

1. *Whisk together the milk, flour, beer, salt, pepper, seasoning, olive oil, and lemon juice in a bowl until smooth. Heat 1 inch of oil in a large, heavy saucepan over moderate heat until a deep-fat fryer thermometer registers 375°F.*

2. *Working in batches of 3 or 4, dip the blossoms in the batter to coat, and fry until golden, about 30 seconds on each side, or 1 to 2 minutes per batch. Transfer to paper towels to drain and sprinkle lightly with salt. (Return the oil to 375°F between batches.)*

3. *Serve at once, while still warm.*

---

ingredients to the bran mixture, stir to incorporate, then add the dry ingredients, stirring just until combined. Do not overmix.

4. Fill each cup half full. Microwave on high power for 5 to 5½ minutes if using a silicone pan, or for 2 to 3 minutes if using stand-alone paper cups. The muffins will be springy when touched. It is best to microwave only 3 muffins at a time.

Cooking Note: If you prefer to bake the muffins in a regular oven, line a standard muffin tin with cupcake papers and bake at 350°F for about 18 minutes, or until a skewer inserted in the center comes out clean.

— Adapted from Produce for Better Health; Fruits & Veggies— More Matters; Centers for Disease Control and Prevention

. . . .

VEGETABLE FRITTATA   SERVES 6 TO 8

3 ounces chopped mushrooms (about 1¼ cups)
4 ounces chopped summer squash (about 1½ cups)
5 tablespoons butter or olive oil, divided
Salt and freshly ground black pepper
12 eggs, beaten and seasoned with salt and pepper
3 ounces grated Parmesan cheese (about 1 cup)
4 ounces shredded cheese (mozzarella, Cheddar, or jack)
4 ounces chopped raw spinach (about 3 cups, packed)

1. Preheat the oven to 325°F.

2. Sauté the mushrooms and squash in 2 tablespoons of the butter, seasoning with salt and pepper, in a nonstick pan over medium heat until they are just softened.

3. Spray a 10-inch cast-iron skillet with nonstick spray. Melt the remaining butter over medium heat and coat the entire inside of the pan. Add the eggs, Parmesan cheese, other shredded cheese, spinach, and squash-mushroom mixture. Stir lightly to make sure all of the ingredients are evenly distributed. Cook for 3 to 4 minutes until the egg mixture starts to adhere to the pan.

4. Bake in the oven for 25 to 30 minutes. (To check for doneness, make sure the eggs are firm in the middle. Insert a toothpick and pull it out; if no runny egg sticks to it, the frittata is done.) Remove from the oven and let it cool for 10 minutes.

5. Using a paring knife, separate the edges of the frittata from the pan. Cover the pan with a dinner plate, use two hot pads to grasp the whole thing firmly, and flip the frittata onto the plate. (If it sticks, turn the pan back over and use a paring knife or rubber spatula to loosen the sides and bottom of the frittata as best you can.) This frittata can be served warm but tastes best at room temperature.

— Davis Farmers Market, Davis, California

Tarragon

ARTEMISIA DRACUNCULUS OR A. DRACUNCULOIDES

Few herbs are so uniquely linked to a specific culture as tarragon, which the French revere and feature prominently in their cuisine. Along with chervil, chives, and parsley, tarragon is one of the four components of fines herbes, that sublime combination that graces so many French chicken, egg, and fish dishes, as well as salad dressings. Tarragon is also a prominent component of the egg-based béarnaise and hollandaise sauces and a favored flavoring for vinegar.

*Fresh tarragon has a strong, robust flavor that combines a mélange of pungency, an anise-like sweetness, and a peppery bite that slightly numbs the tongue. It should be used rather sparingly, as a little goes a long way. The tarragon that is most frequently available in the United States is Russian tarragon (*Artemesia dracunculoides), *which is harsher and more bitter than the French version (*Artemisia dracunculus)*, the one usually called for in cooking. Unfortunately, the latter tends to not produce fertile seeds, so seed companies prefer to distribute the easily propagated Russian variety. Seek out the more subtle French tarragon whenever possible.*

HISTORY

Tarragon is likely a native of the Asian steppes. Despite its close association with European cooking, the herb was probably not widely cultivated or used there until the Tudor family introduced it from Siberia to its royal gardens in England. The Mongols brought the plant to the Near East, where its young shoots were eaten as a cooked vegetable. In fact, honored guests in Syria were often served tarragon. The plant traveled to America with the colonists, along with burnet, horehound, and chamomile.

NUTRITION

Although tarragon is usually not consumed in enough quantity to be a significant source of nutrients, the fresh herb does contain surprising amounts of potassium, iron, calcium, vitamins A, C, and B6, and folate. Two teaspoons contain a whopping 4 calories. Once thought to cure the effects of snakebite in ancient times, tarragon has been used medicinally as a sleep aid, digestive, and breath sweetener.

SEASON

Commercially, tarragon is widely grown and available year-round. You'll find it at its best in farmers markets and CSAs throughout the summer and fall.

SELECTION

When purchasing the raw herb, look for bunches that are uniformly green and fresh looking. Avoid wilted, yellowing, or slimy specimens.

STORAGE

An easy way to store fresh tarragon (and many other cut herbs) is to treat them like flowers; Simply trim the stem ends, strip off the leaves from

The Influence of the Hmong Farmer

Mi Ae Lipe

Although many Americans have never met or even seen Hmong people, their presence is significant at many farmers markets across the country.

Originally of southern Chinese descent, the Hmong are an ethnic group from the mountainous areas that border Vietnam, Laos, China, and Thailand. They led a fairly quiet existence for centuries, farming their land, but everything changed during the Vietnam War. Thousands of Hmong and Laotians were recruited by the American government to resist the North Vietnamese. After Saigon fell in 1975, the United States relocated huge numbers of the Hmong, who faced widespread political persecution from the Vietnamese, to Philadelphia; Providence; Chicago; Des Moines, Iowa; Kansas City; Denver; Tulsa; and Salt Lake City in the late 1970s and early 1980s.

However, this ultimately failed, as the Hmong often encountered violence and hostility in the neighborhoods in which they were settled. Preferring to be reunited with family and clan members, much of the US Hmong population shifted to the Midwest and central California, with Minneapolis–Saint Paul and Fresno, respectively, hosting the biggest populations.

Because the Hmong came from an agricultural background, it was natural for them to turn to farming in their adopted land. But they have not had an easy time of it. In addition to the usual challenges that all American produce farmers face, their troubles are compounded by major language barriers and lack of accessibility to land. Still, we are truly blessed to savor the fruits of their labor in the form of herbs and vegetables not often seen elsewhere, such as pea vines, Thai basil, long

the bottom several inches of the stems, place them in a glass of water, and keep on the counter at room temperature or store in the refrigerator. Or wrap the herb in damp paper towels and place in a plastic bag in the refrigerator vegetable crisper, where it will keep for up to 1 week.

TRIMMING AND CLEANING

Tarragon benefits from a quick rinse under running water to remove all traces of dust and dirt. Gently pat it dry between paper towels and strip the leaves from the stems, discarding the tough stems.

FREEZING

Tarragon leaves, stripped from their stems and chopped or left whole, can be frozen in zipper-lock freezer bags. Or package them using vacuum food sealer-type bags.

A terrific way to freeze tarragon is to chop it finely, mix it into a paste using ⅓ cup of olive oil or cooled melted butter to every 2 cups of herbs, and then freeze the resulting mixture in ice cube trays. To thaw, simply pop out a few cubes into a strainer and let the oil melt away, or just drop them frozen into sauces, soups, stews, casseroles, and other cooked dishes.

DRYING

Tarragon can be dried, but its flavor deteriorates tremendously. Freezing the freshly chopped raw herb in olive oil or butter in ice cube trays yields a far better, full-flavored product (see the Freezing section above), as does preserving it in vinegar.

If you still want to dry the herb, spread a single layer of leaves on a cookie sheet and place the sheet in a warm (up to 180°F) oven for 3 to 4 hours, stirring the herbs periodically until they are thoroughly dry. Or remove the best leaves from the stems and arrange on a paper towel so the leaves do not touch. Cover this layer with another paper towel and add another layer of leaves over the top. Up to five layers may be dried at one time in the oven using this method.

A microwave oven can also be used to dry small quantities of tarragon. Place four or five herb branches layered between paper towels in the microwave. Heat for 1 minute on high power. If the tarragon is not brittle and dry when removed, repeat the microwave drying for 30 seconds more. Note: The heat generated during microwaving removes not only moisture but also some of the oils, so these herbs may not have as intense a flavor as herbs dried by other methods.

MEASURES AND EQUIVALENTS

- 3 teaspoons fresh chopped tarragon = 1 teaspoon dried
- ½ ounce fresh tarragon = ⅓ cup leaves

COMPLEMENTARY HERBS, SEASONINGS, AND FOODS

Artichokes, béarnaise sauce, beef, butter, carrots, chervil, chicken, chives, eggs, fish, lemon, lime, lobster, mayonnaise, melons, mushrooms, mustard, onions, parsley, peaches, potatoes, rabbit, salads, seafood, shellfish, sole, spinach, stuffings, tomatoes, veal, vinaigrette, white beans, wine.

- Tarragon is delicious on fruits like cantaloupe, honeydew melon, and peaches. It is wonderful even on citrus desserts like lime tarts or sorbets.

- Mix 1 tablespoon of chopped fresh tarragon leaves into ½ cup of softened butter to use on grilled or roasted foods.

- Tarragon flavors eggs most wonderfully; use sparing amounts in quiches, frittatas, omelets, and scrambled eggs.

- Tarragon-infused vinegar can be added to salad dressings, soups, sauces, stews, or wherever a hint of tarragon flavor is desired.

- Make a calming tea from tarragon leaves by pouring 1 cup of boiling water over 1 tablespoon of fresh tarragon and steeping for 10 minutes.

- Tarragon combines well with parsley, chives, or chervil. When using tarragon on cooked food, always add it toward the end of the cooking process.

- Tarragon's assertive flavor is fabulous with beef and other robust, hearty meats. Combine with red wine in marinades and gravies.

SUBSTITUTIONS

If you are out of tarragon, try substituting chervil or a dash of either fennel seed or aniseed.

TARRAGON CHICKEN MARINADE   MAKES 1½ CUPS

¼ cup fresh tarragon leaves
¼ cup chopped chives, shallots, or green onions
1 cup dry white wine
½ cup olive oil
About 2 pounds chicken thighs and drumsticks, trimmed

Combine all of the ingredients in a container large enough to hold the chicken pieces. Marinate the chicken thighs and drumsticks at least 1 hour or overnight; then broil, bake, or barbecue the chicken.

— *Jan Taylor, Featherstone Farm CSA member*

EGG SALAD WITH TARRAGON, PARSLEY, AND CHIVES   MAKES ABOUT 2 CUPS

Source Note: With the spring herbs plentiful in the garden, eggs just coming in with the lengthening days, and some very good bread in the house, egg salad suddenly comes into view.

6 farm eggs (small to medium), hard-boiled
1 tablespoon minced tarragon leaves
1 tablespoon finely snipped chives
1 tablespoon minced parsley
3 tablespoons mayonnaise

beans, amaranth, Asian eggplants, bitter melon, Asian brassicas, lemongrass, and Hmong peppers.

And what gorgeous veggies these are! Few self-respecting Hmong farmers would dare think of presenting their wares in haphazard, messy heaps. Instead, their tables are piled high with geometric mounds of lush, succulent specimens, each looking picture-perfect, polished, and almost jewel-like. It is no exaggeration to say that the Hmong have upped the game in selling produce; wherever they have stalls at farmers markets, other vendors scramble to make their displays look as good.

The amazing ability of the Hmong to coax crops that don't ordinarily thrive in diverse climates also applies to flowers. Bouquets of riotous, colorful abundance have put countless smiles on the faces of shoppers toting them home, from Modesto to Madison.

More than 2,000 acres of Asian vegetables are grown in Fresno, which is home to some of the largest Hmong populations in the country. Hmong produce is a fixture at such iconic farmers markets as the Ferry Plaza in San Francisco. According to a 2012 article by the Center for Urban Education about Sustainable Agriculture (CUESA), when the Moua family of **Chue's Farm** started selling in 1992 at the Ferry Plaza, most of their customers were Asian. Today, they are a more heterogeneous group. A few vegetables, such as bitter melon, are still purchased mostly by Asian customers, though they are winning new converts, especially among chefs.

The Twin Cities in Minnesota is where about a quarter of the country's Hmong population resides. According to Pakou Hang, director of the **Hmong American Farmers Association (HAFA)**, an estimated 500 Hmong families sell flowers and vegetables at farmers markets in the metro Minneapolis–Saint Paul region and have been doing so for almost a generation. **Mhonpaj's Garden** near Stillwater was the first Hmong farm operation in Minnesota to be certified organic.

The **HAFA Farm** is a 155-acre research and incubator farm just 15 minutes from Saint Paul. HAFA subleases the land to small family farmers and maintains multiple demonstration plots to teach Hmong farmers how to be better farmers, business operators, and stewards of the environment. HAFA uses numerous sustainable agricultural practices, including farming on the contour, planting pollinators, seeding grass roadways, composting, and using cover crops. HAFA is also the only organization in Minnesota that was started and is led by Hmong-American farmers; it is also the only one singularly focused on the advancement of Hmong-American farmers and their families.

The HAFA CSA is made up of over 30 Hmong-American farmers who primarily live in the Twin Cities but grow their produce on the HAFA Farm. HAFA also partners with various workplace wellness programs to offer a CSA to employees. Historically, Hmong farmers have preferred farmers markets to CSAs. "Literacy and language barrier are the main reasons," says Hang. "If they can't read or write in English, organizing and marketing a CSA is very difficult. A farmers market is much easier. You have your children help you fill out the farmers market application, pay a fee, and you just stand at your stall and sell."

A benefactor purchased the farm in 2014 and leased it to the association with an option to buy it in eight years. The Hmong farmers who grow crops there think it could become a model for other immigrant farmers who want to own land but lack the resources to purchase it. "We're not just about renting land," Hang says. "We are about helping families think long-term about community wealth creation, self-sufficiency, and sustainability."

Sea salt and freshly ground black pepper
1 small shallot, diced
Few drops of tarragon or white wine vinegar
Chive blossoms, to finish (optional)

1. Cook and cool the eggs, then peel and mash them with a fork, leaving some texture. Add the tarragon, chives, parsley, and mayonnaise, and mix well. Taste, add ¼ teaspoon salt, then taste again to see if more is needed.

2. Moisten the diced shallots with the vinegar and let stand for a few minutes. If you have used more than just a few drops of vinegar, drain the shallot before stirring it into the egg salad.

3. Pile the egg salad into a serving bowl and finish with chive blossoms, if desired.

— *Deborah Madison,* Vegetable Literacy

❧ *Cooking Note:* If you need to substitute something else for the tarragon, lovage is always a good choice with eggs. Use young leaves, finely chopped, in place of the tarragon. Dill is another good herb to use with eggs.

CREAMY TARRAGON CHICKEN (OR TURKEY) MEDALLIONS WITH SKILLET SWEET POTATOES AND BEANS   SERVES 4

Source Note: Tangy mustard and sweet honey make this dish high in flavor, yet easy on the salt. Boneless, skinless turkey breast, another lean protein, is a great substitute for the chicken; use the same weight and cut it into four portions.

CHICKEN OR TURKEY MEDALLIONS

1 pound chicken or turkey cutlets
¼ teaspoon freshly ground black pepper
Pinch of salt
2 teaspoons olive oil
¾ cup white wine
½ cup no-salt-added chicken broth
¼ cup whipping cream
2 tablespoons chopped fresh tarragon or 2 teaspoons dried tarragon
1 tablespoon whole-seed mustard

1. Using a meat mallet, flatten the chicken cutlets if they are thicker than 1 inch. Sprinkle with pepper and salt.

2. In a large skillet, heat the olive oil over medium-high heat; brown the chicken, turning once, 6 to 8 minutes. Add the wine and broth;

cover and cook until the chicken is no longer pink inside, about 5 minutes. Transfer to a plate and keep warm.

3. Boil the remaining pan juices until they reduce to ½ cup. Whisk in the cream, tarragon, and mustard; cook until the mixture thickens enough to coat the back of a spoon, about 2 minutes. Serve over the chicken.

SKILLET SWEET POTATOES AND BEANS

2 tablespoons olive oil
2 sweet potatoes, peeled and cut in ½-inch cubes
9 ounces green beans, cut diagonally in 1-inch pieces
1 tablespoon honey
1 tablespoon whole-seed mustard

1. In a nonstick skillet, heat the olive oil over medium-high heat. Cook the sweet potatoes, stirring occasionally, until they turn tender-crisp, about 10 minutes.

2. Add the green beans; cook for 2 minutes. Add ¼ cup water; cover and cook until the potatoes are fork-tender, about 2 minutes. Toss with the honey and mustard. Serve with the chicken.

— Amanda Barnier and The Test Kitchen, Canadian Living Magazine

Transplanting garlic at Featherstone Farm.

"I believe that if ever I had to practice cannibalism, I might manage if there were enough tarragon around."

— James Beard, American chef and food writer

Thyme

THYMUS VULGARIS

Thyme is a hardy Mediterranean herb that is related to mint. It loves arid climates and plenty of sun, which concentrate its aromatic oils. Its elliptical, gray-green leaves are tiny (only about an eighth of an inch long) and arranged along slender, woody stems that are often tipped with pale pink flowers in the summer. Many varieties of thyme exist, each with subtle differences in fragrance (orange, lemon, camphor, and caraway, to name a few). Wild thyme has a character all its own, so different from its cultivated cousins that some European herb references classify it under a separate name altogether, and its honey is sought after the world over for its uniquely herbal sweetness.

Thyme's assertiveness makes it incredibly versatile. Its distinctive, pungent odor and flavor (sometimes described as greenish with an undertone of cloves) melds beautifully with so many herbs and foods that the French consider it an essential ingredient in their famous bouquet garni, that bundle of herbs tied with string that flavors soups, stocks, and stews. Thyme also has a long medicinal history in which it has been used as an aphrodisiac and to treat melancholy, animal bites, and digestive disorders.

HISTORY

The homeland of the common or garden thyme is the western Mediterranean, although other members of the thyme family are native to North Africa and Asia. In its native countries, thyme has been treasured as medicine and a culinary herb since ancient times—Virgil, Hippocrates, and Pliny wrote of its merits in their texts, and the Egyptians used thyme oil to embalm their dead. Thyme grows wild in the Catskill Mountains in New York State, introduced when its seeds were carried in the fleece of sheep imported from England by colonial settlers.

NUTRITION

Two teaspoons of thyme contain a mere 2 calories but over 50 percent of an adult's daily requirement for vitamin K and 20 percent for iron, as well as manganese, calcium, and dietary fiber. Thymol, its primary volatile oil, possesses antioxidant, antibacterial, and antifungal properties. It is sometimes used to treat athlete's foot or is added to commercial mouthwashes and toothpastes.

SEASON

Commercially, thyme is widely grown and in season year-round. You'll find it at its best in farmers markets and CSAs throughout the summer and fall.

SELECTION

Thyme should be fresh looking and uniformly gray green, free from dark spots or yellowish leaves.

Cooking Tip

Soak sprigs of fresh herbs like oregano, thyme, marjoram, sage, or rosemary in water for an hour, shake them partially dry, and lay them on the hot coals of your grill just before cooking meat.

STORAGE

Wrap fresh, unwashed thyme in a damp paper towel in a plastic bag and store in the refrigerator vegetable crisper; use within 1 week.

TRIMMING AND CLEANING

Briefly rinse fresh thyme under running water to wash off any dust, then strip off the leaves from the stems and finely chop.

FREEZING

Thyme can be frozen while still on the branch. Just freeze whole sprigs on cookie sheets, strip off the leaves, and pack them in zipper-lock freezer or vacuum food sealer-type bags. Another easy way to freeze thyme is to place whole sprigs in a zipper-lock freezer bag, freeze, and then run a rolling pin over the unopened bag. This removes many of the leaves from the stems. You can then either continue to store the leaves in the freezer in a small bag or place them in a tightly lidded canning jar. Thyme frozen this way does not need to be thawed before using.

A terrific way to freeze thyme is to chop it finely, mix it into a paste using ⅓ cup of olive oil or cooled melted butter to every 2 cups of herbs, and then freeze the resulting mixture in ice cube trays. To thaw, simply pop out a few cubes into a strainer and let the oil melt away, or just drop them frozen into sauces, soups, stews, casseroles, and other cooked dishes.

Frozen thyme has a flavor that is superior to the dried herb, but its brownish appearance is rather unattractive, so you may want to reserve it for stews, casseroles, or other dishes where aesthetics are not critical.

DRYING

Thyme takes to drying better than most herbs, retaining more of its flavor. Tie fresh, dry sprigs that are free of dew and moisture into a bunch and hang in a cool, dry, dark place with good ventilation. You can cover the bunches with small paper bags to keep dust off them, but make sure the bags have adequate holes for proper ventilation. Once the bunches are dried, seal them tightly in a container with a lid or in a zipper-lock plastic bag and store away from light and heat, where they will keep for about 6 months.

MEASURES AND EQUIVALENTS

- 1 tablespoon fresh = ¾ teaspoon dried
- 1 fresh sprig = 1 teaspoon dried

COMPLEMENTARY HERBS, SEASONINGS, AND FOODS

Basil, beans, beef, carrots, cheese, chervil, chicken, chives, eggs, figs, fish, fruit, garlic, ginger, goat cheese, lamb, lemon, lentils, marjoram, onions, oregano, parsley, parsnips, peas, pork, potatoes, rosemary, rutabagas, sage, salads, savory, seafood, soups, stews, tomatoes, turnips, veal, venison.

SERVING SUGGESTIONS

- Thyme goes beautifully with eggs—sprinkle a little of the fresh herb on omelets, scrambled eggs, and frittatas.
- Thyme is a traditional seasoning, along with sage, in poultry stuffing.

Cooking Tip

Thyme should be added to dishes at the beginning of the cooking time, to allow its flavor to fully permeate the food.

"I know a bank where the wild thyme blows, Where oxlips and the nodding violet grows, Quite over-canopied with luscious woodbine, With sweet musk-roses and with eglantine: There sleeps Titania some time of the night, Lull'd in these flowers with dances and delight. ..."

— *William Shakespeare*, A Midsummer Night's Dream, *Act II, Scene 1*

Thyme to Be Brave

Throughout history, thyme has been associated with courage, and medieval knights setting out for battle wore scarves with embroidered sprigs of thyme.

- Thyme and oregano are a winning combination, wonderful in pasta sauces, pizzas, and other tomato-based dishes.
- Certain fruits pair beautifully with thyme; try oranges, lemons, pineapples, peaches, and mangoes.
- Thyme is excellent in herb butters, either by itself or in combination with marjoram, basil, rosemary, or sage.
- Bruise fresh thyme and tarragon together, and combine with red-wine vinegar and olive oil for a simple yet delicious salad dressing.
- Thyme goes well with many hearty root vegetables: carrots, onions, turnips, parsnips, and rutabagas.
- The woody stems of thyme can be tossed directly onto the grill to impart an aromatic, smoky flavor to meats and poultry.
- Thyme tea makes an effective cough remedy. To prepare, simply place 2 teaspoons of the dried herb in boiling water and steep for 10 minutes. Add sage if your cough is particularly potent.
- Sprinkle a teaspoon of fresh thyme over cottage cheese to add a vibrant, herbal flavor.
- Add freshly chopped thyme, basil, and parsley to cream cheese or sour cream for a delicious dip or baked potato dressing.
- Freezer bouquet garnis are handy: Tie 3 or 4 sprigs of parsley, 2 sprigs of thyme, and 1 bay leaf together with kitchen twine, pack the bouquets into zipper-lock freezer bags, and freeze. Place the garnis in sauces, stocks, soups, or stews toward the end of cooking.
- Cook kidney, pinto, and black beans with thyme.

SUBSTITUTIONS

Basil, marjoram, oregano, parsley, and savory are acceptable substitutes for thyme.

CHICKEN AND MUSHROOM RAGOUT   SERVES 6

Source Note: I developed the recipe so that it is gluten-free. I use tamari when I'm making wheat-free foods, and it's my substitute for soy sauce because soy sauce is made from wheat. If you are not on a gluten-restricted diet, you could easily make a roux out of a couple of tablespoons of all-purpose flour and butter, and use soy sauce instead of the tamari. This is really good with brown jasmine rice.

> 1 tablespoon extra-virgin olive oil
> 1½ pounds boneless and skinless chicken thighs, cut into 2-inch pieces
> ½ teaspoon kosher salt, divided
> ¼ teaspoon freshly ground black pepper
> 1 tablespoon unsalted butter
> ½ medium onion, chopped
> 2 tablespoons tomato paste
> 10 ounces cremini mushrooms, sliced
> 2 cloves garlic, minced

2 tablespoons finely chopped shallot
1 tablespoon chopped fresh thyme
1 tablespoon finely chopped fresh rosemary
2 teaspoons potato starch
2 cups chicken broth
1 tablespoon tamari or soy sauce

1. Over medium heat in a large cast-iron pan or a 3½-quart Dutch oven, add the extra-virgin olive oil. When it is hot and shimmering, add the chicken, ¼ teaspoon of the kosher salt, and the black pepper. Cook until the chicken is no longer pink but not yet cooked through, about 10 minutes.

2. Remove the chicken from the pan. Do not wipe out the pan. Add the butter to the pan, then the onion, tomato paste, and remaining ¼ teaspoon kosher salt; stir to combine. Add the mushrooms, garlic, shallot, thyme, and rosemary.

3. Sauté the vegetables for 2 minutes, then add the chicken back into the pan and sauté with the vegetables until the mushrooms are soft, about 5 minutes.

4. In a separate bowl, whisk the potato starch into the chicken broth. Add the chicken broth mixture into the pan with all of the ingredients. Bring the ragout to a boil. When it boils, turn the heat down to medium low, and simmer. Stir the tamari into the ragout. Continue to simmer for another 10 to 15 minutes, or until the chicken is done.

5. Serve with brown rice, French bread, or slices of tube polenta that have been fried in olive oil and butter.

— *Tram Le*, Nutrition to Kitchen *blog*

. . . .

THYME AND MUSHROOM GRAVY   MAKES ABOUT 2½ CUPS

Author Note: Bragg Liquid Aminos is a liquid protein formula derived from soybeans; it makes a great savory seasoning alternative to soy sauce, which contains gluten. To make a totally gluten-free gravy, substitute potato starch for the regular wheat flour, and use Bragg instead of soy sauce.

2 tablespoons olive oil
1 small yellow onion, sliced
2 teaspoons fresh thyme leaves
1 bay leaf
1 cup coarsely chopped mushrooms
2 tablespoons all-purpose flour or potato starch
½ cup port wine
1 cup vegetable stock
2 tablespoons dark soy sauce or **Bragg Liquid Aminos**

endured by this largely invisible population. Contrary to what some may believe, these people do not come to America simply to glean money. Depending on their home country, their villages and cities are often rife with crime, political persecution, violence, scarce employment opportunities, economic instability, and extreme poverty on a scale unimaginable to most of us. Coming to the United States to work is one way of escaping a life that really has no viable future for themselves or their children. Many of these workers have farms in their own home countries and are already skilled in agriculture, but in a twist of deep irony, unfair trade agreements between the United States and Mexico prevent them from earning enough money from their own farming to make a decent living.

Although legal workers are able to safely enter America, their undocumented counterparts risk their lives and life savings to cross the border. Swimming across rivers and trekking deserts, hundreds die every year from heatstroke, dehydration, and direct violence at the hands of predatory Mexican and American assailants in the borderlands.

Once they have survived the border crossing and managed to not be deported, they often face discrimination at every conceivable level. Depending on the labor hierarchy and management policies of the farms on which they work, they may be abused physically; forced to work without breaks; live in substandard housing with no heating, air conditioning, or barely any running water; and denied medical care or other basic health services. They often cannot advocate for better working or safety conditions, as their employers can play the "deportation card" and threaten to report them to the authorities. They are frequently marginalized and even criminalized in their communities, members of which deliberately (or unwittingly) take advantage of these workers' uncertain legal status to perpetrate systematic human trafficking and subjugation.

As you might imagine, their physical and mental suffering can be profound. They experience severe repetitive-motion issues, joint and muscle problems, and the effects of repeated exposure to toxic pesticides. They are often separated from their families for years at a time, live under the constant psychological threat of potentially being deported (or reported), and endure the rigors and instability of life on the move as seasonal work takes them to different places.

All of this on top of the fact that they are among the very lowest-paid workers in America, below that of even restaurant dishwashers. The average immigrant farmworker makes just $11,000 a year.

We may think that immigrant farmworkers are a fixture just on large-scale, monoculture agricultural operations, such as those in California's Central Valley, but in fact they work everywhere, including on a number of the CSA farms listed in this book. Regardless of the size and type of farm, the need for and importance of these workers is undeniable. Machines simply cannot accomplish many field tasks, especially with delicate crops; an enormous amount of hand labor is required. Without millions of these workers to cultivate and harvest every year, American agriculture and our current food systems—right down to our grocery stores, restaurants, farmers markets, and our own dinner tables—simply couldn't exist.

Farmers and workers alike would like nothing better than for immigrants to have an easier means of obtaining legal status. However, as of 2015, American immigration policy makes it extremely difficult for immigrants to be legal, unless they have high levels of education, money, white-collar employment prospects, or provable evidence of persecution in their home countries. Even

1. Over medium heat, heat the olive oil in a large saucepan and add the onion. Sauté until the onions turn golden.

2. Add the thyme, bay leaf, and mushrooms, and cook until the mushrooms have softened, about 5 minutes. Sprinkle in the flour and stir to combine; then add the wine, vegetable stock, and soy sauce or Braggs. Simmer, stirring until the gravy has thickened slightly, about 3 to 5 minutes.

3. Remove the bay leaf. Pour into a gravy boat and serve.

— *Recipezaar.com*

COMPOUND GARLIC-HERB BUTTER   MAKES 1 CUP

Source Note: This easy compound butter is terrific for steak, corn, turkey, fish, other vegetables, and even bread.

1 cup (2 sticks) unsalted butter, at room temperature
1 tablespoon rosemary, finely chopped
1 tablespoon thyme, finely chopped
5 cloves garlic, finely minced

1. In a large bowl, combine the butter, rosemary, thyme, and garlic. Use a spatula to combine all of the ingredients well.

2. Scoop the mixture onto a sheet of wax or parchment paper. Roll into a log and twist the ends shut.

3. Place in the refrigerator for 2 hours, or until the butter is firm.

Cooking Note: To use for turkey or chicken: Before roasting, carefully lift up the skin on the breast of the turkey and place slices of the compound butter between the meat and the skin. To use for steak: Place the desired amount atop the steaks right after they come off the grill. Allow the butter to melt before serving.

— *Ashley Wagner,* CentercutCook *blog*

ROASTED CHICKEN WITH LEMON AND THYME   SERVES 4

Source Note: There is nothing more satisfying than a simple roasted chicken. Serve with garlic mashed potatoes.

1 lemon
Fresh thyme (5 to 7 large sprigs), leaves stripped from
**   2 to 3 sprigs and finely chopped; other sprigs left whole**
3 tablespoons (about ⅓ stick) softened butter
1 organic whole chicken

Salt and freshly ground black pepper

1. Cut the lemon into quarters and squeeze 2 teaspoons of juice from one of the quarters into a small bowl. Mix the lemon juice with 2 teaspoons of the chopped fresh thyme, then stir both into the softened butter.

2. Preheat the oven to 425°F. Dry the chicken inside and out. Rub the softened butter under the breast skin and all over the outside of the chicken. Season the outside and inside of the chicken with salt and pepper, then place several sprigs of thyme and the remaining three lemon quarters inside the cavity.

3. Place the chicken (your choice of whether to place the breast side up or down) on a baking sheet or shallow-sided roasting pan. Roast it on the middle oven rack for 20 minutes. Reduce the oven temperature to 350°F and continue to roast until the skin is a deep golden brown and the legs move freely when jiggled, about 45 minutes more for a 3½-pound bird. The thickest part of the breast meat should register an internal temperature of 160°F.

4. Let the chicken rest at least 20 minutes before carving.

— *Mariquita Farm, Watsonville, California*

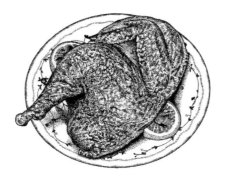

if an immigrant worker has family members who are legal citizens or hold permanent US residency, it is very difficult to get legal status.

There is the federal agricultural guest worker H-2A program, but to participate, both farms and workers must comply with—and prove—a long list of conditions. Red tape and bureaucratic delays are common. In the fields, harvests wait for no one, and many farms simply cannot afford such delay. It results in a horrible situation for both; farmers often want their workforce to be entirely legal and take steps to "do the right thing," but the current system often does not allow for timely execution of this process. And just because workers are legal under the H-2A program does not mean that they are protected by workplace laws and not abused. In fact, the opposite is true, and even over the course of its three decades, the program's protections continue to be so modest as to be essentially ineffectual.

Current American immigration policy means that farms cannot rely on a stable workforce from year to year. Workers live in constant fear of getting caught and deported, and as employers, farms risk breaking the law and incurring huge penalties. Farms frequently cannot find legal alternatives (i.e., drawing from a legal worker pool). Even a couple of missing workers during crucial picking times can mean lost revenue and increased labor for others on many levels. This system works for no one, and it enables labor and humanitarian injustice to continue on an incomprehensible scale.

An immigrant worker was very likely to be the last human to physically touch your blueberry or cherry tomato. Nearly every fruit and vegetable on your plate involved such a worker in some part of the process. It's high time we honor and advocate for these invisible workers in truly respectful, meaningful ways, both big and small.

Tomatoes

Tomatoes are so popular in European and American cuisines that it is easy to forget that at one time (not so long ago in some places) they were considered lethally poisonous. A member of the Solanaceae family, which includes peppers, potatoes, and eggplants, tomatoes were thought to be toxic because of their kinship to the deadly nightshade. Their leaves and stems are indeed poisonous, and apparently few thought to sample the fruit. Thus, for centuries tomatoes were grown strictly for their ornamental value.

Happily, tomatoes are now a staple in many parts of the world. They rank as the number-one vegetable grown in home gardens in the United States, and they are surpassed in commercial cultivation only by the potato, with over three billion pounds harvested annually.

Unfortunately, tomatoes are also a prime example of the follies of commercial production; modern breeding techniques have created tomatoes that are impressively durable and gorgeously appetizing in every way except flavor—we are all familiar with those plastic supermarket beauties that have literally no taste. And these conventionally grown tomatoes are raised with the help of literally tons of pesticides and fungicides, including some of the most toxic in the agricultural industry.

Luckily, this is where farmers markets, CSAs, and home growers fulfill our craving for that ubiquitous yet fleeting summer treat—a deeply colored, richly fragrant tomato ready to explode with juice and flavor.

Technically a fruit rather than a vegetable, tomatoes come in literally thousands of varieties, but they all fall into one of several categories. There are our familiar slicers, the diminutive but sweet cherries, the paste or Roma (a drier variety used for sauces), the lusciously flavorful heirlooms, and yellow and orange varieties, which contain less acid than red varieties. Each has its own characteristics and uses in the kitchen.

Here is a rundown of the most common hybrids, heirlooms, and cherry tomatoes you might find in your CSA box or at your farmers market.

Hybrids or Red Slicers

These are familiar to us as the common supermarket tomato, with uniformly red skins and flesh. Some CSA farmers grow their hybrids directly in the soil, but in greenhouses rather than the field. The greenhouses offer additional protection and an earlier start to the growing season. The skins on these tomatoes can be a bit thick, but the flavor of CSA farm–grown specimens can be wonderful (unlike those tasteless balls in the grocery stores).

Heirlooms

The wild children of the tomato world, heirlooms come in fantastic shapes and colors but have a true tomato flavor that rivals any hybrid. Some heirloom varieties you may find in your box:

- **Aunt Ruby's Green:** This is a large, green slicing tomato with a rich flavor.

- **Brandywine:** This large, pinkish-red variety started the heirloom craze. Its very rich tomato taste is only slightly sweet but has a nice acidic burst.

- **Cherokee Purple:** This is a large, roundish tomato with a red-brown-purple color; a rich, sharp, acidic flavor; and unbelievable body.

- **German Stripe:** This variety has green, yellow, and orange stripes! It is a large, very sweet tomato.

- **Green Zebra:** A small, green-striped tomato, zebras have a unique flavor that some claim is the best in the hybrid world.

- **Red Zebra:** This is the red version of the Green Zebra, with beautiful orange-red-green stripes and a very sweet, true tomato flavor.

- **Roma:** The Romas are long, cylindrical, drier-fleshed tomatoes that are typically used to make sauces and tomato paste. Three of the most common Roma varieties are San Marzano, Amish Paste, and Yellow. The San Marzanos have more flavor than the Amish Paste, but the latter has a better texture for cooking down into paste. The Amish Paste is skinnier than the San Marzanos. The Yellows are, well, yellow with a very mild flavor.

Cherry Tomatoes

These are the sweet, succulent, bite-size red and orange fruits of summer. The modern Sungold variety was developed in Japan, and its distinctive golden yellow-orange fruit bursts in the mouth with startling sweetness and subtle tropical undertones. Hot, dry summers produce the most flavorful, disease-free fruit.

Red grape cherry tomatoes aren't as sweet as the orange Sungolds, but they are very resilient and tasty nonetheless, great for grilling on kebabs, tossing with pasta, or simply eating straight from the box.

HISTORY

Tomatoes originated most likely in South America and Mexico and were possibly cultivated in both areas. When the Spaniards conquered much of the Americas, they found this New World fruit quite palatable and later distributed it to their colonies in the Philippines and the Caribbean. They also introduced it to Europe, where the heat-loving plants thrived in the Mediterranean climate.

Although the English were growing tomatoes for decoration by the beginning of the 1600s, they refused to eat them for many decades, thanks to an herbal text written by an influential physician who knew that tomatoes were eaten in Italy and Spain but still believed they were poisonous. This English belief persisted when the British colonies brought tomatoes to North America in the early 1700s.

With the exception of a few European-cultured people like Thomas Jefferson, Americans grew tomatoes primarily for ornamental value rather than as food. In the 1800s, fortunes turned for the better for tomatoes when farmers began experimenting with different varieties and uses in the kitchen, and the myths of old were finally banished. In 1897, a chemist

Cherry Tomatoes and Pesticides

Conventionally grown cherry tomatoes are on the "Dirty Dozen" list—meaning they are very high in pesticide and herbicide residues.

This residue is particularly harmful to children, as well as to adults with health issues. Purchase organic cherry tomatoes whenever possible.

Cooking Tip

Do not cook tomatoes in aluminum cookware, as their acidity may leach the metal into the food, causing both an unpleasant taste and unwanted health effects.

at the Joseph Campbell & Co. in New Jersey devised a way to efficiently process canned tomatoes and other food ingredients into condensed soups. The rest, as they say, is history.

NUTRITION

The nutritional value of tomatoes has been well-publicized because of studies on their lycopene content. This carotenoid has extensive antioxidant properties, possibly reducing the incidence and severity of many organ cancers, especially prostate. Lycopene is also important to eye health, particularly in warding off macular degeneration. Tomato juice consumption has been shown to reduce blood clotting and inflammation. Cooked tomato products, such as sauce or juice, contain up to five times more lycopene than the raw fruit, because the intense heat breaks down the cell walls and releases this compound. Interestingly, organic red and purple ketchups contain much more lycopene than their nonorganic counterparts.

Tomatoes are also rich in vitamins A, C, and K, as well as potassium, magnesium, dietary fiber, chromium, folate, thiamine, iron, and copper—all for just 37 calories a cup.

SEASON

Commercially, tomatoes are widely grown and in season year-round, much to the regret of many consumers. However, you'll find them at their true best in farmers markets and CSAs throughout the summer and early fall.

SELECTION

For maximum nutritional value, choose tomatoes with the richest, darkest color, which indicates high levels of lycopene. Tomatoes should be uniformly firm with no soft or bruised spots (although ripe specimens should yield slightly to fingertip pressure), no wrinkles, and no signs of decay. Although most books recommend avoiding tomatoes with cracks or splits, many heirloom and beefsteak varieties are naturally prone to cracking, especially if they received inconsistent watering during their development. Cracked tomatoes are still perfectly edible as long as they are not rotting or decaying; they simply will not keep as long, and you should use them right away.

STORAGE

Store tomatoes at room temperature for the best flavor and ripeness; refrigeration tends to make them mealy. If they are not overripe, they will keep for up to 1 week. Tomatoes continue to ripen if stored away from sunlight at temperatures of 60 to 75°F. Tucking an apple or banana among them and storing them in a paper bag hastens ripening, because these fruits release ethylene gas. If you must store overripe tomatoes in the refrigerator, keep them in a warmer section, like the butter compartment.

TRIMMING AND CLEANING

Most tomatoes need little more than a good washing before a bit of trimming to cut out the green stem end. If you want to peel tomatoes easily, blanch them in boiling water for 30 to 45 seconds and then im-

Books

Tomato:
A Fresh-from-the-Vine Cookbook
Lawrence Davis-Hollander,
Storey Publishing LLC, 2010.

The French Kitchen Cookbook:
Recipes and Lessons from Paris
and Provence
Patricia Wells,
HarperCollins, 2013.

The Heirloom Tomato Cookbook
Mimi Luebbermann,
Chronicle Books, 2006.

The Tomato Festival Cookbook:
150 Recipes that Make the Most of
Your Crop of Lush, Vine-Ripened,
Sun-Warmed, Fat, Juicy, Ready-to-
Burst Heirloom Tomatoes
Lawrence Davis-Hollander,
Storey Publishing, 2004.

In Praise of Tomatoes: Tasty Recipes,
Garden Secrets, Legends & Lore
Ronni Lundy,
Lark Books, 2006.

mediately rinse them in cold running water. Insert a paring knife under the skins, which will slip off easily.

STIR-FRYING AND SAUTÉING

Tomatoes make a delicious, healthful addition to your favorite stir-fry. Simply slice and toss in with other vegetables, some olive oil, and fresh herbs; sauté or stir-fry for 5 to 7 minutes over high heat.

BAKING AND ROASTING

Baked tomatoes are a pleasant change of pace as an easy-to-make side dish. Simply preheat the oven to 375°F, halve the tomatoes crosswise (not through the stem), and place them, cut sides up, in a baking dish lined with either cooking parchment paper or a silicone baking mat. Sprinkle them with olive oil, herbs, salt, pepper, and grated Parmesan cheese, and bake uncovered for about 30 minutes. Other variations for toppings include butter, cinnamon, sugar, and breadcrumbs.

To roast tomatoes quickly, preheat the oven to 400°F, halve them crosswise and place them, cut sides down, in a glass pan or parchment-paper–lined metal pan (do not let the tomatoes directly touch the metal). Brush them with olive oil and roast for 30 minutes. Let cool, then peel.

Slow-roasting is a luscious way of cooking tomatoes, since it caramelizes their natural sugars and makes them even more sweet and piquant. To slow-roast, preheat the oven to 225°F; slice the tomatoes crosswise, push out the seeds and juices, and place them on a parchment-paper–lined baking sheet. Sprinkle them with olive oil, salt, pepper, sugar, cayenne pepper, and fresh herbs, and bake for 2 to 4 hours. These roasted beauties will keep for up to 1 week in the refrigerator, or 6 months in the freezer.

BRAISING AND STEWING

Slowly braising tomatoes concentrates their flavors, making a rich-tasting side dish or a great foundation for a vegetable sauce. To braise, place tomatoes (plum or Roma types work best) in a baking pan with enough olive oil to reach halfway up the tomatoes. Cover them with sautéed garlic and onion if desired, and braise them in a 250°F oven for 2½ to 3 hours, turning occasionally.

Or you can stew tomatoes by cutting them into pieces, combining them with salt, pepper, sugar, butter, onion, and bell pepper, if desired, and simmering in a medium saucepan for 15 to 20 minutes, stirring occasionally.

BLANCHING AND FREEZING

Tomatoes can be frozen, although their taste and texture suffer somewhat; the resulting mushy product is best only for sauces or well-cooked tomato dishes. But freezing can be a good, quick way to preserve summer's bountiful harvests when tomatoes are coming in thick and fast.

Raw tomatoes can be frozen whole without blanching or peeling; just wash them, cut away the stem ends, place them on a cookie sheet, freeze, and place them in zipper-lock freezer or vacuum food sealer-type bags, or freezer containers. Squeeze out any excess air and leave 1 inch of headspace (unless you are using the vacuum sealing method). Frozen tomatoes will keep for up to 6 months at 0°F.

The State of the Tomato

The South Arkansas Vine Ripe Pink Tomato was adopted as the Arkansas state fruit and vegetable in 1987. The Pink Tomato Festival is held each year in Bradley County.

V8, Anyone?

Tomato juice is the official state beverage of Ohio.

"It's not hard to breed a tomato that looks great and tastes like hell."

— *Charles M. Rick,*
preeminent US tomato breeder

Tiny and Tubby

The fruits of the smallest species of tomato measure less than ¾ inch in diameter.

The largest is the Ponderosa, the fruits of which regularly weigh in at over a pound.

The heaviest tomato ever recorded weighed a whopping 7 pounds, 12 ounces, of the cultivar "Delicious," grown in Oklahoma in 1986.

Now, That's a Lot of Tomatoes

The largest tomato plant ever recorded was a Sungold that reached 65 feet long, grown by a British hydroponics company.

To peel frozen tomatoes, simply run warm water over the frozen fruit until their skins slip off easily. Or, if you prefer to peel the tomatoes before freezing, dip the raw fruit in boiling water for 30 to 45 seconds; then immediately rinse them in cold running water. Insert a paring knife under the skins, which will slip off like a glove.

DRYING

Dried tomatoes are concentrated summer, with an intense flavor and a versatility that is hard to beat. To get around the priciness of commercial sun-dried tomatoes or if you have an overabundance from your garden, you can dry your own using the sun, a food dehydrator, or your oven. Plum-type or Roma tomatoes work best for drying because of their thicker, meatier walls and fewer seeds. Sungold cherry tomatoes also produce wonderful, candy-like fruits. A pound of fresh fruit will yield about 1 ounce dried.

Drying tomatoes in the sun is easy, but it requires a climate that will kindly oblige with a number of contiguous days of temperatures in the 90s and less than 20 percent humidity. Wash and dry the tomatoes well, and slice them ½- to ¼-inch thick and as uniformly as possible. Plum-type tomatoes should be halved or quartered lengthwise, and cherry tomatoes can be halved or left whole. Arrange the tomato slices in a single layer about 1 inch apart on plastic mesh screens (do not use metal wire ones, as the acid in the tomatoes may react with the metal and produce an off taste). Lay cheesecloth over the fruits to protect them, and place the trays in an area that receives reflective full sun, like a stone patio. Elevate the trays so air circulates underneath them, and bring them indoors every evening or if rain is forecast. The tomatoes should dry to a leathery but soft texture in 3 days to 1 week, depending on their water content, thickness, and the weather. Less moisture present in the final product means less of a possibility of spoilage and bacteria.

Oven-drying in a regular or convection home oven is a convenient method if you live where the weather is uncooperative. Preheat the oven to 140 to 145°F, and place the fruits on a plastic-mesh screen or on a parchment paper–lined baking sheet. Prop open the oven door slightly, check the fruit regularly, and rotate the tray occasionally. Oven-drying can take between 6 and 12 hours, depending on the tomatoes' moisture content. They are done when they are dry, leathery, and pliable, but not sticky.

If you have a food dehydrator, follow the manufacturer's instructions. Good-quality dehydrators usually produce the best, most evenly dried fruits.

Once they are dried, keep the tomatoes in airtight bags in a cool, dry place for up to 6 months, or refrigerated for up to 8 months. They can be rehydrated in water, bouillon, stock, or wine for 1 to 2 hours, or tossed into soups and stews during the last 30 minutes of cooking. Or add them to pastas, sandwiches, sauces, and salads.

MICROWAVING

Core and halve the tomatoes, and dot them with butter or sprinkle with olive oil. Place in a microwave-safe dish and microwave on high power.

- 4 halves = 3 to 4 minutes
- 6 to 8 halves = 5 to 6 minutes

Measures and Equivalents

- 3 to 4 medium globe tomatoes = 1 pound = 2 cups chopped
- 1 large tomato = 1 cup chopped
- 8 small plum tomatoes = 1 pound
- 25 to 30 cherry tomatoes = 1 pound = 2½ cups chopped tomatoes
- 1 pound fresh = 2 cups chopped
- 1 cup canned tomatoes = 1½ cups fresh, chopped, cooked tomatoes
- 1 (16-ounce) can = 2 cups undrained or 1½ cups drained
- 1 (28-ounce) can = 3 cups undrained = 2 to 2½ cups drained
- 1 (6-ounce) can tomato paste = ¾ cup
- ⅜ cup of tomato paste plus ½ cup water = 1 cup tomato sauce

Complementary Herbs, Seasonings, and Foods

Anchovies, arugula, avocados, bacon, balsamic vinegar, basil, bay leaf, beans, beef, breadcrumbs, butter, cheese (Cheddar, cottage, feta, Gruyère, mozzarella, Parmesan), chiles, chives, cilantro, cream, cucumbers, dill, eggplant, eggs, garlic, honey, lemon, lovage, marjoram, mint, mushrooms, nutmeg, olive oil, olives, onions, oregano, parsley, pasta, peppers, potatoes, rosemary, saffron, seafood, shallots, smoked salt, sugar, summer squash, tarragon, thyme, vinegar, zucchini.

Serving Suggestions

- Try serving a traditional English breakfast: Fry up bacon in a pan and reserve the fat to fry thick slices of sourdough or French bread until crisp. Serve with poached eggs and grilled tomato slices on the side.
- Add whole cherry tomatoes to kebabs.
- Top sliced tomatoes with thin slices of Cheddar, American, or mozzarella cheese, and broil until the tomatoes become soft and the cheese is melted and bubbly.
- Who says BLTs are just for sandwiches? Try a bacon, lettuce, and tomato salad, along with hard-boiled eggs and a little of the bacon drippings added to the dressing.
- Stuffed tomatoes are a classic: Fill them with ground beef, bacon, rice, spinach, or, for a vegetarian version, cracked wheat.
- For that quintessential Italian appetizer, bruschetta, top grilled or toasted slices of garlic-and-oil-rubbed baguette with diced fresh, ripe, peeled tomatoes that have been combined with olive oil, salt, pepper, and fresh herbs.
- Combine fresh tomato puree, mint, sugar, champagne, and fresh lemon juice for a refreshing sorbet.
- For a stunning dish that will delight guests, slice and combine different-colored heirlooms on a platter for a "tomato tasting." Try pairing with different flavorful olive oils and balsamic vinegars poured into separate dipping bowls and served on the side.
- One little-known use for tomatoes (and condensed tomato soup) is to add moisture (but not necessarily tomato flavor) to baked goods, like cakes and breads, even puddings.
- Green and yellow tomatoes, with their low acidity and fresh tomato taste, make great toppers for eggs and enchiladas.
- Add zip to tuna salad by adding chopped fresh tomatoes, green onions, and a touch of chopped fresh basil.
- Make salsa!

"It's difficult to think anything but pleasant thoughts while eating a homegrown tomato."

— *Lewis Grizzard, American writer and humorist*

You Are What You Eat

Each man, woman, and child in America consumes almost 80 pounds of tomatoes every year.

We usually don't think about CSAs in the land of paradise, but the same climate that makes people flock to Hawaiian beaches in droves also makes it a natural for farming year-round.

When it comes to food systems, Hawaii is an odd paradox. Imagine a place where, thanks to its warm temperatures, constant rain and sun, and rich volcanic soil, most fruits and vegetables grow like weeds, often producing several harvests a year. Its islands are practically overrun by feral chickens, pigs, goats, and deer, and its oceans teem with a wealth of delicious fish and shellfish.

Why is it, then, that nearly 90 percent of Hawaii's food is imported? Massive container ships and airplanes bring in about 6 million pounds a day to feed the state's residents and visitors at a cost of over $3 billion. Much of this food is highly processed and full of refined sugar, flour, fat, sodium, additives, and preservatives. Not only that, but it is very expensive, thanks to high shipping costs and taxes; bringing it to the islands uses staggering amounts of fossil fuels. And Hawaii's native and local populations are paying the price quite literally with their lives—obesity, diabetes, high blood pressure, and heart disease run nearly as rampant as the wild chickens on Kauai.

For thousands of years, native Hawaiians grew their own food, eating mostly taro, fish, pigs, chickens, breadfruit, bananas, sweet potatoes, and other fruits and vegetables. It was a healthful if somewhat bland diet. With the arrival of both early Europeans and the American military, new foods were introduced and tastes changed. The natives developed an insatiable hankering for salt, fat, and sugar that continues to this day, with disastrous conse-

- Fried green tomatoes are a classic, and a good way to use up those straggler tomatoes of fall that won't ripen before frost.

- Roasted tomatoes are wonderful in little savory tarts. Try using whole cherry tomatoes and Sungolds for a beautiful presentation.

- It's hard to beat the classic Caprese salad. Layer thick rounds of the best mozzarella cheese you can find with slices of vine-ripened tomatoes (heirlooms are amazing for this dish) and leaves of fresh basil, drizzle with a high-quality extra-virgin olive oil, and add a sprinkling of freshly ground black pepper and sea salt. A drizzle of balsamic vinegar is tasty, too.

- Tomatoes are versatile in soups and stews. Try unusual variations with chayotes, bitter melon, cucumbers, curry, and cumin.

- Tomatoes are fantastic in cold vegetable soups. Blend with cucumbers, onions, garlic, jalapeños, cilantro, and olive oil for a refreshing gazpacho on a hot summer day.

- If you're preparing tomatoes and find yourself squeezing out or otherwise removing the seeds, capture those seeds with their juices in a small bowl. Then push them through a fine-mesh strainer. The tasty, acidic juice you collect can enhance your sauce, soup, or salad dressing.

COLORFUL HEIRLOOM TOMATO SALAD   SERVES 6 TO 8

Source Note: The red, yellow, and orange tomatoes make this stunning salad extra flavorful and beautiful.

8 to 10 small heirloom tomatoes, in a variety of colors if possible
2 cloves garlic, finely minced
¼ cup diced sweet onion or purple onion
1 tablespoon chopped fresh parsley
1 tablespoon chopped fresh basil, or 1 teaspoon dried basil
2 tablespoons red wine vinegar
3 tablespoons extra-virgin olive oil
½ to 1 teaspoon salt
¼ teaspoon freshly ground black pepper

Cut the cores from the tomatoes; slice each tomato into 8 to 10 wedges. Combine with the remaining ingredients in a large bowl; toss to blend well. Cover and refrigerate for at least 1 hour before serving. Serve on salad greens, if desired.

— *Teena's Pride CSA, Homestead, Florida*

HEIRLOOM TOMATO SALAD DRESSING   MAKES 3½ CUPS

3 cups chopped yellow or orange heirloom tomatoes
1 generous sprig fresh basil leaves
1 teaspoon salt
⅛ teaspoon cayenne

2 cloves garlic
¼ cup plus 1 tablespoon apple cider vinegar
½ cup organic canola oil

Put all of the ingredients into a blender and blend for a full minute, or until the mixture is creamy. Pour into a narrow-necked bottle and shake well before serving. Refrigerate any leftovers; it keeps about 5 days.

— *Teena's Pride CSA, Homestead, Florida*

TOMATOES STUFFED WITH BLUE CHEESE AND WALNUTS

SERVES 4

2 large tomatoes (about 1 pound)
Salt
¼ pound blue cheese
¼ cup chopped walnuts
¼ cup dry breadcrumbs
1 tablespoon chopped fresh parsley
¼ teaspoon freshly ground black pepper
Olive oil

1. Preheat the oven to 400°F.

2. Cut the tomatoes in half horizontally. Remove the seeds but leave the flesh intact. Sprinkle the tomatoes with salt and let them drain upside down for 30 minutes.

3. Crumble the cheese into a small bowl and stir in the walnuts, breadcrumbs, parsley, and pepper. Pat the tomatoes dry and mound the cheese mixture on top, pushing some into the cavities. Brush the tomatoes with oil, and place them on a lightly oiled baking sheet.

4. Bake until the tomatoes are tender and soft, and their tops are golden brown, about 10 to 12 minutes.

— *Arlayne Fleming*

BAKED HONEY TOMATOES

SERVES 8

Source Note: A lot of people don't realize how well the flavors of tomato and honey go together. These are easy to make, and once cooked may even wait if your timing of some other part of the meal is slightly off.

8 ripe medium tomatoes
½ cup fresh coarse breadcrumbs
2 teaspoons salt

quences to public health.

If any place could develop food independence to help lower costs, improve quality of life, and even weather climate-related catastrophes, it should be Hawaii. But the islands' dependence on external, imported food has left it both extremely vulnerable and unhealthy.

Hawaiian agriculture has traditionally meant sugarcane, pineapple, coffee, and tree fruits grown by multinational corporations running colossal plantations and packing plants. Many of these, however, have been abandoned as globalization has made it impossible for Hawaii to compete with other countries with cheaper labor. Unfortunately, a large proportion of the islands' limited agricultural land acreage is inaccessible because it is either locked up in these defunct plantations or owned by companies like Monsanto that produce genetically engineered crops; they have found Hawaii an ideal place to test new varieties because of its year-round growing season.

In spite of all of this, efforts to grow local, organic food have been flourishing in recent years. It is not easy, as everything from fertilizer to diesel fuel has to be imported at high cost. Sustainable agriculture really requires sustainable energy, and although a few farms have implemented hydroelectricity and other energy sources, progress on a larger scale is often slow.

On Oahu, the Hawaiian government and local farmers have teamed up to transform a former pineapple plantation 20 miles north of Honolulu into the innovative Whitmore Project, a place where fish, vegetables, fruit, and other foods can be raised and produced using shared technology and facilities.

And the taste and demand for local food is burgeoning by leaps and bounds. Restaurant chefs, wholesale grocers, and farmers markets are all doing their part to educate the public and promote and carry local produce as much as possible. It's paying off—supply can hardly keep up with demand in some places.

This book features the story of one unique CSA, **Kahumana Farm** (see pages 384–394), whose origins began in providing transitional housing for Oahu's homeless and disenfranchised. And **Kanalani Ohana Farm** on the Big Island offers Kona coffee and jam CSAs (see the sidebar on page 188).

Because of the difficulty that small, individual farmers and food producers have in efficiently marketing their products on their own, Hawaiian CSAs often take the form of co-ops or larger farms that promote and distribute from smaller entities all over the islands. One such place is **Kula Fields Farmshop** in Maui, which serves the islands of Oahu, Maui, and Lana'i. Kula Fields carries fruits, vegetables, jams, eggs, cheeses, baked goods, meats, coffee and teas, condiments, peanut butter, jams and jellies, sea salts, and honey—all of which are locally grown or produced. They offer local delivery services, or they can ship to the mainland as well.

Another is **Kauai Roots Farm Co-op**, which helps local Kauai farms connect with customers through shared marketing and distribution resources. It also assists farmers in obtaining volume discounts on farm supplies and shipping rates, an ever-present expense in the Hawaiian Islands, and is the first and only farm on the island to take SNAP vouchers (formerly known as food stamps).

The **Mala 'Ai 'Opio Community Food Systems Initiative**, or **MA'O**, was established in 2001 in the Waianae area of Oahu to build community by involving underprivileged youth, sustainable eco-

2 teaspoons freshly ground black pepper
2 tablespoons fresh tarragon or 1 tablespoon dried tarragon
4 teaspoons honey
4 teaspoons unsalted butter

1. Preheat the oven to 350°F. Slice off the stem ends of the tomatoes and carefully scoop out the seeds. Place, open sides up, in a buttered baking dish.

2. Mix the breadcrumbs with the salt, pepper, and tarragon. Drizzle the honey over the tomatoes, rubbing it down into the cavities. Sprinkle the tomatoes with the crumb mixture and dot with butter.

3. Bake, uncovered, for 30 minutes, until the tomato skins begin to wrinkle. Place under the broiler for another 5 minutes, or until the crumbs begin to brown. Serve hot or at room temperature.

— *Lee Bailey*, Lee Bailey's Southern Food

TOMATO, ONION, AND CUCUMBER SALAD

Source Note: This salad is eaten throughout the Mediterranean in slightly different variations. It is easy to make and does not need any particularly exotic ingredients. The only requirements are that its components be the best quality possible, and that the diner appreciates flavors as fresh as the morning sun.

Fresh ripe tomatoes
Fresh cucumbers
White, red, or sweet onion
Extra-virgin olive oil (use the very best quality you can afford)
Sea salt or seasoned salt
Freshly ground black pepper
Fresh basil, torn or chopped

Slice the vegetables in the proportions and shapes desired. Drizzle with olive oil—not too much but not too little, either. Season with salt, pepper, and basil to taste. (When I am about to sneeze is how I know I have put enough pepper on my salad. And then maybe a little more.)

— *Mi Ae Lipe*

GOLDEN GAZPACHO   SERVES 4 TO 6

2 pints (4 cups) Sungold cherry tomatoes
1 cup peeled cucumber chunks

½ cup red or green bell pepper chunks
1 whole scallion (green onion)
1 tablespoon red wine vinegar
2 teaspoons olive oil
1 clove garlic, minced
¼ teaspoon salt

Place all of the ingredients in a blender or a food processor fitted with a steel blade. Cover and process until the mixture is almost smooth but still retains some texture. Chill for at least 1 hour to let the flavors blend.

➤ *Variation:* For a spicier version, add ½ jalapeño pepper or ⅛ to ¼ teaspoon ground red pepper, and a small bunch of fresh, chopped cilantro.

— *Colleen Wolner, Blue Heron Coffeehouse, Winona, Minnesota*

SOUTHWESTERN TOMATO JAM MAKES ABOUT 1 PINT

Source Note: This is a bit of a variation on a theme. The "sweet heat" from the Hatch variety of green chile adds a bit of complexity without being overpowering. Here are a few ideas of what to do with your Southwestern Tomato Jam: spread on toast in the morning; spread on top of your morning eggs; as a condiment on your breakfast sandwich or breakfast burrito; as a layer in a vegetable casserole; as an alternative to tomato paste in meat loaf or hamburger patties; grill a steak with a little salt, pepper, and rosemary, and top with tomato jam; with spicy sausage-stuffed empanadas; married to goat cheese in a fried egg sandwich; glazed on pork ribs; slipped into a BLT sandwich; as a dressing ingredient for a fresh vinaigrette to go with a green salad; and as an excellent glaze for a ham.

    3 pounds diced tomatoes
    1 cup diced Hatch green chiles
    ¾ cup organic brown sugar
    ¼ cup honey (I use Trader Joe's Mostly Mesquite Honey)
    ¼ cup apple cider vinegar
    2 tablespoons grated fresh ginger
    1 teaspoon ground cumin
    1 teaspoon sea salt

1. In a large saucepan, combine the tomatoes and green chiles.

2. Add the remaining ingredients. Bring the mixture to a boil, then simmer on low heat for about 2 hours. Be sure to stir frequently to ensure that it does not start to scorch on the bottom of the pan. The brown sugar lends itself to burning if you aren't careful.

3. After 2 hours, use a stick blender or a hand blender to mix evenly. If you don't have one of these, swirl the contents around the pan, then use a wooden spoon and beat somewhat vigorously until the mixture has an even, smooth consistency.

4. Simmer, stirring, for another hour or so until most of the liquid has cooked off.

5. Remove from heat and let cool. Store in the refrigerator, where it should keep for several weeks.

— *Suzanne Collier, Foodista.com*

Luscious tomatoes from Valley Flora Farm.

CHERRY TOMATO KEBABS   MAKES 4 TO 6 KEBABS

Source Note: My daughter, Miska, is always delighted when we find a little basket of cherry tomatoes in our produce box.

1 basket (about 2 cups) cherry tomatoes, rinsed
1 pound firm tofu, cut into 1-inch chunks and baked
   (see the Cooking Note below)
1 cucumber, sliced
½ pound Cheddar cheese, cut into 1-inch chunks
2 cups green beans, steamed until just tender

Arrange all of the ingredients on toothpicks and serve them on a platter. This is pretty and delicious as an appetizer, good with a vinaigrette dipping sauce. We sometimes make a whole meal of them!

Cooking Note: Start with a block of firm tofu; wrap it in several layers of paper towels and put it on a plate. Cover with a second plate and weigh the whole thing down using a couple of cans of food or a heavy book. Check it in 30 minutes and drain off the liquid. Repeat. Cut the tofu into 1-inch squares. Heat the oven to 400°F. If you'd like, season the cubes with soy sauce, salt, a bit of oil, or other seasonings. Bake for 30 to 40 minutes, or until the cubes are golden brown. Cool.

— *Margaret Trott, Featherstone Farm CSA member*

. . . .

OVEN-ROASTED TOMATO SAUCE   MAKES ABOUT 3 CUPS

8 large tomatoes or 15 Romas (about 3½ pounds)
Salt and freshly ground black pepper
Olive oil
Onions, quartered
Garlic cloves
Green bell pepper, cut into wedges (optional)
Fresh herbs (such as basil, oregano, and parsley)

1. Preheat the oven to 450°F.

2. Core the tomatoes, then cut them in half (in quarters if they are very large). Place them in a 9-by-13-inch baking pan in a single layer. Sprinkle with salt, pepper, and olive oil. Roast them in the oven for 30 minutes.

3. Add some quartered onion pieces, several garlic cloves and, if you like, green bell pepper wedges to the tomatoes. Drizzle again with oil and roast them for about another 30 minutes, or until the vegetables are soft and somewhat charred.

4. To finish the sauce, chop the fresh herbs in a food processor or blender. Add the tomato mixture and blend to a chunky consistency. The sauce is now ready to eat or freeze.

— *Maria Runde*

Tomatillos

PHYSALIS PHILADELPHICA

The small green fruits of the tomatillo, like certain people, are worth getting to know for their perky brightness and distinctive character. They are members of the large Physalis *family, which includes ground cherries and Chinese lanterns, and they are also related to nightshade. Sometimes known as husk tomatoes, jamberries, husk cherries, or Mexican tomatoes, tomatillos sport parchment paper–like husks that enclose the fruits, which resemble large green cherry tomatoes. Although they do look like green tomatoes, tomatillos definitely have their own personality and the two are not interchangeable. Tomatillos have a sharp, lemony, herbal flavor and a slightly gelatinous texture when cooked, making them ideal in sauces, salsas, and Mexican and southwestern dishes of all kinds.*

HISTORY

Tomatillos are native to Mexico and were a staple of Aztec diets as far back as 800 BCE. As with corn, potatoes, tomatoes, and peppers, the Spaniards brought tomatillos to Europe from the New World. To this day they continue to be a mainstay of Mexican and southwestern cuisines, where they are used extensively in green sauces and other dishes.

NUTRITION

As much powerhouses of nutrition as flavor, these little green balls pack vitamins A and C, a surprising amount of potassium, plus some calcium and folic acid—all at only 11 calories for one raw, medium tomatillo.

SEASON

Commercially, tomatillos are widely grown and available year-round. However, they are really a warm-season crop and at their best in farmers markets and CSAs from mid to late summer through early fall.

SELECTION

Tomatillos vary tremendously in size, quality, and flavor. Some can be bitingly sour, whereas others are quite sweet. Generally, the smaller the tomatillo, the sweeter it will be, but size is not always a reliable indicator. As tomatillos ripen, their husks split open, but the fruits remain green until they are fully ripe; then they turn yellow and become surprisingly sweet. Sadly, these specimens are rarely seen in markets. The husks should be clean, fresh looking, and close-fitting, not shriveled or dried up, and the fruits firm, dry, and hard (unlike tomatoes, they do not give).

STORAGE

These little guys are surprisingly long-lasting; they can be stored in the refrigerator for up to 1 month, or even kept out on the counter. Do not store them in airtight containers; they need to breathe. Keep the husks intact, and do not remove them until you're ready to use the fruits.

Trimming and Cleaning

Happily, tomatillos come in their own packaging—their papery green husks protect them quite well. Peel back and remove these inedible husks, and rinse the fruits to remove the sticky film of sap that often coats the skins.

Steaming and Boiling

Tomatillos are not steamed or boiled in the traditional sense like most other vegetables, but they do sometimes need to be gently precooked for certain recipes. This involves either blanching or poaching; both methods are effective in softening the tomatillos, but poaching cooks them more slowly and gently and better preserves their color. To blanch, remove the husks, wash the fruits, and leave them whole. Blanch in rapidly boiling water for 3 to 5 minutes, or until they soften; then plunge them into ice water for 5 minutes to stop the cooking process. Remove and drain.

To poach, place whole, husked tomatillos in a pot with enough cold water to cover them completely. Heat the water until it just barely simmers (it should never approach even a gentle boil) and maintain for 5 to 15 minutes, depending on the size of the tomatillos.

Stir-Frying and Sautéing

Tomatillos take surprisingly well to stir-frying. They have a high water content, so don't add too much liquid to the pan. Simply slice and toss them in with other vegetables, some olive oil or butter, and fresh herbs; sauté or stir-fry for 5 to 7 minutes over high heat.

Baking and Roasting

Tomatillos are exceptional when roasted in the oven, which dries out their copious moisture a bit and concentrates their flavor. One method is to layer them in a casserole dish with herbs and seasonings of your choice, drizzle them with olive oil, and roast them in a 350°F oven for 45 minutes. Or, if you need to prepare less-watery tomatillos quickly for sauces, roast whole, unhusked specimens in a 450°F oven for 10 to 15 minutes. Watch them closely so they do not burst!

Microwaving

Microwaving tomatillos is not advised, as this method destroys nutrients and also compromises their texture somewhat. If you are planning to cook them, it's better to roast, blanch, poach, or even sauté them (see the instructions above).

Blanching and Freezing

Raw tomatillos can be frozen whole without blanching or peeling; just remove their papery husks, wash the fruits, place them on a cookie sheet, and freeze. Put them in zipper-lock freezer or vacuum food sealer-type bags, or freezer containers. Squeeze out any excess air and leave 1 inch of headspace (unless you are using the vacuum sealing method). Frozen raw tomatillos will keep for up to 12 months at 0°F.

You can also precook and peel the tomatillos first by blanching them. Remove the husks, wash the fruits, and leave them whole. Blanch in rapidly boiling water for 3 to 5 minutes, or until they soften; then

Cooking Tip

Tomatillos are naturally high in pectin, which make them ideal for thickening soups and salsas.

Books

Salsas and Tacos:
Santa Fe School of Cooking
Susan D. Curtis,
Gibbs Smith, 2006.

Martha Stewart
www.marthastewart.
com/1013642/tomatillo-recipes/

Yesterday, we took more than 2,000 baby plants to our farm field in West Rutland, ready to be planted into our unheated field greenhouse. The soil inside was nice and warm, but outside posed more of a problem. There was still a heavy snow cover that prevented us from driving to our field, meaning a quarter-mile snowshoe hike dragging our plants in a sled.

Fueled with a morning breakfast of bacon, eggs, sauerkraut, and sourdough toast, I welcomed the first trip, energized to start the season with my hands in the soil. However, by my third trip back to the truck I realized I needed more inspiration. While Scott prepared the beds inside the greenhouse, I channeled the strength of an Eskimo hunter dragging his prey.

I've been reading Weston A. Price's Nutrition and Physical Degeneration, a book that mentions the strength of the Eskimos. Price was a dentist from the Midwest who had a keen interest in nutrition and health. He traveled the world in the 1930s to research native tribes eating traditional diets, in search of their "recipe" for healthy and disease-free lives. He wrote about the jolly nature of Pacific Islanders, whose smiling faces showed true health, as well as the Eskimos, whose average man could carry 300 pounds—100 pounds in each hand and 100 pounds in his jaw.

Despite various climates and cultures, he discovered that people who ate the foods of their ancestors were free from dental disease and cavities, and that their dental arches were perfectly formed to fit all of their teeth without problems. Along with these traits, they also exhibited noteworthy strength and vitality. Aborigines could see move-

plunge them into ice water for 5 minutes to stop the cooking process. Remove and drain. Then pierce the skins of each tomatillo with a knife; they should slip off easily. Package the tomatillos for freezing as in the instructions above.

EQUIVALENTS, MEASURES, AND SERVINGS

- 1 pound fresh tomatillos = 7 medium tomatillos = 1 (11-ounce) can

COMPLEMENTARY HERBS, SEASONINGS, AND FOODS

Avocados, basil, beef, cheese, chicken, chiles, cilantro, cinnamon, cloves, corn, cucumbers, dill, eggs, fish, garlic, grapes, lemons, limes, mint, onions, parsley, peppers, pork, potatoes, salmon, thyme, tomatoes, turkey.

SERVING SUGGESTIONS

- No salsa verde is worth its salt without the tomatillo, which lends a distinctive citrusy acidity that no tomato can give.
- Chop raw tomatillos and add them to fresh salads for a burst of tang and zing.
- Tomatillos are fantastic in cold vegetable soups. Blend them with tomatoes, cucumbers, onions, garlic, jalapeños, cilantro, and olive oil for a refreshing gazpacho on a hot summer day.
- When combined and cooked down with garlic, onion, chiles, cilantro, and seasonings, tomatillos form a versatile green sauce that goes with everything from burritos, enchiladas, chicken, potatoes, and vegetable dishes to huevos rancheros, tacos, roasted meats, baked fish, and even sandwiches.
- Tomatillos make a fun garnish, especially when you pull their papery husks back for a dramatic, windblown look.
- Tomatillos in guacamole? Try it—you might just love it as a zesty alternative to tomatoes.
- Drop in a few sliced tomatillos when making your favorite pork stew.
- Tomatillos are fantastic in margaritas. Puree and juice them through a fine sieve, then combine with lime juice, a simple sugar syrup, white tequila, and crushed ice for an invigorating drink during the dog days of summer.

FRIED GREEN TOMATO FRITTATA

SERVES 4

Source Note: The tart snap of fried green tomatoes really brightens eggs. Fried green tomatoes are terrific, but it's not the only way to go with these firm fruits. These are fried, but then encased within golden-yolked farm eggs. Tomatillos can be treated this way too and used in place of the tomatoes.

2 large green tomatoes, or 6 tomatillos, sliced ⅓ inch thick
½ cup fine cornmeal or corn flour seasoned with salt and pepper
3 to 4 tablespoons olive oil, divided
6 eggs
2 tablespoons chopped fresh parsley or dill
2 tablespoons chives, snipped into small pieces
2 tablespoons grated Parmesan cheese
Sea salt and freshly ground black pepper

1. Preheat the broiler. Dip the tomatoes in the seasoned cornmeal. Heat 2 tablespoons of the oil in an ovenproof skillet over medium heat; fry the slices on both sides until golden but not mushy. Set them on paper towels, wipe out the pan, then add the remaining oil and return it to the stove.

2. Whisk the eggs, herbs, and cheese and season with a few pinches of salt and pepper. Pour the eggs into the skillet, lower the heat, and set the tomatoes on top. Shake the pan gently back and forth a few times to settle the eggs, then cook until set. Set the frittata under the broiler until brown, then slide it onto a serving plate.

— *Deborah Madison,* Vegetable Literacy

. . . .

ENCHILADAS VERDES
SERVES 3 TO 4

1 pound fresh tomatillos (about 7 medium)
2 jalapeño peppers
1 clove garlic
4 large red tomatoes
Olive oil
1 red onion, thinly sliced
Salt and freshly ground black pepper
10 flour tortillas
2 boneless, skinless chicken breasts, cooked and pulled into
      bite-size pieces
1 cup Parmesan cheese, shredded (or use Mexican *cotija* cheese)
1 head iceberg lettuce, washed and shredded (or use other fresh greens)
12 ounces (1½ cups) sour cream

1. In a medium saucepan over medium heat, boil the tomatillos with the jalapeño peppers in enough water to cover until they become soft; remove from the water and drain. Put the tomatillos and jalapeños into a food processor, add the garlic clove, and blend until smooth.

2. Blanch and peel the tomatoes; cut into cubes.

3. In a small frying pan, heat 1 to 2 tablespoons of olive oil over medium heat; add the onion. Add the tomato cubes and cook until the onions become translucent. Add the blended tomatillo mixture and simmer for 10 minutes. Add salt and pepper to taste.

4. Heat more olive oil in a sauté pan over high heat. Lightly fry the tortillas in the hot oil on both sides (or they may be served without frying). Drain on paper towels to absorb the excess oil.

5. Assemble the ingredients on each tortilla shell (chicken, cheese, tomatillo sauce, lettuce, and sour cream). Serve topped with salsa or guacamole.

— *Terhune Orchards, Princeton, New Jersey*

ment at a distance of one mile and confirmed with modern scientists that they could see the moons of Jupiter with their bare eyes. Children of the Swiss Alps happily went barefoot in the snow, and elderly women carried huge stacks of rye on their backs.

Price made a point of visiting a range of people and places. The diets varied greatly, from seafood and oats of Gaelic Irish folk, to blood and milk of the Masai in Africa, to salmon and grizzly bear of Canadian Indians. All of the cultures emphasized special nutrition for pregnant women, incorporating plenty of fat, organ meats, and other nutrient-dense foods. And in every culture with traditional foods, the tribes were truly nourished and the epitome of health.

He studied people who were totally isolated from modern culture, as well as those who had integrated and were striving to keep up with the Joneses. What he noticed was that people who started to eat a modern diet of processed white flour, canned fruits and vegetables, and bakery goods immediately suffered from tooth decay.

He was able to find families with older siblings still eating traditional foods, whose teeth were perfectly healthy, whereas younger siblings eating modern foods had lost many of their teeth to cavities. Furthermore, as soon as parents adopted the modern diets, their children were born with deformed dental arches, meaning that the faces narrowed and the teeth were overcrowded. To put it simply, he discovered that diet had everything to do with dental problems, as well as other modern ailments and diseases like tuberculosis.

The modern foods often appeared in communities before the necessary infrastructure—including dentistry. Without dentists around, the tooth decay often led to toothless mouths and painful abscessed teeth, the only reason for suicide in some of the groups. As modernity crept into the cultures, so too did machine-made clothing and "other novelties that would soon be translated to necessities."

During his travels, Weston Price wrote, "The greatest heritage of the white man today is the accumulated wisdom of the human race." Unfortunately, Americans now spend less of our incomes on food than any other country in the world, and only a tiny fraction of time to prepare that food. Yet many of the diseases we suffer are diet-related. And this is progress?

Although none of us are likely to live off a diet of strictly fish, seaweed, and deer, like native Alaskans, we can incorporate more nutritious foods into our diets and remember that each bite we take is either feeding disease or fighting it. I know when I eat candy that it is providing no nourishment for my body. But when I drink a glass of straight-from-the-cow (raw) whole milk, I can channel the vitality of the isolated Swiss mountain children and their ancestors, and perhaps wander barefoot in the April snow.

HERBED TOMATILLO AND GRAPE SALSA

MAKES ABOUT 1½ CUPS

Source Note: This soft, fruity (and fat-free) green sauce enhances broiled or fried seafood or roasted chicken or turkey. Sweet and mellow, with herbal tones and a light chile snap (use more, if you go for heat), it is smoother and subtler than relish. Either simmer husked tomatillos or roast them unhusked (for somewhat more concentrated flavor), as you prefer. Should a more assertive and crisp salsa be your goal, prepare the raw variation that follows, for sharper taste and color.

¾ pound tomatillos (about 5 medium)
1 to 3 small green chiles, such as serrano or jalapeño, halved and seeded
1 small garlic clove
¼ teaspoon kosher salt
⅓ cup tightly packed cilantro leaves
¼ cup lightly packed basil or mint leaves
½ cup stemmed seedless green grapes
About 1 tablespoon lime juice

1. Barely cover the husked tomatillos with cold water; cook very gently until tender—the time can range from 2 to 15 minutes, depending upon their size and thickness. Check often to prevent bursting. Cool in the liquid.

2. In a food processor, combine 1 chile (or more to taste), the garlic, salt, and half each of the cilantro and basil. Whiz to mince.

3. Drain the tomatillos if needed. Add them to the container, along with the grapes and 1 tablespoon lime juice. Whirl to a chunky puree. Taste for heat and tartness, adding more lime and minced chile to suit. Scoop into a bowl. Cover and chill for at least 1 hour.

4. To serve, mince the remaining cilantro and basil. Stir them into the salsa. Adjust the seasoning.

Variation: For an uncooked version, clean and rinse ½ pound tomatillos. Whiz the chiles, garlic, salt, and half of the cilantro and basil to a fine texture. Add the tomatillos and chop coarsely. Add the grapes and pulse to a medium-coarse texture. Chill. To serve, mince the remaining herbs and stir into the salsa. Adjust the seasoning.

— *Elizabeth Schneider,* Vegetables from Amaranth to Zucchini: The Essential Reference

Tropical Fruits

The wide world of tropical fruits is a wondrous one, and a sheer delight for the senses in terms of colors, shapes, textures, aromas, and of course, jaw-dropping flavors. Their diversity is simply stunning as well, but unfortunately many of them never make it out of their home countries simply because they are too fragile to be shipped. If you happen to live in Hawaii or Florida, you will still have plenty to choose from at your local farmers or roadside market, CSA box, farm stand, or even conventional supermarket. Here are just a few of our most popular favorites.

BANANAS	KIWIFRUITS
CHERIMOYAS	MANGOES
CITRUS	PAPAYAS
COCONUTS	PINEAPPLES

BANANAS MUSA SPECIES

In America, we think of bananas as a ubiquitous sweet, yellow fruit that we peel and munch as a snack, eat for breakfast, or pack in our lunch boxes. But in other parts of the world, they serve as a staple, even a subsistence food.

Bananas are giant herbs, not actual trees in the botanical sense. Nearly a thousand varieties of bananas exist worldwide, but not all of them are edible. Bananas for eating are typically classified in one of two categories: dessert bananas, which are sweet and usually consumed raw (including the familiar, yellow Cavendish type), and cooking bananas, which are starchy and typically cooked (the large, green plantains are an example). A huge percentage of the bananas grown and eaten in Africa, the Caribbean, and Latin America belong to the latter group.

If you live in Hawaii or Florida, you may find profuse bunches of apple or finger bananas at your farmers market or even in your CSA boxes. These little bananas are 4 to 5 inches long, and have thin yellow or dark red skins and firm flesh that is extra-sweet with a complex, tropical flavor. They are truly a treat when you can find them. Plantains may be available as well, but this book contains recipes for dessert bananas only.

HISTORY

Bananas are one of humanity's oldest cultivated food crops; archaeological evidence suggests that they were raised as far back as 8000 BCE in Papua New Guinea. Southeast Asia is the epicenter for banana genetic diversity, but Africa has its fair share of varieties as well. Bananas have a long, fascinating, controversial history deeply intertwined with humans' global travels, exploitation, violence, and greed (the term "banana republic" is not a positive one).

The fruit isn't the only tasty part of the banana plant. In some southern Asian countries, the flowers are eaten raw or steamed as a vegetable; they taste like artichokes.

The tender inner core of the banana plant's trunk is also edible and is a component of a Burmese rice noodle and fish soup called *mohinga*.

Banana leaves also serve major culinary roles in South Asia and India, serving as plates, wrappers in which food is steamed, and as part of the meal itself.

Come Ripen with Me

If you want tomatoes, apples, avocados, and other fruits to ripen, place them in a paper bag with a ripe banana. Bananas give off copious amounts of ethylene gas, a naturally occurring plant hormone that speeds ripening.

And the saga ain't over yet—a virulent, fast-spreading fungal disease that currently has no cure may eventually commercially wipe out the familiar Cavendish, the primary dessert and export banana worldwide. Cultivated bananas are unusual in that they propagate vegetatively rather than from seed, so each plant is an exact genetic duplicate, making it especially vulnerable to disease. Large-scale commercial banana cultivation has traditionally depended heavily on monoculture, with devastating effects when fungi and viruses strike the plantations; in turn this leads to food insecurity for growers and their communities in different countries. Because bananas are innately difficult to breed using traditional hybridizing methods, scientists are working to find genetic engineering solutions through the use of wild banana strains and innovative cell technologies.

NUTRITION

As athletes know, bananas are an excellent source of potassium and natural sugars, but they are also a surprisingly good source of vitamins C and B6, as well as some folate, riboflavin, magnesium, copper, and manganese. A single 7-inch Cavendish banana contains about 100 calories.

SEASON

Bananas are widely grown and available year-round; there is no discernible peak season for them, even in America's tropical regions.

SELECTION

Bananas are typically picked when they are green and starchy; they ripen rapidly off the tree, especially in warm temperatures, and in the process their starches turn to sugars. How you select bananas depends on how long you want to keep them and how you will eat them. Bananas with a greenish tinge will ripen more slowly, but bananas that are fully yellow or have brown spots will become overripe quicker than you can blink. If you intend to cook with them (as in banana pudding or bread), use very ripe ones—and right away. Avoid bananas with major bruising or very large soft spots, although they are fine for cooking or in smoothies.

STORAGE

If you want your bananas to ripen, leave them out at room temperature. They'll keep for 5 to 7 days, depending on how ripe they were to begin with. If you want to slow down the ripening process, refrigerate them; their skins will darken as a result, but their flavor will not suffer. If, however, you put unripe bananas in the refrigerator, they may not ripen properly after they are returned to room temperature.

TRIMMING AND CLEANING

With its own zipped-up wrapper, a banana is about as easy as it gets in this department. Just peel and enjoy!

BLANCHING AND FREEZING

Freezing is a good way to store overripe bananas for future smoothies, breads, and other recipes. Peel them first, then freeze them whole on a tray and store in a zipper-lock freezer bag. Alternatively, mash the bananas, adding 1 tablespoon of lemon juice or ½ teaspoon of ascorbic acid (vitamin C) crystals for each cup of pulp to prevent excessive browning. Package the banana pulp in zipper-lock freezer or vacuum food sealer-type bags, or freezer containers. Squeeze out any excess air and leave 1 inch of headspace (unless you are using the vacuum sealing method). For best quality, use frozen bananas within 2 to 3 months.

EQUIVALENTS, MEASURES, AND SERVINGS

- 1 large banana = 1 cup sliced
- 3 medium bananas = 1 pound = 1 cup mashed
- 2 medium bananas = ½ to 1 teaspoon banana extract

COMPLEMENTARY HERBS, SEASONINGS, AND FOODS

Blueberries, caramel, cherries, chocolate, cinnamon, coffee, cream, ginger, hazelnuts, honey, kiwifruit, mangoes, molasses, nutmeg, papayas, pineapple, raisins, raspberries, rum, strawberry, vanilla, walnuts, yogurt.

SERVING SUGGESTIONS

- Bananas are really tasty fried or made into fritters; make your own batter or use packaged pancake mix. Deep-fry in hot oil until golden brown, then sprinkle with cinnamon and sugar.

- Set your rum-soaked bananas aflame to make bananas Flambeau and bananas Foster. Sauté the bananas in rum, sugar, cinnamon, and butter, then ignite. You can also adapt this slightly to your favorite bread pudding recipe.

- Remember banana pudding from your childhood? The kind where vanilla custard was layered with vanilla wafers or ladyfinger cookies and topped with sliced bananas and whipped cream? Maybe you haven't thought about it in years, but chances are that it is just as good today as it was back then.

- Banana bread is the classic way to use up those overripe bananas sitting on your counter. Try it with nuts (walnuts and pecans are good), raisins, or chocolate chips. This is also a good use for frozen banana puree.

- Make a banana split! Cut a banana lengthwise in half and lay the halves in a long, narrow dish. Place scoops of vanilla, chocolate, and strawberry ice cream between the halves, and top with pineapple, strawberry, or chocolate sauces, chopped nuts, whipped cream, and maraschino cherries.

- Banana cream pie! Must more be said?

- Slice bananas to top your morning cereal, pancakes, waffles, and French toast.

- Combine bananas with kiwi, pineapple, berries, oranges, and other fruits in fruit salad.

- Pureed bananas make a perfect base for many smoothie beverages; mix with yogurt, milks, malted-milk powder, and other fruits.

- An interesting savory curry can be made with sautéed chicken, green apples, bananas, onion, garlic, tomatoes, coconut milk, curry powder, cumin, white wine, and a little flour for thickening.

More about Bananas

Bananapedia.com
www.bananapedia.com

Banana: The Fate of the Fruit
That Changed the World
Dan Koeppel,
Penguin, 2008.

Bananas: How the United Fruit
Company Shaped the World
Peter Chapman,
Canongate, 2009.

FRUIT SHAKE   MAKES 1 LARGE SHAKE

1 cup skim or soy milk
1 cup plain yogurt
1 tablespoon ground flaxseed or flaxseed oil

1 cup berries (strawberries, raspberries, or blueberries)
1 banana
Sugar or honey for sweetening (optional)

Place all of the ingredients in a blender and process well.

— *Kathy Delano,* The Bluff Country Co-op Cookbook

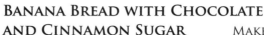

Banana Bread with Chocolate and Cinnamon Sugar
MAKES ONE 8-BY-8-INCH LOAF

Source Note: This lovely stuff comes together in less than an hour, including baking time. And unlike more conventional quick breads, which are best when allowed to cool fully before slicing, this one doesn't suffer when it's eaten warm. That makes it, in my book, a perfect last-minute dessert or afternoon treat. It's a good one to have in the old repertoire.

Oh, and while we're here, let's talk about frozen bananas. I always keep a stash of them in the freezer, and I highly recommend it. I chuck them in there, peel and all, and when I want to use a few, I just pull them out, set them in a bowl, and let them defrost at room temperature for a few hours. It doesn't take long. You can then use them in place of fresh, ripe bananas in any baked item, and they're easier to mash, to boot. The only bad thing is that they look pretty nasty. Think wet, slippery, and slug-like, and don't say I didn't warn you.

Bread

3 very ripe bananas (the size doesn't much matter; medium to large works)
2 large eggs
1½ cups unbleached all-purpose flour
1 cup granulated sugar
1 teaspoon baking soda
2 teaspoons ground cinnamon
1 teaspoon pure vanilla extract
1 cup semisweet chocolate chips

Topping

2 tablespoons granulated sugar
⅛ teaspoon ground cinnamon

1. Preheat the oven to 375°F. Butter or spray an 8-inch square pan.

2. In a medium mixing bowl, mash the bananas well with a fork or potato masher. Add the eggs and stir well to combine. Add the flour, sugar, baking soda, cinnamon, and vanilla, and stir to mix. Add ¾ cup of the chocolate chips, and stir briefly. Pour the batter into the prepared pan, and set aside.

3. In a small bowl, stir together the topping ingredients. Sprinkle the

mixture evenly over the batter, and top with the remaining ¼ cup chocolate chips.

4. Bake for 35 to 40 minutes, or until a toothpick inserted into the center comes out clean. Let cool in the pan on a wire rack for at least 15 minutes before serving.

Serving Suggestion: This bread, like many banana sweets, freezes beautifully. Sometimes I even like to eat it frozen, cut into thick, cold, chewy slices. It's the perfect snack for a hot summer afternoon.

— *Molly Wizenberg,* Orangette *blog*

CHERIMOYAS ANNONA CHERIMOLA

As fruits go, cherimoyas are pretty unforgettable. First there is their distinctive appearance—like stout, apple-green pinecones, their skins embossed with a scale-like pattern. Cut one open and you'll find creamy, juicy, snow-white flesh that is silky-smooth and custardy in texture, punctuated with a number of large black shiny seeds (which are poisonous and must be removed). The fruit's flavor varies somewhat depending on the variety, but its delectability is never questioned— sweet, with hints of pineapple, banana, mango, papaya, and vanilla.

*The nomenclature of cherimoyas and other fruits in the Annona family can be quite bewildering. You may find fresh, frozen, or canned cherimoya labeled under other names—*soursop, sweetsop, sugar apple, custard apple, *atemoya,* mãng cau. *These names are often used to refer to one or more related fruits that bear some resemblance in physical appearance, taste, and texture but are entirely different species. And sometimes the name (especially custard apple) does actually refer to the cherimoya itself. But don't let this complexity intimidate— all of them are quite tasty.*

HISTORY

Cherimoyas are thought to have originated in the Andes, perhaps in the valleys and tropical forests of Ecuador, Colombia, and Bolivia. Ancient Peruvians frequently depicted the fruit in their ceramics and pottery.

They are quite unusual among tropical fruits in that they prefer growing at higher altitudes—from 4,300 to 8,500 feet—and although the trees cannot tolerate snow or frost, they demand periods of cold temperatures or they will go dormant. Cherimoyas are now grown in many regions of the world, including California, Hawaii, southern Italy and Spain, Tunisia, Morocco, and parts of the Middle East.

NUTRITION

Cherimoyas are very high in vitamins C and B6, niacin, thiamine, riboflavin, and folate. The fruits are also a good source of potassium, magnesium, copper, manganese, phosphorus, and dietary fiber. They are quite high in sugar; a single fruit contains about 230 calories.

SEASON

The peak season for cherimoya is typically March through May, although its availability varies, depending on what part of the world it is shipped from—or if it is locally grown.

SELECTION

In spite of their leathery green skins, cherimoyas are quite fragile and very prone to bruising and rotting. They are also extremely sensitive to cold in transit, so avoid specimens with lots of dark splotching, which may indicate such improper exposure. Choose cherimoyas that are firm, heavy, and unblemished. Color is not necessarily an indication of ripeness. If you want to eat the fruit within a day or two, select ones that give slightly when pressed, like an avocado.

STORAGE

Cherimoyas are picked hard to help prevent them from bruising during shipping. Store cherimoyas at room temperature away from direct sunlight, but keep a close eye on them because they ripen very quickly, sometimes in less than 2 to 3 days. Their green skins may turn a bit brownish, which is fine, but don't let them get squishy-soft. Once they are ripe, they can be stored in the refrigerator for 4 to 5 days.

TRIMMING AND CLEANING

Cherimoyas are pretty easy to eat; simply cut them in half lengthwise and scoop the silky white flesh into your mouth for immediate and satisfying gratification. Or peel off the green skins and cut the flesh into cubes, making sure to remove the inedible black seeds.

BLANCHING AND FREEZING

One of the great joys of cherimoyas is that you can pop the whole fruit into the freezer, wait an hour or two, then take it out and scoop the frozen, custard-like flesh right out of the shell with a spoon.

Or you can prepare chunks of the fruit by arranging them in a single layer on a cookie sheet and freezing them. Transfer the frozen pieces into zipper-lock freezer or vacuum food sealer-type bags, or freezer containers. Squeeze out any excess air and leave ½ inch of headspace (unless you are using the vacuum sealing method). Frozen cherimoya should keep for up to 1 year at 0°F.

COMPLEMENTARY HERBS, SEASONINGS, AND FOODS

Balsamic vinegar, blueberries, cherries, chicken, citrus, coconut, cream, ham, honey, ice cream, kumquats, lemons, limes, mangoes, melons, mint, peaches, pears, pineapples, pork, prosciutto, raspberries, rum, seafood, strawberries, vanilla, white pepper, yogurt.

SERVING SUGGESTIONS

- Freeze an entire cherimoya fruit and eat it out of its shell with a spoon for an incredible summertime—or anytime—treat.
- Cherimoya plays well with other fruits; try pears, peaches, strawberries, raspberries, blueberries, kiwis, melons, mangoes, papayas, cherries, and citrus in fruit salads, compotes, smoothies, pies, and tarts.

> "One of the delights of life is eating with friends; second to that is talking about eating. And, for an unsurpassed double whammy, there is talking about eating while you are eating with friends."
>
> — *Laurie Colwin,*
> *American food writer*

- Because of their custard-like consistency, cherimoyas can be easily mashed or pureed and added to desserts, pancake batter, sauces, soufflés, meringues, and crêpes.

- Cherimoyas are a natural made into ice creams, sorbets, and mousses.

- Drink your custard apple! Blend cherimoya with ice, rum, and frozen lemonade concentrate to make divine daiquiris.

CHERIMOYA-ALMOND CAKE
MAKES ONE 10-INCH ROUND CAKE

Source Note: This dense and moist cake has a flavor profile way beyond its simpler cousin, the Galician cake, tarta de Santiago. *Once you pick out all of the seeds in a cherimoya, you are left with a gloopy, yellowy mush. In my opinion, one could use cherimoyas as one would use bananas in baking. So, this recipe is perfect for that cherimoya that is sitting in your fridge, that one you thought was a good idea to buy at the time but now seems like it's rotting. A cherimoya that is beginning to ferment might be your best buddy here. Choose one with barely any green left on its skin. For a cake less dense, just use a bit less butter. This cherimoya cake is gluten-free.*

1 pound almonds or almond flour
1¾ cups (11 ounces) granulated sugar
6 ounces (1½ sticks) butter, plus more for greasing
6 large eggs
1¾ cups cherimoya puree (1 large cherimoya or 2 small ones, seeded), divided
1 lemon, for zest and juice
⅔ cup fresh lavender blossoms, or ½ cup dried (optional)
Powdered sugar, for dusting

1. Preheat the oven to 350°F. Grease a round 10-inch round cake pan (or another pan large enough to hold the batter, such as a springform pan) with soft butter.

2. Puree the almonds in a food processor. You can use a coffee grinder, but it will take much longer and you risk overworking the motor. Alternatively, many stores now sell almond flour in bulk.

3. In a large stand mixer, cream the sugar and butter.

4. Add the eggs and mix until smooth. Add 1¼ cups of the cherimoya puree and mix until smooth. Reserve the rest of the cherimoya for later.

5. Mix in the ground almonds and the zest of half the lemon. Gently fold in the lavender blossoms, if using. The batter should be thick but pourable.

6. Pour the batter into the pan and bake for 45 minutes. When the cake is done, the top should be firm. While the cake is still hot, spoon the rest of the cherimoya puree on top. If you can spread it without damaging the cake, do so, but it is not necessary.

Books

Tropical Fruit Cookbook
Marilyn Rittenhouse Harris,
University of Hawaii Press, 1993.

Kula Fields Farmshop website
(recipes section)
www.kulafields.com

Tastes Like Home:
My Caribbean Cookbook
Cynthia Nelson,
Ian Randle Publishers, 2010.

7. Return the cake to the oven and bake for 20 to 35 minutes more, until the edges are brown and a toothpick comes out clean.

8. Remove from the oven. Let the cake cool for about 10 minutes, then run a knife around the edges to prevent sticking. Carefully remove the cake from the pan, placing it onto a cooling rack. Squeeze lemon juice over the top of the cake, as desired. Let it finish cooling at room temperature. Finish by dusting powdered sugar over the surface.

— *Brian Fink,* The Cascadian Kitchen *blog*

CHERIMOYA, KIWI, AND STRAWBERRY FRUIT SALAD

SERVES 4

1 cherimoya, peeled and seeded, chopped
Fresh lemon juice
1 large kiwi, peeled and sliced
Handful of strawberries, quartered
¼ teaspoon agave nectar

Place the cherimoya in a bowl and toss it with a small amount of lemon juice. Add the remaining ingredients and toss well to combine.

— *Esi Impraim,* Dishing Up Delights *blog*

CHERIMOYA FROZEN YOGURT (MAN CAU)

MAKES ABOUT 1 QUART

10½ ounces frozen cherimoya in sugar and water, defrosted
2 cups plain, whole-milk yogurt
½ cup granulated sugar

1. In a blender, blend all of the ingredients until creamy. Freeze in an ice cream maker according to the manufacturer's instructions.

2. Serve with diced pineapple and butter wafer cookies on the side.

— *Tram Le,* Nutrition to Kitchen *blog*

CITRUS

CITRUS SPECIES

What would our fruit world be like without citrus? The charms of oranges, the versatility of lemons, the zing of limes, the goodness of grapefruit? Not to mention scads of other citrus varieties, like mandarins, tangerines, tangelos, kumquats, citrons, pomelos, and the bizarre-looking Buddha's Hand.

Because citrus is one of the few plant families whose members easily interbreed (peppers are another), this is an enormous genus, with thousands of species and cultivars worldwide. Even mentioning them is a task well beyond the scope of this book; mostly what is covered here is the most basic information for oranges, lemons, limes, and grapefruit.

HISTORY

Citrus are believed to have originated in tropical and subtropical Asia and the Malay Archipelago, where they have been cultivated since antiquity. In spite of the trees' obvious beauty and the fruits' culinary and medicinal value, their spread to other countries was slow; citron (a type of citrus valued for its thick rinds) was the first to reach Europe, recorded in literature around 310 BC, and for centuries it remained the only one. Sour oranges and lemons followed centuries later, spread by the Arabs as the Roman Empire disintegrated.

Christopher Columbus brought citrus to North America in the early 1500s and oranges were introduced into Australia in 1788. By the mid-1800s, citrus was already a thriving commercial industry in both Florida and California, followed by Texas and Arizona in the early 1900s. Periodic, devastating freezes are a part of citrus-growing history in America, with corresponding rises and falls in production in different states.

The modern citrus industry was transformed in the 20th century by faster transportation such as railroads and airplanes, commercial refrigeration, the discovery of vitamin C and its subsequent marketing, and most importantly, the invention of juice concentrates, which began in the late 1940s. By 1963, nearly 80 percent of Florida's orange crop alone was processed into juice.

Our modern greenhouses probably owe much of their existence to the original orangery, a specially heated glass structure popular among the aristocracy of 18th-century Europe for growing citrus fruits and exotic plants in colder climates.

NUTRITION

It is no secret, of course, that citrus fruits are high in vitamin C, but they also contain significant amounts of potassium, folate, calcium, thiamine, niacin, vitamin B6, phosphorus, magnesium, copper, riboflavin, and pantothenic acid. They are rich in phytonutrients, flavonoids, and other antioxidants that are believed to have considerable anticancer and anti-inflammatory properties; higher concentrations of these nutrients lie in the white parts of the peels and the membranes separating the sections. A single large orange contains about 87 calories, and half of a grapefruit has about 50; a whole lemon or lime contains only around 20 calories.

SEASON

The season for commercially grown citrus is a long one, depending on the country of origin and variety. Lemons and limes are available all year; oranges are often at their best from January through March, and grapefruits from mid-October through April. At farmers markets and CSAs, availability will depend on the local growing season. The vast majority of the citrus sold in America is grown in California, Florida, Texas, and Arizona, but you may see fruit from Mexico, Brazil, Argentina, and China.

Eating Tip

The intense tanginess and distinctive flavor of limes makes them a good salt substitute.

Cooking Tip

Lemon or lime juice helps prevent the browning that naturally occurs when certain fruits are cut, such as apples, pears, avocados, and bananas. Dip these fruits into—or spray them with—a mixture of water and lemon or lime juice to help prevent discoloration, especially if the fruit is to be used in salads, as garnishes, or on platters.

"Huge lemons, cut in slices, would sink like setting suns into the dusky sea, softly illuminating it with their radiating membranes, and its clear, smooth surface aquiver from the rising bitter essence."

— *Rainer Maria Rilke, Austrian poet and novelist*

SELECTION

In spite of the huge range of citrus varieties, certain principles for choosing good specimens always apply. Fruits that are heavy for their size are a sure bet, signaling plenty of juice (lightweight fruits are often dry and mealy inside). Avoid fruit with obvious soft, bruised, or moldy areas.

With oranges, glossy, smoother skins usually indicate thinner peels and thus more juicy flesh. Coloration is tricky with oranges, which do not have to be orange to be sweet and delicious; in fact, oranges in many countries remain entirely green on the outside when they are fully ripe, thanks to how climate affects the green chlorophyll in the tree and its fruit. Because consumers in Europe and America associate green fruit with unripeness, some commercially grown oranges are dyed orange.

Lemons should be fully yellow, as green tinges indicate that they are not quite ripe. Limes should be uniformly green; a few brown spots are harmless, but avoid ones with large brownish areas, which may indicate flavor-altering scald. When selecting both lemons and limes, think about how you plan to use them. If you need them immediately, choose ones that are softer, even slightly shriveled, as they'll be juicier. If you don't need the fruits for several days (or if you want the oiliest, most pungent zest), choose harder ones with shiny, bumpier skins. The lemons or limes can sit for 3 to 5 days at room temperature; they'll soften and build up their juice this way.

Grapefruit color varies depending on the variety; yellow types will be uniformly yellow, and pink or red-fleshed fruits should have as yellow skins as possible with slightly rosy blushes.

STORAGE

Citrus fruits prefer lounging at room temperature; they will keep for about 1 week on your countertop, away from sunlight, but monitor them for signs of decay, desiccation, or overripening. Lemons and limes can be stored in the refrigerator crisper for up to 3 to 4 weeks.

TRIMMING AND CLEANING

One of the advantages of citrus is that they come in their own handy wrappers; with most of them, you can just wash the fruit under cold running water, peel, and eat. In the case of kumquats, there's no need to peel—just wash them and pop the entire fruit into your mouth. Citrons are used for their very thick peel and not their dry, unappetizing flesh.

Take a little time someday to teach yourself the technique of segmenting a citrus fruit. Use a sharp paring knife (a 4-inch blade is ideal) to slice off the ends of the fruit. Cut deep enough to expose the orange flesh. Then stand the fruit on one end and slice the peel from top to bottom, following the curve of the fruit and removing the peel and all of the white pith. Hold the fruit in your hand; working over a bowl, use your knife to slice out one individual section of orange, leaving the dividing membrane behind. Go around and around the fruit, doing the same thing until all the sections have been cut away from the membranes. Squeeze any pieces that might yield extra juice. You'll now have beautiful, jewel-like slices for eating and garnishing.

Blanching and Freezing

When citrus is in season, it can be handy to preserve it at its prime by freezing it. The texture may soften slightly and its taste may not be quite as sharp, but in general, frozen citrus holds its shape, color, and flavor quite well.

Squeeze the juice of lemons and limes into ice cube trays, then freeze, pop out the cubes, and store them in zipper-lock freezer bags. Oranges can be frozen either whole or as slices in a syrup of the fruit's own juice, water, and sugar either in jars or freezer containers; although sugar is not absolutely necessary for freezing, it does help preserve the fruit's color, texture, and flavor. Because of their high limonin content, navel oranges may be too bitter to be frozen without sugar, but other orange types are fine.

You can also freeze individual, unsweetened slices by arranging them on a single layer on a cookie sheet and freezing. Transfer the frozen pieces into zipper-lock freezer or vacuum food sealer-type bags, or freezer containers. Squeeze out any excess air and leave ½ inch of headspace (unless you are using the vacuum sealing method). Frozen citrus should keep for 6 to 10 months at 0°F.

Equivalents, Measures, and Servings

Oranges

- 3 medium oranges = 1 cup juice
- 1 medium orange = 2 to 3 tablespoons zest

Lemons

- 1 medium lemon = 2 to 3 tablespoons juice
- 1 medium lemon = 1½ to 3 teaspoons zest

Limes

- 1 medium lime = 1½ to 2 tablespoons juice
- 1 medium lime = 1 to 2 teaspoons zest

Grapefruit

- 1 medium grapefruit = 1 pound = 10 to 12 sections
- 1 medium grapefruit = ⅔ to ¾ cup juice

Complementary Herbs, Seasonings, and Foods

Almonds, apples, apricots, arugula, avocados, basil, berries, black pepper, brandy, brown sugar, cardamom, cherries, chicken, chiles, chocolate, cilantro, cinnamon, cloves, coffee, cranberries, cumin, eggs, figs, fish, ginger, grapes, hazelnuts, honey, mint, nectarines, nutmeg, other citrus, papayas, peaches, persimmons, pineapples, plums, prickly pears, rosemary, salt, seafood, strawberries, vanilla, vegetables.

Serving Suggestions

- As handy, nutritious snacks, it's hard to beat fresh oranges, grapefruit, mandarins, and tangerines. Just peel and enjoy. With kumquats, just pop the whole thing into your mouth—their sweet skins and sour flesh will wake you up in no time and leave you wanting more.

ment, cut-flower production, small-scale poultry production, tree fruit production, and various permaculture activities. Apprentices work 45 to 50 hours a week for approximately 30 weeks. Benefits include a weekly stipend and housing.

At **Hawthorne Valley Farm** (see the "Waldorf Schools" sidebar, page 276) in rural Ghent, New York, apprentices are placed in several types of apprenticeships: whole farm, vegetable field, corner garden vegetable, advanced apprenticeship field vegetable, advanced apprenticeship dairy herd management, and field manager assistant. Positions are for the season or a one- or two-year commitment. Housing is provided, plus a monthly stipend.

Tuition-Based Training Programs

In southern Oregon, the nonprofit **Rogue Farm Corps (RFC)** runs **FarmsNext**, a full-season internship of hands-on training and skill-based education in sustainable agriculture for aspiring farmers and ranchers. Participants receive up to 1,500 hours of field training with a mentor farmer at a host farm, 75 hours of classroom learning through **Oregon State University Extension's Growing Agripreneurs** program, and opportunities for independent study at a network of commercial family farms. Host farms provide a monthly stipend. An advanced, two-season, on-farm training program, **FarmsNOW**, prepares beginning farmers to run a successful farm business. Classes are facilitated by the RFC and **Oregon State University's Small Farms Program**. Host farms provide housing and a monthly stipend.

In Ester, Alaska, **Calypso Farm and Ecology Center's Farmer Training Program** prepares participants to embark on starting their own small farms. They work alongside experienced farmers through the growing season, learning a range of skills, from caring for greenhouse transplants and managing soil fertility to managing pests, caring for farm animals, and operating a CSA. Business planning and homesteading are included, as well as woodworking, basic tool-making, metalworking, and more. Basic housing is provided.

In California, the Apprenticeship in Ecological Horticulture at the **UC Santa Cruz Center for Agroecology and Sustainable Food Systems (CASFS)** provides training in organic gardening and small-scale farming in a six-month program designed to train future organic farmers, gardeners, teachers, and community leaders. About 35 to 40 apprentices annually work with staff in the greenhouses, gardens, fields, and orchards, as well as attend lectures, demonstrations, and field trips. The training location is a 30-acre farm and the 3-acre Alan Chadwick Garden, each with different soils and their own topography, microclimate, and history. Apprentices work 40 hours a week from mid-April to mid-October. Housing is available.

The California Farm Academy in Winters, California, is a program of the **Center for Land-Based Learning**. It offers a seven-month farmer training program that meets part-time in the early evenings and on weekends, and is followed by a farm business incubator component in which qualified graduates are eligible to lease plots of land at less than typical market rates for up to three years. The program does not offer housing.

Farm Beginnings is a 12-month mentored training course for beginning farmers developed by the **Land Stewardship Project**, a nonprofit that advocates for environmental and social justice in rural America. The **Farm Beginnings Collaborative (FBC)** is a national alliance of independent regional groups of farmers and farmer-training support organizations that works together to promote the

- Lemons and limes are nature's all-purpose seasoning; their zinginess enhances the flavors of all sorts of foods, from fish to vegetables to fruit. And be sure to use freshly squeezed juice—the commercial bottled stuff can be quite nasty!

- Key lime pie is that quintessential dessert of summer, made with little more than the juice of Key limes, egg yolks, and sweetened condensed milk, and topped with a meringue of whipped egg whites and sugar.

- Enjoy a glass of freshly squeezed orange juice. If you are making juice mixtures or smoothies, throw the whole, washed citrus fruit into your Vitamix or other juicer to extract the nutritional goodness of the peels, flesh, and all.

- Grapefruit is surprisingly good broiled—and as a hot treat on a cold day. Sprinkle freshly cut halves with a little brown sugar, and set under an oven broiler for 3 to 5 minutes until the sugar browns and starts to caramelize. Yum!

- Perk up the flavor of vegetables, desserts, and fruits with a little finely grated zest from lemons, limes, oranges, or citron. A classic combo is fresh asparagus spears, sautéed or grilled, with a shower of lemon zest grated over them right before serving.

- Pickled or preserved lemons are a major condiment in many Middle Eastern, Indian, and North African cuisines. You can make your own with a brine of water, lemon juice, vinegar, salt, and spices. They are especially good with Moroccan tagines, with rice in Asian dishes, as part of a Cambodian chicken soup called *ngam nguv,* and in cocktails like Bloody Marys.

- Make preserves or marmalade. For the latter, Spanish Seville oranges are traditionally used; they are less sweet than navel or regular eating oranges, they have a high pectin content, and their peel imparts a distinctive, slightly bitter flavor.

- With citrons, it is their thick peel rather than their flesh that is traditionally eaten in candied form or as a lovely pickle. In some Asian and Middle Eastern cultures, it is used as a digestive aid and a hangover cure. Americans usually meet citron in the form of those notorious holiday fruitcakes.

- Citrus was made for refreshing beverages, both spiked and nonalcoholic. Think punches, snappy cocktails, smoothies, teas, homemade sodas, lemonades, limeades…

- Don't throw away those orange, lemon, or lime peels—they are delicious candied or dried and used in desserts, drinks, salads, and as garnishes. Make sure, however, to use fruits that you know have not been sprayed with conventional pesticides or other toxic chemicals.

- Lime juice is ubiquitous in Mexican and South American cooking, where it is used to marinate raw fish in ceviche, combined with guacamole, sprinkled over a multitude of dishes along with chili powder, or as part of margaritas and other alcoholic drinks.

- Oranges and their juice are interesting additions to certain sauces and marinades made with ginger, honey, garlic, cumin, vinegar, hot chiles, and olive oil.

- The blossoms of citrus trees, if you can find them, are also edible, and their taste is reminiscent of their respective fruits. Use them in salads or to garnish drinks and desserts. Be sure to use only flowers that have not been sprayed with toxic chemicals.

- Few things are as soothing for a bad cold as a good homemade chicken soup and a hot drink made with lemons and honey.

- A traditional Greek soup is *avgolemono*, made with eggs, chicken broth, lemon juice, and rice or orzo (a type of pasta that resembles rice).

Lemon Noodles

SERVES 6 TO 8

1 pound linguine
⅓ cup olive oil, plus more for sautéing
¼ cup chopped fresh cilantro
Zest from 1 lemon
Juice from 2 lemons
1 cup sliced portobello mushrooms
3 green onions, thinly sliced
1 cup small green beans (haricots verts), cut into ½-inch segments
Parmesan cheese, finely grated
Salt and freshly ground black pepper

1. Cook the linguine until al dente.

2. Meanwhile, whisk the ⅓ cup olive oil, cilantro, lemon zest, and lemon juice in a large bowl. Add the pasta and toss until well coated. Hold the dressed pasta in a warm place.

3. Heat a tablespoon or two of olive oil in a medium skillet over medium heat. Lightly sauté the mushrooms, green onions, and green beans.

4. Combine the vegetables with the pasta, then garnish with the Parmesan cheese, salt, and pepper.

— *Roxanne Tiffin, Kula Fields, Inc., Kula, Maui, Hawaii*

Kula Fields Easy Key Lime Pie

MAKES ONE 9-INCH PIE

1½ cans sweetened condensed milk
½ cup sour cream
1 tablespoon grated lime zest
½ cup Key lime juice (or to taste)
One (9-inch) prepared or homemade graham cracker crust
Lime slices and whipped cream, for garnish (optional)

1. Preheat the oven to 350°F.

2. In a medium bowl, combine the condensed milk, sour cream, lime zest, and lime juice. Mix well and pour into the graham cracker crust.

3. Bake for 5 to 8 minutes, until tiny pinhole bubbles burst on the surface of the pie. **Important: Do not let this brown!** Remove the pie from the oven.

4. Chill the pie thoroughly before serving. Garnish with lime slices and whipped cream, if desired.

— *Roxanne Tiffin, owner and CEO of Kula Fields, Inc., Kula, Maui, Hawaii*

Farm Beginnings training model. Farm Beginnings began in Minnesota but is also offered in Illinois, Nebraska, North Dakota, South Dakota, Maine, and New York, along with other educational programs. Its programs are nonresidential.

The **North American Biodynamic Apprenticeship Program (NABDAP)** helps aspiring farmers develop the skills and knowledge they need to build successful organic and biodynamic farms. The program combines two years of on-farm training and mentoring on an American or Canadian farm with a course of classroom study in biodynamics. Mentor farms are both organic and biodynamic. Apprentices benefit from a comprehensive training curriculum, carefully selected mentor farms, and access to networking, support, and educational resources. Upon completing their training, apprentices are awarded a certificate in biodynamic farming from the **Biodynamic Association**.

Urban Farming

A growing interest in urban farming is spawning a growing number of training opportunities. The **Urban Farm School (UFS)** in Asheville, North Carolina, is designed for learning about growing resilient food systems in urban environments and beyond. The 716-hour program takes 25 students for a full season that includes a hands-on apprenticeship at one of several working farms in and around Asheville, as well as classes at the **Ashevillage Sanctuary**, a one-acre, eco-urban learning laboratory. Other learning takes place at urban homesteads, community gardens, micro-nurseries, and so on. The tuition includes a permaculture design certificate. **Ashevillage Institute**, the nonprofit parent organization, also offers its **Eco-Urban Homestead Apprenticeship Program** and courses in organic gardening, herbalism, wild edibles, natural building, and more.

CITRUS SALAD WITH FETA AND MINT

SERVES ABOUT 4, DEPENDING ON CHOICE OF FRUIT

CITRUS MUSTARD DRESSING

½ small sweet onion, finely chopped
1 tablespoon apple cider vinegar
1 teaspoon smooth brown mustard
1 tablespoon olive oil
2 teaspoons minced fresh thyme
¼ cup orange juice
1 tablespoon lemon juice

SALAD

5 whole citrus fruits, preferably a mix of different types, such as oranges (different varieties are nice), grapefruits, tangerines, tangelos, kumquats
5 to 6 tablespoons feta cheese, chopped or crumbled
1 tablespoon fresh mint, cut into chiffonade
Salt and freshly ground black pepper

1. Place the onion in a medium bowl. Add the vinegar, mustard, olive oil, thyme, and orange and lemon juices. Stir to combine, and allow the dressing to sit while you cut up your fruit.

2. One at a time, skin the citrus fruits with a knife (if using kumquats just cut them, rind on, into thin rounds). Set the first fruit on the cutting board and slice off the stem end, cutting off just enough to see the pith-free flesh of the fruit. Repeat on the other end. Rest your fruit on one of its now-flat surfaces and begin cutting the peel and white pith off in large, vertical slices as you follow the radius of the fruit. You want the fruit's exterior to be white-free.

3. Turn the fruit back on its side and cut it into ¼-inch-thick wheels, removing any seeds and thick white core as you do. Repeat with the remaining citrus fruits.

4. Once everything is cut, arrange the fruit slices on a platter. (At this point, you may cover the platter with plastic wrap and refrigerate it until ready to serve. Bring the platter out to warm the fruit a little before serving.)

5. Whisk the ingredients in your bowl and drizzle the dressing over the citrus. Sprinkle with the feta, mint, salt, and pepper. Serve immediately.

— *Paul Anater*

Shrimp with Oranges, Black Rice, and Coconut Milk

SERVES 4

Source Note: Weeknight cooking is all about simplicity and speed without sacrificing elegance and flavor. Seafood, as long as you purchase it from a trusted purveyor the day you plan to use it, never fails at being fast and delicious. "Forbidden" black rice is available at Whole Foods Market, Amazon.com, and many specialty food stores.

1½ cups black rice
2¾ cups water
2 teaspoons salt
1 cup freshly squeezed orange juice
2 navel oranges, peeled and cut into segments
1 teaspoon honey
20 jumbo shrimp or prawns (about 2 pounds total), peeled and deveined
Kosher salt and freshly ground black pepper
4 tablespoons neutral-tasting olive oil, divided
1 teaspoon mild curry powder
1 cup coconut milk
2 cups baby spinach leaves

1. Place the rice in a pot (that has a fitted lid) and cover it with the water; add the salt. Bring to a boil, then reduce the heat to very low. Cover and cook for about 30 minutes, or until the water has been absorbed and the rice is cooked through. Spread the rice out on a rimmed baking sheet to cool to room temperature.

2. Pour the orange juice into a small saucepan over medium-low heat. Simmer until it has reduced to ¼ cup. Swirl in the orange segments and the honey; set aside.

3. Pat the prawns dry with a clean dish towel or paper towels. Sprinkle with salt and pepper. Heat a large skillet with enough olive oil to evenly coat the bottom of the skillet (1 to 2 tablespoons). When the oil is shimmering and quite hot, add the prawns in a single layer—you may have to work in batches. Do not move them for 1½ minutes, or until a seared golden crust is formed, and then flip them and cook about 1 minute longer, until just cooked through. Transfer the prawns to a plate.

4. Add about 2 tablespoons of oil to the skillet and add the rice. Cook for 1 minute, stirring frequently, then add the curry powder and coconut milk. Cook for 1 additional minute, then toss in the spinach.

5. Spoon the rice onto individual serving dishes and top with the prawns. Spoon the orange sauce over the prawns and serve immediately.

— *Lauren Mitchell Wilkinson,* Groove Food *blog*

Organic Ag as Job Training Vehicle

*A paid training program not strictly focused on agriculture is offered by **Growing Home**, a social enterprise committed to empowering people and communities affiliated with Chicago's first USDA-certified organic, high-production urban farms. With farms in the Englewood and Back of the Yards neighborhoods, as well as the 10-acre **Les Brown Memorial Farm** in Marseilles, Illinois, Growing Home uses organic agriculture as a vehicle for job training, employment, and community development. The program includes agriculture and horticulture, job readiness training, and job search assistance and placement. Production assistants choose a culinary or landscaping track and are paid an hourly wage for their time in work and in class over 14 weeks.*

Other Training Program Resources

*An excellent resource for education and training in sustainable farming is the **Beginning Farmer section of the website of the National Sustainable Agriculture Information Service** (https://attra.ncat. org/attra-pub/local_food/startup. html). One of the clickable links is to a directory of sustainable farming internships and apprenticeships in the United States and Canada that anyone can browse by state or province for free. Other links take visitors to USDA programs, nongovernmental training programs, and specific resources for immigrants, veterans, and women starting out in farming.*

For all that they offer prospective farmers and the future of family farming, training programs can also be a good reality check for every participant. "So You Want to Be a Farmer," an article by Jesse Hirsch in the fall 2014 issue of Modern Farmer *magazine suggests the need for "negotiating the gap between farm fantasy and reality." The Land*

GRAPEFRUIT AND KIWI SORBET

MAKES ABOUT 2 CUPS

Source Note: *The grapefruits we get tend to be fairly sweet. Their mature sugars make great sorbets while still retaining the gentle tartness that makes grapefruits such a great breakfast snack. This recipe combines them with ripe, organic kiwis and gives the resulting sorbet the perfect blend of exotic sweetness and refreshing tartness.*

I like my sorbets silky smooth, and one of the tricks to keeping them from looking like granitas is to add a little vodka. The vodka lowers the temperature that the sorbet freezes at and keeps large crystals from forming, although it will increase the time it takes for the sorbet to set up. After about half an hour in the ice cream maker, the sorbet should be ready to transfer to a chilled container and into the freezer for another 1 to 2 hours, depending on how firm you prefer your sorbet.

> ½ cup water
> 1 cup sugar
> Juice of 2 grapefruits (about 1½ cups)
> Juice of 2 kiwifruits
> 1 teaspoon grapefruit zest
> 1 tablespoon vodka

1. In a small pan, mix the water and sugar. Bring to a boil, then reduce the heat; simmer until the sugar is completely dissolved. (I prefer the slightly caramel flavor of natural sugar, though it will slightly darken the color of the sorbet.) After the sugar has dissolved, refrigerate the syrup until it is cold.

2. Add the grapefruit and kiwi juice, grapefruit zest, and vodka. Pour the mixture into an ice cream maker and follow the manufacturer's instructions. Transfer the sorbet to a chilled container and freeze until it reaches the desired consistency. That's it!

Cooking Note: If you don't have a juicer for the kiwifruits, use a blender to puree them, then push the puree through a fine-mesh strainer to obtain the juice.

— *Gabriel Avila-Mooney, Full Circle Farm, Seattle, Washington*

FRUIT PIZZA

MAKES ONE 14-INCH PIZZA

Author Note: *This recipe comes from a lovely regional cookbook celebrating 100 years of traditional cooking from the town of Hills, Minnesota, population around 500. In this age of global celebrity chefs and trendy cooking, this book captures the satisfying Midwestern foods and flavors of home, church suppers, potlucks, festivals, and Main Street America. This fruit pizza is a perennial favorite, especially with kids.*

Pizza Crust

1 cup (2 sticks) margarine or butter, at room temperature
1½ cups powdered sugar
1 egg
¼ teaspoon vanilla or almond extract
2½ cups flour
1 teaspoon baking soda
1 teaspoon cream of tartar

Topping

8 ounces cream cheese, at room temperature
½ cup granulated sugar
1 teaspoon vanilla extract

Sauce

¾ cup water
¼ cup lemon juice
1 cup orange juice
1 cup granulated sugar
Pinch of salt
3 tablespoons cornstarch

Fruit

About 3 cups sliced fresh fruit, including halved grapes, strawberries, bananas, kiwifruit, peaches, nectarines, sliced oranges, blueberries, pineapple, etc.

1. In a large bowl, use a wooden spoon or an electric mixer to cream together the margarine, powdered sugar, egg, and vanilla extract. Then stir in the flour, baking soda, and cream of tartar and mix until well combined. Pat the dough into a large disk, wrap, and chill it for several hours.

2. When you're ready to make the crust, preheat the oven to 375°F. Sprinkle some flour onto your work surface, then roll the dough into a circle to fit a 12-to-14-inch pizza pan or cookie sheet. Bake for 15 minutes, then remove the crust from the oven and let it cool.

3. In a bowl, beat the cream cheese, sugar, and vanilla until well combined. Spread it over the cooled crust.

4. To make the sauce, combine the water, lemon juice, orange juice, sugar, salt, and cornstarch in a pan over medium heat. Bring the mixture to a boil, stirring constantly, and remove it from the heat when it starts to thicken. Cool.

5. Arrange the fruit artistically over the top of the pizza; then drizzle the sauce over the fruit.

— *Coleen Martens,* Hills Centennial Cookbook

"In the 1960s, you could eat anything you wanted, and of course, people were smoking cigarettes and all kinds of things, and there was no talk about fat and anything like that, and butter and cream were rife. Those were lovely days for gastronomy, I must say."

— *Julia Child, American chef and TV cooking personality*

COCONUTS

COCOS NUCIFERA

Few plants are as singularly useful to humanity as the coconut palm. The leaves and trunk provide sturdy building materials; the plant's sap can be tapped to make an alcoholic drink; the outer husk of the coconut fruit yields a dry, fibrous material called coir, which is woven into mats and rope; coconut shells are used as containers and carved into ornaments; and of course, the coconut fruit itself produces a multitude of edible products—coconut water (the clear liquid of immature fruits), coconut milk and cream (made from the shredded flesh of mature fruits), the nutritious, white flesh itself (called copra), and its edible oils, which are made into cosmetics, moisturizers, hair-care products, and cooking fat. Even the immature main bud of the plant is edible, a delicacy that kills the tree when harvested.

You are, of course, unlikely to find coconuts in your CSA box, but you will frequently see them at farmers markets in Florida and Hawaii, where, in a matter of seconds, vendors deftly wielding huge machetes whack green coconuts into manageable vessels for sipping the refreshing coconut water within. That said, coconuts are not the easiest fruits to work with at home, unless you have the right tools and plenty of time and patience (see the recipe for making your own coconut milk on page 349). So this book assumes that for cooking, you will be generally relying on commercial dried coconut and canned coconut products.

A lot of culinary attention has been paid to coconuts in recent years in America with the meteoric rise of coconut water, oil, flour, and all sorts of coconut-derived products being touted as healthful alternatives to regular grain and animal dairy foods. As with many such crazes, it remains to be seen if coconuts are simply a passing fad or their popularity will stand the test of time.

HISTORY

The precise birthplace of coconuts is subject to controversy and lost to time—and more likely to the ocean currents in which the fruit often finds itself floating. Most likely the coconut originated in the Malay Archipelago, but it has been so widely dispersed by humans on seafaring journeys both long and short that it is impossible to tell. One fact that is not in dispute, however, is its critical role in the food systems of humans across the Pacific Islands, Asia, and the Americas. Polynesian peoples also brought the coconut, along with sweet potatoes and taro, as much-needed food staples to Hawaii. So valuable was (and still is) the coconut as food, medicine, and shelter that it is called the Tree of Life in several cultures. Currently coconuts are grown in more than 90 countries worldwide, with India and the Philippines among the top producers.

NUTRITION

Coconuts are highly unusual in the plant world for their inordinate fat content, and saturated fat at that. A single medium coconut weighs in at a whopping 1,405 calories and 133 grams of fat, 117 of them saturated. However, the type of saturated fat in coconuts is different from that in meat, and it may have some health benefits. Coconuts also contain significant amounts of vitamins C and B6, protein, calcium, potassium, iron, and magnesium. And some truth does lie behind the marketing hype—coconut water is indeed a rich source of vitamins, minerals, and electrolytes, with minimal fat and calories.

SEASON

Coconut trees bear fruit year-round, so there is no specific season for them. You can readily find green coconuts at farmers markets in tropical regions and often at ethnic food stores. Husked mature coconuts are sometimes carried in regular supermarkets.

SELECTION

To pick out a good coconut, you must know how you are going to use it. If you want refreshing coconut water and the young, gelatinous, jelly-like meat, you must buy young, immature, green coconuts. Pick them up and shake them vigorously; you should hear plenty of sloshing inside, a sign that they may contain at least a cup of fluid. They should be heavy for their size.

If you want firm meat for eating or cooking, or to make white coconut milk or cream, you will need to choose mature, uniformly brown specimens that don't contain much liquid inside; once again, the "slosh" test works well. Avoid coconuts with outer gray areas, especially around their eyes.

Regardless of whether you are buying a coconut green or mature, examine the condition of the three eyes that are always present at one end of the nut. They should be free of mold, grayish coloration, and any protrusions. Fresh coconuts should always have snow-white meat; coconuts past their prime have a yellowish tinge to their flesh.

TRIMMING AND CLEANING

Coconuts are markedly tough to crack; there is a reason why they have flourished for centuries, floating on the world's oceans and used by humans on long voyages as conveniently prepackaged sources of food and liquid. To open mature coconuts, it is best to consult one of the numerous videos or guides on the Internet (WikiHow has an especially good illustrated, step-by-step tutorial), but the basic steps are generally a combination of the following: using a screwdriver to puncture the single eye (of the three) that is soft; loosening the husk by tapping the equator of the coconut with a heavy cleaver or machete while holding it over a bowl to catch any liquid; then whacking it to crack it open. You can also use a hard stone or concrete edge if you don't have a heavy knife or lack the confidence for such potentially dangerous moves.

For green coconuts, you can actually open them with a regular paring knife instead of a machete (although the latter comes in handy for doing the job faster). YouTube has a great video on this detailed process, produced by Okraw (www.okraw.com).

STORAGE

If possible, coconuts should be stored at cooler temperatures in the pantry, refrigerator, or freezer, as they are quite prone to molds and bacteria. Stored this way, whole coconuts will keep for 2 to 3 weeks in the refrigerator and 6 to 8 months in the freezer. Freezing coconuts does change the

No Monkeying Around

Because coconut trees can grow to nearly 100 feet tall and are not noted for their extensive branching patterns, scaling the skinny trunks to pick the nuts is dangerous work, usually reserved for agile kids or men of low social rank or caste in some countries.

Enter the monkeys! In Thailand, Sumatra, India, and other extensive coconut-growing areas, these nimble, pig-tailed macaques are specially trained to climb the trees and twist off the ripe fruits. They are usually controlled by a long rope that is held by their handlers, but some respond simply to voice commands.

According to some coconut farmers, monkeys can pick 500 to 800 fruits a day, compared with just 100 by their human counterparts. And they gladly work for just bananas.

flesh's consistency, making it softer and easier to handle. A coconut at room temperature will keep for only about 1 week.

Dried, shredded coconut should be kept in an airtight container (a lidded jar is perfect) in the refrigerator, where it will last for 6 to 12 months. Fresh, shelled coconut meat keeps in the refrigerator for 4 to 5 days or in the freezer for up to 6 months, and coconut milk can be safely stored in the refrigerator for about 2 days, or in the freezer for up to 2 months.

BLANCHING AND FREEZING

Because of the sheer time and effort involved in processing fresh coconut, the freezer can be your best friend if you want a steady supply of coconut on hand. You can either shred or chunk raw coconut meat, as you prefer. For the chunk method, cut the white flesh into 4 to 8 large chunks and sprinkle them lightly with sugar (this will help them keep better). Place the chunks in zipper-lock freezer or vacuum food sealer-type bags, or freezer containers. Squeeze out any excess air and leave ½ inch of headspace (unless you are using the vacuum sealing method).

For the shredded method, cut the coconut meat into chunks and run it through a food processor, or use a hand grater to shred it. Follow the same steps for packaging it for the freezer as the chunk method above, except that you can pour coconut milk over it, if desired. Coconut preserved this way should keep for up to 6 months at 0°F.

EQUIVALENTS, MEASURES, AND SERVINGS

- 1 medium fresh coconut = 1 pound meat = 3 cups grated
- 7-ounce package dried and flaked = 2½ cups

COMPLEMENTARY HERBS, SEASONINGS, AND FOODS

Allspice, banana, basil, black pepper, Brazil nut, caramel, chocolate, citrus, cumin, curry, fish, garlic, ginger, guava, ice cream, lemongrass, mangoes, passion fruit, pineapple, rice, seafood, shrimp, tomato, turmeric, vanilla.

SERVING SUGGESTIONS

- Creamy coconut milk and coconut cream, because of their fatty richness and distinctive flavor, are the ultimate enhancers in soups, curries, and sauces. They are staples in the cuisines of Southeast Asia, India, Hawaii, Polynesia, the Caribbean, and parts of Africa.

- If you cannot tolerate animal dairy products, use coconut milk to make a delicious yogurt, using full-fat coconut milk, probiotics, and powdered gelatin.

- Dried shredded coconut (either sweetened or unsweetened) is lovely in desserts. Macaroons, those small, circular cookies, are scrumptious—ground almonds, coconut, sugar, and egg whites baked into chewy goodness.

- The simplest pleasures in life are often the best. Open an immature coconut, drink its refreshing water through a straw, and then scoop out chunks of the soft, gelatinous, delicately flavored meat.

- Remember ambrosia, that old-fashioned fruit salad that your grandmother used to make? That original recipe of fresh or canned pineapple, canned mandarin oranges or fresh orange sections, miniature marshmallows, coconut, and whipped cream is still pretty hard to beat.

- Coconut flour can be used in baking as a substitute for regular grain flours for those on gluten-free diets.

- Coconut water (the clear liquid in immature coconuts) is highly nutritious and makes a good base for beverages, juice mixtures, and smoothies instead of regular water. It also makes a refreshing drink on its own.

- Something wonderful happens when you substitute coconut milk for part of the water when cooking rice. As well as the delicious flavor it imparts, the milk gives the rice a richer, chewier texture. Add some grated fresh ginger-root at the start of cooking and chopped cilantro right before serving for even more excitement!

- Coconut cream pie. Bananas. Custard. Habit-forming.

KULA FIELDS MACADAMIA AND COCONUT PIE

MAKES ONE 9-INCH PIE

Source Note: This pie is always a hit. It's also made without corn syrup.

2 eggs
½ cup (1 stick) butter, melted and slightly cooled
1 cup light brown sugar
¼ cup white sugar
1 tablespoon all-purpose flour
1 tablespoon vanilla soy milk (plain cow's milk works just fine too)
1 vanilla bean, seeds scraped, or 1 teaspoon vanilla extract
1 cup chopped macadamia nuts
½ cup shredded coconut
One (9-inch) premade, unbaked piecrust

1. Preheat the oven to 400°F.

2. In a large bowl, beat the eggs until foamy, then stir in the melted butter. Stir in the brown sugar, white sugar, and flour; mix well. Add the milk, vanilla bean (seeds only—save the pod for another use), macadamia nuts, and coconut.

3. Pour the mixture into the piecrust. Bake for 10 minutes at 400°F, then reduce the temperature to 350°F and bake for 30 to 40 minutes, or until the filling is set.

— *Roxanne Tiffin, owner and CEO of Kula Fields, Inc., Kula, Maui, Hawaii*

FRESH COCONUT MILK

Author Note: If you ever wanted to try your hand at making your own coconut milk from fresh coconuts, here's how. It does take some effort; the liquid sloshing around in a green or young coconut is actually a watery juice. In mature coconuts, this liquid has mostly disappeared, and so the creamy coconut milk we commonly think of has to be extracted from the nuts' shredded or grated white meat with hot water and a bit of elbow grease.

"The most remarkable thing about my mother is that for 30 years she served the family nothing but leftovers. The original meal has never been found."

— *Calvin Trillin, American writer*

1. Pare the brown skin and chop or break the inner white meat into small chunks. Measure the meat required by the particular recipe and drop it into the jar of an electric blender. Add an equal number of cups of hot (not boiling) water and blend at high speed for 1 minute. Stop the machine and scrape down the sides of the jar with a rubber spatula. Then blend again until the coconut is reduced to a thick, fibrous liquid. To make the coconut milk by hand, you begin by grating the peeled coconut, piece by piece, into a bowl, then measuring the meat and stirring into it an equal amount of hot (not boiling) water.

2. Then proceed as follows: Scrape the entire contents of the blender jar or the bowl into a fine sieve lined with a double thickness of dampened cheesecloth and set over a deep bowl. With a wooden spoon, press down hard on the coconut to extract as much liquid as possible. Bring the ends of the cheesecloth together to enclose the pulp and wring the ends vigorously to squeeze out the remaining liquid. Discard the pulp. One cup of coarsely chopped coconut meat combined with one cup of hot water should produce one cup of coconut milk. (In the Pacific, the grated coconut is often squeezed with only a few drops of water added, which produces a thicker "cream.")

3. For recipes that specify rich coconut top milk, let the milk stand at room temperature or in the refrigerator for an hour or so until the liquid separates and the richest part rises to the surface. Skim off this top milk with a large spoon. If you do not want to use the top milk separately, stir the liquid well before cooking with it. Tightly covered and refrigerated, coconut milk can be safely kept for about 5 days.

— *Rafael Steinberg,* Time-Life Foods of the World, Pacific and Southeast Asian Cooking

KIWIFRUITS ACTINIDIA DELICIOSA

Few produce items are as recognizable as the little kiwi, an undeniably cute egg of a fruit wrapped in fuzzy, brown skin that, when cut open, reveals startlingly vibrant, juicy green flesh surrounding a dense, cream-colored core. Its refreshing, distinctive, tart-sweet taste is reminiscent of strawberry, watermelon, and citrus. Its numerous seeds surrounding the core are edible.

This cultivar is only one of many varieties of kiwifruit, some of which are no bigger than grapes or have golden rather than green flesh. Kiwis are actually the berries of large, fast-growing vines. The fruit emerged as a darling of the food world in the late 1980s, thanks to savvy marketing and distribution. It also helped that kiwis are a fruit-handler's fantasy come true, partly because they come already packaged in their protective skins. And even when picked hard and unripe, they have phenomenal keeping qualities—sometimes as long as 10 months in commercial coolers. Once they are exposed to warmer temperatures and ethylene gas, they happily ripen within a week's time. About 98 percent of

HISTORY

Kiwis originated in China, where they have been cultivated and enjoyed for centuries. They were introduced in 1906 to New Zealand, where a noted nurseryman developed the familiar Hayward cultivar that makes up nearly all of the US crop today. American servicemen picked up a taste for the fruit when they were stationed in New Zealand during World War II. This prompted the first exports to California in the early 1950s under the unfortunate name of "Chinese gooseberry." Given the rabid anti-Communist spirit of the time, Americans didn't want to buy anything with such a moniker, and the name "kiwifruit" was born, in reference to the fruit's resemblance to New Zealand's famous brown-feathered, flightless bird.

NUTRITION

Kiwis are exceptionally rich in vitamins C and K, and also contain some vitamins E and B6, as well as copper, potassium, and magnesium. They are also a good source of lutein, an antioxidant valued for eye health. The fuzzy, brown skins are perfectly edible if thoroughly washed, and they are an excellent source of dietary fiber. One large kiwifruit contains about 55 calories.

SEASON

Commercially, kiwis are available year-round, with the California crop at its peak between October and May, and New Zealand filling in from June to October.

SELECTION

When selecting kiwifruit, be firm about firmness. A fully ripe kiwi gives slightly under pressure, but one that is too soft may be overripe, mealy, or lacking in flavor.

STORAGE

Unripe kiwis can be ripened by placing them in a bowl at room temperature for a few days, or encasing them in a paper bag with a ripe apple or banana. Once the fruits are ripe and have softened somewhat, store them in the refrigerator. They are not as delicate as they look and can keep for up to 4 weeks in the refrigerator.

TRIMMING AND CLEANING

The skins of kiwis are edible and nutritious, so you can choose to eat them after a thorough washing—or not, as you prefer. Eat them whole, like an apple, or indulge in what the California Kiwifruit Commission affectionately calls "slooping the kiwi"—slicing the fruit in half lengthwise, then scooping out the juicy flesh with a spoon.

BLANCHING AND FREEZING

Kiwifruit can be prepared in a light sugar syrup with ascorbic acid (vitamin C) crystals to better preserve their flavor and color. To make 1 quart

Cooking Tip

Kiwis contain a unique enzyme called actinidin that dissolves proteins, making them natural meat tenderizers; use them in marinades for beef, lamb, pork, and chicken, or spread the pureed flesh or hollowed-out skins directly onto meat that has been pricked a few times with a knife.

These same enzymes also prevent gelatin from setting and can adversely affect milk dishes, so you must either poach or briefly boil the fruit before using it in recipes calling for large quantities of either. Freezing does not inactivate these enzymes.

of syrup, combine 3 cups of sugar with 4 cups of water and 1 teaspoon of ascorbic acid crystals in a pot, stir well, and bring to a boil; cook until the sugar dissolves. Chill, then pour ½ cup of syrup into a freezer container, add the sliced kiwi, and keep adding syrup until the fruit is covered. Leave ½ inch of headspace for pints, 1 inch for quarts.

You can also use a dry sugar pack, with 1 cup of sugar to 1 quart of kiwifruit slices; toss to coat. Or you can freeze individual, unsweetened slices by arranging them on a single layer on a cookie sheet and freezing. Transfer the frozen pieces into zipper-lock freezer or vacuum food sealer-type bags, or freezer containers. Squeeze out any excess air and leave ½ inch of headspace (unless you are using the vacuum sealing method). Frozen kiwi should keep for up to 1 year at 0°F.

EQUIVALENTS, MEASURES, AND SERVINGS

- 1 medium kiwifruit = 5 to 6 slices = ½ cup slices

COMPLEMENTARY HERBS, SEASONINGS, AND FOODS

Apples, bananas, cherries, chicken, chile, citrus, coconut, cream, fish, ginger, grapefruit, ham, honey, lime, mangoes, maple syrup, melons, oranges, pineapples, raspberries, scallops, shrimp, strawberries, watercress.

SERVING SUGGESTIONS

- The kiwi's eye-catching flesh makes it a natural for topping tarts and pies. Peel the fruit and slice it crosswise into thin rounds, or cut it lengthwise into fat wedges.
- Kiwi goes wonderfully with all sorts of fresh fruits in salads and compotes.
- Toss kiwi with ham, chicken, shrimp, or scallops in salads.
- Kiwis can be substituted for oranges in many savory and sweet dishes. Try it with avocado and radicchio for a refreshing, beautiful salad.
- Kiwi makes a fun canapé atop ham and cream cheese on crackers.
- Crush or puree kiwifruit and serve it alongside poached or sliced fresh fruit, or with angel food or pound cake.
- Kiwis can be lovely made into light ices and sorbets.
- Make kiwi jam; try it in combination with other tropical fruits like mangoes, pineapple, and lychees.
- Kiwis and kebabs go together like peas in a pod—skewer chunks with pieces of fish and season with lime and chile powder, or alternate with other fresh fruit like strawberries, melon, and bananas.
- Kiwis and Devonshire cream—an irresistible combination. Make sure to eat this right away, before the enzymes in the fresh kiwi cause the cream to disintegrate.

CALIFORNIA DREAMING KIWI RIBS SERVES 4 TO 6

Author Note: These beef ribs are glazed with a mixture of kiwifruit jam and seasonings for a rich, sweet, savory sauce. Make the kiwifruit jam ahead of time or use a good store-bought version.

2 to 3 racks beef ribs (about 8 pounds)

1 cup Kiwifruit Jam (see the recipe below)
1 large yellow onion, chopped
2 garlic cloves, minced
½ cup apple juice
1 teaspoon dry mustard
1 tablespoon soy sauce
1 teaspoon Worcestershire sauce
¼ cup brown sugar
5 kiwifruit

1. Precook the ribs by baking them in a 350°F oven for 30 minutes. Alternatively, parboil them by cutting the racks into large sections, putting them in a large pot, and covering them with cold water. Bring to a boil, then reduce the heat and simmer for 20 minutes.

2. Prepare the sauce by placing the kiwi jam, onion, garlic, apple juice, mustard, soy sauce, Worcestershire sauce, and brown sugar in a saucepan. Bring to a boil, stir well, then reduce the heat and simmer for 10 to 15 minutes.

3. Heat the oven or your outdoor grill to 275°F.

4. Rub a generous amount of sauce over the precooked ribs. Place the racks on the grill or in the oven and cook for 1½ to 2 hours, or until they are tender and the meat is almost falling off the bone.

5. Cut the ribs into individual portions and pour more sauce over them, saving some sauce for dipping. Place the ribs on a large platter.

6. Peel and slice the kiwifruits and arrange them on the rim of the platter. Have lots of napkins on hand.

— *California Kiwifruit Commission*

KIWIFRUIT JAM   MAKES 8 CUPS

Author Note: This jam is delicious on toast, as an ice cream topping, and as part of a barbecue glaze for ribs (see the California Dreaming Kiwi Ribs recipe above). For more details on correctly and safely making jam, consult a trusted cookbook or follow the instructions included with the pectin.

4½ cups peeled, crushed kiwifruit (about 4 pounds)
1 box (1¾ ounces) powdered pectin
7 cups sugar

1. In a large, heavy kettle, heat the kiwifruit on medium heat, stirring, for 3 minutes.

2. Add the pectin and mix well. Increase the heat to high and stir until the mixture comes to a hard boil.

3. Add the sugar all at once. Bring the mixture back to a full rolling

Since its inception, Growing Power has served as a "living museum" or "idea factory" for the young, the elderly, farmers, producers, and other professionals ranging from USDA personnel to urban planners. Training areas include acid-digestion, anaerobic digestion for food waste, bio-phyto remediation and soil health, aquaculture closed-loop systems, vermiculture, small- and large-scale composting, urban agriculture, permaculture, food distribution, marketing, value-added product development, youth education, community engagement, participatory leadership development, and project planning.

As of 2015, Growing Power has been involved in more than 70 projects and outreach programs in Milwaukee, across the United States, and throughout the world. Will has also trained and taught in the Ukraine, Macedonia, and Kenya, and has plans in place to create community food centers in South Africa, Zimbabwe, and Haiti.

In 2008, Allen was awarded the John D. and Catherine T. MacArthur Foundation's Genius Grant and named a MacArthur Fellow— only the second farmer ever to be so honored. Allen was also one of four national spokesmen who joined First Lady Michelle Obama at the White House to launch her "Let's Move!" initiative to reverse the epidemic of childhood obesity. In May 2010, Time magazine named Allen one of the 100 Most Influential People in the World.

As of 2015, plans include building a five-story vertical farm in Milwaukee that will further support Growing Power's expanding mission as a local and national resource for learning about sustainable urban food production.

To find out more about Growing Power, visit its website at www.growingpower.org, or read Allen's book, The Good Food Revolution: Growing Healthy Food, People, and Communities.

boil; boil hard for 1 minute. Remove the jam from the heat and quickly skim the foam from the surface.

4. Pour the jam into hot, sterilized half-pint jars and seal. Process the jars in a boiling-water bath for 5 minutes. Remove the jars from the water and set them on a rack to cool. When the jam has fully cooled, test the jars to make sure they've all sealed; if there are any that haven't sealed, store them in your refrigerator.

— *California Kiwifruit Commission*

FRENCH TOAST KIWIFRUIT   SERVES 2 TO 3

3 kiwifruit
2 eggs, slightly beaten
2 teaspoons milk
½ teaspoon cinnamon
½ teaspoon vanilla extract
4 to 6 slices bread
3 tablespoons corn oil
2 tablespoons butter or margarine
½ cup confectioner's sugar

1. Rinse and peel the kiwifruit, then slice them into rounds.

2. Whisk the eggs, milk, cinnamon, and vanilla in a shallow dish. Dip the bread slices into the mixture and coat both sides, turning the bread over a few times.

3. Heat the corn oil over medium heat in a nonstick skillet. Place the bread slices in the hot skillet, turning them over until the toast is cooked to a golden color. Transfer to a plate.

4. Spread the butter on each slice of toast, top each piece with several kiwifruit slices, and dust each piece with confectioner's sugar.

— *California Kiwifruit Commission*

LYCHEES   LITCHI CHINENSIS

A beautiful little fruit with a bumpy, raspberry-hued skin and a distinctive, almost floral fragrance, lychees have been enjoyed in China for more than two millennia. To enjoy, just puncture the leathery red shell to reveal the white, succulent, grape-like flesh within, but avoid ingesting the single large, hard brown seed. Fresh lychees are not common in US farmers markets except in Hawaii and Florida, but they are often available in Asian grocery stores and markets. Dried and canned forms of the fruit are also delicious and may be more readily available than fresh.

HISTORY

Lychees originated more than 2,000 years ago in the tropical rainforests and mountain forests in southern China, where they remain a dominant tree species. In fact, Guangdong is called the Kingdom of Lychee, and some villages have trees that are more than a thousand years old. Because of their erratic production, slow growth, and extreme sensitivity to cold temperatures, lychees have never been widely commercially planted in America; nonetheless some 33 varieties are grown, mostly in Florida and Hawaii. In addition to China and Southeast Asia, Australia is a major producer of lychees.

NUTRITION

Lychees are high in vitamins B6 and C, riboflavin, niacin, potassium, copper, and fiber. Each fruit contains about 7 calories; 1 cup contains 125 calories.

SEASON

For the south Florida crop, the peak season for lychees is between May and June; December to February is prime time for the Australian crop.

SELECTION

Choose lychees that are heavy for their size; avoid lightweight specimens with any signs of mold, discoloration, or shriveling.

STORAGE

Lychees are picked fully ripe, as they will not continue to ripen after harvesting. Store lychees in the refrigerator in a perforated plastic bag or container with some ventilation to reduce mold and condensation. They should keep for up to 2 or even 3 weeks, although they may lose some of their fragrance during that time.

TRIMMING AND CLEANING

Not much preparation is needed with a lychee. Simply crack the shell at the stem end with the tip of a knife or a fingernail, then pull it off. Loosen the single glossy seed from the fruit at the stem end, then halve the fruit to remove it. Or just pop the whole fruit into your mouth and spit out the seed.

BLANCHING AND FREEZING

The fruit can easily be frozen right in their skins, or they can be peeled first. The outer skins may turn brown and the fruits' texture will deteriorate during freezing, but this will not affect their flavor. Spread the lychees on a tray in a single layer and freeze. Package the lychees in zipper-lock freezer or vacuum food sealer-type bags, or freezer containers. Squeeze out any excess air and leave 1 inch of headspace (unless you are using the vacuum sealing method). They will keep for up to 1 year at 0°F.

EQUIVALENTS, MEASURES, AND SERVINGS

- 15 to 18 lychees = 1 pound

For More Information

Lychees Online
www.lycheesonline.com

COMPLEMENTARY HERBS, SEASONINGS, AND FOODS

Balsamic vinegar, bananas, basil, blueberries, cherries, chicken, citrus, coconut, ginger, gooseberries, honey, ice cream, lime, mangoes, mint, oranges, passion fruit, pears, pork, raspberries, strawberries, vanilla.

SERVING SUGGESTIONS

- Whole, fresh lychees make a delicious surprise substitute for any recipe calling for whole grapes. Sprinkle them fresh into fruit salads or savory dishes.
- Puree lychees with other fruit and use in homemade ice pops, ice creams, sorbets, and cold fruit soups.
- Spear peeled lychees on toothpicks with baked ham for a fun appetizer, or wrap a little prosciutto strip around each fruit.
- Drop a few lychees into your blender with other fruit when making smoothies and shakes.
- Lychees also go well with stir-fries, especially with chicken.
- Make lychees into a highly perfumed syrup to use in cocktails and mixed drinks.

BASIL-INFUSED LYCHEE-LIME ICE POPS

MAKES 4 TO 5 POPS (DEPENDING ON THE SIZE OF YOUR MOLDS)

Source Note: Lychee, basil, and lime? Yes! They go together perfectly in these ice pops.

⅓ cup water
1 tablespoon sugar
5 large basil leaves
1 (20-ounce) can lychees, drained
Juice and zest from 1 lime

1. Combine the water, sugar, and basil leaves in a small saucepan. Bring to a simmer over medium heat. Remove from the heat and cool to room temperature.

2. Pour the basil syrup through a sieve into a blender or food processor. Discard the basil. Add the lychees, lime juice, and lime zest, and blend until smooth. Pour the fruit mixture into ice pop molds and freeze until solid.

— *Kiersten Frase,* OhMyVeggies *blog*

LYCHEE CHUTNEY
MAKES 6 TO 8 HALF-PINT JARS

Author Note: Lychee vinegar is available online through mail order and specialty food stores. For more details on correctly and safely canning jam and

chutney, consult a trusted cookbook or the USDA website at http://nchfp.uga. edu/publications/publications_usda.html. Or follow the general instructions for Paul's Strawberry Jam on page 100.

1½ cups sugar
1 cup lychee vinegar
1 cup chopped mango
1 cup chopped papaya
2 cups chopped lychees
1 medium onion, chopped
1 bell pepper, chopped
1 lime (peel left on), seeded and chopped
½ cup raisins
1 teaspoon salt
1½ teaspoons ground ginger
¼ teaspoon cayenne
2 whole cloves garlic
A spice bag containing 15 cloves and 1 cinnamon stick

1. Put the sugar and vinegar into a large saucepot and bring them to a boil, stirring to dissolve the sugar. Maintain the boil for 5 minutes; the liquid will reduce and become slightly syrupy. Add all of the remaining ingredients and mix well. Bring the mixture to a boil, reduce the heat, and simmer for 5 minutes.

2. Remove the spice bag and simmer the chutney, uncovered, stirring often, for 30 minutes more. Remove the garlic cloves. Ladle the chutney into hot, sterilized half-pint jars and seal. Process in a boiling water bath for 15 minutes.

3. Remove the jars from the water and set them on a rack to cool. When the jam has fully cooled, test the jars to make sure they've all sealed; if there are any that haven't sealed, store them in your refrigerator. The chutney should be stored in the refrigerator after opening.

— *Lychees Online*

"I come from a family where gravy is considered a beverage."

— *Erma Bombeck, American humorist*

. . . .

SEARED SCALLOPS WITH TROPICAL LYCHEE SALSA

SERVES 4

½ cup diced lychees
½ cup diced mango
½ cup peeled and diced cucumber
½ cup diced red bell pepper
3 tablespoons chopped fresh cilantro
4 teaspoons fresh lime juice
1 jalapeño pepper, seeded and minced
Cooking spray

Salt and freshly ground black pepper
1 pound sea scallops, rinsed and drained

1. Combine the lychee, mango, cucumber, bell pepper, cilantro, lime juice, and jalapeño. Season to taste with salt and pepper, and set aside.

2. Heat a large, nonstick pan over medium-high heat. Coat the pan with cooking spray. Season the scallops with salt and pepper, then add half of them to the pan. Sear until golden brown on both sides, about 2 minutes per side. Transfer the scallops to a warmed plate while cooking the remaining scallops.

3. Spoon the salsa over the scallops, and serve immediately.

— *Lychees Online*

MANGOES MANGIFERA SPECIES

One of humanity's most beloved and widely consumed fruits, the mango is a staple in tropical climates, especially in India, Pakistan, and the Philippines, where it is the national fruit. Mangoes have very distinctive flavors and fragrances, thanks to their numerous resins and acids.

A fruit of staggering diversity, mangoes come in about a thousand varieties worldwide, but in America only six are widely available. Common to all, however, is an elongated fruit with a single pit surrounded by succulent flesh that is usually dripping with sweet, richly fragrant juice (in fact, it is sometimes said that the best place to eat a mango is either in a bathtub or wading in the ocean). They are perhaps at their best eaten fresh, but they're also available dried, making an excellent, energy-rich snack.

HISTORY

People have probably loved mangoes since the day they discovered these sumptuous fruits. Mangoes are native to southern Asia, and India is the epicenter for the fruit's genetic diversity; in these regions they have been cultivated for some 6,000 years. Later the fruit traveled to Brazil, the West Indies, Mexico, Spain, and America. Most of the US crop comes from California and Florida.

NUTRITION

Mangoes are quite nutritious—they provide significant amounts of vitamins A, B6, C, and K, as well as folate, copper, fiber, and potassium. One medium fruit contains about 200 calories.

SEASON

Florida mangoes come into season during the summer, but imported mangoes have a much longer season, from January into fall.

SELECTION

Choose fruits that are heavy for their size and taut, with a yellow or red blush on one side (although color is not always a reliable indicator of ripeness in some varieties). Some blotchiness or brown speckles on the skin is fine. Ripe fruits should give slightly when pressed and will be highly fragrant. Avoid flabby mangoes that have soft spots, wrinkled skins, and a sour, alcoholic aroma.

STORAGE

Keep unripe mangoes at room temperature and avoid refrigerating them before they turn ripe. If you want to hasten the ripening process, place them in a paper bag with a ripe apple or by themselves (the ethylene gas given off by the fruit and trapped inside the bag is what helps them mature faster). Once the mangoes are soft and ripe, place them in the refrigerator to slow down spoilage; they will keep for up to 4 or 5 days.

TRIMMING AND CLEANING

Getting the fibrous, clingy flesh away from the large central pit of mangoes can make them a bit challenging to cut. There are several ways to do this (and Internet demonstration videos abound), but one of the easiest methods is to set the thoroughly washed fruit stem side up in front of you (it's helpful to first cut off enough of the pointy end so that you have a flat surface on which to stand the fruit) and vertically slice about ½ inch to the right of the stem all the way down the length of the fruit so that the knife just clears the pit. Then cut vertically again on the other side. Now you should have two halves (or "cheeks"), still in their skins. Score the flesh into strips or a checkerboard pattern, taking care not to cut through the skin, then use a spoon to scoop out the flesh. The pieces should lift right out.

BLANCHING AND FREEZING

Mangoes freeze well, either in cubed form or as a puree. Package the mangoes in zipper-lock freezer or vacuum food sealer-type bags, or freezer containers. Squeeze out any excess air and leave 1 inch of headspace (unless you are using the vacuum sealing method). They will keep for up to 12 months at 0°F.

EQUIVALENTS, MEASURES, AND SERVINGS

- 1 medium mango = 2 cups prepared fruit

COMPLEMENTARY HERBS, SEASONINGS, AND FOODS

Allspice, apples, bananas, basil, berries, black currants, buttermilk, caramel, carrots, chicken, chiles, chorizo, cinnamon, citrus, coconut, condensed milk, cream, fennel, fish, ginger, ham, ice cream, kiwi, limes, lychees, melons, oranges, papayas, pineapples, pork, quinoa, raspberries, rosemary, sherbet, smoked salt, sorrel, strawberries, tarragon, tomato, vanilla, yogurt.

SERVING SUGGESTIONS

- Try slices of raw mango sprinkled with salt, lime juice, and chile powder for a powerful, refreshing taste kick.

Safety Tip

Mango leaves, sap, and skin contain certain compounds, including urushiol, that can cause swelling and blistering on contact.

Folks allergic to poison ivy or poison oak are most vulnerable, and need to be especially careful when touching and eating mangoes, even in a market setting.

Such individuals may also be allergic to cashews and pistachios, to which mangoes are related.

People with mango allergies can be so sensitive that even dipping their arms in an ornamental pond above which a mango tree drops its leaves can trigger a nasty reaction.

- Who hasn't visited an Indian restaurant and enjoyed a mango lassi? The distinctive flavor and fragrance of mangoes go especially well with cultured dairy products such as yogurt and buttermilk.

- Mango and sweetened condensed milk make a sumptuous topping over shaved ice or as an exotic, simple dessert in its own right.

- Green, unripe mango, like papaya, can be grated and combined with Vietnamese fish sauce and rice vinegar as a salad.

- Mango's sweetness and acid helps tame and mellow the heat of hot peppers, making it ideal for salsas.

- Create a fabulous tropical fruit salad with mangoes, kiwi, pineapple, banana, grapes, lychees, papaya, and coconut.

- Like papayas, mangoes contain enzymes that make them ideal natural tenderizers. Use them in marinades for beef, lamb, pork, and chicken.

. . . .

TROPICAL FRUIT SALSA   MAKES 4 TO 5 CUPS

Source Note: This starts with a base of mild, prepared salsa, to which you add fresh tropical fruits and other ingredients. It's important to use sweet onions like Vidalia or Walla Walla, not the harsher yellow or white onions. Although the quantity seems like a lot, it never lasts long once people break out the chips.

1 (15½-ounce) jar mild prepared salsa
¾ cup finely diced starfruit
¼ cup finely diced mango
¼ cup finely diced pineapple
¼ cup finely diced sweet onion, like Vidalia or Walla Walla
⅛ teaspoon salt
1 medium fresh tomato, peeled, seeded, and finely diced
2 teaspoons minced fresh cilantro
Juice of ¼ lemon
Juice of 1 lime

In a large bowl, thoroughly combine all of the ingredients and let them sit for at least 1 hour before serving to let the flavors blend.

Variation: If you like peppers, you can add ¼ cup each of finely diced red, yellow, and green bell pepper, 1 to 2 teaspoons minced jalapeño pepper, and ¼ teaspoon dried hot pepper flakes.

— *Maureen Cooney,* The Bluff Country Co-op Cookbook

. . . .

CHICKEN WINGS   SERVES 4
WITH MANGO-CHILI SAUCE

3 large mangoes, peeled, pitted, and diced
⅓ cup dark brown sugar

2 teaspoons Worcestershire sauce
1 tablespoon chili paste
1 tablespoon vegetable oil
½ teaspoon dried red pepper flakes
2 cloves garlic, coarsely chopped
2 pounds chicken wings (about 24), wingtips removed
Kosher salt and freshly ground black pepper
Cooking spray
Chopped scallions (green onions), for garnish

1. Place the mangoes, sugar, Worcestershire sauce, chili paste, oil, red pepper flakes, and garlic in a blender. Puree until smooth.

2. Place the chicken wings in a large bowl and season with salt and pepper. Coat the wings with sauce (about ½ cup; reserve the rest for serving). Cover the wings with plastic wrap and refrigerate for 30 minutes to 1 hour.

3. Preheat the oven to 350°F. Line a baking pan with aluminum foil and lightly coat it with cooking spray.

4. Lift the chicken wings out of the sauce, saving the excess marinade. Place the wings on the prepared baking pan and bake for 30 minutes, or until cooked through. Remove the wings from the oven, then move an oven rack to 6 inches from the upper heating element. Preheat the broiler to medium high; place the wings under the broiler, skin side up. Broil for 3 minutes, or until the skin is crispy.

5. While the wings broil, place the reserved sauce (combine the extra sauce you reserved earlier with the marinade from the raw chicken) in a small saucepan and bring it to a boil. Reduce the heat to medium low and simmer until the sauce has thickened, 5 to 10 minutes.

6. Toss the wings in ½ cup of the sauce. Arrange them on a platter and garnish with some chopped scallion. Serve with the remaining mango-chili sauce on the side for dipping.

— *National Mango Board; recipe adapted from Ingrid Hoffmann*

. . . .

MANGO CAPRESE SALAD
SERVES 4

3 large, ripe mangoes, peeled and sliced
8 ounces fresh mozzarella, sliced
3 tablespoons freshly squeezed lemon juice
3 tablespoons extra-virgin olive oil
Sea salt and freshly ground black pepper
Snipped fresh basil
8 slices crusty baguette, toasted

1. Place the sliced mango on a platter, alternating with slices of mozzarella.

We've all heard that sweet corn never tastes better than when it is picked, husked, and thrown into boiling water within minutes of being pulled off the plant. Corn and peas are two vegetables whose sugars start converting to starch the moment they are picked.

But just how many nutrients are actually lost when a fruit or vegetable sits around for a while? What's the difference between conventional produce (grown, say, in central California) and locally grown veggies (i.e., from the farmers market or CSA)? And does it really matter in the grand scheme of things?

According to studies by the University of California, some vegetables can lose 15 to 55 percent of their vitamin C within a week; spinach in particular can lose 90 percent within the first 24 hours after harvest. Levels of some B vitamins, beneficial polyphenolic compounds, and certain enzymes also deteriorate quickly with increased transportation and storage time.

Consider this journey from farm to table: Conventionally grown produce must be picked; transported by truck to huge cold-storage facilities; sit around waiting to be purchased; make another journey by air, land, or sea to the retailer; hang out some more in the grocery store chiller; get put out on display; wait for a shopper to select it and bring it home; and then quite possibly loiter around another week at room temperature or in the refrigerator. Between harvest and consumption, two to four weeks often elapses.

By contrast, it is not unusual for produce in your CSA box or at your farmers market to have been picked in the previous 24 to 36 hours. Needless to say, this makes an enormous difference in flavor, nutrients, and freshness.

2. Drizzle with the lemon juice and oil, and season with salt and pepper.

3. Sprinkle with the basil and serve with the toasted baguette.

— *National Mango Board*

PAPAYAS CARICA PAPAYA

Whereas some fruits impress with their noisy crunch, brazen juiciness, or flamboyant colors, a papaya is all about subtlety. When fully ripe, its golden-orange or reddish flesh is as smooth and melting as the finest butter, and the flavor can be a bit of heaven on earth—sweet, rich, full-bodied, and slightly musky, with hints of melon and berry but with a distinctive tropicalness unique to the species. In some Asian cuisines, the tree's young leaves and flower blossoms are cooked and eaten as a vegetable.

Papayas sprout on fast-growing, small trees that bear prolifically but are odd-looking—the tree consists of a single trunk that never forms bark but is usually covered in maturing fruits and topped with a radiating arrangement of deeply lobed leaves. The trees require exacting, warm conditions to flourish, and most of the US crop is grown in Hawaii.

Depending on where you live, you may find several types of papaya; the most common are the yellow, pear-shaped Kapoho Solos and Rainbows from Hawaii. Much larger are the Mexican red and yellow papayas, which are oblong, can weigh up to 10 pounds, and are not as sweet as the Hawaiian fruits. Occasionally you may see dwarf varieties of papaya in local markets.

HISTORY

Papayas are believed to have originated from southern Mexico and the northern part of Central America. They are grown in nearly every tropical region in the world. In the early 1990s, the papaya industry in Hawaii—and other areas as well—was nearly destroyed by the rapid spread of the ringspot virus. A variety called Rainbow was genetically engineered to be resistant to the devastating disease; at the time of this book's printing, more than two-thirds of Hawaii's crop is Rainbow or Rainbow-derived. The virus-resistant gene in these trees works similarly to a vaccination in people and has been extensively researched for safety. Without it, Hawaii's papaya industry—the state's fifth-largest fruit crop—would have likely become extinct.

NUTRITION

Papayas are outstanding sources of vitamins A and C, and they contain some folate, vitamin E, copper, potassium, and magnesium. They also contain various flavonoids and antioxidants that can help prevent certain cancers. One cup of cubed papaya contains about 55 calories.

SEASON

Commercially, papayas are available year-round, as the trees are able to flower and fruit simultaneously. But its peak season is typically in the spring and fall.

SELECTION

Papayas that are fully tree-ripened always have a richer flavor than those picked green and hard, but given the fruit's fragility in shipping, nearly all of the commercial crop is harvested unripe. If you are lucky enough to live in Florida or Hawaii where these prolific trees grow, you're in for a treat. Different papaya varieties have different colorations, so their feel and sometimes fragrance are more important than their appearance—the surface of the fruit should give like a ripe avocado. A spotted specimen, as long as it has no molding or overly soft areas, can be extra delicious.

STORAGE

Partially ripe papayas can be helped along by placing them in a paper bag with a ripe apple or banana at room temperature (the ethylene gas that is emitted speeds up the ripening process). Once the fruit is ripe and has softened somewhat, store it in the refrigerator. Eat within a day or two, or its fragile flavor will suffer.

TRIMMING AND CLEANING

As fruits go, papayas are pretty simple to prepare. Just cut them in half and scoop out the numerous black seeds. (The seeds are actually edible, but some people find their peppery flavor unpleasant and overpowering.)

BLANCHING AND FREEZING

Papayas freeze well, although their texture will deteriorate somewhat. Remove the rinds and seeds, cut or cube the fruit as desired, and arrange the pieces on a tray in a single layer and freeze. Then package them in zipper-lock freezer or vacuum food sealer-type bags, or freezer containers. Squeeze out any excess air and leave 1 inch of headspace (unless you are using the vacuum sealing method). They will keep for up to 1 year at 0°F.

EQUIVALENTS, MEASURES, AND SERVINGS

- 1 medium papaya = 2 cups cubed

COMPLEMENTARY HERBS, SEASONINGS, AND FOODS

Black pepper, butter, buttermilk, cayenne, chicken, chiles, chili powder, citrus, coconut, cream, ham, honey, ice cream, lemons, limes, mangoes, melons, mint, pineapples, pork, prosciutto, raspberries, rum, seafood, strawberries, vanilla, white pepper, yogurt.

SERVING SUGGESTIONS

- Mild, sweet, and buttery, papaya goes wonderfully with all sorts of fresh fruits (especially acidic ones) in salads and compotes.
- Papaya goes well with ham, chicken, fish, shrimp, scallops, and smoked meats of all kinds.
- Pureed papaya is a lovely surprise ingredient in dressings; add cayenne, ginger, fresh chiles, or a few of its own peppery seeds for a bit of a bite.
- The soft, rich texture of papaya lends itself well to ice creams, sorbets, tarts, pies, and smoothies.
- Alternate cubes of papayas with marinated meats in kebabs. Don't be shy about seasonings.

Get Your Paws Off Me

Papayas are sometimes called papaws or pawpaws, but they should not be confused with the American pawpaw (*Asimina triloba*), a tree found in the eastern, southern, and midwestern United States and adjacent areas of Canada.

Love Me Tender

Papayas contain an enzyme called papain, which breaks down connective tissue and collagen in meat. It is so effective that it is a component in commercial meat tenderizer.

Papain is also used to aid digestion, to reduce pain and inflammation, to treat parasitic worms, and to enhance cosmetics, toothpaste, and enzymatic soft-contact-lens cleaners.

- Surprisingly, cooked papaya does not lose its texture and become a pile of mush like most fruits. Sauté slices with a bit of sugar and lime, and serve as dessert or as an accompaniment to meats and poultry.
- Papayas are handy in that they form their own dishes when halved and scooped out; make fruit salad, pile a generous amount in the depressions, and top with real whipped cream or clotted cream.
- Bake papayas with a little rum, sugar, vanilla, and coconut milk for an incredibly unctuous dessert that looks like it took a lot more effort than it actually did.
- Shaved green papayas with lime juice, garlic, chopped peanuts, chiles, and dried shrimp form a popular salad in Vietnamese and Thai cuisines.

. . . .

PAPAYA, GINGER, AND MINT SMOOTHIE

MAKES 1 SERVING

Source Note: Perfect for breakfast, brunch, or as an afternoon cooler!

> 1 medium strawberry papaya
> 1 cup ice cubes
> 1 apple banana (or regular banana if apple banana is unavailable)
> Freshly squeezed juice from ½ lemon or lime
> 1-inch piece fresh ginger, peeled and grated
> ½ cup coconut milk
> Small handful of spearmint leaves, plus sprigs to garnish

1. Blend all of the ingredients except the mint sprigs in a blender until smooth. Add more coconut milk if the consistency is too thick, and more papaya or banana if the consistency is too thin.

2. Pour into a pretty glass and garnish with spearmint sprigs.

— *Roxanne Tiffin, owner and CEO of Kula Fields, Inc., Kula, Maui, Hawaii*

. . . .

BAKED PAPAYA DESSERT

SERVES 4

Author Note: This recipe comes from Tahiti.

> 2 small ripe papayas (about 12 ounces each)
> ½ cup sugar
> ¼ cup water
> 1½ cups fresh coconut milk made from 1½ cups coarsely chopped coconut and 1½ cups hot water (see the recipe on page 349), or use canned coconut milk

1. Preheat the oven to 375°F.

2. With a small, sharp knife or swivel-bladed vegetable parer, peel the papayas. Cut them in half lengthwise and, with a spoon, scoop out

the seeds. Arrange the papayas cut side up in a shallow baking-serving dish large enough to hold them comfortably in one layer.

3. Sprinkle the fruit with the sugar and pour the ¼ cup of water down the sides of the dish.

4. Bake uncovered in the middle of the oven for 1½ hours, or until the papayas are tender but still intact, basting them every 20 minutes with the syrup that will accumulate in the dish.

5. Raise the heat to 400°F and bake for 5 minutes more until the syrup thickens and brown to a caramel color. Turn off the heat, pour the coconut milk into the cavities of the papayas, and let them rest in the oven for 5 minutes until the milk is warm. Serve at once, or refrigerate and serve chilled.

— *Rafael Steinberg,* Time-Life Foods of the World, Pacific and Southeast Asian Cooking

PINEAPPLES ANANAS COMOSUS

Producing fruits that are nearly synonymous with the tropics, the pineapple belongs to a class of plants called bromeliads. This huge, diverse family has some 3,000 species that often feature spiky, colorful foliage growing in rosettes that trap rainwater and insects for nourishment. Most bear spikes of colorful leaf bracts that sprout forth the actual flowers, which are often tiny and relatively inconspicuous. Pineapples are the only members of the bromeliad family to be commercially cultivated for their fruit.

For centuries, pineapples have been prized by humanity for their intense sweetness, extreme juiciness, and luscious fragrance. With their distinctive looks and melting succulence, they are the epitome of the exotic fruit. And they continue to be sought the world over, the demand for them profoundly changing the economies of the tropical countries where they are farmed commercially.

HISTORY

South America is the pineapple's homeland—probably near southern Brazil or Paraguay, whose native peoples spread the fruit throughout the rest of the continent. From there pineapple was taken to the Caribbean, Central America, and Mexico; the Mayas and Aztecs also cultivated it. In 1493 Christopher Columbus encountered the fruit on the Caribbean island of Guadeloupe and brought it back with him to Spain. The Spanish later introduced it to Africa, Guam, and Hawaii.

Europeans became simply infatuated with pineapples, which require exacting tropical conditions to thrive. After two centuries of attempts to successfully grow this fussy bromeliad, pineapples started being raised in the expensive hothouses of royalty and aristocracy. Because of their rarity, expense, and striking appearance, they soon became symbols of wealth and status, grown more for display at dinner parties than for actual eating.

Bring on the Bromelain

Pineapples contain bromelain, a chemical that contains two enzymes that digest proteins. Bromelain is extracted and used in commercial meat tenderizers and marinade mixtures. It is also commonly converted to pill or capsule form and used to aid digestion and ease joint pain.

For this reason, fresh pineapple will prevent gelatin from properly setting—the bromelain will break the protein links formed in the gelling process as fast as they are made. The enzyme is destroyed by cooking, so canned or cooked pineapple is fine to use in such preparations.

In the Caribbean, Europe, and North America, the pineapple became associated with the return of ships from long voyages and subsequent social entertaining, wherein the hard-to-obtain fruit would be prominently displayed on the dining or parlor table. Thus the pineapple became a symbol of hospitality that continues to this day in folk art, sculpture, home furnishings, and the hotel industry.

Hawaii's commercial pineapple industry began in the early 1900s with the James Dole, Maui Pineapple, and Del Monte companies planting, harvesting, and canning the fruit on an enormous scale for decades. Since the late 1980s, however, Hawaii's pineapple industry has suffered steep declines because of cheaper labor on plantations in Costa Rica and Asia.

NUTRITION

Pineapples are outstanding sources of vitamin C and manganese, and also contain significant amounts of thiamine, vitamin B6, folate, magnesium, potassium, and copper. A 1-cup serving of pineapple chunks contains 83 calories.

SEASON

Commercially, pineapples are often available year-round, but they are at their best from March to July.

SELECTION

Unlike most fruits, pineapples do not ripen any further after picking. Color and size are not necessarily reliable indicators of ripeness, but fragrance is—a truly ripe pineapple practically drips with unmistakable scent. Pineapples should be heavy for their size, and firm and plump, with fresh green crowns. Some varieties (such as Maui Gold) will have a dark gold coloring on their exterior, especially near the base. Avoid specimens with soft areas or mold (especially on the bottom), or that exude an alcoholic, sour smell—which likely means the fruit is overripe and has started fermenting.

STORAGE

Because pineapples are typically picked at their maximum ripeness and shipped quickly, they are quite vulnerable to spoilage. Chances are you won't let yours sit around too long, but if you can't eat it right away, keep it in the refrigerator to help it last longer. Even then, it should be eaten within 2 to 3 days.

TRIMMING AND CLEANING

Trimming a pineapple may seem a bit intimidating at first, but with a little practice you can master it easily with minimum waste. A number of demonstration videos abound on the Internet. My favorite method is this: First cut the top off the pineapple to remove the tuft of spiky leaves. Then stand the pineapple upright, and while holding it firmly with one hand, slice downward into the fruit about ¼ inch, or just enough to remove most of the outer scales. Some "eyes" and other bits may remain, but your main goal should be to preserve as much flesh as possible. Rotate the pineapple as you work your way around it. Once you've removed the outer scales, you can easily slice off the remaining eyes in smaller slivers.

You should now have a cylindrical chunk of completely peeled fruit. Next, locate the circular white core of the pineapple by tapping with the tip of the knife at the fruit's center; it should feel somewhat more fibrous than the tender fruit. See where the outer edges of this core lie, and then cut downward as close to the core as possible to yield slabs of fruit. Once you've worked your way around the core, discard it. Now your pineapple is ready for cutting into thinner slices or bite-size chunks. It may be a bit of work, but no doubt you'll find the effort worth it as soon as you take your first succulent bite.

BLANCHING AND FREEZING

Pineapples freeze well, and this can be a good way to preserve the fruit's fleeting ripeness. Trim the pineapple, slice or cube the fruit as desired, arrange the pieces in a single layer on a tray lined with parchment or wax paper, and freeze. (Or you might prefer to cut the pineapple into chunks, whirl it in a blender, and then freeze the puree.) Then package the fruit in zipper-lock freezer or vacuum food sealer-type bags, or freezer containers. Squeeze out any excess air and leave 1 inch of headspace (unless you are using the vacuum sealing method). Frozen pineapple will keep for up to 1 year at 0°F.

EQUIVALENTS, MEASURES, AND SERVINGS

☛ 1 medium pineapple = 3 cups chunked

COMPLEMENTARY HERBS, SEASONINGS, AND FOODS

Allspice, bananas, basil, berries, caramel, carrots, chicken, chiles, chorizo, cilantro, cinnamon, citrus, coconut, condensed milk, cream, fennel, fish, ginger, ham, ice cream, kiwis, limes, lychees, macadamia nuts, melons, oranges, papayas, pork, quinoa, raspberries, rosemary, sherbet, smoked salt, strawberries, vanilla, yogurt.

SERVING SUGGESTIONS

☛ Fresh, ripe pineapple is a fabulous friend to all sorts of fruits—use it in salads and compotes.

☛ Like most tropical fruits, pineapple goes well with ham, chicken, fish, shrimp, scallops, and smoked meats of all kinds.

☛ The distinctive flavor of pineapple makes refreshing ice creams, sorbets, and smoothies.

☛ Remember that old standby—the Hawaiian pizza, with its topping of Canadian bacon and pineapple chunks? You needn't be ashamed to admit that you still love it!

☛ Pineapples can be halved and scooped out to form their own dishes; fill them with salads that include ham, fruit, nuts, chicken, or whatever you fancy.

☛ Alternate cubes of pineapple with marinated meats in kebabs.

☛ Frozen, slightly thawed pineapple mixed with fruit juice makes a terrific slushy dessert. If you freeze pureed pineapple in ice cube trays, the frozen cubes can be tossed into smoothies, juices, teas, punches, or lemonade.

☛ Make chutney or salsa with fresh or cooked pineapple.

☛ Top yogurt or cottage cheese with crushed or chunked pineapple for a quick, healthful snack.

☛ Pineapple is fantastic grilled, which caramelizes the fruit's sugars and concentrates its flavors. Brush trimmed pineapple spears with a mixture of honey, lime juice, and black pepper, and place the wedges on a preheated grill for about 4 minutes on each side. Check it frequently, as it burns easily.

- ✐ Pineapple and pork were made for each other, along with hot sauces, vinegar, citrus juices, hot chiles, and other spicy seasonings. Be creative!

- ✐ Pineapple juice mixes well with other fruit and vegetable juices for healthful, refreshing beverages.

ABIDJAN CABBAGE SALAD

SERVES 6

4 cups thinly sliced cabbage
1 cup shredded carrot
1 cup pineapple chunks

CITRUS DRESSING
Freshly squeezed juice of 1 lemon
Freshly squeezed juice of 1 medium orange
¼ teaspoon salt
⅓ cup extra-virgin olive oil

1. Place the cabbage, carrot, and pineapple in a large bowl.

2. In another bowl, mix the dressing by whisking all of the ingredients together until creamy, or by combining the lemon and orange juices in a blender, then adding the salt and drizzling in the oil.

3. Thoroughly toss the dressing with the vegetables. Refrigerate to let the flavors mingle, stirring occasionally, or serve immediately.

— *Fooddownunder.com*

PINEAPPLE UPSIDE-DOWN CAKE

MAKES ONE 8-INCH CAKE

Source Note: *This cake is surprisingly easy to make, and I'm sure everyone can do it in no time.*

2 tablespoons unsalted butter, melted
Several tablespoons soft brown sugar, for sprinkling
6 slices canned pineapple, juice reserved (about ¼ cup)
6 tablespoons (¾ stick) unsalted butter, softened
½ cup plus 2 tablespoons caster (fine white) sugar
2 eggs, lightly beaten
1 teaspoon vanilla extract
1 cup self-rising flour, sifted

1. Preheat the oven to 350°F.

2. Pour the melted butter into an 8-inch round cake pan. Brush the base and sides of the pan with the butter, then sprinkle it evenly with the brown sugar.

3. Cut the pineapple slices in half and arrange them nicely in the bottom of the pan.

4. Using an electric mixer, beat the softened butter and sugar till light and creamy, then add the eggs gradually, beating well after each addition.

5. Add the vanilla extract and beat until well combined.

6. At a low speed, fold in the flour alternatively with ¼ cup of pineapple juice (start with half of the flour, then add the juice, and end with the remaining flour). Don't overmix the batter.

7. Spoon the mixture evenly over the pineapple and bake for 40 minutes, or until the cake has pulled away from the sides of the pan and it is set in the center.

8. Leave the cake in the pan for 10 minutes. Place a wire rack on the top of the pan, then swiftly but gently flip the whole thing over. The cake should release from the pan and reveal the pineapple. Note that there may be some drippy juices during this step, so be prepared. Cool before serving.

— *Miss Joan Yu,* Sweetcrumbs *blog*

Buddha overseeing the pond at Kahumana Farm.

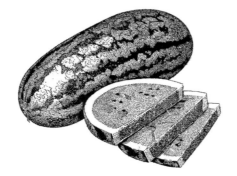

Watermelons   CITRULLUS LANATUS

Along with sweet corn and tomatoes, watermelon is a quintessential sign of summer. Watermelon belongs to the Cucurbitaceae family, which also includes squash, cucumbers, gourds, and pumpkins. All of its members grow as rambling, sprawling annual vines with enormous appetites for space, heat, water, and fertilizer.

Watermelons come in a surprising number of sizes and colors. Most familiar to us are those classic big, oblong red watermelons with striped green skins; Crimson Sweet is a popular variety that averages around 25 pounds. But increasingly popular are icebox melons—smaller, more manageable fruits that you can easily store in your refrigerator. These guys range from 3 to 13 pounds, and feature green or yellow skins; very sweet, brilliant red, yellow, or orange flesh; and often very few or virtually no seeds. Common icebox varieties include Yellow Doll, Sugar Baby, and Mickylee.

You may also find heirloom varieties in your CSA box or at the farmers market; Moon and Stars (named for its constellation of yellow spots on its dark green skin) and Cream of Saskatchewan (with its cream-colored flesh) are just two of hundreds of tasty varieties not seen commercially in large supermarkets.

HISTORY

Watermelon is believed to have originated from Africa's Kalahari Desert, where it grows wild and serves as a convenient source of food and water for indigenous peoples. Ancient Egyptians and Chinese cultivated watermelons, and seeds of the plant were found in Pharaoh Tutankhamen's tomb. The Moors probably introduced watermelon to Europe by the 13th century, and African slaves likely brought the seeds of their beloved native fruit to the United States.

Because of the fruit's surprising fragility, however, watermelons were not a commercially viable, large-scale crop in America until breeding efforts in South Carolina in the 1940s produced a melon with an easy-to-stack shape and harder rind.

NUTRITION

A watermelon consists of … well, mostly water—about 92 percent, which is why these fruits weigh so much when they are ripe. A 2-cup serving of watermelon contains about 30 percent of an adult's daily requirement for vitamin A, 25 percent of vitamin C, and significant amounts of potassium and vitamin B6, all for about 80 calories. Watermelon also contains abundant lycopene, a carotenoid antioxidant that may help prevent certain cancers.

SEASON

Commercially, watermelon is widely grown and in season year-round. You'll find them at their best in farmers markets and CSAs from mid-summer through early fall.

SELECTION

A good watermelon is a heavy, shiny one, with no soft or bruised areas. A ripe melon should sound hollow when thumped, and the skin on the underside that sat on the ground as it ripened should be creamy yellow.

STORAGE

Whole, uncut melons will keep for 7 to 10 days at room temperature. But store them too long, and they will lose flavor and texture. Once a watermelon is cut, it should be tightly wrapped, stored in the coldest part of the refrigerator, and eaten within a day or two.

TRIMMING AND CLEANING

Before cutting, thoroughly wash the melon to avoid introducing contamination from the skin into the flesh. Many modern varieties have very few mature seeds, but if you need to remove them, wash and quarter a whole melon, then cut each quarter into three or four wedges. Cut lengthwise along the seed line with a paring knife and lift off the piece. Using a fork, scrape the seeds from both the removed piece and the remaining flesh on the rind. Save the seeds for spitting and target practice.

To easily cube a watermelon, cut into the flesh in a grid pattern, and tilt—the cubes will practically tumble off.

BLANCHING AND FREEZING

Freezing is a good way to preserve watermelon for those long winters when no decent melons are available or when you have an overabundance of fruit. Frozen watermelon cubes also work well for smoothies. Cut the flesh off the rind, cube, and place in zipper-lock freezer or vacuum food sealer-type bags, or freezer containers. Squeeze out any excess air and leave ½ inch of headspace (unless you are using the vacuum sealing method). Frozen watermelon will keep for up to 9 months at 0°F.

You can also prepare watermelon in a sugar syrup that will help preserve its flavor and color. Peel and cut melons into ½- or ¾-inch cubes or balls. To make the syrup, combine 9 cups of water or fruit juice with 2¼ cups of sugar in a pot, and bring to a boil until the sugar dissolves. Chill, then pour ½ cup of syrup into a freezer container, add the melon, and keep adding syrup until the fruit is covered. Leave ½ inch of headspace for pints, 1 inch for quarts.

EQUIVALENTS, MEASURES, AND SERVINGS

- 1 serving = 1 cup of cubed melon = 6 balls of melon = 1 small, 1-inch-thick wedge of sliced melon
- 100 percent whole watermelon = 70 percent edible watermelon + 30 percent rind

COMPLEMENTARY HERBS, SEASONINGS, AND FOODS

Apples, balsamic vinegar, black pepper, blueberries, coconut, ginger, grapefruit, ham, ice cream, lemon, lime, mango, mint, other melons, pepper, prosciutto, raspberries, salt, seafood, smoked meats, strawberries, sugar, yogurt.

Don't Drop It on Your Foot

The largest watermelon, listed in the Guinness Book of World Records, tipped the scales at 262 pounds, grown by Bill Carson of Arrington, Tennessee, in 1990.

"The true Southern watermelon is a boon apart, and not to be mentioned with commoner things. It is chief of this world's luxuries, king by the grace of God over all the fruits of the earth. When one has tasted it, he knows what the angels eat. It was not a Southern watermelon that Eve took; we know it because she repented."

— Mark Twain, American satirist

Made in China

Over 1,200 varieties of watermelon are grown in 96 countries. China is the world's largest producer of watermelons.

SERVING SUGGESTIONS

- Watermelon is a wonderfully thirst-quenching snack anytime and is surprisingly filling, either by itself or in conjunction with other fruit.
- Kids and adults alike love foods in fun shapes: Cut watermelon, cheese, and sausage into cubes or flat squares, and arrange to create checkerboards or a Rubik's Cube. Serve with toothpicks and a variety of tasty dips and sauces.
- Hollow out a big watermelon shell and fill it with assorted fruits and melon balls tossed in a spicy-sweet, ginger-lemon-honey-mint dressing.
- Mince watermelon and toss with maple syrup to use as a topping on pancakes, waffles, ice cream, and sherbet.
- Use watermelon puree to add a subtle, sweet, fruity flavor to sauces, glazes, and marinades.
- Grill whole shrimp and watermelon cubes on skewers.
- Watermelon is delicious added to summer salads or made into a cold soup.
- A simple, refreshing summer meal is a fruit plate with cut-up watermelon, cantaloupe, pineapple, grapes, and raspberries, accompanied by a selection of fine cheeses like smoked Gouda, Brie, and Stilton, served with sangrias or mimosas.

WATERMELON AND CHICKEN SALAD   SERVES 4

Author Note: Asian noodles come in all sorts of varieties. For this salad, it is best to use a thinner, more delicate noodle like ramen, soba, or rice vermicelli.

SWEET-AND-SOUR GINGER DRESSING

2½ tablespoons rice vinegar
1 tablespoon soy sauce
1 teaspoon sugar
½ teaspoon minced fresh ginger
½ cup soybean oil
2 tablespoons toasted sesame oil

SALAD

1 (3-pound) red watermelon
12 ounces Asian noodles, uncooked
1 pound boneless, skinless chicken breasts, grilled
10 ounces seedless cucumbers, thinly sliced with peel on
2 ounces green onions, thinly sliced
Bamboo shoots, thinly sliced, for garnish
Parsley sprigs, for garnish

1. To prepare the dressing, stir the vinegar, soy sauce, sugar, and ginger until thoroughly mixed; set aside. Combine the soy and sesame oils in a salad dressing shaker; gradually add the vinegar mixture until blended. Shake well before serving.

2. To prepare the salad, remove the rind from the watermelon and cut the flesh into 1-inch cubes. Cover and refrigerate.

3. Cook and drain the noodles; set aside.

4. To make an individual serving, arrange 1 sliced chicken breast on top of about ¾ cup of cooked noodles. Place ¾ cup cubed watermelon and ⅓ cup sliced cucumbers beside the chicken. Sprinkle with green onions. Garnish with bamboo shoots and parsley sprigs, and serve with the Sweet-and-Sour Ginger Dressing.

— *National Watermelon Promotion Board*

Books

Watermelon for Everyone
Martha Rose Woodward,
CreateSpace Independent
Publishing Platform, 2011.

Illiana Watermelon Association
website (recipes section)
www.illianawatermelon.org.

WATERMELON-STRAWBERRY MINT SALSA   SERVES 4

Source Note: For a dynamite combination, serve this salsa with grilled chicken breasts that have been marinated in jerk seasoning before cooking.

1 cup diced watermelon, seeds removed
¾ cup diced strawberries
¼ cup diced red onion
2 tablespoons diced, seeded jalapeño
2 tablespoons finely chopped fresh mint leaves
2 tablespoons olive oil
1 tablespoon lime juice
1 teaspoon sugar

Gently stir together all of the ingredients in a bowl. Let stand to blend flavors, about 1 hour.

— *Chef Marty Blitz, Mise En Place, Tampa, Florida; National Watermelon Promotion Board*

WATERMELON BITS   SERVES 6

1 cup fresh lime juice
½ teaspoon salt
¼ teaspoon hot pepper sauce
6 cups cubed watermelon, seeded

1. In a small bowl suitable for dipping, stir together the lime juice, salt, and hot pepper sauce; adjust the seasoning to taste.

2. Place the bowl in the center of a large platter, arrange the watermelon around the bowl, and serve with toothpicks.

— *Produce for Better Health; Fruits & Veggies—More Matters; Centers for Disease Control and Prevention*

WATERMELON SMOOTHIE   SERVES 2

> 2 cups watermelon, cut into seeded chunks
> 1 cup cracked ice
> ½ cup plain yogurt
> 1 tablespoon sugar
> ½ teaspoon ground ginger
> ⅛ teaspoon almond extract

Combine all of the ingredients in a blender; blend until smooth.

— Produce for Better Health; Fruits & Veggies—More Matters;
Centers for Disease Control and Prevention

WATERMELON GAZPACHO   SERVES 4

Source Note: Surprise your family or guests with this spicy (not sweet) soup! A garnish of thin apple slices adds a special touch.

> 6 cups cubed, seeded watermelon
> 1½ cups chopped Golden Delicious apples
> ½ cup finely chopped onion
> ½ cup finely chopped green bell pepper
> 1 tablespoon chopped fresh basil
> ½ teaspoon salt
> ¼ teaspoon coarsely ground black pepper
> ¼ teaspoon chili powder
> 1 tablespoon cider vinegar
> 1 Granny Smith or other tart apple, thinly sliced, for garnish

1. In a blender, puree the watermelon; pour it into a large mixing bowl.

2. Stir in all of the remaining ingredients except for the apple slices. Refrigerate, covered, at least 1 hour to blend the flavors. Garnish with several pieces of thinly sliced apple.

— National Watermelon Promotion Board

WATERMELON PINEAPPLE PRESERVES MAKES ABOUT 2 CUPS

Source Note: Do not double the recipe, or the mixture may not set.

> 1 cup finely chopped watermelon rind (peeled, all red flesh removed)
> 1 cup sugar

1 (8-ounce) can crushed unsweetened pineapple, with juice
¼ cup water
1 tablespoon grated orange peel
⅛ teaspoon pumpkin pie spice or cinnamon
1 (3-ounce) pouch liquid fruit pectin

1. In a saucepan, stir together the rind, sugar, pineapple with juice, and water. Bring to a boil over high heat, stirring constantly. Decrease the heat and simmer for 15 to 20 minutes, until the rind is tender and translucent.

2. Stir in the remaining ingredients. Increase the heat, bringing the mixture to a full rolling boil, stirring constantly. Boil for 1 minute, stirring constantly.

3. Ladle the preserves into jars; cover. Let stand at room temperature for 24 hours to set. These preserves will keep in the refrigerator for up to 3 weeks.

— *National Watermelon Promotion Board*

William Lee and Kenny Heidtmann showing off some of Sang Lee Farms's summer watermelons.

plants, birds, and bees. No matter your beliefs, the farm is without a doubt divine. Witness the scent of the swallowtail caterpillar, the sight of an iridescent dragonfly, or the brilliant lavender stems of Red Russian kale against the blue sky and you will understand.

Farm, you bring people joy. When the tables are stacked high on market mornings, the customers can't help but be drawn in. The bits of your soil that linger on carrots and beets, the grains of wisdom that you teach, all are handed off to new souls whose bellies, minds, and bodies will be nourished with your fruits. Some will recognize the majestic way that the power of the sun was harnessed. Others will rejoice in the flavors of their dinner. All will absorb the good energy of earth, water, and air, just as naturally as our own bodies are made up of these elements. It can be no other way!

Farm, the lessons you teach resonate to my core. It takes dedication to tend the field, and patience in knowing that growth and change are inevitable but not quick or easy. There are days when we are soaked to the bone, on the brink of exhaustion, or watching hail rip through our crops. But without those days, would the first tomato taste as sweet? Would the red peppers shine so brilliantly? Life is full of both rain and shine, and that is what makes it so beautiful. We learn to be gentle with the plants so that we can learn to be gentle with ourselves and our loved ones, nurturing until at last, nature takes its course and we bloom and thrive.

As Anaïs Nin so wisely mused, "The day came when the risk to remain tight in a bud was more painful than the risk it took to blossom."

Zucchinis

CUCURBITA PEPO

To the home gardener, prolific zucchini are the rabbits of the Cucurbit world, thus earning this summer squash a reputation for being given away to people already weary of too much of a good thing. Zucchinis do not keep, however, and just as quickly as the floodgates of summer open to overflowing armfuls of this succulent green vegetable, they are gone as soon as cold weather nips the vines.

Like many vegetables, zucchini is best as a small package. Zucchinis that are 6 inches long or under are the most succulent. Anything over 8 inches (or a foot long) tend to be tasteless and are more fit for the compost heap than the dinner table.

These vines are astoundingly productive, but if you happen to have one or more in your garden, you can help stem the flow of fruits by indulging in another of life's culinary pleasures—squash blossoms, a delectable treat when stuffed and delicately fried, or made into a quesadilla.

HISTORY

Zucchini was relatively unknown in America until surprisingly recently. Although both summer and winter squashes are one of humanity's oldest foods, zucchini was mostly confined to Europe in general and Italy in particular, where its culinary uses expanded and developed.

In the mid-1900s, Italian immigrants brought this green summer squash to America. From then on, its popularity in the United States grew nearly as quickly as a healthy plant in July.

Like many summer squashes, zucchini was often not well liked in Europe outside of its home country. In particular, the French shunned it until they learned to use just the smallest, most succulent fruits; they call them *courgettes,* which also refers to yellow summer squash.

NUTRITION

Zucchinis are mostly water (over 95 percent) and thus are extremely low in calories (a single cup contains only 36). Like other summer squashes, zucchini contains significant amounts of vitamins A, C, and K, as well as manganese, magnesium, potassium, copper, folate, and dietary fiber.

SEASON

Commercially, zucchini is widely grown and in season year-round. You'll find them at their best in farmers markets and CSAs from midsummer through early fall.

SELECTION

Zucchinis taste best when they are still quite young, tender, and small— about 2 to 8 inches long. Avoid zucchinis that are any bigger, for they may be bitter, tough, and tasteless. Choose firm, plump specimens with unblemished skins and no bruised, shriveled, or watery areas.

STORAGE

Zucchini is a rather perishable vegetable; avoid washing it until just before using, and keep it wrapped in a dry paper towel inside a plastic bag in the refrigerator vegetable crisper for up to 4 days.

TRIMMING AND CLEANING

Like most summer squash, zucchinis need little preparation. Just wash them thoroughly and slice into the desired-size pieces. Peeling their thin skins is usually not necessary.

STEAMING AND BOILING

Zucchini and other summer squashes tend to be watery when cooked, so either choose cooking methods that dry them out a bit, or avoid those that may exacerbate this characteristic. For this reason, steaming zucchini is far preferable to boiling, which yields an incredibly sodden vegetable. Steam 1-inch chunks for 10 to 15 minutes, or until they become tender.

STIR-FRYING AND SAUTÉING

Cut zucchini into thin strips or slices; coat with oil, butter, or soy sauce; and stir-fry or sauté over high heat for 3 to 6 minutes, or until it becomes tender and lightly browned on the edges.

BAKING AND ROASTING

Baking is a good way to prepare zucchini, especially with other vegetables such as onions, peppers, and tomatoes. Layer them in a casserole dish with herbs and seasonings of your choice, drizzle with olive oil, cover, and bake in a 350°F oven for 45 minutes.

GRILLING

Zucchini responds well to grilling, especially the larger fruits. Use about twice what you think you will want, as they will soften and shrink considerably. Trim the ends from about 2 pounds of zucchini; cut them into ¼-inch slabs and slather them with either olive oil (you'll need salt and pepper, too), ½ cup Italian salad dressing, or other vinaigrette if desired. Grill over a medium-hot fire until they are soft and somewhat charred, 2 to 3 minutes per side.

BLANCHING AND FREEZING

Zucchini can be frozen, but like most vegetables, it must be blanched first. Wash, trim off the stem ends, and cut into slices or strips. Blanch in rapidly boiling water for 3 minutes, then plunge the zucchini into ice water for 5 minutes to stop the cooking process. Remove and drain. Package the zucchini in zipper-lock freezer or vacuum food sealer-type bags, or freezer containers. Squeeze out any excess air and leave ½ inch of headspace (unless you are using the vacuum sealing method).

You can freeze shredded zucchini for future batches of zucchini bread. Simply shred the zucchini manually or in a food processor and package it in recipe-size amounts in zipper-lock freezer or vacuum food sealer-type bags. Squeeze out any excess air.

You can also prepare seasoned and breaded zucchini for freezing by cutting the desired number of squash into wedges or sticks. Moisten them

"The trouble is, you cannot grow just one zucchini. Minutes after you plant a single seed, hundreds of zucchini will barge out of the ground and sprawl around the garden, menacing the other vegetables. At night, you will be able to hear the ground quake as more and more zucchinis erupt."

— *Dave Barry, comic writer*

"Vegetables are a must on a diet. I suggest carrot cake, zucchini bread, and pumpkin pie."

— *Jim Davis, American cartoonist*

with water and dredge them in a mixture of cornmeal or breadcrumbs, salt, and pepper. Arrange the sticks on a baking sheet lined with wax paper and place in the freezer. Once the sticks are frozen, package them in a freezer bag. When you are ready to use them, simply take out what you need and deep-fry—no need to thaw them first.

Frozen zucchini will keep for up to 3 months at 0°F.

MICROWAVING

Trim off the stem ends; cut the zucchini into ¼-inch slices and put in a microwave-safe dish with ¼ cup water; cover and cook on high power.

- 1½ cups = 3 to 4 minutes
- 1 pound = 6 to 7 minutes

MEASURES AND EQUIVALENTS

- 3 medium zucchini = 1 pound or about 3 cups sliced or chopped

COMPLEMENTARY HERBS, SEASONINGS, AND FOODS

Basil, beans, breadcrumbs, butter, capers, cayenne, cheese (Asiago, feta, goat, Monterey Jack, Parmesan), chives, cilantro, corn, cream, cumin, curry, dill, eggplant, eggs, garlic, lemons, marjoram, mint, mushrooms, nutmeg, olive oil, onions, oregano, parsley, peppers, pesto, pine nuts, rice, rosemary, sage, salmon, sausage, tarragon, thyme, tomatoes, vinegar, walnuts, yogurt.

SERVING SUGGESTIONS

- Combine with eggs, tomatoes, and basil to make a summer frittata.
- If you find yourself with extra marinated and grilled zucchini, add them to almost any type of sandwich the next day for a burst of smoky flavor.
- Roast zucchini with sliced onions, olive oil, salt, pepper, and other herbs and seasonings.
- Shred zucchini (shred the outer, "meatier" portions only, leaving the seedy interior behind) along with carrots, cucumbers, and cabbage for an unusual coleslaw.
- Sauté coins of zucchini with other summer squashes of contrasting colors—yellow and light green, for instance—and dress with fresh herbs and garlic for a lovely summer dish.
- Add diced, sautéed zucchini to salads and pasta dishes.
- Thinly slice zucchini and use it like cucumbers in sandwiches and hoagies.
- Cut zucchini into thin strips or thin rounds and serve with other fresh vegetables for dipping.
- Roast sliced zucchini that has been brushed with melted butter and sprinkled with lemon pepper at 400°F for 20 to 25 minutes, or until tender.
- Stuff zucchini by coring out the centers of the bigger squash, then stuffing with a mixture of vegetables, ground meat, tofu, cooked garbanzo beans, herbs, and seasonings. Bake, covered, with or without tomato sauce, at 350°F for 45 to 60 minutes.
- Of course, if all else fails, make that old standby—zucchini bread or muffins.

Fat summer squashes from Sang Lee Farms.

. . . .

BAKED CHICKEN AND ZUCCHINI GRATIN   SERVES 4

1 egg
1 tablespoon water
¾ teaspoon salt, divided
⅛ teaspoon pepper
1 cup dry breadcrumbs
4 boneless, skinless chicken breast halves
4 tablespoons olive or vegetable oil, divided
5 medium zucchinis, sliced
4 medium tomatoes, sliced
1 cup shredded mozzarella cheese, divided
2 teaspoons minced fresh basil

1. In a shallow bowl, whisk the egg, water, ½ teaspoon of the salt, and
    pepper.

2. Set aside 2 tablespoons of the breadcrumbs. Place the remaining
    crumbs in a large zipper-lock bag. Dip the chicken in the egg mix-
    ture, then place it in the bag and shake to coat.

3. Preheat the oven to 400°F.

4. In a skillet heated to medium-high, heat 2 tablespoons of the oil.
    Cook the chicken for 2 to 3 minutes on each side, or until it turns
    golden brown. Remove and set aside.

5. In the same skillet, sauté the zucchini slices in the remaining oil until
    they are crisp-tender; drain. Transfer to a greased 9-by-13-inch bak-
    ing dish. Sprinkle the reserved breadcrumbs over the zucchini. Top
    with the tomato slices; sprinkle with ⅔ cup of the mozzarella, the
    basil, and the remaining ¼ teaspoon salt. Top with the chicken.

model with a food assistance mission. Over the course of 18 growing
seasons, it provided the regional
food bank's warehouse with about
half of its annual harvest. In 2009,
the farm shifted its operation to a
partnership with **Mountain View
Farm**, a CSA farm in Easthampton,
Massachusetts, so that it could remain financially sustainable. Today
it provides 100,000 pounds of fresh
produce to the emergency food network each season.

The nonprofit **180 Degree Farm**
in Georgia (see pages 489 and
593) gives away more than 20,000
pounds of organically grown food
annually to people who are ill or
in financial need through partner-
ships with Cancer Treatment Centers of America (CTCA) at Southeastern Regional Medical Center in
Newnan, Georgia, as well as local
churches and food banks. From
the very first day, owners Scott and
Nicole Tyson have had a special
mission: helping people who are
dealing with cancer as their own
family has. Every week they set up
an indoor farmers market at the
Southeastern Regional Medical
Center for staff, patients, and their
families, selling some items and giving others away..

In the rural Methow Valley of
north central Washington State,
farmer Kelleigh McMillan grows
organic vegetables for farmers
markets and seed crops for Uprising Seeds. Concerned about local
poverty and limited access to nutritious food, she decided in 2007
to dedicate an acre of her family
farm, **Sowing Seeds**, to what she
calls **Red Shed Produce**. In 2013,
Red Shed provided more than 3,000
servings of carrots, lettuce, broccoli, green beans, cabbage, summer
squash, and other produce to local
families through Room One, a local
nonprofit health and social service
center, as well as the local Wom-
en, Infants, and Children's (WIC)
program and the Cove Food Bank.
Between November and April, Mc-

6. Cover and bake for 25 minutes. Uncover; sprinkle with the remaining mozzarella. Bake 10 minutes longer, or until the cheese is melted.

— *Mariquita Farm, Watsonville, California*

ZUCCHINI PICKLES   MAKES 3 PINTS

4 medium zucchinis (about 1½ pounds), trimmed
    and thinly sliced
2 small yellow onions, thinly sliced
3 tablespoons salt
Cold water
2 cups distilled vinegar
1 cup sugar
1 teaspoon celery seeds
1 teaspoon anise seeds
2 teaspoons dry mustard

1. Place the zucchinis and onions in a medium bowl. Sprinkle with the salt. Cover with cold water; let stand for 1 hour.

2. Meanwhile, combine the vinegar, sugar, celery seeds, anise seeds, and mustard in a medium saucepan. Heat to boiling, then remove from the heat.

3. Drain the zucchini and onions. Place them in a large pot and pour the hot vinegar liquid over them. Let stand for 1 hour.

4. After the hour, heat the mixture to boiling; simmer for 3 minutes. Remove from the heat and pour into sterilized jars.

— *Bert Greene,* Greene on Greens

ZUCCHINI TEACAKE   MAKES TWO 9-BY-5-INCH LOAF CAKES

3½ cups flour (stir to aerate before measuring)
¾ teaspoon baking powder
1½ teaspoons baking soda
1½ teaspoons salt
1 teaspoon cinnamon
2 cups sugar
1 cup peanut oil (or substitute vegetable oil)
1 teaspoon vanilla extract
4 large eggs
2 cups grated zucchini
1 cup chopped walnuts
1 cup dried currants, rinsed and drained

1. Preheat the oven to 350°F. Grease and flour two standard loaf pans.

2. In a medium bowl, mix together the flour, baking powder, baking soda, salt, and cinnamon.

3. Using a large bowl and a wooden spoon, beat together the sugar, peanut oil, and vanilla until combined. Beat in the eggs one at a time.

4. Use a flexible spatula to fold in the flour mixture, then add the zucchini and combine. Last, stir in the walnuts and currants. Try to stir the mixture just until combined; overmixing may give the cake a chewy texture.

5. Bake for 55 to 60 minutes, or until the loaves crack on top and a skewer inserted in the centers comes out clean.

— *Christina Rude, The 2013 MAJIQal Cookbook*

Zucchinis growing lush at Featherstone Farm.

PICKLED MIXED VEGETABLE SALAD   SERVES 6

Source Note: *This salad is a terrific way to use up all sorts of vegetables that tend to pile up in the lush days of late summer. You can substitute yellow or any young summer squash for the zucchini, or use cucumber, thinly sliced carrots or okra, broccoli, and even Asian eggplant rounds in place of some of the other veggies.*

2 medium zucchinis, thinly sliced
3 or 4 radishes, sliced
½ medium white onion, chopped
⅓ cup coarsely diced green bell pepper
1 cup sliced cauliflower
1 medium tomato, cut into bite-size pieces
3 to 4 sprigs parsley, chopped
1 clove garlic, finely diced and crushed

"Your diet is a bank account. Good food choices are good investments."

— *Bethenny Frankel, American television star*

Several leaves of chopped fresh basil
6 tablespoons extra-virgin olive oil
1 to 2 tablespoons fresh lemon juice
⅔ cup sugar
⅔ cup vinegar
Salt and freshly ground black pepper
Onion or garlic powder
Parmesan cheese, grated

1. Toss the zucchini, radishes, onion, green peppers, cauliflower, tomato, parsley, garlic, and basil together in a bowl. Sprinkle with the olive oil and lemon juice.

2. Dissolve the sugar and vinegar in a saucepan over medium heat. Pour over the salad. Season to taste with salt, pepper, onion powder, and Parmesan cheese.

3. Chill for several hours before serving, stirring occasionally to distribute the juices.

— *Betty Culp,* Daisies Do Tell … A Recipe Book

Fall

AUTUMN CROPS TEND TO FALL INTO TWO CATEGORIES: THOSE THAT ARE PLANTED IN THE SPRING AND TAKE THE FULL LENGTH OF THE SUMMER TO PRODUCE A CROP (WINTER SQUASH, FOR EXAMPLE), AND OTHERS, SUCH AS BROCCOLI AND SALAD GREENS, THAT MAY HAVE BEEN PLANTED AND HARVESTED IN EARLY SUMMER AND ARE THEN REPLANTED FOR A SECOND CROP TO BE PICKED IN SEPTEMBER AND OCTOBER.

MANY FRUITS TRULY COME INTO THEIR OWN IN LATE SUMMER AND AUTUMN—THINK APPLES, PEARS, FIGS, AND SOME BERRIES. AS THE DAYS SHORTEN AND TEMPERATURES FALL, THE NATURAL PLANT RESPONSE IS TO TURN STARCHES INTO SUGARS. BRASSICA CROPS LIKE BROCCOLI, BRUSSELS SPROUTS, CAULIFLOWER, KOHLRABI, COLLARDS, AND KALE BECOME CRISPER AND TASTIER, AND FALL RADISHES TURN FAR SWEETER AND MORE DELICATE THAN THEIR SPRING COUNTERPARTS.

FALL MARKS A TURNING POINT, A BITTERSWEET GOODBYE TO SUMMER'S ABUNDANCE BUT A HELLO TO THE MASSIVE HARVESTS AMONG SOME CROPS YET TO COME. MANY FARMERS ARE JUST BARELY BEGINNING TO CATCH THEIR BREATH AFTER THE CRAZY MONTHS OF SPRING AND SUMMER. BUT FALL CAN BE A TIME OF SUPREME ANXIETY AS WELL—IT IS OFTEN THE LAST HURRAH OF THE SEASON, AND WITH IT THE OPPORTUNITY TO MAKE THE FINAL BIG CASH OF THE YEAR. POOR TIMING OR BAD LUCK WITH FICKLE WEATHER—SUCH AS AN EARLY FROST OR FALL DELUGE—CAN SPOIL THOUSANDS OF DOLLARS' WORTH OF CROPS RIGHT AT THE CRUCIAL MOMENT OF HARVEST.

IT AIN'T OVER TILL IT'S OVER.
WHEN IT IS, IT'S TIME TO CELEBRATE WITH HARVEST AND THANKSGIVING SUPPERS.

Kahumana: When Compassion Meets Community

Kahumana Community

86-660 Lualualei Homestead Road
Waianae, Hawaii, 96792

1-808-696-2655
information@asi-hawaii.org
www.kahumana.org

A warm breeze sweeps across the Pacific, caressing the sweaty faces of thousands of people stretched out on the vast flanks of Waikiki Beach on the Hawaiian island of Oahu. Coconut palms sway in a languid dance as traffic crawls across the third-most congested city in the United States. Throngs of tourists swarm Ala Moana Center, the enormous shopping mecca made famous in iconic television shows like *Hawaii Five-O* and *Magnum P.I.* It's hot, noisy, colorful, crowded, and dirty, full of in-your-face capitalism, like a tropical Las Vegas.

But drive 30 miles west on Highway 93, and it's a completely different world. The lush, manicured vegetation of the resorts surrenders to an arid desert reminiscent of an African savanna or an Australian outback. Here in Waianae, the hotels, developments, and massive suburbs of metropolitan Honolulu fall away to haphazard pockets of run-down neighborhoods and shabby buildings.

It's noticeably hotter here too. Although the ocean is never far away, the heat shimmers almost palpably off the blond, brittle grass. You can hear the birds, the heartbeat of nature in the wind, and the distant waves. You can breathe and relax, without worrying about being peddled something or jostled around by herds of tourists.

But there is something else. It is poverty. Not the sinister inner-city kind that exudes aggression and violence, but a deep-seated systemic weariness that sets in when social service systems fail and humanity starts falling through the cracks of a safety net that was never strong to begin with. You can see it in the wizened faces of people living among clusters of ramshackle tents and bare mattresses on the beaches, and in the rusty tin-roofed shacks and lean-tos dotted along the road. Far from the madding crowd, it may be less frenetic here, but life is far from idyllic.

Turn right onto Lualualei Homestead Road, and the landscape unfolds into a beautiful valley of sharply serrated, windswept volcanic hillsides, with the eroded profile of Mt. Kaʻala in the distance. Gigantic trees flush with tropical flowers and fruit line this quiet country road. And a few miles beyond is another world altogether: Kahumana.

Kahumana's website states its mission simply:

*The way we care for the most vulnerable members of our society determines our mark as a people and a nation. Our mission is to co-create a healthy, inclusive, and productive farm-based community with homeless families, people with disabilities, and youth. We accomplish this through the practice of mindfulness (*makaʻala*), empathy (*aloha*), and working together (*lokahi*).*

Although the land was originally home to a dairy farm, Kahumana's roots began in 1974 from the dire need to provide more effective social services, a legacy of the enormous changes in Hawaii in the 20th century.

From the late 1800s until the mid-1900s, the Hawaiian economy was built on vast plantations of sugarcane, pineapples, coffee, rice, and macadamia nuts, which employed enormous numbers of native Hawaiians, Asian immigrants, and other non-Caucasian populations. When Hawaii attained US statehood in 1959, tourism ballooned on Oahu—and so did real estate prices, making Honolulu one of the most expensive cities in America. At the same time, sugarcane and pineapple-growing operations began closing down and moving to countries with cheaper labor costs. This left many natives and marginalized minorities struggling to subsist on low-wage service jobs in tourism.

This decline in plantations, a lack of living-wage jobs, and skyrocketing rents meant that many found themselves homeless and unable to meet their most basic needs. Even in late 2014, Hawaii had the nation's third-largest homeless population per capita, with more than 7,500 people of all ages living on Oahu's streets. Native Hawaiian populations are especially vulnerable, and Waianae is the epicenter—it has the highest density of Hawaiian natives in the world, as well as numerous Micronesians, Polynesians, and Palauans.

The island's mild climate means that many homeless—including families with children—live outdoors in massive tent camps on public beaches. Even in the 1970s, the need for transitional housing and safe places where families could stay long-term while they underwent job training, psychological counseling, and substance abuse rehabilitation was overwhelming.

Two people, Father Phil Harmon and Chaminade University sociologist Frances Sydow, began discussing how to create meaningful change. In 1974, they founded a unique group home northeast of downtown Honolulu for adults with special needs, one based on a foundation of compassion and intentional community. State case managers soon recognized the effectiveness of their holistic approach and realized that additional space was needed to meet the demand. A few years later, the Kahumana Community was born.

The fruits of the sapsodilla, weighing down the tree's branches.

Today, Kahumana consists of four distinct campuses that cover more than 50 acres in the Lualualei Valley. They include two areas for a combined 118 units of transitional housing for homeless families; the Kahumana Organic Farm and Café, which houses a retreat and learning center, an adult day center, a small bed-and-breakfast, and school demonstration gardens; and 16 acres of newly acquired pristine land that will be used for additional farming and a youth camp. Kahumana also has a commercial, state-certified food service kitchen that provides lunches to Oahu public schools and its transitional housing residents.

Staff and participants of the Hale Lana Team, the program for adults with developmental disabilities, proudly hold up bounty from the fields.

Kahumana's programs for homeless people initially started with 14 units of transitional housing. But as the need to provide more services for disenfranchised people grew urgent, more facilities were built in collaboration with the city and county, from which the land is leased long-term, and through enormous fundraising efforts. In spite of the agricultural zoning that usually imposes strict restrictions on housing, Kahumana, in fulfilling its social service contracts with the state, obtained special city ordinance exemptions.

At any given time, Kahumana is now home to about 130 families and a total of around 600 people—two-thirds of them children under the age of 18. Families may stay as long as 24 months, although most don't remain for the entire two years; many live at Kahumana for only 6 to 18 months.

All of the case managers are employed by Kahumana (not through the state), and each one is responsible for 10 to 20 families. A separate resident manager takes care of each housing site. Partly because of Kahumana's inclusive, close-knit atmosphere, many of the resident managers actually came up through the program themselves—a testament to its extraordinary community strength and effectiveness.

What makes this program unique is the extensive time, attention, and support paid to each person who comes to it. The causes of homelessness are complex, and many factors contribute to an individual's downward spiral. Hawaii has a long history of exploited native populations, and homelessness here is a chronic, generational issue. By learning the background of every child and adult who comes to Kahumana, social workers and case managers are able to customize a care plan and match a network of supportive services and therapies that most effectively fit each person's needs and motivations.

Residents get help with job training, résumé building, parenting, childcare, financial literacy, GED programs, and family counseling, all in a safe environment that emphasizes keeping families together. Kahumana works with 30 to 40 different social service partners and organizations to fill the needs of its residents. It is this level of wrap-around community support, combined with a focus on work and education, that helps residents heal and get back on their feet.

It is not a passive program, and its residents must work hard and be diligent in their efforts. There is zero tolerance for drugs and alcohol. But the goal is that by the time its residents leave, they will have the jobs, stable housing, and life skills to sustain them in the long term.

Funding has become increasingly difficult in recent years; in 2007, the community received 90 percent of its funding from state government contracts, but eight years later, that number has dwindled to about 30 percent. Kahumana is a nonprofit that has no major endowments and runs multiple programs. To help meet the shortfall, it has steadily diversified its business operations by creating an organic farm, its retreat and learning center, a restaurant that is open to the public, and its commercial kitchen. In spite of this diversity, the mission always remains crystal-clear: to empower its community with models for wholeness, wellness, and sustainability, work experience, job training, and a deep sense of inclusivity.

Over the past 40 years, the Kahumana community has served thousands of people, and its efforts have paid off impressively. At least 70 percent of its former residents have reintegrated into society and not returned to the beaches. In fact, the program has been so successful that it has been used as a national model for similar rehabilitative efforts in other parts of the country. Kahumana is always 100 percent full, and there are often as many as 60 families on the waiting list.

To fill the need for fresh food, diversified income, and a workplace for its vocational training programs, Kahumana began its organic farm and café operations around 2008. It now cultivates seven acres, growing salad greens, beets, carrots, chard, broccoli, cauliflower, kohlrabi, herbs, kale, eggplant, black and watermelon radishes, purple-topped turnips, collards, basil, purple onions, leeks, Asian greens, kalumungay leaves, *kalo* (taro), and seasonal fruits such as papayas, oranges, lemons, limes, *lilikoi* (passion fruit), guavas, and Surinam cherries. Its Growing Home Program features closed-circuit systems of aquaponics integrated with vegetable cultivation—an ideal place for its residents to reconnect with the lifegiving *'āina* (land).

The farm also raises some 400 chickens of diverse breeds, ducks, and the occasional turkey for eggs and meat. They are free-range but are cooped at night to protect them from mongooses, which remain a big problem on the island for local bird populations. Kahumana's birds, however, are quite well fed—far more so than probably many of the island's residents.

Watering the transplants in the greenhouse. There are always too many of them waiting to be put out in the field!

A fraction of the farm's 400 chickens, ducks, and turkeys. It's a noisy, free-for-all frenzy at feeding time.

At the local Waianae Farmers Market.

The flower and herb gardens behind the café. In the upper right corner is an enormous mango tree, a common fruit in the islands.

"We give them all-organic feed, all of the leftovers from the café kitchen and farm, and vegetables that are past their prime," says farm manager Christian Zuckerman. "And when we clear fields of our salad mix, we open them up for a week to give them an extra area to go hunting for bugs. They can also scratch around in the big compost pile. They're pretty happy chickens," he adds, grinning. "They've got it pretty good." Plans are in the works to eventually double the number of birds raised.

The farm's tilapia, poultry, eggs, fruits, vegetables, and herbs supply its CSA program, Kahumana residents, the farm café, local farmers markets, and even some area restaurants. At the time of this book's printing, the farm's CSA program was quite small—around 35 shares, all from the Waianae area. Demand is such that it could easily gain another 100 subscribers were it not for production, labor, and delivery challenges (the farm lacks a refrigerated truck, so shareholders must come to the farm to pick up their weekly boxes). It is also the cheapest around—a mere $25 a week.

As you might expect, the farm employs a variety of sustainable growing methods, including biodynamics, composting, permaculture, integrated growing methods to control pests and weeds, crop rotation, and green manure. Natural pesticides are often concocted right on the premises, like a very effective, potent blend of chile pepper, garlic, and neem oil that is strained through cheesecloth and sprayed directly on the plants. For its new 16-acre parcel, Christian is also hoping that the farm will become more self-sufficient and off the grid with its energy usage, turning to solar and desalinization methods rather than depending on fossil fuels.

Composting is also a big deal. The farm works with two companies on the island that collect expired vegetables from supermarkets, food waste from area restaurants, and residuals like guava pulp from juicing operations. It's all combined with chicken manure and water, and the island's heat and moisture work quickly to break it down into black gold.

Since the farm is quite small, it employs only two full-time, long-term workers, and WWOOFers fill in the rest of its paid labor needs (see the sidebar on page 489 for more information). Apprenticeships of 6 to 12 months are available on a limited basis, with food, on-site housing, and a small stipend provided.

The influence of Rudolf Steiner is unmistakable here, both in the architecture of some of the farm's housing and in its community spirit. Steiner was an Austrian philosopher and social reformer who is considered the father of biodynamic agriculture (see the sidebar on page 427 for more information).

Robert Zuckerman, longtime Kahumana member and café manager, relates, "Many therapeutic communities were created based on Steiner's teachings and model for social renewal that date back to the late 1920s and 1930s. Ahead of their time, they were holistic without having to call themselves that. Biodynamic farming is a key component; its agricultural approach recognizes the farm as a living being and its spirituality. The modern dilemma besetting our environment requires healing the macrocosm and the microcosm. Biodynamic farming is not just organic—it embraces an intentional, conscious human process to heal the earth and the environment."

It is not surprising, then, that deeply rooted in Kahumana's philosophy is the integration of people into life at the farm, its café, retreat center, and bed-and-breakfast—whether they're residents, youth, or adult day center visitors. This includes people with developmental disabilities and mental illness. For instance, one young man who is autistic is among the volunteers who participate every morning. He has been getting valuable job training and building his self-confidence and social skills in a warm, loving environment. "Integration" and "inclusivity" are not mere buzzwords here—these people work right alongside regular farmworkers in state-mandated ratios. Organization-wide, Kahumana employs about 80 people, and 20 to 40 more volunteer.

An important part of the farm's income comes from supplying up-scale, trendy restaurants like Roy's, Monkeypod, SEED, Koko Head Café, and Cactus. Such high-end establishments are willing to pay premium prices for produce from farms like Kahumana, which in turn enables farms to charge lower prices at the farmers market to local customers who can't otherwise afford nutritious, local food.

So just what is it like to farm in a tropical place with year-round warmth? There are, in fact, two distinct seasons. October through May marks the cooler and rainier winter season, when daytime temperatures reach the low 80s and nighttime temps drop into the 70s or even 60s. In June through September, however, conditions can be downright miserable—an average of 95+ degrees during the day in the summer with temperatures cooling only to the mid-80s at night. This is on top of intense humidity from brief but almost daily showers that pelt the islands. In the summer, the farm, because it is on the leeward side of the island, gets hardly any rain at all, so it must depend largely on irrigation.

As Christian puts it, "We can grow a broader spectrum of things here, but sometimes it is harder to have more seasonal variety. In some ways I compare our summer to the mainland's winter; we can still grow some crops, but it is much more difficult because of the intense heat—it takes more water and there's a lower survival rate. We grow our baby greens all year, but in the heat of summer, after we've finished our first cut, the second growth that grows back is just not as good, whereas in the winter, that second cut is still excellent, and sometimes we can even get a third cut."

Typically salad greens are harvested year-round, and many of their vegetables are planted in two big, monthly rotations, with brassica crops like broccoli and kohlrabi going into the ground in the fall when the cooler weather begins. Baby salad mix is a staple for the farm, with 10 to 12 different greens included: several varieties of kale, mizuna, tatsoi, three different kinds of mustard, two romaine lettuce varieties, oakleaf and buttercrunch lettuce, and amaranth. The time from seeding to first cutting averages three to four weeks, with one or two cuts of each crop done for salad mix; after that, the rest goes to the chickens. As a small production farm, Kahumana typically harvests an average of 150 pounds of salad mix and about 800 to 1,000 pounds of produce each week.

The intense, tropical climate poses problems for some crops that are taken for granted in other parts of the country. Christian eventually wants to install hoop houses, because they can't grow tomatoes, for instance. "They just get too stung by fruit flies, so unless you constantly spray, they don't turn out well. The weather is great, but it's a bug issue!"

> "We can grow a broader spectrum of things here in Hawaii, but sometimes it is harder to have more seasonal variety. In some ways I compare our summer to the mainland's winter: we can still grow some crops, but it is much more difficult because of the intense heat—it takes more water and there's a lower survival rate."
>
> — *Christian Zuckerman*

The farm's aquaponics system, which raises tilapia in conjunction with vegetables.

The soil is especially fertile here, since the entire area used to be a caldera, formed when a volcano collapsed. "It is such very rich soil that it doesn't need a whole lot of inputs and amendments," says Christian, lapsing into farmer-speak. Some organically approved biological pesticides such as DiPel do need to be used, especially with brassicas, for which neem oil isn't as effective in controlling cabbage moths (see the sidebar on organic pesticides on page 590). DP, as it is often called, works by bacterial action that specifically targets the cabbage worm caterpillars but leaves beneficial insects unharmed. Spraying is generally kept to a minimum, however, and there's more reliance on good soil and growing techniques to grow more bug-resistant plants.

A field of young dragonfruit plants isn't a sight you see at just any CSA farm.

This being Hawaii, fruit plays a bigger part in the farm's offerings than in other parts of the country. The farm has a little orchard that, by Christian's admission, has been a bit undermaintained, but efforts are under way to revitalize it. Here about 15 different fruits are grown, including oranges, lemons, limes, soursops, mangoes, bananas, sapodillas, pomelos, grapefruits, pomegranates, tangerines, and tangelos, all in a permaculture system where cover crops such as buckwheat are cultivated among the trees.

In the face of this organic oasis, it is keenly ironic that just beyond the orchard, literally a stone's throw away, is an enormous basil farm that exemplifies conventional monoculture agriculture. Its huge rows of mammoth, picture-perfect plants are unbelievably lush, thanks to heavy doses of chemical fertilizer and conventional pesticides. An enormous amount of basil is grown in Waianae, but most of it is not organic—indeed, thanks to the area's heat and relatively dry conditions, the industry has boomed in the past 5 to 10 years in Waianae.

"Many of the basil farms are really controversial," says Christian, "because they are run by rural Chinese farmers who have no regard for the environment. They use a lot of non-FDA–approved—thus, illegal—

chemicals, and they've already been busted a few times. Just on a little plot of land they can make up to $100,000 a month because it is such fast production, so there's financial incentive."

In spite of its proximity, Kahumana is in little danger of runoff contamination because it sits on higher ground. Still, on days when the winds are coming from a certain direction, there is some pesticide blow-over. Now that the basil farm's fields surrounding Kahumana are so extensive, Christian plans to build natural barriers of high-growing vines to help block these pesticide residues from reaching their vulnerable fields. He admits that legally, a 25-foot buffer zone is required between organic and nonorganic farming operations, but in the real world, such regulation sometimes doesn't mean much.

One of Kahumana Cafe's delectable signature dishes— the macadamia-nut shrimp pasta dressed with organic homemade pesto with basil, cilantro, kalamungay, garlic, macadamia nuts, sea salt, and olive oil.

Initially, the Kahumana Café began in 2008 as a way to supplement the organization's income after state cuts to Kahumana's funding began. The restaurant has earned quite a reputation for its outstanding food. In a notoriously expensive land, the café's meals are incredibly affordable—the average cost of a full meal, including beverage and dessert, runs about $15 to $20. This is to keep the café's food accessible to people in the local area, who benefit from its healthful approach.

The café serves lunch and dinner five days a week. The menu is based on the farm's daily harvest of fruits, vegetables, herbs, and eggs as well as chicken, duck, tilapia, and local seafood and beef. Vegetarian and vegan options are available, and the café is always happy to accommodate special dietary needs. Signature dishes include a tostada containing macadamia-nut–crusted *ono* (a type of Hawaiian fish) with a Surinam cherry reduction and a cilantro sauce drizzle, served with a side of fresh farm vegetables and brown rice; fresh-caught tilapia pan-fried with a garlic-and-ginger crust; local grass-fed beef shepherd's pie; mixed meat and veggie curries made with the farm's own lemongrass, ginger, basil, cilantro, and coconut milk; and macadamia-nut pasta dressed with organic homemade pesto with basil, cilantro, kalamungay, garlic, macadamia nuts, sea salt, and olive oil. To coin a Hawaiian phrase, it's *ono to da max!*

And of course, you can't slip out without trying Robert's Lilikoi Cheesecake and Supa' Chocolate Brownies—an irresistible combination if ever there was one. A tall glass of crimson-tinted, refreshing hibiscus herbal water or rich, organic coffee magnificently rounds out the meal.

Besides offering delicious, healthful food, the café provides important vocational training in the culinary arts and hospitality industry for Kahumana's residents. Dining at the café helps support that nonprofit mission monetarily as well.

Robert says that his customers come from diverse places and visit for equally varied reasons. "We have people who are local who come here all the time. We feed all of our coworkers, so that means serving 20 to 30 of them for lunch, as well as our own adult day program participants, residents, school groups, and retreat guests. It makes for a vibrant, lively crowd—which ties into our model of wholeness and inclusivity with all age groups and many disparate populations, including the homeless and mentally ill."

"Our setting and the environment are ideal for retreats. People just love being here. We also get a lot of tourists on the island who hear about us through social media. Others may be staying elsewhere, but they make the effort to come all the way out here based on reviews."

— Robert Zuckerman

An example of some of the farm's distinctive, Rudolf Steiner–inspired housing for its permanent staff.

In the lanai of the Kahumana Café.

The menu is equally eclectic. "We have vegetarian dishes, although we are not exclusively so; and we have gluten-free," says Robert. "This is one of the few places where almost everyone who comes in here can find something to eat. And the word gets out, because of social media. One young woman called me about a year ago, and she was so excited to come in. On the phone, she starts pumping me with a thousand questions, just going on and on. Then she came in for dinner, and she kept asking me questions throughout the meal. She can't do dairy, can't eat this, can't have that. We serve our own homemade pesto, and she asked me about every herb, every ingredient. I asked her, 'Why do you need to know all this?' Turns out that cilantro, for instance, would make her right arm go numb. She ended up eating here every day for the whole two weeks she stayed on the island. Then she came back a year later, and I recognized her right away. She just absolutely loves it here, and says there is nowhere else she can go out to eat because of all of her food sensitivities."

He relates the poignant story of another customer who came in with a whole list of foods on her iPhone that she couldn't eat. "No gluten, no dairy, no garlic, no onions, no salt, could eat only steamed foods, no oil. Yet I was able to put a meal together—it was a brown rice pasta with steamed carrots and basil. She was so grateful and said it was the best thing she'd ever had. Turns out that she had caught a parasite in South America years before that nearly destroyed her intestines, and as a result her body has no filter system. All of the foods she formerly enjoyed are like poison to her digestive tract, and if she eats the wrong thing, it's nine hours of agony. Needless to say, she hadn't been able to dine out in years. I was so deeply moved by her gratitude. The point is, we can accommodate."

Meanwhile, the Kahumana commercial kitchen at its Ulu Ke Kukui site a few miles away makes healthful meals for kids. It produces over 5,000 meals per week that are delivered to approximately 35 schools on the west side of Oahu. Some of the *keiki* attending these schools come from households subsisting below the poverty line, and for them, this is often their last substantial—and nutritious—meal of the day, so this school food fills vital dietary needs.

The state-certified kitchen is run by an energetic crew of 20 food-prep workers, cooks, delivery staff, and servers. Many of them came through Kahumana's programs and also from other transitional housing shelters. In fact, the kitchen manager was once a client of the nonprofit when she and her family were homeless.

As a side benefit, many of Kahumana's school clients bring their children to the farm to see where their carrots and baby greens are grown. The farm also offers tours (half-day and daylong), school-to-farm education programs, and overnight camps for students of all ages, from prekindergartners through adults.

Kahumana has also been hosting more farm-stay and retreat experiences to supplement its income and to attract more visitors to its unique area. Their Retreat and Learning Center offers something for everyone, from yoga classes, lectures, and school-to-farm day camps to weeklong wellness retreats. Visitors can learn about organic farming, eat farm-fresh food, meditate and do yoga, or take classes on sustainability and spirituality. The farm also hosts special events like weddings and family reunions.

Kahumana also serves the local community and educational institutions, and on occasion it sponsors retreats for them. "Our setting and the environment are ideal for this," Robert observes, "and people just love being here. We also get a lot of tourists on the island who hear about us through social media. People who stay in this area sometimes come back quite a bit. Others may be staying elsewhere, but they make the effort to come all the way out here based on reviews."

Interestingly, the farm's yoga retreats are very popular with people who come from Japan to attend (Hawaii is a popular tourist destination for the Japanese, since it is a relatively short flight away). "We get a fair number of Japanese tourists because there's a huge interest in this model in Japan—sustainability, holistic, Hawaiiana—and people are looking for alternative things to do. We have been featured in enough Japanese periodicals and magazines that they form a stack about two feet high," Robert says, chuckling. "We get calls all the time from people wanting to do articles and photo shoots. We've even had a couple of videos shot out here. And these are major magazines, the equivalent of Cosmopolitan and Elle, geared for 30- to 40-year-old professional women. One of them is the most-read magazine in Japan right now. And because of these magazines, we often get other Japanese entities interested in us, like travel books and the Hitachi corporation, which expressed interest in our farming model."

Farm-to-school tours are also a very important part of Kahumana's outreach—annually the farm hosts a couple of thousand kids, with 30 to as many as 100 visiting at a time. In fall 2014, students from the Honolulu Waldorf School came and stayed at the farm for 10 days. Split into groups, they worked every day with the farm staff and were assigned different projects, ranging from cultivating to washing to harvesting, thus getting the full farm experience.

It's not all work and drudgery at Kahumana. Recently it started First Friday, at which a movie is screened, the farm hosts live music acts, and local artists display their art and crafts. In 2013, the farm began its own Farm Festival, a free event where the community can come together and enjoy a day of music, food, games, and one another. The festival is also an opportunity for other local farms, restaurants, artists, and musicians to share with the community. Its goal is to promote the ever-growing food-sustainability movement in Hawaii and to give individuals and organizations an opportunity to express their support while enjoying a relaxing day at the farm.

The Kahumana Café serves lunch and dinner five days a week. The menu is based on the farm's daily harvest of fruits, vegetables, herbs, and eggs as well as chicken, duck, tilapia, and local seafood and beef. Vegetarian and vegan options are available, and the café is always happy to accommodate special dietary needs.

Getting ready for packing the CSA boxes for another week at Kahumana.

In fact, the flavor of these kinds of outreach is just one of the many reasons why Kahumana is so special. Born from its founding intent as a place where people from diverse cultural and spiritual backgrounds come together to heal, the sheer love and humanity shared between its staff, residents, and participants is a powerful, palpable force, one that flourishes as rampantly as the veggies, fruits, weeds, and bugs in the island heat and rain.

Apples

MALUS DOMESTICA

It is a paradox that although Americans know and love apples as a ubiquitous food, relatively few of them have ever tasted a truly good one. The world of apples is enormous, with 7,500 varieties grown worldwide, 2,500 of which are grown in the United States and 100 of these commercially. Yet, in spite of this apple abundance, most of us are familiar with only a handful: the classic Red Delicious; the sweet, yellow-skinned Golden Delicious; the tart, green-skinned Granny Smith; the soft, blushing Macintosh; the buttery, spicy Gala; the crisp, golden-pink-skinned Fuji; the supersweet Honeycrisp; and the spicy, tart Braeburn. At one time, the Red Delicious was much superior to what it is now, but coloration profoundly affects flesh quality, and the darker an apple's skin becomes, the more bitter it tastes. The venerable Reds were bred to be an increasingly darker red to appeal to consumers, and so they have come to be fairly inferior as eating apples.

More than 60 percent of the commercial US apple crop is grown in Washington State, although increasingly apples are being imported from abroad, especially from China and Chile. But the varieties you are most likely to see at farmers markets or through your CSA are heirlooms, which are old-fashioned cultivars with distinctive flavors, perfumes, shapes, and skin hues. Often these antique apples are far more complex and nuanced than their commercially popular cousins, which are typically bred for uniformity, longer shipping and storing qualities, and large-scale disease and pest resistance.

It is impossible to list here all of the varieties you might find at your local CSA or farmers market, as heirloom apples are highly regional and particular to certain microclimates. But a few of the names you might see are Winesap, Pippin, Cortland, Empire, Northern Spy, and Winthrop. Often these apples are not as pretty as their commercial counterparts, and if they are organic, they may have significant blemishes, even an occasional wormhole. But if you see them, don't pass up the opportunity to sample this part of America's nearly forgotten—and very tasty—gastronomic history.

HISTORY

Apples have figured richly in human history for thousands of years, with references in religious folklore and mythology in Norse, Greek, and European Christian cultures. Although the apple is famously blamed as the forbidden fruit that tempted Eve in the book of Genesis, it is never actually identified in the Bible. The fruit originated in central Asia, becoming especially genetically diverse in Turkey. Apples were brought to North America in the 17th century, but it wasn't until 300 years later that large-scale cultivation efforts took root, so to speak, in eastern Washington, thanks to massive irrigation efforts.

NUTRITION

"An apple a day keeps the doctor away" is no mere adage; apples are quite nutritious, with vitamins A and C, potassium, phosphorus, highly digest-

You Weren't Going to Eat That, Were You?

Conventionally grown apples are on the "Dirty Dozen" list—meaning they are extra-high in pesticide and herbicide residues. This residue is particularly harmful to children, as well as to adults with health issues.

Purchase organic apples and apple products whenever possible. Even nonorganic apple juice and applesauce have been found to contain significant pesticide levels.

ible sugars, and some dietary fiber. A medium apple contains about 95 calories. Additionally, apples contain significant amounts of phytonutrients and polyphenols that favorably affect levels of blood sugar, digestive bacteria, and blood fats.

SEASON

Commercially, apples are widely grown, and the most common varieties are available year-round. But the crops' peak season is midsummer through frost, and apples are at their best in the fall.

SELECTION

In spite of all the apple varieties that you may encounter, a few standard principles apply to select good ones: They should be smooth-skinned with no signs of desiccation or bruised soft spots, heavy for their size, and firm to the touch. Golden yellow hues or undertones often signal better-tasting, riper fruit.

STORAGE

Apples should be kept as cold as possible under humid conditions. Store them in the refrigerator crisper in a perforated or open plastic bag so they can retain moisture without collecting it. Depending on their condition, they can last from several weeks to a couple of months.

TRIMMING AND CLEANING

Conventionally grown apples may be coated with a food-grade wax. The wax is harmless, but you can remove it by rinsing the fruit under warm water. You can choose to peel the fruit or not, depending on your preference and the dish you're preparing; if you're cooking apples, bits of skin left on can be distractingly tough.

Also be aware that conventionally grown apples tend to have high levels of pesticide residue on their skins, which is why you should always try to buy organic apples if possible. A mixture of 1 part vinegar to 3 parts water can help strip off this residue.

Most apples will turn brown once they are peeled or their flesh is exposed to air; this is mostly harmless, but it may affect their flavor and texture after a while. To prevent this, place the sliced fruit in a bowl of water mixed with some lemon juice.

There is, of course, the matter of the core and the hard little seeds within, which should not be eaten. It's best to core apples before cooking them; an inexpensive apple corer does the trick quite well.

BAKING AND ROASTING

Apples and hot ovens go together—baking softens and caramelizes the fruit, rendering it rich and flavorful. And it's easy too: Just core whole apples; place them in a baking dish; stuff them with a mixture of nuts, butter, and brown sugar; pour a little water in the bottom of the dish to keep them from sticking; and bake in a 375°F oven for 30 to 45 minutes, or until they are soft but not mushy.

MICROWAVING

To bake apples more quickly, you can microwave whole or cut fruit for 3 to 4 minutes on high power.

BLANCHING AND FREEZING

Apples can easily be frozen whole or sliced, although the latter option makes for more convenient use later. Whole apples can be just washed and placed in a large zipper-lock freezer bag, or individually in vacuum food sealer-type bags as desired. To freeze cut apples, peel, core, and slice them; dip them in a bowl of water mixed with lemon juice to prevent them from browning as you work. Drain the slices well, then arrange them in a single layer on a tray lined with parchment or wax paper and freeze. Package them in zipper-lock freezer or vacuum food sealer-type bags, or freezer containers. Squeeze out any excess air and leave 1 inch of headspace (unless you are using the vacuum sealing method). Frozen apples will keep for up to 1 year at 0°F.

EQUIVALENTS, MEASURES, AND SERVINGS

- 1 medium apple = 1½ cups sliced apples = 1 cup chopped apples
- 1 pound apples = 3 medium or 2 large apples =
    4½ cups sliced apples = 3 cups chopped apples =
    1⅓ cups applesauce
- 1 pound dried apples = 4⅓ cups = 8 cups rehydrated apples
- 2 pounds fresh apples = filling for one 9-inch pie
- 4 pounds fresh apples = 4 cups applesauce = 1 pound dried apples

COMPLEMENTARY HERBS, SEASONINGS, AND FOODS

Bacon, beets, brown sugar, butter, caramel, cardamom, celery, cheese (especially Cheddar), chestnuts, cinnamon, cranberries, cream, currants, ginger, goose, hazelnuts, ice cream, mangoes, maple syrup, nutmeg, oatmeal, onions, pears, pork, quince, red cabbage, rosemary, vanilla, veal, venison, walnuts, wild boar.

SERVING SUGGESTIONS

- As the saying goes, nothing is more American than apple pie. This classic dessert is especially good made with different kinds of flavorful apples. A traditional accompaniment is a wedge of aged Cheddar cheese—the sharper, the better. Or a scoop of vanilla ice cream.
- Applesauce is a good way to process and preserve a lot of apples at one time, and it makes an excellent snack, breakfast food, kid treat, or topping for cottage cheese.
- Make caramel apples! Either melt solid, premade caramel or make your own from scratch; dip your apples into the caramel and let cool. Tarter apples like Macintoshes and Granny Smiths help balance the sweetness of the caramel.
- Cut up apples and combine them with other fruits and berries for a fruit salad.
- Sometimes the simple things are best—like apple slices with a little whipped cream, cinnamon, nutmeg, and sugar.
- Baked apples are an easy dessert that taste especially grand on cold winter days. So are apple crisps, crumbles, and cobblers.
- Add apples to vegetable salads for extra crunch and sweetness. They go especially well with nuts, celery, bacon, and beets, and provide a welcome sweet note in coleslaw.
- Make apple butter. This is essentially applesauce that has been cooked and reduced slowly over a long time—caramelizing the fruit's sugars, concentrating its flavors, and thickening it to a viscous consistency.

Cooking Tip

Apples are a great way to infuse moisture into things. Slip half an apple into an airtight container with soft cookies or a cake to help them stay fresher longer.

The same thing works with chicken: Stuff a whole small peeled apple inside a chicken before you roast it; it will help keep it moist and add a subtle fruity flavor.

Have some brown sugar that's hardened into a rock? Place a slice of apple in with the sugar and seal both in an airtight bag. The sugar will absorb the apple's moisture and soften within a few days.

- Apple sandwiches! Try bacon, peanut butter, grilled cheese—with or without the bread!
- Combine julienned apples with finely sliced cabbage and carrots for a refreshing, crunchy slaw. Tart apples work especially well for this dish.
- Make dried apples and apple chips. These make delicious, highly portable snacks for school, work, or athletic activities.

APPLE CRUMBLE   SERVES 8 TO 10

APPLE MIXTURE
**5 to 6 medium apples, peeled, cored, and sliced
   (about 8 to 10 cups)**
1 cup white sugar
1 tablespoon all-purpose flour
1 teaspoon ground cinnamon
½ teaspoon salt
½ cup water

TOPPING
1 cup rolled oats
1 cup all-purpose flour
1 cup packed brown sugar
¼ teaspoon baking powder
¼ teaspoon baking soda
½ cup (1 stick) butter, melted

1. Preheat the oven to 350°F.

2. In a large bowl, prepare the apple mixture by combining the prepared apples, white sugar, flour, cinnamon, and salt. Let it sit for about 5 minutes to allow the apples to sweat and the flavors to combine. Place the apple mixture in a 9-by-13-inch pan, and pour the water over the apple mixture.

3. To make the topping, combine the oats, flour, brown sugar, baking powder, baking soda, and melted butter. Work this mixture together with a fork until it comes to a uniform, crumbly consistency. Sprinkle the topping evenly over the apple mixture.

4. Bake for about 45 minutes. The fruit should be bubbling and the topping browned. Let cool (to allow it to set up) before serving.

— *Paul Anater*

SPICY BALINESE GREEN APPLE SALAD   SERVES 4

Source Note: *The dressing I make for this salad is used commonly throughout Southeast Asia for vegetable and green (unripe) fruit salads, and also as a* *dipping sauce for grilled meats. The green apple juice cocktail I had at my hotel in Bali inspired me to create this green apple salad, which can be eaten on its own or as a accompaniment to grilled meat, or if you are in Bali, perhaps a roast suckling pig. This dish is lovely served with a beverage of freshly pressed green apple, celery, and ginger juice.*

Author Note: Thai bird chiles are very hot, so start with fewer if you'd like to temper the level of heat. Also, handle them with care! Wear gloves while cutting them and avoid touching your eyes or other sensitive areas if you've handled them directly. Last, wash your cutting board thoroughly after slicing the chiles, as it will transfer spicy-hot oils to other foods.

LIME-CHILE DRESSING

⅔ cup freshly squeezed lime juice (from about 6 limes)

2 teaspoons sugar

2 teaspoons fish sauce (if unavailable, substitute about ½ teaspoon salt)

2 teaspoons water

4 Thai bird chiles, thinly sliced

SALAD

2 Granny Smith apples

½ small red onion, thinly sliced

2 to 4 tablespoons crushed roasted peanuts

1. Make the dressing first so the flavors have time to blend. Combine the lime juice, sugar, fish sauce, and water in a bowl and stir well. Add the sliced chiles. Set aside.

2. Core and julienne the apples and immediately combine them with the dressing to prevent them from turning brown.

3. Add the onions and stir well to combine.

4. Just before serving, sprinkle the crushed peanuts on top.

— *Linda Shiue,* Spicebox Travels *blog*

· ·

APPLESAUCE WITH BOURBON, SOUR CHERRIES, AND HAZELNUTS

SERVES 4

¼ cup dried sour cherries

¼ cup plus 1 tablespoon bourbon

4 apples (about 1½ pounds), peeled, cored, and diced

¼ cup water

1 tablespoon butter

3 tablespoons chopped hazelnuts, toasted

1. In a small bowl, cover the cherries with the bourbon and set aside to plump while you prepare the rest of the dish.

With a Little Help from My Friends

Apples emit ethylene gas, a naturally occurring plant hormone. If you have avocados, tomatoes, bananas, kiwis, pears, nectarines, or other fruit that could use a little assistance getting riper faster, place a ripe apple in with them inside a paper (not plastic) bag. They will ripen much more quickly this way.

2. Place the diced apples and water in a medium saucepan over medium-low heat. Cover and cook until the apples are tender enough to smash with the back of a spoon, 15 to 20 minutes.

3. Add the butter. Using a wooden spoon or heavy whisk, beat just enough to smash the apples into a thick, chunky sauce. Stir in the cherries and bourbon and continue cooking until the raw alcohol smell of the bourbon has burned off, about 5 minutes. Stir in the hazelnuts and serve.

— *Russ Parsons,* How to Pick a Peach

NASH'S RAW SLAW   SERVES 8

⅓ cup apple cider vinegar
¼ cup honey
1 tablespoon mustard
2 cups cabbage, shredded
1 cup apples, shredded
2 cup carrots, shredded
⅓ cup chopped fresh dill

1. In a large bowl, whisk the vinegar, honey, and mustard together to make the sauce.

2. Add the rest of the ingredients and mix well.

— *Mary Wong, Nash's Organic Produce, Sequim, Washington*

ROASTED APPLES AND PARSNIPS   SERVES 4

Source Note: This unique combination of sweet apples and earthy parsnips makes a perfect accompaniment to roast pork, chicken, or turkey. A great Thanksgiving side dish too!

1½ pounds (5 medium) parsnips, peeled
1 pound (2 large) Gala or Braeburn apples, peeled and cored

½ teaspoon salt
¼ teaspoon freshly ground black pepper
2 tablespoons extra-virgin olive oil
1 tablespoon coarsely chopped fresh sage

1. Place the oven rack in the upper third of the oven and preheat it to 425°F.

2. Cut the parsnips lengthwise into quarters and then into 2-inch pieces. Cut the apples into quarters and then into 2-inch pieces.

3. Toss the parsnips and apples with the salt, pepper, olive oil, and sage. Spread them in a single layer on a large, shallow baking pan. Roast, turning occasionally, until the parsnips and apples are tender and browned, 20 to 25 minutes.

— *Luisa DePaiva, Purple Rain Vineyard, Vancouver, Washington*

Books

Chez Panisse Fruit
Alice Waters,
HarperCollins, 2002.

The Fruit Hunters:
A Story of Nature, Adventure,
Commerce, and Obsession
Adam Leith Gollner,
Scribner, 2008.

The Apple Lover's Cookbook
Amy Traverso,
W. W. Norton & Company, 2011.

An afternoon with Jack Hedin brings the farm-to-table connection closer and enhances communication about the rewards and challenges of growing great vegetables at Featherstone Farm.

Beets

BETA VULGARIS

Beets are a bargain vegetable, because they are actually two in one: the delicious roots that everyone knows, and also the beet tops or greens, which are extremely nutritious and a wonderful spring treat. Unfortunately, too many adults dislike beets, having eaten (or been forced to eat) poorly prepared specimens as children.

Beets are biennials, meaning that they take two years to grow to maturity. In their first year they develop their familiar swollen roots, and during the second year they flower and seed.

Several types of beets are grown by many CSA farms: the familiar red beet (sometimes called "table beet" or "garden beet"); miniature varieties with roots that may reach a size no larger than a silver dollar; and specialty types raised for their unusual root colors (orange, yellow, or striped) or tasty greens. Chioggia (pronounced kee-oh-ja) is one of the better-known specialty beets, with its striking, concentric red and white rings. Most beets taste pretty similar; the yellow or golden ones are more mellow and earthy, and slightly less sweet than the red varieties.

HISTORY

It is thought that beets originated in the Mediterranean area, possibly Italy, although they have been cultivated since prehistoric times and thus their true origins are unknown. The original beets were closer to chard (a cultivar of the beet family) than the root vegetable we know today, and the early Romans ate only the leaves. Humans and livestock alike have long enjoyed beets and their various cultivars, which include chard, mangel-wurzel, and sugar beets.

Throughout recorded history, beets have been thought to have medicinal powers, combating digestive disorders, lack of sexual interest, and even AIDs.

NUTRITION

Beets have one of the highest sugar contents of all vegetables but are fairly low in calories, at 74 per cup. They are extremely high in folate and manganese and are a decent source of dietary fiber, vitamin C, and potassium. Betacyanin, which gives red beets their distinctive rich pigment, is a powerful cancer-fighting agent and antioxidant.

The roots also contain betaine, supplements of which are sometimes prescribed to lower toxic levels of homocysteine, which can contribute to heart disease and stroke.

SEASON

Commercially, beets are widely grown and in season year-round. You'll find them at their best in farmers markets and CSAs from midsummer through late fall.

SELECTION

Avoid beets that are overly large; they may be old and woody. The smaller beets are, the sweeter they tend to be. The roots should be firm, with no soft or flabby areas, and their tops (if attached) fresh and unwilted.

STORAGE

If you are lucky enough to acquire beets with their greens still attached, cut all but 2 inches of the greens and stems from the roots, so they do not pull moisture away from the roots. Store the unwashed greens in a separate perforated plastic bag in the refrigerator vegetable crisper, where they will keep for about 4 days.

The beetroots should be placed in the coldest place possible. Beets that are unwashed in the refrigerator vegetable crisper will keep for about 3 weeks. Beets also keep quite well in a basement, root cellar, or other place with the proper cool temperature and lack of humidity (for more information, see "Preserving the Bounty" on page 611).

TRIMMING AND CLEANING

Like spinach, beet greens must be very thoroughly washed and rinsed several times, as they usually harbor lots of sand and debris.

To clean the roots, scrub their necks gently with a soft vegetable brush to work off any clinging dirt, but be careful not to break the skin, which will cause them to "bleed." Rinse under cold running water.

To prepare the greens, fill a big sink or bowl full of water, cut the leaves from the roots, and completely submerge them, swishing vigorously. Then rinse them under cold running water, and repeat if necessary. To dry, use a salad spinner or gently pat the leaves dry between a couple of clean dish towels.

STEAMING AND BOILING

Boiling cooks beets quickly, but it tends to leach out nutrients and some color (although red beets usually have plenty of pigment to spare).

To prevent bleeding in red beets when boiling, leave them whole with their root ends and 1 inch of stem attached. Boil for 25 to 30 minutes for small beets; 45 to 50 minutes for medium beets, or until they are tender. Test by piercing them with a knife. Once the beets are cool enough to touch, peel them by rubbing the skins, which should slide off like a glove.

Chioggia beets (the ones with concentric red and white circles) do not bleed. When cooked, their rings will turn orange or rose, or they may fade altogether.

STIR-FRYING AND SAUTÉING

Beet greens adapt well to stir-fries, but add them only during the last 1 to 2 minutes of cooking to preserve their vibrant color and fresh flavor.

Because the roots can be dense and fibrous, they should be parboiled before getting tossed into the wok. You can also julienne them (but cook them separately and add at the very end so they don't bleed all over the rest of the ingredients). If the beets are thinly sliced, stir-fry them for only 2 to 4 minutes.

Beets headed for a sauté should also be thinly sliced (into ⅛- to ¼-inch rounds) and cooked on medium heat for 5 to 7 minutes.

Stanch the Bleeding of Beets

Mi Ae Lipe

Because red beets often "bleed" profusely during cooking and then turn a duller brownish red, it is best to cook them by themselves and add them to other ingredients at the last moment.

To minimize bleeding, wash the beets gently under cool running water, taking care not to tear the skin. This tough outer layer helps keep most of the beet pigment inside the vegetable.

The color of beets can be modified during cooking. Adding an acidic ingredient such as lemon juice or vinegar will brighten the color, whereas an alkaline substance such as baking soda will often cause them to turn a deeper purple. Salt will dull beet color, so add it only at the end of cooking.

Since beet juice can stain your skin, wearing kitchen gloves is a good idea when handling beets. If your hands get stained during the cleaning and cooking process, simply rub some lemon juice on them to remove the stain.

To remove beet stains from clothing, place a piece of white bread soaked in water directly on the stain. The bread will start to absorb the beet pigment almost immediately. Replace the bread if necessary until it picks up no more color, and then rinse the clothing in cold water and treat with a stain remover.

BAKING AND ROASTING

Beets respond very well to slow-roasting in the oven. To prepare, preheat the oven to 375°F. Peel the beets raw, using a vegetable peeler, then slice them into wedges (similar to potatoes). Or if they are very small, leave them whole, and place them in a single layer in a roasting pan or baking dish. Drizzle with oil, then add garlic and seasonings if desired, and roast them for 30 to 40 minutes, or until they are tender when pierced with a fork.

MICROWAVING

Cut unpeeled beets into evenly sized pieces. Place them in a microwave-safe dish and cover with 1 inch of water. Microwave on high power for 8 to 15 minutes, depending on their size and age, or until they are just tender. If you prefer them peeled, rub off their skins right after cooking, while they are still warm.

BLANCHING AND FREEZING

Beets should be fully cooked before freezing, as frozen raw beets will soften undesirably upon thawing. Frozen cooked beets, however, will retain their flavor and texture. To freeze, follow the boiling instructions above. Then plunge them into ice water for 5 minutes to stop the cooking process. Remove and drain. Slice or cube them if desired, and pack in zipper-lock freezer or vacuum food sealer-type bags, or freezer containers. Squeeze out any excess air and leave ½ inch of headspace (unless you are using the vacuum sealing method). Frozen beets will keep for up to 8 months at 0°F, but their texture may diminish considerably by that time.

EQUIVALENTS, MEASURES, AND SERVINGS

- 1 pound = 1¾ cups shredded = 2 cups chopped or sliced

COMPLEMENTARY HERBS, SEASONINGS, AND FOODS

Allspice, apples, bacon, beef, brown sugar, butter, cheese, chestnuts, cilantro, cinnamon, citrus, cloves, cream, cucumber, curry, dill, eggs, fennel, hazelnuts, honey, horseradish, lamb, lemon, lemon basil, mustard, nutmeg, onions, oranges, parsley, pine nuts, pork, potatoes, pumpkin seeds, sherry vinegar, smoked fish, sour cream, tarragon, vinaigrette, walnuts, walnut oil, wine vinegars.

SERVING SUGGESTIONS

- Because of their dense texture and sweet flavor, beets go best with rich meats like pork, beef brisket, duck, and ham, as well as oilier fish like salmon and swordfish.

- Baking and oven-roasting are wonderful ways to accentuate the natural sweetness of beets, because these cooking methods caramelize their sugars.

- Shred beets and carrots for an airy, colorful salad. Toss with raisins and some lemon juice, vinegar, or nut oil.

- Beets can be juiced for beverages, but be sure to use this juice sparingly (or you will have a sugar high unlike any other).

- Beet soup, or borscht, is a perennial Eastern European favorite. Top it with sour cream and serve with pork tenderloin, a green salad, and a dark bread like rye or pumpernickel.

- Shred beets and red cabbage, and cook them together with a little balsamic vinegar, sea salt, and butter.
- Don't forget beet greens—they are incredibly healthful and tasty when sautéed with garlic and a nice olive oil. Try them in stir-fries and soups, or eat them raw in salads. Older beet greens are more flavorful and slightly bitter, which make them a perfect foil for goat cheese, rich soups, stews, meats, and hearty sausages.
- Beets have a special affinity for citrus. Sprinkle cooked beets with the grated zest or juice of lemons or oranges.
- Bake whole beets along with new potatoes in the oven until tender. They are delicious with salt and pepper and served with steak or corned beef.

Books

Beet Recipes: 50 Healthy & Delicious Recipes
Julie Hatfield,
Otherworld Publishing, 2014.

The Essential Root Vegetable Cookbook
Martin Stone,
Clarkson Potter, 1991.

Roots: The Underground Cookbook
Barbara Grunes and Anne Elise Hunt,
Chicago Review Press, 1993.

ICED BEET AND ORANGE SOUP   SERVES 8

Source Note: This soup freezes well if you have any left over.

3 pounds beets, peeled and cut into thin slices
1 cup chopped onions
1 tablespoon chopped fresh basil, or 1 teaspoon dried basil
4 cups chicken stock
2 cups freshly squeezed orange juice

Place all of the ingredients except the orange juice in a saucepan, and simmer over medium heat until the beets are tender, about 15 to 20 minutes. Cool and puree. Add the orange juice and chill.

— *Lee Bailey,* Lee Bailey's Southern Food

MOEN CREEK PICKLED BEETS   MAKES 4 PINTS

Source Note: These will keep in the refrigerator several weeks but may disappear long before. Use as a condiment or a salad topping (chopped or sliced). Delicious as an appetizer with cottage or hard cheeses.

4 pounds beets
3 cups thinly sliced onions
1½ cups cider vinegar
1½ cups water
1½ cups sugar
1 tablespoon mustard seed
1 teaspoon whole allspice
1 teaspoon whole cloves
3 sticks cinnamon, broken
1 teaspoon salt

1. Scrub the beets with a vegetable brush and trim off the tops, leaving 2 inches of the stems attached to the roots. (Young tops can be added

to salads or steamed as a vegetable.) Cover the beetroots with boiling water and cook until they become tender. Lift out the beets and drain. Peel and remove the stems (halve or quarter any roots that are larger than golf-ball size); set aside.

2. Combine the remaining ingredients in a large pot. Bring to a boil, decrease the heat, and simmer for 5 minutes.

3. Add the beets and heat through. Remove the cinnamon sticks, and let the beets sit in the vinegar solution until cool. Store in the refrigerator.

— *FairShare CSA Coalition,* From Asparagus to Zucchini

BORSCHT

SERVES 6

Source Note: Although there are many versions of borscht—the famous Eastern European soup—most are made with beef stock and bacon, with a huge dollop of sour cream on top. If you want a tart topping, you can try a spoonful of soy yogurt, or blend silken tofu with a bit of lemon, a small amount of oil, and some sugar using a hand blender. In this vegetarian version of borscht, I have created a creamy base with the addition of a baked potato for a hearty dinner soup.

½ tablespoon vegetable or olive oil
1 large onion, chopped
4 to 5 cloves garlic, minced or pressed
2 ribs celery, chopped
1 or 2 carrots, sliced
2 tablespoons tomato paste
6 cups water or vegetable stock (or use a combination of the two)
½ tablespoon fresh dill, or ½ teaspoon dried dill
4 cups peeled, sliced beets
Salt and freshly ground black pepper
1 potato, baked
Juice and zest of 1 lemon
1 to 2 tablespoons granulated sweetener

1. Heat a large, heavy-bottomed soup pot over medium heat. Add the oil and onion. Stir, decrease the heat, cover, and "sweat" the onions until they are translucent. Add the garlic, celery, and carrots. Stir and cook for about 5 more minutes. Stir in the tomato paste. Mix well and continue to cook for another minute or two. Add the water, dill, and beets. Bring to a boil. Decrease the heat to a simmer. Cover and cook for 15 minutes or until the beets are tender. Add salt and pepper to taste.

2. In a medium bowl, use a hand blender or electric blender to puree the potato, lemon juice, zest, granulated sweetener, and approximately ½ cup of the soup liquid until it turns smooth and creamy.

Stir into the rest of the soup, and adjust the salt and pepper seasoning. Serve topped with a dollop of plain soy yogurt or the tofu-lemon mixture described above.

— *Debra Daniels-Zeller,* Vegetarian Journal

. . . .

TRINA'S GREEN SALMON

SERVES 2

Source Note: This recipe comes from Trina, the shop manager at Featherstone Farm. This is a perfect fusion of her many lives: her time cooking at her family's restaurant, her work on a CSA in Alaska, and her love of good food. This dish can be found as a first course at many Japanese restaurants, and it is very simple to make. Wasabi paste is available in tubes or packets in Asian grocery and specialty food stores.

> 8 ounces fresh spinach leaves (about 2 bunches), washed
> Handful of beet greens, washed
> 8 ounces salmon (2 medium filets)
> ¼ cup wasabi paste
> Juice from ½ lemon (about 2 tablespoons)
> Salt and freshly ground black pepper

1. Preheat the oven to 300°F.

2. Bring a large pot of salted water to the boil. Add the spinach and beet greens and blanch them (cook quickly, just until they wilt and turn a brighter color). Drain the greens, and when cool enough to handle, spread the leaves somewhat flat, pressing out any excess water.

3. Coat the salmon thickly with the wasabi paste (remove the skin first or leave it on—your choice). Wrap the salmon in the spinach and beet greens and drizzle them with 1 tablespoon of the lemon juice. Sprinkle with salt and pepper.

4. Lay the salmon packages in a small baking dish and bake for 1 hour. Remove from the oven and sprinkle with the remaining lemon juice. Add additional salt and pepper if desired.

— *Trina, Featherstone Farm, Rushford, Minnesota*

Broccoli

Broccoli is a member of the enormous Brassica family, which includes many of the world's familiar vegetables—cabbage, cauliflower, kale, Brussels sprouts, and collards, to name just a few. As with many of its cousins, the mere mention of its name often evokes passionate feelings, either of fond gustatory pleasure or pure disgust and loathing. Broccoli is one of the few plants we savor for its floral abundance, since its distinctive green heads are actually huge clusters of flower buds that are consumed before they open. But the plant's stems make a perfectly respectable vegetable on their own—a tasty, healthful alternative to carrot and celery sticks on the crudité tray or cooked as a sturdy addition to stir-fries.

Broccoli grows best in cool weather, responding to frost by becoming sweeter. Heat drives the plants to bolt—or flower—prematurely, so the best season for broccoli is in the fall and early winter. (For more information on the many different types of broccoli, see the Broccoli Primer sidebar on page 410.)

HISTORY

Broccoli's name suggests that it came from the Mediterranean—particularly Italy, where the ancient Romans knew of it. But since the plant does not grow well in hot climates, it was probably eaten and cultivated long before its mention in the famous Roman cookbook *Apicius,* compiled around the fifth century CE. Possibly the plant originated in Asia. The Italian noblewoman Catherine de' Medici introduced a type of broccoli to France in the mid-1500s, but it remained unfamiliar to English tables until the 1700s. Later, Thomas Jefferson had broccoli planted in his extensive gardens at Monticello, Virginia, where it joined the ranks of other vegetables rare and exotic at that time, like tomatoes and cauliflower.

Broccoli was not commercially cultivated in America until brothers Stephano and Andrea D'Arrigo planted some experimental plots in San Jose, California, in 1922. They shipped a few crates to Boston, where broccoli became a hit in that city's Italian community. In part because of the D'Arrigo brothers' aggressive marketing under their Andy Boy label, broccoli finally became a mainstream vegetable in the United States—and a food of distaste to countless American children.

NUTRITION

Broccoli is one of nature's most nutritious foods, packing formidable amounts of vitamins A, B2, B6, C, and K, as well as folate, dietary fiber, phosphorus, potassium, and manganese. Like other cruciferous vegetables, broccoli contains abundant phytonutrients such as sulforaphane and indoles, which in studies have proven effective in fighting cancer, especially prostate, colorectal, and lung. Broccoli also is a good source of lutein, an antioxidant crucial for eye health.

SEASON

Commercially, broccoli is widely grown and available year-round. But its peak season at farmers markets and CSAs is from October through April.

SELECTION

Choose broccoli that is young and very firm. Supermarket broccoli is susceptible to being dried out; limp florets will lack flavor. The entire head should be a consistent gray-green color. Avoid heads with yellowing buds or opening flowers, which indicate overmaturity.

STORAGE

Store broccoli unwashed in a perforated bag in the coldest part of the refrigerator. It will keep for up to 2 weeks, depending on its original condition.

TRIMMING AND CLEANING

Broccoli florets and stems should be cooked separately to retain their nutrients and optimum texture. Trim the florets from the thicker stems. Unless the stems are very thin, you will probably have to trim their skins with a vegetable peeler and slice them in half or in pieces about 2½ to 3 inches long, so they will cook faster.

STEAMING AND BOILING

Steaming is the best way to cook broccoli to preserve its nutrients; many are leached out or destroyed by boiling and even microwaving. Steam florets for 5 to 10 minutes, or boil for 4 to 7 minutes, depending on your preference for doneness. Remember that the vegetable will continue to cook as it cools down, so it is better to slightly undercook than overdo it.

STIR-FRYING AND SAUTÉING

Divide broccoli florets into small, bite-size chunks with a minimum of the stem attached (since these will be tougher). With the stems, peel them first, then cut them diagonally into thin slices, so they will cook faster. Stir-fry in oil, butter, or water for 3 to 5 minutes on high heat in a wok or large frying pan, or until the pieces are crisp-tender.

For sautéing, it may be better to parboil or steam the broccoli lightly first, so that the pieces cook more evenly. In a large skillet, melt 2 tablespoons of butter until it begins to foam, then add the cooked broccoli along with any herbs, seasonings, or salt desired, and sauté for 2 to 3 minutes.

BAKING AND ROASTING

A nice way to prepare broccoli is to wrap it in aluminum foil with herbs, oil, and chicken broth, and bake it in a 350°F oven for 45 minutes to 1 hour. Roasted broccoli calls for shorter cooking times and a hotter oven—about 17 to 20 minutes at 425°F. Be sure to toss it with a little oil or butter first, so it doesn't burn.

BLANCHING AND FREEZING

For best results, blanch no more than 1 pound at a time. Blanch in boiling salted water for 4 minutes, then plunge into ice water for 5 minutes to stop the cooking process. Remove and drain. Then package the broccoli in zipper-lock freezer or vacuum food sealer-type bags, or freezer containers. Squeeze out any excess air and leave 1 inch of headspace (unless you are using the vacuum sealing method). It will keep for up to 1 year at 0°F.

Cooking Tip

Cut a crisscross incision about an inch deep in the stem of each floret before steaming or boiling. The cooking heat can then penetrate the tougher stem faster.

Cooking Tip

As with all members of the Brassica (cabbage) family, some of the very compounds that make broccoli so healthful also produce a distinctive sulfurous odor.

To minimize the scent, do not overcook. Broccoli that's old and tough will smell more. You can also try adding a few chunks of bread into the cooking water to absorb the smell.

A Broccoli Primer

Mi Ae Lipe

All of the varieties of broccoli available in the markets these days are bound to trigger some confusion for the consumer.

Sprouting broccoli or Calabrese broccoli: *This is the type of broccoli most familiar to us, with a thick central stalk bearing a large head of florets, with some smaller branching stems and florets.*

Purple broccoli: *This variety looks almost identical to the familiar green sprouting broccoli, except that its florets have a purplish cast to them and are often a bit smaller. The chemical compounds responsible for the purple color have additional antioxidant properties. Unfortunately, its attractive purple color tends to fade during cooking.*

Broccolini or baby broccoli: *A cross between broccoli and Chinese kale, these cute stalks look like rather leggy, unkempt versions of our familiar broccoli, with looser florets, narrow but succulent stems, and broad leaves.*

Although it is sometimes called baby broccoli, broccolini is a separate vegetable in and of itself, and not a youthful version of our familiar sprouting type.

Broccoli raab or rapini: *This plant is actually not related to broccoli, but more to the turnip. Still, it bears close-knit tufts of flower buds atop its stalks that closely resemble broccoli. (One way to tell it apart from broccolini is the presence of its distinctive, lacy-edged foliage.) But unlike its sweeter namesake, broccoli raab is a strongly flavored vegetable, pleasantly bitter and aggressive.*

Broccoflower: *This vegetable looks like a green cauliflower, which along with sprouting broccoli is what*

MICROWAVING

Separate the florets from the stems. Peel the largest stalks and cut them into spears. Arrange the pieces in a microwave-safe dish, with florets pointed toward the center. Add 2 tablespoons water, cover, and cook on high power.

- 1 cup = 2 to 3 minutes
- 2 cups = 3 to 4 minutes
- 1 pound = 8 to 10 minutes

MEASURES AND EQUIVALENTS

- ½ pound broccoli = 1 serving
- 1 large bunch = 3 to 4 servings = 1½ to 2 pounds
- 1 pound fresh broccoli = 2 cups chopped and cooked
- 10 ounces frozen broccoli = 2½ cups chopped

COMPLEMENTARY HERBS, SEASONINGS, AND FOODS

Almonds, anchovies, bacon, basil, beef, breadcrumbs, butter, capers, carrots, cheese, chiles, cream, cumin, curry, dill, fish, garlic, ginger, hollandaise sauce, lemon balm, lemon juice, marjoram, mushrooms, mustard, nuts, olives, olive oil, orange, oregano, parsley, peanut oil, peppers, potatoes, rice, sesame, shallots, tarragon, thyme, tofu, vinaigrette.

SERVING SUGGESTIONS

- To make broccoli and other vegetables more appealing to kids (and adults too!), serve bite-size pieces with a variety of dressings and dipping sauces.
- Chop broccoli into small pieces and sprinkle them over pizzas, salads, casseroles, and just about anything that could use color and vegetable crunch.
- Few vegetable dishes beat the simple preparation of steamed broccoli with a little fresh lemon juice, melted butter, and freshly ground black pepper.
- A quick soup: First, blanch cut-up broccoli (florets and stems). Then place the broccoli, cooked potatoes, chicken or vegetable stock, and a couple of garlic cloves and onions (both sautéed in olive oil or butter) into a food processor or blender and puree. Reheat the mixture, and add salt and pepper to taste.
- Broccoli is also great blanched until bright green, then sautéed with garlic, onion, anchovies, and olive oil, and finished with a sprinkling of capers and red pepper flakes. Yum!
- Toss steamed broccoli with butter and herbs. Cool and use in a salad.
- Peeled broccoli stems make a great raw vegetable on their own. Slice them long and serve with carrot and celery sticks on the crudité tray.
- Broccoli goes well with a multitude of Asian and Indian condiments and seasonings. Stir-fry or cook with soy sauce, oyster sauce, black bean sauce, sesame oil, curry powder, cardamom, allspice, and five-spice powder.
- Oven-roasting broccoli mellows and sweetens its strong flavor.
- Add small pieces of sautéed broccoli florets and stems to pasta, rice, and potato dishes.
- Broccoli combines well with other cruciferous cousins; try it with cauliflower, tiny Brussels sprouts, and chopped kale. Good tossed raw or cooked with Italian dressing or balsamic vinegar.
- Finely chop or grate broccoli to use in savory flans, quiches, soups, fillings, and sauces.

☞ Broccoli goes exceedingly well with nuts, mushrooms, and tofu; whether you are a vegetarian or not, be creative!

. . . .

BLASTED BROCCOLI   SERVES 4

Source Note: A few years ago, Food & Wine *editor Tina Ujlaki offered this recipe to a reader who wrote requesting a healthful vegetable side dish. "Blasting" vegetables was in the wind that year. Chefs and home cooks alike were popping asparagus and green beans into hot ovens all over the country, but this recipe captured the mini-trend and codified it. The intense heat ensures that the vegetable is irresistibly crisp, and the trace of bitterness from the browning is trumped by the sweet tang of balsamic vinegar.*

> 4 cups broccoli florets
> 2 tablespoons olive oil
> 1 teaspoon sea salt, or to taste
> 1 tablespoon balsamic vinegar

1. Preheat the oven to 500°F. Rinse the broccoli florets and let them drain in a large strainer or colander.

2. Put the florets in a bowl with the olive oil and toss to coat. Sprinkle with the sea salt and toss again. Spread the seasoned broccoli in a single layer on a baking sheet and pop it in the preheated oven. Bake until the edges of the florets are browned and crisp, about 4 minutes.

3. Put the cooked florets back into the bowl and toss with balsamic vinegar to coat. Taste and add more salt if desired. Serve hot.

— *Greg Atkinson (Adapted from* Food & Wine *Magazine)*

. . . .

THE ENCHANTED BROCCOLI FOREST   SERVES 4 TO 6

> 1 pound broccoli
> 1 tablespoon butter or vegetable oil (plus a little for the pan)
> 1 cup chopped onion
> ¾ teaspoon salt
> 1 large clove garlic, minced
> 2 tablespoons fresh lemon juice
> About 6 cups cooked brown or white rice
> Freshly ground black pepper
> Cayenne pepper to taste
> 2 tablespoons minced fresh dill or 2 teaspoons dried dill
> 3 tablespoons minced fresh mint or 3 teaspoons dried mint
> ¼ cup minced fresh parsley
> ½ cup toasted sunflower seeds (optional)
> 1 packed cup grated Cheddar or Swiss cheese (about ¼ pound) (optional)

makes up its heritage. Raw, it tastes somewhat sweeter than regular white cauliflower, but when cooked, it's much like broccoli.

Chinese broccoli or Chinese kale: This is not a broccoli or kale as we know it, but a whole different subspecies of the vast Brassica family. This vegetable looks distinctively different, with broad, smooth, flat leaves, and very small clusters of floral buds atop their juicy, crunchy, waxy-looking stems. Chinese broccoli tastes milder and sweeter than sprouting broccoli, and it certainly lacks the bitter pungency of broccoli raab. For more information, see pages 123–127.

Romanesco broccoli: Sometimes called Romanesco cauliflower, this exotic-looking plant appears to be from an alien vegetable world. But it is actually another type of green cauliflower, like broccoflower. It is hard to mistake it for any other member of the Brassica family, with its conical, chartreuse heads tightly arranged on a central stalk. (Incidentally, this beautifully geometrical pattern of Romanesco's florets is one of nature's more perfect examples of mathematically accurate fractal design.)

Broccoli sprouts: Last but not least are these little alfalfa-sprout–like veggies, which are simply sprouting broccoli seeds that have germinated.

A little melted butter for the top (optional)

1. Trim the tough bottoms from the broccoli stalks, and cut the tops into smallish spears of whatever size suits you. Cook them in a steamer over boiling water until bright green and just barely tender. Rinse under cold running water, drain well, and set aside.

2. Preheat the oven to 325°F. Lightly grease a 9-by-13-inch baking pan.

3. Melt the butter or heat the oil in a large, deep skillet or a Dutch oven. Add the onion and salt, and sauté over medium heat for about 5 minutes, or until the onion begins to soften. Add the garlic and lemon juice, and sauté for about 2 minutes longer. Stir in the rice, some black pepper and cayenne to taste, the herbs, and the optional sunflower seeds and cheese. Taste to correct the salt, if necessary, and spread into the prepared pan.

4. Now for the fun part. Arrange the broccoli upright in the rice, and, if desired, drizzle with melted butter. Cover loosely with aluminum foil, and bake until just heated through (15 to 20 minutes). Serve right away.

— *Mollie Katzen,* The New Enchanted Broccoli Forest

BASMATI RICE WITH MUSHROOMS, BROCCOLI, AND ONION   SERVES 4

2 tablespoons extra-virgin olive oil
40 pearl onions, peeled and ends removed
    (or substitute 3 cups white or yellow onions, cut into chunks)
1 clove garlic, minced
2 cups uncooked basmati rice
1 tablespoon paprika
½ cup dry white wine
6 cups hot vegetable stock
Salt and freshly ground black pepper
2 cups mushrooms, wild or domestic, sliced
2 cups broccoli florets, blanched
¼ cup chopped chives (or green onions), plus ¼ cup for garnish
¼ cup grated Parmesan cheese, for garnish

1. In a very large nonstick saucepan, heat 1 tablespoon of the olive oil over medium-high heat. Add the onions; cook until they are tender and browned on both sides, about 7 minutes.

2. Add the garlic; cook until it begins to brown, about 2 minutes. Add the rice; heat until it is lightly toasted. Add the paprika and mix well. Add the white wine and cook until all of the liquid is gone, about 3 minutes. Add the hot vegetable stock. Season well with salt and pepper.

3. Cover with a tight-fitting lid and lower the heat to a simmer. Cook until the rice is just about tender, about 15 to 25 minutes, depending upon your choice of rice.

4. Meanwhile, in a large nonstick skillet over high heat, add the remaining 1 tablespoon of oil. Add the mushrooms; cook until they become golden, about 5 minutes. Add the broccoli, cooking until al dente, about 3 minutes.

5. Transfer the mushrooms and broccoli to the saucepan with the rice. Season with salt and pepper. Add ¼ cup of the chives. Cover the pan; remove from the heat and allow to sit for 5 minutes before serving. Spoon onto warm serving plates and sprinkle with the remaining chives and Parmesan cheese, if desired.

— *Fooddownunder.com*

Romanesco broccoli at Sang Lee Farms.

> "No one who cooks, cooks alone. Even at her most solitary, a cook in the kitchen is surrounded by generations of cooks past, the advice and menus of cooks present, and the wisdom of cookbook writers."
>
> — *Laurie Colwin, American food writer*

CHARRED ROMANESCO BROCCOLI WITH ANCHOVIES AND MINT
SERVES 8

Source Note: Getting a good, dark sear on the Romanesco broccoli is critical to the flavor of the dish: There's a nuttiness when you get that color on it.

Author Note: Romanesco broccoli is actually a type of green cauliflower, like broccoflower. It is hard to mistake it for any other member of the Brassica family, with its conical, chartreuse, fractal-patterned heads tightly arranged on a central stalk. It can be cooked like broccoli and cauliflower.

½ cup olive oil, divided
1 large onion, minced

1 large carrot, minced
1 rib celery, minced
4 Fresno chiles or jalapeños, thinly sliced into rounds, seeded
Kosher salt
3 pounds Romanesco broccoli or cauliflower
    (about 2 medium heads), cut into florets
4 anchovy fillets packed in oil, drained
½ cup dry white wine
Freshly ground black pepper
½ cup torn fresh mint leaves

1. Heat ¼ cup of the oil in a medium saucepan over medium heat. Add the onion, carrot, celery, and chiles; season with salt and cook, stirring occasionally, until the vegetables are very soft but not brown, 12 to 15 minutes. Let them cool.

2. Preheat the oven to 450°F. Heat 2 tablespoons of the oil in a large skillet over medium-high heat. Add half of the Romanesco broccoli and cook, undisturbed, until deeply browned, about 4 minutes. Transfer to a roasting pan; repeat with remaining 2 tablespoons oil and remaining Romanesco. Add the anchovies and wine to the roasting pan; season with salt and pepper and toss to combine.

3. Roast, tossing halfway through, until the broccoli is soft and the liquid is mostly evaporated, 25 to 30 minutes; season with salt and pepper and top with mint.

— *Travis Lett,* Bon Appétit

ROASTED BEET SALSA
WITH SKILLET-BROWNED BROCCOLI

SERVES 4

ROASTED BEET SALSA

4 medium golden beets
4 tablespoons extra-virgin olive oil, divided
Salt and freshly ground black pepper
2 teaspoons finely diced shallots
2 teaspoons grated fresh ginger
1 teaspoon finely diced jalapeño pepper
½ teaspoon minced garlic
¼ cup minced fresh mint
¼ cup minced fresh cilantro
2 teaspoons lime juice

1. To roast the beets: Preheat the oven to 375°F. Trim the tops off the beets and drizzle with 1 tablespoon of the olive oil. Season the beets with salt and pepper, wrap them in aluminum foil and roast them until tender (a paring knife slipped into the middle should penetrate easily), about 40 to 50 minutes. Let them cool in the foil.

2. While the beets are roasting, place the shallots, ginger, jalapeño, garlic, mint, cilantro, lime juice, and remaining 3 tablespoons of oil in a small bowl and stir to combine.

3. Peel the beets by slipping the skins off with your fingers. Dice and add them to the salsa mixture, stirring to combine. Taste for seasoning and adjust with salt, pepper, and perhaps a bit more lime juice. Set aside.

BROWNED BROCCOLI

2 large stems broccoli (florets and stalks)
1 large head cauliflower
4 tablespoons extra-virgin olive oil, divided
Salt and freshly ground black pepper
2 to 3 cloves garlic, thinly sliced

1. Slice the broccoli and cauliflower into 1-inch pieces and toss them in a large bowl with 2 tablespoons of the olive oil. Sprinkle with salt and pepper.

2. Heat the remaining 2 tablespoons of oil in a large skillet over medium heat and add the garlic slices.

3. Add the broccoli and cauliflower to the hot skillet, pressing them into the pan with a spatula. Cook them for 5 to 7 minutes, or until nicely browned.

4. Serve hot with the roasted beet salsa.

— *Karolina Tracz, Nash's Organic Produce, Sequim, Washington*

Harvesting broccoli at Featherstone Farm.

Brussels Sprouts

BRASSICA OLERACEA VAR. GEMMIFERA

Ah, the poor maligned Brussels sprout. A sadly frequent childhood gustatory bane and parental weapon from which it has taken some individuals decades to recover, these miniature cabbages spark polarized reactions of love and disgust, often as strong as their smell.

Brussels sprouts are members of the vast Brassica family, which includes cabbage, broccoli, cauliflower, collards, turnips, kale, and kohlrabi. All of these vegetables share in common sulfurous compounds that break down during cooking, resulting in that distinctive odor. Both undercooking and overcooking even for a few minutes exacerbate this problem exponentially. But properly cooking Brussels sprouts that are tiny and young, and preparing them with tasty flavorings, often does wonders.

Brussels sprouts growing on the plant look bizarre; the small, round sprouts cling to heavy central stalks that grow 2 to 4 feet tall. About 98 percent of the commercial US Brussels sprout crop grows in the Monterey coast region of California (New York State grows the remaining 2 percent), and nearly all of it is frozen. Although it is rarely seen in America, there is a cultivar with beautiful purple-red sprouts called Rubine.

HISTORY

As with many of our popular vegetables, the Mediterranean is the most likely homeland for the ancestors of Brussels sprouts; ancient Romans enjoyed them. Their name may have come from the fact that they were commercially grown in Belgium by the 13th century. But it could have also been the presence of the name *Bruxelles* in the local varietal strains available in France and Britain by the late 1800s, a result of a European suburban market gardening tradition that often rooted a vegetable's name and origin to the local areas where it was grown. Brussels sprouts were first commercially cultivated in northern California in the early 1900s.

NUTRITION

A 1-cup serving contains staggering amounts of vitamins B6, C, and K, as well as manganese, folate, dietary fiber, copper, potassium, and iron, all for only 56 calories. Like other members of the Brassica family, Brussels sprouts pack huge amounts of phytonutrients that are believed to have considerable anticancer and anti-inflammatory properties.

SEASON

Commercial Brussels sprouts are available year-round, but they are sweeter and better tasting during the colder winter months when the plant converts more of its energy to sugars. In farmers markets and CSA boxes, you'll probably see them only in the fall and winter.

SELECTION

Brussels sprouts that are very small (½ to 1¼ inches in diameter) are likely to be sweeter and more tender. They should be bright green, tightly furled, and firm, with no signs of yellowing, wilting, or sponginess when squeezed (which could signal desiccation and advanced age). If you are fortunate enough to find sprouts fresh and still attached to their stalk, they will keep better than those cut off. If that stalk still happens to have its huge leaves attached, you can cook those like collards.

STORAGE

Brussels sprouts do not store well, so purchase them right before you plan to cook them. Their flavor deteriorates quickly even after just a few days in the refrigerator, even though their appearance may be unchanged. If you need to store loose sprouts, keep them in a plastic container (put a paper towel inside if they're wet) in the refrigerator. If you buy sprouts on a stalk, trim off the base of the stem and stand the stalk up in a stout container of water in the coolest spot of your house.

TRIMMING AND CLEANING

Trim off the base of each sprout and pull off any outer yellowing or loose leaves. If the sprouts are very small, they can remain whole; otherwise, halving or quartering helps them cook quickly, which is key to minimizing their famous sulfur smell.

STEAMING AND BOILING

Steaming is a terrific way to cook Brussels sprouts, but be careful not to overcook them, which instantly transforms them from a vegetable of delicacy to a smelly, strong-tasting one. Depending on their size, steam for 10 to 15 minutes until the sprouts are tender-crisp, but start checking them at 4 minutes. Brussels sprouts can also be boiled in lightly salted water for 12 to 15 minutes, depending on your preference for doneness; you should be able to pierce them with a fork. Remember that the vegetable will continue to cook as it cools down, so it is better to slightly undercook than overdo it.

STIR-FRYING AND SAUTÉING

Brussels sprouts are best blanched, parboiled, or briefly steamed before stir-frying or sautéing. It is also best to use very young or small sprouts for this purpose, as they are more tender and have better flavor.

For stir-frying and sautéing, halve or quarter the sprouts so they will cook faster. Stir-fry with your other ingredients in oil or butter for 5 to 7 minutes, or until they become tender.

BAKING AND ROASTING

Roasting is perhaps the best way to cook Brussels sprouts, as this cooking method caramelizes their natural sugars rather than releases their sulfurous compounds—it all makes for a far tastier sprout. Toss sprouts with oil, balsamic vinegar, and seasonings, and roast in a 400°F oven for 30 to 35 minutes; this creates sprouts with brown, crispy outer leaves and soft, steamy insides.

"You learn to cook so that you don't have to be a slave to recipes. You get what's in season and you know what to do with it."

— Julia Child, American chef and TV cooking personality

MICROWAVING

Arrange the Brussels sprouts in a microwave-safe dish. Add 2 tablespoons water, cover, and cook on high power. Because individual sprouts vary so much in size, you may need to adjust your cooking times, or halve or quarter the larger sprouts to reduce the time needed (remember that overcooking, even briefly, can bring out the worst in these little green balls).

- 1 pound whole sprouts = 6 to 8 minutes

BLANCHING AND FREEZING

Remove the outer leaves and trim off the stem ends. Blanch in salted boiling water for 3 minutes, then plunge into ice water for 5 minutes to stop the cooking process. Remove and drain. Spread the Brussels sprouts on a tray in a single layer. Cover with plastic wrap to keep the odor out of your freezer, then freeze for 30 minutes. Package the Brussels sprouts in zipper-lock freezer or vacuum food sealer-type bags, or freezer containers. Squeeze out any excess air and leave 1 inch of headspace (unless you are using the vacuum sealing method). Frozen Brussels sprouts will keep for up to 6 months at 0°F.

EQUIVALENTS, MEASURES, AND SERVINGS

- 1 pound whole sprouts = 4 cups cooked
- 1 quart = 1¼ pounds = 5 cups
- 10 ounces frozen = 1½ to 2 cups, cooked = 18 to 24 sprouts

COMPLEMENTARY HERBS, SEASONINGS, AND FOODS

Almonds, apples, bacon, beef, black pepper, buckwheat, butter, caraway seeds, carrots, celery root, celery seed, cheese (blue, Cheddar, Parmesan), chervil, chestnuts, chiles, chives, cream, cumin, dill weed, garlic, ghee, ginger, ham, hazelnuts, hazelnut oil, honey, juniper berries, leeks, lemon, lime, maple syrup, mustard, nutmeg, olive oil, onions, orange, pancetta, parsley, pasta, peanuts, pecans, pepper, pork, potatoes, red wine, sausage, savory, sesame, shallots, smoked paprika, soy sauce, spinach, tarragon, thyme, tofu, vinegar, walnuts, walnut oil, white wine.

SERVING SUGGESTIONS

- Brussels sprouts and nuts or nut oils are a natural pairing; try walnuts, pecans, pine nuts, hazelnuts, almonds, or peanuts.

- Brussels sprouts are often at their best when prepared simply with butter or a little cream. Creamed sprouts make a lovely side dish with hearty meats.

- Very thinly sliced Brussels sprouts add unexpected texture and dimension to soups, combine well with other cooked vegetables such as carrots and beets, and, as a raw vegetable, provide crunch and flavor to salads.

- Brussels sprouts have an incredible affinity with the smoked parts of the pig: bacon, ham, pancetta, lardons—they're all good.

- For something a little different—and for perfectly cooked Brussels sprouts—try oven-roasting them in culinary parchment paper. This method steams them, and you can insert whatever seasonings you fancy inside the paper.

- Although we typically think of only the little green cabbages when it comes to Brussels sprouts, the leaves of the plant are actually quite good eating as well, if you come upon them. Prepare them as you would collards.

- Brussels sprouts can stand up to strong flavors like citrus, mustard, red wine, garlic, celery, pepper, and ginger. Be creative!

. . . .

ROASTED BEET AND BRUSSELS SPROUT SALAD

SERVES 12 AS A SIDE DISH, 4 TO 6 AS A MAIN DISH

½ to 1 pound bacon
6 to 8 beets, cubed
1 pound Brussels sprouts, trimmed
1 medium white onion, thinly sliced
6 cloves garlic, whole
3 teaspoons thyme
Sea salt and freshly ground black pepper
3 tablespoons olive oil, divided
1 to 2 cups mixed salad greens
½ cup almonds, chopped (or substitute your favorite nut)

1. Cook the bacon to your personal preference and set it aside.

2. Preheat the oven at 400°F.

3. In a large roasting pan, add the beets, Brussels sprouts, onion, garlic, thyme, and salt and pepper, and toss with 1 to 2 tablespoons of the olive oil, coating evenly. (If you're using red beets, they will bleed red onto the other vegetables as you mix them. To avoid this, toss the beets separately with oil, salt, and pepper and bake them in another pan—or just keep them to one side of the larger roasting pan.)

4. Roast the vegetables uncovered in the oven until they have softened and browned—approximately 30 minutes.

5. Remove the vegetables from the oven and stir in the bacon. Allow them to cool slightly.

6. Arrange the mixed greens on a serving plate and top with the vegetables. Sprinkle the almonds over the vegetables and finish by drizzling the remaining olive oil over the entire dish.

— *Annie McHale, Nash's Organic Produce, Sequim, Washington*

. . . .

KIELBASA WITH BRUSSELS SPROUTS IN MUSTARD CREAM SAUCE

SERVES 4

Source Note: Any German can tell you that wurst and cabbage go hand in hand. Any Spaniard will say the same of chorizo and beans. But it takes a special international inclination to make the case for kielbasa with Brussels sprouts, white beans, and mustard. I'll tell you that it works wonderfully! The saltiness of the pork combined with the bitter, gentle crunch of the Brussels sprouts and mildness of the beans is well-balanced perfection. Plus, it's cheap, easy, and looks good on a plate!

Friday, and Saturday breakfast. Its menus change weekly and reflect the description on its website: "Seasonal food inspired by the best French and Italian traditions, with our own personal Northwest style."

In 2002, **Nash's Organic Produce** on the north Olympic Peninsula in Washington State rented a small building adjacent to a parcel of its farmland and opened a small produce store featuring products from its farm, other local farms, and local artisans. Next, it began carrying the farm's grains and pork as well as items from an organic produce distributor in Oregon, so that customers could shop for what they needed year-round.

In 2011, a new and much larger **Nash's Farm Store** opened for business where a local creamery had operated a century earlier. Now open daily, it's not only a place to buy local, sustainably grown food, but also a resource for education: talks, workshops, films, and a lending library on topics related to food, agriculture, and the environment. Staff carefully research where to source high-quality local products that are independent of influence from corporate America.

If you visit the farm stand at **Green Gate Farms** in Austin, Texas, on a Saturday morning, you can enjoy a guided tour of the restored historic farm, where you'll be introduced to sheep, pigs, goats, chickens, a children's garden, their incubator farm, and the Big Red Barn, built in 1902.

Just as there are urban farms, there are urban farm stands. One unusual model is **Youthmarket**, a network of about a dozen pop-up seasonal farm stands in New York City developed by the nonprofit GrowNYC to increase access to fresh food in the city while training young people from underserved neighborhoods to operate farm stands as their own small businesses. Food for the farm stands comes from regional farmers and fishers

1 medium shallot
4 large cloves garlic
Extra-virgin olive oil
1½ pounds Brussels sprouts
1 pound pork kielbasa
1½ cups cooked white kidney (cannellini) beans,
    or 1 (10-ounce) can
2 tablespoons coarsely ground mustard
¼ cup heavy cream
Kosher salt
Freshly ground black pepper

1. Preheat the oven to 400°F (I recommend using a toaster oven).

2. Peel the shallot and cut it into quarters. Coat the shallot and garlic with olive oil and a generous pinch of salt. Make a small pouch out of aluminum foil (two layers thick) and place the shallot and garlic inside. Seal the pouch tightly and place it in the oven for 30 minutes.

3. Rinse and clean the Brussels sprouts. Cut each sprout in half, discarding any wilted outer leaves. Steam (or boil, your choice) the Brussels sprouts until they are tender when pierced with a fork. Set aside.

4. Rinse and drain the beans.

5. Slice the kielbasa on a steep bias into ¼-inch rounds. Heat 1 teaspoon of olive oil in a large, heavy-bottomed nonstick skillet over medium-high heat. Arrange the kielbasa rounds and fry until crispy, about 3 minutes per side. Set aside on paper towels to drain.

6. If your skillet is full of porky goodness, keep it there. Add 1 generous tablespoon of good olive oil and keep the heat on medium high. Unwrap the roasted garlic and shallot and smash them using the flat side of your knife. They should be very soft. Add them to the skillet and cook for about 1 minute.

7. Add the mustard and cream to the skillet and stir to combine. Reduce the heat to medium low and add the Brussels sprouts and beans. Toss everything together to coat, then season to taste with a generous amount of salt and black pepper.

8. Plate the kielbasa on top of your Brussels sprouts and beans in a large bowl to serve.

— *Scott Heimendinger, Foodista.com*

BRUSSELS SPROUTS IN HONEY BUTTER WITH CHILI FLAKES

SERVES 4

1 pound Brussels sprouts
1 tablespoon butter, softened
1 tablespoon honey
2 tablespoons water
Red chili flakes
Sea salt

1. Trim any loose or yellow leaves from the Brussels sprouts. Cut the stem off of each sprout and then cut each one in half.

2. In a small bowl, mix the butter with the honey.

3. Heat a wide, flat skillet on medium heat. Add the honey butter and allow it to bubble and melt. Add the Brussels sprouts, tossing to coat them with the butter, then arranging them cut side down in a single layer. Cook for 8 to 10 minutes uncovered, until the cut sides turn golden and a little charred.

4. Sprinkle the chili flakes and sea salt to taste over the Brussels sprouts.

5. Stir the Brussels sprouts around so most of them turn over cut side up. Add the water and cook, covered, for another 3 to 5 minutes until they are soft.

6. Adjust for salt and spice. Serve hot.

— *Nithya Das, Foodista.com*

MAPLE-ROASTED BRUSSELS SPROUTS

SERVES 4

Author Note: The recipe below is from chef Nicole Hoffmann, a graduate of the Western Culinary Institute in Portland, Oregon, who has run the school kitchen at Abernethy Elementary School in southeast Portland and taught in its award-winning School Kitchen Garden program. She says that the kids at Abernethy, before seeing Brussels sprouts in the cafeteria, have in some cases planted, harvested, and written papers about Brussels sprouts grown in the school garden. This super-simple recipe is easy enough for kids to make, and delicious for all ages.

1 tablespoon pure maple syrup
1 tablespoon olive oil
A large pinch of sea salt
1 pound Brussels sprouts, outer leaves removed, cut in half lengthwise

1. Preheat the oven to 400°F.

Books

CookWise: The Secrets
of Cooking Revealed
Shirley O. Corriher,
William Morrow Cookbooks, 2011.

Brilliant Food Tips and Cooking
Tricks: 5,000 Ingenious Kitchen Hints,
Secrets, Shortcuts, and Solutions
David Joachim,
Rodale Books, 2004.

2. In a large bowl, whisk together the maple syrup, olive oil, and salt. Then add the Brussels sprouts, stirring to coat them evenly. Place the sprouts in a single layer on a baking sheet lined with parchment paper.

3. Bake for 10 to 12 minutes, or until the edges of the sprouts are crispy and the insides are soft. Serve immediately.

— *Nicole Hoffmann*

PERFECT BRUSSELS SPROUTS   SERVES NONE

1 pound Brussels sprouts
Salt and freshly ground black pepper, to waste

1. Buy the freshest sprouts you can find. The more tightly packed the leaves, the better.

2. Trim the outer leaves and stem ends from the sprouts, and cut them into quarters. Sprinkle with salt and pepper.

3. Then dump all of them down the garbage disposal.

4. Run the disposal for 5 minutes, just to be extra sure.

5. Get a new disposal, as your first one is bound to be ruined.

— *Ronald Swartz*

Cauliflower

BRASSICA OLERACEA,
BOTRYTIS GROUP

Cauliflower is one of the many members of the Brassica family, which includes cabbage, broccoli, bok choy, kale, and collards. Broccoli and cauliflower are kissing cousins; at one point they were actually identical plants until humans began breeding them for their most desired traits.

Cauliflower is grown for its distinctive heads of modified, undeveloped flowers, called curds, which can be white, green, purple, and even orange. Technically, all parts of the cauliflower plant are edible, although the leaves and stalks are (sadly!) usually ignored.

Like most brassicas, cauliflower thrives in cooler weather, and the crop starts coming into its own in the fall and often remains one of the last vegetables to appear in CSA boxes. It is a slower-growing crop than broccoli and cabbage, but its sweet mellowness, heightened by the season's first frosts, make it well worth the wait.

HISTORY

Cauliflower probably originated in Asia Minor, and there is some evidence that the ancient Romans cultivated it. It was slow to enter the rest of Europe, appearing on French tables only in the 1600s and on American shores about a hundred years later. Cauliflower remains a very popular vegetable in China, India, and Europe.

NUTRITION

A single cup of boiled cauliflower contains about 29 calories and is an extremely good source of vitamins C and K. It also provides folate, dietary fiber, vitamin B6, manganese, and potassium. Along with its other brassica relatives, cauliflower is a cruciferous vegetable, containing phytonutrients that may help prevent cancer.

SEASON

Commercially, cauliflower is widely grown and available year-round. But its peak season at farmers markets and CSAs is in the fall and early winter.

SELECTION

Look for clean, tightly compact heads of uniform color, with no soft or discolored areas, which could indicate rot, extreme age, or sliminess. The size of the heads is not related to quality, but a head that is enveloped in green leaves is likely to be fresher.

STORAGE

Cauliflower should be stored in the refrigerator vegetable crisper, tightly wrapped in a plastic bag, stem side down so as not to trap moisture in the florets. It is not the best keeper, especially cut florets, and should be used within 1 week.

THE CSA FARM COOKBOOK   FALL — CAULIFLOWER   423

TRIMMING AND CLEANING

To prepare, snap off the green leaves surrounding the curds, and cut the entire head in half. Then slice the florets away from the central stem and core. (You can save this stem and core and prepare them like broccoli stems, or use them in soup stocks.) Or you can keep the entire head intact to steam or roast whole.

If you cut the cauliflower and store part of it for later use, the exposed surfaces will probably discolor to a light brown, because of natural oxidation. Just trim these parts away before you next use the cauliflower.

STEAMING AND BOILING

Cauliflower should be cooked at a bare minimum, as its unpleasant sulfurous odor becomes stronger with overcooking. Steaming is far preferable to boiling, which makes the curds watery. Place the florets in a steamer and cook for 5 to 7 minutes. An entire head may take 10 to 12 minutes, depending on its size.

If you simply must boil cauliflower, cook it, covered, as briefly as possible in about 2 inches of boiling, salted water for about 7 to 10 minutes for florets, or 10 to 15 minutes for a whole head.

STIR-FRYING AND SAUTÉING

Break up the florets into small, uniform pieces, with a minimum of stem attached, since the stems will cook unevenly. Stir-fry in oil, butter, ghee, or water for 5 to 7 minutes, or until they become tender.

As with broccoli, cauliflower benefits from parboiling or a brief steaming for a few minutes before to sautéing. Then sauté in butter, oil, and seasonings for 2 to 3 minutes.

BAKING AND ROASTING

Cauliflower is terrific baked and roasted, for this cooking method caramelizes the vegetable's natural sugars. To make the baking go faster, you can steam cauliflower first until it turns tender. Then combine it with breadcrumbs, cheese, herbs, and seasonings, and bake for 10 to 15 minutes in a 375°F oven, or until the top is golden brown.

To roast, separate cauliflower into florets, place them in a lightly greased roasting pan, toss with oil and seasonings, and put in a 400°F oven for 25 to 30 minutes. An entire, intact head may take 1 to 1¼ hours in a 400°F oven.

MICROWAVING

Arrange florets in a microwave-safe dish, with the curds pointed toward the center. Add 2 tablespoons water, cover, and cook on high power. (Depending on your microwave wattage and the size of the pieces, you might need to increase cooking times, as cauliflower often cooks unevenly in the microwave.)

- 1 cup = 2 to 3 minutes
- 2 cups = 3 to 4 minutes
- 1 pound = 8 to 10 minutes
- Whole cauliflower = 11 to 15 minutes

BLANCHING AND FREEZING

Freezing cauliflower affects its texture significantly, causing it to break down. Still, frozen cauliflower is fine for recipes calling for it to be pureed.

For best results, blanch no more than 1 pound at a time. Cut the heads into individual pieces about 1 inch in diameter. Bring a large pot of water to a boil, add the cauliflower, cover, and blanch for 3 minutes. Then drain and plunge the cauliflower into ice water to stop the cooking process. Pack in zipper-lock freezer or vacuum food sealer-type bags, or freezer containers. Squeeze out any excess air (unless you are using the vacuum sealing method); no headspace is necessary. Frozen cauliflower will keep for up to 1 year at 0°F.

EQUIVALENTS, MEASURES, AND SERVINGS

- 1 head = 1½ pounds = 6 cups florets = 1½ cups chopped

COMPLEMENTARY HERBS, SEASONINGS, AND FOODS

Almonds, bacon, basil, béchamel sauce, breadcrumbs, broccoli, brown butter, butter, capers, caraway, cayenne pepper, cheese (Cheddar, Manchego, Gouda, feta, Havarti), chervil, chiles, chives, citrus, cream, coconut milk, coriander, créme fraîche, cumin, curry, dill, garlic, ghee, green olives, green onions, ham, hollandaise sauce, horseradish, leeks, lemon, mushrooms, mussels, mustard, nutmeg, nuts, olive oil, onion, oregano, paprika, parsley, pasta, pepper, potatoes, saffron, tomato sauce, turmeric, walnuts, watercress.

SERVING SUGGESTIONS

- Cauliflower's neutral flavor and color makes it an excellent backdrop for spicy seasonings such as curry. In India, cauliflower is often cooked with turmeric, cumin, and saffron.
- A classic cauliflower dish calls for steamed or boiled florets topped with a cheese or cream sauce.
- Cooked cauliflower can be pureed and used as a soup base, along with cream, seasonings, broth, potatoes, etc.
- Add tiny bits of raw cauliflower to chopped vegetable salads for crunch.
- Use it in casseroles by itself or with broccoli.
- Serve raw cauliflower florets with a variety of taste-tempting dipping sauces.
- Steam cauliflower just until done, dredge in flour and seasonings, and fry until brown.
- Try tossing cauliflower florets with a mixture of butter, sugar, salt, cinnamon, cumin, and pepper, and baking until they are caramelized.
- Marinate steamed cauliflower pieces with other vegetables such as peppers, broccoli, cucumbers, and carrots in a vinaigrette. Serve chilled.
- Cauliflower is fast becoming the new rice. Chop or pulse it in a food processor until it is the consistency of couscous or rice grains. Then sauté it with chopped onions and other seasonings. You can even use it as a base for making a gluten-free pizza crust or even breadsticks.
- Cauliflower can be baked (and blackened) at very high heat similar to broccoli; an entire head of it artfully roasted and seasoned this way can be a most impressive—and delicious—dish.

INDIAN-STYLE ROASTED CAULIFLOWER

SERVES 4 AS A SIDE DISH

Source Note: Roasted broccoli or cauliflower that has been tossed in olive oil, salt, and pepper are side dishes that frequently show up at our dinner table during the week. They are easy and flavorful and always gobbled up by the kids. It proves that you don't need a lot to put together a great meal. I wanted to put a spicy Indian spin on my roasted cauliflower. Now, I was happy just eating a bowlful of this cauliflower with a scoop of steamed rice, but this is a great accompaniment to any meal that needs a kick!

> 1 head cauliflower (about 2 pounds)
> 2 teaspoons ground cumin
> ½ teaspoon ground coriander
> ¼ teaspoon ground turmeric
> ½ teaspoon ground cayenne pepper
> 1 teaspoon kosher salt
> Freshly ground black pepper
> 2 to 3 tablespoons cooking oil

1. Preheat the oven to 400°F.

2. Core the cauliflower, cut it into bite-size florets, and place them in a large mixing bowl.

3. In a small bowl, combine the cumin, coriander, turmeric, cayenne pepper, salt, and black pepper.

4. Add the cooking oil to the cauliflower and toss until the cauliflower is coated. Then add the spices and toss again until the cauliflower is evenly coated.

5. Line a large, rimmed baking sheet with parchment paper. Spread the florets out on the baking sheet so that they are not piled on top of each other; they'll cook more evenly this way.

6. Roast for 25 to 30 minutes, or until lightly browned.

— *Amy Kim,* Kim-Chi Mom *blog*

GREEN CURRY CHICKEN WITH BROCCOLI AND CAULIFLOWER

SERVES 2

> ½ head broccoli
> ½ head cauliflower
> 1 or 2 cloves garlic, chopped
> 2 boneless, skinless chicken breast halves, sliced
> 1 tablespoon olive oil
> 2 tablespoons butter (¼ cube)

3 tablespoons heavy cream
2 to 3 tablespoons green curry paste

1. Cut the broccoli and cauliflower into bite-size pieces and steam until they are tender-crisp. Set aside.

2. In a large skillet over medium heat, sauté the garlic and chicken breast slices in the olive oil. When the chicken is cooked through, push it to the outer edges of the pan.

3. Melt the butter in the center of the pan over low heat. Add the cream and curry paste; blend and stir in the chicken, then turn off the heat. Add the broccoli and cauliflower and stir to coat them with the sauce. Cover, and let the flavors meld for about 5 minutes.

— *Nadine Bayer, The Bluff Country Co-op Cookbook*

CAULIFLOWER FRIED RICE   SERVES 2

Source Note: Occasionally, I have leftover meats and veggies that aren't enough individually to be their own meals, so what better idea than to make fried rice? Here I use grated cauliflower as my "rice," but you literally don't change the order of how you would cook any regular fried rice. It's best to cook all of the other veggies and meats first, and then add the cauliflower last (just like regular fried rice), so it doesn't get mushy.

1 small head of cauliflower
Anything you want in your fried rice (such as onion, garlic, green onions, celery, mushrooms, cabbage, and ham)
Olive oil or bacon fat
1 tablespoon soy sauce
1 egg (optional)
Salt and freshly ground black pepper
Chopped green onions, for garnish

1. Grate the cauliflower using a food processor or blender. If you don't have either, you can use a cheese grater.

2. Dice the other ingredients you want to add to the fried rice.

3. Add several tablespoons of oil to a large sauté pan on medium heat. Add the onions and garlic, and sauté until they turn translucent. Then add the rest of the "anything you want" ingredients (celery, cabbage, ham, etc.). Add the soy sauce and stir to combine.

4. When the vegetables and meat are about done, add the grated cauliflower and combine everything. Cook for another 3 to 4 minutes.

5. Make a hole in the center of the "fried rice" and crack the raw egg into it. Mix everything together—the heat will instantly cook the threads of the egg as you stir.

Biodynamic Principles and Practices

Martha Wagner

*Hundreds of CSA farms likely follow some biodynamic principles and practices, but many of them choose not to go through the biodynamic certification process with **Demeter USA**. LocalHarvest's CSA directory lists more than 200 farms that use biodynamic practices. Technically, an agriculturally or farm-based product can be referred to as "biodynamic" only if it has obtained certification through **Demeter International**, a nonprofit established initially in 1928 in Europe and 1985 in the United States. **The Biodynamic Association**, which promotes education and training opportunities, has been supportive of CSAs since the first American ones started in the 1980s. Wali Via, a co-owner of **Winter Green Farm** in Noti, Oregon, wrote the following explanation of biodynamics for his farm's website:*

What Is Biodynamic Agriculture?

In 1924 the Austrian philosopher and scientist Rudolf Steiner (of Waldorf School fame) gave a series of lectures outlining the principles that have become known as biodynamics. Although there are methods that are unique to biodynamics, I relate to biodynamics not so much as a methodology, but as a training of the farmer to become more sensitive and responsive to the farm.

Steiner referred to the farm as an "individuality" or "farm organism" ("ecosystem" had yet to be coined as a term). This means that the farmer views the farm as an interconnected whole, an entity that is beyond the sum of its parts. A healthy ecosystem is resilient and has a self-sustaining nature. So it is with a farm organism. Ideally there is the right mix of animals and plants, so that the animals provide enough fertility through their

6. Season with salt and pepper, and top with the chopped green onions.

— *Crystal Tai,* HappyChomp *blog*

. . . .

DOROTHY'S CAULIFLOWER SALAD   SERVES 4 TO 6

1 medium head cauliflower, broken into bite-size pieces
¼ cup chopped green onions
2 ribs celery, chopped
½ cup chopped green pepper
10 whole black olives

MAYO-SOUR CREAM DRESSING

½ cup mayonnaise
½ cup sour cream
Italian seasoning (to taste)

1. Combine the cauliflower, green onions, celery, green pepper, and black olives in a large bowl.

2. In a separate bowl, combine the mayonnaise, sour cream, and Italian seasoning to taste.

3. Pour the dressing over the cauliflower mixture and toss until evenly coated. Let the salad sit for a few hours to let the flavors mingle.

Cooking Note: I sometimes add chopped parsley, use the small, brightly colored sweet peppers as well as the green ones, and add sliced black olives (and more of them). If I don't happen to have sour cream on hand, I use just the mayonnaise. Other changes I sometimes make include using hot sauce in place of the Italian seasoning and using less mayonnaise.

— *Esther McRae*

. . . .

ROASTED CAULIFLOWER
WITH ENDIVE AND LEMON   SERVES 4

Source Note: This is an elegant, restaurant-style side dish (or first course) that hails from Quinn's Pub in Seattle, Washington. This popular gastropub offers food that aims to take bar food to the next level—of freshness, of sophistication, and of deliciousness.

½ large head cauliflower (about 1¾ pound whole)
3 to 4 tablespoons extra-virgin olive oil, divided
Salt and freshly ground black pepper

---

manure for the soil to support the plants and in turn there is ample food for the animals and humans as well. This is quite different from chemical agriculture and the majority of organic farms where massive fertility inputs from off-farm sources are necessary.

Biodynamics also recognizes that a farm organism does not stand apart from the rest of the universe but is intrinsically influenced by "cosmic" rhythms. These include the warmth and light of the sun, the phases of the moon, and even the procession of the stars and planets across the sky. Research done by scientists since Steiner's lectures has confirmed that working in harmony with these rhythms reinforces a healthy environment for plant life. By contrast, today most agriculturists look almost exclusively for microscopic solutions to problems (for instance, genetic engineering).

One cannot speak of biodynamics (referred to in short as BD) without speaking of the compost pile. Biodynamic compost is well ripened and no longer resembles its original ingredients. When finished, it is stabilized humus and has the smell and feel of a rich forest soil. Plants growing in composted soils are able to uptake nutrients on an "as-needed" basis, which assures a natural and balanced pattern of growth. Plants fertilized with raw manure and unfinished compost respond similarly to plants fertilized with chemical nitrogen. In these situations, nitrogen is essentially "force-fed" to the plants, creating a lush growth that is more likely to fall prey to fungus and insect attack. Excess nitrogen also leads to runoff and nutrient pollution of waterways.

When making a compost pile, special BD compost preparations are added in homeopathic dosages. These preparations are designed to help strengthen the connection of the soil to the cosmos when the

1 head Belgian endive
1 teaspoon lemon zest
1 teaspoon fresh lemon juice
1 teaspoon champagne or white wine vinegar
2 teaspoons butter
2 to 3 tablespoons chicken or vegetable stock
1½ tablespoons finely sliced fresh mint leaves

1. Place a rack in the center of the oven and heat to 385°F.

2. Cut the cauliflower into medium florets, then cut the florets into thick slices. (They will vary in size, but the idea is to create some flat surfaces that will rest on the pan and caramelize nicely.) Toss the florets with 2 to 3 tablespoons olive oil, a few big pinches of salt, and several grinds of pepper. Spread them, flat sides down, on a heavy baking sheet. Bake for 20 to 30 minutes, or until they are tender and golden brown. Transfer the pieces to a plate and set aside.

3. Meanwhile, trim the Belgian endive and separate it into leaves. Rub the leaves with another tablespoon or so of the olive oil to coat the surfaces. Sprinkle lightly with salt. Place the leaves on the baking sheet that you used for the cauliflower and roast for 5 minutes, or until the leaves are slightly softened and just barely brown around the edges. Remove from the oven. Sprinkle the leaves with the lemon zest, lemon juice, and vinegar. Cover with foil to keep warm.

4. To finish, heat a sauté pan over medium-high heat with the butter and chicken stock. Add the cauliflower pieces and cook, tossing to distribute the butter and stock, until the pan is dry.

5. To finish, sprinkle the fresh mint over the endive leaves. Put the cauliflower into a shallow bowl and tuck the endive leaves onto and around it. Serve immediately.

— *Adapted by Lisa Gordanier from Quinn's Pub, Seattle, Washington*

Cauliflower at Featherstone Farm.

compost is applied to the fields. In a sense, the compost preparations can be seen as medicine for the earth, helping revitalize the life forces in nature that are waning on our planet. Additional preparations are sprayed on the earth and on the growing plants to further promote balanced growth. All of the preparations are made from natural substances and are nontoxic and life-promoting.

If we eat food from a life-force-filled farm, that life force is passed on to us. Steiner believed that our ability to think clearly and direct our will with intention is linked directly with the quality and vitality of the food we eat. Growing the highest-quality produce to feed the bodies, minds, and souls of our members and customers has always been a priority for us at Winter Green.

The study, training, and practice of biodynamics are an ever-evolving lifelong process that heightens one's awareness of our responsibility for healing the Earth. To learn more about biodynamics, visit www. oregonbd.org or www.biodynamics. com, or give me a call at the farm.

Collards

BRASSICA OLERACEA,
ACEPHALA GROUP

The collard is a vigorous member of the rather crowded Brassica family, from which we derive many other vegetables, such as cabbage, broccoli, and Brussels sprouts. It is actually a type of kale, and although both are low-growing plants with robust leaves growing on sturdy stalks, collards are flat and paddle-shaped in contrast to kale's often intricately curled or wrinkled foliage.

Collards are forever associated in American cuisine with Southern soul food. It is thought that African slaves brought seeds of the vegetables they knew and loved from their homeland, including collards, black-eyed peas, and okra. Collards are a staple ingredient in the famous "mess o' greens," that nutritious mass of dark green leaves slow-cooked for hours with that other Southern staple, the pig. Collard's rich, meaty leaves hold up well even to hours of simmering, and make a wonderful foil for robust meats, or as a fulfilling vegetable side dish with rice and beans.

HISTORY

The exact origins of wild cabbage are lost to history, but it's possible that collards are native to the eastern Mediterranean region and Asia Minor. The ancient Greeks were rather unimpressed with them, but the Romans doted on them and their other cabbage brethren, unlike much of the rest of Europe. By the mid-1500s, collards were flourishing in the West Indies and they were growing in Virginia by the early 1600s.

NUTRITION

Dark-green leafy vegetables are among nature's most healthful foods, with abundant amounts of vitamins A and C, folic acid, iron, fiber, and calcium. Per calorie, collards have more calcium than milk, are an excellent source of organic and highly absorbable iron, contain phenomenal amounts of vitamin K, and are also twice as high in vitamin A as carrots. Yet a 1-cup serving of chopped raw collards contains a mere 11 calories. Additionally, like other cruciferous vegetables, collards contain abundant amounts of phytonutrients, which have proved in studies to fight cancer.

SEASON

Commercially, collards are widely grown and available year-round. But the leaves are much sweeter, tastier, and more nutritious when touched by frost, from late fall through early winter.

SELECTION

Collards should be fresh looking, not wilted or yellowing. Younger leaves will be more tender and have a milder flavor.

STORAGE

Collards should not be stored for too long, as their moisture content makes them susceptible to rot or wilting. Wrap collards in a damp paper towel and store in a perforated plastic bag in the refrigerator vegetable

Apply Directly to the Forehead

Southerners believed that a fresh collard leaf hung over the door assured that evil spirits would not enter. (And we always thought garlic was the magic deterrent.)

Some believed that placing a fresh collard leaf on the forehead could chase a headache away.

crisper. They will keep for up to 1 week. Avoid washing them until just before preparation.

TRIMMING AND CLEANING

These greens often host dirt and insects, so they require a thorough washing. One of the best ways to tackle them is to fill the kitchen sink with water, completely submerge the greens, and swish them around several times to dislodge any impurities. Drain the greens in a colander, or if they are small, use a salad spinner. If the water that drains still looks dirty, repeat the washing.

Sturdy greens like collards, kale, and turnip greens have tough central stems or ribs that should be removed from the leaves before cooking, either by hand or by knife.

STEAMING AND BOILING

Steaming is not the best way to cook collards because it gives them a somewhat tough texture. If you want to try it nevertheless, steam using just the greens' own moisture in a covered pan. Collards can be boiled in water or broth for 15 to 30 minutes, but even this cooking method yields a slightly firmer texture. Long, slow simmering over 2 or even 3 hours is the best way to soften these meaty greens and mellow their flavor.

STIR-FRYING AND SAUTÉING

Simmer collards first in a small amount of water for 10 minutes. Then drain them and sauté in olive oil with herbs, spices, or garlic until tender, about 10 minutes.

MICROWAVING

Thoroughly wash the collards; then place the leaves, with water still clinging to them, in a microwave-safe dish. Cover and cook on high power for 7 to 10 minutes, stirring halfway through.

- 2 cups = 2 minutes
- 1 pound = 7 to 10 minutes

BLANCHING AND FREEZING

Collards do freeze well. After washing, trimming, and cutting them into 1-inch pieces, blanch the leaves in rapidly boiling, lightly salted water for 3 minutes. Then plunge them into ice water for 5 minutes to stop the cooking process. Remove and drain. Squeeze out the excess water and place them in zipper-lock freezer or vacuum food sealer-type bags, or in freezer containers. Squeeze out any excess air and leave 1 inch of headspace (unless you are using the vacuum sealing method). Frozen collards will keep for up to 1 year at 0°F.

EQUIVALENTS, MEASURES, AND SERVINGS

- 1 pound = 10 cups pieces = 2 cups cooked
- 2 cups packed raw leaves = ½ cup cooked greens

COMPLEMENTARY HERBS, SEASONINGS, AND FOODS

Asafetida, bacon, basil, beans, black-eyed peas, brown sugar, butter, cardamom, cayenne peppers, chiles, cinnamon, coconut butter, coconut

Books

The Collard Patch
Mary Lou Cheatham and Paul Elliott,
Blue Moon Books Louisiana, 2006.

Fannie Flagg's Original Whistle
Stop Cafe Cookbook: Featuring
Fried Green Tomatoes, Southern
Barbecue, Banana Split Cake, and
Many Other Great Recipes
Fannie Flagg,
Ballantine Books, 1995.

The Soul of a New Cuisine:
A Discovery of the Foods
and Flavors of Africa
Marcus Samuelsson,
Houghton Mifflin Harcourt, 2006.

Afri Chef: African Recipes:
Cooking Real Food from Africa
Michael Tracey, 2003.

Wild about Greens: 125 Delectable
Vegan Recipes for Kale, Collards,
Arugula, Bok Choy, and Other
Leafy Veggies Everyone Loves
Nava Atlas, Sterling, 2012.

Mediterranean Grains and Greens:
A Book of Savory,
Sun-Drenched Recipes
Paula Wolfert, Ecco, 1998.

milk, coriander, cornbread, cream, cumin, curry, dill, garlic, ghee, ginger, ham, hot pepper sauce, lemon, liquid smoke seasoning, mint, miso, molasses, mustard, mustard oil, olives, olive oil, onion, oregano, parsley, pasta, peanuts, pork, potatoes, salt pork, sausage, sesame, smoked meats, smoked paprika, smoked salt, soy sauce, turmeric, vinegar, walnuts, winter squash.

SERVING SUGGESTIONS

- Boiled or pan-steamed greens are tasty seasoned with onion, garlic, and plenty of chopped fresh herbs such as mint, dill, and basil.
- Sauté collards with tofu, garlic, and red pepper flakes for a quick, nutritious, vegetarian meal.
- Serve collards with beans—especially black-eyed peas. An avant-garde approach to spring rolls and sushi: cooked collard greens with black-eyed peas and brown rice.
- Add chopped collards to soups and stews.
- These greens go especially well with ham, bacon, and pork fatback. Sauté chopped greens with a little bacon fat or a hunk of salt pork, sugar, and pepper. Splash liberally with hot pepper vinegar just before serving.
- The liquid left after slow-cooking collards with pork is extremely nutritious and delicious—it's the famed "pot liquor." Drink this broth on its own as a savory soup, or use it as you would vegetable stock.
- Try a vegetarian stew of collard greens, cabbage, sweet bell peppers, garlic, onions, mushrooms, tomatoes, and hot red peppers, seasoned with molasses, vinegar, and seasoned salt.
- Collards work well in most recipes calling for kale. See the serving suggestions for kale on page 444.
- Collards are a staple in Ethiopian and Eritrean cuisines, where they are often cooked with hot peppers and served with butter, cottage cheese, or buttermilk.
- The national dish of Portugal, *caldo verde* (or "green soup"), is traditionally made with kale, broth, potatoes, garlicky pork sausage, olive oil, and salt—but it is just as good with collards.

BRASSICA FRIED RICE   SERVES 6 TO 8

Source Note: Brassicas are cruciferous vegetables, which include cabbage, broccoli, turnips, kohlrabi, collards, mustard, and other greens. I've altered the recipe slightly, substituting in brown rice for white and reducing the amount of soy sauce. This is my personal favorite fried rice recipe, and this dish has made it into weekly rotation at my house, for a Meatless Anyday. Even if you're not a big fried rice or brassica fan, I think this recipe will win you over.

3 tablespoons soy sauce
2 teaspoons rice vinegar
1 teaspoon sesame oil
3 tablespoons vegetable oil, divided
4 eggs, beaten

2 cloves garlic, minced

1-inch knob of fresh ginger, peeled and minced

2 cups slow-cooking ("hard") brassica vegetables such as broccoli, cauliflower, or Brussels sprouts, chopped or sliced into similar shapes and sizes

2 cups quick-cooking ("leafy") brassica vegetables such as collards or chard, torn or sliced if necessary

4 cups cooked brown rice

4 green onions, thinly sliced into rings

Cilantro, Chinese chives, or other herbs for garnish

1. Combine the soy sauce, vinegar, and sesame oil in a small bowl. Set aside.

2. Heat a large pot (a wok is ideal) over high heat. Add 2 tablespoons of the vegetable oil. Add the eggs and scramble them until they turn medium firm. Break them into small pieces with a wooden spoon. Remove and set aside.

3. Wipe out the pot with a paper towel. Add 1 more tablespoon of the vegetable oil. Heat again over high heat.

4. Add the ginger and garlic and stir-fry them until they are fragrant.

5. Add the slow-cooking vegetables and stir-fry them until they are al dente.

6. Add the quick-cooking vegetables and stir-fry them until they are wilted.

7. Add the rice. Stir-fry it for a few minutes.

8. Add the sauce. Then lower the heat to medium and stir-fry until the rice is evenly coated with the sauce.

9. Add the eggs and green onions.

10. Remove the fried rice from the pot and garnish with the herbs.

— *Linda Shiue,* Spiceboxtravels *blog, adapted from a recipe by Joyce Lin-Conrad, Director of Learning at Education Outside*

CITRUS COLLARDS WITH RAISINS   SERVES 6

Source Note: "This is my signature dish," says Chef Bryant Terry proudly. "When it was first published, the recipe was my way of showing you can take traditional cuisine and reinvent it—I grew up on collard greens that weren't considered done unless they'd cooked at least 2 hours."

1½ pounds collard greens, tough stems removed

1 tablespoon olive oil

2 cloves garlic, minced (2 teaspoons)

⅔ cup raisins

½ teaspoon salt

Hazon) offer three-month residential fellowship programs for young adults focused on organic farming and Jewish learning.

New Roots for Refugees, a partnership of Catholic Charities of Northeast Kansas and the Kansas City Center for Urban Agriculture, helps refugee women start their own small farm businesses growing and selling vegetables. Its eight-acre training farm is at Juniper Gardens, a public housing site in Kansas City, Kansas, where many of the participating women—17 in 2014—live with their families, having come from Somalia, Burma, Burundi, Bhutan, and Sudan. New Roots provides training of up to four years for women to build on their strengths and experience while learning English and earning income. New Roots graduates are now farming on their own plots in the area. The training farm uses organic growing methods and its produce is sold at farmers markets throughout the metro area and through a 60-member CSA subscription program.

The Faith-Based Food Hubs Program of Cornell University Cooperative Extension in New York City was set up in 2012 to increase access to New York farm products by New York City churches. Through MarketMaker, a national organization that helps farmers sell their products, churches and faith-based organizations get—at reasonable prices—fresh, healthful produce that they can distribute to parishioners and use in soup kitchens and food pantries. By 2014, 15 hub churches in New York City had formed the core of a network distributing farm products (mostly fruit and vegetables) to 65 churches and faith-based organizations. More than 2,000 New York State farms have participated in the program.

The Interfaith Food & Farms Partnership, a program of Ecumenical Ministries of Oregon, helps churches with projects that pro-

⅓ cup freshly squeezed orange juice
Salt and freshly ground black pepper (optional)

1. Stack several collard leaves atop one another, and roll them into a tight cylinder, like a cigar. Slice it crosswise into strips. Repeat with the rest of the collard greens.

2. Cook the collards in a large pot of boiling, salted water for 8 to 10 minutes, or until they have softened. Drain, and plunge the collards into a large bowl of cold water to stop the cooking process. Drain them again, pressing or squeezing to remove most of the water.

3. Heat the olive oil in a large skillet over medium heat. Add the garlic and sauté for 1 minute. Add the drained collards, raisins, and salt, and sauté for 3 minutes. Stir in the orange juice, and cook for 15 seconds more. Season with salt and pepper, if desired.

— Chef Bryant Terry

STUFFED COLLARD ROLLS WITH CASHEW COCONUT SAUCE   SERVES 4

Source Note: *This Cashew Coconut Sauce, which was adapted from* The Candle Café Cookbook, *is really tasty. Make extra and keep the sauce on hand to lend flavor to all kinds of vegetables. Swiss chard can be used instead of collard greens if you use older, sturdier leaves. The stuffing is also good on its own with vegetables or as a lettuce roll-up. Add coconut milk to turn it into a sauce and serve over warm greens for dinner.*

> 1 bunch collards
> 3 cups broccoli florets
> ½ cup sesame tahini
> 2 tablespoons green onions, sliced
> 1 tablespoon flaxseed, ground (almonds or pumpkin seeds could also be used)
> 1 tablespoon nutritional yeast flakes
> 1 tablespoon wheat-free tamari sauce
> 1 tablespoon prepared mustard
> 2 large cloves garlic, crushed
> 1 tomato, chopped
> 4 green onions, chopped

1. Bring a large pot of water to a boil and heat the oven to 300°F. Trim off the bottom inch or so of the collard stems (removing these wider, tougher stem sections will make it easier to roll them). Place the whole collard leaves in the boiling water for 2 to 3 minutes, until they are wilted but still brightly colored. Lift out with tongs and set aside.

2. To make the filling, put the broccoli florets in the hot cooking water from the collards and let them sit while pulsing the tahini, green on-

ions, flaxseed, nutritional yeast, tamari sauce, mustard, and garlic in a food processor. Remove the slightly cooked broccoli from the pot, add it to the ingredients in the processor, and process until smooth and creamy. Chop the tomatoes and green onions and set aside.

3. Lay a collard leaf flat, place 2 to 3 tablespoons of the filling on the leaf, add some diced tomatoes and green onions, and roll it up. Put the collard rolls in a baking dish, cover with foil, and keep them warm in the oven.

4. When all of the collard rolls have been assembled, spoon the Cashew Coconut Sauce (recipe follows) over the rolls and serve.

— *Kathy Abascal,* The Abascal Way Cookbook

. . . .

CASHEW COCONUT SAUCE   MAKES 2 CUPS

1 cup cashew butter
1 cup coconut milk solids (save the watery part of the milk to thin
    out other dips and sauces)
½ cup brown rice vinegar
¼ cup wheat-free tamari sauce
2 tablespoons chopped cilantro
2 tablespoons chopped fresh mint
1 tablespoon grated fresh ginger
1 garlic clove, minced

Blend all of the ingredients in a food processor until smooth.

— *Kathy Abascal,* The Abascal Way Cookbook

Figs

Figs are oddities in the fruit world, from the way most species reproduce (they must be pollinated by highly specialized wasps that have evolved with the fig) to their extreme fragility in their fresh state, which makes them exceedingly difficult to harvest and ship. Nearly all of the US fig crop is grown in California, which is the largest producer outside Turkey. But if you are lucky enough to live near a farmers market or even subscribe to a warm-climate CSA farm that grows them, you're in for a real treat.

The color of figs varies dramatically depending on the species, and about 150 of them are grown worldwide for their fruit. Here are some of the most common varieties in the United States:

Black Mission
Missions are a very distinctive purplish black with red flesh. They are full-flavored, have a moist and chewy texture, and are best eaten fresh. The dried version is also very useful—for its concentrated flavor, chewy texture, and availability in the winter months.

Kadota
These are medium-sized figs with a yellowish-green thick skin. The sweet, white to amber-pink pulp has relatively few seeds.

Calimyrna
These are large figs, with green skin and white flesh. Their flavor is reminiscent of honey and nuts.

Brown Turkey
These are medium to large figs with a purplish-brown skin and sweet, juicy pulp.

Adriatic
This is the variety most often used to make fig bars. The fruits have a light green skin and pink-tan flesh that has a pronounced flavor when dried.

HISTORY

Figs have a long and storied history with human civilization, and they are frequently mentioned in the Bible and other ancient writings (who could forget Adam's fig leaves when he and Eve were banished from Eden?). Figs originated in Asia Minor but soon spread to the Mediterranean. They were grown in the Hanging Gardens of Babylon and valued in the Phoenician economy. Figs also served as an extremely important food source in Greece and areas of the Middle East where the arid lands and rocky soils could not support grain. In ancient Greek times, figs were even force-fed to geese and hogs alike to fatten their livers for foie gras.

Figs continued charming humanity wherever they were taken, and soon they were growing in the royal gardens of French king Louis XIV,

"Shape is a good part of the fig's delight."

— *Jane Grigson, British food writer*

simmering in the pudding pots of England, and thriving in the warmer parts of the New World, where the Spanish and Portuguese introduced them in the 1500s.

NUTRITION

Figs are a good source of vitamin B6, copper, manganese, potassium, pantothenic acid, and dietary plant fiber. One large fresh fig contains about 47 calories. The dark skins of some fig varieties contain phytonutrients that are believed to have anticancer properties.

SEASON

Figs are truly a seasonal fruit, and most trees bear two crops a year: a small one in late spring or early summer, and another, much bigger one from August through October.

SELECTION

A ripe, plump fig is a most delicate thing—it should be somewhat soft and smell fresh and fragrant. They do not ripen after picking. Overripe or spoiled figs will have a fermented, rank aroma; shriveled specimens should be avoided. The presence of small slits or tears in the fruit is not necessarily a bad thing, as long as the fruit is fresh and there are no signs of mold around the broken skin.

STORAGE

Fresh figs are extremely perishable and should be kept chilled and unwashed in the refrigerator until you're ready to eat them. Even then they should be stored only for a day or two. At room temperature, they can start to spoil after only a few hours of warmth.

TRIMMING AND CLEANING

If your figs have exceptionally thick skins, you can peel them, but most of the time this is unnecessary. Just trim off the tiny bit of stem, and wait to wash them until right before eating.

FREEZING

Fresh figs can be frozen quite easily. Clean and freeze in a single layer on a baking sheet, then pack them into zipper-lock storage bags. Frozen figs will keep for up to 1 year at 0°F.

EQUIVALENTS, MEASURES, AND SERVINGS

- 3 ounces = 1 cup
- 1 pound fresh figs = 9 medium = 12 small
- 1 pound fresh figs = 2⅔ cups chopped
- 1 pound canned figs = 12 to 16 whole figs
- 1 pound dried figs = 3 cups chopped = 44 whole figs

COMPLEMENTARY HERBS, SEASONINGS, AND FOODS

Almonds, anise, balsamic vinegar, beef, black pepper, blue cheese, brandy, caramel, citrus, clove, cream, dates, grapes, ham, honey, lamb, mascarpone, nectarines, onions, oranges, peaches, pistachios, pork, prosciutto, rabbit, raspberries, rum, thyme, vanilla, walnuts, whipped cream, wine.

Getting Figgy with It

Fresh figs contain a chemical that will prevent gelatin from properly setting—it will break the protein links formed in the gelling process as fast as they are made. The enzyme is destroyed by cooking, so cooked figs are fine to use in such preparations.

The popping sensation you feel when chewing fig is actually hundreds of seed capsules bursting between your teeth.

SERVING SUGGESTIONS

- The classic appetizer of figs wrapped in prosciutto is still a great one. Use the best-quality prosciutto or Spanish *jamon* you can find.

- Quarter figs and mash them with a little sugar and rum or brandy, then serve with vanilla ice cream.

- Figs and goat cheese or mascarpone are made for each other. Serve them together in salad or as appetizers.

- Figs take well to stewing or poaching, either by themselves or with other fruits.

- The savory sweetness of figs goes well with hearty meats like ham, lamb, beef, rabbit, and pork; use them in dishes that accompany these meats or as an ingredient in steak sauces or glazes.

- Make figs into rich salsas and surprising chutneys.

- Caramelized onions and figs are a delicious combination that can enhance meats, poultry, and pasta.

- Chopped figs, arugula, and goat cheese make an unexpected topping for homemade pizza.

- Morning oatmeal or Greek yogurt can be made instantly glamorous with chopped figs and a drizzle of orange-blossom honey.

- Skewer figs and grill them lightly for an unexpected taste treat. Or toss halved figs in a mix of honey, chopped fresh thyme, and either water or a sweet white wine like Muscat. Then grill.

- Dried figs can often be used interchangeably in recipes calling for dried apricots, dates, and prunes.

FIG TART WITH FRANGIPANE   MAKES ONE 9-INCH TART

Source Note: Frangipane is a kind of almond paste, and it's really easy to make. Use the leftovers from this recipe to spread on toast or save it for more tarts.

FRANGIPANE
½ cup whole, raw almonds
½ cup sugar
½ cup (1 stick) butter at room temperature
1 large egg

1. Preheat the oven to 350°F. Spread the almonds evenly on a baking sheet and place them in the oven. Roast them for about 10 minutes, or until slightly toasted and fragrant. Transfer to a plate and let cool to room temperature.

2. Put the cooled almonds and the sugar into a food processor and process until fine. Add the butter and egg, and pulse until well combined. If you don't want to use it right away, divide the frangipane into four equal parts, and wrap each tightly in plastic. They will keep in the fridge for a couple of days and up to 1 month in the freezer.

To Make a 9-inch Fig Tart

1 egg
Pastry dough for one (9-inch) pie, made ahead
10 large brown Turkish figs
One quarter of the frangipane from the recipe above

1. Put the egg into a small bowl and add 1 tablespoon of water. Use a whisk to vigorously mix the egg and water so that no whole bits of egg white remain.

2. Preheat the oven to 400°F.

3. Roll out your pastry dough to about a 10-inch diameter. Spread the frangipane on the dough with the back of a spoon, stopping about an inch or so from the outer edge.

4. Quarter the figs and arrange them in concentric circles to cover the frangipane. Fold the pastry edges inward, pinching them a little to make sure they stick. The goal is to make a rather rustic-looking crust. Brush the dough with a coating of the egg wash, and sprinkle sugar over the whole tart.

5. Bake for around 45 minutes, or until the pastry edges are golden brown and the figs have softened and their juices are bubbling. Serve while still warm.

— *Paul Anater*

- -

PITA POCKETS WITH FRESH FIGS AND ROASTED CHICKEN

SERVES 4

¼ cup coarsely chopped walnuts
1 cup shredded roasted chicken breast and thighs (skin removed)
¼ cup chopped onion
1 teaspoon fresh oregano or ¼ teaspoon dried oregano leaves
¾ teaspoon freshly ground black pepper, divided
1 cup mixed baby greens
1 cup sliced fresh figs
½ cup crumbled feta cheese
2 tablespoons extra-virgin olive oil
2 teaspoons white balsamic vinegar
4 white or whole wheat pita rounds, cut crosswise to form pockets

1. Heat a small skillet over medium-high heat. Add the walnuts; cook for 3 minutes or until they are lightly browned, stirring constantly. Set aside to cool.

2. In a large bowl, sprinkle the shredded chicken and red onion with the oregano and ¼ teaspoon of the black pepper. Add the greens, figs, feta cheese, and toasted walnuts; drizzle with the oil and vinegar.

"I am sure that in the story of Adam and Eve, the forbidden fruit was a fig and not an apple, pear or anything else."

— *Yotam Ottolenghi, Israeli chef*

On Friday last week, the forecast added up to a "double whammy" for many of the cold-sensitive crops that we grow in the valley here at Featherstone Farm. Rain all day. Then the clouds parted near sundown, with a widespread frost advisory issued for overnight.

With seven acres of winter squash still out in the "Val shelf" field, I was uneasy to say the least; light frost can burn the tops of fruits—particularly smooth-skinned types like butternut and spaghetti—and take the storage life out of them. And even with the entire crew available to go pick and bring in this crop, it would be slow going, to say the least, in the mud and rain. The forecasted high was in the low 60s at best. Bummer.

But once again the crew picked me up and made light work of a tough challenge. It took a bit to tie up all the other projects early on and to get everyone up there. But by midmorning the entire crew was up there in rainsuits, clipping and collecting squash: a total of 22 Spanish speakers, 6 English speakers (we're depleted in this area after several folks went back to school), and the newest addition to the crew, 4 German-speaking Amish neighbors.

I had a number of loose ends to tie up in the shop myself, and when I came out there in the afternoon, it was an amazing sight. Yellow-jacketed pickers hunched over in long rows, moving through the field. Three tractors pulling long wagons through the deep mud behind them, with other groups of "yellow jackets" tossing and collecting the squash into bins on the wagons. A light but steady rainfall was making everything more trying, to say the least.

What struck me about the scene was that there was such a human

Sprinkle with the remaining ⅛ teaspoon black pepper and toss to mix well.

3. Divide the mixture into eight portions and spoon into the pita pockets. Serve.

— *California Figs*

························

FIG-HONEY GELATO   MAKES ABOUT 4 CUPS

Source Note: Figs add a lovely, luxurious quality to any dish in which they are used. When you taste this gelato, you won't believe that it's made with almost all milk. Figs contain an enzyme called ficin, which can turn milk sour; heating the fruit and sugar to 155°F kills the enzyme.

1 pound fresh figs, quartered
½ cup sugar
2 tablespoons honey
1 tablespoon orange liqueur
⅓ cup mascarpone
1½ cups milk
Pinch salt

1. In a saucepan, heat the figs over medium-high heat with the sugar, stirring roughly so they break apart. Cook, stirring, until the figs have mostly melted and begin to bubble, about 5 minutes.

2. Remove from the heat and stir in the honey, orange liqueur, mascarpone, milk, and salt. Chill well (at least 30 minutes) in the refrigerator; then freeze according to your ice cream maker's instructions.

— *Russ Parsons,* How to Pick a Peach

························

STUFFED BEEF BRISKET   SERVES 8

½ cup chopped dried figs
¼ cup brandy
1 large leek, white and pale green parts only, chopped (½ cup)
3 tablespoons olive oil, divided
1 small pear, cored and finely chopped
2 cloves garlic, minced
¼ cup chopped toasted pecans
2 tablespoons fine matzo crumbs
1 teaspoon finely shredded lemon peel
½ teaspoon dried thyme, crushed (or use 1 teaspoon chopped fresh thyme)
¼ to ½ teaspoon coarsely ground black pepper

1 beef brisket (2 to 2¼ pounds)
Salt and freshly ground black pepper

1. Put the dried figs and the brandy into a small saucepan over low heat, and heat just until hot (do not boil). Remove from the heat; cover and let stand for 15 to 20 minutes, until the fruit is plumped and most of the liquid is absorbed. Drain the fruit, reserving any remaining liquid. Set aside.

2. Meanwhile, in a skillet over medium heat, heat the 2 teaspoons olive oil, then add the leek and cook it until it turns tender. Add the liquid from the drained figs, along with the pear and garlic; stir and cook until tender. Add the plumped figs along with the pecans, matzo crumbs, lemon peel, thyme, and pepper. Let stand off the heat.

3. Cut the beef brisket horizontally, almost in half; spread it open. Lightly pound the entire surface with the flat side of a meat mallet until the brisket is about ½ inch thick. Season lightly with salt and pepper. Spread the fruit mixture over the meat, leaving ½ inch all around. Starting from the long edge, roll up the meat to enclose the fruit mixture; tie the brisket with kitchen twine at 1-inch intervals.

4. Brown the brisket in the remaining 2 tablespoons olive oil in a large ovenproof skillet or Dutch oven. Then roast in the oven at 375°F for about 40 minutes, or until the meat reaches 140°F in the center.

5. Transfer the brisket to a serving platter; cover with foil and let it stand for about 10 minutes before slicing and serving.

— *California Figs*

element present once again. Joel and Mike were moving full trailers out of the field as quickly as they were filled. Abby was chatting up the Amish gals (in their bonnets and aprons, beneath the rain gear!) in a friendly way; Nathan was kidding around with the Gascas, as always. The echo of chatter and laughter floated over the field, heard even through the steady rainfall. Nobody was complaining about the conditions; everyone was bent to a common task with a clear, common goal. Fantastic.

By 5:00 we had brought in 120 bins (800 to 1,000 pounds each) of winter squash of all varieties … butternut, acorn, carnival, spaghetti, and pie pumpkin. What an effort! The crop saved!

To say that I feel humbled by such community efforts at the farm would be an understatement indeed. It is one of the true joys of what I do day-to-day at Featherstone Farm, being part of such a team of dedicated collaborators. I hesitate to use the word "employees" here, to be honest … It doesn't feel like these folks are working for the farm in such a situation; collectively they are Featherstone Farm. I feel so fortunate to be a part of this.

I spent another couple of hours bringing squash trailers under cover on Friday evening, after everyone had left, and putting away the tractors. Then Saturday I woke to a significant frost on the grass around the Peterson house. How would the crops look down below in the valley …, I wondered anxiously, … where the frost settles even harder? *The answer came in the form of another revelation: The previous day's rain had blanketed the valley in a thick fog, holding back all frost and preserving life in the melons, the tomatoes, and the sweet corn that we still have growing near the shop.*

Another miracle!

Kale

In the years since I wrote the first edition of this cookbook, kale has gone from being a largely ignored vegetable in the American kitchen to a darling of the organic food and restaurant scene. How times have changed. That is a terrific thing, and not just because it is one of the most nutritionally packed vegetables in existence. Kale is amazingly versatile, with the lovely trait of retaining its texture and earthy, nutty flavor even when cooked for long periods. Hardy kale loves cold weather, and it becomes sweeter after a frost.

Your CSA boxes may contain one of three different kales: Winterbor (a green, curly kale), Lacinato (a flat, bluish leafy green, also called dinosaur kale, an heirloom variety), and Redbor, which has beautiful red greens. All three varieties can be prepared the same way and share similar nutritional values.

Because of its coarse texture, kale is not pleasant to eat raw in salads, unless its leaves are very small and young; it can be quite prickly in the mouth and tough to chew. Raw kale is best finely shredded in a slaw or as baby leaves; specimens any larger or older should be cooked.

Kale has long been a favorite of the Scots, who likely eat more of it than any other ethnic group, but the Danish and Germans favor it too.

HISTORY

Some people believe that kale is actually wild cabbage and that it may be the ancestor to all of our modern cabbage varieties. Kale is a hardy and hearty green that humans have cultivated for over 2,000 years. It is particularly popular in Scotland, whose cold, damp climate provides ideal growing conditions for this sturdy plant. In the United States, kale is mostly eaten in the South, where, along with collards and turnip leaves, it forms the famous, savory, long-cooked "mess o' greens."

NUTRITION

Few vegetables are as nutrient-rich as kale. A 1-cup serving contains staggering amounts of vitamins A, C, and K, as well as manganese, dietary fiber, copper, B vitamins, potassium, iron, calcium, phosphorus, and vitamin E, all for only 36 calories. Like other members of the Brassica family, kale packs huge amounts of phytonutrients that are believed to have anticancer properties. It is also a rich source of the carotenoids lutein and zeaxanthin, which are known to promote eye health.

SEASON

Commercially, kale is widely grown and available year-round. But it really comes into its best at farmers markets and CSAs from October through the first (or even second) frost.

SELECTION

Choose kale that is fresh looking, crisp, and evenly colored; yellowing or spotted leaves indicate advanced age or poor storage. Smaller leaves will be sweeter and more tender than larger ones.

STORAGE

Kale leaves should not be stored for too long, as their moisture content makes them susceptible to rot and wilting. Kale also tends to become bitter the longer it is stored. Wrap the leaves in a damp paper towel and store them in a perforated plastic bag in the refrigerator vegetable crisper, where they will keep for up to 1 week. Avoid washing until you're ready to use them.

TRIMMING AND CLEANING

Kale's finely curled, crimped leaves provide perfect hiding places for aphids and other insects. The easiest way to flush unwanted critters out is to fill a sink with water and submerge the leaves completely, swishing them back and forth vigorously before draining them in a colander. Rinse and repeat if necessary, pulling the curled leaves apart to inspect them. To prepare kale for cooking, trim the leaves away from the tough stems and discard the stems. If you want the leaves to cook faster, shred or coarsely cut them into strips (the chiffonade method works well).

STEAMING AND BOILING

To prepare kale for steaming, trim the leaves away from their stems with a knife. Place the leaves in a steamer basket and steam them for 5 to 10 minutes, depending on the size of the leaves, or until they become tender and bright green in color. Kale can be boiled for 5 to 15 minutes, or until tender but still bright green.

STIR-FRYING AND SAUTÉING

Kale leaves, stripped from their stems and coarsely shredded, can be stir-fried. For best results, parboil them for 5 minutes, then add to a well-oiled stir-fry pan or wok and cook for an additional 5 minutes.

BRAISING AND STEWING

The sturdy nature of kale takes very well to braising and stewing. One method is to braise coarsely chopped kale in stock or water into which butter, garlic, chiles, herbs, salt, and pepper have been added. Bring to a boil, cover, decrease the heat, and simmer over low heat for 8 to 12 minutes, or until the kale is tender.

Kale can also be stewed; use plenty of liquid such as stock or red wine, and simmer over low to medium heat for 20 to 25 minutes, stirring constantly.

MICROWAVING

Thoroughly wash the kale, then place the leaves, with water still clinging to them, in a microwave-safe dish. Cover, and cook on high power for 7 to 10 minutes, stirring halfway through.

- 2 cups leaves = 2 minutes
- 1¼ pounds = 7 to 10 minutes

BLANCHING AND FREEZING

Unlike many greens, kale freezes well. Blanch the leaves first in rapidly boiling water for 3 minutes, then plunge them into ice water for 5 minutes to stop the cooking process. Remove and drain. Squeeze out the

Cooking Tip

Boiling kale in vegetable or chicken broth adds a hearty flavor to this already substantial vegetable.

How Green Was My Soup

Portugal's national dish is *caldo verde*, or green soup, made from thinly sliced kale strips, light broth, and a little olive oil, topped with slices of garlicky pork sausage.

An Almanac
of Extreme Weather

Jack Hedin
Featherstone Farm Owner
Rushford, Minnesota

November 27, 2010

The news from this Midwestern farm is not good. The past four years of heavy rains and flash flooding here in southern Minnesota have left me worried about the future of agriculture in America's grain belt. For some time, computer models of climate change have been predicting just these kinds of weather patterns, but seeing them unfold on our farm has been harrowing nonetheless.

My family and I produce vegetables, hay, and grain on 250 acres in one of the richest agricultural areas in the world. Although our farm is not large by modern standards, its roots are deep in this region; my great-grandfather homesteaded about 80 miles from here in the late 1800s.

He passed on a keen sensitivity to climate. His memoirs, self-published in the wake of the Dust Bowl of the 1930s, describe tornadoes, droughts, and other extreme weather. But even he would be surprised by the erratic weather we have experienced in the last decade.

Our farm was able to stay in business only after receiving grants and low-interest private and government loans. Having experienced lesser floods in 2004 and 2005, my family and I decided the only prudent action would be to use the money to move the farm over the winter to better, drier ground eight miles away.

This move proved prescient: In June 2008, torrential rains and flash flooding returned. The federal government declared the second natural disaster in less than a year for the region. Hundreds of acres of our neighbors' cornfields were again un-

excess water and place in zipper-lock freezer or vacuum food sealer-type bags, or freezer containers. Squeeze out any excess air and leave 1 inch of headspace (unless you are using the vacuum sealing method). Frozen kale will keep for up to 8 months at 0°F.

EQUIVALENTS, MEASURES, AND SERVINGS

- 1 pound = 2 cups cooked
- 2 cups packed leaves = ½ cup cooked greens

COMPLEMENTARY HERBS, SEASONINGS, AND FOODS

Almonds, anchovies, apples, bacon, balsamic vinegar, beans, black pepper, breadcrumbs, butter, caraway seeds, cheese, chiles, chorizo, cinnamon, cream, fenugreek, garlic, ginger, goat cheese, goose, ham, lemon, mint, miso, mustard, nuts, olive oil, onions, pine nuts, pork, potatoes, red pepper, rice, salt pork, sausage, sesame, smoked paprika, smoked salt, soy sauce, sweet potatoes, tomatoes, vinegar, walnuts, winter squash, yams.

SERVING SUGGESTIONS

- Kale's ability to maintain its texture and flavor makes it ideal for stews, casseroles, and slow-cooking soups.
- For a quick, nutritious meal, stir-fry kale with chunks of tofu and season with garlic, ginger, and red chiles.
- Add kale to your favorite pasta recipe as a substitute for spinach. Especially good with pine nuts!
- Serve boiled or steamed kale with vinaigrette or sesame dressing.
- Slow-cook kale just as you would collards (see page 431). Kale and pork sausage or ham are natural soul mates.
- Scramble eggs with a bit of cooked kale stirred in instead of spinach.
- Chop up plenty of garlic, fry it crisp in olive oil and salt, and sprinkle it over a bunch of steamed kale.
- For another quick and hearty soup, add cooked kale to canned tomatoes, canned white beans, chicken or vegetable broth, parsley, rosemary, and plenty of onion and garlic to taste.
- Add kale to colcannon, that classic Irish dish with mashed potatoes, leeks, and onions.
- Kale is a natural in highly spiced, complex Indian dishes and curries.
- Kale and sweet potatoes make a hearty, highly nutritious combination that is the perfect side or even main dish for cold winter nights.
- Cream helps temper kale's assertive character. Try creamed kale in place of creamed spinach, or puree the two into a silky soup.
- A little acid makes a nice counterpoint to the rich green taste of kale. Stew kale with tomatoes or a little vinegar and red wine, and serve it over pasta.

SIMPLE KALE   SERVES 2

1 bunch kale, leaves cut into thin strips and stems discarded
1 tablespoon olive oil

2 thinly sliced green garlic scapes
1 tablespoon tamari or soy sauce

1. Rinse the kale and toss it, still wet, into a large heated pan. After the kale begins to wilt (about 5 minutes), add the olive oil and green garlic to the pan. Cook until the kale reaches the desired doneness.

2. If you are cooking the kale for a longer time, you will need to add a liquid to ensure that the kale does not burn. Sherry, broth, vermouth, green tea, or water all work well. (I like kale lightly cooked, whereas others prefer it well done. The beauty of kale is that it will not become bitter, even if it is cooked for a long time.)

3. Right before serving, cook off or drain any remaining liquid and add the tamari or soy sauce to the hot greens. Toss, serve, and enjoy.

— Sarah Libertus, former Featherstone Farm CSA manager

GINGER KALE   SERVES 2 TO 4

1 large bunch kale, stems removed and leaves cut into strips
2 tablespoons olive oil
1 tablespoon butter
2 large cloves garlic, minced
1 medium onion, chopped
1 tablespoon minced fresh ginger or 1 teaspoon dried ginger
Juice of 1 fresh lime
Freshly ground black pepper

1. Steam the kale until it wilts slightly.

2. In a large skillet or wok, heat the oil and butter. Then add the garlic, onion, and ginger; sauté until the onion turns soft. Toss in the kale. Cover and cook on low heat until the kale is tender.

3. Sprinkle with lime juice and pepper to taste.

— FairShare CSA Coalition, From Asparagus to Zucchini

RAW KALE SALAD   SERVES 4

Source Note: A less fattening alternative to the typical creamy coleslaw.

1 pound kale, very finely chopped, stems removed
1 medium red onion, diced
3 carrots, grated
1 cup chopped green beans

derwater and had to be replanted. Earthmovers spent days regrading a 280-acre field just across the road from our new home. Had we remained at the old place, we would have lost a season's worth of crops before they were a quarter grown.

The 2010 growing season has again been extraordinarily wet. The more than 20 inches of rain that I measured in my rain gauge in June and July disrupted nearly every operation on our farm. We managed to do a bare minimum of field preparation, planting, and cultivating through midsummer, thanks only to the well-drained soils beneath our new home.

But in two weeks in July, moisture-fueled disease swept through a three-acre onion field, reducing tens of thousands of pounds of healthy onions to mush. With rain falling several times a week and our tractors sitting idle, weeds took over a seven-acre field of carrots, requiring many times the normal amount of hand labor to control. Crop losses topped $100,000 by mid-August.

The most recent onslaught was a pair of heavy storms in late September that dropped 8.2 inches of rain. Representatives from the Federal Emergency Management Agency again toured the area, and another federal disaster declaration was narrowly averted. But evidence of the loss was everywhere: debris piled up in unharvested cornfields, large washouts in fields recently stripped of pumpkins or soybeans, and harvesting equipment again sitting idle.

My great-grandfather recognized that weather is never perfect for agriculture for an entire season; a full chapter of his memoir is dedicated to this observation. In his 60 years of farming, he wrote that only one season—his final crop in 1937—had close to ideal weather. Like all other farmers of his time and ours, he learned to cope with significant, ill-timed fluctuations in temperature and precipitation.

But at least here in the Midwest,

weather fluctuations have been more significant during my time than in his, the Dust Bowl notwithstanding. The weather in our area has become demonstrably more hostile to agriculture, and all signs are that this trend will continue. Minnesota's state climatologist, Jim Zandlo, has concluded that no fewer than three "thousand-year rains" have occurred in the past seven years in our part of the state. And a University of Minnesota meteorologist, Mark Seeley, has found that summer storms in the region over the past two decades have been more intense and more geographically focused than at any time on record.

No two farms have the same experience with the weather, and some people will contend that ours is an anomaly, that many corn and bean farms in our area have done well over the same period. But heavy summer weather causes harm to farm fields that is not easily seen or quantified, like nutrient leaching, organic-matter depletion, and erosion. As climate change accelerates these trends, losses will likely mount proportionally and across the board. How long can we continue to borrow from the "topsoil bank" as torrential rains force us to make ever more frequent "withdrawals"?

Climate change, I believe, may eventually pose an existential threat to my way of life. A family farm like ours may simply not be able to adjust quickly enough to such unendingly volatile weather. We can't charge enough for our crops in good years to cover losses in the ever-more-frequent bad ones. We can't continue to move to better, drier ground. No new field drainage scheme will help us as atmospheric carbon concentrations edge up to 400 parts per million; hardware and technology alone can't solve problems of this magnitude.

To make things worse, I see fewer acres in our area now planted

MUSTARD-BALSAMIC DRESSING

¼ cup olive oil
¼ cup balsamic vinegar
2 tablespoons brown sugar
2 cloves garlic, crushed
1 teaspoon salt
Freshly ground black pepper
1 teaspoon curry powder
2 teaspoons Dijon mustard
Several fresh purple basil leaves, chopped

Thoroughly mix all of the ingredients together, and toss to evenly coat with the dressing. If you like, top with crumbled bacon, vegetarian bacon bits, Gorgonzola cheese, or toasted slivered almonds.

— *Robin Taylor, Featherstone Farm CSA member*

. . . .

CRISPY KALE   SERVES 4

Source Note: This is a "must-try" recipe. It is the ultimate replacement for popcorn. Crispy Kale has a crunch, and then it melts in your mouth, leaving a slightly salty taste. Two variables for success: First, do not mound the kale on the cookie sheet. If you do, it will steam rather than crisp. Second, balance the length of the cooking time with the oven temperature. Temperatures vary from oven to oven. You may need to raise the temperature or you may need to shorten the baking time. It is a good idea to stay in the kitchen during the first few times you make it, as kale can go from crisp to burnt rather quickly.

A Crispy Kale story: One of my friends has a nine-year-old who does not like vegetables. She tried this dish on him. He not only liked it, but began insisting that she include it in his school lunch. One evening, she made a large bowl of Crispy Kale while her husband was preparing vegetables for dinner. She gave her son a small bowl. At dinner, he asked for a refill. She laughed when her husband responded: "No more kale until you finish the vegetables on your plate!"

1 bunch kale
2 tablespoons olive oil
Salt to taste

1. Preheat the oven to 350°F.

2. Wash the kale and shake it mostly dry. Cut out the tough center stem, cut the kale into narrow strips (about ¼-inch wide), and put it into a large bowl. Pour the olive oil over the kale and toss it to coat. Make sure the kale is well-coated in the oil.

3. Spread the oiled kale strips in a single layer on a rimmed cookie sheet and bake for 5 minutes.

4. Remove from the oven and turn them over with a spatula. Return to the oven and continue roasting for 6 to 7 minutes, or until the kale is crisp. Test it to see if it is ready; you do not want it to burn.

5. When it is done, remove it from the oven and sprinkle with salt.

— *Kathy Abascal,* The Abascal Way Cookbook

Kale and Swiss chard at Teena's Pride CSA.

with erosion-preventing techniques, like perennial contour strips, than there were a decade ago. I believe that federal agriculture policy is largely responsible because it rewards the quantity of acres planted rather than the quality of practices employed.

But blaming the government isn't sufficient. All farmers have an interest in adopting better farming techniques. I believe that we also have an obligation to do so for the sake of future generations. If global climate change is a product of human use of fossil fuels—and I believe it is—then our farm is a big part of the problem. We burn thousands of gallons of diesel fuel a year in our 10 tractors, undermining the very foundation of our subsistence every time we cultivate a field or put up a bale of hay.

I accept responsibility for my complicity in this, but I also stand ready to accept the challenge of the future, to make serious changes in how I conduct business to produce less carbon. I don't see that I have a choice if I am to hope that the farm will be around for my own great-grandchildren.

But my farm and my neighbors' farms can contribute only so much. Americans need to see our experience as a call for national action. The country must get serious about climate-change legislation and making real changes in our daily lives to reduce carbon emissions. The future of our nation's food supply hangs in the balance.

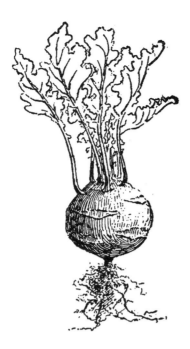

Kohlrabis

BRASSICA OLERACEA, GONGYLODES GROUP

A curious member of the cabbage family, kohlrabi is sometimes called cabbage turnip because its name consists of the German words kohl *(cabbage) and* rabi *(turnip). Some botanists believe that kohlrabi is a hybrid of the two, whereas others maintain that it is actually a variant of mustard; its exact origins are rather mysterious.*

The vegetable's most distinguishing feature is its large, light green (or sometimes purple), globe-shaped swollen stem that grows above ground and is not a root, topped with turnip-like leaves. The plant is grown for this stem, which is crunchy, juicy, sweet, and quite delicately flavored, with a distinct cabbage taste, similar to broccoli stems or turnips.

Most people eat kohlrabi raw, peeling and slicing the vegetable into rounds and sprinkling it with a little salt. But kohlrabi is just as good cooked, braised, steamed, or shredded.

HISTORY

The history of kohlrabi is an elusive one. By some accounts, the vegetable appeared rather suddenly and without explanation in Europe in the middle of the 1500s, but that may be caused more by linguistic confusion than the kohlrabi's actual existence. King Charlemagne ordered kohlrabi grown in his gardens during the Middle Ages, the ancient Romans likely knew of it, and northern and eastern Europeans have consumed it for centuries. In America, kohlrabi is sometimes eaten as part of southern-style mixed greens, and it is popular throughout Africa and Madagascar. Until recently, kohlrabi was not commercially cultivated or available in US supermarkets, and most Americans who wanted to enjoy this unusual vegetable had to grow it in their home gardens. Kohlrabi has also long been cultivated in Europe for livestock food.

NUTRITION

Like other cruciferous vegetables, kohlrabi is very nutritious, containing vitamin C, potassium, iron, thiamine, magnesium, folate, copper, and dietary fiber, all for just 36 calories a cup. Kohlrabi also contains abundant phytonutrients such as sulforaphane and indoles, which have proved in studies to fight cancer, especially prostate, colorectal, and lung. Its green tops are similar to turnip greens in nutrient value and are extremely rich in vitamins A, C, and K.

SEASON

Commercially, kohlrabi is widely grown and available year-round. But it is a cool-season crop and at its best at farmers markets and CSAs in spring and fall.

SELECTION

Choose kohlrabis that are firm, evenly colored, and with fresh green tops. Avoid specimens that are shriveled, cracked, blemished, or have wilted or yellowing leaves. Overly large specimens may be woody.

STORAGE

If their tops are intact, kohlrabi will keep refrigerated in a perforated plastic bag in the refrigerator vegetable crisper for up to 5 days. Detopped bulbs will last longer, keeping for up to 2 to 3 weeks (since the greens deteriorate faster than the roots).

TRIMMING AND CLEANING

Kohlrabi must be peeled before eating. Trim off the tops (save them if desired for cooking), then use a paring knife or a sharp vegetable peeler to cut off the thick outer skin. Wash the leaves thoroughly to remove traces of grit, sand, and insects by submerging them in a sinkful of water and swishing well, then draining.

STEAMING AND BOILING

Steam whole, peeled or unpeeled kohlrabis for 15 to 20 minutes, depending on their size, and sliced kohlrabis for 5 to 10 minutes, or until they are tender when pierced with a fork. Boil cubed, peeled kohlrabis for 15 to 30 minutes, then drain.

STIR-FRYING AND SAUTÉING

Stir-fry or sauté kohlrabi bulbs, cut into ½-inch cubes, in a well-oiled pan or wok over high heat for about 8 minutes, or until crisp-tender. Leeks, jalapeños, and sweet peppers make delicious stir-fry accompaniments. Kohlrabi greens can be sautéed after a quick parboiling for 2 to 7 minutes, depending on their size and thickness.

BAKING AND BRAISING

Bake whole kohlrabis in a 350°F oven for 20 to 30 minutes, depending on their size. Or prepare kohlrabis like oven-roasted potatoes (see the recipe on page 572). To braise, trim and peel the kohlrabis, then cook in butter or pan juices for 10 to 15 minutes over medium heat, or until the kohlrabis are lightly colored and tender.

MICROWAVING

Trim and peel 3 medium kohlrabis, cutting into ¼-inch-thick slices. Place in a covered dish with ¼ cup water and microwave on high power until tender, 10 to 15 minutes, while stirring every 5 minutes. Let stand 5 minutes before serving.

BLANCHING AND FREEZING

Cube or slice kohlrabis into ½-inch-thick pieces, boil for 2 to 3 minutes, and then plunge into ice water for 5 minutes to stop the cooking process. Remove and drain. Package the kohlrabis in zipper-lock freezer or vacuum food sealer-type bags, or freezer containers. Squeeze out any excess air and leave ½ inch of headspace (unless you are using the vacuum sealing method). Frozen kohlrabis will keep for up to 6 months at 0°F.

MEASURES AND EQUIVALENTS

- 4 to 5 medium kohlrabis = 2 pounds = 5 cups chopped

Kohlrabi Kapital

Hamburg Township in Michigan proclaims itself as the Kohlrabi Capital of the world. At its height In 1985, the township's Kohlrabi Festival attracted 600 visitors.

COMPLEMENTARY HERBS, SEASONINGS, AND FOODS

Bacon, béchamel sauce, butter, caraway, chervil, chives, cinnamon, cream, cumin, curry, dill, garlic, ghee, ginger, hollandaise sauce, lemon, lemon thyme, marjoram, mustard, mustard oil, nutmeg, onion, parsley, pork, sausage, thyme, turmeric, vinaigrette dressing.

SERVING SUGGESTIONS

- Boil and mash kohlrabis like potatoes, and serve with butter, salt and pep-per, and other seasonings.
- Combine cubes of kohlrabi with Granny Smith or Yellow Delicious apples and your favorite creamy, sweet or mustard dressing for an unusual, re-freshing summer salad.
- Make a cheesy casserole or gratin with kohlrabi instead of potatoes.
- Try substituting kohlrabi for cabbage in a kohl-slaw.
- Add sliced rounds of kohlrabi to the vegetable relish tray, and serve with your favorite dip.
- Tiny whole kohlrabis or thinly sliced rounds are delicious pickled.
- Prepare kohlrabis cream-style, and pair them with fried chicken and potato salad.
- Roast kohlrabis with other vegetables like carrots, potatoes, turnips, and rutabagas.
- Substitute kohlrabi for cauliflower in an Indian curry.
- Hollow out kohlrabis and prepare like stuffed peppers, filling them with a mixture of ground meat and tomato, or whatever you desire, and baking them in the oven.
- Shred kohlrabis and stir-fry or sauté in fresh herbs and butter.

PARMESAN-BAKED KOHLRABI   SERVES 3 TO 4

> 2 tablespoons breadcrumbs, divided
> 3 medium kohlrabis, peeled and cut into ¼-inch-thick rounds
> 1 tablespoon melted butter
> 2 tablespoons grated Parmesan cheese
> ¼ teaspoon freshly ground black pepper

1. Preheat the oven to 350°F.

2. Butter an 8-inch round pan and dust with ½ tablespoon of the breadcrumbs.

3. In a large pot of salted boiling water, cook the kohlrabi slices until they become just tender, about 7 minutes; drain. Toss with the melt-ed butter.

4. Place the kohlrabi in the prepared pan, and sprinkle with Parmesan cheese, the remaining breadcrumbs, and pepper.

5. Bake for about 1 hour, or until browned.

— Barbara Hunt, mother of Margaret Trott, Featherstone Farm CSA member

A kohlrabi space alien has landed at Sang Lee Farms.

. . . .

Kohlrabi Stuffed with Peppers   Serves 4

Source Note: The slightly sharp flavor of the peppers is an excellent foil for the more earthy flavor of the kohlrabi.

> 4 small kohlrabis (about 6 to 8 ounces each)
> About 1½ cups vegetable stock, heated
> 1 tablespoon olive or sunflower oil
> 1 onion, chopped
> 1 small red bell pepper, seeded and sliced
> 1 small green bell pepper, seeded and sliced
> Salt and freshly ground black pepper
> Flat-leaf parsley, for garnish (optional)

1. Preheat the oven to 350°F.

2. Trim and remove the ends of the kohlrabis, and arrange on the bottom of a medium ovenproof dish. Pour in the stock so it reaches about halfway up the kohlrabis. Cover and braise in the oven for about 30 minutes, until tender. Transfer to a plate and allow to cool, reserving the stock.

3. Heat the oil in a saucepan and cook the onion for 3 to 4 minutes over low heat, stirring occasionally. Add the bell peppers and cook for another 2 to 3 minutes, until the onion is lightly browned (add a bit more oil if the pan seems dry). Add the remaining stock and season with salt and pepper. Simmer, uncovered, over medium heat until the stock has almost evaporated.

4. Holding each kohlrabi gently to keep the outer shell in one piece, use a small spoon to scoop out the flesh. Roughly chop it, then stir the kohlrabi into the onion and pepper mixture. Taste and adjust the seasoning. Arrange the kohlrabi shells in a shallow ovenproof dish.

5. Spoon the filling into the shells. Place them in the oven for 5 to 10 minutes to heat through and then serve, garnished with parsley if desired.

— *Christine Ingram,* Cook's Encyclopedia of Vegetables

7. **Slow-cook a large beef roast, then slice and freeze it** along with its pan juices for serving on busy nights.

8. **A Crock-Pot or a slow cooker is a wonderful timesaver** and is great for making delicious soups, stews, braised meats, and cooked applesauce.

9. **One-pot meals, soups, and stews, frozen in single portions, are great timesavers** and are very versatile. It's easy to freeze single meals in Pyrex or ovenproof glass dishes for later thawing and heating at home or in a microwave oven at work or school.

10. **Prepare fresh-herb ice cubes for instant thawing and seasoning.** Instead of using dried herbs, which often don't have very good flavor or aroma, freeze fresh herbs such as basil, dill, parsley, rosemary, sage, savory, tarragon, and thyme. Chop the herbs finely, mix them into a paste using ⅓ cup of olive oil or cooled, melted butter to every 2 cups of herbs, and then freeze the resulting mixture in ice cube trays. To use, simply pop out however many cubes you need into a strainer and let the oil melt away, or just drop them still frozen into sauces or soups.

 Leeks

Leeks, a member of the onion family, are not popular in North America. This is most unfortunate, because they are a delicious, delicately flavored vegetable. More subtle than onions, leeks are widely adored in France and the British Isles. In Wales, leeks are part of that country's national emblem. Bits of them are worn by Welshmen in their buttonholes on St. David's Day in memory of the victory of King Cadwallader over the Saxons in 640 CE.

Unlike onions, leeks do not form bulbs but instead grow thickened stems, from which sheaths of leaves emerge. The edible part is this stem, which is blanched white by piling soil high around it (trenching), and the light-green portion of the leaves.

In America, the most famous use of leeks is in vichyssoise, that creamy potato-and-leek soup made famous in the mid-1900s by New York City Ritz-Carlton chef Louis Diat, who recalled it from his French childhood. Leeks, however, are very versatile, lending their sophisticated, delicious character to any dish calling for onions.

HISTORY

The precise origin of leeks is a bit contentious. Many sources cite the Mediterranean region, whereas the Irish and other British Isles natives like to claim them for their very own. Shakespeare mentioned leeks in Henry V. On the other side of the globe, the Chinese and ancient Egyptians savored them as far back as recorded history allows. Leeks were described in the Bible as one of the foods that the Israelites missed most when they fled Egypt. The Greek physician Hippocrates prescribed leeks as a cure for nosebleeds, and King Charlemagne had them cultivated in his gardens during the Middle Ages.

NUTRITION

Although not a storehouse of nutrients, leeks do contain manganese, vitamin C, iron, folate, and vitamin B6. A single cup of leeks contains 54 calories. Leeks and other members of the Allium family contain compounds that may reduce the risk of prostate and colon cancer when eaten three or more times a week.

SEASON

Commercially, leeks are widely grown and available year-round. But their peak season at farmers markets and CSAs is from April through September.

SELECTION

Leeks should be firm and fresh looking, with bright green leaves and long thick stalks. Avoid leeks that are split, bruised, or overly large, which signal old age and toughness. Try to select leeks that are all the same size for more consistent cooking if you plan to prepare them whole.

STORAGE

Leeks should be stored unwashed and loosely wrapped in a perforated plastic bag in the refrigerator vegetable crisper. They will keep for up to 1 or 2 weeks this way.

TRIMMING AND CLEANING

Leeks grow in sandy soil that is piled high around their thick stems to make them turn white (and stay mild and tender). As a result, their layered foliage often conceals a surprising amount of grit. Trim off the large, dark-green leaves (save them for making stock) and cut off the root end. Then cut the leek lengthwise into halves and run those exposed areas under running water to rinse away dirt. Another method is to cut the leeks crosswise into small pieces (typically about ¼ inch), then swish the pieces in a bowl of cold water. Let the dirt settle, and lift the leeks out of the water.

STEAMING AND BOILING

Leeks are particularly susceptible to overcooking, which makes them mushy and tasteless. They should be cooked just long enough to be tender but still offer a little resistance when a fork comes to call at their bases. Whole leeks can be steamed for 10 to 15 minutes; sliced leeks for 5 minutes. Avoid boiling leeks, which makes them waterlogged and far less flavorful.

STIR-FRYING AND SAUTÉING

Sauté thinly sliced leeks in a bit of oil or butter on medium heat for 3 to 5 minutes, or until tender. Leeks can be stir-fried over high heat for 2 to 3 minutes.

BAKING AND ROASTING

Roasting leeks in the oven is one of the best ways to prepare this vegetable, as it concentrates their flavor and accentuates their sweetness. Preheat the oven to 400°F, trim and clean whole leeks, slice them in half lengthwise or leave them whole, and brush with olive oil or butter. Place the leeks in an oiled shallow roasting pan, sprinkle with salt and pepper, and roast for 35 to 45 minutes, occasionally basting them with the pan juices or a bit more oil or butter to keep them moist.

BRAISING AND STEWING

To braise or stew leeks, arrange them in a shallow dish or pan and barely cover them with broth or water. Bring to a boil and simmer gently, uncovered, until done, about 20 to 30 minutes for whole leeks and 10 to 15 minutes for sliced or chopped leeks.

MICROWAVING

Whole leeks will not cook evenly in the microwave, so cut them into 1-inch pieces, put them in a microwavable dish, and add 2 tablespoons of water. Cook on high power for 5 to 8 minutes, stirring halfway through.

BLANCHING AND FREEZING

Leeks can be frozen, although freezing destroys some of their taste and texture. Blanch them for 2 minutes in rapidly boiling water, then plunge

No Leeked Secrets

Growing leeks becomes serious business in the North East of England, where an unusual annual contest is held in late September.

No grower worth his leek will reveal the secret of his prizewinning vegetable, which can reach 3½ to 4 inches in diameter.

Rumors fly that the biggest leeks are fed brown sugar and wine. Leeks are marked weeks in advance to prevent cheating and vandalizing.

them into ice water for 2 minutes to stop the cooking process. Remove and drain. Cut them into ½-inch pieces so you can easily pour out what you need, and store them in zipper-lock freezer or vacuum food sealer-type bags. Squeeze out any excess air and leave ½ inch of headspace (unless you are using the vacuum sealing method). Frozen leeks will keep for up to 3 months at 0°F.

Measures and Equivalents

- 1 medium leek = 1 side dish serving
- ½ cup cooked leeks = 1 serving
- 1 pound leeks = 2 cups chopped
- 1¼ pounds leeks = 2 large leeks or 3 medium leeks
- 2 pounds leeks = 1 pound trimmed = about 4 cups chopped = 2 cups chopped and cooked

Complementary Herbs, Seasonings, and Foods

Artichokes, asparagus, bacon, basil, béchamel sauce, beets, breadcrumbs, butter, cabbage, capers, celery, cheese (goat, Cheddar, Gruyère, Parmesan), chervil, chicken, cream, crème fraîche, curry, eggs, fennel, fish, green garlic, ham, hazelnut oil, hollandaise sauce, lemon, mustard, olives, olive oil, Parmesan cheese, parsley, peas, potatoes, red wine, saffron, sage, tarragon, thyme, tomatoes, veal, vinaigrette, walnut oil, white wine.

Serving Suggestions

- Leeks become creamy and subtly sweet when baked. Serve them hot or cold with vinaigrette dressing, or layer them in a dish with ham and cheese and bake until they are hot and bubbling.
- Sprinkle thinly sliced raw leeks atop salads.
- Don't throw away the trimmed darker green tops; they make wonderful soup stock.
- Bake leeks and asparagus together and top with hollandaise sauce for a first-class dish worthy of royalty—or your family.
- Throw oiled and seasoned leeks on the grill along with tomatoes and peppers for a tasty summer treat.
- Braise whole, halved, or chopped leeks in chicken or meat stock until the leeks are soft and glazed.
- Mix finely chopped raw leeks with sour cream, a little pepper, and Worcestershire sauce for a refined chip dip.
- For a delicious, hearty vegetable side dish, place leeks, sweet potato wedges, and whole garlic cloves in a casserole dish and drizzle with olive oil, seasoned salt or Old Bay seasoning, and pepper. Cover and bake in a 375°F oven for about 1 hour, or until the sweet potatoes are tender.
- Braised leeks make a sumptuous accompaniment to rich meats like roast pork, beef, and lamb.
- Sauté leeks with fennel for a tasty, surprise vegetable side dish.

. . . .

Potato Leek Soup   Serves 6

1 tablespoon extra-virgin olive oil
1 tablespoon unsalted butter

3 cups leeks, white and part of the green included, well-washed
    and chopped
½ cup chopped onions
6 cups cubed potatoes (any variety), skins on
1 carrot, diced
1 rib celery, chopped
7 cups vegetable stock or water
1 teaspoon salt
1 cup milk or soy milk
Freshly ground black pepper

1. Heat the oil and butter in a medium soup pot. Stir in the leeks and onions. Cook on low heat, without browning, for 5 minutes.

2. Add the potatoes, carrot, celery, stock, and salt. Bring to a boil, decrease the heat and simmer for 40 minutes, or until the potatoes are fork-tender.

3. Let the soup cool slightly. Puree it in a blender or run it through a food mill.

4. Add the milk. Return the soup to the pot and gently reheat. Do not let it boil, as this will scald the milk. Season to taste with additional salt and pepper, and serve.

— *Tracy, Featherstone Farm CSA member*

CHIOGGIA BEET SLAW
ON A BED OF GRILLED LEEKS   SERVES 4

¼ cup plain Greek-style yogurt
1 tablespoon fresh lemon juice
1 teaspoon finely grated orange zest
3 tablespoons fresh orange juice
5 Chioggia (candy-stripe) beets, julienned or grated (or use
    red or golden beets)
1 medium carrot, julienned or grated
Salt and freshly ground black pepper

Whisk the yogurt, lemon juice, and orange zest and juice in a medium bowl. Add the beets and carrot, and toss to combine. Season to taste with salt and pepper, and set aside to let the flavors blend.

VINAIGRETTE

4 teaspoons Dijon mustard
3 tablespoons white-wine vinegar
½ cup extra-virgin olive oil
⅓ cup finely chopped fresh basil
Salt and freshly ground black pepper to taste

eat is actually imported from Asia and Europe, whereas the vast majority of the Alaskan salmon and Gulf Coast shrimp paradoxically is sent to Asia, never making it into the mouths of Americans.

As consumers, we can and should do something about this. Our most powerful tools are our pocketbooks and personal will.

- *Make an effort to shop local and organic.* Support your local CSA, think twice before buying those melons shipped in from Chile in the dead of winter, and shop at farmers markets when possible. Get to know your local farmers and their growing practices. Keeping your dollars in the local food system helps everyone involved in that system. And buying organic or sustainably farmed food raised or grown without inputs from harmful pesticides and commercial fertilizers means you support a healthier planet and environment.

- *Dine out at restaurants that source their ingredients from local farms and producers.* Let these places know that you appreciate and support their food policies.

- *Don't buy and eat processed food.* About 80 percent of the food items in a typical American supermarket are highly processed and contain refined grains, sugars, hydrogenated fats, preservatives, additives, and artificial colorings, with harmful or unknown long-term health effects. Your body is your temple—why feed it questionable food?

- *Grow your own.* If it is feasible, try raising some of your fruits and vegetables yourself, either in your backyard or in a community garden.

Combine all of the vinaigrette ingredients.

GRILLED LEEKS

12 medium leeks, trimmed to about 7 inches, split lengthwise to within 1½ inches of the root end
Olive oil for grilling

1. Tie the leeks in 4 bundles with kitchen string, and put them in a kettle of boiling salted water. Boil them for 6 minutes or until they are just tender.

2. Cut away the strings and refresh the leeks under cold running water (or drop them into a large bowl of ice water). Arrange them upside down in a colander to drain.

3. Brush the leeks with olive oil and grill them on an oiled rack for 5 minutes on each side, or until they are golden. Transfer the leeks as they are grilled to a platter and keep warm.

4. Drizzle the vinaigrette over the leeks and top with the Chioggia slaw.

— *Karolina Tracz, Nash's Organic Produce, Sequim, Washington*

VEGAN SUN-DRIED TOMATO AND LEEK QUICHE

SERVES 4

Source Note: This sun-dried tomato and leek quiche is a must-have recipe in your repertoire. It is the kind of dish that can be served for any meal at any time of the day; eat it for breakfast or bring it for a simple lunch. For a dinner option, serve this tasty quiche with a light green salad. It is a delicious dish that will satisfy vegans and nonvegans alike. And if you don't have small tart pans, one 9-inch pan will work nicely.

CRUST

1 cup whole wheat pastry flour
¼ cup pine nuts
¼ cup whole almonds
¼ teaspoon baking powder
¼ cup unsweetened almond milk
2 tablespoons olive oil
¼ teaspoon salt

1. Preheat the oven to 350°F.

2. Coat four 5-inch tart pans with cooking spray.

3. Pulse the flour, pine nuts, almonds, and baking powder in a food processor until finely ground.

4. Whisk together the almond milk, olive oil, and salt in bowl. Stir in the flour mixture. Press into the tart pans.

5. Bake for 5 minutes, then cool.

FILLING

4 tablespoons olive oil, divided

1 large leek, washed, white and light green parts chopped (about 2 cups)

12 ounces extra-firm tofu, drained and cut into 1½-inch cubes

2 tablespoons fresh lemon juice

2 teaspoons miso paste

1 clove garlic, minced

¾ teaspoon salt

1 cup panko breadcrumbs

1 teaspoon Italian seasoning (or combine dried thyme and oregano, or use a mix of fresh herbs)

¼ cup chopped, reconstituted sun-dried tomatoes, drained

1. Heat 1 tablespoon of the olive oil in a skillet over medium heat. Add the leek and sauté for 8 minutes, or until softened. Set aside.

2. Bring a large saucepan of water to a boil. Add the tofu, and simmer 5 minutes. Drain and pat dry.

3. Whisk the remaining 3 tablespoons of olive oil with the lemon juice, miso, garlic, and salt in a bowl. Add the tofu and blend until smooth with an immersion blender. Stir in the breadcrumbs, seasonings, sun-dried tomatoes, and leeks. Spoon the filling into the crusts.

4. Bake for 30 to 40 minutes, or until the crusts are browned and the filling has set.

5. Cool for 5 minutes, then unmold.

— *Foodista.com*

Tropical serenity at Kahumana Farm.

Mustard Greens

BRASSICA JUNCEA

Mention mustard greens to different ethnic groups, and you will likely hear them talking about completely different plants. The mustard family, which started as a single species called Brassica juncea, *is now a diverse, confusing one. It has evolved into nearly 20 different subgroups, all with distinct leaf characteristics and flavors, but scattered across various continents.*

The most common mustard green that you will see in your CSA box or at your farmers market is the American or southern (also sometimes called curled) mustard, which has distinctive, large, heavily veined, very curly-edged leaves and a potent, spicy taste. Munch a big leaf and you may think of horseradish (once your sinuses clear and your eyes stop watering). Other mustards are more often seen in Asian markets: wrapped heart mustard, bamboo mustard (sometimes called gai choy), red-in-snow mustard, giant-leafed mustard (also called purple mustard or red mustard), and the diminutive but delicious garlic mustard. Culinarily, these mustards are not interchangeable with the American mustard, as they each have their own characteristics that require individual treatment. This chapter covers American mustard only.

HISTORY

Mustard greens probably originated in the Asian Himalayas; from there they spread to India, China, and the Caucasus regions, where they have been enjoyed for thousands of years. To this day, many of the mustard greens most commonly eaten are Asian varieties that are little known outside their home countries and in Asian markets.

American or curled mustard probably traveled to the New World on African slave ships, where it firmly established itself as an essential part of soul food, with its "mess o' greens" and accompanying pot liquor.

NUTRITION

Mustard greens are outstanding sources of vitamins A, B6, C, E, K, folate, manganese, dietary fiber, calcium, and tryptophan. They are also packed with phytonutrients and beta-carotenes that have antioxidant and possibly anticancer properties. A 1-cup serving of chopped mustard greens contains only 15 calories.

SEASON

Commercially, mustard greens are widely grown and available year-round. But their peak season at farmers markets and CSAs is during the winter months, from December through April.

SELECTION

Look for fresh, crisp bunches with no wilted or yellowing leaves, which indicate mustard well past its prime. Larger, older leaves often pack more heat than very small, young ones, although size is not always a reliable indicator of taste and heat. The only sure way to know is to taste a leaf.

STORAGE

Mustard greens should be stored unwashed in a perforated plastic bag in the refrigerator vegetable crisper, where they will keep for up to 5 days. Mustard prefers high humidity, and benefits from a light misting before storing, or you can wrap the leaves in moist paper towels. Avoid storing mustard greens next to fruits that emit ethylene gas, such as apples, avocados, pears, and bananas, for the gas breaks down chlorophyll and can promote spoilage in green vegetables.

TRIMMING AND CLEANING

Mustard greens should be thoroughly rinsed in several changes of tepid water to flush out hiding insects or lurking soil. Unless the leaves are young and small, the central stem is likely to be quite tough and should be cut away from the foliage and discarded before cooking. An easy way to trim mustard greens and other large flat leaves is to fold them in half lengthwise along the stem, and cut or pull away the leaf part.

STEAMING AND BOILING

Steam mustard greens over rapidly boiling water for 8 to 12 minutes, depending on the leaves' size and age. Mustard greens can also be slow-simmered as you would collards for southern-style greens. Or for faster preparation, cook them in rapidly boiling water for 2 to 4 minutes, then plunge them into ice water to halt the cooking process.

STIR-FRYING AND SAUTÉING

Mustard greens can be stir-fried or sautéed in a little broth or oil, garlic, and seasonings over high heat for about 5 minutes, or until they are wilted.

MICROWAVING

Freshly washed mustard greens can be microwaved with just the water clinging to their leaves. Place them in a microwave-safe dish and cook on high power for 7 to 10 minutes, or until they become tender; stir halfway through cooking.

BLANCHING AND FREEZING

Freezing works well with mustard greens. After washing, trimming, and cutting them into 1-inch pieces, blanch the leaves in rapidly boiling water for 3 minutes; then plunge them into ice water for 5 minutes to stop the cooking process. Remove and drain. Squeeze out the excess water and place them in zipper-lock freezer or vacuum food sealer-type bags, or freezer containers. Squeeze out any excess air and leave ½ inch of headspace (unless you are using the vacuum sealing method). Frozen mustard greens will keep for up to 1 year at 0°F.

EQUIVALENTS, MEASURES, AND SERVINGS

- 1 pound = 2 cups cooked

"The best comfort food will always be greens, cornbread, and fried chicken."

— *Maya Angelou,
American poet and writer*

Zen and the Art of CSA Membership

Katie Sherman
Former Community
Outreach Coordinator
Featherstone Farm
Rushford, Minnesota

What is the CSA experience all about? Often the term itself comes out of nowhere, from a friend, a newspaper article, or an event where you scratch your head and think, "What kind of of initialism is that?" After that, you begin to notice it more. You see advertisements for farms, hear about it on the radio, and find that your neighbor has subscribed to one too. You're now a part of the club. But what happens afterward?

Being a CSA member involves being a savvy, creative individual. You get a boxful of bountiful produce each week, and it's up to you to transform and bring it to your table. It's like an artist with 12 colors staring at an empty canvas! However, being a member also means possessing the dual characteristics of going where the current may lead and acting on something when the time (or the CSA box) arrives. Fortunately you have help from the farm, great ideas on storage and preparation, and the motivation to eat more nourishing food, all of which will be your muse in the kitchen.

Only once you see the contents of your box does the transformative process come into play. Though starting with a whole box of produce was at first a bit overwhelming for me, I learned to slowly put together a puzzle in my mind. The simple thought process goes something like this: Here is what I have in my box, here is what I already have in my refrigerator and pantry, here are my cookbooks; let's make some magic.

After paging through my recipes in books, combing through my tat-

Bacon, balsamic vinegar, black pepper, butter, capers, cashews, chiles, coconut milk, cream, curry, duck, garlic, ginger, goose, ham, lemon, mint, mustard, mustard oil, nuts, olives, olive oil, onions, peanuts, peanut oil, pork, salt pork, sausage, seafood, sesame, shallots, soy sauce, vinegar, walnuts.

SERVING SUGGESTIONS

- Mustard greens are wonderful in curries and other spicy concoctions, especially if tempered a bit with cream or coconut milk.

- Sauté mustard greens and sprinkle with a little lemon juice, walnuts, or pine nuts.

- The next time you make southern-style greens, try combinations of collards, mustard greens, kale, and turnip and beet greens, slow-simmered with ham hocks or salt pork and seasoned with hot peppers and vinegar.

- When you feel yourself coming down with a cold or flu, stir young or finely shredded mustard greens into steaming miso or chicken broth, along with mushrooms and plenty of garlic for a healthful, sinus-clearing alternative to chicken soup.

- The next time you have a large holiday ham, make a most wondrous soup from the leftovers with chopped ham, potatoes, cream, and mustard greens. If you have a genuine country ham like a Smithfield, even better!

- For Chinese-style greens, sauté with fresh ginger, garlic, soy sauce, or oyster sauce. Finish with a little sesame oil or chile paste. Or stir-fry with scallion, garlic, and fermented black beans.

- Larger mustard greens make a piquant, sharp-tasting wrap. Lightly steam or braise the leaves, with or without filling, or wrap them around choice pieces of tuna, cod, or salmon.

- Chop raw or cooked mustard greens and mix them into pasta salads, rice, beans, and casseroles.

- Mix a few young mustard greens in with lettuces and spinach in your next green salad to add a zesty kick.

MUSTARD GREENS WITH PEPPER VINEGAR

SERVES 6 TO 8

> 6 bunches mustard greens
> Salt
> 4 or 5 slices salt-cured hog jowls or thick bacon
> 1 large clove garlic, minced
> 1 teaspoon sugar
> Freshly ground black pepper
> Pepper vinegar (see the Cooking Note below)

1. Wash the greens by stripping the leaves from the stems (discard the stems) and placing them in a sink filled with cold water. Sprinkle a tablespoon of salt over them and swish them around. Allow the sediment to settle, and lift out the greens, shaking off the excess water but not drying them.

2. In a heavy-bottomed pot over medium-low heat, fry the jowls until they become just translucent and curled, about 5 minutes. Add the garlic, being careful not to burn it. Add the wet greens and sugar, and cover. Stir and lift the greens as they wilt during cooking. Cook for 1 hour or until they are tender, stirring occasionally.

3. Taste the cooking liquid ("pot liquor") and add salt and pepper if necessary. Allow to drain slightly as the greens are served. Sprinkle with pepper vinegar.

Cooking Note: Pepper vinegar is made in most places by pouring about one quarter of the vinegar out of a cider-vinegar bottle and then filling it with hot peppers. The peppers are then marinated for several days.

— *Lee Bailey,* Lee Bailey's Southern Food

. . . .

SMOTHERED GREENS WITH TURKEY   SERVES 5

Author Note: Traditionally, pork fatback would be used in this type of dish. If you'd like to experience it, try the fatback—at least once! For a version that is more healthful, use the smoked turkey—it will flavor the dish beautifully as well.

3 cups water
¼ pound skinless smoked turkey breast, chopped
1 tablespoon minced fresh chile, such as jalapeño or serrano
¼ teaspoon cayenne pepper
¼ teaspoon ground cloves
2 cloves garlic, crushed
½ teaspoon fresh thyme
1 scallion (green onion), chopped
1 teaspoon ground ginger
¼ cup chopped onion
2 pounds greens (mustard, turnip, collard, kale, or a mixture)

1. Wash the greens thoroughly, remove the stems, and tear or cut the leaves into bite-size pieces.

2. Place all of the ingredients except the greens into a large saucepan and bring to a boil.

3. Add the greens to the pot.

4. Cook for 20 to 30 minutes, partially covered, or until the greens are tender. Season to taste with salt and pepper.

— *Health.gov*

tered manila folder, or scouring the Internet, the path begins to emerge in what dinners I'll prepare for that week: *Well, yeah, this recipe sounds good, but I don't have any cucumbers (out). Or, Bingo! I've got celeriac and parsnips for this killer soup (in). And maybe it's a, Hmmm … for this one all I need to get is some cheddar at the store (maybe).* And so the process goes. It is starting with basic elements and allowing them to take you where you will be led. For those of us who get great satisfaction from checking off list items, piecing together meals often provides a similar result.

The work has been made even easier lately with cool apps, websites, and small businesses that are enthusiastically jumping on the CSA bandwagon. Companies such as Local Thyme, based out of Madison, Wisconsin, are providing custom menus for specific farms each week CSA members receive a box (including Featherstone!). Then there are websites like Featherstone's, which sorts recipes according to what ingredients you have on hand (even going further to prompt you, "Do you have …?"). Technology has come full circle to give us a major hand in food preparation.

Beyond the dinner-making decision process, CSA membership is also about attitude. Most members I meet are enthusiastic and willing to try new things. When it's October and there is no more basil around, they're game for enjoying a meal with walnuts, roasted beets, and winter squash. They also either already know how to or learn how to plan, using their CSA box as a base and working from there to arrange meals. Even a printable menu plan can be of great assistance.

Lastly, it's about appreciation. Many CSA members speak about their joy at getting strawberries in the box, or the whiff of fresh sweet corn. At Featherstone, it's the sweet fall carrots that do people in. They are joyful, because they know that

CURRIED MUSTARD GREENS AND GARBANZO BEANS WITH SWEET POTATOES   SERVES 4

2 medium sweet potatoes, peeled and thinly sliced
1 tablespoon chicken or vegetable broth, plus up to
    ½ cup additional
1 medium onion, halved and thinly sliced
2 medium cloves garlic, sliced
½ teaspoon curry powder
¼ teaspoon turmeric
2 cups mustard greens, rinsed and chopped
1½ cups cooked garbanzo beans (chickpeas), or 1 (15-ounce) can,
    drained
1 (15-ounce) can sodium-free diced tomatoes
Salt and freshly ground white pepper
2 tablespoons extra-virgin olive oil

1. Steam the sweet potatoes for approximately 5 to 8 minutes.

2. While steaming the potatoes, heat 1 tablespoon of the broth in a 12-inch skillet. Sauté the onion in the broth over medium heat for 4 to 5 minutes, stirring frequently, until it turns translucent. Add the garlic, curry powder, turmeric, and mustard greens. Cook, stirring occasionally, until the mustard greens are wilted, about 5 minutes. Add the garbanzo beans, diced tomatoes, salt, and pepper. Cook for another 5 minutes.

3. Mash the steamed sweet potatoes with the olive oil, and season to taste with salt and pepper. If you need to thin the potatoes, add a little more broth. Serve the mustard greens with the mashed sweet potatoes.

— Produce for Better Health; Fruits & Veggies—More Matters; Centers for Disease Control and Prevention

Pears

In this age of hyper-hybridized produce for large-scale cultivation and shipping, the pear is a rare fruit that has been mercifully left alone; the varieties you see in markets today are pretty much unchanged from over a century ago. About 3,000 varieties exist worldwide. Pears require quite specific conditions to thrive and are very vulnerable to disease and blights; thus, nearly 95 percent of the US crop is grown in the drier climes of California, Oregon, and Washington.

Pears are quite unusual among fruits in that they ripen from the inside out; this explains why we often get pears that look ripe and delicious on the outside but reveal disappointing mushy, brown rottenness radiating from their cores. For this reason, pears need to be picked when they are still hard, and ripened afterward; tree-ripened fruit is almost always spoiled. Still, guessing that exact moment when pears are at their sweetest, juiciest, and most flavorful is an elusive, frustrating art; as Ralph Waldo Emerson once said, "There are only ten minutes in the life of a pear when it is perfect to eat."

Although the modern American experience of pears lies in eating them fresh and cooked, there is a long, storied tradition (especially in France and England) of making pears into hard cider, pear brandy, and another alcoholic drink called perry. In fact, many heirloom pear varieties are grown in Europe strictly for making these distinctive beverages, which are as complex and distinctive as many wine varietals. Colonial America used both apples and pears to make ciders and perry, but the tradition waned once safe drinking water became available and other beverages became more popular. Now that artisan hard ciders are making a comeback on the American gastronomic scene and US distilleries have picked up on the trend, we hope it is only a matter of time before a new generation gets to taste pears in this delectable form.

Here are a few types of pears you might find in your CSA box or at your farmers market.

Anjou
This is a large, slightly squat pear that comes in either red or bright green. Its flesh is on the firmer side, with a mellow, slightly spicy flavor and a smooth, juicy texture. It is great for cooking as well as for eating raw.

Asian
Contrary to popular belief, Asian pears are not crosses between apples and regular pears, even though their characteristics might lead you to believe otherwise. Many Asian pears have the rounded shape of apples, and their flesh is crisp, not melting. However, their flavor is distinctively pear-like, with some notes of honey and spice, and they can be quite juicy.

Bartlett
This greenish-gold or red fruit epitomizes classic pear flavor and shape. When ripe, its flesh is meltingly soft, very juicy, and fragrant, with citrusy

notes. It is fantastic for eating fresh (indeed it is hard to imagine consuming it any other way), but it's also a popular canning and baking pear.

Bosc

This variety has a very distinct russet brown skin and a slender, tapered neck. Its sweet flesh has assertively smoky, almost musky notes, and its firmness makes it outstanding for poaching and baking, since it doesn't fall apart in cooking.

Comice

Often considered the queen of pears, the Comice is unrivaled in peardom for its complex flavor, buttery texture, floral fragrance, and dripping juiciness. The season for these squat, wide-bottomed green gems is always eagerly awaited and way too brief.

Concorde

This variety resembles a green Bosc, with a long, tapering neck. It's a pleasant pear, sweet with vanilla notes, and good for baking and poaching. Its flesh does not brown in the air as quickly as other pears, making it especially good in salads and as a garnish.

Seckel

These tiny, chubby pears are uncommon, but well worth pouncing on if you come across them. They range from dark green with a maroon blush to nearly all red, with very dense, super-sweet flesh that has a rich, winey, spicy taste. They make excellent poached pears and, because of their petite size, make beautiful individual servings.

HISTORY

The exact origin of pears is debated, but evidence exists that European and Asian varieties evolved separately in parts of the Old World, North Africa, and Asia. Pears are one of humanity's oldest foraged and cultivated foods, dating back to prehistoric times. Throughout history the fruit has been revered, with frequent mentions in religion, literature, and folklore. In 19th-century France, England, Belgium, and America, an interest in growing and breeding pears exploded. Interestingly, two of the most popular pears today, the Seckel and Comice, were discovered by chance in Philadelphia and France, respectively; as with many fruits that go on to be commercially successful, they were likely mutants growing in the orchards of curious farmers who knew great fruits when they tasted them.

NUTRITION

To anyone who has ever savored a pear in its full glory, it won't be any surprise that pears are very high in fruit sugars. But they also contain significant amounts of vitamins C and K, as well as some riboflavin, folate, magnesium, potassium, manganese, and copper. A single medium pear contains about 100 calories.

SEASON

Pears are one of the few fruits and vegetables that, even as a commercial crop, has a specific season. The Anjou is typically available year-round, but September is when the Bartletts, Boscs, and Comices show up, and October is really when pears hit their peak.

SELECTION

Different pear varieties vary widely in texture, color, flavor, and degree of firmness at their prime, but all good pears should be smooth-skinned, heavy for their size, and plump with no signs of desiccation or large bruised areas (although pears with soft spots are often just fine for cooking). Two signs of perfect ripeness: if a pear gives slightly just below its stem, and a profuse perfume.

STORAGE

Pears ripen very well at home, so there's no need to worry if the pears you find at the market or in your CSA box are as hard as rocks. Keep them at room temperature until they start to soften. You can hasten their ripening by placing them in a paper bag with a ripe apple or banana; their combined ethylene gas will do the trick. Once the pears have ripened to the point you like, store them in a perforated plastic bag in the refrigerator.

TRIMMING AND CLEANING

You can choose to peel the fruit or not, depending on your preference and the dish you're preparing. (But also be aware that conventionally grown pears tend to have high levels of pesticide residue on their skins, which is why you should always try to buy organic pears if possible. A mixture of 1 part vinegar to 3 parts water can help strip off some of this residue.)

Most pears will turn brown once they are peeled or their flesh is exposed to air; this is mostly harmless, but it may affect their flavor and texture after a while. To prevent this, place the sliced fruit in a bowl of water mixed with some lemon juice.

There is, of course, the matter of the narrow central core and the hard little seeds within, which should not be eaten. It's best to core pears before cooking them.

BAKING AND ROASTING

Baking softens and caramelizes pears, rendering them rich and flavorful. And it's easy too: Just cut them in half, scoop out their cores, and place them in a baking dish; top them with cinnamon, nuts, and brown sugar or honey; pour a little water in the bottom of the dish to keep them from sticking; and bake in a 350°F oven for 30 to 40 minutes, or until they are soft but not mushy.

MICROWAVING

To bake pears more quickly, you can microwave whole or cut fruit for 3 to 4 minutes on high power.

POACHING

Pears and poaching go together even better than babies and diapers. Poaching involves long, very gentle cooking and is an excellent method of preparing pears with less-than-optimal flavor. Use firmer pears like

They also help neighborhoods plant new trees and orchards and rehabilitate neglected trees. Surplus fruit is donated to local food distribution programs. You just register your tree, its location, type of fruit, and when it's ripe, and volunteers will show up to pick it.

If you have fruit in your backyard, sometimes it is tough to know whom to call for help in picking it. *Falling Fruit* is a global online resource that lists organizations growing food in public urban spaces (such as food forests and public orchards), picking food (urban foraging and farm gleaning), or distributing food (swaps and donations). Organizations are listed by country, state or province (if applicable), and city.

Falling Fruit is a massive, collaborative map of the urban harvest. Uniting the efforts of foragers, foresters, and freegans everywhere, the map points to more than half a million food-producing locations around the world. It relies on a rapidly growing user community to continuously explore, edit, and add to the map.

Although Falling Fruit lists far more than just fruit-picking resources, it can be handy place to start. And sometimes that's all you need.

Boscs, Seckels, or Anjous; softer varieties like Bartletts and Comices will fall apart. Quarter the pears and submerge them in a pot with enough cold water to cover them completely (note that many recipes call for using white or red wine as part of the poaching liquid, a step that will increase the complexity of flavors). Add spices and sweeteners to taste, such as cinnamon, ginger slices, black peppercorns, allspice berries, lemon, star anise, vanilla beans, wine, honey, and sugar (use about 1⅓ cups sugar per quart of water). Heat the water until it just barely simmers; then maintain for 15 to 25 minutes—depending on the size and firmness of the pears—until the pears are soft and completely cooked through. The cooking liquid will reduce considerably in the process; you can further concentrate the flavors after poaching by removing the pears, straining out the spices, and then cooking the liquid over medium-high heat until it becomes a thick syrup. This is absolutely scrumptious drizzled over the poached pears.

BLANCHING AND FREEZING

Pears can easily be frozen for enjoying all year long. Wash, core, and thinly slice them. To prevent them from turning an unsightly brown, dip each slice in a bowl of water mixed with either ascorbic acid (vitamin C crystals) or lemon juice, or brush them with the mixture. Arrange them in a single layer on a tray lined with parchment or wax paper and freeze. Package the slices in zipper-lock freezer or vacuum food sealer-type bags, or freezer containers. Squeeze out any excess air and leave 1 inch of headspace (unless you are using the vacuum sealing method). Frozen pears will keep for up to 1 year at 0°F.

You can also freeze pears using a sugar syrup. To make the sugar syrup, dissolve 2 cups of sugar in 3 cups of cold water in a pot and bring to a boil. Place the pear slices in the boiling syrup for 1 to 2 minutes, then drain and cool. Package them in zipper-lock freezer bags, jars, or freezer containers. Squeeze out any excess air, and leave ½ inch of headspace for pints, 1 inch for quarts. These frozen slices will keep for up to 6 or 8 months at 0°F.

EQUIVALENTS, MEASURES, AND SERVINGS

- 1 pound = 4 medium pears = 2 cups slices

COMPLEMENTARY HERBS, SEASONINGS, AND FOODS

Allspice, almonds, almond extract, anise, apples, apricots, arugula, bacon, beets, berries, black pepper, brown sugar, butter, caramel, cardamom, cheese (blue, feta, goat, Parmesan, cream cheese), chestnuts, chocolate, cinnamon, citrus, cranberries, cream, currants, fennel, figs, ginger, goose, ham, hazelnuts, honey, ice cream, lemon, maple syrup, nutmeg, oatmeal, pine nuts, pork, quince, rosemary, vanilla, veal, walnuts.

SERVING SUGGESTIONS

- Pears are wonderful in pies and tarts, either by themselves or with other fruits like apples and quince. Brown sugar, maple, vanilla, cinnamon, nutmeg, almond extract, and lemon are terrific flavor complements.

- Instead of applesauce, make pear sauce! This is a good way to process and preserve a lot of pears at one time, and it makes an excellent snack, breakfast food, kid treat, or topping for cottage cheese.

- Cut up pears and combine them with other fruits and berries for a fruit salad.
- Sometimes the simple things are best—like pear slices with a little whipped cream, cinnamon, nutmeg, and sugar. Or poached pears drizzled with warm chocolate sauce.
- Baked or poached pears are an easy dessert that taste especially grand on cold winter days. So are pear crisps, crumbles, and cobblers.
- Add pears to vegetable salads for extra crunch and sweetness. They go especially well with nuts, celery, bacon, and beets.
- If you have a perfectly ripe Comice pear, not much can—or should—be done to improve it. Serve it with fresh walnuts, a little blue cheese, and some port or sherry, and your day will improve by leaps and bounds.
- Use halved, scooped-out pears as handy holders for oatmeal or fruit.
- Pears are lovely in jams, jellies, chutneys, and fruit salsas; take advantage of their brief season to cook and prepare them in ways for savoring long after the fresh fruit is a distant memory.

. . . .

PEAR AND WATERCRESS SALAD

SERVES 4

Source Note: The lemon juice and truffle oil make a delicious vinaigrette for coating the salad.

2 firm ripe pears
2 tablespoons fresh thyme leaves, chopped
2 teaspoons white truffle oil (you can substitute olive oil)
1 teaspoon salt
2 tablespoons pine nuts, toasted
2 teaspoons fresh lemon juice
1 teaspoon freshly ground black pepper
2 bunches watercress, rinsed, dried, large stems removed
Small chunk Parmigiano-Reggiano (Parmesan) cheese, shaved

1. Peel the pears if you'd like, then remove the cores and slice the pear pieces into small, julienned strips.

2. In a bowl, combine the thyme, truffle oil, salt, pine nuts, lemon juice, and pepper.

3. Add the watercress to the bowl and toss everything together. Finish with shavings of Parmesan cheese.

— *Esther McRae, adapted from Greg Atkinson*

. . . .

PAUL'S BARTLETT PEAR AND BLACK PEPPER PIE

ONE 9-INCH PIE

Source Note: The black pepper gives the pears just enough of an edge to make guests wonder what delightful thing they're eating.

Paul's Blue-Ribbon Pie Dough

▸ *Cooking Note:* I use lard because I think it yields the flakiest pastry. You can substitute butter or any solidified vegetable shortening. Additionally, I do this by hand, but that's just me. This same recipe will work in a food processor so long as you're using the dough blade and not the metal cutting blade. This amount will yield more than enough dough for a two-crust pie.

2½ cups all-purpose flour
1 teaspoon salt
½ teaspoon sugar
1 cup cold lard
½ cup ice water

1. Put all of the ingredients, including the bowl in which you'll make the dough, in the refrigerator for 1 hour before you start making it.

2. After chilling, mix the flour, salt, and sugar together in the cold bowl. Cut the chilled lard into small pieces and work it into the dry mix with a fork. When the lard and the dry mixture are blended, it will have the consistency of coarse meal. Remember to work quickly, because you can't allow the mixture to warm up.

3. Add the ice water in small drips and work the dough after every addition of water. After you have ¼ cup of the water worked in, slow down and start to test the dough after each time you add more water. Test the dough by squeezing a pinch between your fingers. If it's crumbly, then add more water. When it holds its shape and approaches the consistency of modeling clay, stop adding water. Work the dough into a ball with your hands and wrap it in plastic wrap. Put the dough back in the refrigerator.

4. After an hour or so, cut the ball into two halves.

Pie Filling

Pie dough for a two-crust pie (recipe above)
⅓ cup brown sugar (or a mixture of white and dark brown)
3 tablespoons all-purpose flour
1 tablespoon butter, melted
1 tablespoon freshly squeezed lemon juice
½ teaspoon salt
1 teaspoon cinnamon
½ teaspoon nutmeg
1 teaspoon finely ground black pepper
3 pounds Bartlett pears, peeled, cored, and cut into ¾-inch pieces or thinly sliced
Coarse sugar, for sprinkling
Spray bottle filled with water

1. Move a rack to the bottom shelf of your oven. Heat the oven to 425°F.

2. Roll the dough into two crusts, each about ⅛ inch thick. Line a 9-inch pie pan with one crust, leaving at least ½-inch overhang. Keep the crusts refrigerated while you prepare the filling.

3. In a large bowl, mix the brown sugar, flour, butter, lemon juice, salt, cinnamon, nutmeg, and pepper. Add the pears and mix gently to coat.

4. Place the pears on top of the bottom crust and spread evenly in the pan. Wet your fingertip with water and run it over the edge of the lower crust. This will help form a seal between the two crusts. Lay the top crust on, then fold the overhang under to make a thick rim around the pie. Crimp the edge with your fingertips or a fork. Cut five or six symmetrical holes in the top crust to allow steam to vent. Spray the top crust with a fine water mist and then sprinkle it with the coarse sugar. The water allows the sugar to stick to the crust.

5. Set the pie on a baking sheet and bake it for 15 minutes at 425°F. Then reduce the heat to 350°F and bake about 1 hour more.

6. Stick a thin knife through a slit in the crust to test the pears, which should be very tender. Use a metal pie rim protector (or aluminum foil) around the edges if the crust is browning too fast. Let cool for at least 45 minutes before serving.

— *Paul Anater*

. . . .

PEAR, FENNEL, AND WALNUT SALAD   SERVES 4 TO 6

1 teaspoon butter
⅓ cup walnut halves
1 medium fennel bulb
2 Bartlett pears
Juice of 1 lemon
3 tablespoons walnut oil
½ teaspoon salt

1. In a small sauté pan, heat the butter until melted. Toast the walnut halves in the butter over low heat until lightly browned.

2. Trim the top and bottom off the fennel bulb. Cut it in half lengthwise and slice very thinly.

3. Peel the Bartlett pears if you like (but it is not necessary). Remove the cores, then slice the pears very thinly.

4. In a large bowl, toss the fennel and pear with 1 tablespoon of the lemon juice. In a small bowl, whisk the walnut oil with the remaining lemon juice and the salt until the dressing is smooth.

USDA standards. This process and its associated costs usually have to be repeated every year to keep the organic certification current.

For farmers, the advantages of being certified can be huge; they can access additional markets with far more credibility and gain many more customers in the process. Most larger wholesale buyers require certification—and will pay higher prices—to meet customer demand for verified products. And the certification process may not be as difficult for some farmers as they think, and sometimes the fees are not as high as anticipated (some can be reimbursed by the USDA if eligible).

But many farmers think that the process of organic certification is too cumbersome and expensive, and just not worth the significant time and labor required to keep up with all the documentation and procedures. This is especially true for very small farms, which simply may not produce on a large enough scale to make it worth it. Farmers may also want to use certain products that are not on the USDA's National Organic Program list, such as biodegradable plastic mulch versus regular plastic, and think that the fiscal and labor outcome of using such products outweighs potential negative consequences. Sometimes the way in which such products are classified is also vague. Each farm's situation and motive are highly contextual, often in ways that are not obvious to the lay consumer who is unfamiliar with farming challenges.

That said, don't necessarily think that just because a CSA farm or producer is not certified or using the official USDA Organic seal that they are not dedicated to organic and sustainable growing methods—most are, and will be happy to explain their methods and reasoning if you ask. This is a great opportunity to get to know those who grow or produce your food, and communicating about it benefits both sides.

"The biggest thing you can do is understand that every time you're going to the grocery store, you're voting with your dollars. Support your farmers market. Support local food. Really learn to cook."

— *Alice Waters, American chef*

5. Arrange the fennel and pears on 4 to 6 plates, and drizzle each portion with dressing. Sprinkle the toasted walnuts on top and serve immediately.

— *Helsing Junction Farm, Rochester, Washington*

🞜 🞛 🍁 🞻

Pumpkins

CUCURBITA PEPO

Few plants symbolize fall (and fun) in America as much as pumpkins, which are actually a type of gourd. Pumpkins belong in the same family as cucumbers, melons, and squashes, developing on rambling vines that demand huge amounts of water, fertilizer, and space.

In the United States, millions of pumpkins are carved every autumn into fanciful jack-o'-lanterns, their flesh baked to make pumpkin pie, and their seeds roasted as a seasonal snack. Post-Halloweeners that didn't sell get sent to feed livestock. In Europe, Latin America, the Caribbean, and parts of Asia, however, pumpkins are used more widely in cooking, especially as a stand-alone dish or in stews. Shelled, roasted pumpkin seeds are commonly found in Latin American markets as pepitas.

Some CSA farms grow pie pumpkins, sometimes known as sugar pumpkins or sugar pie pumpkins. These fruits are especially bred for cooking and baking, with a higher sugar content and more convenient size than the larger pumpkin varieties.

HISTORY

The pumpkin probably originated in Central America; seeds from its ancestors have been found in Mexico and carbon-dated to 5500 BCE. Native American peoples used pumpkin as a staple food along with other squashes, maize, and beans, and introduced the plant to European settlers in the 17th century. (Incidentally, throughout history, pumpkins have been constantly confused with and referred to interchangeably with other gourds and hard-skinned squashes.)

The tradition of jack-o'-lanterns began in the British Isles, when various hollowed-out vegetables like turnips, mangel-wurzels, beets, and potatoes were used as lanterns. Irish folklore has it that a lazy, stingy farmer named Jack strikes a deal with the devil to never let him into hell. When Jack dies, he is refused admittance into heaven, and the devil keeps his promise, leaving Jack no choice but to forever wander the earth, carrying a carved-out turnip with a candle inside it to light his way.

Legend aside, the term "jack-o'-lantern" originally referred to a night watchman. When the Irish arrived in America in the 1800s, they presumably found pumpkins easier to hollow out than turnips.

NUTRITION

Pumpkins are among the richest plant sources of vitamin A, which comes in the form of beta-carotene. They also contain potassium and vitamin C. A single-cup serving contains 30 calories. The seeds are even greater nutritional powerhouses, with ¼ cup containing 72 calories, plus half of the adult daily requirement for manganese, 45 percent for magnesium, and 40 percent for phosphorus, and significant amounts of tryptophan, iron, copper, zinc, vitamin K, protein, and monounsaturated fat.

Cooking Tip

Freshly made pumpkin puree is much more watery than the commercially canned stuff.

You will need to drain or evaporate this moisture before using it for baking, either by spooning off the pooled liquid that forms on the top of the puree or letting the pumpkin drip overnight through a cheesecloth-covered strainer over a bowl in the refrigerator.

Black Gold

Austria commercially produces pumpkin seed oil, extracted from the seeds of the Styrian oil pumpkin; this dark, viscous oil is especially prized for its high levels of monounsaturated fat and vitamin E.

SEASON

Pumpkins are, of course, carefully timed to be in markets in early fall, with peak harvests in late September and October—just in time for the Halloween holiday.

SELECTION

Choose heavy fruits that are uniformly hard, with no soft, shriveled, or bruised areas. Steer clear of pumpkins developing moldy patches, and check the undersides or spots on which they are resting for potential problem areas. Discoloration or scabbing is not necessarily a sign that the flavor is affected; just inspect for softening or rot.

STORAGE

Pumpkins are best stored in cool, dry places, such as a basement or a root cellar with the proper temperature and lack of humidity. (For more information, see "Preserving the Bounty" on page 611.)

The cooler the temperature, the longer pumpkins will keep. At room temperature they can last for several weeks, or at 40°F to 50°F for several months. They should remain unwashed until ready to use. Refrigerate after cutting.

TRIMMING AND CLEANING

If you are carving a pumpkin, you will be cutting off its top and scooping out its seeds. Scrape the flesh clear of seeds and their associated stringy pulp, and cut into 1½-inch chunks.

If you won't be making a jack-o'-lantern, then cut the entire pumpkin into wedges and remove the flesh in large sections with a heavy, sharp knife. Then boil the chunks until tender (see Steaming and Boiling, below).

STEAMING AND BOILING

Steam 1½- to 2-inch chunks for 15 to 20 minutes. Or boil 1½-inch chunks in rapidly boiling salted water for 8 to 10 minutes, or until they become tender. This pumpkin is then ready to use as-is, or it can be pureed or mashed like potatoes. Because freshly cooked pumpkin tends to be quite watery, draining is a must; place mashed pumpkin in a fine-meshed colander suspended over a bowl and refrigerate for at least 1 hour.

STIR-FRYING AND SAUTÉING

It may surprise you that not only can pumpkin be stir-fried, but it is a popular dish in Southeast Asia. Cut pumpkin into ½-inch or bite-size pieces and stir-fry with mustard oil, red chiles, ginger, sugar, turmeric, coriander, cumin, and salt for 3 to 5 minutes, or until the pumpkin is tender but still slightly al dente.

BAKING AND ROASTING

Large jack-o'-lantern pumpkins are not the best candidates for baking, as they are bred for large size rather than appetizing flavor and texture. Sugar or pie pumpkins are better for home baking, as they average about 4 to 8 pounds and their flesh is sweeter and far less stringy. Because hacking through the skin of a raw pumpkin sometimes requires tools like keyhole saws and wood gouges (according to Martha Stewart), baking the whole pumpkin to soften it first makes life far more pleasant (and safer).

To prepare, use a sharp chef's knife to make a shallow cut between the stem and blossom end on both sides. Penetrate slowly and carefully until the two halves start to separate, then cut the rest of the way through and pull apart. Cut off the stem, scoop out the seeds, and slice the pumpkin halves crosswise in half.

Arrange the pumpkin pieces in a shallow roasting pan or a baking sheet with a high rim. Pour in 1½ cups of water and bake at 375°F, uncovered, for 1 to 1½ hours or until very tender.

Sugar pumpkins can also be baked whole. Pierce the skin in several places with a sharp knife (exploding pumpkins are not much fun in the kitchen), then place the pumpkin on a baking sheet and bake for about 2 hours at 350°F, or until the flesh can be easily pierced with a knife or fork.

MICROWAVING

Cut the pumpkin into sections and place, skin side up, on a microwavable dish or platter. Microwave on high power for 7 minutes per pound, turning the pieces every few minutes so they cook evenly.

BLANCHING AND FREEZING

Pumpkin freezes well, but it requires a thorough cooking first, not just a regular blanching. Follow the above instructions to boil, steam, or bake; then cool and remove the seeds. Scoop out the flesh and run it through a food mill or processor to puree it. Then pack the pureed flesh in convenient amounts for preparing pie or other recipes into zipper-lock freezer or vacuum food sealer-type bags or freezer containers, leaving ½ inch of headspace.

Frozen pumpkin puree will keep for up to 5 months at 0°F. Thaw it in the refrigerator the day before you plan to use it, and drain the excess moisture through a cheesecloth-covered sieve.

EQUIVALENTS, MEASURES, AND SERVINGS

- One 4-pound sugar pie pumpkin = 1½ to 2 cups pureed

COMPLEMENTARY HERBS, SEASONINGS, AND FOODS

Apples, brown sugar, butter, cheese, cinnamon, cloves, cream, curry, eggs, ginger, honey, maple syrup, molasses, nutmeg, persimmons, quinces, rosemary, sage, salt, squash, sugar, thyme, walnuts.

SERVING SUGGESTIONS

- For a twist on tomato-basil soup, try adding pureed pumpkin for a smooth, creamy texture.
- Cook pie pumpkins in the half shell until creamy, scoop out, season, bake in a pie shell, top with whipped cream, and call in the neighbors.
- Whip up a batch of pumpkin dip, using canned or fresh pumpkin puree, brown sugar, cinnamon, ginger, nutmeg, and cream cheese. Great with crackers, carrots, gingerbread, or molasses cookies.
- Use pureed pumpkin in your favorite pancake recipe.
- Substitute lightly sweetened, cooked pumpkin in recipes calling for sweet potatoes. Whip pureed pumpkin into mashed potatoes, or finely shred pumpkin and potatoes for a twist on hash browns.

The Greatest Pumpkin

The biggest pumpkin ever recorded tipped the scales at 1,502 pounds, grown in Rhode Island in 2006.

And You Should've Seen the Size of That Oven

The world-record pumpkin pie was baked by the New Bremen Giant Pumpkin Growers at New Bremen, Ohio, on October 8, 2005, and weighed 2,020 pounds (after baking).

- Combine pumpkins with other seasonal autumn fruits like apples, persimmons, and quinces to make thick, almost cakelike puddings.

- An unusual side dish is to sauté thin slices of pumpkin with onion rings and cooking apples, and top with freshly grated ginger, honey, or maple syrup.

- A very popular Argentinian dish is *carbonada en zapallo,* a savory beef stew cooked in a pumpkin shell, calling for beef cubes, potatoes, kabocha squash, onions, tomatoes, corn, sweet potatoes, and peaches.

- Use hollowed-out pumpkins as decorative containers for soups and stews, saving the stem end as a lid!

TWICE-ROASTED MINIATURE PUMPKINS   SERVES 6

Source Note: At Thanksgiving, these filled pumpkins make a nice vegan or vegetarian option for members of the party who don't enjoy turkey. Served with green beans, mashed potatoes, and whatever other side dishes are part of the feast, these miniature pumpkins provide a focal point. For people who do eat meat, they provide a whimsical side dish with turkey, pork, or chicken.

6 miniature pumpkins, about 8 ounces each
1 medium onion, peeled and finely chopped
¼ cup (½ stick) butter
1 teaspoon fresh thyme leaves or ½ teaspoon dried thyme
1 teaspoon kosher salt, or to taste
½ teaspoon pepper, or to taste
¼ teaspoon nutmeg (optional)
1 cup fresh breadcrumbs
1 egg

1. Preheat the oven to 375°F. Roast the miniature pumpkins until fork-tender, about 30 minutes.

2. While the squash is roasting, sauté the chopped onion in butter or oil until it turns soft and translucent. Stir in the thyme, salt, pepper, and nutmeg and cool the mixture to room temperature.

3. When the pumpkins are tender, use a very sharp knife to cut a lid from each one. With a teaspoon, scoop out the seeds and the stringy fibers, but leave the thick walls of the little pumpkins intact.

4. Combine the breadcrumbs with the egg and the cooled sautéed onion. Fill each pumpkin with the prepared stuffing. (The pumpkins may be made ahead up to this point and refrigerated for up to a day in advance.)

5. Bake the filled pumpkins until they are heated through, about 20 minutes; serve hot.

— *Greg Atkinson,* Northwest Essentials: Cooking with Ingredients
    That Define a Region's Cuisine

For More Information

Pumpkin Nook
www.pumpkinnook.com

The Pumpkin Patch
www.pumpkin-patch.com

ROASTED PUMPKIN SEEDS   SERVES 2

Author Note: These seeds are quite delicious and great fun for kids. Some people like to chew the seeds, then spit out the hulls; others eat the whole seed, hull and all. Either way is fine, and up to your personal preference.

Unfortunately, this recipe involves that traumatic step immortalized in Charlie Brown's The Great Pumpkin: *killing the pumpkin.*

1. Slice open one pumpkin, and scoop out the seeds. Separate the seeds from the pulp, rinsing thoroughly under running water to remove as much of the flesh and stringy fibers as possible.

2. Preheat the oven to 350°F.

3. Place the seeds in a bowl and sprinkle them with lots of seasoned salt, a little flavored oil, soy or Worcestershire sauce, minced fresh garlic, or any other flavoring you prefer. (Garlic salt, a little pepper, Tabasco sauce, Old Bay, Tex-Mex, or cheese-flavored popcorn seasoning are good too.) Mix well.

4. Grease a baking sheet with a thin film of vegetable oil. Spread the seeds out in a single layer on the baking sheet.

5. Bake the seeds for about 20 minutes. Then stir the seeds and sample them for doneness by taking out a few, letting them cool, and munching. Add more seasoning and roasting time, if necessary.

Cooking Note: The seeds will continue to roast for a little while after removing them from the oven, so take them out a little ahead of the time you think they will be done.

Variation: For sweet-flavored pumpkin seeds, use sugar, cinnamon, nutmeg, ground cloves, salt, and a little honey for a sweet and salty treat.

— *Mi Ae Lipe*

PUMPKIN PIE WITH
SPICED WALNUT STREUSEL   SERVES 10

Source Note: The piecrust dough can be made 2 days ahead; keep it chilled until you are ready to use it, and let it soften slightly at room temperature before using.

BUTTER PIECRUST DOUGH
1¼ cups all-purpose flour
½ tablespoon sugar
½ teaspoon salt

Books

The Compleat Squash: A Passionate Grower's Guide to Pumpkins, Squashes, and Gourds
Amy Goldman,
Artisan, 2004.

Pumpkin, a Super Food for All 12 Months of the Year
Dee Dee Stovel,
Storey Publishing, 2005.

Pumpkin, Butternut & Squash: 30 Sweet and Savory Recipes
Elsa Petersen-Schepelern,
Ryland Peters & Small, 2003.

What's in That Can?

Most commercially canned pumpkin is not true pumpkin at all, but the richer, more full-flavored flesh of *C. maxima*, a type of winter squash. Delicious and Boston Marrow are two varieties often used in canning.

½ cup (1 stick) chilled unsalted butter, cut into ½-inch cubes
3 tablespoons (or more) ice water

1. Blend the flour, sugar, and salt in a food processor. Add the butter and cut in, using on-off turns, until a coarse meal forms. Add 3 tablespoons water. Using on-off turns, blend just until moist clumps form, adding more water by half-tablespoonfuls if the dough is dry.

2. Gather the dough into a ball; flatten it into a disk. Wrap it in plastic and refrigerate 1 hour. Let it soften slightly at room temperature before rolling.

STREUSEL

⅓ cup all-purpose flour
¼ cup firmly packed brown sugar
1 tablespoon minced crystallized ginger
1 teaspoon ground cinnamon
¼ teaspoon ground nutmeg
2 tablespoons (¼ stick) chilled, unsalted butter, cut into cubes
⅓ cup walnuts, coarsely chopped

PUMPKIN FILLING

15 ounces cooked pumpkin
1 cup white sugar
½ cup firmly packed brown sugar
3 large eggs
½ cup (1 stick) unsalted butter, melted
1 teaspoon vanilla extract

Sweetened whipped cream

1. Roll out the butter piecrust dough on a lightly floured surface to create a 13-inch round. Transfer to a 9-inch-deep glass pie dish. Trim the overhang to ½ inch. Fold the overhang under; crimp the edges decoratively. Refrigerate 1 hour.

2. Preheat the oven to 375°F. Line the crust with aluminum foil and fill it with dried beans or pie weights. Bake until the edges begin to brown and the crust is set, about 17 minutes. Take it out from the oven, and remove the foil and beans. Then continue to bake until the crust turns golden brown, pressing it with the back of a fork if the crust bubbles, about 5 minutes longer. Transfer to a wire rack to cool, and maintain the oven temperature.

FOR THE STREUSEL

Mix the flour, sugar, ginger, cinnamon, and nutmeg in a medium bowl. Add the butter, rubbing it in with your fingertips until a coarse meal forms. Stir in the walnuts.

FOR THE PUMPKIN FILLING

Whisk the pumpkin and white and brown sugars together in a medium bowl. Whisk in the eggs, one at a time. Whisk in the melted butter and vanilla. Pour the mixture into the prepared crust.

TO COMPLETE THE PIE

Sprinkle the streusel over the filling. Bake the pie until the streusel is golden and the filling is set, about 45 minutes. Cool on the wire rack for at least 2 hours at room temperature. (The pie can be made up to 6 hours ahead.) Serve with sweetened whipped cream.

— Bon Appétit, *November 2003, as appeared on Epicurious*

Pumpkin harvest at Featherstone Farm.

CHICKEN PUMPKIN CHILI   SERVES 6

Source Note: *For a peppier version, try this with the quantities of jalapeño, garlic, coriander, and cilantro doubled.*

2 tablespoons olive oil
2 cups chopped onion
2 cups chopped red bell pepper
3 tablespoons minced jalapeño pepper
1 clove garlic, minced
1 cup beer
1 cup chicken broth
¼ cup sliced black olives
3 tablespoons chili powder
1 teaspoon ground coriander
½ teaspoon salt
1 (28-ounce) can diced tomatoes, with juice
1 pound boneless, skinless chicken breasts, cubed
2 cups cooked pumpkin or butternut squash, peeled and cubed

The Pumpkin Must Go On

The Circleville Pumpkin Show, held in Circleville, Ohio, is the largest annual US festival dedicated to the pumpkin.

It has taken place every year since 1903, even during the 1918 influenza epidemic, with the exception of three years during World War II.

2 tablespoons chopped cilantro
1 tablespoon unsweetened cocoa powder
1½ cups cooked pinto beans, or 1 (16-ounce) can, drained
6 tablespoons sliced scallions (green onions)
1½ ounces (about ½ cup) shredded Cheddar cheese
6 tablespoons sour cream

1. Heat the oil in a Dutch oven over medium heat. Sauté the onions until they are lightly browned, about 8 minutes. Add the bell pepper, jalapeño, and garlic. Sauté for 5 minutes more.

2. Add the beer, broth, olives, chili powder, coriander, salt, tomatoes, and chicken. Bring the mixture to a boil, decrease the heat, cover partially, and simmer for 15 minutes.

3. Stir in the pumpkin, cilantro, cocoa powder, and beans. Cook for 5 minutes.

4. Serve in individual bowls, topped with scallions, cheese, and sour cream.

— *Mimi Hiller, Epicurean.com*

. . . .

PUMPKIN-GINGER SOUP   SERVES 2

Source Note: For an even easier variation, use frozen, already-cooked squash.

1 small cooking pumpkin
½ cup cashew pieces (not roasted or toasted)
1 tablespoon finely grated fresh ginger (or to taste)
Salt

1. Preheat the oven to 350°F.

2. Cover the cashews in water and soak them for several hours. This step is optional, but it helps them blend better.

3. Cut the pumpkin in half, remove the seeds, and bake cut-side down until very tender (45 minutes to 1 hour). When the pumpkin has cooled, scrape the flesh from the peel (hold the pumpkin over a bowl while doing this to keep any accumulated juices) and puree in a blender in batches. Put the pureed pumpkin into a large soup pot.

4. Drain the cashews, then blend them in a blender until smooth and add them to the pumpkin puree. Rinse the blender with a little water and pour it into the pot. Add a little more water if the pumpkin-cashew mixture is too thick. Add ginger and salt to taste, and heat gently for a few minutes to blend the flavors.

— *Melinda McBride*

Radishes

RAPHANUS SATIVUS

Most Americans associate radishes with their roots, but this is not necessarily so in other parts of the world. In fact, this vegetable is cultivated for not only its nether regions but also its leaves, seeds (for oil), and deliciously crunchy seedpods (produced long after the roots have ceased to be appetizing).

Anyone who has sampled the zippy leaves and roots of radishes will not be surprised that it is a close relative of the mustard and turnip families. Radishes come in many different forms. In Europe and America, small red, white, pink, and purple globe-shaped table radishes are enjoyed as a snack on buttered bread or as a welcome addition to the hors d'oeuvres tray. But in Asia, huge, thick-rooted winter radishes, such as the Japanese daikon, may grow to 3 feet long and weigh up to 60 pounds. Such radishes constitute a full-fledged food, used extensively raw, cooked, and pickled. Black radishes are yet another variety, very different from Asian or table radishes, with their dry, dense, assertively potent flesh. India grows the rat-tailed radish, a variety noted for its seedpods, which can grow eight to twelve inches long and are often pickled.

When they are at their best, table radishes can be irresistibly succulent and crunchy, with an appealing blend of both peppery and sweet flavors. Yet they are equally susceptible to being lifeless, pithy, wormy, bitter, and spicy if their growing conditions are too dry or hot. These radishes are best enjoyed as either a late-spring or fall crop, but decidedly not as a height-of-summer one.

Fall table radishes tend to be much sweeter than their spring counterparts; the cool weather allows their sugars to develop slowly, giving them a sweet and mild flavor. Radish greens can also be a treat when they are young and tender. Older leaves tend to be tough and prickly, but they are still suitable for long, slow cooking, like turnip or mustard greens.

HISTORY

Humans have cultivated different species of radishes since antiquity, but they most likely originated in the Far East, possibly China. In ancient Egypt, radishes were so prized for their seeds, which yielded an extremely expensive oil, that the Roman author Pliny complained that farmers ceased to grow grain in favor of radishes.

The modest radishes most of us are familiar with today seem to be a relatively recent and historically insignificant edible. Enormous, thick-rooted winter specimens (of which the Japanese daikon is one) were the most commonly eaten radishes in northern and southern Europe in medieval and Renaissance times, but they have since disappeared from those cuisines. Radishes reached Great Britain in the mid-1500s, and the Spanish and Portuguese introduced the plant to the Americas around that time.

NUTRITION

Radishes are well known as a diet food, with three radishes averaging just 8 calories. They also contain vitamin C, folate, riboflavin, potassium, calcium, magnesium, manganese, and dietary fiber. Like other brassica crops, radishes have sulfurous compounds that may help fight cancer but also sometimes contribute to flatulence.

SEASON

Commercially, radishes are widely grown and available year-round. But the crop has two peak seasons at farmers markets and CSAs—from April through June and again from October through January.

SELECTION

Selecting good radishes can be a challenge, for size (or the lack of it) does not necessarily indicate quality. More reliable factors include season (early spring and fall radishes taste the best) and whether fresh-looking greens are still attached. Choose radishes that are uniformly hard, with absolutely no signs of shriveling or give when firmly pressed. Their skins should be smooth and unbroken, with a slight sheen. Sampling is the only sure-fire way to tell a radish's true character.

STORAGE

Table radishes do not store well, even in the refrigerator. Keep them unwashed in a plastic bag in the refrigerator vegetable crisper for only a few days if you plan to eat them raw; if they are destined for the cooking pot, they will keep for up to 1 week.

TRIMMING AND CLEANING

Given their proximity in their native environment, dirt tends to be a radish's best friend. Give them a thorough scrubbing with a soft vegetable brush; leaves must be submerged and vigorously swished in water as long as it takes to remove all traces of sand.

STEAMING AND BOILING

Radishes transform into a surprisingly sweet and mild vegetable when cooked. Quarter or slice them, then steam, covered, over rapidly boiling water for 5 minutes or until they just turn tender.

STIR-FRYING AND SAUTÉING

Radishes and their greens are delicious stir-fried or sautéed lightly in a little butter or olive oil, garlic, and salt. Cook radishes on moderately high heat for about 10 to 12 minutes, or until crisp-tender; the greens for about 5 minutes, or until wilted but still bright green.

BAKING AND ROASTING

Roasting radishes tames their pungency and makes a surprisingly good vegetable side dish. Toss sliced radishes with olive oil and seasoning, then spread them on a baking sheet or roasting pan, and roast for 30 to 45 minutes in a 425°F oven.

MICROWAVING

Place radishes in a covered microwave-safe container with 2 to 3 tablespoons of water, and microwave on high power for 8 minutes, or until they are tender when pierced with a fork.

BLANCHING AND FREEZING

Radishes do not make good candidates for freezing, as they lose their flavor and crispness upon thawing.

EQUIVALENTS, MEASURES, AND SERVINGS

½ pound = 1⅔ cups sliced

COMPLEMENTARY HERBS, SEASONINGS, AND FOODS

Asparagus, bread, butter, carrots, chicken, crab, fish, garlic, ginger, greens, ham, lemons, mushrooms, onions, oranges, peas, pea shoots, prosciutto, rice vinegar, salami, salmon, salt, scallops, seafood, sesame, shrimp, smoked salt, snap peas, soy sauce, spinach, thyme, turnips, watercress.

SERVING SUGGESTIONS

- Make radish soup with chicken stock, rice vinegar, sugar, cayenne pepper, ginger, shrimp, sliced radishes, spinach, and green onions.
- Serve braised, roasted, or grilled radishes with savory meats like roast pork, beef, lamb, or chicken.
- For a dainty hors d'oeuvres, serve tea sandwiches made with layers of very thinly sliced radishes and raw mint leaves on white bread spread with a mixture of mayonnaise, lemon juice, and sour cream.
- Add chopped radish to your favorite salsa recipe.
- Stir-fry radish greens with soy sauce, sesame seeds, and garlic.
- In Korea, daikon radishes and pears are combined to create a highly prized white kimchi, or pickled vegetable. Try this combination in an unusual salad with sliced table radishes, crisp Asian or Bartlett pears, watercress, shredded napa cabbage, ginger, and a touch of green onion or chives.
- Add chopped or sliced radishes to your favorite potato, egg, tuna, or ham salad recipe.
- Thinly slice radishes and pickle them in the refrigerator as you would cucumbers (see Barely Pickled Cucumbers on page 175).
- Toss lightly cooked or raw radishes in your favorite vinaigrette.
- Combine and puree radish tops with other spring greens like arugula, lettuce, and spinach; finish with cream and chicken stock for a lovely spring soup.

When Woodcarvers Get Bored

Every December 23, since 1897, the town of Oaxaca, Mexico, celebrates Noche de Rabanos (Night of the Radishes), a festival in which enormous daikon-like radishes are carved into unbelievably elaborate scenes and figures and displayed around a zocalo.

Often the intricate carvings depict saints, conquistadors, and nativity scenes.

RADISH, MANGO, AND APPLE SALAD   SERVES 4

Source Note: With its crisp, clean tastes and mellow flavors, this salad goes well with smoked salmon, ham, or salami.

DRESSING

½ cup sour cream
2 teaspoons creamed horseradish
1 tablespoon chopped fresh dill
Salt and freshly ground black pepper
Sprig of dill, for garnish

As consumers of supermarket produce, we have grown accustomed to eating pretty much any vegetable or fruit all year-round, rather than waiting for certain crops to come into season. This concept of eating something in season and what this means to me as a farmer—pulling leaves off broccoli, eating green beans at different times of the year, harvesting the perfect radish—grows increasingly important as the years pass.

To me, seasonality is not just when something is available, but when it is good, and dependably so. Weather, climate, and soil conditions enormously impact the quality of both fruits and vegetables.

We humans tend to perceive the seasons as how we experience weather when we are out and about (always during the day). Plants, on the other hand, experience seasons as night and day: dew sets that occur because of humidity, moisture, wind (or the lack of them), and temperatures.

In particular, here in southeast Minnesota, temperature differences during the day and night can range in June from 45 degrees Fahrenheit at night to 86 degrees during the day. In August, that nighttime temperature might not get below 70 degrees.

Moisture in the field and how soil and its organic matter retains moisture in the root zone are also extremely important factors. Dewfalls play critical roles too. Every single morning in August, the fields will be completely soaked. When the sun rises, even if it is brightly shining, its solar energy goes first into drying things out, not into the leaves to make energy,

Such fluctuations really affect

10 to 15 radishes, ends removed
1 apple, peeled, cored, and thinly sliced
2 celery ribs, thinly sliced
1 small ripe mango, peeled and cut into small chunks
Dill sprigs, for garnish

1. To prepare the dressing, blend the sour cream, horseradish, and dill in a small jug or bowl and season with a little salt and pepper.

2. Thinly slice the radishes. Place them in a bowl with the apple and celery.

3. Cut through the mango lengthwise, on either side of the pit. Make even, crisscross cuts through each section, cutting through the flesh but keeping the skin intact. Take each one and bend it back to separate the cubes. Remove the mango cubes with a small knife and add to the bowl.

4. Pour the dressing over the vegetables and fruit, and stir gently so that all of the ingredients are coated in the dressing. When ready to serve, spoon the salad into an attractive bowl and garnish with a dill sprig.

— *Christine Ingram,* The Cook's Encyclopedia of Vegetables

SOUTHWESTERN RADISH SALAD   SERVES 4

ORANGE-SALSA DRESSING
1 cup prepared salsa
½ cup orange juice, preferably freshly squeezed
2 tablespoons cider vinegar
1 teaspoon grated orange zest

SALAD
6 cups lettuce, cut into 1-inch strips
1½ cups sliced radishes
3 hard-boiled eggs, cut into wedges
1½ cups cooked red kidney beans, or 1 (16-ounce) can, rinsed and drained
1 (7-ounce) can corn kernels, drained
1 cup Monterey Jack cheese, cut into 1-inch cubes
½ cup crumbled cooked bacon or bacon bits
¼ cup sliced green onions

1. Thoroughly combine all of the dressing ingredients.

2. Combine all of the salad ingredients, toss with the dressing, and serve immediately.

— *Featherstone Farm, Rushford, Minnesota*

RADISHES WITH SALT AND BUTTER   SERVES 4

Author Note: This is a popular snack in France, eagerly devoured by young and old alike. Sometimes the radishes are sliced and eaten atop thick slices of generously buttered French bread, open-faced, and finished with a shake of the salt grinder.

12 radishes, trimmed and washed
Sweet cream butter, unsalted
Coarsely ground sea salt and freshly cracked black pepper

Dab each radish with a generous dollop of butter, sprinkle with sea salt and pepper, and enjoy.

— *Mi Ae Lipe*

SAUTÉED RADISHES AND SUGAR SNAP PEAS WITH DILL   SERVES 6

Source Note: This side dish pairs beautifully with roast lamb or salmon.

1 tablespoon butter
1 tablespoon olive oil
½ cup thinly sliced shallots
12 ounces sugar snap peas, trimmed and strings removed
2 cups thinly sliced radishes (about 1 large bunch)
¼ cup orange juice
1 teaspoon dill seeds
1 tablespoon chopped fresh dill

1. Melt the butter with the oil in a large nonstick skillet over medium heat. Add the shallots and sauté until golden, about 5 minutes. Add the sugar snap peas and radishes; sauté until crisp-tender, about 5 minutes.

2. Add the orange juice and dill seeds; stir 1 minute. Season with salt and pepper. Stir in the chopped dill. Transfer to a bowl, and serve.

— Bon Appétit, *April 2004, as appeared on Epicurious*

RADISH TOP SOUP   SERVES 4

Source Note: This earthy soup made from radish greens and roots should persuade you to keep your throwaways. It can also be made with the tops and roots of turnips, daikon radishes, rutabagas, or black radishes. It's also a great way to use up lots of greens. And it is truly delicious!

how a melon ripens in the field, for instance. Squash and melons need accumulated heat to ripen. That means that they do not start to ripen until all of their leaves are dry, so those dewfalls in the valley hugely impact how these crops develop.

Having worked on farms in California, I often think in terms of the conditions of where a crop is grown in that agricultural state, where so many different microenvironments exist.

Here in our valley in southeastern Minnesota, the nightly dew sets mimic the coastal fogs of California's heavily cultivated Salinas Valley, which is why we grow so much leaf lettuce and broccoli. Both prefer cool soils and plenty of moisture.

One of the most striking examples of the divide between the consumer perception of seasonality and actual seasonality occurs with radishes. When we come to the farmers market in June, everyone lines up to get radishes because they are psyched up for it.

What is happening in the field, however, is that the lengthening days are causing the radishes to grow so fast in May and June that they get pithy and hollow inside. When the soil reaches above 65 degrees, the roots lose crunch, juiciness, and sweetness, and turn very spicy. What people perceive as peak radish time in early June is, in my mind, a pretty risky season.

Although radishes can be good at this time, what I believe people are really responding to is the lack of fresh fruits and vegetables during the previous six or eight months. They are not necessarily looking for radishes; they are seeking something good, and even though these radishes might be fresher than those from California, they are nothing like the fall radishes we harvest.

In September and October, the radishes are growing so much more slowly. The nights are cooler, and we get unbelievably good radishes at this time of year; they are what I think of as an in-season radish. But this timing is so contrary to what most people think about radishes.

The same is true for lettuce. Our initial goal was to cultivate all of the leaf lettuce one could eat during the entire growing season, which runs from May 20 to November 1. But the lettuce is superb for only a short time, between May 20 and June 20. After that, we do not grow lettuce in July and August, for it quickly turns bitter once the soil becomes hot and dry.

Another example of seasonality occurs with broccoli. Because of our scale, we do not want to grow many acres of a certain crop until we know it will have a high success rate. In the case of broccoli, we need 80 to 90 percent of our crop to have both high eating quality and be aesthetically superior.

Here in southeastern Minnesota, it is possible to harvest broccoli every day from June 20 to November 10. But broccoli loves cool weather and even frost; if the temperatures are not falling below 30 degrees at night, it won't be as sweet. As a result, our broccoli is best only about eight to ten weeks of that time, from about September 10 to October 20.

Broccoli could be in every CSA basket during the summer and fall, but in times of hot days, warm nights, and dry soil, it will be stringy and tough. If it looks any good at all, the heads are likely to be bitter. Even though we could sell and market it, this poorer-quality vegetable is not what we want to promote as a grower.

1 tablespoon vegetable oil
Fresh greens from 2 bunches radishes or from 1 bunch turnips, daikon radishes, or rutabagas, washed and roughly chopped
Roots from those radishes (or turnips, etc.), cut into bite-size chunks
3 medium scallions (green onions) or 1 medium onion, chopped
2 potatoes, diced
4 to 6 cups vegetable or chicken broth
Salt and freshly ground black pepper

1. Heat the oil in a large pot over moderate heat. Add the greens, roots, scallions, and potatoes. Toss until the greens are wilted. Add 4 cups of the broth. Simmer, covered, over low heat until the potatoes and roots are soft, about 20 minutes.

2. Blend with an immersion blender or with a food processor until smooth. Return the soup to the pot and stir in more broth until the soup is the desired consistency. Season with salt and pepper.

— *Philippe Waterinckx, Tucson CSA*

Handful of fresh radishes at Sang Lee Farms.

Sage

SALVIA OFFICINALIS

A member of the vast mint family, sage is nearly synonymous with poultry stuffing in American cuisine, but its uses go much further than that. Sage has a long and storied history as a highly effective medicinal herb, both internally and externally, and indeed sage's volatile oils contain several effective antiseptic and antispasmodic compounds.

Sage comes in many different varieties, but the one we are most familiar with is the common or broadleaf type, with its silvery-gray, velvety leaves. But there is pineapple sage, with its fruity scent, red sage, white sage, lavender sage, Mexican sage, Jerusalem sage, and Cleveland sage, to name but a few. Not all of them are used culinarily, but all are powerfully fragrant.

HISTORY

Sage is one of the oldest herbs used by humans; Egyptians used it as a fertility drug, the ancient Greeks wrote of its healing properties, and the Druids thought it could even revive the dead. Sage reached the height of reverence during the Middle Ages, where it was used to combat the effects of poison and many sources of malaise, from sore throats to rheumatism.

NUTRITION

Normally, sage is not consumed in large enough quantities to make it nutritionally significant, but the herb does contain significant amounts of vitamin K and vitamin A. It is a rich source of volatile oils and phenolic acids that act as antioxidants. Two teaspoons of the dried herb contain 4 calories.

SEASON

Commercially, sage is widely grown and in season year-round. But it is typically at its best at farmers markets and CSAs in the fall and winter months.

SELECTION

Fresh sage should be uniformly green with plump, firm leaves, with no signs of wilting or shriveling.

STORAGE

Treat fresh sage sprigs like any living flower or plant cutting; just snip off the stem ends, place them in a glass of water, and store them at room temperature on the counter or in the refrigerator. Or you can wrap the sprigs in damp paper towels and store them in a plastic bag in the refrigerator vegetable crisper, where they will keep for 3 to 4 days.

TRIMMING AND CLEANING

Wash the sprigs under running water, and strip the leaves off the stems. Pat dry with a soft towel.

A European superstition holds that sage will not flourish in your garden if your money affairs are in bad order.

FREEZING

To prepare sage for freezing, thoroughly wash and dry the sage sprigs. Strip the leaves from the stems, place them loosely in a zipper-lock freezer or vacuum food sealer-type bag, and gently squeeze out the air.

A terrific way to freeze sage is to chop it finely, mix it into a paste using ⅓ cup of olive oil or cooled melted butter to every 2 cups of herbs, and then freeze the resulting mixture in ice cube trays. To thaw, simply pop out a few cubes into a strainer and let the oil melt away, or just drop them frozen into sauces, soups, stews, casseroles, and other cooked dishes. Frozen sage will keep for up to 1 year at 0°F.

DRYING

Sage takes longer to dry than other herbs because of its high oil content. Tie fresh, dry sprigs that are free of dew and moisture into a bunch and hang in a cool, dry, dark place with good ventilation. You can cover the bunches with small paper bags to keep dust off them, but make sure the bags have adequate holes for proper ventilation. Once the bunches are dried, seal them tightly in a container with a lid or in a zipper-lock plastic bag and store away from light and heat.

Or you can oven-dry sage by spreading a single layer of leaves on a cookie sheet and placing it in a warm (up to 180°F) oven for 2 to 4 hours, stirring the leaves periodically until they are thoroughly dry.

A microwave oven can also be used to dry small quantities of sage. Place 4 or 5 sprigs in the microwave between paper towels. Heat for 2 minutes over high power. If the sage is not brittle and dry when removed, repeat the microwave drying for 30 seconds more. (Be aware that the heat generated during microwaving not only removes moisture but also some of the oils, so sage dried this way may not have as intense a flavor.) Store dried sage in a tightly sealed glass container away from light and heat; it will keep its potency for about 6 months.

EQUIVALENTS, MEASURES, AND SERVINGS

- 2 teaspoons fresh, minced = 7 leaves = 1 teaspoon dried

COMPLEMENTARY HERBS, SEASONINGS, AND FOODS

Anchovies, apples, bacon, beans, bread, butter, cheese, chestnuts, chicken, croutons, duck, eggs, garlic, goose, ham, honey, lamb, lemon, liver, lovage, mint, olive oil, onions, peas, pasta, pineapple, polenta, pork, potatoes, rosemary, sausage, squash, thyme, trout, tuna, turkey, veal, watermelon.

SERVING SUGGESTIONS

- When using raw sage leaves in a dish, remember that they are, by nature, quite thick and chewy—and not that pleasant to gnaw your way through. Chop fresh sage leaves finely, especially before adding them to delicate dishes.
- Sage is a perennial favorite in breadcrumb-based stuffings for turkey, goose, and roast chicken.
- Try mixing sage with other herbs to make compound herb butter.
- Freshly minced sage brightens up egg dishes, including frittatas.
- Combine and simmer cooked navy or white beans with olive oil, sage, and garlic as a side dish, or serve with toasted crusty bread such as bruschetta.

- Sage leaves, bell peppers, cucumbers, and sweet onions make a delicious, refreshing summer salad.
- Tuck sage leaves under the skin of raw chicken or fish to add a lovely flavor.
- Crisp-fried sage leaves are a delightful topping or accompaniment to many savory dishes.
- Infuse honey with sage; this is especially good with pineapple sage.
- Roll up thin slices of honey-cured ham with slivers of crisp red onion and a leaf or two of fresh sage. You should really like sage for this one!
- Use sage with parsley, rosemary, and thyme in tomato-based dishes and sauces.
- If you're making homemade sausage, fresh sage is indispensable.
- Sage and Cheddar cheese are an unlikely—but tasty—combination in biscuits.
- Combine sage with pork and apples to make delicious burgers.

CLASSIC BREAD STUFFING WITH SAGE, PARSLEY, AND THYME   SERVES 10 TO 12

Source Note: For an easy yet memorable stuffing, one key is the right bread. To make a light stuffing with a crisp exterior and moist interior, choose crusty Italian- or French-style loaves. Take the time to air-dry the bread cubes. Adding a couple of eggs with the broth helps the bread cubes cling together. Finally, the stuffing benefits from a two-step cooking process: Bake it covered until it becomes hot and steamy, then uncover it and bake until it develops an appealingly crusted top. Baking the stuffing separately allows it to cook through without overcooking the bird.

> One (1-pound) loaf crusty Italian or French bread,
>   cut into ½-inch cubes (10 to 12 cups)
> 4 tablespoons (½ stick) butter
> 2 medium onions, diced (about 2 cups)
> 2 medium ribs celery, diced (about 1 cup)
> ¼ cup minced fresh parsley
> 2 teaspoons fresh minced sage, or 1 teaspoon dried rubbed sage
> 2 teaspoons fresh thyme, or 1 teaspoon dried thyme
> ¾ teaspoon salt
> ½ teaspoon freshly ground black pepper
> 2 cups chicken broth
> 2 large eggs, lightly beaten

1. Spread the bread cubes in a single layer on two large baking sheets and let dry for a couple of hours at room temperature or overnight.

2. Adjust the oven racks to lower- and upper-middle positions. Heat the oven to 400°F.

3. Bake the bread for 12 to 15 minutes, until it is toasty and dry, switching the pans halfway through the baking. Remove the bread from the oven and set aside. Reduce the heat to 350°F.

lemons, avocados, figs, peaches, apples, plums, fava beans, onions, collards, Swiss chard, parsnips, turnips, and artichokes, to name a few. The produce also includes foods that are culturally appropriate for the Latino, African-American, and Korean people who are the primary residents of the housing project.

The farm also has an aquaponics system that raises both food fish and plants in a closed-loop system. The grounds and extensive demonstration gardens provide a training space for educational events, workshops, and tours. The Growing Experience also hosts seasonal events that feature music, site tours, children's activities, and local chefs cooking the farm's produce.

In addition to growing healthful food, the urban farm offers programs for at-risk youth, who learn not only farming but many life and job skills. As of 2013, more than 75 youth had gained their first employment opportunity by participating in the program, made possible through the California Green Jobs Corps Initiative and Summer Youth Employment Training Program in conjunction with the City of Long Beach. And more than 90 resident participants have been trained at The Growing Experience; as a result, several residents have moved from public housing to purchase their own homes.

Ng has been the farm's project manager from the beginning; much of its success has been the result of his vision, dedication, contagious enthusiasm, and patience that has nurtured the garden through its long evolution. The farm has received widespread accolades and numerous awards and grants for its innovation in urban agriculture and its mission to serve Los Angeles residents. Among them, The Growing Experience has received recognition from the Ford Foundation and the John F. Kennedy School of Government at Harvard University as one of the most innovative programs in American government.

4. Meanwhile, melt the butter in a large skillet over medium-high heat. Add the onions and celery; sauté until soft, 8 to 10 minutes.

5. Transfer the sautéed vegetables to a large bowl, and add the bread and remaining ingredients. Turn them into a greased 3-quart baking dish.

6. Cover the dish with foil and bake until steamy hot, about 30 minutes. Remove the foil and continue to bake until the top is crusty, about 10 minutes longer. Serve immediately.

— *Pam Anderson,* Perfect Recipes for Having People Over

Sage, thyme, and oregano from Steel Wheel Farm at the farmers market.

FRIED SAGE LEAVES   SERVES 10 TO 12

Source Note: If you've never had fried sage leaves as a garnish on your soup or pasta, you're missing out. They're delicious, healthful, and quite easy to make. If you have a sage plant in your garden, no doubt you've been looking for ways to use up the leaves. I always have to fry up extra because I snack on them while dinner is finishing up!

1 large knob of unsalted butter (preferably organic pastured butter; see the Cooking Note below)
A handful of fresh sage leaves (any size works, but the small ones are less intensely flavored than the big ones)
A sprinkling of freshly ground sea salt

1. Melt the butter in a cast-iron skillet over medium heat. When the butter has melted, throw in the sage leaves and cook, stirring occasionally until they stop sizzling. Remove the crispy sage leaves from the pan and let them drain and cool on a paper-towel-lined plate.

Volunteer Opportunities

Martha Wagner

Wanna volunteer on a farm to learn about growing methods, work with animals, help with events, or fill CSA boxes? Volunteer opportunities at farms across the country and abroad are abundant and diverse. Many farms rely on volunteers and even welcome families and work groups!

B.U.G. (Backyard Urban Garden Farms) in Salt Lake City, Utah, is one of many farms that offer some type of work trade in exchange for a CSA share. Its work-share volunteers commit to working four to six hours per week on the same day each week for the length of the season in exchange for a full-size vegetable CSA share. At the end of a work shift, they're thanked with a home-cooked farm lunch. Most of the work is harvesting, processing, and packing vegetables; sometimes it's weeding or prepping beds for planting. Prior farming or gardening experience is not required. At Community Crops in Lincoln, Nebraska, work-share members contribute three hours of work each week during the season for a discount on their CSA share.

Farms with large volunteer programs typically provide opportunities for drop-by help as well as scheduled weekly positions. At Waltham Fields Community Farm in Waltham, Massachusetts, volunteers come en masse to help with weeding on several Crop Mob Saturdays. People available for a committed volunteer position join the Steward, Greenhouse, and Harvest Program and come to the farm one day a week to tend or harvest a specific crop. Groups of seven or more can sign up for volunteer tasks listed on a monthly online calendar.

At Zenger Farm in Portland, Oregon, volunteers assist with the children's gardens maintenance and

2. You'll be left with sage brown butter in your skillet, which is quite a treat in itself. It's wonderful drizzled on top of soup or pasta and is at its best when enjoyed over pumpkin or butternut squash ravioli.

Cooking Note: A large knob of butter is ¼ to ⅓ cup or so, depending on the size of your skillet. I use an 8-inch skillet and between ⅛ and ¼ inch of butter in it.

— *Susy Morris,* ChiotsRun *blog*

....

SAGE-APPLE PORK BURGERS WITH CARAMELIZED ONIONS SERVES 4

Source Note: Not your average backyard fare, these thick, juicy burgers, dressed up with lettuce and thinly sliced apple, are fancy enough for casual entertaining. And since you can make the patties and the caramelized onions ahead, they might become a weeknight grilling favorite, too.

CARAMELIZED ONIONS

1 tablespoon vegetable oil
1 large onion, thinly sliced
1 tablespoon granulated sugar
1 tablespoon wine vinegar
¼ teaspoon salt
¼ teaspoon freshly ground black pepper

In a skillet, heat the oil over medium-high heat; fry the onion, stirring occasionally, until turning golden, about 8 minutes. Sprinkle with the sugar and vinegar; lower the heat to medium and cook, stirring occasionally, until deep golden, about 10 minutes. Sprinkle with the salt and pepper.

BURGERS

1 egg
¼ cup apple juice
2 green onions, chopped
¼ cup dry breadcrumbs
1 tablespoon finely chopped fresh sage or ½ teaspoon dried
½ teaspoon salt
½ teaspoon freshly ground black pepper
1 pound lean ground pork

1. In a bowl, beat the egg with the apple juice. Stir in the green onions, breadcrumbs, sage, salt, and pepper; mix in the pork.

2. Shape into four ½-inch-thick patties. (To make these ahead, cover and refrigerate for up to 6 hours. Or layer between waxed paper in an airtight container and freeze for up to 1 month; thaw in the refrigerator.)

activities, the community livestock project (chickens, bees and worms), farm visits by school groups, and special events. They also lead cooking and nutrition education classes for the farm's Healthy Eating on a Budget program (see the "Zenger Farm" on page 92).

The nonprofit **180 Degree Farm** in Georgia works with five colleges in the Southeast to coordinate its Alternative Spring/Fall Break program for groups of college students to come work at the farm.

Another piece of the volunteering picture is team-building events for work groups. Eleven-acre **Full Circle Farm** in Sunnyvale, California, hosts such events for nearby Silicon Valley employers such as NetApp, Hewlett Packard, Intel, SAP, Applied Materials, Yahoo, Intuit, Deloitte, and Google.

People who want a future in farming have usually considered or completed a volunteer stint through **WWOOF (Worldwide Workers on Organic Farms)**. Founded in 1971, the organization has branches in 50 countries. Through Internet listings, farms and related businesses (ranches, vineyards, agritourism inns, etc.) find willing volunteers and vice versa, usually from two weeks up to six months. In most countries the exchange is based on four to six hours of help in exchange for a full day's food and accommodation. Volunteer tasks run the gamut from planting and harvesting to milking, fencing, wine or cheese making, and more.

Farm supporters who want to help but have physical or time limitations have alternative options, such as writing a check. **Community Crops** in Lincoln, Nebraska, is one of many farms that take donations for CSA scholarships for families in need. Recipients of its Share-a-Share program pay a portion of their share through SNAP benefits (a federally administered supplemental nutrition program, formerly known as food stamps).

3. Place the patties on a greased grill over medium-high heat; close the lid and cook, turning once, until they are no longer pink inside, about 10 minutes.

ASSEMBLING THE BURGERS

4 onion or plain hamburger buns
4 leaves leaf lettuce
1 red-skinned apple, thinly sliced

1. Cut the buns in half; place them, cut sides down, on the grill and toast until golden, 1 to 2 minutes.

2. Place the lettuce, apple, meat patties, and caramelized onions on the bottom buns; then sandwich with the top buns.

— *Canadian Living Test Kitchen,* CanadianLiving.com

Closeup of lettuce at Featherstone Farm.

Winter

Mid November Through March

During the winter months of December through March, a surprising amount of farm produce is available. In addition to whatever fruits of summer have been preserved in the freezer, dehydrator, and canner, a number of crops store well, including cabbage, winter squash, root vegetables, apples, onions, dried beans, and garlic. Others, such as kale and parsnips, can even be harvested in the frigid depths of January and February. Some CSAs offer substantial winter shares, including grains.

Winter on a farm is typically a well-deserved time of rest, a respite after the frenetic planting, cultivating, and harvesting of spring, summer, and fall. In most places, the ground sleeps frozen under a layer of snow. And it means an opportunity for equipment and facilities to finally be repaired, and catching up on longstanding chores awaiting a less hectic time. But in the milder West and South, cooler temperatures and increased rains just mean a slowdown in growth, not a suspension of it.

In tropical areas such as Hawaii and Florida, however, November marks the start of the CSA season in earnest, when temperatures are at last cool enough to grow decent greens and veggies.

Winter is also a time for reflection for many farmers, a chance to strategize about the next season, take stock in what they might do differently, and dream when the seed catalogs arrive in January. It's a time of hope and starting anew for CSA membership sign-ups, sowing seeds in the greenhouses for spring plantings, preparing fields, and rallying the energy to start another year. A farmer's work is never done.

Teena's Pride: Tomatoes and Dreams

Teena's Pride All Locally Grown Produce

20025 SW 270th Street
Homestead, Florida 33031
305-216-2336
www.teenaspridecsa.com

SAFFFE (Save American Family Farms from Extinction)

www.safffe.com

At a time when most fields around the country are buried under several feet of snow, the ground is suspended in deep-freeze, and temperatures are hovering in the single digits, operations at Teena's Pride All Locally Grown Produce are buzzing. South Florida in January is hot and humid, but nothing like the roiling steam bath it will become in July and August, when even heat-loving tomatoes wither.

And Florida is known for its tomatoes. They may not necessarily all be good-tasting tomatoes, but there sure are a lot of them. In the 2013–2014 season, Florida's commercial crop totaled more than 890 million pounds and was worth nearly $350 million, much of it destined for supermarkets, food-service companies, and canning industries. In fact, the state is the country's leading grower of this ubiquitous vegetable, with California coming in at a distant second.

The city of Homestead sits about 35 miles southwest of Miami, 25 miles north of Key Largo, and 10 miles east of Everglades National Park. It originally got its name when railroad construction began around 1900 and the land was opened up for homesteading. It's a small city, with a population of about 62,000 people as of 2012 and a total land area of only 14.4 square miles. Its daytime temperatures average between 88° and 92°F in the summer and 68° and 80°F in the winter. However, this is tropical monsoon country, with a hot, wet season that lasts from mid May to early October.

Like much of Florida, Homestead is flatter than a roadkill pancake, but its rich soils, ever-present sun, and mild climate make it ideal for agriculture, which forms the backbone of its economy. According to the South Dade Chamber of Commerce, Miami-Dade County's agricultural operations represent a nearly $1 billion annual industry but occupy just 6 percent of the county's land. Since the late 1800s, the area has supplied America with much of its year-round and winter produce, including sweet potatoes, squash, beans, taro, okra, eggplant, herbs, Asian vegetables, mangoes, avocados, carambolas, lychees, longans, mamey sapotes, bananas and plantains, cherimoyas, coconuts, sapodillas, jackfruit, and passion fruit.

The area is home not just to food plants but an enormous nursery industry as well (the second-largest in America), with some 1,500 state-certified nurseries cultivating 13,000 acres of palms, trees, shrubs, ornamentals, bedding plants, orchids, bromeliads, and houseplants destined for homes, offices, malls, and hotels across North America and abroad. Tourists passing through on their way to Miami or the Florida Keys often see signs inviting them to stop by roadside greenhouses or farm stands to grab an orchid or enjoy a taste of tropical fruit to take home with them.

In spite of Homestead's rich history as "America's Salad Bowl" and "Winter Bread Basket" for more than a century, many of its vegetable farms are in serious jeopardy because the economics of global competition have completely changed their business landscape in recent years. In 1994, the North American Free Trade Agreement, or NAFTA, opened trade between the United States, Mexico, and Canada. The consequences have proved devastating for many farmers on both sides of the borders.

Large- and small-scale food systems, agricultural policy, and international trade are complicated matters that intertwine government subsidies, powerful multinational corporations, artificial price distortions, the rise and fall of commodity surpluses, and political forces that work to maintain the status quo. Mexican and American farmers have been unfairly pitted against one another by market economics that ruthlessly favor the cheapest labor and production costs—and the greatest profits for large wholesale buyers and food manufacturers—over the quality of the actual produce itself, or what's truly sustainable for the farmer and the environment.

Few have felt this devastation more than Florida's tomato and vegetable farmers, who have seen a meteoric rise in production and imports from Mexico. Every year this less expensive produce from south of the border displaces more and more American-grown fruits and vegetables. And unlike their colleagues who grow commodity crops like corn and soybeans, American produce farmers have absolutely no access to government subsidies, financial assistance, or other economic safety nets.

❄

It wasn't always like this. In the 1970s, a very young Teena (originally Martina) traveled from her native fishing village in Newfoundland, Canada, to South Florida, where she met Steven Borek, a Homestead vegetable farmer. The couple married and had two sons, Steven Jr. and Michael. But when their sons were toddlers and her husband was killed at the age of 24 in an accident, Teena had to decide whether to sell the 500-acre farm or keep it. In the face of tragedy, she chose the latter in hopes of eventually passing the farm on to her sons when they grew up.

In spite of Homestead's rich history as "America's Salad Bowl" and "Winter Bread Basket" for more than a century, many of its vegetable farms are in serious jeopardy because the economics of global competition have completely changed their business landscape in recent years.

Steven Borek with his young bride Teena.

Teena with her sons Michael and Steven Jr.

"The local farmers were awesome.
Before Steven died, I never had to
do anything on the farm other than
help at harvest time, but after he
was gone, I learned really quick.
I had old Italian guys telling me
how to make my squash grow.
And you know, you think farmers
are competition, but they're not.
The farmers were great and never
discriminated against me."

— Teena Borek

Over the past 40 years, Teena has remained a remarkable figure in the Miami-Dade County farming community. Her accomplishments and accolades are many. At one time, she was the area's only female row-crop farmer. She graduated from the Wedgworth Leadership Institute for Agriculture and Natural Resources and is a charter member of the Florida Agricultural Promotional Campaign and a past president of the Dade County Farm Bureau.

In addition to serving on the board of directors of the Florida Tomato Committee and the Florida Fruit and Vegetable Association, Teena was chosen as Agriculturist of the Year in Homestead in both 1985 and 2011. She was named 2004 Woman of the Year in Agriculture by Agriculture Commissioner Charles Bronson and the Florida Department of Agriculture. And both Miami-Dade County and the cities of Homestead and Florida City have proclaimed "Teena Borek Day" in her honor.

Over her decades as a farmer, Teena's resilience, ability to adapt, and fierce work ethic have served her well. She was the first farmer in Dade County to use a linear irrigation system and the first vegetable farmer in Homestead to use a computer in her work. For years she partnered with researchers to experiment with higher-yielding, more nutritious varieties. Teena has also steered her farm through several devastating freezes. And when Hurricane Andrew struck the Homestead area in August 1992, she wasted no time in rebuilding the farm and planting 60 acres of seed corn just days after the storm blew out all the windows in her house and destroyed most of her farming equipment.

Did Teena ever encounter any prejudice as a woman farmer in a male-dominated profession? "I hadn't intended to ever go into farming," Teena says, "but after my husband's death, I just took over because that's just what you did. We had farm debt even back then, and I kept the farm going with the help of his family." Early on, she tried to obtain farm loans from the USDA's Farmer's Administration agency and was refused, even though she knew male farmers who were getting loans who didn't deserve them.

"But the local farmers were awesome," she adds. "Before Steven died, I never had to do anything on the farm other than help at harvest time, but after he was gone, I learned *really* quick. I had old Italian guys telling me how to make my squash grow. And you know, you think farmers are competition, but they're not. The farmers were great and never discriminated against me.

"I remember one night when we had a freeze, and I had potatoes that year. I burnt tires underneath power lines, and the man from Florida Power and Light called me up and said, 'Little girl, stop it, because I can tell you that those potatoes are never gonna pay enough money for you to pay me after you put out my transformers!'" She laughs heartily at the memory.

The proverbial bounty flows from the fields and greenhouses at Teena's Pride. The farm has always specialized in tomatoes, particularly heirlooms, those succulent bastions of flavor—it grows nearly 30 varieties. But it also raises heritage eggplant, peppers, sweet corn, arugula, chard, cauliflower, beets, summer and winter squash, cucumbers, kale, lettuces, micro-greens, basil, cilantro, dill, bay, lemongrass, rosemary, mint, stevia, okra, celery, spinach, mint, radishes, edible flowers, sunflower sprouts, and wheatgrass, to name a few.

Its CSA program began in 2011 and now has around 250 members. The farm has nine full-time employees, some of whom have been working for Teena for more than 20 years.

The farm hosts a monthly open house when the general public can stop by to see what truly superior vegetables and fruits taste like. A chef is on hand to cook produce from scratch, and visitors tour the greenhouses and get to sample right from the plants as they go, so they can see the direct connection between how the vegetables are grown and what makes them so delicious. Educating the consumer with this kind of outreach is absolutely crucial if family farms are to survive, Teena says, because most shoppers don't have a clue about where their food comes from or how it gets to them. And it's working—more than 100 people usually show up at these open houses.

Kids and parents touring the greenhouse.

This colorful array of red, green, yellow, and orange heirloom tomato slices might be the most incredibly delicious tomatoes you ever taste, should you be lucky enough to be in Homestead during one of the monthly open houses at Teena's Pride.

A special section of the greenhouse is reserved for kids, who are often thrilled when they get to pull their own radishes. "We try to teach parents and children how good fresh vegetables taste," Teena says. "I had a little kid whose parents called me back later and said, 'You know, when I got home, she made me cut up that beet and she wouldn't let anyone else eat it because she pulled it herself.'"

Teena's Pride also participates in a local farmers market in which all of the produce and food products (like honey and jam) come from within a 10-to-15-mile radius. Teena's Pride makes and sells its own pesto and salsa, featuring its basil and tomatoes. The farm is both federal and state food-safety–certified, meaning that, among other things, all of its employees participate in the food safety training program provided by the University of Florida. The farm undergoes third-party audits and routine inspections to ensure proper handling as well as field sanitation. And its 10,000-square-foot packinghouse is certified by the Florida Department of Agriculture.

Teena's sons did indeed go on to take over the family business; Michael is now a third-generation owner of the farm, and his brother Steven Jr. raises sweet corn and snap beans in northern Florida. But in this day and age—one that has changed completely since her young husband was a farmer—Teena's not sure it was such a good idea.

Kids eagerly pulling their own radishes.

Teena with some of her signature heirloom tomatoes fresh off the vine.

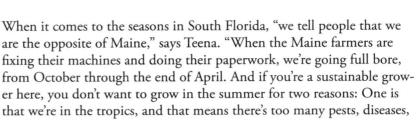

When it comes to the seasons in South Florida, "we tell people that we are the opposite of Maine," says Teena. "When the Maine farmers are fixing their machines and doing their paperwork, we're going full bore, from October through the end of April. And if you're a sustainable grower here, you don't want to grow in the summer for two reasons: One is that we're in the tropics, and that means there's too many pests, diseases, blights, and funguses during that rainy time. You'd be putting too many chemicals on your crops. The other thing is that all of the other farms up north during the summer are growing and harvesting, and they can do that a lot cheaper than we can because of all the crop care required here. So it's just smarter to stay in our own market window."

There are other reasons too. Although herbs can be grown in South Florida, the muggy, rainy climate makes it nearly impossible to grow basil outdoors. Celery and cilantro have their own seasons and simply will not grow here except in the dead of winter. And then there is the simple need for rest. "During the winter, farmworkers are putting in long days seven days a week," Teena says, "so by the time summer comes, they are exhausted and need 30-hour weeks just to recover."

The farm's soils consist of coral rock, which produces awesome tomatoes, corn, and green beans—crops that thrive on its high calcium content. Teena is also strict about doing regular crop rotations to avoid wearing out the soil and employing integrated pest management methods. The farm uses an enormous number of natural predators like ladybugs and praying mantises to keep the plant-loving bugs at bay.

Plant-based green chemistry is another important growing technology, and Teena's Pride applies natural insecticides like Spintor that target only certain pests. "I used to love parathion—you just spray it once and everything dies!" Teena says, chuckling. "But it's so poisonous that they don't allow that anymore. But because there are no broad-based natural alternatives available, if you have thrips, whitefly, and worms on the same plant, you have to use three or four different natural chemicals to be just as effective. In using this new chemistry, growers are spraying a lot more than usual."

In spite of these more frequent applications, Teena says that there are definite advantages. "Back when we could use broad-based chemicals, that would take care of all the bugs at once, but they also killed the beneficial insects as well. And this new plant-based chemistry is really safe—the reentry time [from application to when workers can go back in without protective clothing] is only three to four hours."

The farm uses separate types of fertilizers for their hypdroponic operations and fields. Because it is a food-safety–certified farm, the state does not allow it to use organic fertilizers because they are animal waste–based. These regulations are very strict, and not even compost can be used.

"We can't even keep a dog or cat on the premises. We have traps for rats set all over our farm—not that I think that a rat could even fit in there—" jokes Teena, "and every month inspectors come and check to see if they contain any rats. Can you imagine a farm that doesn't have a cat?"

"We try to teach parents and children how good fresh vegetables taste. I had a little kid whose parents called me back later and said, 'You know, when I got home, she made me cut up that beet and she wouldn't let anyone else eat it because she pulled it herself.'"

— Teena Borek

According to Teena, south Dade County's agricultural output is enormous—and undervalued. "If America has a freeze (and it has happened)," she says, "south Dade has the capability to grow enough vegetables to supply the whole country. We currently ship all over America and quite a bit to Canada, but unfortunately it's always priced low because of our competition from Mexico."

This deeply worries Teena. "NAFTA absolutely sold the farmers of Dade County down the river because the government wanted it for the big grain farms up north. Because we're considered specialty farmers in that we don't grow commodity crops, we're very expendable."

Teena shakes her head. "We used to grow thousands upon thousands of acres of tomatoes here in the county, and now there's less than a thousand total. We're losing more and more family farmers here because everyone is choosing to buy foreign produce. There's no farmers really making any money any more. Used to be that in the wintertime, farmers could make enough to sustain themselves for the whole year, but now the profit margin is just not there. We have more food safety laws, more paperwork, and additional things we have to do and pay for. My son Michael has to pay $10,000 a year to comply with mandatory food safety regulations, and it doesn't come back to us—it's all overhead."

Teena relates the story of a third-generation Italian farmer of squash and green beans who was honored as the local Farmer of the Year a few years ago. At his acceptance speech, he told everyone, "I'm telling you all, I'm quitting before I go broke."

What's especially frustrating is that it's not a level playing field, according to Teena. "Our government makes organic, sustainable American farmers comply with all of these laws and regulations, while Mexican farmers, who do not have our employee labor laws or may use pesticides that are banned in the United States, are allowed to ship their produce into the US and compete unfairly with our family farms.

Okra seedlings flourishing in the greenhouse.

"The biggest thing I tell my CSA members is that if you want to be really sustainable, and you're buying certified organic from China, Chile, or Mexico, you really have no idea what you're actually getting. China alone has been fined hundreds of thousands of dollars for falsifying organic-certification documents. There is this misconception that the USDA is checking all of these imports, but that's just not true. Less than 2 percent of all imported produce from Mexico is actually inspected, and out of that 2 percent, more than 80 percent of it at any given time can fail, because of illegal pesticide use or the smuggling of drugs in the shipments."

Because labor and production costs are so much less in Mexico, American farmers simply cannot compete. There have been years when Teena's son Michael has had to let tomatoes rot in his fields because prices for his crop fell so low that he literally could not afford to harvest them. Major food-service companies and individual consumers alike see Mexican produce selling for a fraction of the prices of local produce, are assured by their organic labels, and blindly buy, not realizing or caring that their actions are driving the nails into the coffins of local farms.

In response to this crisis and to address consumer ignorance of the issues at hand, Teena started SAFFFE, Save American Family Farms from

Michael keeping an eye on tomato plants early in the season.

Extinction. One of its biggest missions is to educate children through its Kids 2 Farm 2 Table Children's Program, which is based on an experiential education model (by doing, reflecting, and applying). By involving them in gardening and tasting experiences that build their knowledge and understanding through inquiry and reflection, kids learn firsthand about food and the natural world on a working farm. With the help of volunteer chefs and fresh-food advocates, this program is part of a growing movement to transform the way nutrition is taught. The instruction follows a "rainbow on your plate" philosophy that promotes a diet incorporating a diverse set of colorful, whole foods. This approach ensures that students learn to eat a balanced diet.

Thanks to a partnership with Slow Food of Miami, many children are brought in to see Teena's Pride farm. But Teena is working to obtain grants to create a separate SAFFFE farm in a different location that can accommodate two busloads of kids five days a week, especially those from inner cities. This new farm will contain separate areas for row crops, herb gardens, greenhouses, and a pond with catch-and-release trout. The whole idea is to get parents and children alike more knowledgeable and invested in their local farmers and food—and eat more healthfully for life.

With the bottom having fallen out of the wholesale business in recent years, Teena's Pride has turned to local restaurants, and now fully half of its total income comes from this profitable revenue stream. The incredibly rich flavors and aromas, juiciness, freshness, and superb quality of Teena's Pride heirloom tomatoes, herbs, vegetables, edible flowers, micro-greens, and sprouts have caught the eye of many high-end area chefs from Miami to Coral Gables to Key Largo. Restaurants like Michael's Genuine Food and Drink, the Four Seasons Hotel Miami, Essensia Restaurant, A Little Taste of the Keys Catering, Ocean Reef Club, and Norman's 180 are just a few of the many establishments that proudly serve Teena's Pride produce. Diners often ask for the farm's products by name.

"Teena and Michael's produce is simply amazing," says Executive Chef Aaron Brooks of the Four Seasons. "It's a true pleasure to work with them and be able to showcase their product on our menus. When our guests taste the herbs, tomatoes, or veggies that come from the farm, they are simply blown away with how tasty the product is."

Chef Julie Frans of Essensia Restaurant agrees. "I always joke around with our guests that Teena's Pride produce makes my job as a chef too easy! It all starts with the ingredients, and the care that goes into creating great-tasting, high-quality produce. When I have these amazing ingredients to work with, I don't need to do too much to them—I mainly strive just to provide them to guests in a way that showcases their true nature and flavors. As a chef, using this amazing produce, my job becomes more about highlighting the natural product and working the flavors to marry and compliment one another, rather than having to change or tweak them or mask them too much."

In March 2014, Teena's Pride got a visit from none other than Emeril Lagasse, restaurateur, cookbook author, and television personality, when he toured South Florida for his Cooking Channel's *Emeril's Florida* show.

Emeril and Philippe Reynaud, executive director of Culinary Operations at the Ocean Reef Club, toured Teena's Pride farm. While walking the greenhouses with Teena, Emeril taste-tested baby arugula, kale, cucumbers, lemon sorrel, and living micro-greens. Michael guided Emeril through his heirloom tomato greenhouses, and they enjoyed a final stop at a white linen-covered table set by the farm team with a variety of heirloom tomatoes. Emeril also experienced delicious, bite-sized samples of Teena's own ultra-fresh vegetables prepared by students from the Robert Morgan Educational Center's culinary arts program.

Chef and television personality Emeril Lagasse posed with the crew when he visited the farm to film an episode of his Emeril's Florida show. Teena's son Michael is in the center row, far right.

"The show is about what this great state offers," said Emeril. "So it's not just about cooking, and it's not just restaurants, although that's a nice chunk of it. But it's about the beaches, it's about fishing, it's about farming, it's about the agriculture."

The long-term future of the farm remains uncertain. Because of recent market contractions, Teena's Pride as of 2015 has shrunk from its original 1,000 acres of tomatoes, potatoes, and sweet corn to a mere 10 acres of greenhouses and 20 acres of heirloom tomatoes. Even in just a year's time, Teena and Michael went from growing more than 400 acres of sweet corn and 100 acres of tomatoes to a mere fraction of that because of plummeting wholesale demand and their inability to compete with foreign produce. "The market at the end of 2014 killed everything," Teena says.

"We used to grow thousands upon thousands of acres of tomatoes here in the county, and now there's less than a thousand total. We're losing more and more family farmers here because everyone is choosing to buy foreign produce. There's no farmers really making any money any more.

People are so far removed from farms since they no longer visit them anymore to see relatives. And since they have no idea of the hard work involved, they have no compassion for family farmers. But on the flip side, they all do want to save farmland.

Thing is, you can't save the farmland—you have to save the farmers by giving them a decent price for their crops. The farmland is not going to be any good if there are no growers."

— Teena Borek

Sweet corn on a beautiful Florida day.

"You have to sell your product and make a profit," she rightly contends. "Farmers can't just grow because they like to. And CSAs do not make profits; subscribers expect more than their money's worth when they get their boxes because they're getting their produce straight from the farm. And what we do is hand-plant, hand-weed, and hand-harvest everything. We don't use herbicides in our greenhouses, we do everything manually, and the cheapest labor we can get is $9 an hour. So it is extremely difficult. More than half of the money from our CSA boxes goes just to labor costs.

"And farming is a continuous education process—you have to be learning all of the time," she continues. "You have to be on top of all of the laws, the technology, the crop care, the paperwork, and so much more than people who work regular jobs."

As of spring 2015, the Florida Tomato Committee is working on drawing up a more reasonable trade agreement between Mexico and the United States. "The way things are going, I don't see any Dade County farmer surviving, unless something drastic happens," says Teena. In her four decades as a farmer, Teena has seen seismic shifts in government attitudes toward domestic farming and foreign produce, more regulations and paperwork introduced, and an increasing disconnect between corporations, consumers, and food.

"People are so far removed from farms since they no longer visit them anymore to see relatives. And since they have no idea of the hard work involved, they have no compassion for family farmers. But on the flip side, they all do want to save farmland. Thing is, you can't save the farmland—you have to save the farmers by giving them a decent price for their crops. The farmland is not going to be any good if there are no growers."

Compounding the problem is the fact that the government does not make distinctions in the levels of food-safety regulations and paperwork required for different sizes of growers. With these associated costs, a big commodity farm, a major food manufacturer, or a corporation may pay only half a cent on a package of product—hardly enough for them to notice—whereas a small family farmer can easily be forced to pay many times that amount to comply, thus cutting into profit margins that were perhaps nonexistent to begin with. It isn't that regulations and high standards shouldn't be required; it's the injudicious enforcement and expectation without a proper sliding scale that is so detrimental. "The further that people are removed from knowing where their food comes from," says Teena, "the more they demand from something they don't know anything about."

So what can the average consumer do? "People need terribly to be educated," Teena says. "If they see sweet corn in Whole Foods, and some comes from my son's local sustainable farm and the other says it's certified-organic from China, they need to be educated that the latter is not necessarily as safe or better, even if it is cheaper. And they need to support family farmers through their wallets and local legislators, and by letting their stores and restaurants know they need to carry local produce."

In spite of everything, Teena is still hopeful. "People are really waking up to the fact that they want their food from their own country. It's starting a great movement. And if they go to a restaurant, they want to know that restaurant's buying from local farmers. It is making a big difference."

Beans (Shell)

PHASEOLUS AND
VIGNA SPECIES

Beans, beans, the musical fruit—the more you eat, the more you toot. Nursery rhymes and rude jokes aside, shell beans, or "shellies" as they are known in old-time southern lingo, are one of the loveliest vegetables around. The term "shell beans" refers to bean varieties with mature, fat seeds that are typically shelled (removed) from their pods and eaten either fresh or dried, as opposed to pole beans such as string, snap, and wax, whose tender pods and immature seeds are eaten fresh.

The digestive difficulties of beans are legendary, and for several reasons. In their raw state, all shell beans except favas and soybeans contain natural plant toxins that can result in food poisoning–like symptoms (see page 503 for more details), and so they must be properly cooked before eating. They also contain complex sugars that some people lack the digestive enzymes to break down, which results in the infamous bloating and flatulence; over-the-counter supplements like Beano work by providing that natural enzyme. Proper soaking, draining, and cooking are also instrumental to easing unpleasant gut explosions.

But don't shy away from shellies—they are delicious, versatile, extremely nutritious, and should be eaten more often. Shell beans cooked fresh from their pods are a creamy, truly seasonal treat—don't pass them up when you see them.

An extremely diverse plant family, shell beans come in a wondrous variety of sizes, shapes, and colors; you never know what lovely heirloom types might show up in your fall or winter CSA box or farmers market. Below are some of the most common varieties; for more information on fava beans, see pages 37–42.

Black
These little deep-black beans, sometimes called turtle beans, are common in Latin American, Caribbean, and American southern cuisines. They have a mild, sweet, earthy flavor.

Black-Eyed Pea or Cowpea
Most people outside of the American South have never tasted these firm, nutty, full-flavored legumes from Africa, which require long, hot summers to grow. They go by many names, including blackeye, southernpea, field pea, or crowder pea, and come in many varieties, colors, and shapes. If you are lucky enough to find them, don't pass them up—they have a more assertive culinary personality than most beans and are worth getting to know.

Cannellini
These large, white Italian kidney beans have a nutty flavor and a pleasing, creamy texture. They hold their shape well in cooking and are among the best beans for salads.

Cranberry, Horticultural, and Borlotto

These are among the most common shell beans you'll find in your CSA box or farmers market, with beautiful pods splashed with brilliant red or rose; cradled within are ivory beans flecked with similar markings that disappear in cooking. They are nutty-tasting and are especially popular in Mediterranean cuisines. Some varieties you may encounter by name are Tongue of Fire, Dragon's Tongue, Vermont Cranberry, or French Horticultural.

Garbanzo or Chickpea

These little round yellow or beige seeds are a staple in Middle Eastern and Indian cuisines; they are the primary ingredient in hummus and in falafel patties. They have a nutty flavor and a buttery texture.

Great Northern

These familiar flat, kidney-shaped white beans have a mild, delicate personality that takes on the flavors of whatever they are cooked with. They are the classic bean of American baked beans and the French cassoulet.

Lima and Butter

These beans come in many sizes, forms, and colors, from diminutive baby limas to meaty, larger butter beans. If you have bad memories of being forced to eat your limas as a child or of mediocre succotashes, put them aside and try them again—limas can be rich, buttery, and delectable.

Kidney

These large, kidney-shaped beans vary from light to dark red and have a full, robust flavor, along with somewhat thick skins. They are popular in Caribbean and Spanish dishes and are the classic bean in red beans and rice, as well as American chili.

Navy

These little white, oval-shaped beans are sometimes called pea beans. Their mild flavor makes them excellent in soups and stews. They are most often used in the classic American dish of pork and beans.

Pinto

Pintos are medium-sized, with mottled beige and brown seeds. Their earthy flavor and powdery texture make them a favorite in refried beans and in Tex-Mex and Mexican dishes.

Soybean

Not until the rise of Japanese restaurants did fresh, green soybeans become popular among Americans in the form of edamame, which are served boiled in their pods and nibbled before a meal. Bred especially to be eaten at an immature stage, this soybean is a cousin of the yellow variety that's grown on a huge scale in the United States for livestock feed, oil, and food products.

HISTORY

Beans are among humanity's oldest food crops, cultivated since prehistoric times in remarkably diverse parts of the planet. They've been found in Asian archaeological sites dating as far back as 9750 BC, in 4,000-year-old Egyptian tombs, and in remnants of civilizations from around 7000 BC in the Middle East, Mexico, and Peru. It is thought that beans and grains are among the plants that helped humans make the transition from nomadic hunter-gatherers to more settled agrarians. Indeed, beans and grains contain complementary proteins when eaten together, and combinations of them have been historically linked both in the field and in the kitchen (think red beans and rice, lima beans and corn, garbanzo beans and couscous, and the Native American triumvirate of "three sisters"—corn, beans, and squash).

NUTRITION

Shell beans are nutritional powerhouses, packing significant amounts of protein, complex carbohydrates, vitamins B6, E, and K, calcium, thiamine, folate, iron, magnesium, phosphorus, potassium, zinc, copper, manganese, and selenium. They are also high in dietary fiber, which helps you feel satiated. A one-cup serving of cooked beans contains around 250 calories.

SEASON

Commercially, dry beans are available year-round. Fresh shell beans start showing up in CSA shares and farmers markets in July and are available into the fall months (favas are an exception, appearing in the spring). Dry beans are a substantial part of many winter CSAs.

SELECTION

Fresh shell beans should be plump and bumpy, fat with mature seeds. Pods that are heavy for their size are a good bet. They should strike a balance between looking freshly picked and yet beginning to dry out—if they are too young, the seeds are likely to be immature and very difficult to extract. Depending on the variety, pod color can indicate quality; very yellow or brownish pods tend to be past their prime. Shell beans both fresh and dried should be completely dry and free from any signs of mold, sprouting, or undue desiccation (although some varieties may have a slightly shriveled appearance). Also avoid pods with holes or obvious punctures, which may be a sign of insect damage.

STORAGE

Fresh shell beans, either in their pods or shelled, are quite perishable; store them unwashed in a paper bag or a basket (but not in plastic) in the refrigerator for only a few days at the most. Dry beans should be stored in airtight containers in a cool, dry place away from sunlight. If properly stored, they will last indefinitely, but they will start to lose their moisture after a year or two; beans older than a couple of years may need to be soaked and cooked longer. Commercially packaged dry beans have a sell-by date that denotes a time to use them for best quality, not safety—so they are fine to use after this date.

TRIMMING AND CLEANING

One of the simple pleasures in life is having a huge pile of pods to shell; it can be a most satisfying task to do with friends, children, or even by yourself. To shell, twist the pods to pop out the beans; or use a fingernail

---

Safety Tip

Fresh shell beans should not be eaten raw or even nibbled on while being prepared for cooking because they contain phytohaemagglutinin (PHA), a natural plant toxin that interferes with digestion and can cause severe vomiting and diarrhea. Small children have died from eating just a few raw seeds.

This is totally unrelated to the flatulence commonly associated with beans, which is the result of some people lacking the enzymes and gut bacteria to properly break down the beans' sugars.

Kidney beans contain the highest levels of PHA, while favas and soybeans do not contain any. Some people are allergic to favas, however; see page 41 for more details. Limas also contain linamarin, which forms a cyanide compound. Proper cooking renders both PHA and linamarin harmless.

Cooking below the boiling point has been known to actually increase PHA levels with dry beans. To be on the safe side, it's best to vigorously boil dry beans (especially kidney, cannellini, and butter beans) for at least 10 minutes before using them in recipes involving a slow cooker. Cook fresh shell beans for at least 10 minutes (although hard boiling is not necessary as for dry beans).

For More Information

US Dry Bean Council
www.usdrybeans.com

The Bean Institute
www.beaninstitute.com

"Beans are highly nutritious
and satisfying, they can also be
delicious if and when properly
prepared, and they posses over all
vegetables the great advantage of
being just as good, if not better,
when kept waiting, an advantage
in the case of people whose
disposition or occupation makes it
difficult for them to be punctual
at mealtime."

— *Andre Simon,*
The Concise Encyclopedia
of Gastronomy

to nick open the pod's seam, then run your thumb down to extract the beans. With limas, it's often easier to use scissors to snip the pods open.

Tiny pebbles, twigs, and other bits of unwanted debris often lurk among dry beans, so it is worth picking them over before cooking. It's a good time to remove any shriveled or damaged beans as well. And always rinse them before soaking and cooking, as they are often dusty.

SOAKING (DRY BEANS)

Although it is not absolutely necessary, dry beans do benefit from a good soaking before cooking to rehydrate them, reduce their cooking times, and make them more digestible (fresh shell beans don't require it). Long soaking is traditionally done, but you can do quicker versions if you lack the time, according to the US Dry Bean Council. For the traditional soak, pour the beans in a bowl or pot, and add at least three times the amount of water (thus, 2 cups of beans requires 6 cups of water). Discard any beans that float to the surface. Soak them for 8 hours or overnight. By now the beans will have absorbed most of the water and swollen to several times their original size. Drain the beans in a colander, discard the soaking water, and rinse with fresh, cool water. It's normal for the beans to appear wrinkled after this kind of rehydration.

For a quick soak, place the beans in a large pot and add 10 cups of water for every 2 cups of beans. Bring them to a boil and keep boiling for 2 to 3 minutes. Then drain and discard the soaking water, and rinse with fresh, cool water.

Or you can hot-soak them, which reduces cooking time and consistently produces tender beans. Place the beans in a large pot and add 10 cups of water for every 2 cups of beans. Bring them to a boil and keep boiling for 2 to 3 minutes. Then remove the beans from the heat, cover, and let them stand for 4 to 24 hours. Drain and discard the soaking water, and rinse with fresh, cool water.

STEAMING AND BOILING

FRESH SHELL BEANS

Personal preferences run deep when it comes to cooking fresh shellies; some folks swear by gentle simmering and believe that boiling toughens the beans and potentially overcooks them. Some people like their beans firmer and drier, and others prefer a more pliant vegetable; still others want them soft and creamy, almost mooshy. To complicate matters, cooking times vary tremendously with different types of beans, their state of dryness, the mineral content of their cooking water, and even the altitude at which they are prepared. They should, however, be cooked long enough to deactivate a natural toxin that can interfere with digestion—at least 10 minutes.

Adding aromatics to the cooking water or using broth or stock instead of water helps flavor the beans—leeks, onions, garlic cloves, bay leaf, sage, rosemary, thyme, oregano, even a little bacon or salt pork all work wonders. Salt in the cooking water hardens the beans' skins, and longer cooking times or vigorous boiling will split them, so keep this in mind when deciding what texture you want the beans to have in the finished dish.

Smaller or younger fresh shell beans take about 10 to 15 minutes of steaming, simmering, or gentle boiling, whereas larger beans may require

20 to 30 minutes. Taste them often to test their texture—they are often at their best when they're tender but still a bit firm. Take care to add warm water as necessary while the beans expand and cook, and stir them occasionally to keep them from sticking.

DRY BEANS

Soak and drain dry beans, as outlined in the soaking instructions above. Fill the pot with enough fresh water or stock to cover them, add aromatics if desired, and gently simmer or boil. A tablespoon of vegetable oil or a bit of butter stirred into the cooking liquid prevents the beans from foaming and boiling over (the brownish foam is not dirt—just coagulated proteins).

Taste them often to test their texture. Add warm water as necessary while the beans expand and cook, and stir them occasionally to keep them from sticking. Refrain from adding any ingredients high in acid or calcium, such as lemon juice, vinegar, tomatoes, ketchup, molasses, or wine, until the beans are fully cooked, as their presence can prevent the beans from becoming tender.

The cooking times listed below are estimates only; exact times depend on the age and condition of your dry beans, how long they've soaked, and your preferences in texture. These times also assume you are cooking them on the stove at a gentle simmer. Because beans vary so much, it's best to cook them for 30 minutes, then taste them and do a "bite" test. If the beans are still chalky inside, set a timer for 10 or 15 minutes, then test them again.

Pressure cooking is one of the fastest ways to cook dry beans, sometimes in as little as 20 minutes; consult the manufacturer's instructions for more information.

- Black: 60 to 90 minutes
- Black-eyed peas: 60 to 90 minutes
- Cranberry and horticultural: 45 to 60 minutes
- Garbanzo (chickpeas): 60 to 90 minutes
- Great Northern: 45 to 60 minutes
- Lima and butter: 60 to 90 minutes
- Kidney and cannellini: 90 to 120 minutes
- Navy: 90 to 120 minutes
- Pinto: 60 to 90 minutes

MICROWAVING

Place fresh shell beans in a microwave-safe dish, add 2 tablespoons water, and cook on high power.

- 2 cups fresh shell beans = 4 to 8 minutes, depending upon their size

Microwaving is not recommended for preparing dry beans unless it is to reheat already cooked beans.

BLANCHING AND FREEZING

Fresh shell beans freeze beautifully (as do cooked dry beans). Blanch them in boiling water for 2 to 3 minutes. Drain, then plunge them into ice water for 5 minutes to stop the cooking process. Remove and drain. Package

Winter CSA Shares

Martha Wagner

Farmers have plenty of work to do year-round, even if their CSA programs are not year-round. If you live in Florida or southern Arizona, your CSA season might run from November through May, then close down for the summer, but in most parts of the country, the majority of CSA programs close down for at least a few months in the winter.

A growing number of farms are selling winter shares, however, with once- or twice-monthly pickups or deliveries. Some CSAs are selling a large, one-time, end-of-season box of storage crops—onions, potatoes, and other root veggies, plus winter greens and other extras. Some end-of-season CSA programs are designed specifically for home canners and preservers, with large quantities of cucumbers, green beans, tomatoes, garlic, and basil ready for pickling, canning, and freezing.

Unless you live in a temperate climate, a typical winter CSA share will not look like a summer share, but there is no shortage of taste and variety for the willing cook. **Full Moon Farm** *in Hinesburg, Vermont, offers a 23-week winter CSA share consisting primarily of root crops, plus leeks, spinach, cabbage, Brussels sprouts, collards, kale, lettuce mix, and more. Its website bluntly advises, "You must cook or at least be open to the idea of it. If you don't cook, juice or love raw vegetables, this share is not for you."*

At **Quail Hill Farm** *in Amagansett, New York, winter shares are picked up at the farm twice a month and are likely to include such veggies as broccoli, bok choy, cauliflower, kale, collards, potatoes, winter squash, turnips, carrots, sweet potatoes, beets, wheat berries, and greenhouse herbs and greens.*

In southwestern Pennsylvania, winter shares from **Penn's Corner**

them in zipper-lock freezer or vacuum food sealer-type bags, or freezer containers. Squeeze out any excess air and leave ½ inch of headspace (unless you are using the vacuum sealing method). Frozen shell beans will keep for up to 6 months at 0°F.

EQUIVALENTS, MEASURES, AND SERVINGS

Typically, dry beans slightly more than double in weight and volume when cooked, so plan on using about half the specified amount of cooked beans in a recipe. Garbanzos (chickpeas) and black-eyed peas may triple in size. The following estimates are approximate, depending on the type of bean.

- 2 pounds fresh pods = about 1 cup fresh shell beans (but pod waste varies considerably with the type of bean)
- 1 pound dry beans = 2 cups dry = 2 to 3 pounds (4 to 5 cups) cooked
- ¾ cup dry beans = about 1½ to 2 cups cooked = one 15-ounce can
- 1½ cups dry beans = 3 to 4 cups cooked beans = two 15-ounce cans
- One 15-ounce can, drained = 1½ cups cooked
- One 19-ounce can, drained = 2¼ cups cooked
- One 28-ounce can, drained = 3 to 3¼ cups cooked

COMPLEMENTARY HERBS, SEASONINGS, AND FOODS

Apples, arugula, bacon, basil, bay leaf, black pepper, chicory, chiles, cinnamon, coconut milk, corn, cream, cumin, dill, eggs, epazote, escarole, greens, fennel, fish, garlic, ginger, goose, ham, honey, horseradish, kale, lard, leeks, lemon, marjoram, milk, molasses, mustard, nutmeg, olive oil, onions, oregano, Parmesan cheese, pasta, pork, raisins, rosemary, sage, savory, scallions, shallots, squash, tahini paste, thyme, tomatoes, tuna.

SERVING SUGGESTIONS

- Like many good things, fresh shell beans are best when cooked as simply as possible. Finishing touches include a great olive oil, a little butter or cream, slivers of ham, a sprinkling of fresh herbs or garlic, salt and pepper, or lemon juice.
- Fresh shell beans are also delicious cold in salads. Serve with vinaigrette, tuna, fresh herbs, onion, celery, and cold sliced chicken or ham.
- An extremely delicious soup can be made from just fresh shell beans, whole milk, bacon, salt and pepper, and green onion. Coconut milk makes an interesting nondairy substitute.
- Canned beans are a perfectly acceptable (and timesaving) substitute for cooked dry beans in most recipes; just drain and rinse.
- Try succotash, that classic American dish of lima beans and corn. This is especially good when both crops are in season and at their sweetest succulence. You can also use green soybeans (edamame) instead of limas.
- Puree cooked fresh or dried beans to make rich, unctuous soups.
- Make hummus! This Mediterranean dip is typically made with garbanzos (chickpeas), but you can use cranberry, horticultural, green soybeans (edamame), or other beans as well. Serve with pita bread or raw vegetables.
- When the weather turns nippy, few dishes are as hearty and filling as traditional Boston baked beans, with or without the pork. And it's a great dish to make in the slow cooker.

- Instead of chips or sweets, reach for some freshly boiled green soybeans (edamame). These make a highly nutritious, filling, fun snack for kids and grownups alike.

- Shell beans and bitter, hearty greens like chicory, endive, collards, escarole, kale, dandelion, and mustard have a great affinity for one another, either in salads or cooked dishes. Try this combination with a little honey and black pepper for seasoning.

- Four-bean salad is another perennial favorite. This sweet-and-sour marinated salad traditionally contains a mixture of green and yellow (wax) string beans, kidney beans, and garbanzos (chickpeas), but fresh shell beans and limas are also delicious; feel free to experiment.

- Pasta and beans were made for each other, both in cold salads and hot dishes. White beans such as cannellini, borlotto, and cranberry are delicious with small shell, ditalini, miniature penne, orecchiette, or radiatore pasta. Combined with tomatoes, olive oil, sausage, and a little cheese, this makes a quick, easy, healthful, one-dish meal.

- Refried beans are popular in Mexican, Latin American, and Tex-Mex cuisines as both a side dish and a filling in burritos. This concoction of cooked, mashed beans is usually made with pintos, which give the dish a distinctively sweet earthiness, but black beans, garbanzos (chickpeas), or just about any shell bean can be used. Cooking the beans with aromatics such as onions, garlic, and fresh herbs (epazote is a traditional Mexican one) is especially key to making flavorful refried beans, as is the choice of fat (lard is the most popular, but vegetable oil, bacon drippings, and even butter can be good).

- For a stunning fall salad or hot dish, try the combination of cranberry beans, butternut or delicata squash, kale or broccoli raab, bacon or pancetta, cranberries, and nuts.

- Cassoulet is a rich, slow-cooked French stew of white beans, sausages, goose, duck, and plenty of goose fat. It takes some time to prepare, but oh, how it's well worth it.

- Beans are surprisingly tasty in sweet as well as savory dishes. Try them in baked goods such as bread, bars, muffins, and cookies, or slow-cooked with apples, pears, cinnamon, honey, nutmeg, and molasses. Beans that are neutral in color and taste, such as Great Northern or navy, are good ones to experiment with.

Farm Alliance, a farmer-owned co-operative, include eggs, cheese, and honey as well as canned tomatoes, salsas, and jams from its 30 member farms.

In Junction City, Oregon, **Lonesome Whistle Farm** actually has no summer CSA, although it does sell at several farmers markets. The farm specializes in heirloom dry beans and grains, plus open-pollinated vegetable and flower seeds. It also offers a one-time annual CSA distribution of 80 pounds of heritage grains, polenta, popcorn, and dry beans in December. Its grains include emmer farro, Red Fife wheat berries, flint whole-kernel corn and polenta, hard red wheat, dark northern rye flour, vintage pink beans, and Dakota black heirloom popcorn.

SUPER-QUICK BLACK BEAN SALAD

SERVES 4 AS A SIDE DISH
OR 2 AS A MAIN DISH

Source Note: This dish will keep well for several hours without refrigeration. I often take it to potlucks or for a meal on long airline flights. You can use canned black beans (this is one case where canned beans work just as well as cooked dried beans).

> 1½ to 2 cups cooked black beans (simmered until done but not soft or mushy), or one (15-ounce) can, drained and rinsed
> 1 avocado, peeled and chopped
> 1 red bell pepper, chopped, or 1 cup chopped, vine-ripened tomatoes (or you can use both)

Bean soup has been on the menu of the United States Senate Dining Room in Washington, DC every day since around 1904, with the exception of September 14, 1943, when World War II rationing left the Senate kitchen without the soup's signature navy beans for a single day.

The soup's exact origins are unknown. Although the original included mashed potatoes, celery, and garlic, the current recipe uses Michigan navy beans, water, ham hocks, butter, onions, and salt and pepper.

The late Senator Everett Dirksen of Illinois had this to say about the soup in 1963: "It has ... become an inviolate practice and a glorious tradition that the humble little bean should always be honored. I venture the belief that the marathon speakers of the Senate ... would agree the little bean had much to do with [their] sustained torrent of oratory."

2 tablespoons extra-virgin olive oil
¼ to ½ cup fresh lemon or lime juice
Salt and freshly ground white pepper

1. Combine the drained beans with all of the chopped ingredients.

2. Add the oil and toss; add the lemon juice and toss again. Season to taste with the salt and pepper.

3. Serve at room temperature.

— Marianne Streich

. . . .

WHITE BEAN AND BASIL SALAD   SERVES 4

DRESSING

2 tablespoons olive or safflower oil
2 tablespoons lemon juice or salad vinegar
1 or 2 cloves garlic, crushed
Several leaves chopped fresh basil, or 2 teaspoons dried basil
Pinch of salt
Freshly ground black pepper

SALAD

2 cups cooked Great Northern or cannellini beans, or one
**   (15-ounce) can, drained and rinsed**
1 cucumber, peeled, quartered, and sliced into small chunks
1 sweet red or green bell pepper, chopped
Several sprigs fresh parsley, chopped
1 small red onion, or 2 to 3 green onions, chopped

1. In a medium bowl, mix the dressing ingredients, grinding the garlic and salt into the oil with the back of a spoon.

2. Add the salad ingredients and stir. This salad tastes best when refrigerated for an hour or two before serving.

— Robin Taylor, Featherstone Farm CSA member

. . . .

HARLOW HOUSE BAKED BEANS   MAKES 3 QUARTS

Source Note: These beans are baked uncovered for the last hour to crisp the pork. Pork sausages, frankfurters, beefsteak, and baked ham glazed with brown sugar and studded with cloves are all delicious with baked beans. This recipe is adapted from The Plimoth Colony Cook Book.

2 to 3 quarts water
4 cups (2 pounds) dry pea beans or Great Northern beans

1 large onion, peeled, plus 2 large onions, peeled and each pierced
    with 2 whole cloves
1 teaspoon plus 1 tablespoon salt
¾ cup dark molasses
½ cup dark brown sugar, divided
1 tablespoon dry mustard
1 teaspoon freshly ground black pepper
½ pound salt pork in one piece, with rind left on

1. In a heavy 4- to 5-quart casserole, bring 2 quarts of water to a boil over high heat. Drop in the dried beans and boil them for about 2 minutes. (The water should cover the beans by at least 2 inches; add more if necessary.) Turn off the heat and let the beans soak for 1 hour. Then add the peeled onion and 1 teaspoon of salt and bring to a boil again. Reduce the heat to low and simmer, partially covered for about 1 hour, or until the beans are tender. Check them from time to time, and add more boiling water to the pot if necessary. (The beans should be covered with water throughout the cooking.) Drain the beans through a fine sieve set over a bowl, pick out and discard the onion, and reserve the cooking liquid. There should be about 2 quarts; add water if necessary.

2. In a deep bowl, mix the molasses, ¼ cup of the brown sugar, the dry mustard, the remaining 1 tablespoon salt, and the pepper. Pour in about ½ cup of the bean liquid and blend the ingredients well. Stir in 4½ cups of bean liquid, then add the beans, stirring them gently with a spoon until they are evenly coated. The beans should be covered by ½ inch. Add more bean liquid if necessary, and mix gently.

3. Preheat the oven to 250°F. Place the clove-pierced onions in the bottom of a 4- to 5-quart bean pot and ladle the bean mixture over them. Score the fatty side of the salt pork by making crisscrossing diagonal cuts about ½ inch deep and ½ inch apart all over the surface. Push the salt pork down into the beans, letting only the top edge protrude above them. Cover the pot with a piece of foil and set the lid securely in place.

4. Bake the beans in the middle of the oven for 5 hours, adding more bean liquid if they become dry. Then remove the lid and foil, spread the remaining ¼ cup of brown sugar evenly over the beans, and bake for 1 hour longer. Serve the beans at once, directly from the pot. Leftover beans may be refrigerated in the same pot, tightly covered with foil or plastic wrap. They can safely be kept for about 1 week. The beans will continue to absorb the cooking liquid as they stand; add a little water to the pot before reheating the beans in the oven.

— *Jonathan Norton Leonard,* Time-Life Foods of the World:
    American Cooking: New England

"There is a growing market today for local, organic foods produced by small farmers. And farmers markets have played a large role in making that happen."

— *Eric Schlosser*, Fast Food Nation

SWEET ONION–APRICOT LIMAS

SERVES 8

Source Note: Sweet onion and tart apricots complement the buttery taste of lima beans. This can be served hot, as a side dish, or cold, as a relish.

⅔ cup dry baby lima beans, or one (15-ounce) can, rinsed
    and drained
1 medium sweet onion (such as Walla Walla), sliced
1 cup sliced dried apricots
1 teaspoon salt
5 cups water
½ cup honey

1. In a large saucepan, place the beans in 3 cups of water. Soak overnight, or boil for 2 minutes and let stand for 1 hour.

2. Drain the beans, then combine them with the onion, apricots, salt, and water in a saucepan. Cover and simmer for 1 hour, or until the beans are very tender but not mushy.

3. Add the honey and simmer for 5 minutes longer. Serve as a hot dish or cold relish with turkey, chicken, or pork.

— *US Dry Bean Council*

RAISIN–PINTO BEAN MUFFINS

MAKES 12 MUFFINS

Source Note: These high-fiber, low-cholesterol bean muffins are moist, flavorful, and packed with protein.

1 cup cooked pinto beans, or 1 cup canned, rinsed and drained
¾ cup milk
2 egg whites
¼ cup vegetable oil
½ cup firmly packed brown sugar
1½ cups all-purpose flour
    (or ¾ cup whole wheat flour plus ¾ cup all-purpose flour)
2 teaspoons baking powder
½ teaspoon baking soda
½ teaspoon salt
½ teaspoon cinnamon
¼ teaspoon nutmeg
¼ teaspoon cloves
½ cup raisins

1. Preheat the oven to 400°F. Line a 12-cup muffin tin with papers, or smear the cups with butter or vegetable oil.

2. In a blender or food processor, puree the beans with the milk until smooth; transfer to a large bowl.

"Create a garden; bring children to farms for field trips. I think it's important that parents and teachers get together to do one or two things they can accomplish well— grow a teaching garden, connecting with farms nearby, weave food into the curriculum.

— *Alice Waters, American chef*

3. Beat in the egg whites, oil, and brown sugar until well combined.

4. In a separate bowl, combine the flour, baking powder, baking soda, salt, cinnamon, nutmeg, cloves, and raisins.

5. Using a rubber spatula, fold the flour mixture into the bean and egg mixture, mixing just until all the dry ingredients are moistened.

6. Spoon the batter into the muffin cups.

7. Bake for 15 to 18 minutes, or until golden brown. A skewer inserted into the centers should come out clean.

— *US Dry Bean Council*

....

DAL MAKHANI (INDIAN LENTILS AND BEANS)   SERVES 8

Source Note: Garam masala is a blend of ground spices used in Indian cooking. Mixtures vary depending on the locale and type of dish in which they are used, but traditional mixes usually include cinnamon, roasted cumin, cloves, nutmeg, and green cardamom seeds or black cardamom pods. Commercial mixtures may contain less expensive spices such as dried red chile peppers, dried garlic, ginger powder, sesame, mustard seeds, turmeric, coriander, bay leaves, cumin, and fennel. The combination shown here is a favorite one that I've developed over the years.

3 tablespoons vegetable oil
2 large onions, chopped
1 to 4 large cloves garlic, crushed
1 jalapeño pepper, minced (optional)

SPICE MIXTURE (GARAM MASALA)

2 tablespoons ground coriander
1 teaspoon ground cumin
1 teaspoon ground ginger, or 1 tablespoon minced fresh ginger
1 tablespoon turmeric
1 to 2 teaspoons curry powder
1 teaspoon cumin seeds (optional)
1 teaspoon commercial garam masala (optional)

6 cups water (more if necessary)
2 cups lentils, sorted and rinsed
1 tablespoon vegetable or chicken bouillon paste
1½ cups cooked kidney beans, or one (15-ounce) can, drained and rinsed
One (6-ounce) can tomato paste
Salt
½ cup to 1 cup cream or half-and-half, for finishing (optional)
Chopped fresh cilantro, for garnish

Books

Bean By Bean: A Cookbook: More than 175 Recipes for Fresh Beans, Dried Beans, Cool Beans, Hot Beans, Savory Beans, Even Sweet Beans!
Crescent Dragonwagon.
Workman Publishing Company, 2012.

Heirloom Beans: Great Recipes for Dips and Spreads, Soups and Stews, Salads and Salsas, and Much More from Rancho Gordo
Steve Sando and Vanessa Barrington.
Chronicle Books, 2008.

1. In a large stewpot, heat the oil on medium heat. Add the onions, garlic, and jalapeño pepper; sauté until wilted.

2. Combine all of the spice ingredients in a small bowl, then add the mixture to the pan and stir to combine; sauté until it becomes fragrant. (Feel free to experiment with the spices, and don't hesitate to make the dish anyway if you are missing one or two of those suggested. Try something else instead!)

3. Add the water, lentils, and bouillon paste, and cook for 20 minutes. Add the kidney beans and tomato paste and simmer for another 30 minutes, stirring occasionally, adding more water if necessary so that the beans do not stick. Add salt to taste.

4. For nonvegans, stir in 1 to 2 tablespoons of cream or half-and-half per serving, if desired, which makes this dish more like the traditional version. (If you're using half-and-half, don't boil the finished soup—it will break and look less than lovely.) Garnish with the chopped cilantro.

— Robin Taylor, Featherstone Farm CSA member

ITALIAN WHITE BEAN SOUP   SERVES 6 TO 8 AS A MAIN DISH

Source Note: Serve this simple but delicious winter soup with a green salad and delicious artisan bread and butter. It will thicken on the second day. You can add water to thin it out, or serve it as-is for a side dish.

¼ cup flavorful, extra-virgin olive oil (Greek is good)
¼ to ½ cup chopped Italian or curly leaf parsley
3 large cloves of garlic, minced
1 pound cannellini beans, washed, sorted, soaked, cooked, and drained
Salt and freshly ground white pepper

1. Sauté the parsley and garlic in olive oil over medium heat for a few minutes.

2. Add the cooked beans and water to cover. Bring to a boil, reduce the heat, and simmer for 6 minutes. Remove from the heat while you mash about a cup of the mixture with a fork, or put in a blender until it is the consistency of mashed potatoes.

3. Return the mashed mixture to the pot and cook for 6 more minutes. Season to taste with salt and pepper, and serve immediately.

— Marianne Streich

Cabbages

Often disliked for its strong smell when cooking and regarded for centuries as a poor person's food, cabbage is one vegetable desperately in need of a public relations spin doctor. Despite its humble profile, cabbage is one of the most versatile, widely grown and consumed vegetables around—it is eaten raw, cooked, and pickled in cuisines all over the world.

You'll find both the familiar head cabbage in red and green colors; savoy cabbage, with its super-crinkly leaves; and the napa cabbage, which resembles romaine lettuce with its oblong head and loosely packed, wrinkled, light-green leaves on wide, white stems. Napa cabbage (sometimes called Chinese cabbage) has a sweeter, milder flavor than its head cousins, making it a good alternative for diners who prefer a less potent cruciferous presence in their food.

HISTORY

Cabbage is one of humankind's earliest foods, but some skepticism exists about where it originated. The ancient Romans enjoyed it, but it seems unlikely that such a cool-weather-loving plant would be native to the toasty Mediterranean climate. Perhaps the Celts introduced it from northern Europe to the southern portions of the continent around 600 BCE and possibly to Asia about 300 years later. The savoy variety was developed in Italy in the 1500s. Cabbages were almost certainly brought to North America by the earliest European colonists.

NUTRITION

Cabbage is one of the most nutritious vegetables available, packing formidable amounts of vitamins C, K, and folate, as well as dietary fiber, vitamins B2 and B6, phosphorus, potassium, and manganese. A 1-cup serving of shredded raw cabbage contains 22 calories. Like other cruciferous vegetables, cabbage contains abundant phytonutrients, such as sulforaphane and indoles, which have proved in studies to fight cancer, especially prostate, colorectal, and lung.

SEASON

Commercially, cabbage is widely grown and in season year-round. But it is typically at its best in the fall and winter months. Cabbage can be a substantial part of winter CSA shares.

SELECTION

With head cabbage, choose firm, tightly packed heads with uniform color and a heavy weight for their size. Large yellowish areas on the outer leaves may signal that the cabbage is old or has not been properly stored. Napa cabbage should have compact heads with tightly closed, crisp leaves with no signs of yellow or brown discoloring.

STORAGE

To help cabbage stay fresh longer, do not wash it until you are ready to

That's a Lot of Vinegar

Americans consume about 387 million pounds of sauerkraut annually.

use it. Store cabbage in the refrigerator vegetable crisper. Avoid slicing or shredding cabbage in advance, as this will cause it to lose a significant amount of vitamin C. Napa cabbage should be kept in a plastic bag, as it tends to absorb odors; it will keep for 4 to 5 days. Most head cabbages will keep for 1 week to 10 days, but their flavor and aroma may become stronger as they get older.

If you must shred cabbage an hour or more before cooking, place it in a plastic bag, seal tightly, and refrigerate in the vegetable crisper until ready to use. If you cut into the head, cover it with plastic for storage.

TRIMMING AND CLEANING

For head cabbage, strip off the outer leaves if they are wilted or yellowing. If you are not shredding the cabbage, store it whole or in large pieces; ultimately you should remove the core since it is bitter and not tasty. If you want to keep the outer leaves intact for wrapping or stuffing, boil the entire head for 1 to 2 minutes to make it easier to peel off the leaves.

STEAMING AND BOILING

Steaming cabbage results in a less waterlogged vegetable than boiling. Head cabbage can be steamed for about 20 minutes, if you like it with a little crunch, or longer if you prefer it more tender. The more delicate napa and savoy varieties do not need to be steamed as long as head cabbages—10 to 12 minutes.

Cabbage has a bad rap because it is often overcooked, which releases more of the vegetable's sulfurous compounds and makes it strong smelling—yet another reason not to overcook it!

STIR-FRYING AND SAUTÉING

Napa cabbage takes well to a quick stir-fry; just shred and cook it in a heated, oiled wok on medium heat for 2 to 3 minutes, or until wilted but still crisp-tender. Green or red head cabbages, cut into ½-inch ribbons, may need a little longer, depending on their toughness and age.

BAKING AND ROASTING

Cabbage can be tasty sliced and combined in a casserole dish with other vegetables, bacon or other meat, and seasonings, then topped with plenty of butter, covered with aluminum foil, and baked for 30 to 40 minutes in a 325°F oven.

BLANCHING AND FREEZING

As with almost all vegetables, cabbage must be blanched before freezing. Coarsely shred it, submerge it in rapidly boiling salted water for 2 minutes, then plunge it into ice water for 5 minutes to stop the cooking process. Remove and drain. Package the cabbage tightly in zipper-lock freezer or vacuum food sealer-type bags, or freezer containers. Squeeze out any excess air and leave ½ inch of headspace (unless you are using the vacuum sealing method). Frozen cabbage will keep for up to 1 year at 0°F.

MICROWAVING

Chop or shred, add 2 tablespoons water, place in a microwave-safe dish, and cook on high power.

Cooking Tip

Red cabbage will often turn an unappetizing blue while cooking because the compound that gives it its characteristic hue, anthocyanin, reacts with alkaline minerals in tap water.

To bring back its red color, add a little lemon juice or vinegar (a teaspoon may be enough), or cook the red cabbage with something acidic, like apples.

- 2 cups = 5 to 7 minutes (chopped or shredded)
- 4 cups = 6 to 8 minutes (chopped or shredded)

MEASURES AND EQUIVALENTS

HEAD OR SAVOY CABBAGE

- 1 medium head cabbage = about 2 pounds = 4 cups raw shredded = 4 servings
- 2 pounds head cabbage = about 10 cups shredded
- 1 pound raw cabbage = 2 cups cooked = 4 servings cooked

NAPA CABBAGE

- 1 head = 6 cups shredded

COMPLEMENTARY HERBS, SEASONINGS, AND FOODS

Anchovies, apples, arugula, bacon, béchamel sauce, beef, beets, black pepper, butter, caraway, carrots, celery root, celery seed, cheese (Cheddar, feta, Gruyère, Parmesan, pecorino), chervil, chestnuts, chicken, chiles, chives, cilantro, coconut, corned beef, cream, dill, duck, eggs, fish, garlic, ginger, goose fat, ham, horseradish, juniper berries, lamb, leeks, lemon, lime, mint, mushrooms, mustard, nutmeg, olive oil, onions, parsley, pork, potatoes, rosemary, sausage, savory, sesame, soy sauce, spinach, tarragon, thyme, tofu, tomatoes, vinegar.

SERVING SUGGESTIONS

- Try cutting up small wedges of raw cabbage and serving them with your favorite dip or salad dressing. Kids especially love eating cabbage (and many other raw veggies) this way.
- Bake cabbage with cheese at 350°F for 30 to 40 minutes for a filling, savory vegetable treat.
- Stuffed cabbage dishes abound around the world. Some delicious fillings include combinations of bacon, onions, ground beef, sausage, lamb, tomatoes, mushrooms, or sauerkraut.
- Braise red cabbage with apples, a little red wine, and cinnamon or cloves.
- Cabbage is one of the staples of the New England boiled dinner, where it is cooked with corned beef, potatoes, carrots, and onions.
- Napa cabbage is ideal for stir-fries; cut it into strips and toss in with garlic, ginger, sesame oil, and soy sauce.
- Thinly shred napa cabbage and add to very hot, clear beef or chicken broth. Sprinkle with soy sauce and top with tofu, thinly sliced mushrooms, and green onions for a delicate soup.
- Make homemade kimchi, the potent Korean condiment of pickled cabbage fermented with hot chiles, green onions, garlic, and anchovies or oysters. More and more evidence appears every day of fermented foods' tremendous health benefits.
- Coleslaw, that staple dish of summer picnics and potlucks, can be made with lots of different vegetables; it is a good way to use up not only cabbage, but also carrots, apples, radishes, kale, Asian pears, and other produce.
- Kugel is a baked pudding or casserole that is commonly made with egg noodles or potato. Numerous variations exist, but popular additions include fruit, broccoli or cabbage, mushrooms, and carrots.

"Cabbage as a food has problems. It is easy to grow, a useful source of greenery for much of the year. Yet as a vegetable it has original sin, and needs improvement. It can smell foul in the pot, linger through the house with pertinacity, and ruin a meal with its wet flab. Cabbage also has a nasty history of being good for you."

— *Jane Grigson*, Vegetable Book

Cooking Tip

The cylindrical shape of napa cabbage makes it naturally easy to cut up: Position the cabbage horizontally, cut off the top, and then proceed to make thin cuts down the body of the cabbage.

This will produce a perfect shred for salads or stir-fries. Cut only the amount that you need, and loosely wrap the rest in plastic wrap. This cabbage should stay fresh for up to 2 weeks in your crisper.

Something Smells in Here

Russia has the highest annual consumption of cabbage at 44 pounds per person, followed by Belgium at 10 pounds, the Netherlands at 8.8 pounds, Americans at 8.6 pounds, and Spain at 4.2 pounds.

- Cabbage is a frequent, welcome vegetable in many Indian dishes. Use it in raitas (a creamy condiment made with yogurt), muthias (steamed dumplings), parathas (stuffed Indian bread), spicy soups, and *aloo patta gobhi*, a classic Indian dish of potatoes and cabbage cooked together with spices.

- Cabbage loves sausage. Kielbasa, bratwurst, blood sausage, frankfurters, knackwurst, weisswurst, American hot dogs—they're all good.

- Make sauerkraut!

Savoy cabbage at Steel Wheel Farm.

PASTA WITH SAVOY CABBAGE AND GRUYÈRE   SERVES 4

Source Note: An inexpensive and simple dish with a surprising texture and flavor. The cabbage is cooked so that it has plenty of "bite" to it, contrasting with the softness of the pasta.

    2 tablespoons butter, plus more for greasing the dish
    1 small savoy or green head cabbage, thinly sliced
    1 small onion, chopped
    12 ounces dry, uncooked pasta (such as tagliatelle, fettuccine, or penne)
    1 tablespoon chopped fresh parsley
    1¼ cups vegetable or chicken stock

⅔ cup light cream
2 ounces Gruyère or Cheddar cheese, finely shredded
Salt and freshly ground black pepper

1. Preheat the oven to 350°F and butter a large casserole dish. Place the cabbage in a mixing bowl.

2. Melt the 2 tablespoons butter in a small pan and fry the onion until it softens. Stir the onions into the cabbage in the bowl.

3. Cook the pasta according to the package instructions, until al dente. Drain well and stir into the bowl with the cabbage and onion. Add the parsley, mix well, and then pour the mixture into the prepared casserole.

4. Heat the vegetable stock in a medium saucepan. Beat together the cream and cheese, and then stir them into the hot stock. Season well and pour over the cabbage and pasta, so that the sauce comes about halfway up the casserole. (If necessary, add a little more stock.)

5. Cover tightly and cook in the oven for 30 to 35 minutes, until the cabbage is tender and the sauce is bubbling. Remove the lid during the last 5 minutes of the cooking time to brown the top.

— *Christine Ingram,* The Cook's Encyclopedia of Vegetables

. . . .

ASIAN FUSION SLAW

SERVES 6 TO 8

Source Note: This has become a staple in my potluck repertoire. It is easy and beautiful and offers a fresh twist on a classic.

DRESSING

½ cup vegetable oil
2 tablespoons toasted sesame oil
¼ cup rice vinegar
1½ tablespoons finely minced fresh ginger
2 teaspoons soy sauce

SLAW

6 cups thinly sliced napa cabbage
2 bell peppers (any color), sliced into sticks
1 bunch green onions, finely chopped
Salt
1 cup chopped salted peanuts
1 cup minced cilantro

1. Whisk the dressing ingredients in a small bowl.

2. In a big bowl, toss together the cabbage, peppers, and onions. Pour the dressing over the cabbage mixture and toss. Add salt to taste.

"Cabbages, whose heads, tightly folded see and hear nothing of this world, dreaming only on the yellow and green magnificence that is hardening within them."

— *John Haines, American poet*

3. Add the peanuts and cilantro right before serving. (This salad tastes better on the second day, but wait to sprinkle the peanuts over it until just before serving, or else they will soak up the dressing and get soft.)

— *Sarah Libertus, former Featherstone Farm CSA manager*

WARM RED CABBAGE–BACON SALAD   SERVES 4

Author Note: This recipe uses turkey bacon as a more healthful alternative to regular bacon. If fat and cholesterol are not an issue, you can use regular bacon instead.

    3 slices reduced-fat turkey bacon
    1½ tablespoons olive oil
    ½ large onion, peeled and chopped
    3 large ribs celery, sliced
    ⅓ cup cider vinegar
    3 tablespoons sugar
    ½ teaspoon celery seed
    ½ large head red cabbage, shredded (about 6 cups)
    Salt and freshly ground black pepper (optional)
    2 tablespoons chopped fresh parsley, for garnish

1. Cut the bacon slices into 1-inch pieces and sauté them over me-dium-low heat in a very large, deep skillet until they are crisp but not overdone. Transfer them to absorbent paper towels and reserve. Drain off all of the bacon fat from the pan, wipe it clean, and re-place with the olive oil.

2. Heat the oil in the skillet over high heat. Add the onion and celery and sauté briefly. Add the vinegar, sugar, and celery seed. Heat until the mixture boils, then immediately add the cabbage and bacon pieces all at once. Stir and toss for about 1 minute, or until the cab-bage is warm but not cooked. Season to taste with salt and pepper.

3. Serve the salad immediately while it is still very warm, with a garnish of chopped parsley.

— *Produce for Better Health; Fruits & Veggies—More Matters;*
    Centers for Disease Control and Prevention

SPICY CABBAGE   SERVES 16

Source Note: I don't know what it is with me and pickles, but I love them. This recipe reminds me of a trip to Korea and all of the kimchi eaten there. Unlike that ubiquitous Korean accompaniment, this pickled cabbage is not

nearly as pungent, although the small Asian-style chiles do give this recipe a kick. You could expand the pickle by adding carrots, daikons (mild Asian radishes), and cucumbers.

1 head green cabbage or napa cabbage (about 2 pounds)
2 to 3 red bird's-eye chiles, seeded and diced
    (see the Cooking Note below)
1 (3-inch-long) piece fresh ginger, peeled and julienned
1 tablespoon ground turmeric
½ cup chopped fresh cilantro leaves
4 cloves garlic, chopped
2 teaspoons Thai fish sauce
1 cup rice vinegar
⅛ cup soy sauce

1. Cut the cabbage into eighths and remove the core. Place the pieces in a 1-gallon glass or ceramic container with a nonmetallic lid. (If you use a plastic container, you will never get the smell of this pickle out of it, so be prepared to dedicate that container to this recipe.)

2. In a 4-cup saucepan, bring all of the other ingredients to a boil over medium heat, and simmer for 10 minutes. Pour this hot mixture over the cabbage.

3. Cover and store in the refrigerator for 3 days to 1 week before you start to enjoy it. It will keep for 1 to 2 months.

Cooking Note: These chiles are very, very hot, so wear gloves when seeding and dicing them.

— *Richard Ruben,* The Farmer's Market Cookbook

. . . .

COLESLAW

SERVES 6 TO 8

Source Note: This is the coleslaw served at the famous Driesbach's Restaurant in Grand Island, Nebraska. Very tasty!

3 ounces half-and-half
3 tablespoons sugar
½ cup grated carrots
¾ head green cabbage, shredded
½ cup red head cabbage, shredded
½ teaspoon celery seed
Salt and freshly ground black pepper to taste

Combine everything and toss well.

— *Shirley Holt,* The Schoenleber Family Cookbook

That's when the two landowners discovered that there was a problem with the local office of the Farm Service Administration, the Agriculture Department branch that runs the commodity farm program, and it was going to be expensive to fix.

The commodity farm program effectively forbids farmers who usually grow corn or the other four federally subsidized commodity crops (soybeans, rice, wheat, and cotton) from trying fruit and vegetables. Because my watermelons and tomatoes had been planted on "corn base" acres, the Farm Service said, my landlords were out of compliance with the commodity program.

I've discovered that typically, a farmer who grows the forbidden fruits and vegetables on corn acreage not only has to give up his subsidy for the year on that acreage, but is also penalized the market value of the illicit crop, and runs the risk that those acres will be permanently ineligible for any subsidies in the future. (The penalties apply only to fruits and vegetables. If the farmer decides to grow another commodity crop, or even nothing at all, there's no problem.)

In my case, that meant I paid my landlords $8,771—for one season alone! And this was in a year when the high price of grain meant that only one of the government's crop-support programs was in effect; the total bill might be much worse in the future.

In addition, the bureaucratic entanglements that these two farmers faced at the Farm Service office were substantial. The federal farm program is making it next to impossible for farmers to rent land to me to grow fresh organic vegetables.

Why? Because national fruit and vegetable growers based in California, Florida, and Texas fear competition from regional producers like myself. Through their control of congressional delegations from those states, they have been able to virtually monopolize the country's fresh produce markets.

That's unfortunate, because small producers will have to expand on a significant scale across the nation if local foods are to continue to enter the mainstream as the public demands. My problems are just the tip of the iceberg.

Last year, Midwestern lawmakers proposed an amendment to the farm bill that would provide some farmers, though only those who supply processors, with some relief from the penalties that I've faced—for example, a soybean farmer who wanted to grow tomatoes would give up his usual subsidy on those acres but suffer none of the other penalties. However, the congressional delegations from the big produce states made the death of what is known as Farm Flex their highest farm bill priority, and so it appears to be going nowhere, except perhaps as a tiny pilot program.

Who pays the price for this senselessness? Certainly I do, as a Midwestern vegetable farmer. But anyone trying to do what I do on, say, wheat acreage in the Dakotas or rice acreage in Arkansas would face the same penalties. Local and regional fruit and vegetable production will languish anywhere that the commodity program has influence.

Ultimately, of course, it is the consumer who will pay the greatest price for this—whether it is in the form of higher prices I will have to charge to absorb the government's fines or in the form of less access to the kind of fresh, local produce that the country is crying out for.

Farmers need the choice of what to plant on their farms, and consumers need more farms like mine producing high-quality fresh fruits and vegetables to meet increasing demand from local markets—without the federal government actively discouraging them.

VEGETARIAN STIR-FRY SERVES 4

Source Note: This recipe gives you a delicious and easy way to receive the many health benefits of vegetables in just 20 minutes. The cooking method makes it even more healthful by not using heated oils. Feel free to add other vegetables you may have on hand to this dish.

- 1 tablespoon vegetable broth
- 1 medium onion, cut in half and sliced medium thick
- 1 red bell pepper, cut into ½-inch pieces
- 1 cup thinly sliced fresh shiitake mushrooms, stems removed
- 4 medium cloves garlic, pressed
- 1 tablespoon minced fresh ginger
- 2 cups thinly sliced green cabbage
- 5 ounces extra-firm tofu, cut into ½-inch cubes
- 2 tablespoons soy sauce
- 1 tablespoon rice vinegar
- 2 tablespoons chopped fresh cilantro
- Salt and freshly ground white pepper
- 1 tablespoon sesame seeds, for garnish

1. Heat the broth in a stainless-steel wok or a 12-inch skillet. Stir-fry the onion for about 2 minutes in the broth over medium-high heat, stirring constantly.

2. Add the red bell pepper and mushrooms. Continue to stir-fry for another 2 minutes. Add the garlic and ginger and continue to cook, stirring for another 2 to 3 minutes.

3. Add the rest of the ingredients, season to taste with the salt and pepper, and cook for another 2 minutes. Sprinkle with sesame seeds.

— *World's Healthiest Foods*

WILTED BUTTERY ESCAROLE WITH RED CABBAGE AND SHIITAKE MUSHROOMS SERVES 2 TO 3

Source Note: Escarole is probably not a common vegetable in most American kitchens. Unless one is a foodie, the tendency for most shoppers is to purchase familiar produce. If this is your first time trying escarole, the recipe below was created with you in mind. The strong, sharp notes are mellowed by the butter.

- 1 to 2 teaspoons minced fresh ginger
- 4 tablespoons extra-virgin olive oil, divided
- 4 tablespoons (½ stick) unsalted butter, divided
- 2 tablespoons chopped chives

4 roasted garlic cloves, chopped or 4 raw garlic cloves, minced
6 ounces escarole, coarsely chopped (about 4 inches long)
Sea salt and freshly ground black pepper
1 cup thinly sliced shiitake mushrooms
1 cup thinly sliced red cabbage

1. In a saucepan, add the ginger, 2 tablespoons of the olive oil, 2 tablespoons of the butter, chives, and the roasted garlic. Let the flavors
   infuse while stirring for about 2 minutes.

2. Add the escarole, season it with salt and pepper, and stir until the
   leaves are wilted. Remove from the heat and transfer it to a serving
   platter. Keep warm.

3. In another saucepan, add the remaining 2 tablespoons olive oil and
   2 tablespoons butter. Add the mushrooms and cook them until they
   are soft and slightly shriveled. Season to taste with salt and pepper.

4. To serve, arrange the raw red cabbage on the center of the escarole
   platter, topped by the mushrooms and ginger.

Cooking Note: In the winter, I sometimes stir the minced ginger into
the olive oil and butter before sautéing the mushrooms.

— *Luisa DePaiva, Purple Rain Vineyard, Vancouver, Washington*

Cabbage in the morning sun at Featherstone Farm.

Carrots

DAUCUS CAROTA

Ah, the common carrot. This ubiquitous vegetable, long a mainstay on tired crudité trays, a flavoring staple in the stew and soup pot, a ridiculed diet food, and a juicing favorite, really deserves higher regard as a vegetable of beauty and delicacy in its own culinary right.

For a long time the only carrots we knew were orange ones. Originally, wild carrots were purple, and now we are coming full circle; CSAs and farmers markets are now growing and selling "rainbow" carrots—roots of brilliant purple, reddish orange, golden yellow, creamy ivory, bright maroon, even white. They are all equally delicious, and healthful too—the same chemical compounds that give these carrots their beautiful colors also contain valuable phytonutrients and antioxidants.

Botanically, carrots are members of the same plant family as Queen Anne's lace, parsley, dill, fennel, chervil, parsnip, and cilantro, to name a few. All of the members of the Umbelliferae *or* Apiaceae *families are characterized by their fernlike foliage and distinctive flower heads that resemble lacy, upside-down umbrellas.*

In recent years, the phenomenon of the bagged baby carrot has emerged in our supermarkets. These little guys are not true juvenile carrots; they were actually invented by a California farmer in the late 1980s who was seeking a way to use his blemished, imperfect specimens. He adapted a commercial green-bean cutter and a potato peeler to cut and peel regular-size carrots into uniform lengths. The resulting product, as we all know, has been an astounding commercial success.

HISTORY

Humans have been eating carrots for an awfully long time; classical Greek and Roman texts mention these edible roots and seeds, which were used as medicine. Carrots originated in Asia Minor (probably Persia), and these wild versions, with their skinny white or purple roots, looked nothing like the plump orange specimens we're familiar with today. Carrots were first domesticated in what is likely modern-day Iran and Afghanistan. The first orange carrots were not documented until the 15th and 16th centuries in Europe. Although wild carrots still grow throughout the world, plant breeders continue to select for strains with greater sweetness, less bitterness, a more uniform size, different shapes, and longer keeping qualities.

NUTRITION

It is little secret, of course, that carrots are low in calories and very rich in vitamin A (at least the orange ones). But they are also great sources of biotin; vitamins C, K, and B6; potassium; manganese; and dietary fiber. What gives them their distinctive color is beta-carotene, an antioxidant renowned for its benefits to cardiovascular and eye health. One medium carrot contains about 25 calories.

The World Carrot Museum

This peculiar museum is a virtual one only, a website that is operated out of England. If you're interested in carrot history, trivia, and varieties, it's definitely worth a trip—and no airfare!

www.carrotmuseum.co.uk

SEASON

Commercially, carrots are widely grown and in season year-round. But they are typically at their best at CSAs and farmers markets in the late summer and fall months.

SELECTION

Look for hard, fresh specimens with no signs of shriveling or rubberiness, which means they are old and past their prime. Carrots with tops that are still green are a sign of freshness; look for these at your farmers market. With packaged, full-size carrots, be aware that some may be overly large with tough cores; if you want consistency, it is best to pick out your own single ones.

So-called baby carrots packaged in bags are a handy, timesaving alternative. Avoid bags that contain too much water inside; this excess moisture can hasten deterioration and cause them to be a bit slimy. It's a good idea to give your baby carrots a little love when you get them home: Empty the bag into a large bowl of cold water and swish them around vigorously. This will remove any slippery residue or stale flavors. Lay them out on a cloth and, when mostly dry, store them in the refrigerator.

STORAGE

Carrots keep well unwashed in a perforated plastic bag for up to 2 weeks or more in the refrigerator vegetable crisper. Remove the tops before storing.

TRIMMING AND CLEANING

For regular-size whole carrots: Give them a good scrubbing to remove dirt and sand. Slice off the ends, removing any greenish areas, then peel them lengthwise with a good, sharp vegetable peeler. Packaged baby carrots need no peeling or washing; a quick rinse if desired is all that is necessary.

As with many vegetables and fruits, the greatest concentration of nutrients lies within the outer skin of carrots. If your carrots are conventionally grown, then they should be peeled, as this is where the most pesticide residue lurks as well. But if they are organic, you can skip the peeling. The outer skins can be slightly bitter and have a stronger carrot flavor, so keep this in mind if you're preparing them as ingredients in other dishes.

STEAMING AND BOILING

Carrots can be steamed over rapidly boiling water until they are just tender.

- 8 to 10 minutes for ¼-inch rounds
- 5 to 7 minutes for strips
- 8 to 10 minutes for baby carrots

The sturdy nature of the carrot makes it a better candidate for boiling than many vegetables. Cook 1 pound of carrots covered in lightly salted, boiling water until they are crisp-tender.

- 7 to 9 minutes for ¼-inch rounds
- 4 to 6 minutes for strips
- 8 to 10 minutes for baby carrots

STIR-FRYING AND SAUTÉING

Although most of us don't think of sautéing carrots, they are delicious prepared this way. Thinly slice them (a diagonal cut works best to increase the surface area), place them in a pan with water and seasoning if desired, and bring to a boil. Sauté on medium heat for about 7 to 8 minutes or until tender; then toss them with a little butter or oil and continue to cook until all of the water has evaporated, another 1 to 2 minutes.

BAKING AND ROASTING

Like other root vegetables, carrots are lovely roasted, which concentrates their natural sugars and caramelizes them. Place cut carrots or baby carrots in a shallow pan, toss them with oil and seasonings as desired, cover them, and bake them in a 425°F oven for 30 minutes. Remove the cover, stir them, and finish roasting uncovered for another 5 to 10 minutes until they are tender and beginning to show golden caramel colors.

MICROWAVING

For 1 pound of carrots, place in a microwave-safe dish, add 2 tablespoons water, and cook on high power until crisp-tender.

- 6 to 9 minutes for ¼-inch rounds
- 5 to 7 minutes for strips
- 7 to 9 minutes for baby carrots

BLANCHING AND FREEZING

Scrub the carrots, peel them, and cut into thin rounds, ¼-inch cubes, or lengthwise strips. Very small carrots can be left whole. Blanch in lightly salted, boiling water—small whole carrots for 5 minutes, diced or sliced rounds for 2 minutes, and lengthwise strips for 2 minutes. Then plunge into ice water for 5 minutes or until cooled. Remove and drain. Spread the carrots on a tray in a single layer and freeze for 30 minutes. Package the carrots in zipper-lock freezer or vacuum food sealer-type bags or freezer containers. Squeeze out any excess air and leave ½ inch of headspace (unless you are using the vacuum sealing method). Frozen carrots will keep for up to 6 months at 0°F.

EQUIVALENTS, MEASURES, AND SERVINGS

- 1 pound carrots = 3 to 3½ cups sliced, chopped, or grated
- 1 pound carrots = 1½ cups pureed = 3 to 4 servings
- ¾ pound peeled carrots = approximately 3 cups chopped carrots

COMPLEMENTARY HERBS, SEASONINGS, AND FOODS

Anise, apples, balsamic vinegar, beets, burdock, butter, caraway, cayenne, chervil, chicken, cilantro, cinnamon, citrus, coconut, coconut oil, cream, crème fraîche, cumin, dill, fennel, ginger, green onions, honey, lemon, lime, lobster, maple syrup, mint, mushrooms, olive oil, onions, orange, paprika, parsley, parsnips, peas, potatoes, sesame oil, shallots, soy sauce, thyme, vinegar.

SERVING SUGGESTIONS

- Serve raw or lightly steamed on a plate with a variety of dipping sauces: mayonnaise, melted butter, salad dressing. A favorite with children.

- Carrots Vichy is a classic French dish where the vegetable is cooked in water with a little sugar to create a glaze. Modern versions sometimes add sherry vinegar, honey, shallots, and fresh thyme.

- A Pennsylvania Dutch treat is barbecued carrots, the signature of which is the Amish "stickin' sauce," a toothsome combination of chile powder, molasses, onions, oranges, cider vinegar, Worcestershire sauce, raisins, ketchup, dried red pepper flakes, and ground cloves; this concoction is delicious with all sorts of meats as well as vegetables.

- Sausage, shallots, and carrots combined are the filling for a traditional Russian pie.

- Make a savory pudding using cooked carrots, chicken stock, butter, milk, nutmeg, black pepper, cayenne, and rice.

- Carrots, of course, are exceptional for juicing. They contain a lot of natural sugar, so be careful if pairing carrots with apple and beet juices to avoid overly sweet concoctions—and massive sugar highs.

- Like potatoes, carrots are the workhorses of the kitchen. Add them to soups, stews, casseroles, steaks, roasts, and a wide variety of other dishes for color, flavor, and nutrients.

- Raw carrots julienned in salads are a delight.

- Carrots are one of the traditional fillings for pasties, those little baked pastry shells filled with beef, potatoes, onions, turnips, or rutabagas.

- Carrot cake is a perennial favorite; use finely shredded carrots with cinnamon, mace, lemon peel, raisins, and chopped nuts.

- Pickled carrots can be quite an unexpected treat. Pickle with dill, mustard, and peppercorns.

- Along with celery and onion, carrots are one of the key ingredients in France's *mirepoix*, a flavoring base for all respectable soups and many other dishes. Finely chop all three vegetables, and use twice as much onion as carrot and celery.

- Sometimes the simplest of vegetable dishes are the best. Braise whole baby vegetables like carrots, turnips, fennel, and pearl onions in butter, along with chicken stock, chervil, dill, and fresh shelled peas.

- Culinarily, carrots have a huge affinity for other members of their plant family. Cook them with dill, cumin, parsley, anise, cilantro, parsnips, and fennel.

PETER RABBIT'S BIRTHDAY SOUP   SERVES 8 TO 10

2 pounds carrots, peeled and chopped
4 cups chicken stock or water (or a combination)
1½ teaspoons salt
1 medium potato, chopped
1 cup onion, chopped
1 to 2 small cloves garlic, crushed
⅓ cup chopped cashews
3 to 4 tablespoons (about ½ stick) butter
¾ cup sour cream
½ to 1 teaspoon finely chopped fresh thyme
Toasted nuts and extra sour cream (optional)

parsnips and beets that need to be washed week to week.

It truly is awesome to look back and see how much we have done over the last few months, but we couldn't have done it without the help of the entire farm team. We are constantly receiving help from the office team, the shop guys, and a group of Amish girls who come in and help us a couple of days a week. And, of course, thank you to our customers across the state. We are extremely grateful for all of your support.

From left to right: Jennifer Breitlow, James Mabry, and Nathan Manfull.

As the end of February approaches and we look into our empty coolers where once 1,000 bins of produce were stacked to the ceiling, we will celebrate the victory of another winter conquered. Then we will convert our washroom into the seed room and begin the seeding process of the 2015 season.

But until that day, we keep our nose to the grindstone and wash the unspeakable amount of mud off of these damn little orange roots and dream of the days to come. To our CSA subscribers and loyal customers, I cannot say thank you enough for your continued support of Featherstone Farm. Thank you for making everything we do possible. You rock!

1. In a large saucepan, bring the carrots, chicken stock, salt, and potato to a boil. Cover and simmer for 12 to 15 minutes, or until the vegetables are very soft. Let cool.

2. Meanwhile, in a separate pan, sauté the onion, garlic, and cashews in the butter until the onions turn translucent.

3. Puree everything together in a blender until the soup is smooth. Return the puree to a pan or double boiler, and whisk in the sour cream. Heat very slowly and season with the thyme. Garnish with the toasted nuts and more sour cream, if desired.

— *Maureen Cooney,* The Bluff Country Co-op Cookbook

. . . .

MOROCCAN CARROTS IN VINAIGRETTE · SERVES 4

Source Note: This dish should be served slightly warm or at room temperature. Adapted from Recipes from An Ecological Kitchen: Healthy Meals for You and the Planet.

2 pounds carrots, scrubbed and cut into ½-inch rounds

VINAIGRETTE
⅔ cup olive oil
2 tablespoons fresh lemon juice
2 tablespoons red wine or balsamic vinegar
1½ teaspoons sweet paprika
1 teaspoon ground cumin
1 large clove roasted garlic, mashed or 1 small clove raw garlic, minced
¼ teaspoon or pinch cayenne
⅓ cup minced fresh parsley or cilantro

1. Put the carrots in a saucepan, barely cover with water, and bring to a boil. Reduce the heat and simmer until they are tender.

2. In a jar, combine all of the other ingredients and shake well. Add more lemon juice or vinegar to taste.

3. Drain the carrots and add the dressing while the carrots are warm.

— *Kathy Abascal,* The Abascal Way Cookbook

. . . .

SUNFLOWER SEED AND MILLET CAKES · MAKES 12 CAKES
WITH SPICY TAHINI SAUCE · OR 6 BURGERS

Source Note: These cakes feature sunflower seeds, ground almost to a powder in a food processor. Then in goes cooked millet (or quinoa or rice if you prefer) and a host of other ingredients to give your cakes flavor and texture. This is where you can draw on the creativity of your inner cook. I like mine

with caramelized onions, grated carrots, and plenty of fresh herbs. I've also made them with chopped sun-dried tomatoes and golden raisins. I can vividly imagine them with diced, sautéed mushrooms. This recipe makes about 12 cakes, or you can shape them larger and have burgers.

Feel free to experiment with the vegetables, which you can readily change to use what's in season. I recently served these cakes with yogurt mixed with smoked-jalapeño kraut. I hope readers will feel inspired to be creative with the recipe, because there are infinite ways to experiment with it!

They keep well, so I make them at the beginning of the week and mightily praise my foresight when hunger hits and there is a quick, tasty, filling snack at my disposal. The best part is the crispy golden crust that's formed when you sear the cakes in your favorite cast-iron skillet, so don't skimp on that part.

> 1 cup millet, rinsed
> 2 cups vegetable stock or water
> ½ teaspoon turmeric
> ¼ teaspoon red chile flakes
> 1 bay leaf
> Sprig of fresh thyme
> 2 cups raw sunflower seeds
> 1 teaspoon ground coriander
> 2 cloves garlic, finely minced, or 1 teaspoon garlic powder
> ¾ cup caramelized onions (see the instructions below this recipe)
> 1 cup grated carrot
> ½ cup chopped flat-leaf parsley
> Sea salt and freshly ground pepper
> ¼ cup vegetable oil suitable for high-heat frying, such as canola or safflower

1. First, cook the millet: Preheat the oven to 350°F. Place the millet, stock, turmeric, red chile flakes, bay leaf, and thyme in an oven-safe pot with a fitted lid, and heat on the stove over medium-high heat. When the stock comes to a boil, remove the pot from the heat, cover it, and place it in the oven. Cook for 20 to 25 minutes, or until the stock is absorbed and the millet is cooked through (it will still have a pebbly texture). Fluff it with a fork and set aside to cool to room temperature.

2. Meanwhile, make the cakes: Place the sunflower seeds, coriander, and garlic in the bowl of a food processor fitted with the metal blade. Process until the sunflower seeds are finely ground—they will have the texture of breadcrumbs. Add the cooked millet, caramelized onions, grated carrot, and chopped parsley to the processor, season with salt and pepper, and pulse a few times to combine all the ingredients. Do not overprocess or the mixture will get gummy.

3. Shape the mixture into cakes, using about ¼ to ⅓ cup of the mixture for each cake (½ to ¾ if you're making burgers). Chill the cakes in the refrigerator for an hour or more so they set.

4. When you are ready to cook the cakes, preheat the oven to 400°F.

Grocery Manufacturers Association, the Food Marketing Institute, and the National Restaurant Association. In four years since its creation in 2011, the FWRA has already engaged over 30 leading companies to take part. Simple techniques such as clarifying expiration dates and selling food in smaller portions have made a significant difference. So has channeling manufacturing and restaurant food waste into operations that create compost, which in turn can be used to grow crops in urban areas.

In Germany, an innovative, non-profit website called **Foodsharing. de** allows people who have leftovers or extra food to get it to those who are hungry or in need. Soup, produce, eggs, baked goods, extras from a party—any and all of it can be given away. Users sign up on the site as members and list "baskets" with approved food items available for pickup, and they can find a "basket" if they are looking for specific foods. Anyone who is about to cook and is short on a certain ingredient may also use this system to locate others with that food. Since its inception, Foodsharing.de has connected thousands of members in over 200 German cities, Austria, Switzerland, Mexico, Israel, and the United Kingdom. Bakeries and restaurants are using the site as well. A similar concept is behind US-based **Leftoverswap**, a mobile app that links hungry people with those with victuals to give away.

Of course, this kind of foodsharing may not be for everyone, and naturally, some question its hygiene and food safety. Leftoverswap uses a social rating system similar to Airbnb and Uber to help self-police its community. Incidents of unsafe food have been extremely rare, and foodsharing organizations always advise vigilance and common sense—if it seems off or just not right, don't accept or eat it.

Food is being rescued in ingenious ways. **Boulder Food Rescue** in Col-

Set out a rimmed baking sheet. Heat 1 to 2 tablespoons of the oil in a cast-iron or nonstick skillet over medium heat. Use enough oil to generously cover the bottom of your pan. Cook the cakes in batches, searing on each side for 1 to 3 minutes, until a golden crust forms. Transfer the cakes to the baking sheet.

5. Slip the baking sheet into the oven for 7 minutes to allow the cakes to cook through. Serve immediately with Spicy Tahini Sauce (recipe below), or save them for later (the best way to reheat the cakes is in the oven; however, I'm happy to eat them cold or at room temperature—yes, they are that good).

Variations: This recipe is ripe for experimentation. A few other ideas for add-ins are grated sweet potato, green onion, capers, and minced jalapeño peppers.

TO CARAMELIZE THE ONIONS

Slice 2 large onions into ¼-inch half moons. Heat 2 tablespoons olive oil in a heavy, medium saucepan over medium heat. Add the onions and stir to coat with the olive oil. Cook for a few minutes, stirring so as not to burn them, then turn the heat to medium low. Season with a generous pinch of salt and several grindings of black pepper. Cook the onions, stirring from time to time, for 45 to 70 minutes, or until they are deeply golden and shrunken down in size. Make sure to watch the heat so they do not burn; you can add a splash of water if they are sticking to the pan.

— *Lauren Mitchell Wilkinson,* Groove Food *blog*

SPICY TAHINI SAUCE   MAKES 1½ CUPS

⅓ cup tahini (sesame seed paste), **preferably raw**
⅓ cup water
¼ cup freshly squeezed lemon or lime juice
1 tablespoon chopped jalapeño
1 clove garlic, chopped
¼ cup chopped cilantro (optional)
Sea salt and freshly ground black pepper

Place all of the ingredients in a blender and blend until well combined, about 1 minute.

— *Lauren Mitchell Wilkinson,* Groove Food *blog*

COPPER PENNY CARROTS   SERVES 4

2 pounds carrots, sliced and cooked

1 onion, chopped
1 green pepper, chopped
1 can condensed tomato soup, undiluted
¼ cup vegetable oil
¼ cup vinegar
¾ cup sugar
1 teaspoon Worcestershire sauce
Salt and freshly ground black pepper
1 teaspoon prepared mustard
Dash of hot pepper sauce

Put the carrots, onion, and green pepper into a large bowl. Thoroughly mix all of the remaining ingredients and pour the mixture over the carrots. Let stand overnight. Serve hot or cold as a salad or a vegetable side dish.

— *Betty Elbers,* Hills Centennial Cookbook

Bountiful rainbow carrots at Sang Leel Farms.

CARROT SLAW   SERVES 2

Source Note: This is especially tasty served with the recipe for Caramelized Cabbage on page 183.

1 small bunch carrots, shredded
1 tablespoon fresh lemon juice
¼ teaspoon kosher salt
¼ teaspoon freshly ground white pepper

Thoroughly combine all of the ingredients, and place the slaw in the refrigerator for at least ½ hour to let the flavors blend. You can also make this slaw the night before.

— *Karolina Tracz, Nash's Organic Produce, Sequim, Washington*

Rising production costs and razor-thin margins mean that many farmers can't afford to waste their crops either. One huge problem is that consumers have gotten so conditioned to picture-perfect produce that they won't buy a misshapen tomato, a lightly crushed berry, or a splotchy apple, even if the rest of the fruit or veggie is perfectly good. So more farms have taken to producing their own jams, jellies, sauces, and other products to use up their blemished crops. And yet many large-scale agricultural growers, some of whom discard as much as 30 percent of their crop because of blemishes, spoilage, and tricky distribution logistics, find that donating food is just not economically worth it—the incentive is just not there yet.

Another interesting twist is California-based **Cropmobster**, a website that allows farmers to use social media and instant messages to post the word about excess crops that might otherwise be sent to the compost bin.

Three-legged carrots and tumorous tomatoes are having their day in the spotlight as large grocery store chains like Raley's are proudly selling less-than-perfect produce as a way to educate their customers about food waste. Organizations like **Imperfect Produce** and **End-FoodWaste.org** (founder of the **@UglyFruitandVeg** campaign) are also raising consumer awareness.

And a brand in the Netherlands called **Kromkommer** is introducing a line of soups made from misshapen root vegetables. So far it's been a hit with consumers who enjoy its wonkiness and potential for social and economic change, even if it is just one bowl at a time.

It's a win-win situation—it and similar products could result in farmers commanding prices for their imperfect produce similar to those for their more photogenic counterparts, plus more for everyone to eat. And that's good for all of us in the long run.

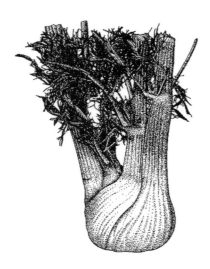

Fennel

FOENICULUM VULGARE

Folks in Mediterranean Europe have been eating the good stuff for centuries: olive oil, artichokes, cardoons, fresh sardines, whole-grain pastas, anchovies, red wine—and fennel. The distinctive Florence fennel, with its feathery foliage and plump, slightly flattened white bulbs (which are actually thickened leaf stems), is a relative newcomer to the American gastronomic scene, but better late than never.

A botanical relative of dill, cumin, anise, and carrots, fennel has long been savored in its home countries for its delicately sweet, anise flavor, which is quite pronounced in the vegetable's raw, crunchy, celery-like form but mellows considerably when the bulb is cooked. Humans have long consumed fennel in myriad ways—the bulbs and leaves as a vegetable and herb in cooking; the pollen as a potent, sweet, anisey seasoning; and the seeds as a flavoring agent in foods, teas, and the alcoholic spirit absinthe.

Bulb fennel is a fall and winter vegetable, a welcome addition to the table when more starchy vegetables dominate and the delicate delights of summer have dissolved into a distant memory. In some parts of the country, especially in California, you may see a baby version as well.

Unlike Florence fennel, the domesticated sweet and bronze fennels and wild fennel do not form bulbs but instead feature lush, powerfully aromatic foliage and highly prized edible pollen. Wild fennel can sometimes grow as tall as 7 or 8 feet, and in many dry, coastal areas and roadsides it has become an invasive weed, especially in the western United States and Australia. But both sweet and wild fennel are often far more intensely flavored than their Florence cousin; the wild fennel is well worth foraging, if you can find pollution-free specimens.

HISTORY

Fennel is thought to have originated in Mediterranean Europe. Ancient Romans and Greeks cultivated it for both culinary and medicinal purposes and considered it a source of strength and victory in battle. The Roman writer and philosopher Pliny assigned no fewer than 22 remedies to the herb, including the ability to cure bad vision, and even King Charlemagne had it grown in his gardens for its healing properties. Bunches of fennel were sometimes hung over doorways in medieval times to ward off ghosts and evil spirits and bring good luck.

In later centuries, the seeds were used by the English as an appetite suppressant during periods of religious fasting and by the American Puritans as a way to keep stomachs from rumbling during interminably long church sermons (along with dill, they were known as "meetin' seeds"). Fennel has also been a popular herb and seasoning since antiquity in the cuisines of India, Pakistan, Iran, and Afghanistan.

NUTRITION

Fennel contains significant amounts of vitamin C, potassium, manganese, molybdenum, and copper. It's a good diet food as well—a single

BOUNTY FROM THE BOX

cup of sliced raw fennel contains a mere 27 calories and some good dietary fiber, helping fill you up. And with its sweet, licorice flavor, it's far more appealing than celery sticks—and healthful than the candy!

SEASON

Commercially, fennel is widely grown and in season year-round. But it is typically at its best in the fall and winter months.

SELECTION

Look for fennel bulbs that are fresh, white, pearly, and plump, with no signs of dullness, splitting, brown edges, or shriveling, which could indicate soft or pulpy flesh within. Avoid very flat, elongated bulbs; these indicate that the plant is starting to bolt and will have an inferior flavor and tougher texture. Specimens with vibrant, unwilted fronds are more likely to be extra-fresh, crisp, and juicy—plus, these leaves pack exceptional fennel flavor! Bulbs of all sizes are just as tasty, although keep in mind that with the prerequisite trimming involved, there's more waste with smaller bulbs.

STORAGE

Bulb fennel prefers to stay unwashed in a plastic bag in the refrigerator vegetable crisper, but not for too long—only 3 to 4 days at most, as it dries out and loses flavor quickly. The fronds of sweet, bronze, and wild fennels, however, will keep much longer—up to 2 weeks wrapped in plastic in the refrigerator.

TRIMMING AND CLEANING

With bulb fennel, cut off the fronds, if any are present, then trim off the stalks and tough outer layers. (Don't throw away these valuable leaves and trimmings—save them for flavoring soups and broths, roasting with meats and poultry, and using in other dishes.) Leave about ⅛ inch of the root base on to keep the vegetable intact during cooking, then rinse thoroughly under running water to remove any lodged dirt. Then halve or quarter the bulbs for braising or roasting, or cut the raw fennel into long slices or diced pieces. There is a core that in old or overgrown specimens is sometimes woody and may need to be removed, but usually it is perfectly tender and need not be fretted over.

STEAMING AND BOILING

Whole trimmed fennel bulbs can be steamed or boiled for 20 to 25 minutes, depending on their size, or until they are just tender.

STIR-FRYING AND SAUTÉING

Fennel can be delicious stir-fried and sautéed, making for a surprise vegetable of sorts that blends well with a variety of seasonings and sauces. Thinly slice or julienne strips from around the core of a single bulb, place them in a pan with butter or oil and a little garlic or onion, and sauté on medium heat for 5 to 7 minutes, or until they turn tender and start to caramelize. For more fennel flavor, stir in 1 or 2 tablespoons of the finely minced fronds at the end of cooking time.

Books

Chez Panisse Vegetables
Alice Waters,
HarperCollins, 1996.

Mariquita Farm Fennel Recipes
http://www.mariquita.com/recipes/
fennel.html

The Glorious Vegetables of Italy
Domenica Marchetti and Sang An,
Chronicle Books, 2013.

BRAISING AND STEWING

Braising is a terrific way to cook fennel, rendering it tender and silky. It is best to sauté it first in butter or oil for 15 minutes, then braise in broth or water into which vermouth, garlic, herbs, and seasonings have been added. Bring to a boil, cover, decrease the heat, and simmer over low heat for 15 to 25 minutes, or until the fennel is tender.

BAKING AND ROASTING

Fennel responds beautifully to roasting, which concentrates and caramelizes its natural sugars. Place cut wedges in a shallow pan, toss them with oil and seasonings as desired, cover them, and bake in a 400°F oven for about 20 minutes. Remove the cover and roast for another 10 to 20 minutes, until they are cooked through and nicely caramelized.

GRILLING

Fennel turns out lovely on the grill, especially when quartered and seasoned first with just good olive oil and salt and pepper, or with a marinade of mustard, garlic, olive oil, and lemon juice. (Another way is to cut the bulbs lengthwise into thick slices, leaving the core intact to hinge the leaves together.) Grill them cut side down on medium heat for 5 to 10 minutes, depending on their size, until they become lightly charred and tender. Then turn them over and repeat on the other side. Take care that they don't burn, which can happen rather easily. Sprinkle with Parmesan cheese and you have a mighty sublime vegetable on your hands.

MICROWAVING

Place 2 trimmed bulbs (each about 12 ounces) in a microwave-safe dish, add ¼ cup water, and cook on high power for 8 to 10 minutes.

BLANCHING AND FREEZING

Fennel does not take well to freezing, as it will become a mushy mess upon thawing.

EQUIVALENTS, MEASURES, AND SERVINGS

- 1 pound fennel with 1-inch stalk = about 12 ounces trimmed
- 1 pound fennel = 2½ to 3 cups chopped or sliced = 2¼ cups cooked

COMPLEMENTARY HERBS, SEASONINGS, AND FOODS

Apples, bacon, bay, beans, butter, celery, celery root, cheese (Parmesan), chicken, cream, duck, eggs, fennel seeds, eggs, fish, garlic, ginger, green olives, ham, juniper, lemon, olives, olive oil, onions, oranges, pancetta, parsley, pasta, pastis, pork, potatoes, prosciutto, rice, risotto, sausage, saffron, shellfish, shrimp, star anise, thyme, turkey, tomatoes, veal.

SERVING SUGGESTIONS

- Raw fennel thinly sliced and served with fruity, peppery olive oil, freshly ground black pepper, and sea salt is a traditional snack in Italy. Thinly sliced raw leeks, shavings of Parmesan cheese, olives, and orange sections also make excellent company.
- Serve raw or lightly steamed on a plate with a variety of dipping sauces: mayonnaise, melted butter, salad dressing. A favorite with children.

- Combine fennel with shrimp in a creamy risotto.

- Fennel and oranges go together like Bogart and Bacall, and they are both at their peak in the winter months. Use this combination (and timing) in a refreshing, light salad that is a great foil for richer, heavier meats and winter dishes.

- Combine plenty of finely chopped fennel leaves, seeds, or pollen when making your own Italian sausages or sausage dishes.

- Looking for a dessert idea? Try slicing fennel into long strips and pairing it with soft goat cheese, figs, and vin santo (an Italian dessert wine).

- Wrap raw fennel slices in prosciutto; pair slices with smoked salmon; or serve iced raw fennel slices with generous shavings of Parmesan cheese. All make lovely appetizers.

- Fennel's strong character mellows with cooking and braising. Stir-fry or sauté slices to add to other vegetables in poultry stuffings or for baking inside a whole fish.

- Deep-fried fennel makes for a surprise vegetable that is nutty and sweet; it's especially good with tomatoes and grilled fish.

- Fennel and fish have an affinity for each other; they are divine in that quintessential French fish stew, bouillabaisse, combined with saffron, orange peel, and plenty of garlic.

- Combine with cream and potatoes to make a delicious, filling soup.

- Braise or roast the quartered wedges and serve as a distinctive vegetable side dish, a change from the usual carrots or potatoes.

- Cooked fennel, combined with potato and run through a food processor, makes a surprisingly tasty Hungarian bread. Add fennel seeds as well for an extra burst of fennel flavor.

- Pan-fry fennel, potatoes, and bacon for a tasty hash.

BRAISED FENNEL WEDGES WITH SAFFRON AND TOMATO

SERVES 4

Source Note: Fennel is a natural with seafood, so you might pair this dish with halibut or seared scallops. But it's also good with rice, and black rice makes for an especially dramatic—and delicious—pairing. Be sure to leave the core in the fennel bulb; it's what holds the wedges together.

2 large fennel bulbs
2 to 3 tablespoons olive oil
1 onion, thinly sliced
2 teaspoons fennel seeds
Good pinch of saffron threads
½ teaspoon dried thyme
1 garlic clove, crushed
3 tablespoons tomato paste
1½ cups fennel stock, chicken stock, or water
Sea salt
1 tablespoon butter
Freshly ground black pepper
Minced fennel greens or fresh flat-leaf parsley

six one-week Summer Farm & Science Camp sessions at the nonprofit **Crown Point Ecology Center**, which is affiliated with its 115-acre CSA farm in Bath, Ohio. The camps explore such themes as who's eating whom in the Children's Garden and following your food from field to plate, with opportunities to harvest and prepare snacks. Crown Point staff work with youth groups, Scout groups, and schools.

Green Gate Farms in Austin, Texas, offers farm camps and workshops for children and adults through its nonprofit affiliate, New Farm Institute. The institute's mission is to engage people of all ages and abilities in learning about healthful foods and sustainable farming, as well as to inspire a new generation of sustainable farmers. Programs include a weeklong farm camp for kids, half-day farm camps for adults, and a workshop called Creating the Farm of Your Dreams, for "wannabe farmers."

Farm tours for school groups are also offered by numerous farms, often tailored to the needs of the classroom teacher, as at the **George Jones Farm**, a 70-acre farmstead owned by Oberlin College in Ohio and leased by the New Agrarian Center as a cooperative farm incubator and educational center. At **Sauvie Island Center**, a nonprofit established by **Sauvie Island Organics** in Portland, Oregon, field trips might include a farm lunch and planting something in the Grow Lunch Garden. Scholarships are available to Title One low-income schools to cover the cost of the field trips. More than half of the approximately 1,700 students who visit the farm on field trips are from such schools.

The **Shambala Permaculture Farm** on Camano Island in Washington State has a plant nursery and serves as a go-to resource for permaculture education: workshops and classes, hands-on certification programs, food forest garden and farm animal tours, and edible landscaping and permaculture design services. It also offers permaculture design certification programs and works with public and private educational institutions to offer some of its courses.

Youth Programs

Planting seeds and tasting what grows from them can change a child's relationship with food for years to come. Teens and young adults can benefit from farm education programs in many more ways that can make a difference in their lives. In Boulder, Colorado, the **¡Cultiva! Youth Project** engages kids 12 to 19 in running an organic farm that's part of **Growing Gardens**, a nonprofit that oversees diverse urban agricultural projects, from community gardens to a horticultural therapy program for seniors and people with disabilities. ¡Cultiva! participants plant, tend, harvest, and sell weekly produce shares to CSA members. They also help with other tasks, such as gleaning produce from the Boulder Farmers Market. The project employs 50 to 60 teenagers annually, most receiving a stipend and a weekly box of produce, and 10 of them earning an hourly wage while serving as youth mentors.

The **OutDoor High School** in Eugene, Oregon, a private school established by **Northwest Youth Corps (NYC)** in 1997, offers a combination of hands-on learning, conservation work, applied science, and academics. The fully accredited school prepares youth for the workplace by emphasizing basic skills and career readiness, while providing the academic foundation needed for students planning on a college education. The school property includes **Laurel Valley Education Farm & Garden**, a two-acre nonprofit organic farm run by AmeriCorps volunteers with help from students. Each year, the

1. Trim off the stalks and greens from the fennel bulbs. (Mince the greens for a garnish. If there are none, you can use parsley.) If the thick outer leaves of the bulbs look tough and scarred, as they often do, take a slice off the base to loosen them and set them aside for another use.

2. Halve each bulb lengthwise and cut the halves into wedges about 1½ inches at the widest part.

3. Heat the olive oil in a wide sauté pan over medium-high heat. When hot, add the onion and fennel seeds, crumble in the saffron and thyme, and then cook until the steam releases the color from the saffron, after several minutes.

4. Add the fennel wedges and cook them until golden, turning them and the onions occasionally. Once they are well colored, add the garlic, stir in the tomato paste, and then add the stock and 1 teaspoon salt.

5. Scrape the pan to release the juices, then cover and simmer until the fennel is tender, another 15 minutes.

— *Deborah Madison,* Vegetable Literacy

FENNEL SALAD WITH POMEGRANATE SEEDS, FETA, AND SUMAC   SERVES 4

Source Note: This salad is a little festival in itself. The fennel and tarragon, with their echoing flavors, form a solid base on which stronger colors and flavors—pomegranate, feta, sumac—manifest themselves without overwhelming the whole salad. It is distinctly fresh and goes well with roast meats and grilled fish. Crusty bread is almost obligatory to soak up the juices from the plate.

Try substituting dried cranberries or sour cherries for the pomegranate. The fennel for this salad should be the round and bulky variety; it is crisper and sweeter than the long one.

½ pomegranate
2 medium fennel bulbs
1½ tablespoons olive oil
2 teaspoons sumac, plus extra to garnish
Juice of 1 lemon
4 tablespoons fresh tarragon leaves
2 tablespoons coarsely chopped flat-leaf parsley
Salt and freshly ground black pepper
2½ ounces Greek feta cheese, sliced

1. Start by releasing the pomegranate seeds. The best way to do it is to halve the pomegranate along its "belly" (you only need half a pomegranate here), then hold the half firmly in your hand with the seeds facing your palm. Over a large bowl, start bashing the back of

the fruit with a wooden spoon. Don't hit too hard or you'll bruise the seeds and break the skin. Magically, the seeds will just fall out. Pick out any white skin that falls in.

2. Remove the leaves of the fennel, keeping a few for garnish later, and trim the base, making sure you leave enough of the root still attached to hold the slices together. Slice very thinly lengthwise (a mandoline would come in handy here).

3. In a bowl, mix the olive oil, sumac, lemon juice, tarragon, parsley, and some salt and pepper. Add the fennel and toss well. Taste for seasoning but remember, the feta will add saltiness.

4. Layer the fennel, then the feta, and then the pomegranate seeds in individual serving dishes. Garnish with the reserved fennel leaves, sprinkle with a bit more sumac, and serve immediately.

— *Yotam Ottolenghi and Sami Tamimi*, Ottolenghi: The Cookbook

....

FENNEL AND TORPEDO ONION SALAD   SERVES 4

Source Note: This salad is a perfect accompaniment to very simply grilled or pan-fried fish of your choosing.

Author Note: Tropea onions are delectable, oblong, torpedo-shaped red onions named for the glamorous beach town in Calabria, Italy, where they originated. If you don't have access to Tropeas, any sweet, mild red onion will suffice nicely in this dish.

> **2 small or medium fennel bulbs, trimmed, halved, and sliced**
> **1 Tropea onion, trimmed, halved, and sliced thinly**
> **1 to 2 carrots, cut into matchsticks or julienned**
> **Juice of 1 lemon**
> **Olive oil**
> **Salt and freshly ground black pepper**
> **2 teaspoons capers, chopped (optional)**
> **2 ounces feta cheese**

1. If you are sensitive to the biting taste of raw onions, you can soak the sliced onions in a small bowl of ice water for 10 minutes, then drain well, pat dry, and then proceed. Soaking reduces the bite quite a bit and gives the onions a nice crunch.

2. Combine the fennel, onions, and carrots in a large bowl. Toss with the lemon juice, olive oil, salt and pepper, and capers. Taste and adjust the seasoning, keeping in mind that the feta will add saltiness. Add the feta, gently toss, and taste again.

— *Katherine Deumling of Cook With What You Have via*
Sauvie Island Organics, Portland, Oregon

farm supplies hundreds of pounds of fresh produce to NYC trail crews, the OutDoor High School's Culinary Arts program that makes the school lunch, and a 20-share CSA.

Common Good City Farm, a nearly half-acre farm on the grounds of a closed elementary school in Washington, DC, provides hands-on training in food production, healthful eating, and environmental sustainability, which promotes a local food system that bridges race, class, and age. Youth education programs at the farm include a six-week paid summer youth employment program for young people ages 14 to 17. Participants learn many aspects of vegetable production, visit other nearby farms, help prepare weekly community lunches, and attend workshops on issues of diversity awareness, hunger, homelessness, and sustainable agriculture. Youth who complete this program are eligible to return for a six-week paid fall and spring internship.

Farm-to-School Programs

Just what are farm-to-school programs? The term encompasses efforts that bring local or regionally produced foods into school cafeterias; hands-on learning activities such as school gardening, farm visits, and culinary classes; and the integration of food-related education into the regular, standards-based classroom curriculum. The latest trend: farm-to-preschool programs in settings as varied as Montessori and Head Start to private preschools, some with their own gardens, others subscribed to a CSA farm. Why preschool? Leaders in this movement believe that attitudes toward food are formed before children enter kindergarten, and many preschoolers consume most of their daily nutrients in child-care settings.

Much of the credit for what's become a movement can be traced to chef and cookbook author Al-ice Waters, one of the pioneers in seasonal, local, organic eating, first known as founder of the highly ac-claimed **Chez Panisse Restaurant and Café** in Berkeley, California. In 1996, her commitment to food education led to the creation of **The Edible Schoolyard** at Berke-ley's Martin Luther King, Jr. Middle School, a one-acre garden with an adjacent kitchen-classroom and an "eco-gastronomic" curriculum.

Today the **United States De-partment of Agriculture (USDA) Farm to School Program** includes research, training, technical assis-tance, and grants. Initial USDA Census results from 1,500 school districts during the 2011–2012 school year show that 23.5 million kids participated in farm-to-school activities at more than 40,000 schools in all 50 states, and more than $385 million was spent on lo-cal food for schools.

How much difference do these programs make? They can change lives, and they can be as creative as the teachers and others involved have the imagination to pursue. For example, in central Oregon, where many kids have long been involved with raising animals through FFA (formerly known as Future Farm-ers of America), the Bend-LaPine School District is using farm-to-school grant money to fund a unique "piglet to plate" program. FFA students at one high school are raising pigs on the school farm, while students, food service staff, and culinary teachers at anoth-er high school learn how to break down a side of pig into various cuts and make the best use of the meat for school district cafeterias.

A Corps at the Core of Farm to School

The recent growth of the farm-to-school movement may be partly caused by the work of **FoodCorps**, a national nonprofit organization

FENNEL, SAUSAGE, AND WHITE BEAN HASH   SERVES 2

Source Note: Fennel and sausage—two foods born to be together—form the major flavor components of this dish, while filling, creamy cannellini beans make a perfect bridge between the two. We like to make this recipe heavy on the fresh fennel and slightly lighter on the sausage. (Italian sausage usually contains fennel seeds, so it's a natural choice, but any tasty sausage—pork, chicken, or even vegetarian—will work great.) This hash can come together in a jiffy on a weeknight. Add a refreshing green salad to complement the bold flavors of the hash—and don't cheat yourself by skipping the crusty toast!

1 tablespoon extra-virgin olive oil
1 large fennel bulb (about 10 ounces)
2 links fresh Italian sausage, or 5 ounces fresh bulk sausage
1 cup cooked or canned white beans, such as cannellini, drained
2 to 3 green onions, chopped
Salt and freshly ground pepper
1 tablespoon chopped flat-leaf parsley or other fresh herbs
2 tablespoons cream, sour cream, or yogurt (optional)
2 thick slices crusty Italian or sourdough bread

1. If there are still feathery green fronds attached to the fennel bulb, cut them off and chop them for later use. Trim away any dried or brown areas. If the outer surface of the bulb seems fibrous, use a vegetable peeler to remove some of it; this will make that outer layer much more tender and usable. Cut the bulb into quarters and remove the inner core that keeps all the leaves attached (it's great for munching!). Slice the fennel into long strips.

2. Heat the olive oil in a large sauté pan over medium heat. Remove the sausage from its casings and crumble it into the pan, spreading the pieces so they cook evenly. Cook without moving the sausage for several minutes, until one side has a crispy brown crust. Add all of the fennel and stir. Continue cooking until the fennel has softened about halfway.

3. Meanwhile, butter or oil the bread slices. Toast them (your oven broiler works great for this) until the top side is golden and crunchy. Set aside and keep warm.

4. Add the cannellini beans and green onions to the pan; stir to com-bine. Season to taste with salt and pepper. Cook until all the ingredi-ents are hot and the fennel has softened a bit more. Add the parsley and fennel fronds. If you'd like to add more moisture and richness, add the cream. Place a piece of the crusty toasted bread on each plate and spoon the hash on top.

— Lisa Gordanier

TERHUNE ORCHARDS VEGETABLE SOUP   SERVES 4

¼ cup barley, uncooked
1 large onion, chopped
1 bunch celery, plus leaves
4 tomatoes, peeled and quartered, or 1 (15-ounce) can stewed
    whole tomatoes
1 pound carrots
2 zucchinis, sliced
1 green bell pepper, cleaned and chopped
1 fennel bulb, chopped (including enough fronds to make
    2 tablespoons)
4 chicken bouillon cubes dissolved in 4 cups water
4 cups chicken broth (or replace 2 cups of the broth with
    2 cups of tomato juice)
1 bunch fresh thyme, leaves stripped and chopped

1. Cook the barley by putting it in a small saucepot along with 1½ cups
    of lightly salted water. Bring to a simmer, cover, and cook for about
    40 minutes, or until the barley is cooked through but still a little
    chewy. You may discard any extra water or use it as part of the liquid
    in the soup.

2. Put all of the ingredients in a stockpot and bring to a boil. Turn the
    heat down to low and simmer for 45 minutes to 1 hour, or until the
    vegetables are cooked but not too soft.

— *Terhune Orchards, Princeton, New Jersey*

Chow time for the chickens of Kahumana Farm.

founded in 2009 that places young leaders in communities to help educate kids about healthful foods, build and tend school gardens, and bring local food into school cafeterias. A part of the AmeriCorps Service Network, FoodCorps has, as of September 2014, 182 service members placed at 145 sites in 16 states and Washington, DC.

Six young leaders in the food movement developed the concept of FoodCorps and announced their plans on Earth Day 2009, the day President Obama signed the Kennedy Serve America Act into law. This legislation signaled an opportunity to engage AmeriCorps in building a more sustainable, healthful, and equitable food system.

FoodCorps sprang from the grassroots up: a national initiative that thousands of local voices shaped according to their needs. Service members serve one year. Service sites are the grassroots nonprofits, public schools or districts, and community-based organizations that supervise them, such as the **Johns Hopkins Center for American Indian Health** in Arizona, the **Mississippi Roadmap to Health Equity**, and the **University of Maine Cooperative Extension**.

FoodCorps is a grantee of AmeriCorps—receiving a portion of funding from it—and a member of a service network that includes Habitat for Humanity, City Year, and Teach for America. Its service members are considered AmeriCorps service members and receive the benefits accorded with that program, including a monetary education award upon successful completion of the service term.

Garlic

ALLIUM SATIVUM

Few plants attract such polarizing opinions as garlic. Whether you consider it a delectable flavor or a rambunctious stink bomb, garlic is used almost universally in the world's cuisines. Garlic is the most pungent member of the large Allium family, which gives us such kitchen favorites as onions, leeks, shallots, and chives.

Garlic, as most of us know, is actually the plant's mature bulb, which consists of numerous cloves clustered around a central stem. The very young, tender shoots, stems, and flower buds that emerge from sprouting cloves in early spring are sold as "green garlic," "scapes," or "whistles." They are a fleeting favorite in farmers markets in early spring (see pages 47–52 for more information).

Garlic is classified as either hardneck or softneck, and literally hundreds of heirloom varieties exist, with bulbs whose personalities range from soft and mellow to very spicy and pungent. Hardnecks produce flower spikes, tend to be mild in flavor, grow well in northern climates, contain 6 to 11 cloves per bulb, and can be stored for 3 to 6 months. Softneck varieties (sometimes known as braiding garlic) usually lack flower spikes, have a spicier taste, thrive in warmer climates, contain 12 to 20 cloves per bulb, and can be stored up to a year. The papery white garlic bulbs you see at your grocery store are usually softnecks.

HISTORY

Garlic's exact origin is unclear, although many sources list Asia as its homeland. References to the aromatic bulb exist in so many ancient cultures and cuisines that it is impossible to be certain where it was first enjoyed by humans. (Not helping is the fact that it may have been confused with its Allium sibling the leek.)

One thing is certain, however: Over the ages, garlic has been both adored and shunned, and whether you were a garlic lover or hater often depended on your socioeconomic standing and geographical location. Southern Europeans, especially in Italy and France, practically lived on it, whereas northern Europeans found it quite distasteful. The Greeks treated it as an important vegetable in its own right, and Egyptian pyramid builders ate it as part of their food rations. Garlic was probably brought to America from the Old World by the Spaniards, but Native Americans likely had been consuming their own native wild garlic for centuries.

NUTRITION

Garlic is legendary for its nutritional and medicinal benefits, which humans have been employing for hundreds of years. The sulfurous compounds that give garlic its characteristic odor also have healthful benefits, especially allicin, which is released in greater amounts when the garlic is chopped or mashed rather than left whole. Regular garlic consumption may lower blood pressure and reduce the buildup of atherosclerotic plaques and the incidence of certain cancers. Both garlic and onions contain significant anti-inflammatory and antibacterial properties, even

The Aroma of the Windy City

The city of Chicago got its name from the Native American word *chicagaoua*, for the wild garlic that grew on the shores of Lake Michigan.

against antibiotic-resistant strains. Garlic is also a good source of manganese, vitamin B6, vitamin C, tryptophan, and selenium. A single teaspoon contains 4 calories.

Esteban at Featherstone Farm trims and cleans garlic to prepare it for curing.

SEASON

Commercially, garlic is widely grown and in season year-round. But it is typically at its best from late July through early winter. Cured garlic (garlic that is partially dried for long-term storage) is often a significant part of many winter CSAs.

SELECTION

Choose bulbs that are fresh, dry, and plump, with unbroken skins. Squeeze the bulbs lightly to check that they are firm, with no large gaps beneath the skin, which could mean shriveled, dehydrated garlic well past its prime. Garlic that is beginning to sprout green shoots is still edible, but it is not the most ideal for culinary purposes. If you have kids, try planting it in the backyard or in a large pot—a fun exercise in gardening!

STORAGE

Keep garlic in the refrigerator or continue to cure it by storing it in a dry, dark, well-ventilated place. Moisture and light will trigger the bulb to sprout. Although sprouting garlic is still edible, it tends to be bitter and less digestible. Whole garlic bulbs can keep from 2 weeks to several months, depending on the variety and storage conditions.

They will also keep quite well in a basement, root cellar, or other place with the proper cool temperature and lack of humidity (for more information, see "Preserving the Bounty" on page 611).

TRIMMING AND CLEANING

Before you can use garlic, you must first separate and peel the cloves from the bulb, unless you plan to roast the bulbs whole. To peel, place the clove flat side down on a hard surface, then firmly press or rock the blade of a wide knife against the clove to split the skin. Then you can use either your fingers or a smaller knife to peel it off. Sometimes peeling the cloves is easier if the very tips from both ends are sliced off.

Allicin Lives Here After All

The compound that gives garlic its pungency (and many of its health benefits) is allicin, which whole garlic does not actually contain. What forms it is alliin and the enzyme allinase, which garlic stores in different cells.

When the garlic clove is crushed, these compounds combine to form allicin.

Waiting a few minutes after chopping, mashing, or crushing garlic before cooking with it increases the allicin production, and also its characteristic flavor.

Cooking Tip

If at all possible, avoid using garlic powder or dried garlic granules. These forms of garlic often have an unpleasantly acrid, metallic taste, and they can also worsen digestion and bad breath.

Stick to using fresh garlic whenever possible!

Bet You Can't Stop at Just One

Restaurants in Korea serve raw garlic cloves in bowls for munching, like peanuts.

This habit may partly account for why Koreans have the highest garlic consumption per capita in the world (a whopping 22 pounds annually, compared with the US average of about 2.5 pounds).

Sources

The Garlic Shoppe
www.garlicdude.com

The Garlic Store
www.thegarlicstore.com

Gilroy Garlic Festival
www.gilroygarlicfestival.com

A word about garlic presses and gadgets: Some work very well, and others are a waste of money. If you regularly prepare garlic in large quantities, investing in a good-quality press or peeler can be worth it. One major caveat: You can't press garlic and then let it sit in the air, waiting for cooking to happen. If you do so, its sulfurous gases will go to town and the whole kitchen gets stinky. What does work is to press your cloves directly into your sauté pan or other cooking vessel (thus into the warming oil), so the pureed garlic doesn't come into as much contact with the air. Likewise, you can press it directly into, say, the vinaigrette you're making, or into hot pasta.

STEAMING AND BOILING

Peeled garlic cloves can be dropped either whole or sliced into soups, stews, or other cooked dishes. The degree of garlic flavor you want dictates the cooking time and how finely sliced the cloves are; the longer garlic cooks, the more mellow and less pungent it will be in the finished dish. Finely chopped or mashed garlic will taste much stronger than unbroken cloves. Whole garlic cloves require about 20 to 25 minutes of rapid boiling to become a mild, sweet vegetable.

STIR-FRYING AND SAUTÉING

Garlic is delicious stir-fried and sautéed, but care must be taken so it does not burn, or it turns unpleasantly bitter. Always use plenty of cooking oil or butter when stir-frying or sautéing garlic; chicken broth can also be used when the pan becomes too dry or if you are watching calories. Warm up a wok or frying pan over medium-high heat, add 1 or 2 tablespoons of oil, add the chopped fresh garlic, and stir-fry for about 1 minute, or until it becomes fragrant, before adding the rest of your ingredients.

BAKING AND ROASTING

Garlic responds wonderfully to slow-roasting in the oven, losing its ornery pungency to become a sweet and mellow creature. You can easily prepare a whole bulb by cutting off its top (the pointed end) to expose the cloves and then placing the head in a baking dish or wrapping it in aluminum foil. Sprinkle with olive oil or butter, if desired, then bake at 350°F for about an hour. When it's done, gently squeeze the soft, roasted garlic directly onto toasted French bread, or scoop out the flesh with a knife and spread over the food of your choice. Delicious!

MICROWAVING

Passable roasted garlic can be prepared in the microwave: Just cut off the tips from whole garlic heads and put the heads, along with ⅓ cup of chicken broth and 3 tablespoons of olive oil, into a microwave-safe dish (glass absorbs fewer odors than plastic). Cover tightly with microwave-approved plastic wrap and cook on high power for 6 to 8 minutes. Let stand, covered, for 10 minutes, and peel the cloves after they have cooled.

To microwave peeled garlic, place cloves in a microwave-safe glass dish with enough chicken broth or water to submerge them. Cover the dish with plastic wrap and microwave on high power for 5 to 10 minutes, or until the garlic is soft.

BLANCHING AND FREEZING

Garlic can be frozen, although this method can affect its flavor. Since garlic is almost always available raw and its taste is far superior fresh, freezing garlic is not recommended. Still, if you want to preserve an abundant harvest or a specialty type that spoils easily, you can freeze unpeeled whole cloves in a zipper-lock freezer or vacuum food sealer-type bags. Squeeze out any excess air. Garlic frozen this way will keep for up to 3 months at 0°F.

You can then simply prepare the number of cloves you need by peeling them, then pureeing or chopping them in a food processor with a bit of oil. Use this garlic immediately; *do not store it at room temperature because of the possibility of botulism contamination* (see the Safety Tip on page 543).

EQUIVALENTS, MEASURES, AND SERVINGS

- 1 small clove = ½ teaspoon minced = ⅛ teaspoon garlic powder
- 1 large clove = 1½ teaspoons minced = ½ teaspoon garlic powder
- 1 head = 8 to 15 cloves

COMPLEMENTARY HERBS, SEASONINGS, AND FOODS

Beans, beef, beets, bread, butter, cabbage, chicken, eggplant, eggs, fish, ginger, greens, hot pepper, lamb, lentils, mayonnaise, mushrooms, olive oil, onions, pasta, pesto, pork, potatoes, poultry, rice, rosemary, sesame, shellfish, soy sauce, spinach, tomatoes, veal, vegetables, zucchini.

SERVING SUGGESTIONS

- Puree fresh garlic, canned garbanzo beans (chickpeas), tahini, olive oil, and lemon juice to make hummus, that classic Middle Eastern dip. Serve with pita bread, naan, or fresh raw vegetables such as baby carrots, celery, radishes, broccoli, and cauliflower.
- Sauté thinly sliced or chopped garlic cloves with steamed spinach and sprinkle with red pepper flakes.
- Roast garlic in a fragrant nut oil, then add to your favorite chocolate chip cookie recipe. It might sound horrid, but garlic after it has been roasted loses its pungency; it gives the cookies a savor that is noticeable but not garlicky. Don't tell anyone—see if they can guess the secret ingredient.
- Add garlic to sauces, soups, stews, and casseroles.
- Insert thin slivers of garlic and sprigs of fresh herbs directly into meat or under the skin of poultry to be roasted.
- Top your favorite pizza with very thin slices of garlic. A must for garlic lovers, not so for garlic haters!
- Add garlic to your favorite pesto, marinade, and salsa recipes.
- Pickle whole garlic cloves in soy sauce or vinegar.
- Add finely chopped garlic and fresh herbs to ground beef for out-of-this-world hamburgers, meat loaf, and meatballs.
- Roast whole garlic bulbs, then squeeze them and spread the resulting paste onto slices of thick-cut French or sourdough bread instead of butter.
- Sprinkle vegetables that will be oven-roasted, like potatoes, sweet potatoes, turnips, onions, and carrots, with a combination of olive oil, chopped garlic, fresh herbs, and salt and pepper.
- Stage a garlic-themed dinner. If you're going to wreck your breath, you might as well go all out. Invite like-minded friends and family.

Elephant Garlic

Mi Ae Lipe

Elephant garlic is an entirely different species of Allium, more closely related to the leek than regular garlic.

Its cloves are enormous—a single clove can be as large as a whole bulb of ordinary garlic, and entire elephant bulbs sometimes weigh over a pound. Some people assume from its size that elephant garlic is more strongly scented, but actually the opposite is true—its flavor is much more mild, delicate, and sweet.

It can be prepared the same way as regular garlic, but its mildness does not make it a true substitute for the real McCoy. It is best used in recipes where a subtle hint of garlic is desired, but not an overpowering presence. Don't be put off, though—roasted elephant garlic is truly delectable in its own right.

THE CSA FARM COOKBOOK   WINTER — GARLIC   541

Taking a Breather

To deal with the unpleasant breath that consuming garlic tends to cause, the easiest way is to simply associate with others who like garlic just as much.

Barring that, chlorophyll is quite effective in temporarily absorbing the distinctive odor; chew sprigs of raw parsley or mint for several minutes after eating a garlicky dish.

- Make garlic bread! Toast slices of French baguette or Italian bread in an oven broiler, toaster oven, or regular oven, then rub cut cloves of garlic over the bread. The rough surface of the bread acts like a grater on the garlic.
- Caesar salad is one of the best things that ever happened to lettuce, anchovies, and garlic.
- In Spain, a very popular soup is made from just water, garlic cloves, and bread—the venerable *sopa de ajo* (see the recipe on page 544).
- Make aïoli, the classic garlic mayonnaise. It is delicious with vegetables, salads, meats, or anywhere a light, creamy garlic flavor is desired.

CHICKEN WITH 40 CLOVES OF GARLIC   SERVES 4 TO 6

Source Note: Do not be alarmed at the quantity of garlic in this traditional French dish. Baking the garlic in the oven along with the bird softens and mellows it to a piquant, sumptuous sweetness, with none of the harsh pungency of the raw bulb. As you eat, squeeze the contents of the garlic cloves onto the chicken.

FRESH HERB RUB

1½ tablespoons fresh thyme
1½ tablespoons finely chopped fresh sage
1 tablespoon finely chopped fresh rosemary
4 large cloves garlic, finely minced
2 teaspoons salt
1 teaspoon freshly ground black pepper

CHICKEN

1 large frying or roasting chicken (3½ pounds)
¼ cup olive oil
1 medium lemon, cut into quarters
Sprigs of fresh rosemary or thyme (optional)
40 cloves garlic, separated but not peeled
1½ cups white wine
½ cup chicken stock
2 tablespoons fresh basil or parsley, minced, for garnish

1. Thoroughly mix the herb rub ingredients together.

2. Rinse the chicken thoroughly and pat it dry with paper towels. Rub the skin with 1 tablespoon of the olive oil. Apply the herb rub evenly over the chicken, including within the cavity. Place the lemon quarters in the cavity along with the herb sprigs. Refrigerate and allow to marinate for at least 2 hours.

3. Preheat the oven to 375°F.

4. In a saucepan, sauté the remaining olive oil and garlic cloves over medium heat for 3 to 4 minutes. Add the wine and stock and cook for 3 minutes longer.

5. In an ovenproof casserole dish large enough to hold the chicken, add the garlic-wine-stock mixture. Place the chicken in the casserole, cover, and bake for 25 minutes. Uncover, raise the oven temperature to 400°F, and bake for 40 to 50 minutes longer, or until the juices run clear when the thigh joint is pierced. (Be sure that some liquid always remains in the bottom of the casserole to prevent scorching. If it is evaporating away, add a little more wine or stock—you don't want the garlic cloves to get dry and burn.)

6. Remove the chicken, let it rest in a warm place for 15 to 20 minutes, and cut it into serving pieces. Place the pieces on a warm platter and spoon the pan juices over the top. Arrange the garlic cloves around the chicken, and garnish with minced basil or parsley.

— *Fooddownunder.com*

· ·

ROASTED GARLIC HUMMUS

SERVES 2 TO 3

Source Note: The roasted garlic gives this hummus a subtler flavor than raw garlic. Even though it is time-consuming, removing the skins from the chickpeas (garbanzo beans) makes the hummus smoother, especially if you are pureeing it with a mortar and pestle. Go easy on the tahini, and adjust the spices as you see fit. This hummus is delicious with baby carrots, pretzels, tortilla chips, warmed pita bread, pita chips, or celery.

1 head garlic
1½ cups cooked garbanzo beans (chickpeas), or 1 (20-ounce) can
    with liquid
Juice of 2 lemons
¼ cup tahini (sesame paste)
1½ teaspoons ground cumin
1 teaspoon freshly ground black pepper
1½ teaspoons salt
¾ teaspoon cayenne pepper
1 tablespoon extra-virgin olive oil, plus more for garnish

1. Preheat the oven to 375°F. Cut the top (the pointed end) off the head of garlic and wrap the head in aluminum foil. Roast for 45 minutes.

2. Meanwhile, drain the chickpea liquid into a small saucepan. Simmer over low heat for 5 minutes. Pour the chickpeas onto a plate, then pinch off and discard their skins, adding each chickpea to the saucepan.

3. When the garlic is done roasting, squeeze the pulp into a medium mixing bowl and discard the skins.

4. Remove the chickpeas from their liquid and puree them with a mortar and pestle or in a food processor until they are smooth. Put the puree into the mixing bowl along with the garlic, add the remaining ingredients, and stir until combined. Use the remaining chickpea liq-

Safety Tip

Never store raw garlic in oil at room temperature; even in the refrigerator this is chancy, as sulfurous compounds in garlic provide ideal conditions for breeding botulism, the most deadly natural toxin known to humans.

However, garlic can be safely stored in wine and vinegar if refrigerated; the high acid content of these mixtures prevents the formation of botulism.

5. Serve the hummus at room temperature, garnishing with a bit more cayenne pepper and drizzling with extra-virgin olive oil.

— *Justin Watt,* Justinsomnia *blog*

....

SOPA DE AJO (TRADITIONAL SPANISH BREAD SOUP) SERVES 4

Source Note: *There is a certain austerity to many traditional Spanish dishes that I find utterly appealing.* Sopa de ajo *(literally "garlic soup") is one of those dishes—an example of the great cuisine of bread, the kingdom of leftovers, and the audacity to make the best out of what's in the larder.*

You can find soups made with bread throughout Spain, from north to south, from Majorca to Andalucía, cold and hot, thick and light, meaty or full of vegetables. The recipe below is perhaps the best-known version, where only four ingredients (bread, garlic, olive oil, and paprika) are able to convey childhood memories and a bit of daydreaming on a dull winter evening.

Seasonal Hint: *Because of the lack of meat, this soup has traditionally been a Lenten dish; in fact, the whole concoction is plain and clear frugality. Rejoice.*

> **5 to 7 ounces (3 to 4 thick slices) of stale, dense, good-quality white bread, crusts retained**
> **3 to 5 cloves of garlic, sliced**
> **3 teaspoons paprika (the best you can find—my favorite is smoked bittersweet Pimentón de la Vera)**
> **½ cup extra-virgin olive oil (again, try to find good oil: dense, deep and fragrant)**
> **⅔ cup water or stock**
> **4 eggs (optional)**

1. Traditionally in Spain you would use a clay pot for this recipe, but any deep pot will do. Fry the garlic in a bit of the olive oil until it turns golden. Remove the garlic from the pan and set it aside so it doesn't burn and turn bitter.

2. Now place the bread in the pan and fry it in the remaining oil (it will soak up part of the oil). Take the pot off the stove, add the paprika, and stir it with the bread and oil, making sure it doesn't burn; otherwise it will lose its wonderful fragrance and turn bitter.

3. Add the water and garlic, and let it simmer for 10 to 15 minutes. At the very beginning, it will probably not look like the most appetizing of meals, but just be confident—time will bind the soup, and the result will be simply delicious.

4. Some people like to have their *sopa de ajo* really thick and dry (some

---

Events, Education, and Recreation

Martha Wagner

Many small farms are running multiple businesses today, diversifying their income through numerous visitor activities, from farm tours to farm stay accommodations to special events. Visitors can try their hand at milking goats or making cheese, or learn about composting, permaculture, beekeeping, or ecology. They're also visiting farms for events such as music festivals, hoedown dances, and benefit dinners.

Green Gate Farms, *a family farm near Austin, Texas, offers camps and workshops for children and adults through its nonprofit affiliate, New Farm Institute. The Institute's mission is to engage people of all ages and abilities in healthful foods and sustainable farming, as well as to inspire a new generation of sustainable farmers in central Texas. Programs include a weeklong farm camp for kids and workshops on topics such as beekeeping and fermentation. The farm also hosts community-building activities for schools, businesses, and nonprofits.*

The nonprofit ***Calypso Farm and Ecology Center*** *in Alaska is all about education. The School-Garden Initiative offers hands-on classes at local schools, and the Learning Ecology and Alaskan Farming (LEAF) program offers summer camps. The Farmer Training Program attracts young people from around the country to gain the skills, inspiration, and experience needed to embark on starting their own small farm. Workshops at the farm offer visitors a huge range of skill- and knowledge-building opportunities, including blacksmithing, preserving with fermentation, sheep shearing, beginning spinning, composting, drip irrigation basics for home gardens, starting a home garden CSA, and raising and butchering meat birds.*

even finish it in the oven). I prefer to keep mine just on the creamy side of the term "soup," with thick blobs of creamy bread that melt in your mouth. Once the soup has thickened, and while I set the table, I like to take the pot off the stove and use the remaining heat to poach one egg per person. Once at the table, the yolk will break in each guest's bowl, taking the *sopa de ajo* experience to its very limit, so to speak. Sometimes I also sprinkle on a bit of ground cumin. Feel free to add anything you like.

— *Ibán Yarza, as appeared on Johanna Kindvall's* Kokblog *blog*

. . . .

GARLIC SPINACH   SERVES 3 TO 4

Author Note: This is a decidedly robust dish. After consuming it, don't have a job interview or plan to meet the Queen of England the next day.

> 1 tablespoon olive oil
> 3 to 8 cloves garlic, or 4 to 6 green garlic scapes
> Many shakes of freshly ground black pepper
> Several spritzes of Tabasco sauce
> 2 pounds (2 to 3 large bunches) spinach leaves

1. Heat the olive oil in a large skillet or wok on medium heat. Mince or chop the garlic (I use a miniature food processor) and add it to the oil. Sauté for 1 to 2 minutes, until the garlic begins to heavily perfume the kitchen (but be careful not to let it burn, or it will turn bitter).

2. Add the pepper and Tabasco sauce to the sizzling oil and garlic and let cook for about ½ minute. Then add enough spinach to fill the pan, stirring in more as it wilts and shrinks. Cook the spinach on medium-high heat for another 2 to 3 minutes, or until it has all wilted but is still a healthy green color.

3. Remove from the heat immediately and serve while piping hot.

— *Mi Ae Lipe*

Kids and adults have many farm tours and classes to choose from at the **Green Mountain Girls Farm** in Vermont. Visitors can also stay overnight in the Barn Guesthouse or the new, luxurious, three-bedroom Farmhouse Inn—both of them well suited for people who want a longer on-farm experience or who want to ski and explore nearby. Overnight guests are treated to a guided farm tour to visit the gardens and meet the animals (pigs, chickens, goats, and more), as well as learn about the farm's practices and philosophy.

Many states have agritourism or farm stay websites. If you're interested, check out the website www.farmstayus.com for listings in the United States.

The **Shambala Permaculture Farm** in Washington State has a plant nursery and serves as a go-to resource for permaculture education: workshops, classes, food-forest garden and farm animal tours, and edible landscaping and permaculture design services and certification programs. The farm is unusual in offering wild foraged foods as well as typical vegetables and fruits. It hosts events such as weddings, too.

Many farms invite their CSA members to workdays and open houses. **Helsing Junction Farm** in Washington State throws open its farm gate every September for an open house, inviting its 1,200 CSA shareholders. It also hosts an annual camping sleepover with a local record company. The festival features more than a dozen different K Records acts, independent films, homemade organic food, swimming in the river, and two nights of camping in the farm's orchard and fallow fields. More than 300 people come out to the farm for what has become a tradition, paying a modest charge for the weekend.

Jerusalem Artichokes

HELIANTHUS
TUBEROSUS

No one is sure just how Jerusalem artichokes got their name, because they are neither native to Jerusalem nor related to the more familiar green globe artichokes. Misnomers aside, the knobby tubers of this member of the sunflower family are quite possibly one of the more delicious vegetables you might ever eat, and definitely worth trying should they show up in your CSA box or at your farmers market. Their flavor is nutty and sweet, and when raw, their texture is delightfully crisp, like jicama or water chestnuts. Cooked, they become rich and creamy, a nice change from the usual potatoes, for which they can be used culinarily almost interchangeably. They are also known as sunchokes.

HISTORY

Jerusalem artichokes are native to the New World and were a staple food of Native Americans in both North and South America. Later, European explorers brought them back to their home countries in the 1600s, where they became popular, especially in France.

NUTRITION

Jerusalem artichokes are excellent sources of potassium, iron, copper, and thiamine; they also contain smaller amounts of vitamins A, C, and E. These tubers are curious in that they are rich in protein, contain no fat and very little starch, are low in calories, and are one of the best natural sources of dietary fiber. They are unusual in that their primary carbohydrate is inulin, which makes them an excellent food for diabetics, who can better tolerate this form of fructose. (Note that inulin should not be confused with the hormone insulin.) This characteristic also makes Jerusalem artichokes difficult to digest for some people, who may experience bloating and flatulence; go easy on them the first time you try them.

SEASON

Commercially, Jerusalem artichokes are widely grown and in season year-round. But they are typically sweetest and best from October to April.

SELECTION

Look for Jerusalem artichokes that are fresh and plump looking, with no signs of shriveling or decay. They can be tricky to clean, so choosing specimens that are as smooth as possible with the fewest protrusions can save you some work. Also avoid Jerusalem artichokes that are tinged with green or are blotchy or sprouting.

STORAGE

Store Jerusalem artichokes by wrapping them unwashed in a plastic bag and refrigerating them in the vegetable crisper until ready to use. They will keep for up to 1 week.

Trimming and Cleaning

Some vegetables are a snap to clean, but Jerusalem artichokes are not one of them. Scrub them vigorously with a vegetable brush to remove the dirt that tends to hide out among the bumpy tubers. Peeling is optional and not necessary; the skins are tender and perfectly edible. If you do peel them, drop them in water to which a bit of acid has been added, such as lemon juice, to keep them from discoloring.

Steaming and Boiling

Jerusalem artichokes can be steamed either peeled or unpeeled over rapidly boiling water for 12 to 20 minutes, depending on their size. They continue to cook for some time after they are removed from the pan, and they overcook quite easily, turning into mush. With that in mind, remove them as soon as they feel tender when pricked with a knife; either serve them at that point or drop them into a bowl of cold water to slow further cooking.

Stir-Frying and Sautéing

Jerusalem artichokes take well to sautéing. Thinly slice them (a mandoline works like a charm, especially considering their irregular size and shape) and drop them into acidulated water to keep them from darkening. When you are ready to cook them, drain and dry the pieces. Sprinkle them lightly with kosher salt or sea salt, and sauté on medium-high heat in oil or butter for about 5 minutes, or until they are light brown on the outside and tender on the inside.

Baking and Roasting

These tubers are fantastic roasted, which concentrates their natural sugars and caramelizes them. Place them whole, unpeeled, in a pan, drizzle a little oil or melted butter over them (plus a dash of salt), and roast them in a 350°F oven for 30 minutes, or at 400°F for about 20 minutes, for medium-size chokes. Their exact cooking time will depend on their size and your oven temperature. If you need to cook chokes of different sizes, place the larger ones in the oven first and the smaller ones 5 to 10 minutes later. You can also cut them all into more uniform chunks for more even roasting.

Microwaving

Slice, add 2 tablespoons water, place in a microwave-safe dish, and cook on high power.

- 1 pound = 5 to 6 minutes (whole; time depending on size)

Blanching and Freezing

Jerusalem artichokes should not be frozen. Freezing turns them black and destroys their texture.

Equivalents, Measures, and Servings

- ¼ pound sunchokes = 3 to 4 whole = 1 serving
- 1 pound peeled, thin-sliced sunchokes = 3 cups raw
- 1 pound raw sunchokes = 1 pound chopped
     = 2 cups cooked = 1½ cups mashed

Drinking Your Artichokes

In Baden-Württemberg, Germany, over 90 percent of the Jerusalem artichoke crop is used to produce a type of fruity, nutty-sweet brandy called Topinambu or Rossler.

COMPLEMENTARY HERBS, SEASONINGS, AND FOODS

Anchovies, anise, artichokes, bacon, bay, butter, cardamom, cardoons, carrots, celery, celery root, cheese (Gruyère, Fontina, Gouda), chestnuts, chicken, chile, cream, garlic, ginger, hazelnuts, hazelnut oil, leeks, mint, mustard, onions, parsley, pasta, pistachios, potatoes, radicchio, rosemary, shallots, sunflower seeds, sweet potatoes, thyme, walnuts, walnut oil.

SERVING SUGGESTIONS

- Puree Jerusalem artichokes like you would potatoes and use them to make creamy, delicate soups.
- Roasted Jerusalem artichokes are hard to beat, either by themselves or with other root vegetables. The next time you decide to oven-roast your standard assortment of winter veggies, add some sunchokes to the mix. They're really quite sociable.
- Dice Jerusalem artichokes and add them to stir-fries and sautés.
- Finely shredded Jerusalem artichokes are terrific fried with plenty of onions, then mixed into savory pancakes and fritters.
- Pickle Jerusalem artichokes with mustard seed, celery seed, hot peppers, and allspice; their crispy texture makes a refreshing pickle.
- Jerusalem artichokes make great au gratins.
- Steam or boil Jerusalem artichokes and serve with vinaigrette, hollandaise sauce, or simply with butter and lemon.
- The crunchy texture and slightly sweet, nutty flavor of raw Jerusalem artichokes makes them an unexpected taste treat on the crudité tray.
- Serve raw Jerusalem artichokes with a variety of dips and dressings—quite a hit with kids.
- Jerusalem artichokes make a satisfying vegetable side dish with fish, poultry, pork, beef, lamb, and veal.
- Add chunks of Jerusalem artichokes to stews, just like potatoes.
- Thinly slice Jerusalem artichokes and deep-fry like potato chips.
- Bake Jerusalem artichokes unpeeled along with your favorite roast and other root vegetables for a hearty, one-dish meal.
- It's not every day that one pulls out the deep fryer, but if you have some nice sunchokes, it's worth the trouble! (Think potato chips with a sweet, complex flavor and perfectly crisp texture.) Slice thinly, fry just until golden, then sprinkle with fine sea salt.

JERUSALEM ARTICHOKE FRITTERS

SERVES 4 AS AN APPETIZER

½ pound Jerusalem artichokes, scrubbed
1 carrot, peeled
3 shallots, thinly sliced
2 tablespoons yellow cornmeal
¼ cup flour
½ teaspoon salt
½ teaspoon baking powder
Freshly ground black pepper to taste

Tabasco
2 eggs, lightly beaten
3 tablespoons chopped chives
½ cup sour cream
1 tablespoon fresh lime juice
Peanut oil for frying

1. Heat the oven to 250°F. Grate the Jerusalem artichokes and carrot into a mixing bowl. Add the shallots. In a separate bowl, stir together the cornmeal, flour, salt, and baking powder, then add the dry ingredients to the vegetables, mixing well. Season with pepper and Tabasco to taste. Add the eggs, and mix thoroughly.

2. Combine the chives, sour cream, and lime juice, and set aside.

3. Pour the oil ½ inch deep into a large skillet. Heat over medium-high heat until sizzling. Carefully drop the mixture in by tablespoons, flattening them slightly. Fry until crisp and golden brown, turning once. Transfer to the oven on a baking sheet lined with paper towels while frying more. Serve with the sour cream mixture.

— *Regina Schrambling,* The New York Times

. . . .

JERUSALEM ARTICHOKE SOUP WITH TOASTED PISTACHIOS AND PISTACHIO OIL
SERVES 8

Source Note: How can this gnarled and knobby vegetable offer such elegance? This soup deserves a pedestal, as the creamy alabaster liquid mingles with the equally regal pistachio oil and brilliant green toasted pistachios. The soup elicits looks of surprise from guests, followed by sounds of happy pleasure.

2 quarts whole milk
2 teaspoons fine sea salt
2 pounds Jerusalem artichokes, scrubbed
¼ cup salted pistachios, toasted, for garnish
Best-quality pistachio oil, such as Leblanc brand, for garnish

1. Rinse a large saucepan with water, leaving a bit of water in the pan (this will prevent the milk from scorching and sticking to the pan). Pour the milk into the pan and add the salt.

2. Trim and peel the Jerusalem artichokes, and chop them coarsely, dropping them into the milk as you work (this will stop the vegetable from turning brown as it is exposed to the air). When all of the Jerusalem artichokes are prepared, place the pan over medium heat and cook gently until they are soft, 35 to 40 minutes. Watch carefully so the milk does not boil over. The milk may curdle, but that will not alter the texture or flavor of the final soup.

3. Transfer the mixture, in small batches, to a blender or food processor. Do not place the plunger in the feed tube of the food processor

marketing and distribution of their certified organic produce, including a communal farm stand and participation in a summer CSA organized by **Growing Washington**. This incubator is not designed for first-time farmers but for people with experience who are ready to launch a farm business. Many are Latinos. Viva helps farmers further their education through certificate programs in sustainable agriculture offered by local colleges. Its funding comes from multiple sources, including foundations, government, and social impact loans.

For some farmers, incubators represent not only a way to establish a successful business but also a means of finding stability in a new country. The **Minnesota Food Association (MFA)** in Marine on St. Croix and **New Roots for Refugees** in Kansas City, Kansas, both provide farm incubator programs for immigrant refugees displaced by war, political upheaval, and human rights persecution. Many of the participants were successful farmers in their home countries but face the added challenges of navigating a new country with its unfamiliar language, regulations, and climate. The MFA's training program at **Big River Farms** works primarily with Hmong farmers from Southeast Asia.

New Roots for Refugees (see the Food and Faith Connections sidebar on page 432) is a partnership of Catholic Charities of Northeast Kansas and the Kansas City Center for Urban Agriculture. It trains refugee women farmers primarily from Somalia, Myanmar (otherwise known as Burma), Burundi, Bhutan, and Sudan on an eight-acre farm at Juniper Gardens, a public housing site in Kansas City, Kansas. Many New Roots graduates are now farming on their own plots in the area. The training farm uses organic methods, and its produce is sold at farmers markets throughout the metro area and through a 60-member CSA program. The CSA is unique in that it pairs every sub-scriber with one farmer, allowing that farmer to experience having her own business.

Not all farmers participating in incubator programs succeed in establishing their own farms, but many do. Some other notable in-cubators are **Green Gate Farms** in Austin, Texas; the **New Agrari-an Center** in Oberlin, Ohio; **Tilian Farm Development Center** in Ann Arbor, Michigan; and **Community Crops** in Lincoln, Nebraska.

or in the lid of the blender, or the heat will create a vacuum and the liquid will splatter. Puree until the mixture is perfectly smooth and silken, 1 to 2 minutes.

4. Return the soup to the saucepan and reheat gently. Taste for sea-soning. Transfer it to warmed, shallow soup bowls, shower with the pistachios, and drizzle with pistachio oil.

— *Patricia Wells*, The French Kitchen Cookbook

. . . .

CABBAGE AND SUNCHOKE SLAW   SERVES 4

3 cups cabbage (or substitute any Asian head cabbage,
    such as napa)
Salt
¼ pound coarsely shredded sunchokes (Jerusalem artichokes)
    (or substitute jicama, apple, or daikon radish)
Juice of ½ large lime or 1 Mexican lime
1 teaspoon celery seed
¼ cup finely minced red onion
½ to 1 teaspoon toasted sesame oil, walnut oil, or pistachio oil
Freshly ground black pepper
¼ cup finely minced cilantro or dill
1 teaspoon rice wine vinegar (optional)

1. Coarsely shred the cabbage and place it in a colander over a medium bowl. Toss it thoroughly with the salt and let it sit and drain for 30 to 60 minutes. Toss from time to time.

2. Shred the sunchokes and immediately transfer them to a separate bowl. Toss them with the lime juice and minced onion.

3. When the cabbage has wilted, rinse it and place it on towels to press it dry. Combine it with the sunchoke-onion mixture. Taste, and then add the sesame oil. Toss with black pepper to taste, and top it with the chopped herbs. If the slaw is not sour enough from the lime juice, add the rice wine vinegar to taste.

— *Lorraine Glazar, Tucson CSA, Tucson, Arizona*

Onions

Like its Allium cousin garlic, a gastronomic life without onions is nearly unimaginable. Few vegetables have so many versatile personalities and are equally good sautéed, baked, braised, roasted, stuffed, steamed, grilled, and of course, deep-fried. The pungent, distinctive flavor of onions melds well with so many ingredients, both flesh and vegetable, that this bulb is truly a workhorse in kitchens around the world.

Do not confuse onions with other members of the large Allium family; although they may seem similar at first glance, shallots, leeks, ramps, green onions, garlic, chives, and garlic chives all have varying complexities and potencies of flavor that profoundly affect finished dishes, and they should not be used interchangeably.

Onions themselves come in diverse forms and degrees of pungency. Farming them can be surprisingly difficult, as they grow slowly, need to be kept free of weeds during their long juvenile period, and can be quite fickle, sometimes going to seed without ever actually forming their bulbs. As many farms know, just because onions did well one year in a certain field doesn't ensure success the next, so farmers often grow several varieties at a time to help hedge their bets. If you see a beautiful, well-formed onion in your CSA box or on the farmers market table, rejoice!

CSA farms grow many different types of onions. They generally fall into one of the following categories, listed here in the order of their seasonal appearance:

Green Onions or Scallions

These are actually regular onions that haven't grown up yet; they are slim, green, very immature plants with a delicate flavor, best used raw or in dishes involving brief cooking (see their chapter on pages 225–231 for more information).

Spring-Summer Onions (includes Bunching Onions)

As their name suggests, these onions are typically available between March and August. They have a delicate flavor and equally delicate, thin skins and thus are not suited for long storage—some cultivars will last for only a few weeks. They come in yellow, red, or white varieties.

Pearl, Stewing, or Boiling Onions (includes Cipolline)

These little onions come in a variety of shapes and colors (including white, yellow, and red), but common to all is their compact size—less than 2 inches in diameter. They are actually regular onions that stay small thanks to being grown in very tight quarters and picked early. They are ideal for stewing, braising, boiling, roasting, and pickling.

Sweet or Mild Onions (includes Walla Walla, Vidalia, Sweet Spanish, and Bermuda)

These onions tend to be exceptionally sweet, juicy, and mild, which

Cooking Tip

To help lessen or rid the scent of onions on your hands, try washing them with salt or lemon juice.

Rubbing your fingers on a stainless steel surface (like a spoon or even a soap-sized steel block made just for this purpose) also helps.

For More Information

National Onion Association
www.onions-usa.org

comes from their low sulfur content (about half that of an ordinary yellow onion). These types are best for eating raw or lightly cooked, as their delicate flavor dissipates when cooked too long. They have thin skins, must be refrigerated, and are not suitable for long storage.

Fall-Winter Onions

These onions come from the same plants as the spring-summer ones, but are left in the ground a few weeks longer to build their flavor and size; they're typically available between August and May. They have much thicker skins and a lower water content, and thus have a much longer shelf life than spring-summer onions. They come in yellow or white varieties.

HISTORY

Precisely where humans ate their first onions remains a matter of some dispute. Several wild species exist, and these were probably foraged by ancient peoples long before domestication occurred. The first known record of them is in Mesopotamia.

The ancient Egyptians valued onions not only as food but as currency, for the pyramid builders were partially paid with these aromatic vegetables along with garlic. Onions quickly spread throughout the rest of Europe and were often associated with the lower classes, who depended on them as a staple in their frugal diet.

Although the United States has several native wild species, nearly all of the onions eaten and cultivated today are descended from specimens brought from the Old World and planted in Massachusetts in the mid-1600s.

NUTRITION

A tidbit that may come in handy at your next cocktail trivia party: A 1-ounce cup of onions contains 20 percent of an adult's daily requirement for chromium. Onions also have vitamins C and B6, dietary fiber, manganese, molybdenum, tryptophan, folate, and potassium. A single medium onion contains 44 calories. As with other members of the Allium family, the chromium and sulfurous compounds in onions may have beneficial effects against heart disease, diabetes, and high blood cholesterol.

SEASON

Commercially, onions are widely grown and in season year-round. But green and small bunching onions typically make their appearance at CSAs and farmers markets in the spring and summer, whereas larger bulb onions are at their peak in the late summer, fall, and even winter months. Fall-winter onions can be a substantial part of winter CSA shares.

SELECTION

When choosing any type of onion, look for fat, firm specimens with no signs of shriveling, sliminess, soft or dark spots, or moisture at the neck, which could signal decay. Onions past their prime also may be sprouting. (Although they are still edible, their flavor may be off.)

STORAGE

Cured storage onions (onions that are partially dried for long storage) can be kept in a wire hanging basket or a perforated container with a raised base so that air can circulate freely underneath. They keep best in an area like a basement, root cellar, or other place with the proper cool temperature and lack of humidity (for more information, see "Preserving the Bounty" on page 611).

For the best flavor, mature onions (including pearl or cipolline onions) should not be stored in the refrigerator but at room temperature. Green and bunching onions should be kept tightly wrapped in a paper towel inside a plastic bag in the refrigerator crisper, as they can wilt and spoil quickly.

Do not store onions next to potatoes; the former produces gases that will hasten the spoilage of the latter. Also avoid storing them with apples, celery, and pears, as they will absorb one another's odors.

Cut onions should be wrapped very tightly (aluminum foil is quite effective) or kept in an airtight container and used within a couple of days, as they oxidize quickly and lose flavor and nutrients.

TRIMMING AND CLEANING

To prepare onions, trim about ¼ to ½ inch from both ends, but avoid cutting off the root stub entirely, as it keeps the onion from falling apart. Cut a slit in the outer skin and peel off this first layer. Now your onion is ready for slicing into thin rounds or wedges, or for chopping.

STEAMING AND BOILING

Onions can be quickly steamed as a side dish on their own. Cut large onions into ½-inch-thick rounds or quarter them into wedges, place them over a steamer rack, add aromatic herbs such as rosemary or oregano branches to the steaming water, and steam for 15 to 25 minutes, depending on the size of the onion, or until they become tender.

To boil onions, cut off the very ends, remove just enough of the outer layers to eliminate the tough skins but not so much that they fall apart, and place them in a pan, covering with water. Boiling times will vary widely, depending on the size of the onion, but it will be around 10 to 20 minutes. Avoid overcooking, and boil just until tender. Drain and serve with melted butter and seasonings.

STIR-FRYING AND SAUTÉING

One of the most common ways to prepare onions is sautéing or stir-frying. (Indeed, many of the recipes in this book begin with sautéing onions.) Preheat oil or butter in a pan over medium-high heat, slice or chop the onions thinly, and sauté until the onions turn limp and begin to turn translucent, 3 to 5 minutes. If you want to use the onions for a quiche or as a filling in another dish, cook them slowly on lower heat; they will caramelize and develop a much richer flavor.

BAKING AND ROASTING

Onions take to roasting like a duck takes to water. Keep their skins on, as they will prevent the onions from drying out. Cut the root ends down so that they have a flat surface to stand on, and rub the outside with a little

"If you hear an onion ring, answer it."

— *Anonymous*

"The onion is the truffle of the poor."

— *Robert J. Courtine, French gourmet*

oil. Prick them with a fork to allow steam to escape, and pour a little oil or butter on the bottom of a baking pan to prevent scorching. Roast in a 375°F oven for 50 minutes to 1½ hours, depending on the size of the onions, until they become tender.

GRILLING

Both sweet onions and yellow and white storage onions turn out juicy and terrific when grilled whole. Peel the outer skin off each onion and slice just enough off one of the ends to create a flat surface for placing on the grill. Wrap each onion in aluminum foil, set them on the grill, and cook for 20 to 30 minutes, depending on their size, or until they become tender. Then turn them over and roast the other side for another 20 minutes. Peel and separate the onion layers, seasoning to taste.

As a variation, some people carve out a hole within the onion, taking care not to pierce all of the way through, and fill the hole with butter, a little beer, or Coca-Cola to add flavor.

BRAISING AND STEWING

Small onions take very well to braising and stewing. One method is to braise white onions in broth, wine, or water into which butter, herbs, salt, and pepper have been added. Bring to a boil, cover, decrease the heat, and simmer over low heat for 15 to 25 minutes, or until the onions are tender.

An alternative method is to sauté the onions in butter first until they brown, then add the broth mixture and cook as described in the paragraph above. These browned onions can then be added to a roast toward the end of its cooking time.

MICROWAVING

To microwave, peel the onions while leaving them whole, place them in a microwave-safe dish, add 1 tablespoon of water, cover, and cook on high power.

- 3 medium onions (about 1 pound) = 4 minutes (for stuffing) = 5 minutes (to soften)
- 1 pound small white onions = 6 minutes

BLANCHING AND FREEZING

Onions can be frozen without blanching. Simply peel and chop them into ½-inch pieces. Then package them in zipper-lock freezer or vacuum food sealer-type bags, or freezer containers. Squeeze out any excess air and leave ½ inch of headspace (unless you are using the vacuum sealing method). Frozen onions will keep for up to 12 months at 0°F. They do not require thawing before using.

EQUIVALENTS, MEASURES, AND SERVINGS

- 1 large onion = 1 to 1½ cups chopped
- 1 pound = 3 medium onions = 3 to 4 cups chopped
- 1 tablespoon dried minced onion = 1 medium chopped onion
- 1 teaspoon onion powder = 1 medium chopped onion

COMPLEMENTARY HERBS, SEASONINGS, AND FOODS

Apples, bacon, basil, beef, butter, cheese (blue, Cheddar, Gruyère, mozzarella, Parmesan), chiles, cinnamon, cloves, cream, cucumbers, garlic, liver, mushrooms, nutmeg, olives, olive oil, paprika, parsley, pepper, pork, poultry, raisins, red wine, rice, sesame, sherry, soy sauce, taco mix, thyme, tomatoes, vegetables, vinegar, Worcestershire sauce.

SERVING SUGGESTIONS

- Try an unusual and tasty "coleslaw" made with thinly sliced red onion, fennel, and a tangy vinaigrette dressing.

- Make this quintessential Italian summer salad: vine-ripened tomatoes, sliced onion rings, cucumber slices, and mozzarella cheese, drizzled with olive oil, chopped fresh basil, and freshly ground sea salt and pepper.

- The French slow-simmer very thinly sliced onions in butter and red wine to create a confit that is tasty with beef, pork, and lamb dishes.

- Chopped onions add flavor to just about any vegetable or side dish you can imagine.

- Make French onion soup. (Be sure to use the highest-quality beef broth you can find and the proper cheese, or the soup may disappoint.)

- A simple but delicious lunch or snack idea: Roll up thinly sliced onions inside a slice of deli honey ham or honey turkey, along with a leaf or two of fresh herbs like basil, sage, or dill. This is a delicious, nutritious treat that especially appeals to kids, especially if the onions are the sweet, mild kind, like Vidalias or Walla Wallas. You can also spread a little soft cream cheese on the meat to help the flavors blend and also glue the onion and herbs better to the meat.

- Small halved red onions are absolutely delicious brushed with olive oil and cooked on the griddle, then finished with balsamic vinegar, and salt and freshly ground black pepper.

- Thinly sliced caramelized onions and apples make an interesting topping on puff pastry.

- Pickled onions are tasty, versatile, and add zip to many a meal; they are essential in the British ploughman's lunch, along with honest bread, hard cheese like Cheddar or Stilton, butter, robust ham, and a solid ale or stout. Cipolline or little pearl onions are ideal for pickling.

- Fry up some onion rings—one for each finger!

- Make salsa or pico de gallo. Although the classic ingredients are chiles, onions, cilantro, garlic, and tomatoes, feel free to mix it up (so to speak) a bit with finely chopped cucumbers, mangoes, papayas, apples, jicama, and even radishes.

- Spring or bunching onions deserve to be regarded as a delectable vegetable in their own right, not just seasoning. Combine with asparagus, morels, fava beans, fiddlehead ferns, and other young, tender vegetables of the season. Keep the preparation simple—the freshness and succulence of these springtime treats should shine through.

- Liver and onions, anyone? It really can be delicious, provided that the liver is not overcooked to the consistency of shoe leather.

- Serve roasted onions with a warm bacon dressing or vinaigrette.

- Little pearl onions are just the right size for throwing into stews or cooking along with roasts. They make lovely vegetable side dishes in their own right creamed or gratinéed, too.

> "I crawled into the vegetable bin, settled on a giant onion and ate it, skin and all. It must have marked me for life for I have never ceased to love the hearty flavor of onions."
>
> — *James Beard,*
> *American chef and food writer*

> "Onion skins very thin,
> Mild winter coming in.
> Onion skins very tough,
> Coming winter very rough."
>
> — *Old English rhyme*

Books

The Elegant Onion:
The Art of Allium Cookery
Betty Cavage,
Storey Communications, 1987.

Onions, Onions, Onions:
Delicious Recipes for the World's
Favorite Secret Ingredient
Linda Griffith and Fred Griffith,
Houghton Mifflin, 2002.

The Onion Harvest Cookbook
Barbara Ciletti,
Taunton Press, 1998.

- Onions and potatoes may not store well together, but that changes when they are cooked.

- Onions, especially the milder, sweeter ones, have an affinity for pineapple. Try this combination on tacos, pizza, and savory tarts. It may sound a little odd, but you will probably be convinced after your first bite.

- Sweet onions are terrific in salads; as a pizza topping; as thick, fresh rings in hamburgers or sandwiches; or as a quiche filling.

. . . .

STUFFED AND BAKED SWEET ONIONS   SERVES 4

4 green bell peppers
4 medium sweet onions
12 plum tomatoes, seeded and chopped
1 tablespoon capers
2 tablespoons chopped fresh basil, or 1 tablespoon dried
2 tablespoons chopped fresh thyme, or 1 tablespoon dried
¾ cup balsamic vinegar
1 teaspoon salt
1 teaspoon freshly ground black pepper
Fresh thyme sprigs, for garnish

1. Preheat the oven to 400°F on the broil setting.

2. Place the bell peppers on an aluminum foil–lined baking sheet, and with the oven door partially open, broil them 5 inches from the heat source, turning, for 5 minutes, or until their skins blister. Remove the peppers and let them cool slightly. Place them in a paper bag, close it, and let them stand 10 minutes to loosen their skins. Peel, seed, and chop them. Set them aside.

3. Cut a thin slice from the bottom of each onion, forming a base for the onions to stand on. Cut about one third off the top of the onion; remove the onion centers, leaving ½-inch-thick shells. Reserve the top and centers for other uses.

4. Stir together the bell peppers, tomatoes, capers, basil, thyme, vinegar, salt, and pepper; spoon the mixture into the onion shells.

5. Place the onions in a baking dish and bake, covered, for 50 minutes, or until the onion is quite soft but not collapsing. Garnish with fresh thyme sprigs.

    — *Barbara Hunt, mother of Featherstone Farm CSA member Margaret Trott*

. . . .

PORK TENDERLOIN PITAS   SERVES 4

1 cucumber, peeled and diced
1 cup nonfat sour cream
1 teaspoon fresh dill, or ½ teaspoon dried dill

8 ounces pork tenderloin, trimmed

2 teaspoons Dijon mustard

3 tablespoons olive oil, divided, or nonstick cooking spray

1 tablespoon fresh lemon juice

1 clove garlic, minced

1 teaspoon fresh oregano, or ½ teaspoon dried oregano

1 green bell pepper, thinly sliced

1 red onion, thinly sliced into rings

1 cup shredded spinach

4 pita breads, halved

8 cherry tomatoes, halved

1. In a small bowl, combine the cucumber, sour cream, and dill. Refrigerate until needed.

2. Cut the pork across the grain into ½-inch cutlets, then slice each piece into thin strips. In a large bowl, combine the mustard, 1 tablespoon of the olive oil, lemon juice, garlic, and oregano. Add the pork and toss well to coat all of the pieces. Let stand about 10 minutes.

3. Coat a large nonstick frying pan with some of the remaining olive oil and place it over medium heat for 3 minutes. Working in batches to avoid overcrowding the pan, add the pork and sauté it for about 3 minutes, or until it is cooked through (pork tenderloin can overcook easily, so sauté it just until the pink color disappears). Transfer it to a plate and wipe the pan clean.

4. Place the bell peppers and onions in a 9-inch glass pie plate. Cover the plate with vented plastic microwave wrap and microwave on high power for 3 to 4 minutes, or until the peppers and onions soften. Add them to the pan and sauté them in a bit more oil for 3 minutes, or until they are lightly browned.

5. Line the pita pockets with the spinach. Add the pork, then top it with the peppers and onions. Top each sandwich half with a cherry tomato and some cucumber sauce.

— *Produce for Better Health; Fruits & Veggies—More Matters; Centers for Disease Control and Prevention*

FRENCH ONION SOUP

SERVES 8

Source Note: *This recipe calls for beef bones, but a perfectly respectable stock can be made with vegetarian beef-flavored soup base. However, the following recipe is richer than the vegetarian one. Either way, the real trick in this soup is to caramelize lots of onions.*

5 pounds beef soup bones

8 cups water

¼ pound (1 stick) unsalted butter

to the improvement of water quality in a major salmon-bearing river, the Snoqualmie.

About 80 miles west of Oxbow Farm, the mission of **Nash's Organic Produce**—in addition to growing organic food and educating customers about healthful food systems—includes protecting the local agricultural land base, the environment, and open-pollinated organic seed. For more than 30 years, Nash Huber and his staff have farmed on a growing number of acres (now 450) in the Sequim-Dungeness Valley on the north Olympic Peninsula. This area's unique microclimate allows the year-round production of vegetables, grains, and pork that the farm sells to the public at its retail store and to local restaurants, farmers markets, and its 300-member CSA. Huber has helped to save hundreds of acres of local farmland and important wildlife habitat through his work with the **PCC Farmland Trust**, the **North Olympic Land Trust**, **Clallam Citizens for Food Security**, and **Friends of the Fields**, which he helped found.

Huber's farm is certified "Salmon-Safe" by a nonprofit that recognizes farms and other entities working to protect water quality and salmon habitat. Its conservation efforts include planting grasses and trees to ensure high-quality habitat for migratory waterfowl, as well as using a chemical-free pest-control management program to deal with insects naturally without harm to the environment. An extensive composting program improves soil using natural by-products from dairy farms, fish-processing plants, and Nash's own vegetable-packing operations.

In northeastern Ohio, the **George Jones Farm** is one of 20 farms growing food for the City Fresh CSA. The 70-acre farmstead is owned by Oberlin College and is notable for diverse habitats that include wetlands, ponds, wood-

1 tablespoon vegetable oil
1 tablespoon olive oil
1 loaf French bread, sliced into ¾-inch-thick rounds
3 pounds white or yellow onions, sliced into half-moon strips (use Vidalia or Walla Walla onions, if available)
1 tablespoon sugar
2 tablespoons flour
1 cup dry or semi-dry white wine (chenin blanc, Chablis, dry vermouth, or white table wine)
½ teaspoon freshly ground black pepper
1½ teaspoons salt
Enough slices of Swiss or Gruyére cheese to cover each bowl of soup

1. In a roasting pan, roast the soup bones in a preheated 450°F oven for about 35 minutes. While roasting the bones, bring the water to a boil and maintain the boil, covered, until the bones are ready. Add the roasted bones to the boiling water, discarding the rendered fat that will have collected on the roasting pan. Simmer the bones, covered, for a minimum of 2 hours.

2. While the bones are simmering, melt the butter and both oils in a large frying pan or brazier. Brush the tops of the bread slices with the butter mixture, spread the slices on a baking sheet, and put them in a preheated 300°F oven to toast, for about 20 minutes. Set aside to cool. (These will become the croutons to be used later in the soup.)

3. In a large frying pan or heavy-bottomed pot, sauté the onions in the remaining butter-oil mixture over medium-high heat until they become soft and translucent. Add the sugar, and continue to cook until the onions caramelize (they will turn golden brown). This should take about 30 minutes. Do not leave the onions during this stage, but stir them steadily. When the onions turn a deep golden brown, stir in the flour until it disappears. Remove the pan from the heat and set it aside.

4. Remove the bones from the broth with a slotted spoon. Using a gravy separator or soup skimmer, strain out all of the fat from the broth. Transfer the onion mixture to the broth. Add the wine, pepper, and salt. Adjust the seasonings to taste.

5. Preheat your oven broiler to high. Place 1 crouton on the bottom of each soup bowl. (This soup should be served in individual crock-style bowls, with a narrower width, rather than in a large serving bowl or wide-mouthed soup bowls.) Ladle the soup over the croutons, filling the bowls to ½ inch from the top. Float another crouton on top. Cover the bowls with sliced cheese. Place the bowls under the broiler (or into a hot oven if you don't have a broiler) long enough for the cheese to melt over the top of the soup. Serve immediately.

— *Peter Reinhart,* Sacramental Magic in a Small-Town Café

BEEF BOURGUIGNON (FRENCH BEEF STEW)   SERVES 4

Source Note: Bouquet garni (French for "garnished bouquet") is a little bundle of herbs that is tied with string or enclosed in a sachet. It is used to flavor soups, stews, and stock during cooking and is then removed before serving. Although there is no precise formula for bouquet garni, it usually includes parsley, peppercorns, thyme, and bay leaves. Basil, burnet, celery leaves, chervil, rosemary, savory, and tarragon may also be used. This recipe involves marinating the beef overnight, so plan ahead accordingly.

Marinade

1 large carrot, cut into ½-inch pieces
1 onion, cut into ½-inch pieces
1 rib celery, cut into ½-inch pieces
2 cloves garlic
Bouquet garni (see the Source Note above)
¼ cup brandy
10 black peppercorns
6 cups good red wine
2 tablespoons vegetable oil, plus more for browning the beef

Stew

2 pounds beef chuck steak, trimmed and cut into 1½-inch cubes
Oil and butter for browning the beef
1 heaped tablespoon tomato paste
2 tablespoons all-purpose flour
1½ cups beef stock
32 small boiling onions, peeled
About 3 tablespoons unsalted butter, for sautéing and melting
2 teaspoons sugar
Salt and freshly ground pepper
5 ounces mushrooms, cut into quarters
2 tablespoons chopped garlic
8 ounces slab or sliced bacon, cut into cubes or short batons
2 slices white bread, crusts removed and cut into triangles
2 tablespoons chopped fresh parsley, for garnish

1. Place all of the ingredients for the marinade in a bowl with the cubes of beef. Cover and refrigerate for about 12 hours, or overnight, stirring occasionally.

2. Strain the marinade into a saucepan, then remove the beef and set it aside, keeping the vegetables and bouquet garni separate. Bring the marinade to a boil, skim off the foam, and cook for 6 to 8 minutes. Strain through a fine sieve.

3. In a large, heavy-bottomed flameproof casserole or Dutch oven, heat a little oil and butter. Pat the meat dry and brown it on all sides in

lands, and college research ponds. The property is leased by the nonprofit New Agrarian Center (NAC) and managed from an ecosystem perspective, with a focus on restoring topsoil, wetlands, forests, and meadows.

The farm was previously leased to commodity grain producers until 2002, when the NAC began its work of restoring the ecosystem after years of degradation by industrial farming methods. In just six years, it converted 40 acres of soybean fields into a complex of market gardens, learning spaces, sustainably designed buildings, and restored wetland, prairie, and woodland habitat. Today the farm serves as an incubator for young and beginning farmers from Oberlin High School, Lorain Community College, Oberlin College, and the wider community.

Land trusts have also played a major role in saving family farms from the pressures of housing and other development. The 164-acre **Denison Farm** in Schaghticoke, New York, was one of the first farms to be settled after the Revolutionary War and has been tended since then by generations of farmers. Since purchasing the property in 2005, Brian and Justine Denison have developed the existing CSA operation into a thriving business with more than 500 subscriber families.

When a high-tech plant opened 16 miles away, the Denisons worried about the pressure to sell and approached the **Agricultural Stewardship Association (ASA)**. This land trust in upstate New York helped them obtain a conservation easement that bars any development on their land unrelated to farming and also ensures that the property remains available and affordable for future farmers. The family raised much of the $173,000 needed for the easement through grants and donations, but ASA helped with the final $27,000.

What Happens on a Farm During the Winter?

Grace Ward
intern
S&S Homestead Farm

Right now at S&S, much of our time is spent caring for the animals: our sheep, chickens, and dairy and meat cattle. Abby the dairy cow is milked twice every day. We keep most of the milk to consume ourselves or process into cheese and yogurt, but some is fed back to Abby's two month-old calf, Embla.

Milking Abby is a multistep operation that begins with grooming and ends with decanting and processing what she produces. The milk Abby provides is essential to life on the farm, and so we try to honor and thank her by giving her extra love and care. We also need to ensure that her milk is collected and processed in such a manner that it can be shared with the public. The milking area is cleaned daily, as well as the room in the dairy kitchen where we decant and chill the milk.

Our cow herds can be tough on pasture during a wet winter. In order to combat mud and evenly distribute manure, we rotate grazing areas and alternate where we feed hay. This means the cows are regularly on the move, shifting from

batches; remove and keep to one side. Add the well-drained vegetables from the marinade (don't add the bouquet garni), lower the heat slightly, and cook, stirring occasionally, until they are lightly browned.

4. Heat the oven to 400°F. Return the meat to the pan, add the tomato paste, and stir over medium heat for 3 minutes. Sprinkle the meat with the flour and place it in the oven for 6 to 8 minutes; then carefully remove the hot pan and mix in the flour. Place the pot over medium heat again, add the marinade, and bring it to a boil, stirring constantly. Then add the beef stock and bouquet garni.

5. Lower the oven temperature to 325°F. Return the stew to a boil, cover, and transfer it to the oven. Cook for 1½ to 2 hours, or until the meat is very tender. Check occasionally to make sure the mixture isn't boiling; you want to maintain just a very low, bubbling simmer.

6. Meanwhile, place the onions, some of the butter, sugar, and some salt in a deep skillet and pour in enough water to cover. Cook over medium heat until the water has almost evaporated, then swirl the skillet until the onions are golden. Fry the mushrooms in some sizzling butter until they turn golden; season and drain them and add to the onions. Fry the garlic and bacon in a little oil, drain, and add to the onions and mushrooms.

7. Melt a little more butter, brush the bread with it, and toast the slices in the oven for 3 to 5 minutes, or until brown.

8. Once the beef is fork-tender, skim off the excess fat. Transfer the beef to a clean, flameproof casserole or serving dish, cover, and keep warm. Strain the sauce and return it to the pan, discarding the vegetables and bouquet garni.

9. Bring the sauce to a boil and simmer for about 15 minutes, skimming frequently, until the sauce coats the back of a spoon. Season to taste with salt and pepper, strain it once more over the meat, and add the onions, mushrooms, and bacon. Simmer just until hot, about 5 minutes.

10. Dip a corner of each bread crouton into the sauce, then into the parsley. Sprinkle the remaining parsley over the stew, and serve with the croutons on the edge of the dish or on the side.

— *Meryle, Epicurean.com*

ONION LOVER'S DIP

MAKES 3 CUPS

Source Note: *Quark is a type of fresh, mild, unaged cheese, similar to cottage or ricotta cheese. The variety available in plastic tubs usually contains some whey and has the consistency of sour cream.*

¼ cup olive oil, preferably extra-virgin

4 large shallots, peeled, halved, and thinly sliced

1 pound (2 cups) quark (or 8 ounces cream cheese at room
   temperature mixed with 8 ounces sour cream)

2 tablespoons fresh lime juice

1 teaspoon kosher salt

¼ teaspoon freshly ground black pepper

Pinch of sugar

6 medium scallions (green onions), trimmed and thinly sliced

1 small red onion, peeled and finely diced

Chips and assorted cut-up raw vegetables, for serving

1. Heat the oil in a heavy-bottomed skillet over medium-high heat until
    hot but not smoking. Add the shallots and cook, stirring often, until
    they turn brown and crisp. Transfer them to paper towels to drain
    and cool.

2. In a large bowl, stir together the quark, lime juice, salt, pepper, and
    sugar until smooth. Stir in the scallions, red onion, and reserved
    shallots.

3. Cover and refrigerate for 1 hour to let the flavors blend. Serve with a
    variety of chips and raw vegetables.

— *Joel Patraker and Joan Schwartz*, The Greenmarket Cookbook

. . . .

MEAT LOAF: YES, VIRGINIA, THERE IS A GREAT MEAT LOAF!

SERVES 4

*Source Note: This is absolutely delicious meat loaf and sauce. Those who
claim they don't believe there can be such a thing as a great meat loaf will love
this. A second batch of sauce served hot is good to serve with the meat loaf.*

1½ pounds ground beef (ground shoulder roast is good)

1 slice bread, torn or chopped finely

1 egg

1 small Vidalia onion (or other type of sweet onion,
   such as Walla Walla), finely chopped

1 teaspoon salt

¼ teaspoon freshly ground black pepper

¼ cup ketchup

½ to ⅔ cup milk or half-and-half

SAUCE

4 tablespoons apple cider vinegar

2 to 4 tablespoons firmly packed dark brown sugar

½ cup ketchup

1. Preheat the oven to 350°F.

paddock to paddock across the pasture. We use electric lines to delineate each paddock and keep the herd together in one area.

Sigurd the bull spends time with both herds, depending on which cows are cycling at any given time. We monitor his behavior with the cows in order to know which of them might be pregnant and when we can expect a calf. This planning and observation is part of what makes winter special here, a time of latent growth and expectation.

All of our ewes are currently pregnant, so, in addition to hay, we feed the sheep herd a mixture of grain and molasses to provide better nutrition for the lambs who will be born later this spring. Just like in the cow pastures, we try to distribute the manure and compaction that occurs in areas where the sheep eat by rotating where we place the hay. Pasture health is essential to ensuring that we can feed our animals from season to season without relying on outside food sources.

On a biodynamic farm like S&S Homestead, the farm is considered to be a whole, self-contained organism. This approach necessitates careful planning. To this effect, we recently went over the work plan for the entire coming year, discussing garden layouts, plans for the CSA, public workshops, animal reproduction, and the many other details that are part of life at S&S.

Though most of the garden beds are resting right now, the farm is still full of energy and requires constant care. Each chore, even raking up uneaten hay or gathering fallen leaves, ensures the survival of the farm during this quiet, inward season.

2. Combine the meat loaf ingredients in a large bowl; stir them gently so as not to compact the mixture too much. Place the mixture into a loaf-shaped baking dish, patting it so the sides of the mixture don't quite touch the sides of the pan. Smooth out the top.

3. Combine the sauce ingredients, varying the amount of brown sugar according to your taste, and pour the sauce over the top and sides of the meat loaf.

4. Bake for 1 to 1¼ hours, or until the meat loaf is nicely browned; there should not be juices pooled in the pan by this point.

— *Nita Holleman, Food.com*

GLAZED PEARL ONIONS   SERVES 4 TO 6

Source Note: These sweet, tangy red pearl onions in a red-wine vinegar and honey glaze are a great side dish for Thanksgiving.

1 cup red pearl onions
1 teaspoon honey
2 tablespoons red wine vinegar
1 tablespoon olive oil

1. This is the easiest way to peel pearl onions: Bring a pot of water to a rapid boil and add the unpeeled pearl onions. Boil for 1 minute, strain, and place the onions in a bowl of ice water to stop the cooking process. Using a sharp knife, slice off the root end of the onions. Squeeze from the top, and your onion should slide right out.

2. Whisk together the honey and red wine vinegar. Set aside.

3. In a skillet, heat the olive oil over medium high heat. Add the peeled onions and sauté for 3 to 4 minutes, swirling the pan, until they begin to brown.

4. Pour the honey and vinegar mixture over the onions and stir to evenly coat them. Lower the heat to medium low and continue to sauté the onions until the sauce is reduced to a syrup.

5. Serve warm.

— *Kris, Foodista.com*

Parsnips

PASTINACA SATIVA

As a sturdy winter root vegetable that shares seasonal space and a role in sustenance along with potatoes, rutabagas, turnips, and carrots, parsnips have survived centuries of being loved and shunned alike according to culinary fashion and nutritional need. This is puzzling, because parsnips can be truly delicious, both raw and cooked—they are one of those gems of the vegetable world that modern cooks and gardeners ought to get to know much better.

The parsnip is a relative of the vast Apiaceae family, which includes the familiar carrot, fennel, parsley, and dill. The vegetable retains herbal hints of its aromatic cousins, but it charms with a mellow, sometimes spicy, nutty sweetness all its own. Parsnips are hardy roots that can be left in the ground after the first frost arrives or even over the winter, for harvesting the following spring. The longer parsnips stay out in the cold, the sweeter they become—almost like candy. In the kitchen, they are just as versatile as carrots and potatoes, and indeed the three make an ideal root triumvirate in many dishes.

HISTORY

Parsnips originated in Eurasia and have been eaten since ancient times in Europe. Early Romans considered the vegetable fit for aristocracy, and in medieval Europe parsnips were used as a sweetener, since honey and sugar were both rare and expensive. It was also a valuable starch crop, as the Spaniards had not yet brought potatoes from the New World; after the latter was introduced, parsnips' popularity began to wane. Parsnips came to America with the colonists but never really caught on; however, a recent US resurgence in seasonal vegetables and fine cooking and dining has meant that the lowly parsnip is finding opportunities to enthrall a new generation of eaters.

NUTRITION

Parsnips are surprisingly high in vitamin C and also contain significant amounts of vitamin E, thiamine, folate, manganese, magnesium, phosphorus, copper, potassium, and dietary fiber. A ½-cup serving of cooked parsnips contains 55 calories.

SEASON

Commercially, parsnips are widely grown and in season year-round. But they are typically at their best from fall to spring, especially when they have been nipped by frost, which makes them sweeter. Parsnips are often a significant vegetable in winter CSA shares.

SELECTION

Look for fresh, firm specimens with no signs of shriveling or rubberiness, which means they are old and past their prime. Size is not an indication of toughness or sweetness; big roots can be just as tender and flavorful as small ones—the only true test is to nibble a raw piece. And be careful that what you are getting at the market is indeed actually parsnip; parsley root

"If barley be wanting to make into malt, we must be contented, and think it no fault; for we can make liquor to sweeten our lips, of pumpkins and parsnips and walnut-tree chips."

— "Forefathers' Song," early American ballad, circa 1630

looks almost identical, but you can tell the difference by sniffing (parsnips don't smell like parsley) and also by the presence of foliage attached to the root. Parsnips are never sold with their tops still on, because sap from the leaves contains a photosensitive chemical that can trigger nasty rashes and blisters on human skin when exposed to sunshine (as some home gardeners have found out the hard way when coming into contact with their plants on hot days).

STORAGE

Parsnips keep well unwashed and wrapped in a paper towel in a perforated plastic bag for up to several weeks in the refrigerator vegetable crisper.

TRIMMING AND CLEANING

Commercial parsnips are often already thoroughly washed, but, like children, ones from your CSA box or farmers market often need a good scrubbing to remove dirt and sand. Slice off the ends, removing any greenish areas, then peel them lengthwise with a good, sharp vegetable peeler. If you will be pureeing them, you do not need to peel them if they are thin-skinned, fresh, and preferably organic.

Parsnips (especially large, older specimens) have a central core that is often tough and woody, and sometimes bitter. Unless you're cutting the parsnips into thin rounds, remove the cores before cooking; otherwise you'll end up with chewy, fibrous strands in the finished dish. If the parsnips are very young, their cores may be tender enough to leave in.

STEAMING AND BOILING

Peeled parsnips can be cut into chunks, logs, or batons and steamed over rapidly boiling water. Exact times depend on their widest diameter and how done you prefer them. They cook faster than you might expect, so be vigilant.

- 8 to 10 minutes for 1- to 1½-inch chunks, or small whole parsnips 1 to 1½ inches wide and 6 inches long
- 12 to 15 minutes for pureeing
- 5 to 8 minutes for 3-inch logs or batons about ½ inch thick

Boiling is a quick way to cook parsnips, although it will yield a less flavorful vegetable than roasting or sautéing; this method is ideal if you are planning to puree them. Cook them covered in lightly salted, boiling water. Exact times depend on their widest diameter and how done you prefer them. They cook very quickly, so watch them carefully.

- 5 minutes for 1- to 1½-inch chunks
- 8 to 10 minutes for pureeing
- 4 to 5 minutes for 3-inch logs or batons about ½ inch thick

STIR-FRYING AND SAUTÉING

Although most of us don't think of sautéing parsnips, they are quite delicious prepared this way and couldn't be easier. Thinly slice them, place them in a pan with butter and seasoning as desired, and sauté on medium heat for 5 to 8 minutes, depending on the thickness of the slices. If you want them a little softer, reduce the heat, cover the pan, and let them steam for another 1 to 2 minutes.

BAKING AND ROASTING

Like other root vegetables, parsnips are simply divine roasted, which concentrates and caramelizes their natural sugars. Place peeled, cut parsnips in a shallow pan, toss them with oil (try coconut oil for a pleasant change) and seasonings as desired, and bake in a 400°F oven for 30 to 45 minutes, turning them at least once or twice during the cooking process. They are done when browned and tender when pierced with a knife; cooking times vary widely, depending on the size and condition of the parsnips.

MICROWAVING

For 1 pound of parsnips, cut into 1-inch chunks, place in a microwave-safe dish, add 2 tablespoons of water, and cook on high power until tender.

- 1 pound = 4 minutes
- 6 minutes, if pureeing

BLANCHING AND FREEZING

Peel and cut the parsnips into ½-inch cubes. Blanch in boiling water for 2 minutes, then plunge into ice water for several minutes to stop the cooking process. Drain. Spread the parsnip pieces on a tray in a single layer, then freeze for 30 minutes. Package the parsnips in zipper-lock freezer or vacuum food sealer-type bags or freezer containers. Squeeze out any excess air and leave ½ inch of headspace (unless you are using the vacuum sealing method). Frozen parsnips will keep for up to 12 months at 0°F.

Or you can boil parsnips (see the instructions above), puree them, and freeze them that way. Leave ½ inch of headspace.

EQUIVALENTS, MEASURES, AND SERVINGS

- 1 pound parsnips = 4 servings = 4 to 6 small parsnips
- 1 pound = 3 cups chopped parsnips

COMPLEMENTARY HERBS, SEASONINGS, AND FOODS

Allspice, anchovies, anise, apples, bacon, basil, beef, brown sugar, butter, cardamom, carrots, chicken, cilantro, cinnamon, citrus, cloves, coconut, coriander, cranberries, cream, cumin, dates, dill, figs, fish, ginger, ham, hazelnuts, honey, horseradish, leeks, lemon, maple syrup, mustard, nutmeg, onions, oranges, oxtails, parsley, peas, pork, potatoes, quinces, rosemary, rutabagas, sour cream, sunflower oil, tarragon, thyme, toasted breadcrumbs, truffles, turmeric, turnips, walnuts, winter squash.

SERVING SUGGESTIONS

- Parsnips are a delicacy when prepared with cheese, butter, and cream in concoctions like vichyssoise, au gratins, and creamy soups.
- Parsnips make an interesting substitute for potatoes. Try them deep-fried, mashed, or baked; in soups and stews; or on their own as a side dish.
- The light sweetness of parsnips makes them dynamite with fruits like apples, oranges, cranberries, dates, and figs.
- Baking and roasting caramelize the parsnip's natural sugars, bringing out its delicate flavors gloriously.

niche in providing certified-organic transplants to farmers in the Midwest and beyond.

One 2011 innovation of GOE farm manager Linda Halley was a farmers market CSA card that can be used at two weekend farm stands where GOE produce is sold; this enables customers to support the farm by paying it forward and to select the items they want. Customers purchase a CSA card for $50 and receive $55 worth of fresh, certified-organic produce from GOE as they need it, until they are ready to buy another card.

*Meanwhile, **Roanoke Natural Foods Co-op** was working with the city of Roanoke, Virginia, to find property to develop its own farm. In 2012, after 38 years in the grocery business, the 3,700-member co-op purchased 17.5 acres from the city and leased another 7.4 acres with an option to purchase. The co-op's board of directors and staff, as well as a few key city officials, spent 10 years looking for a site suitable for creating an urban farm that could serve the co-op and also strengthen the local food infrastructure in southwest Virginia.*

*Located near the banks of Tinker Creek, the land for **Heritage Point Urban Farm** most recently served as home to the city's mounted police program until 2009. It includes a deluxe 2,500-square-foot barn as well as a historic cabin. Plans call for a fruit orchard, honey, cut flowers, and nursery and bedding plants. Free-range chickens supply the co-op with egg production and fertilizer for the farm. Hoop houses allow for off-season growing, an underdeveloped yet suitable practice for southwest Virginia. At 25 acres, Heritage Point is currently the largest contiguous urban farm in the United States.*

A staff of five manages the farm. Although the terrain is hilly and 18 different easements make it difficult to plant more than about 12 acres, a significant portion of the long-

term income from Heritage Point is projected to come from the sale of fruit and perennials, including a U-pick operation with strawberries, blueberries, asparagus, and more. A farm store is open six days a week during the primary growing season. At the time of this writing, Heritage Point was projected to generate a profit by 2015.

- Use parsnips as a filling for pasties and pies, along with other root vegetables such as carrots and potatoes.

- Try parsnips as a surprise vegetable in curries; the mild, sweet flavor is a nice foil for the spice.

- Coconut, ginger, honey, and parsnips are an unexpectedly delicious combination—try them as a cake, as a mashed or whole vegetable side dish, or as a creamy soup.

- Slice crisp, raw, sweet parsnips into long thin strips and serve with dips or dressing for a light snack or appetizer. Good with carrot and celery sticks too! (Note that young, tender, very fresh parsnips are best for eating raw—older, larger ones not so much.)

- Parsnips have an affinity for the sweet spices we associate with fall and winter desserts: cinnamon, cloves, nutmeg, allspice.

PARSNIP-CARROT BISQUE   SERVES 6

2 small potatoes
3 parsnips
3 carrots
1 tablespoon vegetable oil
1 bunch green onions, chopped
1-inch piece fresh ginger, peeled and grated
1 teaspoon ground coriander
1 (13½-ounce) can coconut milk
A pinch of nutmeg, plus more for garnish
Salt and freshly ground black pepper

1. Peel the potatoes, parsnips, and carrots as desired, then chop them into small pieces.

2. In a large saucepan, heat the oil over medium-high heat. Add the potatoes, parsnips, carrots, green onions, and ginger. Stir to coat. Add the coconut milk, plus 1 can of water. Stir, then bring to a boil; lower the heat and simmer for about 20 minutes, or until the veggies are tender. Add the nutmeg, salt, and pepper.

3. Puree the soup in a blender in small batches. Garnish with nutmeg before serving.

— *Sara Jones, Tucson CSA, Tucson, Arizona*

PARSNIP AND PEAR PANCAKES   SERVES 2 TO 3
WITH HORSERADISH SOUR CREAM   YIELDS 6 TO 7 PANCAKES

Source Note: I am a huge fan of potato pancakes from way back, so when I came across this recipe for parsnip and pear latkes, I was practically out the door to buy a pear in the next second. And oh my, they are so good—crispy, a little sweet from the pear, salty, and delicious.

I added bacon, onion, and rosemary to the original recipe ingredients, and if that works for you, I highly recommend it. If not, even without bacon, I can't imagine these still not being amazing. Just sauté the onion in a little olive oil and continue on from there.

Note that these are a little tricky to keep together. You can either add an extra egg white or a whole egg to the batter, or just be very gentle with flipping them over; be prepared to be okay with one or two pancakes falling apart.

1 slice bacon
1 teaspoon chopped fresh rosemary, plus more to garnish
1 small shallot, diced
1 medium (about 6 ounces) underripe Bosc pear, quartered
    and cored
1 large (about 8 ounces) parsnip, peeled and cut into 1-inch pieces
1 large egg, beaten
1½ teaspoons prepared horseradish
½ teaspoon salt
½ cup panko (Japanese breadcrumbs)
Freshly ground black pepper
Vegetable, peanut, or olive oil, for frying

For serving:
½ cup sour cream or low-fat Greek yogurt
1 to 2 teaspoons prepared horseradish
Pinch of salt

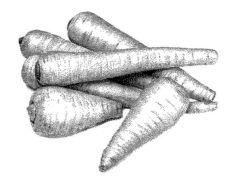

1. In a small skillet, cook the bacon. When it is cool enough to handle, crumble it into a medium mixing bowl. Add the chopped rosemary. Meanwhile, add the diced shallot to the pan of bacon grease and cook it for several minutes over medium heat until it turns golden and soft. Add it to the bacon and rosemary.

2. Use a box grater to grate the pear. Transfer the pear to paper towels; squeeze very dry and then transfer it to the bowl with the bacon. Grate the parsnip and add it to the pear. (You can also use a food processor to grate the pear and parsnip, if you'd like.)

3. Next, mix in the egg, horseradish, and salt, then mix in the panko and a sprinkle of black pepper.

4. Heat a medium nonstick skillet over medium heat and coat the bottom with oil. Drop the batter by packed ¼ cupfuls into the skillet; flatten to ½-inch thickness. Sauté until brown and cooked through, about 4 minutes per side. Drain on paper towels.

5. In a small bowl, mix the sour cream and horseradish. Season with a little salt. Serve the parsnip pancakes with the horseradish sour cream and use more rosemary leaves to garnish, if you'd like.

— *Michelle Abendschan,* Je Mange le Ville *blog (recipe adapted from* Bon Appétit *magazine)*

Parsnips Whipped with Potatoes

SERVES 6

Source Note: *Parsnips have a nutty, sweet potato–like flavor. Pureed with potatoes and chives, they lend a gentle root-vegetable sweetness.*

1 pound (4 to 6 small, or 2 to 3 medium) parsnips
¾ pound (about 1 large) baking potato
½ cup heavy cream
2 shallots, minced
1 tablespoon thinly sliced fresh chives
2 tablespoons unsalted butter
Salt and freshly ground black pepper

1. Peel the parsnips and potatoes and cut them into ½-inch chunks. Bring a large pot of salted water to a boil over high heat. Add the parsnips and potatoes and cook until tender, 8 to 10 minutes.

2. While the vegetables are boiling, combine the cream, shallots, and chives in a small saucepan and bring to a simmer; cook 1 minute, then adjust the heat to keep them warm but not simmering.

3. Drain the parsnips and potatoes in a sieve and shake them dry. Rest a food mill on the edges of the warm, dry pot the vegetables were boiled in. Pass the vegetables through the mill directly into the pot. (If you don't have a food mill, push the soft vegetables through a coarse sieve or mash them well with a fork. Don't use a food processor or blender, as it will give the potatoes a gluey texture.)

4. Using a wooden spoon, beat in the butter and warm cream mixture. Season well with salt and pepper. Serve immediately.

— *Luisa DePaiva, Purple Rain Vineyard, Vancouver, Washington*

Potatoes   SOLANUM TUBEROSUM

One of the planet's most versatile, staple foods, the potato is the number-one vegetable crop internationally, cultivated in 130 of the world's 167 countries, and the fourth most-grown food plant, after rice, wheat, and maize. It is also one of the most genetically diverse plants—at least 5,000 varieties were once known to the Andean peoples. Today, only a fraction of these have survived, and scientists at Peru's International Potato Center are desperately trying to save the remaining rarer species.

The potato is a member of the Solanaceae family, which includes tomatoes, eggplants, and the deadly nightshade. Because of this association, potatoes were not widely trusted as food plants outside of their native Peru and Andes regions until the 17th and 18th centuries. Eventually recognizing their value as a high-starch, high-yielding crop that would thrive in soils too poor to grow other food plants, governments of different countries employed fascinating tactics to entice their populations to consume this unfamiliar tuber. Today, the average American eats about 140 pounds of potatoes annually.

New potatoes are typically dug by hand in July and early August. These potatoes are so delicate that, to protect their skins, the sand is not washed off. Unlike cured potatoes, which are partially dried to increase their storage life, these newbies need to be refrigerated. Later in the season, mature potatoes are machine-dug and cured as finished potatoes, to be used from September to New Year's.

About 100 different potato varieties are grown in the United States, but they all fit into one of seven major categories: red, white, Russet, yellow, blue-purple, fingerling, and petite. Here are a few varieties you may find in your CSA box:

All Blue
A curious-looking blue (obviously) variety that is sure to attract attention in salads and french fries, All Blue has a deep bluish-purple hue that extends from its skin all the way through the center of its flesh. This potato has an excellent flavor, wonderful for baking, frying, and mashing. When boiled, the flesh turns a lighter blue.

Bintje
This is an extremely popular, creamy, yellow-fleshed variety from the Netherlands. Its versatile, waxy flesh is excellent for making french fries and potato salads.

Désirée Pink
This variety has pastel pink skin and pale-yellow, almost white flesh that has a creamy texture and a mild flavor, excellent for boiling, baking, mashing, and roasting, but not for frying.

Langlade White
This is a white-fleshed variety that is a good, all-purpose spud.

Conventionally grown potatoes are on the "Dirty Dozen" list—meaning they are extra-high in pesticide and herbicide residues. This residue is particularly harmful to children, as well as to adults with health issues.

Purchase organic spuds whenever possible—especially if you intend to eat the nutrient-rich skins.

Red Norland

These reds are excellent for roasting, boiling (think potato salad), and frying (potato chips, anyone?), but not so good for baking—they are far more soggy and wet than Russets.

Russet Burbank

This large, brown-skinned beauty is the classic baking potato, with a dry, mealy texture that also makes it excellent for boiling and mashing.

Russian Fingerling

Russian Fingerlings are skinny (like a finger) and creamy, with tender skins. Try leaving these unpeeled; doing so will add texture, color, and nutrition. These are terrific for roasting and ideal for potato salad.

Yukon Gold

Yukons are an all-purpose yellow potato with golden, waxy, buttery flesh that is ideal for boiling, baking, and roasting. Their creamy texture makes outstanding mashed potatoes and soups.

HISTORY

Potatoes are native to the mountainous Andes regions of Bolivia and Peru in South America, where they have been domesticated for over 7,000 years. The earliest wild potatoes were small, wrinkled, and extremely bitter, which challenged the native peoples to find ways to make these tubers edible. In the 16th century, Spanish explorers introduced the potato to Europe and other countries that they colonized.

Despite their obvious value as a potentially nutritious, easily cultivated sustenance crop, potatoes were not welcomed with open arms in most of Europe. In part this was due to a predictable resistance to strange, new foods and also because of the potato's kinship to the deadly nightshade. Indeed, contact with the plant's toxic leaves can produce skin rashes, and before advanced medical science proved otherwise, it was believed that potatoes could spread leprosy. The fact that one of Queen Elizabeth I's chefs, inexperienced in the way of the potato, mistakenly cooked and served the poisonous leaves instead of the tubers for a royal banquet certainly did not help.

Even after confusion over which part of the plant to eat was cleared up, much of Europe regarded the tuber with disdain, calling it suitable only for lowly riffraff. However, many governments, wanting to take advantage of this economical food source, practically ordered their citizenry to eat these unfamiliar roots or devised ingenious psychological means to overcome public resistance to them.

By the 1800s, potatoes were being widely consumed across Europe. The degree to which humans can be dependent on a single food source was dramatically and tragically demonstrated during the Irish Potato Famine of 1845–49. A blight triggered by severe plant inbreeding caused a total crop failure, which (along with the forced exports of other foodstuffs from Ireland to England) led to the starvation of nearly a million people and a massive immigration of a million more Irish to American shores.

Ironically, despite the potato's origins in the New World, it was the Scotch-Irish who brought potatoes to America. Today, Idaho is the top potato-growing state in the United States, which annually produces 45.6 billion pounds valued at over $2.6 billion.

NUTRITION

Potatoes are unfairly maligned nutritionally, usually because of how they are prepared—deep-fried into french fries, made into potato chips, or mashed and adorned with plenty of high-fat toppings such as butter, cheese, bacon, and sour cream. Actually, potatoes by themselves are extremely healthful for you; they're high in fiber, low in calories, and rich in vitamins C and B6, as well as copper, potassium (more than bananas), manganese, and trypto-phan, all for just 132 calories per cup. In addition, researchers have recently identified compounds called kukoamines, which may help lower blood pressure. For maximum nutrients, leave the skins on your potatoes, where most of the tuber's vitamins, minerals, and fiber reside.

SEASON

Commercially, potatoes are widely grown and available year-round. But the peak season for new potatoes at farmers markets and CSAs is from April through July; mature potatoes are at their best from October through April, and are often a staple in winter CSAs.

SELECTION

Potatoes of any type should be smooth and firm, with no signs of shriveling or soft or green spots.

STORAGE

New potatoes should be stored in a perforated plastic bag in the refrigerator vegetable crisper and used within 1 to 2 weeks. Mature, cured potatoes do best kept quite cool (around 45°F) in a well-ventilated, dark place that is out of direct sunlight, which will trigger the formation of sprouts. Do not store potatoes next to onions; the latter produces gases that will hasten the spoilage of the former. Mature potatoes may keep for up to 2 months, depending on the temperature and humidity levels.

If the potatoes start to sprout or develop isolated green patches on their skins as a result of being exposed to light and warm temperatures, they may still be edible. If, however, the green portion is widespread throughout the surface of the potato or within its flesh, discard such specimens.

Potatoes can also keep quite well in a basement, root cellar, or other place with the proper cool temperature and lack of humidity (for more information, see "Preserving the Bounty" on page 611).

TRIMMING AND CLEANING

The most preparation that properly stored new and mature potatoes alike usually require is a thorough scrubbing with a vegetable brush—and peeling, if desired. If a potato has begun to sprout, simply cut away the eyes (undeveloped buds) and peel away any green areas on or just under the surface of the skin.

STEAMING AND BOILING

New and mature potatoes alike take well to steaming; those of average size typically take from 15 to 20 minutes to become tender throughout.

Cooking Tip

Potato varieties that are high in starch make good baked and mashed spuds, because they are drier and lower in moisture.

Low-starch varieties are firmer in texture and are best-suited for boiling, sautéing, and using in potato salads.

When making oven fries,
chill the potatoes, unpeeled,
in the refrigerator for a day
or two to make them browner.

"For me, a plain baked potato is
the most delicious one …
It is soothing and enough."

— M. F. K. Fisher,
American food writer

Steaming can be a good alternative to boiling, which tends to make potatoes soggy and leach out their flavor. Average-size potatoes usually require 20 to 30 minutes of boiling time, but accurate cooking times are impossible to generalize because they depend on the variety and size of the potato. Always test cooked potatoes with an inserted fork or knife to be sure of their doneness. Also, if the potatoes will be used in a chilled salad, take care to halt the cooking while they are still firm; they will continue to cook for a while after they are removed from the heat.

STIR-FRYING AND SAUTÉING

Stir-frying and sautéing are usually not the first cooking methods that come to mind when preparing spuds, but potatoes can be quite delicious prepared this way, either by themselves or in combination with other vegetables. Waxy or new potatoes work better for this purpose than baking types.

For these cooking methods, the potatoes cook faster and more evenly if they are sliced quite thinly (or julienned, shredded, or cut into small cubes). Soaking potatoes beforehand in cold water helps to leach out their starch and make them cook up more crisply. Some recipes recommend parboiling potatoes first.

Stir-fry or sauté on medium-high heat in oil or butter (use 4 to 6 tablespoons for every 2 pounds of spuds) for 5 to 7 minutes, or until they reach the desired tenderness and are golden brown. Potatoes cut into rounds or small chunks will take 10 to 15 minutes to cook.

BAKING AND ROASTING

Baked potatoes are an old, trusty standby, and they are also wonderfully simple to prepare. Resist the urge to wrap potatoes in aluminum foil; this only results in steamed potatoes with soggy, wet skins and flesh.

Place washed potatoes in a baking pan or directly on the oven rack, and pierce their skins several times to allow steam to escape (unless you want an explosion to enliven your day). Baking times can vary immensely, depending on the potato variety and size, but a large baking-type potato will usually take 40 to 50 minutes in a 425°F oven; new potatoes take nearly as long—typically 30 to 40 minutes. Test by inserting the point of a large, sharp knife into the center of the spud; if the blade meets no resistance, the potato is done.

Roasting potatoes concentrates their flavor, which can be accentuated with seasonings. (I personally love roasting potatoes with onions, shallots, or even garlic cloves along with olive oil and chopped fresh rosemary.) Some cooks recommend parboiling potatoes for 5 minutes first to soften them, then rubbing them with oil and seasoning, and placing them in a 400°F oven for 30 to 40 minutes, or a 350°F oven for 45 to 55 minutes. Turn them occasionally to prevent scorching.

For a real treat, make crispy potato skins. Scoop out the flesh from baked potatoes, cut the skins into strips, spread butter and sprinkle salt over them, and bake them in a 450°F oven until they turn crisp.

MICROWAVING

To prepare potatoes for microwaving, puncture them a few times with a fork to prevent explosions; then place them on a paper towel or directly on the oven plate. Microwave on high power.

At the end of the cooking time, insert a knife into the center of the potato. If the knife sticks or meets resistance, cook another 1 or 2 minutes, and then let them stand for 5 minutes. They will finish cooking during the standing time. If you're running behind schedule getting dinner on the table, you can start the spuds in the microwave and partially cook them on high power for 4 minutes. This gives them a good head start. Then bake them at a high temperature in the regular oven to finish them and dry them out.

NEW POTATOES

- 6 to 8 (about 1 pound), plus 3 tablespoons water = 8 to 12 minutes
- 2 pounds new potatoes in a covered dish with ¼ cup water = 10 to 12 minutes
- 6 small new potatoes in a covered dish with ¼ cup water = 8 to 10 minutes

MATURE POTATOES

- 1 to 2 medium potatoes (6 to 8 ounces) = 4 to 6 minutes
- 4 large baking potatoes = 16 to 18 minutes

BLANCHING AND FREEZING

Raw potatoes do not respond well to freezing; they will discolor and their texture will deteriorate. Boiled potatoes do not fare much better, unless they are frozen along with other ingredients, as in a stew.

Potatoes to be frozen must be blanched first by boiling them in salted water for 4 to 5 minutes, then plunging them into ice water for 2 minutes to stop the cooking process. Remove and drain. Package the potatoes in zipper-lock freezer or vacuum food sealer-type bags, or freezer containers. Squeeze out excess air and leave ½ inch of headspace (unless you are using the vacuum sealing method). Sliced, lightly fried potatoes can also be frozen. Frozen potatoes will keep for up to 6 months at 0°F.

EQUIVALENTS, MEASURES, AND SERVINGS

- 3 medium to large potatoes = 1¾ cups mashed
- 1 pound = 2 to 3 medium Russet or 6 to 8 new = 3 to 3½ cups chopped, sliced, or cubed = 1¾ to 2 cups cooked and mashed

COMPLEMENTARY HERBS, SEASONINGS, AND FOODS

Arugula, bacon, basil, beef, butter, cabbage, capers, caviar, cayenne, celery root, chard, cheese, chervil, chicken, chives, cod, corned beef, cream, créme fraîche, dill, duck, fennel, fish, garlic, goose, ham, herring, horseradish, kale, lamb, leeks, lettuce, lovage, mint, mushrooms, mustard, nutmeg, olives, olive oil, onions, paprika, parsley, parsnips, pepper, pork, sage, salt, sausages, savory, smoked salmon, sour cream, squash, steak, sweet potatoes, thyme, turnips, watercress.

SERVING SUGGESTIONS

- Combine diced potatoes with green and red peppers, onions, olives, slices of chorizo or other sausage, and diced ham to add to your favorite omelet, scrambled eggs, or frittata for an easy, nutritious, one-dish meal.
- Leftover mashed potatoes can be reincarnated in breads, doughnuts, and cakes.
- Potatoes are one of the traditional fillings for pasties, those little baked pastry shells filled with beef, carrots, onions, turnips, or rutabagas.

Books

The Potato: How the Humble Spud Rescued the Western World
Larry Zuckerman,
North Point Press, 1999.

The Ultimate Potato Book: Hundreds of Ways To Turn America's Favorite Side Dish into a Meal
Bruce Weinstein and Mark Scarbrough,
William Morrow Cookbooks, 2003.

For More Information

Washington State Potato Commission
www.potatoes.com

Idaho Potato Commission
www.idahopotato.com

The United States Potato Board
www.healthypotato.com

- Make hash browns by finely shredding potatoes and frying them, covered, in butter or oil over low heat for 10 minutes. Then remove the cover, turn them over, and continue to fry until they become crispy.

- Enjoy new potatoes boiled simply and topped with butter, salt, cheese, garlic, and dill or other fresh herbs.

- Make oven fries by cutting potatoes into wedges, drizzling them with oil and seasonings of your choice, and baking in a 375°F oven for 30 minutes.

- Use pureed potatoes to thicken soups, or to make that cold leek-potato soup, vichyssoise.

- Finely shred potatoes to make potato latkes or pancakes.

- For new potatoes like Russian Fingerlings, toss the washed potatoes in oil, salt, pepper, and an herb or spice of your choice (rosemary, tarragon, and sage are nice complements, as are smoky paprika and curry powder). Then roast them at 375°F until they are fork-tender, about 45 minutes to 1 hour.

- Prepare garlic mashed potatoes by pureeing roasted garlic, potatoes, and olive oil together. (This is also fantastic with bacon bits!)

- Potatoes are a key ingredient in one of Sweden's most popular dishes, Jansson's Temptation, a casserole of sliced potatoes, onions, and anchovy fillets that is finished with plenty of freshly ground black pepper, butter, and light cream. Tempting as sin, indeed!

- Who could forget shepherd's pie? This is essentially a savory beef stew covered with a thick layer of mashed potatoes baked to a delicious brownness.

- Oven-roast fingerling potatoes and serve with spicy ketchup, *romesco*, or sriracha mayonnaise. A great alternative to fries!

. . . .

VEGETABLE CORNMEAL CRÊPES

SERVES 6
(2 CRÊPES PER SERVING)

CRÊPES

1 cup all-purpose flour
⅓ cup yellow cornmeal
1 tablespoon sugar
2½ teaspoons baking powder
3 tablespoons grated Parmesan cheese
1¾ cups skim milk
2 tablespoons margarine or butter, melted
1 egg
2 egg whites
Vegetable cooking spray

FILLING

1 pound new potatoes, cut into ½-inch pieces, cooked
1 cup sliced mushrooms
½ medium red bell pepper, chopped
1 to 2 tablespoons olive or vegetable oil
2 small zucchini, coarsely shredded
2 cups broccoli florets, steamed until crisp-tender
3 tablespoons grated Parmesan cheese

"Potatoes are to food what sensible shoes are to fashion."

— Linda Wells

2 teaspoons finely chopped fresh thyme,
   or ½ teaspoon dried thyme
⅛ teaspoon salt
¼ teaspoon freshly ground black pepper
6 tablespoons reduced-fat sour cream
Parsley sprigs, for garnish

FOR THE CRÊPES

1. In a medium bowl, mix the flour, cornmeal, sugar, baking powder, and cheese. Then whisk in the milk, margarine, egg, and egg whites until smooth. (A blender also works very well to thoroughly combine and smooth the batter.) Chill the batter for about 30 minutes before using.

2. Spray a crêpe pan or small, 6-inch nonstick skillet with cooking spray; heat over medium heat. Stir the batter gently to recombine the ingredients. Spoon 3 tablespoons of the crêpe batter into the skillet, rotating the pan quickly so that the batter covers the bottom of the pan in a thin layer. Cook over medium heat until the crêpe turns light brown on the bottom. With a spatula, loosen the edges of the crêpe; turn and cook momentarily, until other side is light brown. Because the heavier ingredients will tend to settle to the bottom, stir the batter gently between making each crepe.

3. Stack the crêpes between sheets of waxed or parchment paper, and cover loosely with a clean kitchen towel.

FOR THE FILLING

1. In a large skillet, sauté the cooked potatoes, mushrooms, and bell pepper in the oil until the potatoes begin to brown, about 5 minutes.

2. Stir in the zucchini and broccoli; sauté until the zucchini turns tender, about 3 minutes.

3. Stir in the cheese, thyme, salt, and pepper. Spoon the vegetable mixture into the center of the crêpes (about ⅓ cup per crêpe). Roll the crêpes and place, seam sides down, on the plates.

4. Garnish with dollops of sour cream and some parsley.

— *Produce for Better Health; Fruits & Veggies—More Matters;
Centers for Disease Control and Prevention*

. . . .

PEPPERY POTATO AND ZUCCHINI PACKETS ON THE GRILL
SERVES 4

1½ pounds potatoes (about 6 medium), scrubbed and thinly sliced
1 zucchini, thinly sliced
1 medium onion, thinly sliced
1 tablespoon olive oil
1 teaspoon fresh thyme, or ½ teaspoon dried thyme

One Potato, Two Potato

Celebrity chef Wolfgang Puck prefers Yukon Golds for making his signature mashed potatoes.

The Russet Burbank variety was developed by famed horticulturist and plant breeder Luther Burbank in the early 1870s. The primary potato used in American french fries, it is the number-one crop in Idaho and the most widely cultivated commercial potato variety.

Cooking Tip

Steaming instead of boiling the potatoes makes a less watery mashed product.

½ teaspoon salt

1. Heat the grill.

2. Mix all of the ingredients in a bowl. Divide the mixture among 4 pieces of aluminum foil, placing the mixture near one end. Fold in half to form a packet; then fold the edges to seal completely.

3. Grill the packets 25 to 30 minutes, turning over once, until the potatoes are tender when pierced.

— *Featherstone Farm, Rushford, Minnesota*

YUKON GOLD POTATO SOUP   SERVES 6

Source Note: Served cold, this would be vichyssoise; served hot, it is sometimes called soup bonne femme, or "good housewife" soup. Whatever it is called, it is inexpensive, satisfying, and very, very good. Thin-skinned Yukon Gold potatoes need not be peeled. In fact, the skins almost disappear when the soup is pureed, but their memory lends the soup more character.

**2 pounds (4 to 6 medium) Yukon Gold potatoes
2 large leeks (whiter ends only)
¼ cup butter
4 cups chicken or vegetable broth
2 teaspoons kosher salt, or to taste
1 teaspoon ground white pepper
1 cup organic whipping cream
Chives, for garnish**

1. Cut the potatoes into 1-inch chunks. Split the leek ends in half lengthwise and rinse out any soil trapped between the layers; slice them crosswise into ¼-inch half-rounds.

2. In a large soup pot with a thick base, melt the butter over medium heat and cook the sliced leeks, stirring often until they are very tender but not brown, about 10 minutes. Add the cubed potatoes, broth, salt, and pepper and bring the soup to a boil. Cover and decrease the heat to low. Simmer gently for 15 minutes, or until the potatoes are very tender. (The soup may be served as a rustic country soup at this point, but it is even better when it is pureed.)

3. In a blender, puree the soup in small batches. Cover the top of the machine with a kitchen towel and process, using short pulses at first so that the hot mixture does not overflow when the machine is turned on. Bring the cream to a gentle simmer in the soup pot and stir in the pureed soup. Serve the soup hot with snipped chives on top.

— *Greg Atkinson,* Northwest Essentials: Cooking with Ingredients That Define a Region's Cuisine

MOM'S LEFSE

MAKES ABOUT 2 DOZEN

Source Note: Lefse is a traditional soft, thin, Norwegian flatbread that is made with leftover potatoes, flour, butter, and sometimes milk or cream and cooked on a griddle. Special tools are needed to prepare lefse, such as a lefse stick—a long wooden instrument that resembles an extra-long paint stir stick—and a circular lefse board, for rolling out paper-thin sheets.

Traditionally lefse was eaten with lutefisk, a type of preserved cod that is not always a favorite of the younger generation. But there are plenty of other ways to enjoy this Scandinavian favorite—spread 'em with butter, sprinkle them with sugar, or top them with jam. They can be used as a crepe or rolled around all sorts of fillings like a wrap. They can be eaten hot or cold, or eaten on the side with a meal just like bread. The possibilities are endless!

5 cups cooked, mashed or riced potatoes (Russet potatoes are best)
1 teaspoon salt
2 tablespoons butter
2 cups all-purpose flour

1. While the potatoes are hot, combine them with the salt and butter in a stand mixer or a large bowl. Mix or stir until no lumps remain (think of smooth mashed potatoes).

2. Let stand covered until the potatoes are cool, then add the flour. Work the flour into the potatoes by hand, kneading it in thoroughly, or use a stand mixer with the dough hook attached. (You can use a rotary eggbeater as well.)

3. Preheat an electric griddle to 450°F (you can also use a 12-inch cast-iron skillet if you don't have a griddle). Spread out a big bath towel or flour-sack dish towel on the counter or table (avoid using towels that are laundered with scented detergent or dryer sheets).

4. Form patties of the dough, each about the size of a tennis ball (a measuring cup can be useful for making sure the resulting lefse sheets are all the same size). Place one patty at a time on a generously floured lefse board, pastry cloth, or other large, flat surface. Roll out the dough into a 12-inch circle, making sure it is evenly thin throughout.

5. Carefully slide a lefse stick under the middle of the lefse sheet, making sure to keep the end of the stick down so it doesn't poke through the dough. Lift the stick gently from the board. Matching the edge of the sheet to the edge of the griddle, lay the sheet down and unroll it onto the griddle in one smooth, quick motion.

6. Bake the lefse until small brown spots appear on the underside and bubbles appear on top like a pancake, 1 to 2 minutes. Then flip and repeat on the other side. Lefse cooks very quickly; don't ignore it too long or it will burn before you know it!

7. Transfer the finished lefse onto the towel. You can stack several sheets on top of one another in a shingle pattern, then start another layer

has over 100 human-made chemicals in our bloodstream. Some of these pollutants are EPA- or FDA-approved and it would be difficult to restrict them, but we CAN control the ones we put in our mouths.

According to the 2009 Annual Report of the President's Cancer Panel, "Exposure to pesticides can be decreased by choosing, to the extent possible, food grown without pesticides or chemical fertilizers and washing conventionally grown produce to remove residues. Similarly, exposure to antibiotics, growth hormones, and toxic runoff from livestock feedlots can be minimized by eating free-range meat raised without these medications, if it is available."

"If you're talking about pesticides, the evidence is pretty conclusive. Your chances of getting pesticide residues are much less with organic food," says John Reganold, professor of soil science at Washington State University in Pullman, Washington.

The amount of human-made pesticide residues found in conventional foods is still well below the level that the Environmental Protection Agency has deemed unsafe. But the real issue is whether these small doses, over years and decades, add up to an increased health risk down the line and what they contribute to the cocktail of chemicals already in our bodies from other sources.

If you can't always afford organic, do spend the extra money when it comes to what the Environmental Working Group calls the "dirty dozen": peaches, strawberries, nectarines, apples, spinach, celery, pears, sweet bell peppers, cherries, potatoes, lettuce, and grapes. These fragile fruits and vegetables often require more pesticides to fight off bugs compared to hardier produce such as asparagus and broccoli. Download a list of produce ranked by pesticide contamination at www.foodnews.org.

and stack those. Then cover them with a thin cloth or another towel, and set them aside to cool.

8. When they have completely cooled, fold the lefse in half, then half again so you have a round-edged triangle. Store them in zipper-lock freezer bags. They will keep in the freezer for at least 6 months.

— *Erma Schubbe,* Hills Centennial Cookbook

....

SOUR CREAM POTATO SALAD   SERVES 10

Source Note: This is a real favorite. It is even better when refrigerated a day ahead to give the flavors a chance to blend.

7 medium red or white potatoes, cooked in their jackets, peeled and sliced (6 cups)
⅓ cup Italian salad dressing
¾ cup sliced celery
⅓ cup chopped scallions (green onions), white sections and green tops (plus extra for garnish, if desired)
4 hard-cooked eggs
1 cup Miracle Whip
½ cup sour cream
1½ teaspoons prepared horseradish mustard (or use 1 teaspoon prepared mustard and ½ teaspoon horseradish)
Salt
Celery seed
⅓ cup diced cucumber

1. While the potato slices are still warm, pour the Italian dressing over them; toss gently to coat, then chill for 2 hours.

2. Add the celery and scallion.

3. Chop the egg whites and sieve or mash the egg yolks, reserving some yolk for garnish if desired. Combine the remaining sieved yolk with the Miracle Whip, sour cream, and horseradish mustard. Fold into the salad. Add salt and celery seed to taste.

4. Chill the salad for at least 2 hours.

5. Gently fold in the diced cucumber just before serving. Garnish with the reserved sieved yolk and sliced onion tops.

— *Matthew George Looper,* The Schoenleber Family Cookbook

LaVerne's Potato Candy

SERVES 8

Author Note: This is an unusual, old-fashioned candy recipe that uses potatoes in a very different way, and I've included it for historical interest. Note that this candy is super sweet, maybe overly so for some palates, although the peanut butter balances it somewhat. Creamy peanut butter will spread and roll easier than chunky, so use it if possible.

Source Note: As a child this was one of our favorite treats. My mother made potato candy for my siblings and me while we were growing up in the small company railroad and coal town of Delano, Pennsylvania. Potato candy still is often served as a special treat, because everyone likes it. Often it is made for social affairs at the local firehouse and church because it sells well and serves as a good fundraiser. Although it is hard work to make it, it's worth the effort because kids and adults like its taste.

1 medium, cooked Russet potato (about 6 ounces), mashed
1 tablespoon of butter
Dash of vanilla
1¼ pounds powdered sugar, plus more as needed
Peanut butter, preferably salted

1. Mix the mashed potato with the butter, keeping it to a dough-like consistency, similar to pie dough. (Or instead of mashed potatoes, soften 4 ounces of cream cheese and combine with 1 tablespoon of butter.)

2. Add a dash of vanilla and the powdered sugar to the potatoes. Mix well; add more sugar until the mixture becomes quite stiff—about the texture of cookie dough. Cover and chill for about 30 minutes.

3. Roll out the dough on wax paper using some flour so the dough will not stick.

4. After you have rolled out the dough until it is somewhat smooth and to the desired thickness (about ¼ inch), spread a layer of peanut butter over the top.

5. Then roll up the dough like cinnamon rolls, using the wax paper to help lift it. You can also make small individual rolls. Refrigerate until chilled and slice into pieces of candy.

6. Enjoy eating this Pennsylvania Dutch treat!

— *Library of Congress, American Memory Project,* Immigration … The Great American Potluck

---

plan their year's crops around what the restaurants want. They can also command higher prices for their produce, which the restaurant passes on to their diners, who are usually glad to pay extra for it.

It goes beyond the farmer and the restaurant, though; diners get to know local farms and producers by name whom they might not otherwise encounter, which raises general community awareness.

The farm-to-table movement has also triggered cases of fraud, with some restaurants caught proclaiming that some of their items came from farms when in actuality they didn't. The motive is higher profit—restaurants can charge a lot more for such dishes. Such "farm-to-fable" dishonesty has compelled farmers to walk into restaurants to confront chefs, or even issue invoices for fraudulently using their names. Other chefs can be quick to call out dishonest colleagues, and it is often a very small world, indeed.

Interestingly, another related trend is emerging: the CSR, or community-supported restaurant. Built on the business model of the CSA farm, CSRs allow customers to pay a membership fee in exchange for extra dining credit, special events, in-home gourmet dining opportunities, and more. Such a restaurant benefits from customer loyalty, financing without being at the mercy of a bank, and free advertising from members, whose friends and family can often dine at no extra cost.

But such a restaurant has to have extremely good business and marketing acumen to pull this off. In this era of crowd-funded enterprises, however, many consumers are more willing than ever to invest in a membership ranging from $250 to $5,000 to support a worthy cause. Notable CSRs include **Braise** in Milwaukee, Wisconsin; **Lenoir** in Austin, Texas; and **The Gleanery** in Putney, Vermont.

Rutabagas

It is perhaps sadly fitting that a vegetable whose name literally means "root bag" in Swedish is among the most mistrusted, disliked, and even vilified of vegetables, along with cabbage and turnips. Is it their earthy rootiness, their decidedly unhandsome external appearance, their sometimes intimidating size, or their distinctly musky brassica aroma that repulses? Or all of the above? More likely than not it was the way they were traditionally cooked—boiled in gallons of water for an eternity, which is precisely how not *to cook a rutabaga, or pretty much any vegetable, for that matter—and the fact that they have been traditionally thought of as a lowly subsistence food.*

A curious cross between a cabbage and a turnip, rutabagas play a major role in many northern European cuisines, where they tend to be adorned with plenty of heavy cream, butter, and hearty broth. These sturdy root vegetables have dual personalities in the kitchen: One takes to the expected baking, roasting, and mashing like other root vegetables. The other is more surprising—as a thinly sliced, crisp, delicate, slightly sweet raw vegetable. Either way, their butter-yellow flesh is smooth-textured and quite beautiful, especially in combination with other vegetables. Some may be strong tasting and somewhat bitter, whereas others are mild and delicate; the roots vary widely depending on their size, age, and growing conditions.

HISTORY

No one really knows exactly where rutabagas came from, but most likely they originated in Russia or Scandinavia, where they continue to be very popular to this day. They seem to be relative latecomers to England and America, not making their appearance until the 18th and 19th centuries, respectively. However, the venerable roots were a part of Halloween festivities in the British Isles, where they were once carved into lanterns to ward off evil spirits and as hideous masks for children to wear.

Rutabagas have typically been a staple food for the poor and desperate, which has done little to improve their culinary image. People of certain generations in Germany and France endured severe food rationing and shortages in World Wars I and II, during which time rutabagas in particular were commonly made into thin, watery stews; bad associations and memories still persist, and to this day some Germans prefer kohlrabi to rutabagas.

NUTRITION

Like nearly all brassicas, rutabagas are quite nutritionally redeeming, with significant amounts of B vitamins, vitamin C, phosphorous, manganese, magnesium, calcium, potassium, and dietary fiber. A single cup of mashed rutabaga contains about 100 calories.

SEASON

Commercially, rutabagas are widely grown and in season year-round.

But this fall-winter vegetable is typically at its best from October through March. Rutabagas are often a significant vegetable in winter CSA shares.

SELECTION

Choose rutabagas that are firm and heavy, with no shriveled, soft, cracked, or pitted areas. Supermarket rutabagas are usually coated with a food-grade wax to help them keep longer, but ones from CSAs and farmers markets typically are not waxed.

STORAGE

Rutabagas are famous for keeping for months under the right conditions. Place them in a basement, root cellar, or other place with the proper cool temperature and lack of humidity (for more information, see "Preserving the Bounty" on page 611). If you don't have such a storage area, wrap them unwashed in a plastic bag and keep them in the refrigerator crisper for 3 to 4 weeks.

TRIMMING AND CLEANING

Rutabagas have thick skins that must be peeled before eating, but their extremely dense, hard flesh can make cutting into them a rather dangerous challenge (and waxed specimens can be slippery). A very sharp, heavy cleaver works best, and it is easier to peel the vegetable when it is quartered or cut into chunks rather than whole. If the rutabaga is unwaxed, you can put it in the microwave for 1 or 2 minutes to soften it enough to cut into chunks. Then it's easy to use a paring knife or a sharp vegetable peeler to remove the outer skin.

STEAMING AND BOILING

Peel and cut rutabagas into 2½-inch cubes and steam them for 25 to 30 minutes, or until tender when pierced with a fork. Boiling is not the best way to prepare rutabagas (braising, roasting, or steaming are better), but if you must, boil cubed, peeled rutabagas for 20 to 35 minutes, or until tender when pierced with a folk, then drain well.

STIR-FRYING AND SAUTÉING

To stir-fry or sauté rutabagas, cut them into very thin strips or into ½-inch cubes and cook them in a well-oiled pan or wok over high heat for about 8 minutes, or until crisp-tender.

BAKING AND ROASTING

Slice rutabagas into ½-inch-thick rounds and bake in a 400°F oven for about 30 minutes, depending on their size. For a taste treat, baste them with butter and honey twice during the baking. Or cut them into 1½-inch chunks, brush with melted butter or oil, and bake for 30 to 45 minutes in a 350°F oven. Or prepare them like oven-roasted potatoes (see the recipe on page 572).

BRAISING

Because of their size and sturdy nature, rutabagas are an ideal candidate for braising. Cut them into uniform pieces and place them in a skillet with enough liquid (such as chicken or vegetable broth) to generously

Tatties and Neeps, Anyone?

Rutabagas are called many things—Swedes, yellow turnips, snadgers, narkies, and neeps.

Tatties and neeps (potatoes and rutabagas) is a popular Scottish dish in which the vegetables are boiled separately, then mashed together and served with the infamous national Scottish dish, haggis—a savory pudding containing sheep's organ meats minced with onion, oatmeal, suet, spices, salt, and stock, and traditionally encased in the animal's stomach.

Believe it or not, it's more delicious than it sounds.

cover the bottom. Cook at a gentle simmer for 15 to 20 minutes, or until the rutabagas can be easily pierced with a knife.

MICROWAVING

Cut 2 pounds of trimmed rutabaga into ½-inch cubes. Place them in a covered dish with ¼ cup water and microwave on high power until tender, stirring occasionally, for about 12 minutes.

BLANCHING AND FREEZING

Peel and cube the rutabaga. Blanch in boiling water for 3 minutes, then plunge into ice water for 3 minutes or until cooled. Drain thoroughly. Then spread the rutabaga pieces on a tray in a single layer and freeze them for 30 minutes. Package the rutabaga in zipper-lock freezer or vacuum food sealer-type bags or freezer containers. Squeeze out any excess air and leave ½ inch of headspace (unless you are using the vacuum sealing method). Frozen rutabaga will keep for up to 8 months at 0°F.

Or you can steam rutabagas (see the instructions on page 581), drain and mash them, and freeze them that way. Leave ½ inch of headspace.

EQUIVALENTS, MEASURES, AND SERVINGS

- 1 medium rutabaga = 2 to 3 pounds = 5 cups cubed

COMPLEMENTARY HERBS, SEASONINGS, AND FOODS

Allspice, apples, apple cider vinegar, bacon, bay, beef, beets, black pepper, butter, caraway, carrots, coriander, cranberries, cream, cumin, fennel, garlic, ginger, green onions, ham, honey, kale, lamb, lemon, maple syrup, mushrooms, mustard, nutmeg, onions, paprika, parsley, parsnips, pork, potatoes, rosemary, shallots, smoked salt, soy sauce, squash, sweet potatoes, turnips, vinegar.

SERVING SUGGESTIONS

- A classic winter vegetable trio is rutabagas, potatoes, and carrots, which can be mashed with plenty of butter or cream.
- Take advantage of rutabagas' beautiful yellow color and cook them, julienned, with broccoli stems, carrots, and turnips to create a lovely vegetable side dish.
- Add rutabagas to soups, stews, casseroles, and other hearty winter dishes.
- Lightly sauté very thinly sliced rutabagas in a little butter, salt, and seasonings for a surprisingly delicate vegetable side dish.
- Purée rutabagas for creamy soups and bisques.
- Rutabagas are lovely thin-sliced and combined with cream and cheese, au gratin–style.
- Bake rutabagas slowly to caramelize them—they're absolutely delicious with bacon.
- With their sturdy, earthy nature, rutabagas are lovely accompaniments to roasts of pork, beef, or lamb.
- Oven-roast rutabagas with other root vegetables, like carrots, potatoes, parsnips, sweet potatoes, turnips, and beets.
- Rutabagas are one of the traditional fillings for pasties, those little baked pastry shells filled with beef, carrots, onions, potatoes, or turnips.

- Make pickles! Rutabagas take very well to this method, especially if made with apple cider vinegar, honey, lemon juice, cumin seeds, mustard seeds, coriander seeds, paprika, and cayenne.
- Rutabagas make surprisingly light, delicate pies. Combine pureed rutabaga with apple, pear, honey, ginger, and coriander.
- Grate raw turnips and rutabagas for a delicious slaw seasoned with mint, parsley, and green onions.
- If you're making vegetable soup, add rutabagas for color and delicious flavor.

. . . .

MEXICAN RUTABAGA AND SWEET POTATO   MAKES 5 CUPS

Source Note: This mixture provides the base for one of our go-to vegetarian meals. We roast the rutabaga and sweet potatoes, sauté some onions and kale, and throw it all into a tortilla with some beans on the side. Yum!

2 large rutabagas
2 sweet potatoes
Olive or sunflower oil
Cumin, to taste
Chili powder, to taste
Pinch of oregano

1. Preheat the oven to 375°F.
2. Cube the sweet potatoes and rutabaga into bite-size pieces. Coat them with the oil, salt, pepper, and spices, then put them into a large baking dish.
3. Bake for about 45 minutes or until tender, stirring occasionally.

— *Alchemy Gardens, West Rutland, Vermont*

. . . .

ROASTED ROOT VEGETABLES FROM GRETA'S KITCHEN   SERVES 6

3 pounds various root vegetables, including carrots, potatoes, beets, rutabaga, turnips, parsnips, celeriac, and daikon radish, peeled and chopped into ½-inch cubes
2 tablespoons olive oil
2 tablespoons soy sauce or Bragg Liquid Aminos
2 tablespoons maple syrup
Salt and freshly ground black pepper
Fresh or dried thyme, to taste (optional)
Grated ginger, to taste (optional)

1. Preheat the oven to 400°F.
2. Place all of the cubed veggies in a 9-by-13-inch baking pan (you should have about 8 cups).

The Bitter Gene

To some people, rutabagas taste bitter. This means they have a special gene that affects the taste receptor called TAS2R38. Folks with this gene also can't stand Brussels sprouts, cabbage, kale, turnips, and other brassicas.

3. Mix the olive oil, soy sauce, and maple syrup. Add the salt and pepper, as well as the thyme and ginger. Season according to your mood.

4. Cover the pan with aluminum foil and bake for 40 to 55 minutes, depending on the size of the vegetable cubes. The vegetables will be tender, and a fork should easily pierce the largest vegetable cube in the pan. Be careful when you're removing the foil so as not to get a steam burn.

— *Greta Sikorski, Featherstone Farm, Rushford, Minnesota*

. . . .

SHEPHERD'S PIE   SERVES 8

1 pound ground pork or beef
1 onion, chopped
2 carrots, cut into small cubes
2 rutabagas (or turnips), cut into small cubes
1 bunch chopped greens, such as kale or spinach, or ½ small
**   shredded cabbage, or 2 bulbs fennel, cored and sliced (optional)**
1 teaspoon Worcestershire sauce, or 1 tablespoon mustard
Salt
Freshly ground black pepper (or use chili flakes)
1 cup water or broth
1½ pounds potatoes, quartered
4 tablespoons (½ stick) butter, softened
½ cup milk
1 pinch ground nutmeg

1. Sauté the meat in a skillet on medium heat for about 5 minutes until it has browned, making sure to break the meat up as it cooks.

2. When the meat has released its fat, add the onion, carrots, rutabagas, greens (if using), Worcestershire sauce, salt, and pepper. Cover and reduce the heat to low and cook for another 5 minutes, stirring occasionally. Add the water, stir, and simmer, covered, for another 15 minutes.

3. Meanwhile, place the potatoes in a large pot of cold water. Bring them to a boil and cook for 20 minutes, or until quite soft. Drain and mash the potatoes with the butter, milk, and nutmeg. Season to taste with salt and pepper.

4. Preheat the oven to 400°F.

5. Place the meat and vegetable mixture in a large ovenproof dish and cover it evenly with the mashed potatoes. Finish by drawing a fork across the top of the potatoes in the pattern of your choice. Bake for 30 minutes, or until the potatoes begin to brown and the mixture is hot throughout.

— *Philippe Waterinckx, Tucson CSA, Tucson, Arizona*

VEGETABLE FRITTERS

MAKES ABOUT 18 FRITTERS

Source Note: Vegetable fritters are an innovative way to use up any leftovers from Christmas dinner. Whether you have carrots, turnips, butternut squash, or broccoli, they can all be easily converted into fritters with a beaten egg and some flour. The leftover mashed potatoes act as a binder to hold the cakes together. Feel free to add some extra turkey or ham.

1 zucchini, shredded
3 cups mashed potatoes
2 cups leftover cooked vegetables (butternut squash, carrots,
    parsnips, rutabaga, and celery root are all good choices)
¼ cup all-purpose flour
½ cup sharp Cheddar cheese
1 egg, beaten
Kosher salt and freshly ground black pepper
Vegetable oil, for cooking

1. Using a food processor or hand grater, shred the zucchini. Squeeze the grated zucchini between two paper towels to remove any excess liquid.

2. In a large bowl, place the grated zucchini with the mashed potatoes, leftover cooked vegetables, flour, cheese, and egg. Mix until well combined. Season with salt and pepper and carefully mix again.

3. Coat the bottom of a large frying pan with oil and heat it over medium-high heat. Once hot, add several large spoonfuls of the mixture to the pan. Flatten slightly until the fritters appear round and flat, about ½ inch thick. Cook for 2 to 3 minutes on each side until golden brown. Remove the fritters from the pan and allow them to drain on paper towels. Continue to do this until all the batter is gone.

4. Serve hot with crème fraîche or sriracha cream (2 teaspoons of sriracha hot sauce mixed into ¼ cup of mayonnaise).

— Foodista.com

mate. All of the big seed companies are developing new varieties in the laboratory through genetic modification rather than in the field, as farmers have for centuries.

With consolidation, many seed varieties and heirloom seeds have been phased out. Heirloom seeds are those that have been passed down through the generations for at least 50 years and are now in some danger of extinction. They are all open-pollinated (meaning pollinated naturally through insects, birds, and wind).

Many heirloom seeds come from immigrants who brought seed from "the old country" to add cultural, culinary, and agricultural diversity to their new worlds. "Because of consolidation and concentration in the seed industry, there has been loss of variety and loss of heirloom varieties," according to Matthew Dillon, a founder of the **Organic Seed Alliance** of Port Townsend, Washington. "But the real concern from our perspective was that the skills of working with seed are being lost even more than the seeds themselves. The work of farmers and gardeners who created the diversity we have today is no longer being regenerated—selecting varieties, seeing anomalies you like, and saving it" (Edible Seattle, March–April 2011, page 30).

Gardeners as well as farmers may lose the ability to plant what they want because seed diversity is so diminished under the current system of consolidation. Interested individuals should contact the **Seed Savers Exchange** in their area.

Today, more and more organic farmers realize that they must take responsibility for their own seed production. They must cooperate to share seed, get training in seed selecting, work to restore seed varieties from the past, and keep current and future varieties vigorous. The Organic Seed Alliance is a great resource for farmers for information about seed.

Squashes (Winter)

CUCURBITA MAXIMA,
C. MOSCHATA,
AND C. PEPO

With so many members, variations, and lineages, the world of squashes is vast and frequently confusing. Cucurbita pepo includes several varieties: the yellow-ivory-skinned Delicata, various gourds, and summer squash. These fruits are typically ribbed and available earlier in the season. They are also one of the oldest domesticated species (traces have been found in Mexican caves dating before 7,000 BCE).

Cucurbita moschata represents such varieties as butternut, cushaw, winter crooknecks, Japanese pie, and large cheese pumpkins. Cucurbita maxima includes well-known varieties such as Hubbard, Delicious, marblehead, Boston marrow, and turban.

Literally hundreds of different varieties belong to these three species, representing fruits that weigh from 1 to 50 pounds and come in amazingly diverse shapes and colors. But they all share in common a thick, outer rind and dense, fairly dry flesh that allows them to be stored far longer than their summer squash cousins. All winter squashes thrive in hot weather, but because they take a long time to mature, they are at their best in the fall months. If properly stored, some winter squashes can hold for as long as six months.

Here are several varieties of winter squash you may find weighting down your CSA box or displayed at your farmers market:

Acorn *(Cucurbita pepo)*
Acorn squash, with its distinctive shape and dark-green skin, has yellow flesh that is mildly sweet and slightly nutty in flavor. A smallish squash that measures 5 to 8 inches long, it will keep in a cool, dark, well-ventilated place for months. Remember, however, that the Acorn is an early-ripening squash, so it will not last through the winter.

Buttercup *(C. maxima)*
This old classic has distinctive, dark-green roundish fruits that wear "beanies" as they mature. Averaging 5 to 7 pounds, this is a superb squash with deliciously sweet orange flesh that becomes dry and fine-textured when baked, creamy and smooth when steamed. Buttercups make wonderful soup or pie.

Butternut *(C. moschata)*
One of the most popular of the winter squashes, this is a pear-shaped, dependably good squash with an elongated neck, tan skin, and plenty of dense, sweet, orange flesh. This squash is best baked, used in soups, or sliced and made into casseroles. It also works well, prebaked and pureed, in custards and pies (try substituting it for pumpkin). This squash can be stored for 3 to 6 months.

Carnival *(C. pepo)*

The Carnival is a striking, heart-shaped, smallish to medium squash whose diameter ranges from 5 to 7 inches and usually weighs 1 or 2 pounds. A cross between the Acorn and Delicata, the Carnival has ivory skin that is heavily splotched with green ribs and veins but adds bright splashes of orange and yellow to its middle. Its somewhat coarse flesh is sweet, with pleasant, nuanced flavors. It is good baked, pureed to make soup, or hollowed out and stuffed.

Heart of Gold *(C. pepo)*

This beauty is a cross between the Acorn and Sweet Dumpling. It is the size and shape of the Acorn, but the fruit has the sweetness and dramatically striped skin of the Dumpling. Sweet and rich, this squash is excellent baked, steamed, or mashed. It is a good storage squash that should keep until January.

Kabocha *(C. maxima and C. moschata)*

The name of this roundish green squash is something of a misnomer, for *kabocha* is a generic term for all winter squash bred in Japan, but rarely is any distinction awarded to the several types available in America. Weighing an average of 3 pounds, all kabochas, regardless of the cultivar, possess delicious, honey-sweet, deeply flavored flesh that is the texture of custard when cooked. It is superb steamed and fantastic in recipes calling for sweet potatoes or pumpkin.

Red Kuri *(C. maxima)*

A kabocha-type squash that resembles an orange pumpkin without the ridges, it weighs from 5 to 10 pounds. Its pale orange flesh tends to be firm, with a mellow flavor somewhat reminiscent of chestnuts. This is a good squash for baking, braising, steaming, or pureeing into soups.

Spaghetti *(C. pepo)*

This compact, oblong-shaped squash has solid yellow or orange skin and typically weighs from 4 to 8 pounds (although there is a miniature cultivar that averages a mere 1 to 2 pounds and is perfect for serving one hungry eater or a couple). When cooked, its pale, mild flesh can be fluffed into pleasantly crunchy strands with a fork, like spaghetti noodles. Topped with your favorite sauce, this squash is a fun, filling, low-calorie alternative to pasta.

Sweet Dumpling *(C. pepo)*

This is a rather small, apple-shaped squash that averages only 4 to 5 inches in diameter and weighs about 1 pound. The Sweet Dumpling is delicately colored, with tan skin and pale green stripes. Its pale yellow flesh is more starchy than some squashes but is quite sweet, with some corn flavor undertones. This squash makes a fine dish steamed, baked, or stuffed.

Pie Pumpkin

See the Pumpkin section on pages 471–478.

Books

The Compleat Squash: A Passionate
Grower's Guide to Pumpkins,
Squashes, and Gourds
Amy Goldman,
Artisan, 2004.

The Classic Zucchini Cookbook:
225 Recipes for All Kinds of Squash
Nancy C. Ralston, Marynor Jordan,
and Andrea Chesman,
Storey Publishing, 2002.

Pumpkin, Butternut & Squash:
30 Sweet and Savory Recipes
Elsa Petersen-Schepelern,
Ryland Peters & Small, 2003.

HISTORY

Winter squashes and pumpkins are native to South and Central America, ranging from Mexico to northern Argentina. These heat-loving plants tend to be popular in warm climates and have never been commonly cultivated in northern Europe or places with short or cool summers. Winter squashes were unknown in the Old World until the 1500s, when European explorers imported them to their home countries. Later they were introduced to other continents, including Asia and Africa.

The earliest squash fruits were not valued so much for their flesh, which tended to be extremely bitter and sparse, but rather for their protein- and oil-rich seeds. As they were domesticated, humans began selectively breeding them for size, flavor, and proportion of flesh to seeds.

NUTRITION

Most winter squashes are packed with nutrients. Depending on the variety, a 1-cup serving may contain about 80 calories and nearly 150 percent of the adult daily requirement for vitamin A, over 30 percent of vitamin C, and over 20 percent of potassium, manganese, and dietary fiber. In addition, winter squashes contain significant amounts of folate, omega-3 fatty acids, vitamin B1, and copper. Squashes with darker shades of orange flesh contain more beta-carotene and phytonutrients, which may play a role in helping prevent certain cancers.

SEASON

Commercially, the most common varieties of winter squash are widely grown and available year-round. But typically they are at their best at CSAs and farmers markets from early fall through winter. They can be a major component of winter CSA offerings.

SELECTION

Winter squashes are hardy and sturdy by nature, so choosing a good specimen would not appear to be difficult. However, if you are seeking a squash with maximum flavor and storage potential, look for a specimen that is rock-hard, with absolutely no soft or moldy spots. Its stem should be intact, and its skin relatively dull (shiny skins may mean that the squash is immature or that it has been waxed to mask its true condition). Keep in mind that winter squashes are at their best in the fall and early winter. Although they are often available year-round in the supermarket, they are likely to be tasteless at other times.

STORAGE

Winter squash are surprisingly prone to decay, and should be stored in a cool, dry, well-ventilated place, preferably with temperatures of 45°F to 50°F and 65 to 70 percent humidity. Many varieties will keep, properly stored, from 2 weeks to 6 months in a basement, root cellar, or other place with the proper cool temperature and lack of humidity (for more information, see "Preserving the Bounty" on page 611).

Mildew may become a problem if your storage area is not dry enough. If you suspect that your storage area is too damp, prepare your winter squash by sanitizing and sealing it: Wipe your squash with a solution of 1 part chlorine bleach to 9 parts water (or use hydrogen peroxide solution). Then air-dry the squash completely, rub its exterior with salad oil, and store on a piece of cardboard with plenty of air circulation around each individual squash. This method cuts down on the number of squashes lost to rotting and molding.

TRIMMING AND CLEANING

Rarely are the tough outer rinds of winter squash edible, and thus they require removal before eating. Peeling or cutting them away when the squash is uncooked, however, can be quite challenging, requiring an implement akin to a machete or an ax. Some of the smaller squashes have tender enough skins that their rinds can be peeled fairly easily with a very sharp knife or a good-quality vegetable peeler, but you may be better off (and safer) by baking others whole in the oven until they soften (see the instructions below under "Baking and Roasting") before you attempt to peel. Alternatively—and easiest of all—you can also just fully bake the squashes and then scoop the cooked flesh out of their shells.

Be sure to thoroughly wash the outside of all winter squashes before cutting into them, to avoid contamination from the skin into the flesh. Warm or cold running water and a little mild soap do the job just fine.

A final note on trimming: If you are baking a whole squash, pierce it several times with a knife or fork to prevent explosions, and saw down its stem if it is too tall (a squash nearly caught on fire in my oven once because its woody stem was inadvertently touching the upper heating element).

STEAMING AND BOILING

Squashes that are very hard or starchy make good candidates for steaming. Halve or quarter the squash, remove its seeds, and set the pieces on a steamer rack or in a basket. Cover and steam over rapidly boiling water for 15 to 30 minutes, depending on the size and variety. Chunks cut into 2-inch pieces require only about 15 minutes, but test all squash for doneness by piercing each one with a knife or fork.

STIR-FRYING AND SAUTÉING

An unusual method for preparing winter squash is to stir-fry or sauté it. The key to making this work is to cut the squash into pieces small enough so that they will cook evenly and all the way through. Peel the skins from the squash, cut into pieces 1 inch long and ½ inch thick, and sauté over high heat for 7 to 10 minutes, or until they become tender. Or you can reduce this time by baking or otherwise cooking the squash ahead, then quickly finishing it in your sauté pan.

BAKING AND ROASTING

Baking and roasting are the best ways to prepare winter squash, as these methods caramelize their natural sugars and concentrate their flavors. To bake whole squash, follow the directions above for washing, trimming, and pricking. Place the squash on a baking sheet or pan. If it is too big, you may halve or quarter it and place the pieces on the pan, cut sides down. Most squashes weighing 1 to 1½ pounds will take about 45 minutes in a 350°F to 375°F oven; 3-pounders require 1½ to 2 hours.

In the last third of the cooking time, check constantly for doneness by inserting the point of a sharp knife into the center of the squash. If the knife blade passes through easily with no resistance, then the squash is done. Extract the seeds and surrounding stringy pulp, and scoop out the flesh into another container. Season to taste and reheat if necessary.

Or you can peel and cube squashes such as butternut, then toss the cubes with olive oil, salt, and pepper. Roast at 385°F, turning once, until caramelized and tender.

MICROWAVING

Place halves or quarters, cut sides down, in a shallow, microwave-safe dish; add ¼ cup water or apple juice. Or pierce whole squash several times with a fork and place in a microwave-safe dish. Cover tightly and microwave on high power for 6 minutes per pound, or until the flesh softens.

Most Winter Squash Types

- 1½ cups cubed = 3 to 4 minutes
- 1 pound = 6 to 7 minutes
- 1 squash (4 to 5 pounds) = 15 to 20 minutes

Spaghetti Squash

- 1 whole squash (1 to 6 pounds) = 6 to 12 minutes, depending on size

BLANCHING AND FREEZING

To properly freeze winter squash, it must first be thoroughly cooked, not just briefly blanched, as with most vegetables. Steam, boil, or bake the squash as described above, and then scoop out the flesh, discarding the seeds, stringy surrounding pulp, and skins. Mash the flesh, or run it through a food processor, or press it through a sieve. You can also cube, peel, and steam the flesh.

Pack the pureed or cubed squash in zipper-lock freezer or vacuum food sealer-type bags, or freezer containers. Squeeze out any excess air and leave ½ inch of headspace (unless you are using the vacuum sealing method). Frozen winter squash will keep for up to 3 months at 0°F.

MEASURES AND EQUIVALENTS

- 1 pound peeled, trimmed squash = 2 cups cooked = 1½ cups mashed = 2 to 3 servings
- 2½ pounds whole squash = 1½ pounds, 10 ounces cut-up pieces = 2¾ to 3 cups pureed squash
- 12 ounces frozen squash = 1 to ½ cups
- Spaghetti squash: 1 medium squash = 5 pounds = 6 to 6½ cups strands

COMPLEMENTARY HERBS, SEASONINGS, AND FOODS

Ancho chiles, apples, bacon, black pepper, brown sugar, butter, carrots, celery root, cheese (Cheddar, feta, Fontina, Gruyère, Parmesan), chiles, cinnamon, cloves, coconut milk, cream, cumin, curry, garlic, ginger, hazelnuts, honey, maple syrup, marjoram, mint, miso, nutmeg, nuts, olive oil, onions, oranges, pears, pecans, pine nuts, quinces, rosemary, sage, sherry, tamari, walnuts.

- Boil or mash winter squash just as you would potatoes.
- Add peeled squash cubes to your favorite soups, stews, beans, gratins, and vegetable ragouts.
- Steam cubes of winter squash and dress with olive oil, garlic, tamari, and ginger for a savory dish, or with apples and ginger for a sweeter dish.
- Bake squash, cut into halves, and stuff with seasoned meat, rice, bread-crumbs, or a favorite stir-fry recipe.
- Make shredded strands of spaghetti squash into an au gratin, with butter and cheese.
- Very tender, sweet winter squashes can be finely shredded to make an un-usual slaw, along with raisins, mayonnaise, vinegar, cream, and sugar.
- Incorporate mashed or finely shredded squash into pancakes, much like potato pancakes, or deep-fry like hash browns.
- Purée cooked squash and blend with sugar, cinnamon, honey, nutmeg, maple syrup, and cream for a luscious dessert.
- Substitute sweet-flavored winter squash in any recipe calling for pumpkin.
- Dress cooked winter squash with butter and herbs, a cream sauce, cheese sauce, maple syrup and nuts, marinara sauce, or stewed fruit.
- Use cooked, mashed squash in breads (especially cornbread), muffins, custards, and pies. Be sure to compensate in the recipe for the squash's extra moisture.
- Peel and cube butternut squash, then toss the cubes with olive oil, salt, and pepper. Roast at 385°F, turning once, until caramelized and tender. Serve as is or toss the cubes with sautéed chard, kale, or roasted bell pepper strips.

GINGER-SQUASH SOUP   SERVES 4

Source Note: Steaming allows the butternut squash to stay moist while retaining its vitamins. This soup is made with heavy cream, so how can it be bad?

1 medium butternut squash (about 2 pounds), halved and seeded
1 tablespoon finely grated fresh ginger
2 tablespoons unsalted butter, softened
About 4 cups chicken or vegetable stock
Salt and freshly ground black pepper
¼ cup heavy cream
¼ cup chopped, toasted pecans

1. Steam the butternut squash for 30 minutes, or until it is fork-tender. Scoop the flesh out and run it through a food processor. (Or you may use a blender, but the processor works better.)

2. Add the ginger and butter, and process. The squash will be a bit thick, so add stock until the soup reaches the desired consistency.

3. Place the soup in a large stockpot and heat. Add more stock to thin as necessary. Add salt and pepper to taste. (You can also add more

---

types of vegetable oils, and herbal essential oils such as rosemary and mint.

In the words of one organic farmer, "To prevent tomato blight, a conventional farmer uses a fungicide that enters the plant through the leaves and fights the blight internally. Organic farms, on the other hand, use a copper spray that is applied after the rain falls. It has a short life span but requires monitoring, or it can affect copper levels in the soil; too much copper harms our soil by killing off beneficial organisms.

"The downside of an organic spray program is the number of times these pesticides must be applied. Since all of the sprays we use remain only on the surface of the plant, they break down very quickly. When I began farming organically, I was surprised at the amount of spraying it involves. But the majority of organic customers don't want the holes caused by beetles and worms in their arugula or cabbage. If people see worms on our crops at the farmers market, they won't buy our produce.

"So we try very hard to grow healthy plants that are able to repel pests in the first place, to reduce the amount of spraying needed. But knowing we do have the ability and resources to spray allows us to maintain a balance between the beneficial insects and the more harmful ones."

Because the quantities of organic pesticides and fungicides typically required are so much larger than their conventional counterparts, the results of some recent studies have raised concerns about overall toxicity and residue. Although this is no reason to shun organic produce as a whole, the complexity of this issue is another example of why getting to know your local farmers is so important. Ask them about their pesticide usage and growing practices; learning about their methods can help you understand the issues and stay informed.

Hospitals across the country are responding to a growing awareness that our conventional industrial food system is not aligned with US dietary guidelines and relies on methods of food production and distribution that negatively affect both physical and environmental health. Because of their large-scale purchasing power, institutions—from hospitals to prisons to colleges—can have a significant effect on supporting family farmers and reducing reliance on the industrial food system when they source directly from local farms.

Jefferson Healthcare, a small hospital in Port Townsend, Washington, committed to a focus on more healthful food and local sourcing when it hired Arran Stark, a former restaurant and catering chef, as executive chef in 2011. First he persuaded the hospital administrators to expand its kitchen and let him provide more training for longtime cooks. Next, they gave him the go-ahead to develop what he calls an institutional CSA, which allowed him to buy food from five area farms, including Nash's Organic Produce in Sequim (see pages 168 and 558).

Stark has made it his mission to change the nature of institutional food, finding it ironic that hospitals have become synonymous with bland, unhealthful fare. "Hospitals should be the places that serve the most nutritious and organic food," he says.

In February 2014, the hospital invested $14,000 of seed money in these farms in return for wholesale vouchers that Stark can use for farm purchases throughout the growing season. Nash's supplies triticale, wheat berries, ground pork, an occasional whole pig, and assorted vegetables. The meal program feeds

ginger if you wish, but remember to go slowly—it is more difficult to take away a strong flavor than it is to add.)

4. Before serving, add the heavy cream and reheat, taking care not to let the soup boil. Ladle into bowls and top with toasted pecans.

— *Sarah Libertus, former Featherstone Farm CSA manager*

STUFFED SQUASH   SERVES 2

Source Note: This delicious, colorful, stuffed winter squash dish—bursting with nuts, plenty of herbs, and dried fruit—is hearty enough to be a main course. It's also an excellent accompaniment to golden, roasted chicken or grilled pork or lamb chops.

> 2 acorn squash, halved and seeded
> 4 tablespoons butter or olive oil
> 1 cup chopped onion
> 2 ribs celery, chopped
> ½ cup walnuts
> ½ cup sunflower seeds
> 2 large cloves garlic, minced
> 2 teaspoons fresh sage, or 1 teaspoon dried sage
> 2 teaspoons fresh thyme, or 1 teaspoon dried thyme
> 2 teaspoons fresh marjoram, or 1 teaspoon dried marjoram
> 2 cups coarsely crumbled whole wheat bread
> Juice of 1 lemon or orange
> Salt and freshly ground black pepper
> ½ cup raisins or dried cranberries
> 1 cup grated Cheddar cheese

1. Preheat the oven to 375°F.

2. Oil a baking dish that can snugly fit the squash halves. Place the squash, flesh side down, in the dish and pour in 2 cups of water. Bake until it is fork-tender, about 20 minutes.

3. Meanwhile, heat the butter or oil in a frying pan and sauté the onions until they turn translucent. Add the celery, walnuts, sunflower seeds, and garlic. Cook over low heat until the nuts are browned. Add the sage, thyme, and marjoram. Stir in the breadcrumbs, lemon juice, salt, pepper, and raisins; then cook over low heat for 5 to 8 minutes. Remove from the pan and stir in the cheese.

4. Lower the oven temperature to 350°F. Pack the stuffing into the squash cavities and cover with aluminum foil. Bake, flesh side up, for 25 minutes. Then uncover and cook for 5 to 8 minutes longer to brown.

— *Featherstone Farm, Rushford, Minnesota*

Roasted Squash
with Potatoes and Garlic

SERVES 8

Source Note: The squash may be peeled if desired.

4 cloves garlic, peeled and crushed

3 tablespoons olive oil

1 large sprig rosemary, finely chopped, plus 1 more for garnish

2 tablespoons balsamic vinegar

1 unpeeled acorn squash (1 to 1½ pounds), washed, halved, seeded, and cut into 12 equal pieces

4 to 5 medium potatoes (about 2 pounds), unpeeled, washed, and quartered

1. Preheat the oven to 425°F.

2. Combine the garlic, olive oil, chopped rosemary, and vinegar in a large bowl. Add the squash and potato pieces and toss well to coat; season to taste with salt and pepper.

3. Arrange the squash and potatoes in a single layer in a large, shallow baking pan (use two pans if necessary). Drizzle with the garlic-oil mixture, and add salt and pepper to taste. Top with the second rosemary sprig.

4. Bake for 35 minutes, switching the pans halfway through the cooking time for even baking. After the vegetables have browned on one side, turn them over, lower the heat to 350°F, and then bake for 20 minutes more, or until the squash and potatoes are easily pierced with a fork.

— *Produce for Better Health; Fruits & Veggies—More Matters;
Centers for Disease Control and Prevention*

Butternut Surprise

SERVES 4

1 butternut squash

3 tablespoons butter

1 cup small fresh or canned pineapple chunks

Parsley, finely chopped

1. Preheat the oven to 375°F.

2. Halve the butternut squash lengthwise. Scoop out the seeds and the stringy, surrounding pulp. Make several horizontal and vertical slits in the squash. Rub the butter into each squash half, place the pineapple chunks in the hollowed-out part of the squash, and sprinkle with parsley.

---

hospital staff and visitors as well as patients. The hospital dining room is now known by locals as one of the best places to eat in this small tourist town, says Stark.

Healthier Hospitals Initiative

*In Southwest Florida, **Lee Memorial Health System** has been ramping up its emphasis on fresh produce supplied by local growers in its meal service for patients and outpatient programs and striving to offer more organic choices. Out of $10 million spent annually on food, buying locally means that the $800,000 spent on produce has stayed in local business hands to help sustain the agricultural community. Lee Memorial is the largest public hospital system in the state with 1,423 inpatient beds and more than 10,000 employees. The hospital is also taking part in a national campaign called the Healthier Hospitals Initiative, in which healthcare systems commit to serving healthier foods, reducing energy waste, recycling more, using safer chemicals, and buying more environmentally friendly products.*

*The **Healthy Food in Health Care Pledge**, another national initiative, was launched in 2006 by **Health Care without Harm**. The pledge outlines steps hospitals can take to improve the health of patients, communities, and the environment. By 2014, more than 500 hospitals and a number of food service contractors had signed the Pledge, which works to improve hospital meal programs by upholding nutrition standards and encouraging local sourcing.*

Farms Come to the Hospital

*In Newnan, Georgia, **180 Degree Farm** (see pages 379 and 489), partners with the **Cancer Treatment Centers of America (CTCA) at Southeastern Regional Medical Center**, where it sets up an indoor market every Wednesday, selling its organic produce to staff, patients,*

3. Bake until soft (30 to 45 minutes). Serve immediately.

— *Nickolas Vassili*

. . . .

JOHN'S WINTER SQUASH SOUP
WITH VANILLA ICE CREAM
SERVES 6

8 cups winter squash (butternut or Hubbard), peeled, seeded, cubed
4 tablespoons olive oil, divided
2 cups sliced onion
1 garlic clove, minced
2 cups peeled, sliced carrots
1 cup sliced celery
1 bay leaf
4 (14½-ounce) cans of chicken or vegetable stock
1 pint Ben & Jerry's vanilla ice cream, divided
2 tablespoons chopped nuts (walnuts, almonds, pecans, etc.)
Salt and freshly ground black pepper

1. Preheat the oven to 350°F.

2. In a large bowl, toss the squash with 2 tablespoons of the olive oil to coat. Place the squash in a roasting pan or on a sheet pan covered with foil. Roast in the oven for 25 minutes, or until soft.

3. Meanwhile, in a 4-quart soup pot over medium heat, heat the remaining olive oil and sauté the onions until they turn translucent. Add the garlic and cook for 15 seconds more, stirring constantly to avoid burning. Add the carrots, celery, bay leaf, and chicken stock; bring to a simmer and cook uncovered for 45 minutes to 1 hour, until approximately half of the liquid has evaporated. Remove the bay leaf and discard.

4. In a blender or food processor, puree the vegetables and stock (if using a blender, remove the center part of the lid so that the hot liquid can safely emit steam). Add the cooked squash cubes and puree until very smooth. Put the puree into the pot and add ½ pint (1 cup) of the ice cream. Simmer over low heat to warm the mixture thoroughly.

5. Season to taste with salt and pepper, and serve with a dollop of vanilla ice cream and some chopped nuts sprinkled over the top.

— *Ben & Jerry's Homemade Ice Cream*

. . . .

STUFFED SPAGHETTI SQUASH LASAGNA-STYLE
SERVES 6

1 large spaghetti squash (about 6 pounds)
Olive oil
Salt and freshly ground black pepper

---

and families of patients and offering dry goods such as beans and grains at no charge. Farm owners Scott and Nicole Tyson started their nonprofit farm after their young son was diagnosed with cancer and they chose dietary change as an alternative to chemotherapy. The farm also supplies produce to the hospital's restaurant. Cancer patients from CTCA visit the farm for tours and to fish in its pond.

*Another CTCA facility, this one located at the **Western Regional Medical Center** near Phoenix, Arizona, actually established an organic farm in 2011 specifically for the purpose of providing its patients with healthier food. As the first cancer hospital in the country to raise organic produce on-site and year-round on 25 acres of its campus, CTCA partnered with **McClendon's Select**, a large family-run, certified-organic farm in Peoria, Arizona. Thanks in part to the dedication of CTCA nutrition director Sharon Day and executive chef Frank Caputo, this unique arrangement enables the farm and the hospital's nutrition therapy department and culinary services program to work together to provide fresh, nutrient-rich produce to help keep patients strong during cancer treatment.*

*Hospitals and other healthcare facilities also connect the public with locally grown food by serving as host sites for local farmers markets, as **Kaiser Permanente** has done in many states, and through partnering with CSA farms for purchase of shares by their staff. In Portland, Oregon, **Sauvie Island Organics**, a 700-member CSA farm offers share pickup for **Providence Health & Services** employees at four locations, two of which are open to nonemployees with season shares as well. Staff can pay for full-season CSA shares through automatic payroll deductions.*

As institutions seek to increase their percentage of locally grown

1 pound Italian sausage (we like to mix spicy and sweet varieties)
2 cups of your favorite pasta sauce (or make the Simple Red Sauce recipe below)
½ cup ricotta cheese
½ cup shredded mozzarella cheese (plus extra for topping)
2 tablespoons chopped fresh basil

1. Preheat the oven to 400°F.

2. Wash the spaghetti squash, cut off the stem, and slice the squash lengthwise. Scoop out the seeds and stringy fibers. Brush the inside of the squash with the olive oil, season with salt and pepper, and place it, cut side down, in a 9-by-13-inch baking dish with a little water in the bottom of the dish. (As the squash cooks, you can add more water if the pan gets dry.)

3. Roast the squash for 45 to 60 minutes, depending on the squash's size, or until the inside is soft and easily fluffs with a fork (it will look like very tiny spaghetti noodles).

4. While the squash is roasting, brown the Italian sausage in a large skillet (if you're using sausage links, remove the meat from the casings) over medium heat. Remove the sausage from the pan and set aside, but save the drippings in the pan for the next step.

5. If you are using a jarred pasta sauce, add it to the pan now and bring it to a simmer. (If you chose to make the sauce recipe below, use the drippings in the pan instead of the olive oil to start your sauce.) Add the sausage back into the sauce and simmer it for 15 to 30 minutes to let the flavors blend.

6. In a bowl, combine the ricotta, mozzarella, and basil. Set aside.

7. When the squash is tender, remove it from the oven. Using a fork, scoop, fluff, flake, and scrape to get the inside of the squash to look like spaghetti noodles. You don't have to get at all of the squash—you can scoop more later when you're enjoying it for dinner.

8. Now to fill them! Start with a scoop of the red sauce, followed by a layer of the cheese mixture (you can add extra mozzarella on each layer too). Repeat the layers until you've overfilled your squash, ending with a layer of red sauce and then topping each half with more mozzarella.

9. Turn the oven to the broil setting. Place the squash back into the oven until the cheesy top bubbles and turns brown. Cut each half into three pieces and serve.

SIMPLE RED SAUCE

2 to 3 tablespoons extra-virgin olive oil
1 small yellow onion, diced
1 rib celery, diced
2 garlic cloves, minced
1 (28-ounce) can crushed tomatoes

food, they can get sourcing help through regional food hub organizations located across the country. Some of the best expertise on hubs comes from the National Good Food Network, which comprises producers, buyers, distributors, advocates, investors, and funders working together "to create a community dedicated to scaling up good food sourcing and access."

Books

Local Flavors: Cooking and Eating
from America's Farmers' Markets
Deborah Madison,
Broadway Books, 2002.

The Broad Fork: Recipes
for the Wide World
of Vegetables and Fruits
Hugh Acheson, Clarkson Potter, 2015.

The CSA Cookbook: No-Waste
Recipes for Cooking Your Way
Through a Community Supported
Agriculture Box, Farmers' Market, or
Backyard Bounty
Linda Ly, Voyageur Press, 2015.

From Asparagus to Zucchini:
A Guide to Cooking Farm-Fresh
Seasonal Produce
FairShare CSA Coalition
and Doug Wubben,
FairShare CSA Coalition, 2004.

The Farmer's Kitchen:
The Ultimate Guide to Enjoying Your
CSA and Farmers' Market Foods
Julia Shanks and Brett Grohsgal
CreateSpace, 2012.

Farm-Fresh and Fast: Easy Recipes
and Tips for Making the Most of
Fresh, Seasonal Foods
FairShare CSA Coalition,
FairShare CSA Coalition, 2013.

Cooking Your Local Produce:
A Cookbook for Tackling Farmers
Markets, CSA Boxes, and
Your Own Backyard
Greta Hardin,
Ward Street Press, 2013.

The Farmer's Market Cookbook:
Seasonal Dishes Made from Nature's
Freshest Ingredients
Richard Ruben,
The Lyons Press, 2000.

4 ounces (½ cup) tomato sauce
Salt and freshly ground black pepper
3 fresh basil leaves, chopped

1. Heat the olive oil over medium-high heat.

2. Add the onion and celery and sauté for 4 to 5 minutes, until they start to soften. Add the garlic and sauté for 30 seconds, stirring frequently. Stir in the tomatoes and tomato sauce. Season to taste with salt and pepper. Reduce the heat and simmer while roasting the squash (probably 30 to 45 minutes), or until the sauce has thickened and the flavors have come together.

3. Add the fresh basil at the very end of cooking.

— *Sarah Nielsen,* Celiac in the City *blog*

Bins of winter squash at Featherstone Farm.

SPAGHETTI SQUASH PAD THAI   SERVES 2

Source Note: This is a great idea from one of our volunteers. Although the texture of spaghetti squash is not really spaghetti-ish, it is quite similar to Thai rice noodles. In this recipe, the squash actually makes a decent stand-in for the noodles. Add sautéed greens to the dish if you like.

2 tablespoons lime juice
2 tablespoons fish sauce
1 tablespoon soy sauce
1 to 2 tablespoons brown sugar
1 tablespoon chili sauce
½ cup dry-roasted peanuts, finely chopped, divided,
    plus more for garnish
1 tablespoon vegetable oil
1 large handful bean sprouts

½ medium onion, thinly sliced
2 cloves garlic, minced
2 eggs, beaten
½ medium spaghetti squash, cooked and separated into strands
Cilantro, for garnish
Lime wedges, for garnish

1. In a bowl, mix together the lime juice, fish sauce, soy sauce, sugar, chili sauce, and half of the peanuts. Set aside.

2. In a large saucepan, heat the oil over medium heat. Stir-fry the bean sprouts, onion, and garlic for 1 to 2 minutes. Move the vegetables to the side of the pan and pour in the beaten eggs. Wait until the eggs are mostly set and then stir them to scramble.

3. Add about half of the lime juice mixture to the pan; once it begins to bubble, add the squash. Toss gently to coat. Taste for seasoning, adding more of the lime juice mixture as needed. Garnish with extra peanuts, cilantro, and lime wedges, and serve immediately.

— *Sara Jones, Tucson CSA, Tucson, Arizona*

Sweet Potatoes   IPOMOEA BATATAS

When it comes to sweet potatoes in the United States, misconceptions and even culinary abuse abound. One issue is that both fresh and canned forms are commonly mislabeled as yams. True yams are botanically unrelated; they are massive, starchy tubers that bear little resemblance to sweet potatoes and can weigh as much as 150 pounds each. Yams are also rarely seen outside Africa and Latin America. Sweet potatoes are also totally unrelated to regular potatoes. As anyone who has seen flowering sweet potato plants might suspect, they are part of the morning glory family (Convolvulaceae), whereas potatoes are members of the tomato family (Solanaceae), which also contains eggplants, peppers, tobacco, and deadly nightshade.

Too often in the American kitchen, sweet potatoes are not allowed to shine on their own, meaning that many recipes featuring them also call for massive quantities of sugar, honey, syrup, and molasses. Although the sugar content of sweet potatoes can vary widely, the moist-fleshed varieties (more on that in a minute) are usually consistently sweet enough that they don't need much assistance in that department. Adding more sugary ingredients can therefore result in an effect that is heavy and cloying, not complementary.

In America, sweet potatoes are used as animal feed, a source of commercial starch, and a vegetable that humans enjoy. "Sweets" for people typically are classified as either moist-fleshed or dry-fleshed, which is really an indicator of how sweet or starchy (respectively) they taste rather than their actual moisture content. Both types come in a range of colors—the traditional orange-fleshed American varieties (the most common, with orange or garnet skins), Japanese and Korean ivory-fleshed cultivars (sometimes with red and rose skins), and miscellaneous white-fleshed varieties whose flavor varies from honey-like to fairly bland. A Hawaiian variety features flesh that turns lilac when cooked, and in Florida you may find the boniato, a knobby red-skinned tuber that is quite starchy (similar to regular potatoes) and is used mostly in savory dishes.

HISTORY

Sweet potatoes hail from Central America, where they were cultivated for many thousands of years before Christopher Columbus brought them (along with corn and regular potatoes) back with him to Spain; from there, they traveled to the rest of Europe. Whereas it took 200 years for regular potatoes to catch on, sweet potatoes became an immediate hit. Interestingly, the sweet potato was cultivated in Polynesia, Hawaii, and New Zealand long before European contact, probably as a result of the Polynesians' maritime explorations to South America and back. In both colonial and Civil War times, the sweet potato was often one of the only foods to fill Americans' empty bellies. Along with peanuts and rice, sweet potatoes have been a staple crop in the South for generations. Nowadays Asia and Africa are major growers, with China alone producing 90 percent of the global crop, much of it for livestock feed.

Pigs and People Know a Good Leaf When They Eat One

In China, over 60 billion pounds of sweet potato plant leaves are used annually just to feed pigs.

Sweet potato leaves are tasty to humans, too, and very nutritious. They are cooked like spinach but are more tender and mild-tasting. Look for them at farmers and Asian markets, especially in the American South, Hawaii, and Florida.

NUTRITION

Sweet potatoes are nutrition powerhouses. Not surprisingly, orange-fleshed varieties contain enormous amounts of beta-carotene—and thus vitamin A. They are rich in vitamin C, most of the B vitamins, calcium, iron, magnesium, phosphorus, potassium, copper, and manganese; they also contain significant amounts of protein and dietary fiber. A single-cup serving of baked sweet potato contains 180 calories.

SEASON

Commercially, sweet potatoes are widely grown and available year-round. But their peak season at farmers markets and CSAs is in the fall. Sweet potatoes may be one of the staples in your winter CSA share.

SELECTION

A good sweet potato is heavy for its size and free from any signs of shriveling or soft or moldy spots. Apart from these factors, it's pretty tough to tell a great sweet potato from a mediocre one—size, sheen (or the lack of it), and color are not necessarily reliable indicators of density and sweetness.

STORAGE

Raw sweet potatoes do not store as well as you might think. They should not be put in the refrigerator, as this actually hastens their spoilage. If you have a dark, cool, well-ventilated place where you won't forget about them, stash them there. Or keep them at room temperature; in either case, use them as soon as possible. If sprouts develop, just rub or cut them out, and use the rest of the sweet right away.

TRIMMING AND CLEANING

The most preparation that sweet potatoes usually require is a thorough scrubbing with a vegetable brush—and peeling, if desired, although their flavor is better if they are baked in their skins.

STEAMING AND BOILING

Place whole, washed, unpeeled sweet potatoes in a steamer basket over rapidly boiling water and steam them for 40 to 50 minutes, or until tender when pierced with a fork. Alternatively, quarter unpeeled sweet potatoes and steam for about 20 minutes. You can also boil whole unpeeled sweet potatoes for 35 to 45 minutes, but keep in mind that boiling tends to leach out flavor and produces a more watery vegetable. Exact cooking times vary widely, depending on the size and shape of the sweet potato; always test cooked sweets with an inserted fork or knife to be sure they are done.

STIR-FRYING AND SAUTÉING

Stir-frying and sautéing are usually not the first cooking methods that come to mind when preparing sweet potatoes, but they are delicious prepared this way, either by themselves or in combination with other vegetables and plenty of fresh herbs and spices.

For these cooking methods, sweet potatoes cook faster and more evenly if they are sliced very thinly, julienned, or shredded. Stir-fry or

One Potato, Two Potato … Then 500

The African-American scientist and educator George Washington Carver developed hundreds of uses for the humble sweet potato, including 73 dyes, 17 wood fillers, 14 candies, 5 library pastes, 5 breakfast foods, 4 starches, 4 flours, and 3 varieties of molasses.

Books

The Sweet Potato Lover's Cookbook: More than 100 Ways to Enjoy One of the World's Healthiest Foods Lyniece North Talmadge. Cumberland House, 2010.

Louisiana Sweet Potato Commission website (recipes) www.sweetpotato.org

sauté on medium-high heat in oil or butter (use 4 to 6 tablespoons for every 2 pounds of sweets) for 5 to 7 minutes, or until they reach the desired tenderness and are golden brown.

BAKING AND ROASTING

Baking turns sweet potatoes into rich, creamy, sweet gold, and they are incredibly simple to prepare. Resist the urge to wrap sweet potatoes in aluminum foil; this only results in steamed potatoes with soggy, wet skins and flesh.

Place whole, scrubbed, unpeeled sweet potatoes in a baking pan or directly on the oven rack, and pierce their skins several times to allow steam to escape (unless you want a possible explosion to enliven your day). Baking times vary, depending on the sweet potato's size, but a large sweet will usually take 40 to 50 minutes in a 400°F oven. Test by inserting the point of a sharp knife into the center of the potato; if the blade meets no resistance, the hapless tuber is done.

Roasting sweet potatoes concentrates their flavor and further caramelizes their sugars. Some cooks recommend parboiling sweets for 1 to 3 minutes first to soften them. Then toss them with oil and seasoning and place them in a 425°F oven for 30 to 40 minutes, or a 350°F oven for 45 to 55 minutes. Turn them occasionally to prevent scorching.

MICROWAVING

Microwaving is not the best way to prepare sweet potatoes; baking or roasting is really preferable, as these cooking methods yield a drier, more flavorful vegetable. However, it can be much quicker to use the microwave if you are in a hurry or are preparing sweets for pureeing.

To prepare whole sweet potatoes for microwaving, puncture them a few times with a fork to prevent explosions; then place them on a paper towel or directly on the oven plate. Microwave on high power. At the end of the cooking time, insert a knife into the center of the potato. If the knife sticks or meets resistance, cook the potatoes for another 1 or 2 minutes, then let them stand for 5 minutes. They will finish cooking during the standing time. Alternatively, cut them into chunks, toss them with melted butter or oil, place them in a covered dish, and microwave on high power until tender.

- 1 whole sweet potato = 8 minutes
- 1 pound chunks cut into 1½-inch pieces = 5 minutes

BLANCHING AND FREEZING

Raw sweet potatoes do not respond well to freezing; they will discolor and their texture will deteriorate. Mashed sweet potato, however, does freeze splendidly. Boil, steam, or bake the sweets as indicated in the instructions above and remove the skins. Mash the pulp or run it through a food processor, then package the potatoes in zipper-lock freezer or vacuum food sealer-type bags, or freezer containers. Squeeze out any excess air and leave ½ inch of headspace (unless you are using the vacuum sealing method). Frozen sweet potatoes will keep for up to 12 months at 0°F.

EQUIVALENTS, MEASURES, AND SERVINGS

- 3 sweet potatoes (about 5 inches long by 2 inches wide) = 1 pound
- ½ pound sweet potatoes = 2 cups grated
- 1 pound sweet potatoes = 1 to 1¼ cups pureed

COMPLEMENTARY HERBS, SEASONINGS, AND FOODS

Allspice, anise, apples, apple cider vinegar, black pepper, bourbon, brown sugar, butter, cardamom, carrots, chiles, cilantro, cinnamon, coconut butter, coconut milk, coriander, cranberries, curry, fennel, garlic, ginger, hazelnuts, honey, horseradish, kale, lamb, lime, maple syrup, miso, molasses, nutmeg, onions, oranges, peanuts, peanut oil, pork, raisins, rosemary, rum, sage, sesame, shallots, shrimp, smoked salt, tangerines, thyme, vinegar, walnuts, yogurt.

SERVING SUGGESTIONS

- A plain baked sweet potato adorned with a little seasoning of one's choice is one of life's simple pleasures. It makes a handy snack, small meal, or lunchbox treat.

- Puree sweet potatoes to make thick, unctuous soups.

- Although we often associate sweet potatoes with dishes flavored with maple syrup, cinnamon, and marshmallows, don't be afraid to try them with savory ingredients too, like horseradish, black pepper, chiles, and leafy greens.

- Finely shred raw sweet potato and add it as a garnish to soups and salads, as you would carrots.

- Make pie with sweet potatoes, similar to pumpkin; both have an affinity with the same sweet spices. Try lime as a surprise flavoring.

- Indian cuisine makes use of sweet potatoes in curries containing beef and pork; season them with curry powder, cloves, cinnamon, chiles, and cardamom.

- Thinly slice sweet potatoes and fry them into crisp chips.

- Cooked sweet potatoes are surprisingly good as the main ingredient in ice cream. Use sugar, dark rum, vanilla extract, egg yolks, milk, and heavy cream to complete the recipe. Or combine sweet potatoes with coconut milk, sugar or honey, and vanilla for delicious ice pops.

- Make yummy pancakes from sweet potatoes—add the pureed potatoes to your favorite pancake batter along with sweet spices for a breakfast surprise. It works great for waffles too!

- Sweet potatoes are delectable as an ingredient in beignets, those light, elegant balls of fried dough that are half cruller, half fritter. They are also versatile in cakes, biscuits, and breads.

- Combine with leftover mashed white potatoes and fry in butter for potato cakes.

- Sweet potatoes and tomatoes together make a delicious, unusual soup.

MOTHER AFRICA'S SPICY KALE AND YAM   SERVES 4

Author Note: The term "yam" is something of a misnomer; in America it refers to an orange-fleshed, moist, sweet potato, whereas the rest of the world knows yams as enormous tubers that measure several feet long, can weigh over

---

GMOs: A Complicated Issue

Mi Ae Lipe

Few topics elicit such immediate and polarizing opinions as GMOs, or genetically modified organisms. The topic is a complicated one that deserves more rational, constructive debate than it is often afforded.

First, what exactly are GMOs? They are organisms (both plants and animals) in which genetic material has been artificially inserted, deleted, or mutated using biotechnology.

In a sense, there is nothing new about gene tinkering; humans have been selectively breeding plants and animals to develop desirable traits in appearance, taste, resistance to disease, and climate adaptation for thousands of years. What makes genetic modification different is that it exponentially speeds up the laborious and time-intensive breeding process, and it also allows genes of completely nonrelated species to be combined, such as those of spiders with goats, or anchovies with tomatoes.

The uses of GMOs go beyond the obvious; they trigger many biological processes that help create food ingredients, medicines, biofuels, growth hormones, and enzymes. Zebrafish and salmon were the first patented animals to be genetically engineered for use as food and environmental sensors, respectively.

Since their inception in the 1970s, GMOs have stirred immense controversy. GMOs are far less regulated in the United States than in most other countries, including those in the European Union, Japan, and Australia, where they are either banned or severely restricted. Nearly 90 percent of the corn and up to 94 percent of the soybeans grown in America are genetically modified. Food ingredients derived from these two crops alone are present in nearly all the processed foods in the United States, but many consumers are unaware of them.

So what, exactly, is the big fuss? There is the widely held belief that GMOs are innately more harmful to our health. As of 2015, results of major scientific studies have not borne this out, although GMO opponents point out that some of this research is funded by the very companies that profit from GMO creation and sales. Much more—and unbiased—research remains to be conducted, especially over the long term.

Much of the controversy over GMOs lies in their development, distribution, and regulation, and the lack of transparency therein. It is important to remember that most GMOs in and of themselves are not harmful; in fact, many of them can effect significant good, such as providing additional nutrients (increased beta-carotene in strains of rice) and offering vaccine-like resistance to devastating diseases that have no cure (papayas in Hawaii).

But the ethics and integrity of GMOs are seriously compromised when the financial motives of multinational agricultural companies drive their regulation, distribution, and marketing. It is no surprise that these corporations make enormous profits from GMO crop development and the sale of seed, sometimes to farmers who are not entirely informed of the consequences and drawbacks. Along with powerful food manufacturers and related entities that have a stake in GMO products, the lobbying power of these companies in pushing regulation—and scientific research—that favors them is formidable indeed.

In the late 1990s, Monsanto developed varieties of soybeans and corn that are resistant to the herbicide Roundup (which it also developed). This means that farmers can use Roundup to control weeds in their fields without harming their crops, but because these GMO plants are sterile, farmers must buy new seed every year from Monsanto instead of being able to save seed from their previous year's crop. In

100 pounds, and have a firmer, drier, creamy white flesh. The garnet yams in this recipe are sweet potatoes with distinctive purplish-red skins.

Nama shoyu is a type of unpasteurized soy sauce that is naturally aged for several years in cedar kegs, giving it a much more full-bodied flavor and complex bouquet than regular soy sauce. It can be found in natural foods stores and through online retailers.

If you plan to serve this dish a day or two after preparing it, wait to add the yams until just before heating and serving. They tend to discolor and appear brownish as all the vegetables sit together.

1 large bunch kale, thickest stems removed
    (about 4 cups chopped and firmly packed)
1½ pounds garnet yams, peeled, rinsed, and chopped
    (about 4 cups)
1½ tablespoons olive oil
1½ cups chopped onion
1 tablespoon minced garlic
1 tablespoon peeled, minced fresh ginger
1 teaspoon seeded, diced serrano chile
2 cups sliced purple cabbage
3 tablespoons *nama shoyu* soy sauce (or use regular soy sauce)
1 teaspoon sea salt, or to taste
Abba's African Hot Sauce (recipe below)

1. Rinse and drain the kale well. Steam the kale until it is soft but still colorful, about 5 minutes. Steam the yams until they're cooked through (they should retain some firmness).

2. While the kale and yams are steaming, heat the olive oil in a large saucepan over medium-high heat. Add the onion, garlic, ginger, and serrano chile. Cook for 5 minutes, stirring frequently.

3. Add the cabbage and cook for 5 more minutes, stirring frequently. (Add small amounts of water if necessary to prevent sticking.)

4. Place the cabbage mixture in a large bowl with the soy sauce and salt; add the kale and mix well. Add the yams and gently mix. Serve with Abba's African Hot Sauce (recipe follows).

— *Gladys, The Recipe Link*

. . . .

ABBA'S AFRICAN HOT SAUCE   MAKES ABOUT 2 CUPS

Author Note: If you want to make a milder sauce, increase the amount of green bell pepper in proportion to the amount of hot peppers suggested—or, if you'd like to bump up the heat, add one or two habanero peppers. This sauce is really tasty and versatile; it would be just as perfectly delicious with scrambled eggs or beef tacos as it is with the African vegetable dish above.

1 cup filtered water or stock

8 to 10 assorted hot peppers, chopped
   (such as serrano or jalapeño, about ½ cup total)
1 medium green bell pepper, diced (about ¾ cup)
1½ teaspoons minced garlic
⅓ cup chopped shallots, or ½ cup chopped green onions
¼ cup tomato paste
2 tablespoons apple cider vinegar, preferably raw
1 teaspoon freshly ground black pepper
1 teaspoon sea salt
¼ teaspoon cardamom powder
¼ teaspoon cayenne powder

Place all of the ingredients in a blender and blend until smooth. Place in a small saucepan on low heat and cook for about 20 minutes, stirring frequently, until the sauce has thickened and darkened a bit.

— *Gladys, The Recipe Link*

SWEET POTATO CUSTARD

SERVES 6

Source Note: Sweet potatoes and bananas combine to make a flavorful, low-fat custard made with evaporated skim milk and no added fat.

1 cup cooked, mashed sweet potato
½ cup mashed banana (about 2 small)
1 cup evaporated milk
2 tablespoons packed brown sugar
2 egg yolks, beaten, or ⅓ cup egg substitute
½ teaspoon salt
Nonstick cooking spray
¼ cup raisins
1 tablespoon sugar
1 teaspoon ground cinnamon

1. Preheat the oven to 325°F.

2. In a medium bowl, stir together the sweet potato and banana.

3. Add the milk, blending well. Add the brown sugar, egg yolks, and salt, mixing thoroughly.

4. Spread a thin coat of butter in a 1-quart casserole or spray it with nonstick cooking spray. Transfer the sweet potato mixture to the casserole dish.

5. Combine the raisins, sugar, and cinnamon; sprinkle over the top of the sweet potato mixture.

6. Bake for 40 to 45 minutes, or until a knife inserted in the center comes out clean.

— *Health.gov*

this scenario, it is not hard to piece together a profit motive. And recent cases of Monsanto aggressively penalizing non–GMO-crop farmers whose fields were found to have their individual GMO plants growing in them as a result of wind contamination have been well-publicized. Also questionable is Monsanto's incentivizing of farmers in developing countries such as India to grow its crops, which often results in financial exploitation.

Opponents of GMOs rightly criticize these strong-arm tactics and shaky ethics, as well as corporate influence on regulatory agencies. As consumers, we should be wary of such practices. And we should remember that this goes for any entity that has a part in raising, processing, or manufacturing the food we eat—not just GMO companies.

Another big problem with GMOs is cross-contamination of non–GMO-crop fields via wind-carried pollen. It is difficult enough to find suitable land for farming, but many organic farmers seeking certification find it impossible if their fields are next to GMO farms.

Supporters of GMOs point out their tremendous potential in feeding the world's rapidly increasing population, particularly in the face of climate change, less arable land, and the changing diets of emerging middle-class populations in developing countries. These are very real issues that are not within the realm of the abstract; millions of people suffer from chronic malnutrition and die of starvation annually.

The question of whether GMOs should be labeled as such is a major issue, one that draws lightning from both sides. On the one hand, labeling advocates say the public deserves to know what is in their food, and that extends to whether it contains GMO crops or ingredients, which may or may not prove to have harmful health and environmental effects. On the other hand, opponents fear that consumers who haven't educated themselves about GMOs will needlessly boycott whole categories of foods based on knee-jerk reactions and rumor.

An interesting issue with GMOs was brought up by one CSA farmer featured in this book. He spoke about trying to "do the right thing" in growing non-GMO sweet corn versus another strain that had been genetically modified to be inedible for a certain type of earworm that, although harmless, lives in and disfigures the ears. This would not be a problem if he were growing the corn for canning or other applications where it would be processed. But customers do not react well when they see live caterpillars curled up in their food; they have become accustomed to picture-perfect fruits and vegetables and demand product that matches expectations.

When this farmer tried growing the non-GMO corn, he found that about six applications of pesticide were required to combat the earworm. Because his customers expect to enjoy sweet corn over a number of months, he grows it in staggered plantings over several fields. His farmworkers had to track how often they needed to spray all their cornfields—and then actually apply it numerous times. Soon they began worrying about the health effects of such repeated exposure, not to mention the pesticide residues for consumers eating that corn. Was it really worth it just for the sake of being GMO-free?

The debate about GMOs often comes down to fundamental disagreements on what food systems are truly sustainable to meet the needs of our planet and humanity, as well as financial motive, greed, and mistrust. Public opinion, fueled by misinformation and rumor-mongering, often trumps objective science and rational debate. World hunger and sustainable food systems will need to be addressed through a variety of solutions—no single method will solve them all.

SWEET POTATO AND CARROT LATKES   MAKES 25 LATKES

Author Note: This is a different take on the savory potato pancake known as the latke, using sweet potatoes and carrots.

1 pound sweet potatoes, peeled and coarsely grated
1 to 2 carrots, finely grated
½ bunch cilantro, finely chopped
3 scallions (green onions), finely chopped
½ cup all-purpose flour
2 large eggs, lightly beaten
½-inch piece peeled ginger, finely diced
¾ teaspoon salt
½ teaspoon black pepper
Pinch of cinnamon
½ cup vegetable oil, plus more as needed

1. Combine the grated sweet potatoes and carrots, then add the cilantro, scallions, flour, eggs, ginger, salt, pepper, and cinnamon. Mix everything together until the mixture has a sticky but not gluey consistency. You may have to adjust the flour and egg quantities, depending on how big your eggs are.

2. Heat the oil in a deep 12-inch nonstick skillet over moderately high heat until hot but not smoking. Using a slotted spatula and working in batches of 4, spoon 2 tablespoons of the potato mixture per latke into the oil and flatten it to a 3-inch round. Reduce the heat to moderate and cook until golden, about 2 minutes on each side. Transfer the latkes to paper towels to drain.

3. Repeat until the batter is used up, adding more oil as needed. Remember to bring the oil back up to a fairly hot temperature before adding more latkes; if the oil isn't hot enough, they'll cook more slowly and soak up more oil.

4. If you plan to serve the latkes warm, shuttle them to a preheated 300°F oven. Serve with homemade applesauce!

— *Lucy, Sang Lee Farms, Peconic, New York*

Turnips

BRASSICA RAPA, RAPIFERA GROUP

Like their cruciferous cousins cabbage and rutabagas, turnips have a ways to go before they reach the gastronomical cachet of, say, artichokes or asparagus. This is a shame, because they can make a fine root vegetable provided that they are not too tough or cooked too long, which tends to render them smelly, watery, and tasteless.

The turnips that are most familiar to Americans (and about the only ones commercially available in the United States) have white roots whose upper third portion is tinted a light purple. But beautiful heirloom turnips exist whose skins come in a multitude of colors, from gold and green to rose and nearly black.

Rutabagas and turnips are often confused with each other, for their roots may share nearly identical exterior coloring. Turnips, however, tend to be smaller and smoother, with flesh that usually cooks up pure white, whereas rutabagas are thicker and more elongated, with rough-textured skin and flesh that is golden yellow when cooked.

The root is not the only edible part of the turnip; its greens are a nutritional powerhouse and a proper vegetable in their own right. They are, however, a bit too fuzzy to eat raw and should be added to stir-fries or soups, or slow-cooked southern-style with salty, cured parts of the savory pig.

HISTORY

The turnip is believed to have originated in northern Europe over 4,000 years ago, and even back then, it was soon relegated to the tables of the poor. In fact, around 1500 BCE, the Aryans passed a law that the turnip should never soil the lips of the noble classes (along with beans, garlic, onions, and mushrooms). Over the centuries Europeans used lowly turnips as livestock food, as weapons to be hurled at outcasts, and as sustenance food. But in India, China, and the Middle East, the vegetable was treated with far more respect, often pickled, sun-dried, and sautéed in savory dishes.

By the early 1600s, turnips were already growing in Virginia and Massachusetts. Subsequently the Native Americans took such a liking to them that an American general destroyed an extensive turnip field in New York in 1779 as a tactical raid into their territory.

NUTRITION

Like other cruciferous vegetables, both turnip greens and roots are extremely nutritious, containing vitamin C, potassium, iron, thiamine, magnesium, folate, copper, and dietary fiber. Turnips also contain abundant phytonutrients such as sulforaphane and indoles, which have been proven in studies to fight cancer, especially prostate, colorectal, and lung. Turnip greens are extremely rich in vitamins A, C, and K. A single medium turnip contains 34 calories.

SEASON

Commercially, turnips are widely grown and in season year-round. But they are typically at their best in the fall and spring months, when they are smaller and sweeter. Turnips are frequently offered in winter CSA shares.

SELECTION

Choose turnips that are firm and evenly colored, with fresh green tops. Avoid specimens that are shriveled, have wilted or yellowing leaves, or have cracked or blemished roots. Overly large specimens may be woody.

STORAGE

Turnip greens should be detached from their roots (if they come together) and stored separately, tightly wrapped in a plastic bag and stored in the refrigerator vegetable crisper. The greens will keep for a few days this way, whereas the roots may keep for up to 1 to 2 weeks.

The roots will also keep quite well in a basement, root cellar, or other place with the proper cool temperature and lack of humidity (for more information, see "Preserving the Bounty" on page 611).

TRIMMING AND CLEANING

Turnips must be peeled before eating. Trim off the leafy tops (save them for cooking later, if desired), then use a paring knife or a sharp vegetable peeler to cut off the thick outer skin. To remove traces of grit, sand, and insects lurking in turnip greens, the leaves must be thoroughly washed by submerging them in a sinkful of water and swishing well, then draining and rinsing again if necessary.

STEAMING AND BOILING

Steam whole, peeled or unpeeled turnips for 15 to 20 minutes, depending on their size, and sliced turnips for 5 to 10 minutes, or until tender when pierced with a fork. Boil cubed, peeled turnips for 15 to 30 minutes, then drain. Some cooks add a whole peeled potato to the boiling water to absorb the bitter flavor that older turnips often have.

STIR-FRYING AND SAUTÉING

Stir-fry or sauté turnips, cut into ½-inch cubes, in a well-oiled pan or wok over high heat for about 8 minutes, or until crisp-tender. Turnip greens can be sautéed after a quick parboiling for 2 to 7 minutes, depending on their size and thickness.

BAKING AND ROASTING

Bake whole, peeled turnips in a 350°F oven for 20 to 30 minutes, depending on their size. Or prepare and season like oven-roasted potatoes (see the instructions on page 572).

BRAISING AND STEWING

To braise turnips, trim and peel them, cut them into uniform sizes, and cook in butter or pan juices for 10 to 15 minutes over medium heat, or until they are lightly colored and tender.

Microwaving

Trim and peel 2 cups of turnip, cutting into ¼-inch-thick slices. Place them in a covered dish with ¼ cup water and microwave on high power until tender, 10 to 15 minutes, stirring every 5 minutes. Let stand 5 minutes before serving.

Blanching and Freezing

Cube or slice the turnips into ½-inch-thick pieces, boil for 2 to 3 minutes, then plunge them into ice water for 5 minutes to stop the cooking process. Remove and drain. Package the turnips in zipper-lock freezer or vacuum food sealer-type bags, or freezer containers. Squeeze out any excess air and leave ½ inch of headspace (unless you are using the vacuum sealing method). Frozen turnips will keep for up to 6 months at 0°F.

Equivalents, Measures, and Servings

- 3 medium turnips = 1 pound = 2½ cups chopped

Complementary Herbs, Seasonings, and Foods

Apples, bacon, bay, beef, broccoli raab, butter, carrots, cheese (Gruyère, Gorgonzola, Gouda, Cheddar), chicken, chives, cider, cinnamon, cream, cream sauces, duck, fennel, garlic, ghee, lamb, leeks, lemon, lemon thyme, maple syrup, miso, mushrooms, mustard, nuts, onions, paprika, parsley, peas, pork, potatoes, rosemary, sausages, sherry, squash, sugar, sweet potatoes, tarragon, thyme, turmeric, vinaigrette, vinegar, watercress.

Serving Suggestions

- Turnips pair best with hearty meats and vegetables; they are especially good slow-cooked by braising, baking, stewing, or roasting (this last method caramelizes the natural sugars and best brings out turnips' delicate flavors). Duck, pork, and beef are especially good with turnips.

- Prepare turnip greens southern-style, simmering for a couple hours with a piece of country ham, fatback, or salt pork.

- Add a little variety to the traditional corned beef and cabbage or a New England boiled dinner by adding turnips and celery root to the potatoes, carrots, and cabbage.

- For a twist, try preparing turnips with a cream sauce.

- Prepare turnips as you would mashed potatoes, mixing in plenty of butter, cream, and a touch of horseradish, cinnamon, or nutmeg if desired.

- Pair turnips with beets and potatoes, drizzle with olive oil mixed with garlic and fresh herbs, and bake them slowly in a 375°F oven for 45 minutes to 1 hour.

- Add cubes of turnips to beef and lamb stews.

- Slice very young, tender, raw baby turnips into thin rounds or sticks to add to the vegetable relish tray.

- Grate raw turnip into salads or slaws.

- Turnips are one of the traditional fillings for pasties, those little baked pastry shells filled with beef, carrots, onions, potatoes, or rutabagas.

- Pickling turnips is a delicious way to prepare this vegetable, especially combined with beets and hot peppers. This is a popular Middle Eastern dish.

- Indian and Pakistani cuisines make good use of turnips with vibrant seasonings, including *shaljam salan* (turnip curry), masala, and *poriyal*. Experiment and try something totally different!

"The turnip is a capricious vegetable, which seems reluctant to show itself at its best."

— *Waverley Root*, Food

Books

Roots: The Definitive Compendium with More than 225 Recipes
Diane Morgan,
Chronicle Books, 2012.

Vegetables, Revised: The Most Authoritative Guide to Buying, Preparing, and Cooking, with More than 300 Recipes
James Peterson,
Ten Speed Press, 2012.

POTATO AND TURNIP AU GRATIN WITH LEEKS   SERVES 6

1 cup whole milk
1 cup heavy cream
3 large cloves garlic, minced
Salt and freshly ground black pepper
2 tablespoons butter, divided
3 leeks (white section only), thoroughly washed and thinly sliced
1 pound Russet potatoes, peeled and thinly sliced
1 pound turnips, peeled and thinly sliced
2 cups shredded Gruyère cheese

1. Preheat the oven to 365°F.

2. In a saucepan set to medium heat, combine the milk, cream, and garlic; season to taste with salt and pepper. Do not boil. Decrease the heat and simmer for another 5 minutes, then set aside. (Do not be shy on the salt—it will help flavor the potatoes and turnips.)

3. In a small pan over medium heat, melt 1 tablespoon of the butter and add the leeks. Cook for 7 to 8 minutes, until the leeks start to brown, stirring frequently; then set aside.

4. Spread the remaining butter around a 9-by-13-inch baking dish, covering the bottom and sides. Arrange half of the potatoes, then half of the turnips in the dish, lightly seasoning each layer with salt and pepper. Add 1 cup of the Gruyère cheese and the cooked leeks on top of this layer. Pour enough of the cream mixture over the top to just barely cover.

5. Repeat with the remaining potatoes and turnips, again seasoning lightly with salt and pepper. Top with the remaining cheese, and drizzle the rest of the cream mixture on top, making sure to moisten everything evenly.

6. Bake for 40 to 45 minutes, until the top is golden brown and the vegetables can be pierced easily with a sharp knife.

— *David Cannata, Yolo Catering; Davis Farmers Market, Davis, California*

HAKUREI TURNIP SALAD   SERVES 2

Source Note: Hakurei turnips are a small, round, white Japanese variety. They have a crispy sweet peppery taste with a hint of a fruity flavor. They pair well with pears, apples, dried fruits, and nuts. I prefer to eat them raw in a salad, but they are also good roasted. If you don't have all of the ingredients for this salad, improvise with what you have.

DRESSING

2 tablespoons balsamic vinegar
1 tablespoon honey
Sea salt and freshly ground black pepper
3 tablespoons extra-virgin olive oil

SALAD

1 cup pecans
2 tablespoons maple syrup
Hakurei turnip greens, coarsely chopped
Other mixed salad greens (optional)
1 bunch Hakurei turnips, peeled and thinly sliced

1. To make the dressing, mix together the balsamic vinegar, honey, sea salt, and pepper. Slowly whisk in the olive oil until the dressing thickens. Set aside.

2. Preheat the oven to 375°F. In a bowl, add the pecans and maple syrup. Mix well. Place the pecans in a single layer on a cookie sheet and bake until they are golden and crispy. Transfer the pecans to a plate, spread them into a single layer, and place them in the freezer (this step enhances their texture). Be sure to seal the nuts in an airtight container—this will help avoid stickiness as they thaw.

3. To serve, place a single serving of the greens on plates, add the turnips, and drizzle the dressing over the top. Lastly, sprinkle some of the baked pecans over the salad.

— Luisa DePaiva, Purple Rain Vineyard, Vancouver, Washington

BROCCOLI WITH BABY WHITE TURNIP AND GARLIC SCAPES DRESSING

SERVES 4

1 bunch baby white turnips
1 bunch garlic scapes, finely chopped
½ cup olive oil, divided
Salt and freshly ground black pepper
1 bunch sautéed broccoli, for serving

1. Preheat the oven to 375°F.

2. Wash the turnips and cut off the leaves (chop them coarsely and reserve them for using later on in the recipe).

3. Place the scapes and turnips on a cookie sheet. Drizzle 2 tablespoons of the olive oil over the turnips and scapes, and roast for 45 minutes. (If the scapes are browning faster than the turnips, remove them when they're golden brown and continue roasting the turnips until soft.)

With the exception of tomatoes, we grow mostly hybrids at Featherstone. Hybrids provide several big advantages to us as growers. For example, because less natural variability exists in hybrid seed genetics, our crops tend to mature more evenly in the field. This is important with, say, broccoli, where we have many succession plantings in the fall and need to be able to predict how much will be ready to pick in each successive patch every week.

Another example is traditional sweet corn, which is not naturally very sweet and tends to lose its sugars extremely quickly after harvesting. Our modern hybrids not only contain far more sugar, but they retain it for days after picking—something we all enjoy!

Also, do not underestimate cosmetic appeal—whether we like it or not, we depend on aesthetics for 80 percent of our sales at stores and even farmers markets.

Hybrid development can have very positive consequences as well. Consider the Sungold cherry tomato. It was originally bred in Italy for one trait only—its sublime sweet flavor with slight citrus undertones. This plant has no disease resistance, and its thin-skinned fruit routinely cracks and splits. For this reason, Sungolds never became commercially viable in California, because it could not be shipped for long distances—they split and leak even when they are in their boxes. So we started growing them for local markets and the CSAs with great success. Now a new hybrid—Sunsugar—has been developed, which is indistinguishable from the Sungold except that it sports a thicker skin that makes the fruit ship better. We are trying both—let's see if anyone notices the difference!

Heirloom tomatoes are all the rage now—we usually grow six to eight varieties in a given year, and they are extremely popular with our CSA subscribers and at the farmers markets. Again, the big advantage is flavor, which is often very distinct from variety to variety. Striped Germans and Brandywines are rich and sweet, while Cherokee Purples are more sharp and acid.

No doubt that the potential exists for heirlooms to be much better eating than the more typical hybrid reds, but growing conditions matter a lot too. During cool, wet summers, for example, heirlooms might not be as tasty. And there is the ever-constant problem with cosmetic appearance and shipping—heirlooms ripen much faster than hybrids—so careful, more time-consuming handling is even more important.

We continue to be open to trying more heirlooms in other crops—if our customers want them. Growing more would add more management effort for us—and hybrids work well for us on a mass scale. In many ways, from a strictly commercial cultivation standpoint, heirlooms seem basically better suited for the home gardener, where their special qualities and charms can be better appreciated.

4. Once the turnips and scapes are roasted and cooled, place them in a blender with the remaining olive oil and turnip leaves. Blend to a smooth consistency, add salt and pepper to taste, and serve over the sautéed broccoli.

— *Karolina Tracz, Nash's Organic Produce, Sequim, Washington*

ULTIMATE ROOT SOUP

SERVES 8

2 large leeks
1 large onion
3 ribs celery
1 large carrot
½ pound (2 medium) turnips
3 small Russet potatoes, peeled
4 tablespoons (½ stick) butter
3 cups shredded cabbage
Handful of chopped green garlic scapes
1½ teaspoons salt
1 pound (3 to 4 medium) beets, scrubbed, unpeeled
1 cup canned diced tomatoes
3 bay leaves
1 tablespoon sugar
8 cups water
Salt and freshly ground black pepper
3 tablespoons white or red wine vinegar
½ cup sour cream
1 tablespoon prepared horseradish
Finely chopped fresh dill

1. Wash, peel, and dice the leeks, onion, celery, carrot, turnips, and potatoes.

2. Melt the butter in a large pot over medium heat and add all of the diced vegetables, along with the cabbage and garlic scapes. Toss with the salt and cook for 20 minutes, or until the vegetables are tender. Set aside.

3. Julienne the beets, then place them in a 4-quart saucepot along with the tomatoes, bay leaves, and sugar. Add the water and simmer for 15 to 20 minutes, or until the beets are tender.

4. Add the beets to the other cooked vegetables. Season with salt and pepper to taste, and stir in the vinegar.

5. In a small bowl, mix the sour cream and horseradish until smooth. Serve the soup hot or cold, with a spoonful of the sour cream–horseradish mixture on top and a sprinkling of fresh dill.

— *Featherstone Farm, Rushford, Minnesota*

Preserving the Bounty

This section is by Larisa Walk, former bookkeeper and wholesale sales coordinator for Featherstone Farm. She is the author of A Pantry Full of Sunshine—Energy-Efficient Food Preservation Methods, *and the inventor of the Walk Solar Food Dryer. Her website is at www.GeoPathfinder.com.*

Frost, freeze, snow—all elements of the cycle of seasons here in Minnesota. But they do not have to signal the end of eating our locally grown delectables. By using a few tricks to mimic nature's goal of reproduction and survival, you can have fresh produce in winter that isn't trucked in from warmer climes.

Root cellaring is an age-old food preservation method that holds foods in a state of suspended animation or hibernation. For some veggies, this dormancy is part of their biennial life cycle, in which their second summer triggers seed production after wintering over in the ground, as long as the soil does not freeze hard. This is the case with carrots, beets, cabbage, celery, and onions, among others. For crops like potatoes, the dormant spuds remain viable, as this plant's strategy is to reproduce as clones from the tubers themselves. Squashes remain intact containers for their clusters of seeds until they are opened and dispersed by humans or other critters. If you understand a bit of botany, you can help the plant preserve itself.

Most people picture a root cellar as a structure set into a north-facing hillside, maybe with stone masonry work and a heavy, oak-plank door. While this would be an ideal set-up, how many of us have the location, space, materials, and building know-how to take advantage of the earth's natural coolness? While almost nobody has this resource available, most Americans already own a root cellaring device—an ordinary picnic cooler works wonderfully for temporary, portable, versatile, and flexible food storage options. Most coolers aren't used over the winter months anyway, and if you don't already own one, they are relatively inexpensive or can be found at garage sales. (If you get into this, you may want more than one—I have eight.)

Here is how to operate a cooler as a root cellar: For potatoes, carrots, beets, and other root crops (or apples), place your produce in the cooler and set it outside in the fall in a cool, shady spot, like the north side of your house, in a porch, or an unheated garage. This will work even when the nights are below freezing but are getting above 32°F during the day. When winter really starts to take hold, move the cooler to a less cold spot. An unheated entryway, outside cellar stairs, buried in a hole in the ground and covered with leaves, or an unheated basement—you may have to get creative to make use of the resources at hand. You can monitor the conditions inside your cooler by sticking an indoor/outdoor thermometer probe into the drain plug (stick some crumpled paper or fabric into the gap around the wire). Ideally the temperature should be 32°F to 40°F with a humidity level of 80 to 90 percent.

By shuffling your cooler to various positions around your abode, you can keep potatoes and other roots all winter (it is early June as I write this and I still have a few beets left). If things aren't spoiling, shriveling from lack of moisture, or sprouting from being too warm, then you are doing things right.

I use the term root cellaring loosely, as some fall veggies are not strictly roots, nor do they store well under cellar conditions. Squash do best in a warmer and drier setting, about 50°F to 60°F, with 60 percent humidity. These conditions can often be found in a spare room that is closed off from the rest of the house—a guestroom with some squash under the bed works well for some folks. Onions and garlic require the same humidity as squash, but prefer a bit cooler temperatures.

Do not worry if your conditions are not ideal—even fair conditions are going to extend your harvest longer than doing nothing. Go through your bins regularly and use veggies before they spoil. The point of this exercise is to eat the food, not horde it. So remember to have fun with your food and let nature be the guide on your food storage trip. Here's wishing you the best on your squirrelly endeavor.

SOLAR FOOD DRYING

Using the sun to preserve foods that its energy provided is a great way to increase your use of local foods year-round. Although I have "invented" a solar food dryer that works well in the humid Midwest and written a book on the subject, you do not need to invest in any special equipment to do solar drying on a small scale.

In fact, I would like to encourage you to use the solar food dryer that, like most Americans, you already own—your car. Here is how to use your dryer on wheels: Park the car in the sun with the largest sloped pane of glass facing south (this may be the front windshield or rear window of the car, depending on the model). You will need something on which to place the food—cookie sheets, dryer screens from an electric dryer, baskets, or cotton dish towels will work. Just make sure that whatever you use is material that is safe for contact with food.

Arrange your veggies on the food tray and place it in the south-facing window if possible (or it could be elevated above the seats with some kind of spacer—books, boxes—be creative). Since you are trying to remove the water from food, you will need adequate airflow around, if not through, your trays to accomplish this task.

Next, put a dark piece of fabric, kitchen towel, or even a bandanna (black, navy blue, brown, or another dark color) on top of the food to keep the sunlight

from bleaching out its nutrients and to help it heat up. Lastly, open your car windows about one inch, more or less depending on the air temperature outside and wind conditions. You will want your car to be at 100°F to 140°F, depending on what you are drying (you can use a thermometer to monitor conditions if you want). If things have not completed drying by day's end, they can be left in the car overnight to finish the next day.

This way, you can have your "dryer" and drive it too! I have a friend who would drive her car to work and set up the trays of food. Maybe with the rising cost of gas, more cars will be used as food dryers on sunny days and people will take to the streets on their bikes instead. That would be the healthier option in terms of fitness and nutrition. Cutting-edge new trend? We will see.

For more information on food drying techniques, check out my book, *A Pantry Full of Sunshine*, available on my website: www.GeoPathfinder.com.

Recipes by Type of Dish

Spiced Okra and Tomatoes over Toasty
    Cracked Wheat, 223
Strawberry and Goat Cheese Pizza, 98
Stuffed Beef Brisket, 440
Stuffed Collard Rolls with Cashew Coconut Sauce,
    434
Stuffed Spaghetti Squash Lasagna-Style, 594
Sunflower Seed and Millet Cakes with Spicy
    Tahini Sauce, 526
Sweet Potato and Carrot Latkes, 604
Swiss Chard Wonton Raviolis, 104
Trina's Green Salmon, 407
Triticale Berries with Baby Artichokes, Baby Bok
    Choy, and Dill Oil, 121
Vegan Sun-Dried Tomato and Leek Quiche, 456
Vegetable Cornmeal Crêpes, 574
Vegetable Frittata, 300
Vegetable Fritters, 585
Vegetarian Paella with Brown Rice, 255
Vegetarian Stir-Fry, 520
Veggie-Stuffed Bell Peppers, 254
Walnut-Mushroom Burgers, 68

MUSHROOM DISHES

Asparagus and Morels, 29
Basmati Rice with Mushrooms, Broccoli, and Onion,
    412
Boneless Lamb Sauté with Olives and Mushrooms, 69
Chicken Salad with Mushrooms and Walnuts, 67
Creamy Green Bean and Mushroom Soup, 143
Mushroom, Snow Pea, and Spinach Salad, 73
Thyme and Mushroom Gravy, 309
Vegetable Cornmeal Crêpes, 574
Walnut-Mushroom Burgers, 68
Wilted Buttery Escarole with Red Cabbage
    and Shiitake Mushrooms, 520

PASTA DISHES

Basic Lo Mein, 144
Fava-Studded Pasta with Ricotta Cheese,
    Pancetta, and Lemon, 40
Gallagher's Bar Spaghetti, 267
Kahumana Café Pasta with Macadamia Nut
    Pesto Sauce, 33
Lemon Noodles, 341
Oregano and Zucchini Pasta, 235
Pasta with Arugula, 21
Pasta with Savoy Cabbage and Gruyère, 516
Shrimp Pad Thai, 229

Spaghetti Squash Pad Thai, 596
Spaghetti with Cilantro, Corn, and Tomatoes, 161
Spaghetti with Spring Vegetables, 29
Stuffed Spaghetti Squash Lasagna-Style, 594

PICKLES

Barely Pickled Cucumbers, 175
Japanese Pickled Garlic Scapes, 51
Moen Creek Pickled Beets, 405
Okra Pickles, 222
Pickled Mixed Vegetable Salad, 381
Spicy Cabbage, 518
Zucchini Pickles, 380

POTATO (BAKING AND NEW) DISHES

Baby Potatoes with Lemon and Chives, 45
Eggplant, Tomato, and Red Potato Casserole, 192
Green Garlic Mashed Potatoes, 49
LaVerne's Potato Candy, 579
Mom's Lefse, 577
Mylar's Rosemary Potato Wedges, 281
Parsnip-Carrot Bisque, 566
Parsnips Whipped with Potatoes, 568
Peppery Potato and Zucchini Packets on the Grill, 575
Potato and Bacon Pierogies with Caramelized
    Shallots and Walnuts, 291
Potato and Turnip au Gratin with Leeks, 608
Potato Leek Soup, 454
Roasted Root Vegetables from Greta's Kitchen, 583
Roasted Squash with Potatoes and Garlic, 593
Salade Niçoise, 146
Shepherd's Pie, 584
Sour Cream Potato Salad, 578
Ultimate Root Soup, 610
Yukon Gold Potato Soup, 576

POULTRY DISHES

Baked Chicken and Zucchini Gratin, 379
Chicken and Mushroom Ragout, 308
Chicken Pumpkin Chili, 477
Chicken with 40 Cloves of Garlic, 542
Chicken Wings with Mango-Chili Sauce, 360
Chicken Salad with Mushrooms and Walnuts, 67
Creamy Tarragon Chicken (or Turkey) Medallions
    with Skillet Sweet Potatoes and Beans, 304
Green Curry Chicken with Broccoli and Cauliflower,
    426

SALSAS

Corn Salsa, 170
Herbed Tomatillo and Grape Salsa, 328
Homemade Salsa, 164
Roasted Beet Salsa, 414
Spicy Cantaloupe Salsa, 151
Tropical Fruit Salsa, 360
Watermelon-Strawberry Mint Salsa, 373

SANDWICHES

Bacon, Lettuce, and Cantaloupe Sandwich, 151
Blossom Tea Sandwiches, 203
Pork Tenderloin Pitas, 556
Vegetable Subs, 176

SAUCES AND GRAVIES

Applesauce with Bourbon, Sour Cherries,
    and Hazelnuts, 399
Abba's African Hot Sauce, 602
Cashew Coconut Sauce, 435
Gallagher's Bar Spaghetti Sauce, 268
Jalapeño Cream Sauce, 268
Macadamia Nut Pesto Sauce, 33
Mustard Cream Sauce, 419
Oven-Roasted Tomato Sauce, 323
S. Nardecchia's Spaghetti Sauce, 234
Spicy Tahini Sauce, 526
Thyme and Mushroom Gravy, 309

SEAFOOD DISHES

Asparagus and Shrimp Salad, 27
Balachaung (Burmese Dried Shrimp Relish), 293
Deviled Eggs with Salmon and Basil, 34
Gravlax (Salmon Marinated in Dill), 184
Lemongrass Halibut, 212
Maine Lobster Chowder with Coconut,
    Corn, and Lemongrass, 211
Mylar's Lettuce Wraps, 59
Rosemary-Roasted Salmon, 282
Salmon, Cucumber, and Dill Salad, 182
Seared Scallops with Tropical Lychee Salsa, 357
Shrimp Pad Thai, 229
Shrimp with Oranges, Black Rice, and Coconut Milk,
    343
Trina's Green Salmon, 407

SIDE DISHES

Asparagus and Morels, 29
Asparagus and Shrimp Salad, 27
Baby Potatoes with Lemon and Chives, 45
Baked Chicken and Zucchini Gratin, 379
Baked Honey Tomatoes, 319
Ballistic Baby Bok Choy and Fried Tofu, 122
Basmati Rice with Mushrooms, Broccoli, and Onion,
    412
Blasted Broccoli, 411
Braised Fennel Wedges with Saffron and Tomato, 533
Brassica Fried Rice, 432
Broccoli with Baby White Turnip and Garlic
    Scapes Dressing, 609
Brussels Sprouts in Honey Butter with Chili Flakes,
    421
Butternut Surprise, 593
California Dreaming Kiwi Ribs, 352
Caramelized Cabbage, 183
Carrot and Red Lentil Curry
Cauliflower Fried Rice, 427
Chard with Raisins and Almonds, 103
Charred Romanesco Broccoli with Anchovies
    and Mint, 413
Cherry Tomato Kebabs, 322
Chicken Wings with Mango-Chili Sauce, 360
Chinese Broccoli in Sesame-Sichuan Vinaigrette, 126
Citrus Collards with Raisins, 433
Classic Bread Stuffing with Sage, Parsley, and Thyme,
    487
Copper Penny Carrots, 528
Crispy Kale, 446
Curried Mustard Greens and Garbanzo Beans
    with Sweet Potatoes, 462
Dal Makhani (Indian Lentils and Beans), 511
Delicious Green Beans, 147
Eggplant, Tomato, and Red Potato Casserole, 192
Enchanted Broccoli Forest, The, 411
Fava-Studded Pasta with Ricotta Cheese,
    Pancetta, and Lemon, 40
Favorite Baked Summer Squash, 298
Fried Sage Leaves, 488
Fried Squash Blossoms, 299
Garlic Spinach, 545
Gomae (Sesame Spinach), 90
Ginger Kale, 445
Glazed Pearl Onions, 562
Grandma's Spinach Soufflé, 89
Green Beans in Basil-Walnut Vinaigrette, 35
Green Curry Chicken with Broccoli and Cauliflower,
    426

SNACKS

SOUPS AND STEWS

STIR-FRIES

TOFU DISHES

Recipes by Ingredient

Onions (Green) (Scallions)

Oranges and Orange Juice

Oregano

Vegetarian, Vegan & Gluten-Free Recipes

VEGETARIAN

None of the vegetarian recipes listed here contain non-optional meat, seafood, or poultry, but they may contain eggs and dairy. They may also contain chicken or meat-based broth, but you should assume that you can substitute vegetable or vegan broth. Many of the other recipes in this book may be altered to be vegetarian by omitting meat, chicken, and seafood, and substituting vegetable stock for chicken or beef broth.

VEGAN

None of the vegan recipes listed here contain nonoptional meat, seafood, poultry, eggs, or dairy. They may contain chicken or meat-based broth, but you should assume that you can substitute vegan broth. Many of the recipes in this book may be altered to be vegan by omitting meat, chicken, and seafood; substituting vegetable stock for chicken or beef broth; and using dairy substitutes, like products made from rice, soy, nuts, coconuts, and seeds.

GLUTEN-FREE

None of these recipes contain nonoptional gluten, including wheat, barley, rye, and oats (i.e., bread, pasta, cereals, biscuits, crackers, cakes, pastries, and pies). Be aware that many prepared and processed foods often contain flour or gluten-containing components, including canned meats, cold cuts, chips, sausages, processed cheese products, milkshakes, canned soups, bouillon cubes, many commercial broths and salad dressings, soy sauce, self-basting turkey, some candies, fried foods, imitation fish, malt, matzo, Worcestershire sauce, miso, and some vinegars. People who follow a gluten-free diet should always check food labels for additives or thickeners that may contain gluten, such as hydrolyzed vegetable protein (HVP).

Contributors and Bibliography

This list contains the names of farms, organizations, individuals, and publications that either contributed content to or were mentioned in this book.

AGRIHOODS

Agritopia, Gilbert, Arizona
Bucking Horse, Fort Collins, Colorado
Harvest, Northlake, Texas
Hidden Springs, Boise, Idaho
Kukul'ula, Kauai, Hawaii
Prairie Crossing, Grayslake, Illinois
Serenbe, Chattahoochee Hills, Georgia
Skokomish Farms, Union, Washington
South Village, South Burlington, Vermont
Willowsford, Aldie, Virginia

· ·

BOTANICAL GARDENS

Chicago Botanic Garden, Glencoe, Illinois

· ·

COMMUNITY ORGANIZATIONS

AmeriCorps, Washington, DC
GrowNYC, New York, New York

· ·

COOKBOOKS

1,001 Hot & Spicy Recipes
Dave DeWitt, Agate Surrey, 2010.

The 2013 MAJIQal Cookbook
Self-published, MAJIQ, 2013.

Afri Chef: African Recipes: Cooking Real Food from Africa
Self-published, Michael Tracey.

The Alcoholic's Cookbook
J. Michael Gallagher, self-published, 2011.

Bluff Country Co-op Cookbook
Bluff Country Co-op, 2002.

Cooking with Fruit
Rolce Redard Payne and Dorrit Speyer Senior, Crown Publishers, 1992.

The Cook's Encyclopedia of Vegetables
Christine Ingram, Lorenz Books, 2001.

CookWise
Shirley Corriher, HarperCollins Publishers, 1997.

Daisies Do Tell … A Recipe Book
Betty Culp, self-published, date unknown.

From Asparagus to Zucchini: A Guide to Cooking Farm-Fresh, Seasonal Produce
FairShare CSA Coalition, 2003.

Greene on Greens
Bert Greene, Workman Publishing Company, Inc., 1984.

Hills Centennial Cookbook
Kathryn Erickson, editor. Crescent Publishing, Inc., 1989.

How to Pick a Peach
Russ Parsons, Houghton Mifflin Harcourt, 2007.

Northwest Essentials: Cooking with Ingredients That Define a Region's Cuisine
Greg Atkinson, Sasquatch Books, 2005.

Ottolenghi: The Cookbook
Yotam Ottolenghi and Sami Tamimi, Ten Speed Press, 2013.

Perfect Recipes for Having People Over
Pam Anderson, Rux Martin/Houghton Mifflin Harcourt, 2005.

Sacramental Magic in a Small-Town Café
Addison Wesley Peter Reinhart, 1994.

Southern Food and Plantation Houses
Lee Bailey, Clarkson Potter/Publishers, 1990.

The Abascal Way Cookbook
Kathy Abascal, Tigana Press, 2011.

The Farmer's Market Cookbook
Richard Ruben, The Lyons Press, 2000.

The French Kitchen Cookbook
Patricia Wells, William Morrow Cookbooks, 2013.

The Garden Fresh Vegetable Cookbook
Andrea Chesman, Storey Publishing, 2005.

The Greenmarket Cookbook
Joel Patraker and Joan Schwartz, T. Viking Penguin, 2000.

The New Enchanted Broccoli Forest
Mollie Katzen, Tante Malka, Inc., and Ten Speed Press, 1982, 1995, 2000.

The Schoenleber Family Cookbook
edited by Lura Looper, self-published, 1993.

Time-Life Foods of the World, Pacific and Southeast Asian Cooking
Rafael Steinberg, Time-Life Books, 1970.

Time-Life Foods of the World, The Cooking of Provincial France
M. F. K. Fisher and Julia Child, Time-Life Books, 1969.

Time-Life Foods of the World: American Cooking: New England
Jonathan Norton Leonard, Time-Life Books, 1971.

Time-Life Foods of the World: The Cooking of Scandinavia
Dale Brown, Time-Life Books, 1974.

Uncommon Fruits & Vegetables
Elizabeth Schneider, Harper & Row Publishers, Inc., 1986.

Vegetable Literacy
Deborah Madison, Ten Speed Press, 2013.

Vegetables from Amaranth to Zucchini: The Essential Reference
Elizabeth Schneider, William Morrow Cookbooks, 2001.

Vegetarian Classics
Jeanne Lemlin, HarperCollins Publishers, 2000.

Vegetarian Cooking for Everyone
Deborah Madison, Broadway Books, 1997.

• •

COOKING AND FOOD WEBSITES

Foodista
www.foodista.com

The Chamomile Times and Herbal News
www.chamomiletimes.com

The Garlic Store
www.thegarlicstore.com

The Recipe Link
www.kitchenlink.com

Fooddownunder.com
www.fooddownunder.com

Epicurean.com
www.epicurean.com

CD Kitchen
www.cdkitchen.com

World's Healthiest Foods
www.whfoods.com

Okraw
www.okraw.com

Food.com
www.food.com

Razzle Dazzle Recipes
www.razzledazzlerecipes.com

Ben and Jerry's Homemade Holdings, Inc.
www.benandjerrys.com

Renee's Garden
www.reneesgarden.com

Cooks Illustrated
www.cooksillustrated.com

Greatist
www.greatist.com

Texas Monthly
www.texasmonthly.com

Betty Crocker
www.bettycrocker.com

Bon Appétit
www.bonappetit.com

Vital Choice Seafood
www.vitalchoice.com

The New York Times
www.nytimes.com

Canadian Living Magazine
www.canadianliving.com

Epicurious
www.epicurious.com

Centers for Disease Control & Prevention's Fruits and Veggies—More Matters
www.fruitsandveggiesmatter.gov

Home of the Office of Disease Prevention and Health Promotion
www.health.gov.

The Great American Potluck, Library of Congress
www.loc.gov/teachers/classroommaterials/presentationsandactivities/presentations/immigration/ckbk

• •

CSA ORGANIZATIONS

FairShare CSA Coalition, Madison, Wisconsin
Healthy Food For All, Ithica, New York
Local Harvest, Santa Cruz, California
Portland Area CSA Coalition (PACSAC), Portland, Oregon

• •

EDUCATIONAL INSTITUTIONS AND SCHOOLS

Association of Waldorf Schools of North America, Longmont, Colorado
Farm to School Program, USDA, Washington, DC
Hawthorne Valley Waldorf School, Ghent, New York
Kimberton Waldorf School, Kimberton, Pennsylvania
Learning Ecology and Alaskan Farming (LEAF) (Calypso Farm and Ecology Center), Ester, Alaska
Martin Luther King, Jr. Middle School, Berkeley, California
Northwest Youth Corps (NYC), Eugene, Oregon
Oregon State University Extension Service, Corvallis, Oregon
OutDoor High School, Eugene, Oregon
Sauvie Island Center, Portland, Oregon
School Garden Initiative (Calypso Farm and Ecology Center), Ester, Alaska
Summerfield Waldorf School, Santa Rosa, California
Sunfield Farm and Waldorf School, Port Hadlock, Washington
The Edible Schoolyard, Berkeley, California
University of Maine Cooperative Extension, Orono, Maine
University of California-Santa Cruz Center for Agroecology and Sustainable Food Systems (CASFS), Santa Cruz, California

• •

FARMS AND COMMUNITY GARDENS

Asheville Sanctuary, Asheville, North Carolina
¡Cultiva! Youth Project, Boulder, Colorado
180 Degree Farm, Sharpsburg, Georgia
Adaptations, Inc., Captain Cook, Hawaii
Afton Field Farm, Corvallis, Oregon
Alchemy Gardens, West Rutland, Vermont
B.U.G. (Backyard Urban Garden Farms), Salt Lake City, Utah
Big River Farms, Marine on St. Croix, Minnesota
Blue Turtle Botanicals, Tucson, Arizona
Bray Family Farms, Powder Spring, Georgia
Calypso Farm and Ecology Center, Ester, Alaska
Cedar Circle Farm & Education Center, East Thetford, Vermont
Cherry Tree House Mushrooms, Twin Cities, Minnesota
Chino Farm, Del Mar, California
Chue's Farm, Clovis, California
CityGrown Seattle, Seattle, Washington
Clay Bottom Farm, Goshen, Indiana
Cleveland Crops, Cleveland, Ohio
Common Good City Farm, Washington, DC
Community Crops, Lincoln, Nebraska
Countryside Produce, Lagrange, Indiana
Crown Point Ecology Center, Bath, Ohio
Dandelion Spring Farm, Newcastle, Maine
Denison Farm, Schaghticoke, New York
Employer Sponsored Gardens, Minneapolis, Minnesota
Essex Farm, Essex, New York
Featherstone Farm, Rushford, Minnesota

Food Bank Farm, Hadley, Massachusetts,
For the Love of Dandelions, Cambridge, Minnesota
Full Circle Farm, Seattle, Washington
Full Circle Farm, Sunnyvale, California
Full Moon Farm, Hinesburg, Vermont
Fungi for the People, Eugene, Oregon
Garden City Harvest, Missoula, Montana
Gardens of Eagan, Farmington, Minnesota
Gathering Together Farm, Philomath, Oregon
George Jones Farm, Oberlin, Ohio
Gila Farm Cooperative, Phoenix, Arizona
Green Gate Farms, Austin, Texas
Green Mountain Girls Farm, Northfield, Vermont
Greyrock Farm, Cazenovia, New York
Growing Experience, The, North Long Beach, California
Growing Gardens, Boulder, Colorado
Growing Power, Milwaukee, Wisconsin
Growing Washington, Everson, Washington
HAFA Farm, Vermillion Township, Minnesota
Hawthorne Valley Farm, Ghent, New York
Helsing Junction Farm, Rochester, Washington
Herbal Revolution, Lincolnville, Maine
Heritage Point Urban Farm, Roanoke, Virginia
Idexx Laboratories, Westbrook, Maine
Intervale Community Farm, Burlington, Vermont
Kahumana Farm, Waianae, Oahu, Hawaii
Kaiser Permanente, Oakland, California
Kanalani Ohana Farm, Honaunau, Hawaii
Kauai Roots Farm Co-op (KRFC), Kalaheo, Kauai, Hawaii
Kimberton CSA, Kimberton, Pennsylvania
Kula Fields Farmshop, Kula, Maui, Hawaii
Lancaster Farm Fresh Cooperative (LFFC), Leola, Pennsylvania
Laurel Valley Education Farm & Garden, Eugene, Oregon
Les Brown Memorial Farm, Marseilles, Illinois
Lonesome Whistle Farm, Junction City, Oregon
Mala 'Ai 'Opio Community Food Systems Initiative (MA'O), Waianae, Oahu, Hawaii
Mariquita Farm, Watsonville, California
McClendon's Select, Peoria, Arizona
Mhonpaj's Garden, Grant, Minnesota
Morgan Botanicals Herbal CSA, Loveland, Colorado
Mountain View Farm, Easthampton, Massachusetts
Moutoux Orchard, Purcellville, Virginia
Mycoterra Farm, Westhampton, Massachusetts
Nantucket Mushrooms LLC, South Chatham, Massachusetts
Nash's Organic Produce, Sequim, Washington
New Roots for Refugees, Kansas City, Kansas
Niman Ranch, Alameda, California
North Spore Mushroom Company, Portland, Maine
Oakhill Organics, Grand Island, Oregon
Penn's Corner Farm Alliance, Pittsburgh, Pennsylvania
Pioneer Valley Heritage Grain CSA, Amherst, Massachusetts
Prairie Crossing Learning Farm, Grayslake, Illinois
Providence Health & Services, Renton, Washington

Provisions Mushroom Farm, Olympia, Washington
Quail Hill Farm, Amagansett, New York
R-evolution Gardens, Nehalem, Oregon
Rainshadow Organics, Terrebonne, Oregon
Red Shed Produce, Twisp, Washington
Robin Hollow Farm, Newport, Rhode Island
S&S Homestead Farm, Lopez Island, Washington
Sang Lee Farms, Peconic, New York
Sauvie Island Organics, Portland, Oregon
Sawyer Farm, Worthington, Massachusetts
Schreiber & Sons Farm, Eltopia, Washington
Seabreeze Organic Farm, San Diego, California
Seed and Thistle Apothecary, Portland, Oregon,
Shambala Permaculture Farm, Camano Island, Washington
Siskiyou Sustainable Cooperative CSA, Jacksonville, Oregon
Sowing Seeds Farm, Twisp, Washington
Teena's Pride All Locally Grown Produce, Homestead, Florida
Terhune Orchards, Princeton, New Jersey
Tucson CSA, Tucson, Arizona
The Youth Farm, Missoula, Montana
University of California-Santa Cruz Center for Agroecology
    and Sustainable Food Systems (CASFS), Santa Cruz,
    California
Valley Flora Farm, Langlois, Oregon
Vanderpool Gourmet Gardens, China Spring, Texas
Viva Farms, Mount Vernon, Washington
Waihuena Farm, Haleiwa, Oahu, Hawaii
Waltham Fields Community Farm, Waltham,
    Massachusetts
Whitmore Project, Wahiawa, Oahu, Hawaii
Winter Green Farm, Noti, Oregon
Zenger Farm, Portland, Oregon

FARM ORGANIZATIONS AND INCUBATORS

Biodynamic Association, Milwaukee, Wisconsin
California Farm Academy, Winters, California
Center for Land-Based Learning, Winters, California
Center for Rural Affairs, Lyons, Nebraska
Center for Urban Education about Sustainable Agriculture
    (CUESA), San Francisco, California
Community Crops, Lincoln, Nebraska
Demeter International, Darmstadt, Germany
Demeter USA, Philomath, Oregon
Farm Beginnings Collaborative (FBC), Minneapolis,
    Minnesota
Farm Hack, Essex, New York
Farms Program, Burlington, Vermont
FarmsNext, Ashland, Oregon
The Greenhorns, Essex, New York
GrowFood (defunct)
Growing Home, Chicago, Illinois
Grow Portland, Portland, Oregon
Growing Agripreneurs, Central Point, Oregon
Hmong American Farmers Association (HAFA), Saint Paul,
    Minnesota

Intervale Center, Burlington, Vermont
Land Stewardship Project, Minneapolis, Minnesota
National Young Farmers Coalition, Hudson, New York
New Agrarian Center, Oberlin, Ohio
Oregon State University Southern Oregon Research and
    Extension Center, Central Point, Oregon
Prairie Farm Corps, Grayslake, Illinois
Rogue Farm Corps, Ashland, Oregon
Tilian Farm Development Center, Ann Arbor, Michigan
Urban Farm School (UFS), Asheville, North Carolina
Women, Food, and Agriculture Network (WFAN), Ames, Iowa
Worldwide Workers on Organic Farms (WWOOF),
    San Francisco, California

FARMERS MARKETS, FARM STANDS, AND FOOD CO-OPS

Bluff Country Co-op, Winona, Minnesota
Boulder Farmers Market, Boulder, Colorado
Davis Farmers Market, Davis, California
Farm Stand, Philomath, Oregon
Nash's Farm Store, Sequim, Washington
Roanoke Natural Foods Co-op, Roanoke, Virginia
Wedge Co-op, Minneapolis, Minnesota
Youthmarket, New York City, New York

FOOD BLOGS

The Cascadian Kitchen blog, Brian Fink
www.cascadiankitchen.com

Celiac in the City blog, Sarah Nielsen
www.celiacinthecity.wordpress.com

CenterCutCook blog, Ashley Wagner
www.centercutcook.com

Dishing Up Delights blog, Esi Impraim
www.dishingupdelights.blogspot.com

ChiotsRun blog, Susy Morris
www.chiotsrun.com

Girlichef blog, Heather Schmitt-Gonzalez
www.girlichef.com

Groove Food blog, Lauren Mitchell Wilkinson
groovefood.typepad.com

Happy Chomp blog, Crystal Tai
www.happychomp.com

Je Mange le Ville blog, Michelle Abendschan
www.jemangelaville.com

Justinsomnia blog, Justin Watt
www.justinsomnia.org

Kim-Chi Mom blog, Amy Kim
www.kimchimom.com

Mission: Food blog, Victoria
www.mission-food.com

Nutrition to Kitchen blog, Tram Le
www.nutritiontokitchen.com

Oh My Veggies blog, Kiersten Frase
www.ohmyveggies.com

Orangette blog, Molly Wizenberg
www.orangette.blogspot.com

Spicebox Travels blog, Linda Shiue
www.spiceboxtravels.com

Sweet Crumbs blog, Joan Yu
www.sweetcrumbs.blogspot.com

. . . .

FOOD DELIVERY

Brooklyn Bike Armada, New York, New York
Fork + Frame, Seattle, Washington
Loaded Bikes, Chicago, Illinois
Metro Pedal Power, Boston, Massachusetts
One Revolution, Burlington, Vermont

. . . .

FOOD MAGAZINES

Old Fashioned Living
Brenda Hyde

Vegetarian Journal
The Vegetarian Resource Group/Vegetarian Journal

. . . .

FOOD ORGANIZATIONS

Bayfield Food Producers Cooperative, Wisconsin
Boulder Food Rescue, Boulder, Colorado
City Fruit, Seattle, Washington
Clean Greens Farm and Market, Seattle, Washington
Cropmobster, San Francisco Bay Area, California
EndFoodWaste.org, Oakland, California
Falling Fruit, Boulder, Colorado
Farmers Ending Hunger, Salem, Oregon
FlashFood, Scottsdale, Arizona
Food Bank of Western Massachusetts, Hatfield,
    Massachusetts
The Food Project, Lincoln, Massachusetts
Food Waste Reduction Alliance (FWRA), Washington, DC
FoodCorps, Portland, Oregon
Foodsharing.de, Berlin, Germany

The Gleaners Coalition, Olympia, Washington
Imperfect Produce, Emeryville, California
Just Food, New York, New York
Know Thy Food, Portland, Oregon
Kromkommer, Rotterdam, the Netherlands
Local Thyme, Madison, Wisconsin
Minnesota Food Association (MFA), Marine on St. Croix,
    Minnesota
Mother Hubbard's Cupboard, Bloomington, Indiana
Organic Consumers Association, Finland, Minnesota
Plate & Pitchfork, Portland, Oregon
Produce for People, Portland, Oregon
Santa Cruz Fruit Tree Project, Santa Cruz, California
Slow Food USA, Brooklyn, New York
Strolling of the Heifers, East Dummerston, Vermont

. . . .

FOOD TRADE ORGANIZATIONS

California Artichoke Advisory Board, Castroville, California
California Avocado Commission, Irvine, California
California Figs, Fresno, California
California Kiwifruit Commission, Sacramento, California
California Strawberry Commission, Watsonville, California
Lychees Online, West Palm Beach, Florida
Maine Lobster Promotion Council, Portland, Maine
National Mango Board, Orlando, Florida
National Watermelon Promotion Board, Springs, Florida
US Dry Bean Council, Pierre, South Dakota

. . . .

HEALTHCARE ORGANIZATIONS
AND INITIATIVES

Cancer Treatment Centers of America (CTCA) at
    Southeastern Regional Medical Center, Newnan,
    Georgia
Cancer Treatment Centers of America (CTCA) at Western
    Regional Medical Center, Goodyear, Arizona
Center for American Indian Health, Baltimore, Maryland
Health Care without Harm US, Reston, Virginia
Healthy Food in Health Care Pledge, Reston, Virginia
Jefferson Healthcare, Port Townsend, Washington
Lee Memorial Health System, Cape Coral, Florida
Mississippi Roadmap to Health Equity, Jackson, Mississippi
Providence Health & Services, Renton, Washington

. . . .

INDIVIDUALS AND CHEFS

Anush Oganesian and Lida Hovhannesyan
Arlayne Fleming
Bryant Terry
Esther McRae
Ibán Yarza

Jacob Wittenberg
Jen Vassili
Jim Richards
Julie Ridlon
Katherine Deumling (via Sauvie Island Organics)
Larisa Walk
Lisa Gordanier
Maria Runde
Marianne Streich
Melinda McBride
Nelda Danz
Nickolas Vassili
Nicole Hoffmann
Paul Anater
Rich Hoyle
Ronald Swartz
Tom Douglas

INDIVIDUALS FROM FEATHERSTONE FARM CSA AND NEWSLETTER

Allison
Amy Chen
Greta Sikorski
Heather
Judy
Margaret Houston
Margaret Trott
Mi Ae Lipe
Pam Garetto
Robin Taylor
Ruth Charles
Sarah Libertus
Tracy
Trina

LAND TRUSTS AND STEWARDSHIP

Agricultural Stewardship Association (ASA), Greenwich, New York
Connecticut Farmland Trust, Hartford, Connecticut
Maine Farmland Trust, Belfast, Maine

NURSERIES AND SEED COMPANIES

Adaptive Seeds, Sweet Home, Oregon
Appalachian Seeds Farm and Nursery, Asheville, North Carolina
Open Oak Farm, Sweet Home, Oregon
Organic Seed Alliance (OSA), Portland, Oregon
Seed Ambassadors Project, Sweet Home, Oregon
Seed Savers Exchange, Decorah, Iowa

Uprising Organics, Bellingham, Washington
Wild Garden Seed, Philomath, Oregon

RELIGIOUS INSTITUTIONS

Adamah, Falls Village, Connecticut
Catholic Charities of Northeast Kansas, Overland Park, Kansas
Ecumenical Ministries of Oregon, Portland, Oregon
Hazon, New York, New York
The Faith-Based Food Hubs Program, New York, New York
The Interfaith Food & Farms Partnership, Portland, Oregon
Urban Adamah, Berkeley, California

RESTAURANTS

Blue Heron Coffeehouse, Winona, Minnesota
Braise, Milwaukee, Wisconsin
Chez Panisse Restaurant and Café, Berkeley, California
The Gleanery, Putney, Vermont
Fire & Ice Café, Midleton, County Cork, Ireland
Kahumana Café, Waianae, Oahu, Hawaii
Lenoir, Austin, Texas
Purple Rain Vineyard, Brush Prairie, Washington

URBAN AGRICULTURE

Growing Gardens, Boulder, Colorado
Growing Power, Milwaukee, Wisconsin
Kansas City Center for Urban Agriculture, Kansas City, Kansas

OTHER

City University of Hong Kong, Hong Kong
The Climate Group, New York, New York

SUGGESTED ADDITIONAL RESOURCES

The following books, magazines, organizations, and recipe websites are not direct contributors to this book, but they are nonetheless some of my favorite cooking and food-related resources.

About.com
www.about.com/food

All Around the World Cookbook
Sheila Lukins, Workman Publishing, 1994.

The All-Purpose Joy of Cooking
Irma S. Rombauer, Ethan Becker, and Marion Rombauer Becker, Scribner Book Company, 1998.

Allrecipes
www.allrecipes.com

The Art of Eating (book)
M. F. K. Fisher, John Wiley and Sons, 2004.

The Art of Eating (magazine)
www.artofeating.com

The Artful Eater: A Gourmet Investigates the Ingredients of Great Food
Edward Behr, Art of Eating, 2004.

Ballymaloe Cookery School
www.cookingisfun.ie

The Breath of a Wok: Unlocking the Spirit of Chinese Wok Cooking Through Recipes and Lore
Grace Young, Simon & Schuster, 2004.

Brilliant Food Tips and Cooking Tricks: 5000 Ingenious Kitchen Hints, Secrets, Shortcuts, and Solutions
David Joachim, Rodale Inc., 2001.

The Chile Pepper Encyclopedia: Everything You'll Ever Need to Know About Hot Peppers, With More Than 100 Recipes
Dave DeWitt, Diane Publishing, 2003.

Chow
www.chow.com

A Clove of Garlic: Garlic for Health and Cookery: Recipes and Traditions
Katy Holder and Gail Duff, Chartwell Books, 1997.

Cooking Basics for Dummies
Bryan Miller and Marie Rama, 3rd Edition, IDG Books Worldwide, 2004.

The Cook and the Gardener: A Year of Recipes and Writings for the French Countryside
Amanda Hesser, W. W. Norton & Company, 2000.

Cooksrecipes
www.cooksrecipes.com

Diet for a Small Planet
Frances Moore Lappé, Ballantine Books, 1991.

Fast Food Nation: The Dark Side of the All-American Meal
Eric Schlosser, Houghton Mifflin Company, 2002.

The Flavor Bible: The Essential Guide to Culinary Creativity, Based on the Wisdom of America's Most Imaginative Chefs
Karen Page and Andrew Dornenburg, Little, Brown and Company, 2008.

Food by Waverley Root: An Authoritative and Visual History and Dictionary of the Foods of the World
Waverly Root, Simon and Schuster, 1980.

The Food Network
www.foodnetwork.com

The Food Reference Website
www.foodreference.com

Garlic Central
www.garlic-central.com

The Garlic Lover's Cookbook
Gilroy Garlic Festival, Celestial Arts, 2005.

Gastronomica
www.gastronomica.org

Gilroy Garlic Festival
www.gilroygarlicfestival.com

Good Things (revised)
Jane Grigson, Bison Books, 2006.

Greens Glorious Greens: More Than 140 Ways to Prepare All Those Great-Tasting, Super-Healthy, Beautiful Leafy Greens
Johnna Albi and Catherine Walthers, St. Martin's Griffin, 1996.

Heal with Food
www.healwithfood.org

The Heirloom Tomato Cookbook
Mimi Luebbermann, Chronicle Books, 2006.

The Herbfarm Cookbook
Jerry Traunfeld, Scribner, 2000.

Herbs & Spices: The Cook's Reference
Jill Norman, DK Adult, 2002.

Home Cooking: A Writer in the Kitchen
Laurie Colwin, Harper Perennial, 2000.

Homemade Baby Food Recipes
www.blog.homemade-baby-food-recipes.com

In Search of the Perfect Meal: A Collection of the Best Food Writing of Roy Andries De Groot
Roy Andries De Groot, St. Martins Press, 1986.

James Beard's American Cookery
James Beard, Little, Brown and Company, 1972.

The Kitchn
www.thekitchn.com

Local Flavors: Cooking and Eating from America's Farmers' Markets
Deborah Madison, Broadway Books, 2002.

Mediterranean Vegetables: A Cook's ABC of Vegetables and Their Preparation in Spain, France, Italy, Greece, Turkey, the Middle East, and North Africa, with More than 200 Authentic Recipes for the Home Cook
Clifford A. Wright, The Harvard Common Press, 2001.

National Center for Home Food Preservation
www.uga.edu/nchfp/index.html

The New Moosewood Cookbook
Mollie Katzen, Ten Speed Press, 2000.

The Omnivore's Dilemma: A Natural History of Four Meals
Michael Pollan, Penguin Press, 2006.

On Food and Cooking: The Science and Lore of the Kitchen
Harold McGee, Scribner, 2004.

One Bite Won't Kill You: More than 200 Recipes to Tempt Even the Pickiest Kids on Earth
Ann Hodgman, Houghton Mifflin Company, 1999.

Onion: The Essential Cook's Guide to Onions, Garlic, Leeks, Spring Onions, Shallots and Chives
Brian Glover, Lorenz Books, 2001.

Onions, Onions, Onions: Delicious Recipes for the World's Favorite Secret Ingredient
Linda Griffith and Fred Griffith, Houghton Mifflin, 2002.

A Pantry Full of Sunshine—Energy-Efficient Food Preservation Methods
Larisa Walk, www.geopathfinder.com

The Pumpkin Patch
www.pumpkin-patch.com

Recipe Encyclopedia: A Complete A–Z of Good Food and Cooking
Random House Publishing, 1997.

Recipes for a Small Planet
Ellen Buchwald Ewald, Ballantine Books, 1985.

Recipes from a Kitchen Garden
Renee Shepherd and Fran Raboff, Ten Speed Press, 1993.

The Recipe Link
www.recipelink.com

Recipe Tips
www.recipetips.com

The Rhubarb Compendium
www.rhubarbinfo.com

Rodale's Illustrated Encyclopedia of Herbs
Rodale Press, 2000.

Saveur
www.saveur.com

Seasonal Chef: Buying and Using Produce from Farmers Markets
www.seasonalchef.com

Seed Savers Exchange
www.seedsavers.org

Serious Eats
www.seriouseats.com

South Wind Through the Kitchen: The Best of Elizabeth David
Elizabeth David, Penguin Books Ltd., 1998.

Specialty Produce
www.specialtyproduce.com

The Splendid Table
www.splendidtable.org

A Taste of the Far East
Madhur Jaffrey, BBC Books, 1993.

The Tomato Festival Cookbook: 150 Recipes that Make the Most of Your Crop of Lush, Vine-Ripened, Sun-Warmed, Fat, Juicy, Ready-to-Burst Heirloom Tomatoes
Lawrence Davis-Hollander, Storey Publishing, 2004.

The United States of Arugula: The Sun-Dried, Cold-Pressed, Dark-Roasted, Extra Virgin Story of the American Food Revolution
David Kamp, Broadway, 2007.

United States Department of Agriculture (USDA)
www.recipefinder.nal.usda.gov

Vegan Mos
www.veganmos.com

The Vegetarian Flavor Bible: The Essential Guide to Culinary Creativity with Vegetables, Fruits, Grains, Legumes, Nuts, Seeds, and More, Based on the Wisdom of Leading American Chefs
Karen Page, Little, Brown and Company, 2014.

Veggie Desserts: From the Garden to the Cake Stand blog
www.veggiedesserts.co.uk

The Victory Garden Cookbook
Morene Morash, Alfred A. Knopf, 1982.

Whole Food Facts: The Complete Reference Guide
Evelyn Roehl, Healing Arts Press, 1996.

Whole Foods Market
www.wholefoodsmarket.com

World Spice at Home: New Flavors for 75 Favorite Dishes
Amanda Bevill, Sasquatch Books, 2014.

Permissions and Additional Credits

Grateful acknowledgment is made to all those who granted permission to reprint their material in this book. Every effort has been made to properly credit, trace, and contact copyright holders; if any error or omission has been made, please contact me, and I will be glad to remedy it in future printings of this book.

....

COOKBOOKS

- Artichokes Stuffed with Ham and Pine Nuts; Applesauce with Bourbon, Sour Cherries, and Hazelnuts; Fig-Honey Gelato; and Nectarines and Blackberries in Rose Geranium Syrup. Recipes from *How to Pick a Peach* by Russ Parsons. Copyright © 2007 by Russ Parsons. Reprinted by permission of Houghton Mifflin Harcourt Publishing Company. All rights reserved.

- The Enchanted Broccoli Forest and Dilled Vegetable-Barley Soup by Mollie Katzen from *The New Enchanted Broccoli Forest*. Copyright © 1982, 1995, 2000 by Tante Malka, Inc., and Ten Speed Press. Reprinted with permission from Mollie Katzen.

- Tender Tatsoi with Sesame Oil Vinaigrette and Sabzi (Herb Salad) from *Vegetarian Cooking for Everyone* by Deborah Madison. Copyright © 1997 by Deborah Madison. Used by permission of Broadway Books, an imprint of the Crown Publishing Group, a division of Random House LLC. All rights reserved.

- Wilted Greens with Coconut; Grilled Summer Corn and Sugar Snap Pea Salad; Spicy Cabbage; and Swiss Chard Wonton Raviolis from *The Farmer's Market Cookbook* by Richard Ruben. Copyright © 2000 by Richard Ruben. Used by permission of The Lyons Press, Guilford, Connecticut.

- Jerusalem Artichoke Soup with Toasted Pistachios and Pistachio Oil (pp. 76–7) from *The French Kitchen Cookbook* by Patricia Wells. Copyright © 2013 by Patricia Wells, Ltd. Reprinted by permission of HarperCollins Publishers.

- Basic Lo Mein adapted from *The Garden Fresh Vegetable Cookbook* by Andrea Chesman. Copyright © 2005 by Andrea Chesman.

- Egg Salad with Tarragon, Parsley, and Chives; Fried Green Tomato Frittata; and Braised Fennel Wedges with Saffron and Tomato from *Vegetable Literacy: Cooking and Gardening with Twelve Families from the Edible Plant Kingdom, with Over 300 Deliciously Simple Recipes* by Deborah Madison. Used by permission of Ten Speed Press, an imprint of the Crown Publishing Group, a division of Random House LLC. All rights reserved.

- Classic Bread Stuffing with Sage, Parsley, and Thyme from *Perfect Recipes for Having People Over* by Pam Anderson. Copyright © 2005 by Pam Anderson. Reprinted by permission of Houghton Mifflin Company. All rights reserved.

- Strawberry Shortcake and Pea Pods with Raspberries by Rolce Payne and Dorrit Senior, *Cooking with Fruit*. Copyright © 1992 by Rolce Redard Payne and Dorrit Speyer Senior. Used by permission of Crown Publishers, a division of Random House, Inc., New York, New York.

- Mustard Greens with Pepper Vinegar; Baked Honey Tomatoes; and Iced Beet and Orange Soup from *Lee Bailey's Southern Food and Plantation Houses* by Lee Bailey, copyright © 1990 by Lee Bailey. Used by permission of Clarkson Potter/Publishers, an imprint of the Crown Publishing Group, a division of Random House LLC. All rights reserved.

- Tossed Mesclun Salad (p. 62) and Vegetable Subs (pp. 143–4) from *Vegetarian Classics* by Jeanne Lemlin. Copyright © 2001 by Jeanne Lemlin. Reprinted by permission of HarperCollins Publishers.

- Mexican Hot Dish by Janie Helgeson; Copper Penny Carrots by Betty Elbers; Fruit Pizza by Coleen Martens; and Mom's Lefse by Erma Schubbe. All from *Hills Centennial Cookbook*, edited by Kathryn Erickson. Copyright © 1989. Crescent Publishing, Inc., Hills, Minnesota.

- Green Curry Chicken with Broccoli and Cauliflower by Nadine Bayer; Jesse's Chicken Stew by Jesse Smith; Fruit Shake by Kathy Delano; Boursin Dip; Marco's Caesar Salad; Tropical Fruit Salsa; Peter Rabbit's Birthday Soup; and S. Nardecchia's Spaghetti Sauce by Maureen Cooney. Reprinted from the *Bluff Country Co-op Cookbook*. Copyright © 2002 by Bluff Country Co-op, Winona, Minnesota. All recipes used by permission of Bluff Country Co-op or the individual authors.

FOOD MAGAZINES

- Summer Savory Soup and Black Bean Soup with Garlic and Summer Savory by Brenda Hyde, *Old Fashioned Living*, www.oldfashionedliving.com. Copyright © 2005 by Brenda Hyde. Used by permission of Brenda Hyde.

- Borscht by Debra Daniels-Zeller, *Vegetarian Journal*, September 2000. Copyright © 2000 by The Vegetarian Resource Group/Vegetarian Journal. Used by permission of The Vegetarian Resource Group/ Vegetarian Journal, Baltimore, Maryland, www.vrg.org.

FOOD TRADE ORGANIZATIONS

- Pork and Baby Artichoke Sauté with Apple Brandy and Lemon Artichoke Soup, from the California Artichoke Advisory Board, www.artichokes.org.

- California Avocado Hummus by Marji Morrow and Classic Guacamole from the California Avocado Commission, www.californiaavocado.com. Recipes courtesy of the California Avocado Commission.

- Pita Pockets with Fresh Figs and Roasted Chicken and Stuffed Beef Brisket by California Figs, www.californiafigs.com.

- California Dreaming Kiwi Ribs; Kiwifruit Jam; and French Toast Kiwifruit by the California Kiwifruit Commission, www.kiwifruit.org.

- Strawberry Nachos by Roz Kelmig and Strawberry and Goat Cheese Pizza from the California Strawberry Commission, www.calstrawberry.com.

- Lychee Chutney and Seared Scallops with Tropical Lychee Salsa, from Lychees Online, www.lycheesonline.com.

- Maine Lobster Chowder with Coconut, Corn, and Lemongrass, by Pamela Eimers, *Simply Seafood*, 1998, courtesy of the Maine Lobster Promotion Council, www.lobsterfrommaine.com.

- Chicken Wings with Mango-Chili Sauce and Mango Caprese Salad, from the National Mango Board, www.mango.org.

- Watermelon Pineapple Preserves; Watermelon and Chicken Salad; and Watermelon Gazpacho from the National Watermelon Promotion Board. Watermelon Strawberry Mint Salsa by Chef Marty Blitz, Mise En Place, Tampa, Florida. All recipes reprinted from www.watermelon.org and used by permission of the National Watermelon Promotion Board.

- Sweet Onion–Apricot Limas and Raisin–Pinto Bean Muffins from the US Dry Bean Council, www.usdrybeans.com.

FOOD BLOGS

- Compound Garlic-Herb Butter by Ashley Wagner, *CenterCutCook* blog, www.centercutcook.com.

- Cherimoya, Kiwi, and Strawberry Fruit Salad by Esi Impraim, *Dishing Up Delights* blog, www.dishingupdelights.blogspot.com.

- Shrimp with Oranges, Black Rice, and Coconut Milk and Sunflower Seed and Millet Cakes with Spicy Tahini Sauce, by Lauren Mitchell Wilkinson, *Groove Food* blog, groovefood.typepad.com.

- Stuffed Spaghetti Squash Lasagna-Style by Sarah Nielsen, *Celiac in the City* blog, www.celiacinthecity. wordpress.com.

- Basil-Infused Lychee-Lime Ice Pops by Kiersten Frase, *Oh My Veggies* blog, www.ohmyveggies.com.

- Japanese Pickled Garlic Scapes and Cherimoya-Almond Cake, by Brian Fink, *The Cascadian Kitchen* blog, www.cascadiankitchen.com.

- Indonesian Avocado and Chocolate Shake; Brassica Fried Rice; and Spicy Balinese Green Apple Salad by Linda Shiue, *Spicebox Travels* blog, www.spiceboxtravels.com.

- Roasted Garlic Hummus by Justin Watt, *Justinsomnia* blog, www.justinsomnia.org.

- Shrimp Pad Thai and Armenian Steak Tartare (Chi Kofte) by Victoria, *Mission: Food* blog, www.mission-food.com.

- Banana Bread with Chocolate and Cinnamon Sugar by Molly Wizenberg, *Orangette* blog, www.orangette. blogspot.com.

- Blackberry-Lavender Popsicles by Heather Schmitt-Gonzalez, *Girlichef* blog, www.girlichef.com.

- Chicken and Mushroom Ragout and Cherimoya Frozen Yogurt (Man Cau) by Tram Le, *Nutrition to Kitchen* blog, www.nutritiontokitchen.com.

- Pineapple Upside-Down Cake by Miss Joan Yu, *Sweet Crumbs* blog, www.sweetcrumbs.blogspot.com.

- Fried Sage Leaves by Susy Morris, *Chiot's Run* blog, www.chiotsrun.com.

- Indian-Style Roasted Cauliflower by Amy Kim, *Kim-Chi Mom* blog, www.kimchimom.com.

- Parsnip and Pear Pancakes with Horseradish Sour Cream by Michelle Abendschan, *Je Mange le Ville* blog, www.jemangelaville.com.

- Cauliflower Fried Rice by Crystal Tai, *Happy Chomp* blog, www.happychomp.com.

....

INDIVIDUALS AND CHEFS

- Fava-Studded Pasta with Ricotta Cheese, Pancetta, and Lemon; Flavored Butters for Fresh Corn (Chipotle Chile Butter, Curry-Lime Butter, and Miso Butter); Tabbouleh; Harissa; and Fennel, Sausage, and White Bean Hash by Lisa Gordanier. Raw Corn Summer Salad with Apples and Jicama and Lavender-Mint Tea Punch by Lisa Gordanier and Mi Ae Lipe. Rainy Night Chili by Lisa Gordanier and Jim Richards; Roasted Cauliflower with Endive and Lemon by Lisa Gordanier, adapted from Quinn's Pub.

- Chicken Salad with Mushrooms and Walnuts and Delicious Green Beans, by Anush Oganesian and Lida Hovhannesyan.

- Poached Eggs with Pancetta and Tossed Mesclun by Julie Ridlon.

- Spanakopita (Greek Spinach Pie) by Jen Vassili.

- Paul's Strawberry Jam; Fennel and Celery Salad with Asiago Cheese; Parsley Salad with Olives and Capers; Citrus Salad with Feta and Mint; Apple Crumble; Fig Tart with Frangipane; and Paul's Bartlett Pear and Black Pepper Pie by Paul Anater.

- Favorite Baked Summer Squash and Super-Quick Black Bean Salad by Marianne Streich.

- Maple-Roasted Brussels Sprouts by Nicole Hoffmann.

- Perfect Brussels Sprouts by Ronald Swartz.

- Green Onion Pancakes by Tom Douglas, www.tomdouglas.com.

- Dorothy's Cauliflower Salad and Pear and Watercress Salad by Esther McRae.

- Citrus Collards with Raisins by Bryant Terry.

- Sopa de Ajo (Traditional Spanish Bread Soup) by Ibán Yarza, as appeared on Johanna Kindvall's *Kokblog* blog.

- Eggplant, Tomato, and Red Potato Casserole by Nelda Danz. Courtesy of Nelda Danz.

- Summer Fruit in Wine Dessert and Pumpkin-Ginger Soup by Melinda McBride. Courtesy of Melinda McBride.

- Easy-as-Pie Rhubarb Pie by Rich Hoyle. Courtesy of Rich Hoyle.

- Fried Squash Blossoms and Butternut Surprise by Nickolas Vassili. Courtesy of Nickolas Vassili.

- Boneless Lamb Sauté with Olives and Mushrooms by Jacob Wittenberg. Courtesy of Jacob Wittenberg.

- Tomatoes Stuffed with Blue Cheese and Walnuts by Arlayne Fleming. Courtesy of Arlayne Fleming.

- Oven-Roasted Tomato Sauce by Maria Runde. Courtesy of Maria Runde.

....

COOKING AND FOOD WEBSITES

- Saag Paneer; Malaysian Sambal Kangkong (Water Spinach with Sambal); Vegetable Fritters; Vegan Sun-Dried Tomato and Leek Quiche; Classic Wedge Salad; Julia Child's Buttered Peas with Mint; and Iced Green Tea with Lemongrass and Ginger. Fruit Kebabs by Noviceromano; Honeydew Bubble Tea; Glazed Pearl Onions; and Potato and Bacon Pierogies with Caramelized Shallots and Walnuts by Kris; Sweet Corn Pudding by Marybeth; Moroccan Mint Tea by MsAnthea; Balachaung (Burmese Dried Shrimp Relish) by Evelyn Ong; Southwestern Tomato Jam by Suzanne Collier; Kielbasa with Brussels Sprouts in Mustard Cream Sauce by Scott Heimendinger; Brussels Sprouts in Honey Butter with Chili Flakes by Nithya Das. All from Foodista, www.foodista.com.

- Creamy Dill Dressing by Amanda Formaro, *The Chamomile Times and Herbal News*, www.chamomiletimes.com.

- Garlic Scape Pizza by David Sutton; Garlic Scape Soup; and Green Garlic Mashed Potatoes. All from the Garlic Store, Fort Collins, Colorado. www.thegarlicstore.com.

- Mother Africa's Spicy Kale and Yam and Abba's African Hot Sauce by Gladys, the Recipe Link, www.kitchenlink.com.

- Basmati Rice with Mushrooms, Broccoli, and Onion; Abidjan Cabbage Salad; Bacon, Lettuce, and Cantaloupe Sandwich; Blackberry-Walnut Mesclun Salad; Mesclun with Maple Mustard Tofu Points from *The New Soy Cookbook: Tempting Recipes for Soybeans, Soy Milk, Tofu, Tempeh, Miso and Soy Sauce* by Lorna Sass, 1998; Baby Potatoes with Lemon and Chives; Chive and Parmesan Popcorn; Chicken with 40 Cloves of Garlic; Miso Broth with Tatsoi-Enoki Salad; Spinach, Rocket, and Mizuna Salad; French Cream of Lettuce Soup; Honeydew and Cucumber Salad with Sesame; Iced Honeydew and Gewürztraminer Soup; and Salade Niçoise. All recipes reprinted from Fooddownunder.com, www.fooddownunder.com.

- Chicken Pumpkin Chili by Mimi Hiller; Beef Bourguignon by Meryle. Both from Epicurean.com, www.epicurean.com.

- Rosemary-Lemon Crockpot Chicken by Harmony; Rosemary- or Basil-Infused Oil by Kylan. Reprinted from CD Kitchen, www.cdkitchen.com.

- Salmon, Cucumber, and Dill Salad; Marinated Bean Salad; and Vegetarian Stir-Fry. From World's Healthiest Foods, www.whfoods.com.

- Meat loaf: Yes, Virginia There Is a Great Meat loaf! by Nita Holleman; Thyme and Mushroom Gravy by Food.com. Reprinted from Food.com, www.food.com.

- Crockpot Chocolate-Raspberry Strata. Razzle Dazzle Recipes. Reprinted from www.razzledazzlerecipes.com.

- John's Winter Squash Soup with Vanilla Ice Cream by Ben & Jerry's. Copyright © 2006 by Ben and Jerry's Homemade Holdings, Inc. Reprinted from www.benandjerrys.com. Used by permission of Ben & Jerry's Homemade Holdings, Inc., South Burlington, Vermont.

- Green Beans in Basil-Walnut Vinaigrette and Blossom Tea Sandwiches, by Renee Shepherd, Renee's Garden, www.reneesgarden.com.

- Gallagher's Bar Spaghetti and Jalapeño Cream Sauce by J. Michael Gallagher, *The Alcoholic's Cookbook*, self-published, 2011.

- Arugula and Grilled Goat Cheese Salad; Kohlrabi Stuffed with Peppers; Radish, Mango, and Apple Salad; and Pasta with Savoy Cabbage and Gruyère by Christine Ingram, *The Cook's Encyclopedia of Vegetables*. Copyright © 2001 by Christine Ingram. Used by permission of Anness Publishing Ltd, London.

- Roasted Artichokes for Two, from Cooks Illustrated. Used by permission of Cooks Illustrated.

- Dark Chocolate Avocado Cookies from Greatist, adapted from *Cooking with Dia* by Kate Morin, www.greatist.com.

- Cantaloupe Pie adapted from Edward Pierce's original recipe, originally from *Fort Worth Star-Telegram* article.

- Okra, Corn, and Tomatoes adapted from Betty Crocker, www.bettycrocker.com.

- Charred Romanesco Broccoli with Anchovies and Mint by Travis Lett, *Bon Appétit Magazine*, December 2013. Spiced Rhubarb Chutney from *Bon Appétit Magazine*, April 1994. Reprinted by permission from Condé Naste.

- Lemongrass Halibut and Rosemary-Roasted Salmon by Vital Choice Wild Seafood and Organics, www.vitalchoice.com. Reprinted by permission of Vital Choice.

- Jerusalem Artichoke Fritters by Regina Schrambling and Cold Cream of Tomato and Peach Soup by Mark Bittman, *The New York Times*. Reprinted by permission of The New York Times and PARS International Corporation.

- Creamy Tarragon Chicken (or Turkey) Medallions with Skillet Sweet Potatoes and Beans by Amanda Barnier and The Test Kitchen, *Canadian Living Magazine*, March 2013; Sage-Apple Pork Burgers with Caramelized Onions by the Canadian Living Test Kitchen, www.canadianliving.com.

- Farmers Market Green Salad with Fried Shallots from *Gourmet*, June 1999; Pumpkin Pie with Spiced Walnut Streusel; and Sautéed Radishes and Sugar Snap Peas with Dill. All from Epicurious, www.epicurious.com.

- Spaghetti with Spring Vegetables by Jeanette Mettler Cappello; Warm Red Cabbage–Bacon Salad; Corn Chowder; Baba Ghanoush (Eggplant Dip); Pork Tenderloin Pitas; Vegetarian Paella with Brown Rice; Baked Rhubarb with Raspberries; Balsamic Rhubarb Compote; Homemade Salsa; Watermelon Bits; Watermelon Smoothie; Roasted Squash with Potatoes and Garlic; Savory Summer Squash Muffins; Vegetable Cornmeal Crêpes; Curried Mustard Greens and Garbanzo Beans with Sweet Potatoes; Low-Fat Ranch Dip; Seedless Cucumbers, Yogurt, Mint, and Garlic

Salad from Produce for Better Health Foundation. All recipes reprinted from the Centers for Disease Control & Prevention's Fruits and Veggies—More Matters website at www.fruitsandveggiesmatter.gov.

- Smothered Greens with Turkey and Sweet Potato Custard, Health.gov.

- LaVerne's Potato Candy from American Memory Project's Immigration … The Great American Potluck, Library of Congress, 2006. Reprinted from www.memory.loc.gov/learn/features/immig/ckbk/.

• •

FARMS AND RESTAURANTS

- Roasted Apples and Parsnips; Parsnips Whipped with Potatoes; Hakurei Turnip Salad; and Wilted Buttery Escarole with Red Cabbage and Shiitake Mushrooms by Luisa DePaiva, Purple Rain Vineyard, www.purplerainvineyard.com.

- Agua de Pepino (Cucumber Limeade) by Gary Masterson, Fire & Ice Café, Midleton, County Cork, Ireland, www.fireandicecafe.ie.

- Marinated Tofu with Mizuna or Swiss Chard by Seabreeze Organic Farm, San Diego, California, www.seabreezed.com.

- Mizuna and Summer Squash; Herbed Rice Salad; Roasted Chicken with Lemon and Thyme; Baked Chicken and Zucchini; Shallot Salad Dressing by Julia Wiley. All from Mariquita Farm, www.mariquita.com. Used by permission from Mariquita Farm, Watsonville, California.

- Spicy Cantaloupe Salsa; Grilled Eggplant Quesadillas by Marc Casale of Dos Coyotes Border Café, Davis, California; Vegetable Frittata; and Potato and Turnip au Gratin with Leeks by David Cannata of Yolo Catering. All recipes from Davis Farmers Market, Davis, California; reprinted from www.davisfarmersmarket.org, and used under the Creative Commons Attribution License.

- Creamy Green Bean and Mushroom Soup; Spicy Roasted Vegetable Soup; Golden Gazpacho; Spinach and Warm Sungold Salad; and Sungold Salad with Feta and Cumin-Yogurt Dressing by Coleen Wolner, Blue Heron Coffeehouse, Winona, Minnesota. Creamy Green Bean and Mushroom Soup and Spicy Roasted Vegetable Soup reprinted from the *Bluff Country Co-op Cookbook*. Recipes used by permission of Colleen Wolner and the Bluff Country Co-op, Winona, Minnesota.

- Enchiladas Verdes and Terhune Orchards Vegetable Soup from Terhune Orchards, Princeton, New Jersey. www.terhuneorchards.com.

The following Featherstone CSA members generously donated recipes for the farm's CSA newsletters and this cookbook.

- Amy Chen—Corn Salsa.

- Allison—Carrot and Red Lentil Curry.

- Greta Sikorski—Roasted Root Vegetables from Greta's Kitchen.

- Heather—Heather's Quinoa Sauté.

- Jan Taylor—Tarragon Chicken Marinade.

- Judy—Spinach, Nuts, and Cheese.

- Margaret Houston—Grandma's Spinach Soufflé and Ratatouille Niçoise.

- Margaret Trott—Cherry Tomato Kebabs; Parmesan-Baked Kohlrabi and Stuffed and Baked Sweet Onions (by Barbara Hunt).

- Mi Ae Lipe—Roasted Bacon-Wrapped Asparagus; Deviled Eggs with Salmon and Basil; Mylar's Lettuce Wraps; Garlic Spinach; Barely Pickled Cucumbers; Mylar's Rosemary Potato Wedges; Tomato, Onion, and Cucumber Salad; Oregano and Zucchini Pasta; Roasted Pumpkin Seeds; Radishes with Salt and Butter; Polka Dot Clouds; and Wake-Up Tuna Salad.

- Pam Garetto—Seasonal Salad with Vinaigrette.

- Robin Taylor—Rhubarb Crisp; Mexican Black Bean and Tomato Salad; White Bean and Basil Salad; Raw Kale Salad; and Dal Makhani (Indian Lentils and Beans).

- Ruth Charles—Pasta with Arugula and Chard with Raisins and Almonds.

- Sarah Libertus—Simple Kale and Ginger Squash Soup, Stuffed Squash, and Asian Fusion Slaw.

- Tracy—Potato Leek Soup.

- Trina—Trina's Green Salmon.

- From Featherstone Farm newsletters: Ultimate Root Soup; Citrus Butter Salad; Gomae (Sesame Spinach); Roasted Eggplant Salad with Beans and Cashews; Peppery Potato and Zucchini Packets on the Grill;

Southwestern Radish Salad; and Stuffed Squash with Basil and Honey.

The following recipes are courtesy of other CSA farms.

- Kahumana Café Pasta with Macadamia Nut Pesto Sauce by Robert Zuckerman, Kahumana Farm Café, Waianae, Oahu, Hawaii.

- Arugula Pesto; Fava Bean Pesto with Romaine; Caramelized Cabbage; Triticale Berries with Baby Artichokes, Baby Bok Choy, and Dill Oil; Chioggia Beet Slaw on a Bed of Grilled Leeks; Carrot Slaw, Roasted Beet Salsa with Skillet-Browned Broccoli, and Broccoli with Baby White Turnip and Garlic Scapes Dressing by Karolina Tracz; Fava Bean Borscht and Nash's Raw Slaw by Mary Wong; and Roasted Beet and Brussels Sprout Salad by Annie McHale. All from Nash's Organic Produce, Sequim, Washington.

- Pear, Fennel, and Walnut Salad from Helsing Junction Farm, Rochester, Washington.

- Grilled Romaine with Poached Eggs and Green Goddess Dressing; Veggie-Stuffed Bell Peppers; and Sweet Potato and Carrot Latkes from Sang Lee Farms, Peconic, New York.

- Cantaloupe and Cucumber Salad and Grapefruit and Kiwi Sorbet by Gabriel Avila-Mooney, Full Circle Farm, Seattle, Washington.

- Colorful Heirloom Tomato Salad and Heirloom Tomato Salad Dressing from Teena's Pride CSA, Homestead, Florida.

- Radish Top Soup and Shepherd's Pie by Philippe Waterinckx; Parsnip-Carrot Bisque and Spaghetti Squash Pad Thai by Sara Jones; and Cabbage and Sunchoke Slaw by Lorraine Glazar. All from Tucson CSA, Tucson, Arizona.

- Fennel and Torpedo Onion Salad by Katherine Deumling (via Sauvie Island Organics, Portland, Oregon), Cook With What You Have, www.cookwithwhatyouhave.com.

- Lemon Noodles; Kula Fields Easy Key Lime Pie; Papaya, Ginger, and Mint Smoothie; and Kula Fields Macadamia and Coconut Pie by Roxanne Tiffin, Kula Fields, Inc., Kula, Maui, Hawaii.

- Mexican Rutabaga and Sweet Potato by Lindsay Arbuckle Courcelle, Alchemy Gardens, West Rutland, Vermont.

. . . .

- Information on drying tomatoes adapted from "Drying Tomatoes" article by Shila Patel; excerpted from www.doityourself.com.

- Information on freezing and blanching adapted and reprinted from Pick Your Own (www.pickyourown. org) and the University of Illinois Extension (www. urbanext.uiuc.edu).

- Some nutritional information adapted from World's Healthiest Foods at www.whfoods.com.

- Partial information on chives adapted from article by Susan Mahr, the Department of Horticulture, the University of Wisconsin-Madison.

- Information on food weights, equivalents, conversions, and measurements adapted and reprinted from About. com (www.about.com); RecipeZaar (www.recipezaar.com); GourmetSleuth.com (www.gourmetsleuth.com), and *The Victory Garden Cookbook* by Morene Morash, Alfred A. Knopf, 1982.

. . . .

GRAPHICS CREDITS

- Photographs throughout book courtesy of Sang Lee Farms (Lucy Sensenac), Featherstone Farm, Kahumana Farm, Teena's Pride CSA, S&S Homestead Farm, and Valley Flora Farm.

- Illustrations from Clipart.com, iStockphoto.com, and Dreamstime.com.

- Front and back cover illustrations by Mary Woodin, www.marywoodin.com.

General Index

Items in **boldface** indicate fruits and vegetables with their own sections in the book. Items in *italics* indicate book and magazine titles. Recipe titles are in title case.

H

Halley, Linda, 565
Hands-On Learning—on the Farm and at School sidebar, 532–537
Hang, Pakou, 303, 304
HappyChomp blog, 428
Harmon, Father Phil, 385
Harmony, CD Kitchen, 282
Harrison, Betsy, 280
Harvest agrihood, 153
Harvesting Our Potential (HOP), 342
Hawaiian CSAs sidebar, 318–321
Hawthorne Valley Association, 277
Hawthorne Valley Farm, 277, 339
Hawthorne Valley Waldorf School, 277
Hazon, 432
healthcare organizations and food programs, 592–595
Health.gov, 461, 603
Healthy Food For All, 162
Hedin, Jack, 47, 108–115
    sidebars authored by, 48, 220, 233, 440, 444, 482, 518, 608
Hedin, Oscar, 48–51
Heimendinger, Scott, 420
heirloom plants, seeds, and foods
    Ark of Taste sidebar, 284
    Consolidation of the Seed Industry and Loss of Heirloom Varieties Sidebar, 584–585
    Heirlooms Versus Hybrids: A Farmer's Perspective sidebar, 608–610
Heirlooms Versus Hybrids: A Farmer's Perspective sidebar, 608–610
Helgeson, Janie, 270
Helsing Junction Farm, 189, 380, 470, 545
Herbal Revolution, 191
herb CSAs, 190–191
herbs. *See also* basil, chives, cilantro, dill, marjoram, mint, oregano, parsley, rosemary, savory, tarragon, thyme, and sage
    herb CSAs, 190–191
    using fresh versus dried, xvii
Herbfarm, The, 578
Heritage Point Urban Farm, 565
hibiscus, 196
Hidden Springs agrihood, 152
Hiller, Mimi, 478
Hills Centennial Cookbook, 270, 345, 529, 578
Hmong farmers, 302–304
Hmong American Farmers Association (HAFA), 303–304
Hoffmann, Ingrid, 361
Hoffmann, Nicole, 422
Holcomb, Bridget, 281
Holleman, Nita, 562
hollyhock, 196
Holt, Shirley, 519

homelessness in Hawaii, 384–386
honeydew melons, 205–208
    recipes
        Fruit Kebabs, 207
        Honeydew and Cucumber Salad with Sesame Dressing, 207
        Honeydew Bubble Tea, 208
honeysuckle (Japanese), 196
Hong Kong City College, 528
hot peppers. *See* peppers (hot)
Houston, Margaret, 89, 255
Hovhannesyan, Lida, 67, 147
How to Choose a CSA That's Right for You sidebar, 72–74
How to Pick a Peach book, 15, 249, 400
Hoyle, Rich, 77
Huber, Nash, 168, 558
hummus, list of recipes, 614
Hunt, Barbara, 450, 556
hybrids, 608–610
Hyde, Brenda, 286
hyssop, 196

I

¡Cultiva! Youth Project, 534
Idexx Laboratories, 39–40
immigrant farm workers
    An Inconvenient Truth: Immigrant Farm Workers sidebar, 308–311
    Gratitude sidebar, 233–237
    Jack and Oscar Go to Mexico sidebar, 48–51
Immigration … The Great American Potluck, 579
impatiens, 196
Imperfect Produce, 529
Impraim, Esi, 336
Incubators: Nurturing a New Crop of Farmers sidebar, 548–550
Ingram, Christine, 23, 451, 482, 517
ingredients, using the best, xvii
International Rutabaga Curling Championship, 582
Intervale Center, 548
Intervale Community Farm, 135
Iowa Female Farmer Veteran Network Project, 342

J

Jack and Oscar Go to Mexico sidebar, 48–51
jams and preserves, list of recipes, 615
jasmine, 196
Jefferson Healthcare, 592
Je Mange le Ville blog, 567
Jerusalem artichokes, 546–550
    brandy from, 547
    recipes
        Cabbage and Sunchoke Slaw, 550
        complete list of recipes, 630

W

Wagner, Ashley, 310
Wagner, Martha
  sidebars authored by, 38, 64, 72, 78, 92, 131, 134, 143, 152, 162, 167, 180, 188, 216, 254, 276, 279, 367, 378, 418, 432, 488, 506, 532, 544, 548, 557, 564, 592
Waihuena Farm, 321
Waldorf Schools: Integrating Education and the Natural World sidebar, 276–277
Walk, Larisa, 611
Waltham Fields Community Farm, 488
Ward, Grace
  sidebar authored by, 560
watercress
  complete list of recipes, 645
Waterinckx, Philippe, 484, 584
watermelons, 370–375
  China as producer, 372
  recipes
    complete list of recipes, 645
    Watermelon and Chicken Salad, 372
    Watermelon Bits, 373
    Watermelon Gazpacho, 374
    Watermelon Pineapple Preserves, 374
    Watermelon Smoothie, 374
    Watermelon-Strawberry Mint Salsa, 373
Waters, Alice, 82
water spinach, 133–135
  complete list of recipes, 645
  recipes
    Malaysian Sambal Kangkong (Water Spinach with Sambal), 135
Watt, Justin, 544
Wedge Co-op, 564
Welcome to the Agrihood! sidebar, 152–153
Wells, Patricia, 550
WFAN (Women, Food, and Agriculture Network), 281, 342
What Happens on a Farm During the Winter? sidebar, 560–561
What Is Community-Supported Agriculture (CSA)? sidebar, 14
Where Did CSAs Come From? sidebar, 15
Whole-Diet CSAs sidebar, 143–145
Whole Foods, 110, 113
Wild Farm Alliance, 557
Wild Garden Seed, 169

Wiley, Julia, 294
Wilkinson, Lauren Mitchell, 343, 528
Will Allen, xi–xii
Willowsford agrihood, 153
Winter at the Farm sidebar, 524–525
Winter CSA Shares sidebar, 506–507
Winter Green Farm, 427
winter squash. *See* squash (winter)
Wiscoy Community Co-op, 109
Wittenberg, Jacob, 69
Wizenberg, Molly, 333
Wolner, Colleen, 93, 228, 257, 321
Women Caring for the Land, 342
Women, Food, and Agriculture Network (WFAN), 281, 342
Women, Infants, and Children's (WIC), 379
Women in Farming Today sidebar, 279–282
Wong, Mary, 42, 400
World Carrot Museum, 522
World's Healthiest Foods, 183, 236, 520
Worldwide Workers on Organic Farms (WWOOF), 282, 388, 489
WWOOF. *See* Worldwide Workers on Organic Farms (WWOOF)

Y

Yarza, Ibán, 545
Yolo Catering, 608
Youth Farm, The, 254
Youthmarket, 419
yucca, 199
Yu, Miss Joan, 369

Z

Zen and the Art of CSA Membership sidebar, 460–462
Zenger Farm, 92–93, 378, 488
Zephyr Valley Land Community Co-op, 109
zucchinis, 376–382
  recipes
    Baked Chicken and Zucchini Gratin, 379
    complete list of recipes, 645
    Pickled Mixed Vegetable Salad, 381
    Zucchini Pickles, 380
    Zucchini Teacake, 380
Zuckerman, Christian, 388–391
Zuckerman, Robert, 34–39, 388–391
ZVCC. *See* Zephyr Valley Community Land Co-op

ABOUT THE AUTHOR

Born in South Korea, Mi Ae Lipe grew up in the San Francisco Bay Area, where she first became interested in food and gardening. A self-taught artist and illustrator, she lived and worked in Wisconsin and Minnesota for 13 years, and during this time she met Jack Hedin, owner of Featherstone Farm. After doing a logo project for the farm, she became one of its CSA subscribers, which inspired her to create first cookbook, *Tastes from Valley to Bluff: The Featherstone Farm Cookbook*, published in 2008. She now resides in Seattle, where she works as a freelance book editor, designer, and publications consultant; you can find her portfolio on www.whatnowdesign.com.

When not regularly indulging in eating (a favorite hobby), Mi Ae lives another life as a traffic safety advocate. She blogs about driving on her website Driving in the Real World at www.drivingintherealworld.com and regularly collaborates with car clubs, American and international driving instructors, nonprofits, government agencies, private companies, and others. Her particular interest is in holistic, experiential solutions rooted in common sense, social sciences, and psychology to improve road safety awareness, traffic culture, and driver training, especially in the United States.

Love to Hear From You!

What do you think about this book?
Thoughts? Questions? Feedback?

Let me know!
Please send your comments and ideas:

Mi Ae Lipe
206-349-2038
miae@bountyfromthebox.com

And thank you!

**Don't forget to visit Bounty from the Box
on Twitter, Facebook, Pinterest, and Google+**

Find and share recipes, CSA farms, and lots of other goodies
on the Bounty from the Box website!

www.bountyfromthebox.com